HITT · IRELAND · HOSKISSON

Strategic Management

Concepts

Competitiveness and Globalization

Strategic Management

Concepts

Competitiveness and Globalization

8th Edition

Michael A. Hitt
Texas A&M University

R. Duane Ireland
Texas A&M University

Robert E. Hoskisson
Arizona State University

Australia • Brazil • Canada • Mexico • Singapore • Spain • United Kingdom • United States

Strategic Management: Competitiveness and Globalization (Concepts) 8th Edition

Michael A. Hitt, R. Duane Ireland, and Robert E. Hoskisson

VP/Editorial Director: Jack W. Calhoun

VP/Editor-in-Chief: Melissa Acuña

Senior Acquisitions Editor: Michele Rhoades

Developmental Editor: Rebecca Von Gillern—Bookworm Editorial Services

Executive Marketing Manager: Kimberly Kanakes

Marketing Manager: Clint Kernen

Marketing Coordinator: Sara Rose

Senior Content Project Manager: Colleen A. Farmer

Technology Project Editor: Kristen Meere

Manufacturing Coordinator: Doug Wilke

Production Service: LEAP Publishing Services, Inc.

Compositor: ICC Macmillan, Inc.

Senior Art Director: Tippy McIntosh

Photo Manager: Sheri I. Blaney

Photo Researcher: Marcy Lunetta

Printer: Transcontinental

Internal & Cover Designer: Craig Ramsdell, Ramsdell Design

Cover Image: © Don Hammond/Design Pics/Corbis

Library of Congress Control Number: 2007940878
Student Edition ISBN 13: 978-0-324-58112-6
Student Edition ISBN 10: 0-324-58112-2

Instructor's Edition ISBN 13: 978-0-324-58122-5
Instructor's Edition ISBN 10: 0-324-58122-X

Concepts and Cases ISBN 13: 978-0-324-65559-9
Concepts and Cases ISBN 10: 0-324-65559-2

South-Western Cengage Learning
5191 Natorp Boulevard
Mason, OH 45040
USA

Cengage Learning products are represented in Canada by Nelson Education, Ltd.

For your course and learning solutions, visit **academic.cengage.com**

Purchase any of our products at your local college store or at our preferred online store **www.ichapters.com**

Printed in Canada
1 2 3 4 5 6 7 11 10 09 08 07

To Shawn and Angie. I have been blessed to have two wonderful children. You have always been highly important to me; I love you very much and I am proud of your accomplishments.

—**MICHAEL A. HITT**

To my beloved Grandmother, Rowena Steele Wheeler Hodge (1905–2007). You have been such a strong beacon of guiding light for me for so long. You are a treasured blessing. Rest in peace. I love you, Grandma.

—**R. DUANE IRELAND**

To my dear wife, Kathy, who has been my greatest friend and support through life, and I hope will remain so into the eternities.

—**ROBERT E. HOSKISSON**

Brief Contents

Contents

2: The External Environment: Opportunities, Threats, Industry Competition, and Competitor Analysis 32

3: The Internal Organization: Resources, Capabilities, Core Competencies, and Competitive Advantages 68

Part 2: Strategic Actions: Strategy Formulation 95

4: Business-Level Strategy 96

5: Competitive Rivalry and Competitive Dynamics 126

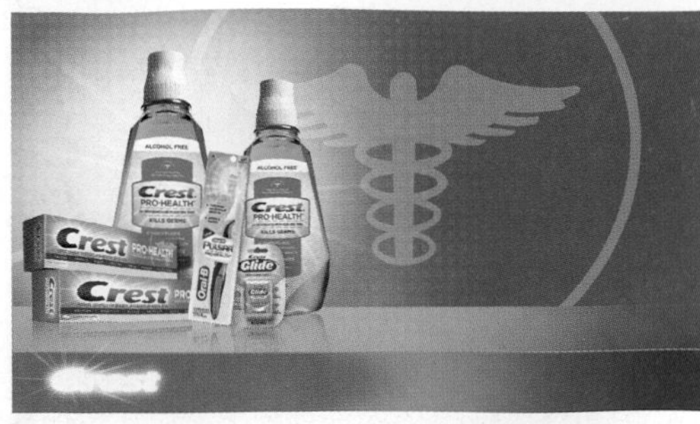

6: Corporate-Level Strategy 152

7: Acquisition and Restructuring Strategies 180

IBM

11: Organizational Structure and Controls 306

12: Strategic Leadership 338

Google
Google

Preface

Our goal in writing each edition of this book is to present a new, up-to-date standard for explaining the strategic management process. To reach this goal with the 8th edition of our market-leading text, we again present you with an intellectually rich yet thoroughly practical analysis of strategic management.

With each new edition, we are challenged and invigorated by the goal of establishing a new standard for presenting strategic management knowledge in a readable style. To prepare for each new edition, we carefully study the most recent academic research to ensure that the strategic management content we present to you is highly current and relevant for organizations. In addition, we continuously read articles appearing in many different business publications (e.g., *Wall Street Journal, BusinessWeek, Fortune, Financial Times,* and *Forbes,* to name just a few); we do this to identify valuable examples of how companies use the strategic management process. Though many of the hundreds of companies we discuss in the book will be quite familiar to you, some companies will likely be new to you as well. One reason for this is that we use examples of companies from around the world to demonstrate how globalized business has become. To maximize your opportunities to learn as you read and think about how actual companies use strategic management tools, techniques, and concepts (based on the most current research), we emphasize a lively and user-friendly writing style.

Several *characteristics* of this 8th edition of our book will enhance your learning opportunities:

- This book presents you with the most comprehensive and thorough coverage of strategic management that is available in the market.
- The research used in this book is drawn from the "classics" as well as the most recent contributions to the strategic management literature. The historically significant "classic" research provides the foundation for much of what is known about strategic management; the most recent contributions reveal insights about how to effectively use strategic management in the complex, global business environment in which most firms operate while trying to outperform their competitors. Our book also presents you with many examples of how firms use the strategic management tools, techniques, and concepts developed by leading researchers. Indeed, this book is strongly application oriented and presents you, our readers, with a vast number of examples and applications of strategic management concepts, techniques, and tools. In this edition, for example, we examine more than 600 companies to describe the use of strategic management. Collectively, no other strategic management book presents you with the *combination* of useful and insightful *research* and *applications* in a wide variety of organizations as does this text. Company examples range from the large U.S.-based firms such as Wal-Mart, IBM, Kodak, Whole Foods, and Google to major foreign-based firms such as Toyota, Nokia, Hyundai, and Shanghai Automotive Industry

Corporation (SAIC). We also include examples of successful younger and newer firms such as Caribou Coffee and Mustang Engineering.

- We carefully *integrate* two of the most popular and well-known theoretical concepts in the strategic management field: industrial-organization economics and the resource-based view of the firm. Other texts usually emphasize one of these two theories (at the cost of explaining the other one to describe strategic management). However, such an approach is incomplete; research and practical experience indicate that both theories play a major role in understanding the linkage between strategic management and organizational success. No other book integrates these two theoretical perspectives effectively to explain the strategic management process and its application in all types of organizations.
- We use the ideas of prominent scholars (e.g., Raphael [Raffi] Amit, Kathy Eisenhardt, Don Hambrick, Constance Helfat, Ming Jer-Chen, Rita McGrath, Michael Porter, C. K. Prahalad, Richard Rumelt, Ken Smith, David Teece, Michael Tushman, Oliver Williamson, and numerous others) to shape the discussion of *what* strategic management is. We describe the practices of prominent executives and practitioners (e.g., Bill Gates, Jeffrey Immelt, Steven Jobs, Anne Mulcahy, Indra Nooyi, Howard Schultz, Meg Whitman, and many others) to help us describe *how* strategic management is used in many types of organizations.
- We, the authors of this book, are also active scholars. We conduct research on different strategic management topics. Our interest in doing so is to contribute to the strategic management literature and to better understand how to effectively apply strategic management tools, techniques, and concepts to increase organizational performance. Thus, our own research is integrated in the appropriate chapters along with the research of numerous other scholars.

In addition to our book's *characteristics,* there are some specific *features* of this 8th edition that we want to highlight for you:

- **New Opening Cases and Strategic Focus Segments.** We continue our tradition of providing all-new Opening Cases and Strategic Focus segments. In addition, new company-specific examples are included in each chapter. Through all of these venues, we present you with a wealth of examples of how actual organizations, most of which compete internationally as well as in their home markets, use the strategic management process to outperform rivals and increase their performance.
- **Strategy Right Now.** A new feature for this edition, Strategy Right Now is used in each chapter to highlight companies that are effectively using a strategic management concept examined in the chapter. In Chapter 3, for example, Volkswagen AG's effective use of a global mindset is described as the foundation for the success the firm is achieving today as a result of its decision to establish manufacturing facilities in Slovakia before competitors chose to do so. In Chapter 4, both Cemex and Target are signaled as firms that effectively use the strategic management process to create excellent business-level strategies. This feature is a valuable tool for readers to quickly identify how a firm is effectively using a strategic management tool, technique, or concept. We follow up with the most current research and information about these firms by using Cengage Learning's Business Company and Resource Center (BCRC). Links to specific current news articles related to these companies can be found on our Web site (academic.cengage.com/management/hitt). Whenever you see the Strategy Right Now icon in the text, you will know that current research is available from the BCRC links posted to our Web site.

- **An Exceptional Balance** between current research and applications of it in actual organizations. The content has not only the best research documentation but also the largest amount of effective real-world examples to help active learners understand the different types of strategies that organizations use to achieve their vision and mission.

- **29 All-New Cases** with an effective mix of organizations headquartered or based in the United States and a number of other countries. Many of the cases have full financial data (the analyses of which are in the Case Notes that are available to Instructors). These timely cases present active learners with opportunities to apply the strategic management process and understand organizational conditions and contexts and to make appropriate recommendations to deal with critical concerns.
- **All-New Enhanced Experiential Exercises** to support individuals' efforts to understand the use of the strategic management process. These exercises place active learners in a variety of situations requiring application of some part of the strategic management process. The exercises in this edition are creative and enriched relative to previous editions.
- **All-New Access to Harvard Business School (HBS) Cases.** We have developed a set of assignment sheets and assessment rubrics to accompany 10 of the best selling HBS cases. Instructors can use these cases and the accompanying set of teaching notes and assessment rubrics to formalize assurance of learning efforts in the capstone Strategic Management/ Business Policy course. The cases are Adolph Coors in the Brewing Industry, Cola Wars Continue: Coke vs. Pepsi in the 1990s, Nucor at a Crossroads, Marks & Spencer: The Phoenix Rises, Crown Cork & Seal in 1989, Bitter Competition: The Holland Sweetener Company vs. NutraSweet, The Brita Products Company, Wal-Mart Stores in 2003, Callaway Golf Company, and Sampa Video, Inc.
- **Lively, Concise Writing Style** to hold readers' attention and to increase their interest in strategic management.
- **Continuing, Updated Coverage** of vital strategic management topics such as competitive rivalry and dynamics, strategic alliances, mergers and acquisitions, international strategies, corporate governance, and ethics. Also, we continue to be the only book in the market with a separate chapter devoted to strategic entrepreneurship.
- **Full four-color** format to enhance readability by attracting and maintaining readers' interests.

To maintain current and up-to-date content, new concepts are explored in the 8th edition.

Chapter 6 illustrates an interesting trend towards small unrelated diversified firms that are buying "castoffs" from large diversified firms that are restructuring their operations. For instance, Jarden Corporation has acquired Coleman Camping Goods, Ball Canning Jars, Bicycle Playing Cards, and Crock-Pot Cookers. Jarden was able to acquire these firms at relatively low prices. The larger firms felt pressure to divest assets unrelated to their core operations as a path to improving their performance.

One of the interesting ideas introduced in Chapter 8, the International Strategy chapter, concerns the effect of country institutional environments on multinational firm strategies. Factors such as country laws and regulations, political systems, economic growth, and physical infrastructure (e.g., roads, airline flights, telephone lines) can have a major impact on how multinational firms operate in a country as well as the results of their competitive efforts in those countries. One example regards intellectual property rights laws and enforcement mechanisms. Multinational firms with operations in China and India have called for stronger laws to protect their intellectual property in those countries. Interestingly, many of India and China's companies are beginning to emphasize innovation instead of imitating other multinationals' products; therefore, these companies are emphasizing stronger patent protections for intellectual property because they provide more basic innovation that leads to first-mover advantages.

We expanded our discussion of international entrepreneurship in Chapter 13. We did this because of the increasing importance of international entrepreneurship on a global scale for the success of individual firms and different nations' economies. For example, 40 percent of the adult population in Peru is involved in entrepreneurial activity (the largest percentage of any country globally). The lowest percentage of the population involved in entrepreneurship is in Belgium (3 percent). Slightly more than

10 percent of the U.S. adult population engages in entrepreneurship. Entrepreneurship also is becoming quite important in former centrally planned economies such as China and Russia.

Supplements

Instructors

IRCD (0-324-58118-1) Key ancillaries (Instructor's Resource Manual, Instructor's Case Notes, Test Bank, ExamView™, PowerPoint® and Case Analysis Questions Using Business & Company Resource Center) are provided on CD-ROM, giving instructors the ultimate tool for customizing lectures and presentations.

Instructor Case Notes (0-324-58121-1) All new expanded case notes provide details about the 29 cases found in the second part of the main text. These new expanded case notes include directed assignments, financial analysis, thorough discussion and exposition of issues in the case and an assessment rubric tied to AACSB assurance of learning standards that can be used for grading each case. The case notes provide consistent and thorough support for instructors, following the method espoused by the author team for preparing an effective case analysis. The case notes for the 8th edition have been written in great detail and include questions and answers throughout along with industry and company background and resolutions wherever possible.

Instructor's Resource Manual (0-324-58124-6) The Instructor's Resource Manual, organized around each chapter's knowledge objectives, includes teaching ideas for each chapter and how to reinforce essential principles with extra examples. The support product includes lecture outlines, detailed answers to end-of-chapter review questions, instructions for using each chapter's experiential exercises, and additional assignments.

Certified Test Bank (0-324-58126-2) Thoroughly revised and enhanced, test bank questions are linked to each chapter's knowledge objectives and are ranked by difficulty and question type. We provide an ample number of application questions throughout and we have also retained scenario-based questions as a means of adding in-depth problem-solving questions. With this edition, we introduce the concept of certification, whereby another qualified academic has proofread and verified the accuracy of the test bank questions and answers. The test bank material is also available in computerized ExamView™ format for creating custom tests in both Windows and Macintosh formats.

ExamView™ (Available on IRCD: 0-324-58118-1) Computerized testing software contains all of the questions in the certified printed test bank. This program is an easy-to-use test creation software compatible with Microsoft Windows. Instructors can add or edit questions, instructions, and answers, and select questions by previewing them on the screen, selecting them randomly, or selecting them by number. Instructors can also create and administer quizzes online, whether over the Internet, a local area network (LAN), or a wide area network (WAN).

All-New Video Program (0-324-58129-7) You spoke and we listened! For our 8th edition we have a selection of 13 brand-new videos that relate directly to chapter concepts. Provided by Fifty Lessons, these new videos are a comprehensive and compelling resource of management and leadership lessons from some of the world's most successful business leaders. In the form of short and powerful videos, these videos capture leaders' most important learning experiences. They share their real-world business acumen and outline the guiding principles behind their most important business decisions and their career progression.

PowerPoint® (0-324-58118-1) An all-new PowerPoint presentation, created for the 8th edition, provides support for lectures emphasizing key concepts, key terms, and instructive graphics. Slides can also be used by students as an aid to note-taking.

WebTutor™ WebTutor is used by an entire class under the direction of the instructor and is particularly convenient for distance learning courses. It provides Web-based learning resources to students as well as powerful communication and other course management tools, including course calendar, chat, and e-mail for instructors. See http://webtutor.thomsonlearning.com for more information.

Product Support Web Site (academic.cengage.com/management/hitt) Our product support Web site contains all ancillary products for instructors as well as the financial analysis exercises for both students and instructors.

The Business & Company Resource Center (BCRC) Put a complete business library at your students' fingertips! This premier online business research tool allows you and your students to search thousands of periodicals, journals, references, financial information, industry reports, and more. This powerful research tool saves time for students—whether they are preparing for a presentation or writing a reaction paper. You can use the BCRC to quickly and easily assign readings or research projects. Visit http://academic.cengage.com/bcrc to learn more about this indispensable tool. For this text in particular, BCRC will be especially useful in further researching the companies featured in the text's 29 cases. We've also included BCRC links for the Strategy Right Now feature on our Web site, as well as in the Cengage NOW product. Finally, we have incorporated data from BCRC into the exercises for financial analysis to facilitate students' research and help them focus their attention on honing their skills in financial analysis (see Web site).

Resource Integration Guide (RIG) When you start with a new—or even familiar—text, the amount of supplemental material can seem overwhelming. Identifying each element of a supplement package and piecing together the parts that fit your particular needs can be time-consuming. After all, you may use only a small fraction of the resources available to help you plan, deliver, and evaluate your class. We have created a resource guide to help you and your students extract the full value from the text and its wide range of exceptional supplements. This resource guide is available on the product support Web site. The RIG organizes the book's resources and provides planning suggestions to help you conduct your class, create assignments, and evaluate your students' mastery of the subject. Whatever your teaching style or circumstance, there are planning suggestions to meet your needs. The broad range of techniques provided in the guide helps you increase your repertoire as a teaching expert and enrich your students' learning and understanding. We hope this map and its suggestions enable you to discover new and exciting ways to teach your course.

Students

Financial analyses of some of the cases are provided on our product support Web site for both students and instructors. Researching financial data, company data, and industry data is made easy through the use of our proprietary database, the Business & Company Resource Center. Students are sent to this database to be able to quickly gather data needed for financial analysis.

Acknowledgments

We express our appreciation for the excellent support received from our editorial and production team at South-Western. We especially wish to thank Michele Rhoades, our Senior Acquisitions Editor; Rebecca von Gillern, our Development Editor; Kimberly

Kanakes and Clinton Kernan, our Marketing Managers; and Colleen Farmer, our Content Project Manager. We are grateful for their dedication, commitment, and outstanding contributions to the development and publication of this book and its package of support materials.

We are highly indebted to the reviewers of the seventh edition in preparation for this current edition:

Brent Allred,
The College of William and Mary

Jame Bronson,
University of Wisconsin, Whitewater

Daniel DeGravel,
California State University, Los Angeles

Steve Gove,
University of Dayton

Peggy Griffin,
New Jersey City University

Franz Kellermans,
Mississippi State University

Frank Novakowski,
Davenport University

Finally, we are very appreciative of the following people for the time and care that went into the preparation of the supplements to accompany this edition:

Brian Boyd,
Arizona State University

Judith Gebhardt,
Catholic University

Steve Gove,
University of Dayton

Dana Gray,
Rogers State University

Michael A. Hitt
R. Duane Ireland
Robert E. Hoskisson

About the Authors

Michael A. Hitt

Michael A. Hitt is a Distinguished Professor and holds the Joe B. Foster Chair in Business Leadership at Texas A&M University. He received his Ph.D. from the University of Colorado. He has co-authored or co-edited 26 books and 150 journal articles.

Some of his books are *Downscoping: How to Tame the Diversified Firm* (Oxford University Press, 1994); *Mergers and Acquisitions: A Guide to Creating Value for Stakeholders* (Oxford University Press, 2001); *Competing for Advantage* 2nd edition (South-Western College Publishing, 2008); and *Understanding Business Strategy* (South-Western College Publishing, 2006). He is co-editor of several books including the following: *Managing Strategically in an Interconnected World* (1998); *New Managerial Mindsets: Organizational Transformation and Strategy Implementation* (1998); *Dynamic Strategic Resources: Development, Diffusion, and Integration* (1999); *Winning Strategies in a Deconstructing World* (John Wiley & Sons, 2000); *Handbook of Strategic Management* (2001); *Strategic Entrepreneurship: Creating a New Integrated Mindset* (2002); *Creating Value: Winners in the New Business Environment* (Blackwell Publishers, 2002); *Managing Knowledge for Sustained Competitive Advantage* (Jossey-Bass, 2003); *Great Minds in Management: The Process of Theory Development* (Oxford University Press, 2005), and *The Global Mindset* (Elsevier, 2007). He has served on the editorial review boards of multiple journals, including the *Academy of Management Journal, Academy of Management Executive, Journal of Applied Psychology, Journal of Management, Journal of World Business,* and *Journal of Applied Behavioral Sciences.* Furthermore, he has served as Consulting Editor and Editor of the *Academy of Management Journal.* He is currently a co-editor of the *Strategic Entrepreneurship Journal.* He is president of the Strategic Management Society and is a past president of the Academy of Management.

He is a Fellow in the Academy of Management and in the Strategic Management Society. He received an honorary doctorate from the Universidad Carlos III de Madrid and is an Honorary Professor and Honorary Dean at Xi'an Jiao Tong University. He has been ackowledged with several awards for his scholarly research and he received the Irwin Outstanding Educator Award and the Distinguished Service Award from the Academy of Management. He has received best paper awards for articles published in the *Academy of Management Journal, Academy of Management Executive,* and *Journal of Management.*

R. Duane Ireland

R. Duane Ireland holds the Foreman R. and Ruby S. Bennett Chair in Business from the Mays Business School, Texas A&M University where he previously served as head of the management department. He teaches strategic management courses at all levels (undergraduate, masters, doctoral, and executive). His research, which focuses on diversification, innovation, corporate entrepreneurship, and strategic entrepreneurship, has been published in a number of journals, including *Academy of Management Journal, Academy of Management Review, Academy of Management Executive, Administrative Science Quarterly, Strategic Management Journal, Journal of Management, Strategic Entrepreneurship Journal, Human Relations, Entrepreneurship Theory and Practice, Journal of Business Venturing,* and *Journal of Management Studies,* among others. His recently published books include *Understanding Business Strategy, Concepts and Cases* (South-Western College Publishing, 2006), *Entrepreneurship: Successfully Launching New Ventures* (Prentice-Hall, Second Edition, 2008), and *Competing for Advantage* (South-Western College Publishing, 2008). He is serving or has served as a member of the editorial review boards for a number of journals, including *Academy of Management Journal, Academy of Management Review, Academy of Management Executive, Journal of Management, Journal of Business Venturing, Entrepreneurship Theory and Practice, Journal of Business Strategy,* and *European Management Journal,* and more. He has completed terms as an associate editor for *Academy of Management Journal*, as an associate editor for *Academy of Management Executive*, and as a consulting editor for *Entrepreneurship Theory and Practice*. He is the current editor of *Academy of Management Journal*. He has co-edited special issues of *Academy of Management Review, Academy of Management Executive, Journal of Business Venturing, Strategic Management Journal, Journal of High Technology and Engineering Management*, and *Organizational Research Methods* (forthcoming). He received awards for the best article published in *Academy of Management Executive* (1999) and *Academy of Management Journal* (2000). In 2001, his co-authored article published in *Academy of Management Executive* won the Best Journal Article in Corporate Entrepreneurship Award from the U.S. Association for Small Business & Entrepreneurship (USASBE). He is a Fellow of the Academy of Management. He served a three-year term as a Representative-at-Large member of the Academy of Management's Board of Governors. He is a Research Fellow in the National Entrepreneurship Consortium. He received the 1999 Award for Outstanding Intellectual Contributions to Competitiveness Research from the American Society for Competitiveness and the USASBE Scholar in Corporate Entrepreneurship Award (2004) from USASBE.

Robert E. Hoskisson

Robert E. Hoskisson is a Professor and W. P. Carey Chair in the Department of Management at Arizona State University. He received his Ph.D. from the University of California-Irvine. Professor Hoskisson's research topics focus on corporate governance, acquisitions and divestitures, corporate and international diversification, corporate entrepreneurship, privatization, and cooperative strategy. He teaches courses in corporate and international strategic management, cooperative strategy, and strategy consulting, among others. Professor Hoskisson's research has appeared in over 90 publications, including the *Academy of Management Journal, Academy of Management Review, Strategic Management Journal, Organization Science, Journal of Management, Journal of International Business Studies, Journal of Management Studies, Academy of Management Executive* and *California Management Review*. He is currently an Associate Editor of the *Strategic Management Journal* and a Consulting Editor for the *Journal of International Business Studies,* as well as serving on the Editorial Review board of the *Academy of Management Journal*. Professor Hoskisson has served on several editorial boards for such publications as the *Academy of Management Journal* (including

Consulting Editor and Guest Editor of a special issue), *Journal of Management* (including Associate Editor), *Organization Science, Journal of International Business Studies* (Consulting Editor), *Journal of Management Studies* (Guest Editor of a special issue) and *Entrepreneurship Theory and Practice*. He has co-authored several books including *Understanding Business Strategy* (South-Western/Thomson), *Competing for Advantage,* 2nd edition (South-Western College Publishing, 2008), and *Downscoping: How to Tame the Diversified Firm* (Oxford University Press).

He has an appointment as a Special Professor at the University of Nottingham and as an Honorary Professor at Xi'an Jiao Tong University. He is a Fellow of the Academy of Management and a charter member of the Academy of Management Journals Hall of Fame. He is also a Fellow of the Strategic Management Society. In 1998, he received an award for Outstanding Academic Contributions to Competitiveness, American Society for Competitiveness. He also received the William G. Dyer Distinguished Alumni Award given at the Marriott School of Management, Brigham Young University. He completed three years of service as a representative at large on the Board of Governors of the Academy of Management and currently is on the Board of Directors of the Strategic Management Society.

Part 1 Strategic Management Inputs

Strategic Management and Strategic Competitiveness

1

Studying this chapter should provide you with the strategic management knowledge needed to:

1. Define strategic competitiveness, strategy, competitive advantage, above-average returns, and the strategic management process.
2. Describe the competitive landscape and explain how globalization and technological changes shape it.
3. Use the industrial organization (I/O) model to explain how firms can earn above-average returns.
4. Use the resource-based model to explain how firms can earn above-average returns.
5. Describe vision and mission and discuss their value.
6. Define stakeholders and describe their ability to influence organizations.
7. Describe the work of strategic leaders.
8. Explain the strategic management process.

Boeing and Airbus: A Global Competitive Battle over Supremacy in Producing Commercial Aircraft

right: © AP Photo/Boeing, left: © AP Photo/Oliver Fantitsch

Boeing has historically been a global leader in manufacturing commercial airplanes. However, in 2001, Airbus had more orders than Boeing for the first time in their competitive history. But, in 2006, Boeing regained its supremacy with 1,044 versus 790 orders for commercial aircraft. The main turnaround in this battle for competitor orders has been most visible in the super jumbo category with Airbus's A-380 versus Boeing's 787.

Apparently in 1992, Boeing and Airbus's parent EADS agreed to a joint study on prospects for a super jumbo aircraft. The impetus for the study was the growing traffic in China and India. However, Airbus and Boeing reached different conclusions concerning the market trends, and the joint effort was disbanded.

Boeing's 787 Dreamliner design focused on long-range efficient flight, capable of transporting 250 passengers, whereas Airbus's strategy focused on long-haul flights with the A-380 offering 550-plus seats. In their diverging strategies, Airbus focused on flying to larger airports that use the hub-and-spoke system, whereas Boeing concentrated more on a point-to-point system in which smaller airports are more abundant. In reality, the Airbus A-380 aircraft, because of its size and weight, is currently able to land at approximately only 35 airports. The Boeing aircraft, on the other hand, can land at many more airports around the world and the number is growing in emerging economies, such as throughout Eastern Europe where smaller airports desire international connections.

Airbus won the competitor battle that occurred between 2001 and 2005 because it focused on the midsized market as well, using the A-320 strategy, which competes with Boeing's 737 and 757 aircraft. The A-320 was more efficient than the aircraft used by Boeing, and Boeing did not respond to customer demands to create new, efficient aircraft. In fact, it had slowed its innovation process in regard to new models. Besides the lack of new models, the commercial aircraft business was sluggish; new orders significantly ebbed due to the complications of the terrorist attacks and the subsequent recession. It was a bleak time for Boeing relative to Airbus.

More recently, Boeing's strategy in regard to overall design with the 787 Dreamliner is winning the day, as far as the order battle goes. It has also realized success by implementing a different strategy in regard to the production process. It has been able to speed up the process by creating an efficient global supply chain that involves many potential customers around the world, including Japan, China, and others. Moreover, Airbus is behind in its schedule to produce the A-380 and its midsized plane, the A-350, has also had redesign issues. The midsized A-350, comparable to the Boeing 787, is behind schedule and Airbus has had to provide significant incentive discounts to increase future orders.

Also, Airbus has been forced to produce more of its plane parts in European countries because governments have significant ownership and provide subsidies to Airbus. Accordingly, these governments—Spain, France, Germany, and the United Kingdom—want to maintain employment levels in these countries, and thus Airbus must continue to produce primarily in European countries. "Boeing outsources 85 percent of the work for its 787 'Dreamliner' aircraft. The corresponding figure for Airbus's A380 is 15 percent." As a result of the design and development delays, Airbus's development costs for the A-380 have risen to $14 billion versus the $8 billion invested by Boeing for the 787.

In making its decision to move ahead with the 787 Dreamliner versus a more jumbo aircraft comparable to the A-380, Boeing made a more concerted effort in connecting and getting input from its airline customers, as well as the ultimate customers, the passengers. Overwhelmingly the passengers in particular, and thereby the airlines, preferred smaller aircraft which would enable them to get to smaller airports quickly, without as many transfers on a point-to-point system. Additionally, Boeing followed up with the ultimate creditors, the leasing agents, and asked what they would prefer as far as risks were concerned. Again, the leasing agents preferred a smaller aircraft which would reduce their risks in financing versus the large super jumbo A-380. These business-level strategies have created an obvious advantage in the near-term for Boeing.

Interestingly, Boeing only receives 50 percent of its revenue from the commercial aircraft division as a result of its diversification strategy. The other 50 percent of its revenue comes from military contracts, as well as business from space satellite launching. Some crossover takes place in the technology used between military aircraft and commercial aircraft, which indirectly contributes to lower commercial aircraft development costs. This argument is used by Airbus when Boeing confronts it regarding the subsidies from local European governments. The ultimate battle will continue between these two firms, but currently Boeing has the winning edge and it looks like that will continue. Boeing's orders are now so plentiful, it will not be able to deliver all that are ordered in 2007 until the 2012–2013 range.

Sources: J. Bruner & G. Maidment, 2007, Breaking up Airbus, *Forbes*, http://www.forbes.com, March 20; N. Clark & L. Wayne, 2007, Airbus hopes its planes, not its setbacks, will stand out, *New York Times*, http://www.nytimes.com, June 18; G. Colvin, 2007, Boeing prepares for takeoff, *Fortune*, June 11, 133; C. Matlac & S. Holmes, 2007, Airbus revs up the engines, *BusinessWeek*, March 5, 41; D. Michaels, J. L. Lunsford, & M. Trottman, 2007, Airbus seals US Airways order in big boost for A350 jetliner, *Wall Street Journal Online*, http://www.wsj.com. June 18; D Michaels & J. L. Lunsford, 2007, Airbus faces wide game in A-350 orders, *Wall Street Journal*, June 13, A3; J. Newhouse, 2007, Boeing versus Airbus: The inside story of the greatest international competition in business, Toronto, Canada: Alfred A. Knoph; L. Wayne, 2007, A U.S. star turn for the jumbo of jets, *New York Times*, March 20, C1; D. Q. Wilber, 2007, Boeing's 2006 Jet orders surpass Airbus, *Washington Post*, January 18, D03; 2007, Boeing vs. Airbus: battle of the skies, *CNN*, http://www.cnn.com, May 7; D. Michaels, R. Stone, & J. L. Lunsford, 2006, Airbus superjumbo jet could be delayed further, *Wall Street Journal*, September 13, A3.

Strategic competitiveness is achieved when a firm successfully formulates and implements a value-creating strategy.

A **strategy** is an integrated and coordinated set of commitments and actions designed to exploit core competencies and gain a competitive advantage.

As we see from the Opening Case, Boeing began outperforming Airbus in 2006, whereas Airbus was winning the competitive battle between 2001 and 2006. The basic reasons for this turn of events is the strategic decisions both firms have made. Both firms analyzed their similar competitive environments and made decisions that fit with their view of the facts. We can be confident in believing that both firms want to be highly competitive (something we call a condition of *strategic competitiveness*) and want it to earn profits in the form of *above-average/returns.* Firms seek to accomplish these important outcomes when using the strategic management process (see Figure 1.1). The strategic management process is fully explained in this book. We introduce you to this process in the next few paragraphs.

Strategic competitiveness is achieved when a firm successfully formulates and implements a value-creating strategy. A **strategy** is an integrated and coordinated set of commitments and actions designed to exploit core competencies and gain a competitive advantage. When choosing a strategy, firms make choices among competing alternatives. In this sense, the chosen strategy indicates what the firm intends to do, as well as what it does not intend to do. As the opening case indicates, Airbus chose to focus on super jumbo jets (550-plus person capacity) as the preeminent strategy in betting on its future, while Boeing focused on medium capacity (250 people) but with longer range and better

Figure 1.1 The Strategic Management Process

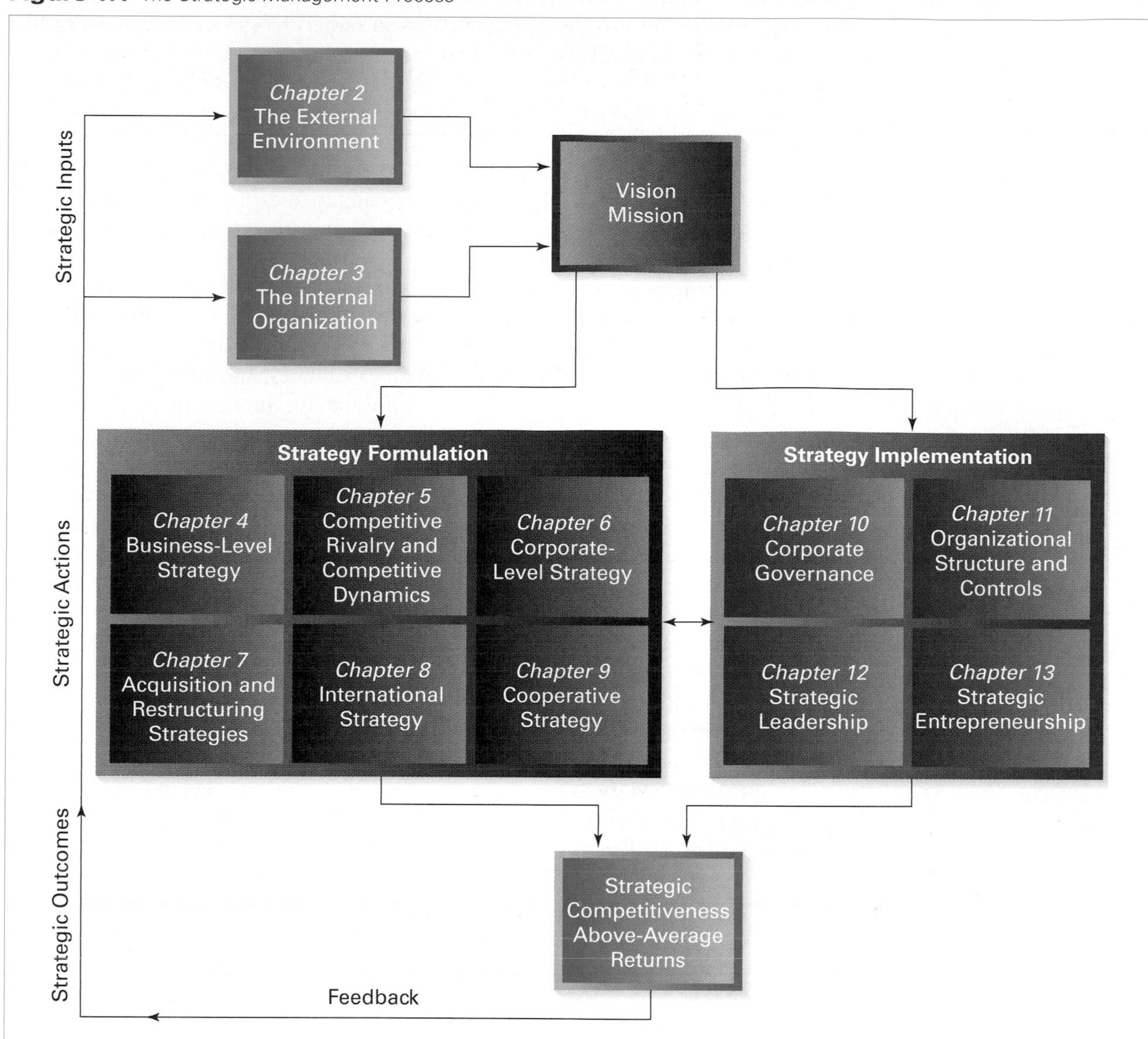

efficiency than current versions. While the battle continues, Boeing's decisions and associated strategy seem to be winning.

A firm has a **competitive advantage** when it implements a strategy competitors are unable to duplicate or find too costly to try to imitate.[1] An organization can be confident that its strategy has resulted in one or more useful competitive advantages only after competitors' efforts to duplicate its strategy have ceased or failed. In addition, firms must understand that no competitive advantage is permanent.[2] The speed with which competitors are able to acquire the skills needed to duplicate the benefits of a firm's value-creating strategy determines how long the competitive advantage will last.[3]

A firm has a **competitive advantage** when it implements a strategy competitors are unable to duplicate or find too costly to try to imitate.

Above-average returns are returns in excess of what an investor expects to earn from other investments with a similar amount of risk. **Risk** is an investor's uncertainty about the economic gains or losses that will result from a particular investment.[4] Returns are often measured in terms of accounting figures, such as return on assets, return on equity, or return on sales. Alternatively, returns can be measured on the basis of stock market returns, such as monthly returns (the end-of-the-period stock price minus the beginning stock price, divided by the beginning stock price, yielding a percentage return).

Above-average returns are returns in excess of what an investor expects to earn from other investments with a similar amount of risk.

Risk is an investor's uncertainty about the economic gains or losses that will result from a particular investment.

In smaller, new venture firms, performance is sometimes measured in terms of the amount and speed of growth (e.g., in annual sales) rather than more traditional profitability measures,[5] because new ventures require time to earn acceptable returns on investors' investments.[6] Understanding how to exploit a competitive advantage is important for firms that seek to earn above-average returns.[7] Firms without a competitive advantage or that are not competing in an attractive industry earn, at best, average returns. **Average returns** are returns equal to those an investor expects to earn from other investments with a similar amount of risk. In the long run, an inability to earn at least average returns results in failure. Failure occurs because investors withdraw their investments from those firms earning less-than-average returns.

Average returns are returns equal to those an investor expects to earn from other investments with a similar amount of risk.

The **strategic management process** is the full set of commitments, decisions, and actions required for a firm to achieve strategic competitiveness and earn above-average returns.

The **strategic management process** (see Figure 1.1) is the full set of commitments, decisions, and actions required for a firm to achieve strategic competitiveness and earn above-average returns. The firm's first step in the process is to analyze its external and internal environments to determine its resources, capabilities, and core competencies—the sources of its "strategic inputs." With this information, the firm develops its vision and mission and formulates its strategy. To implement this strategy, the firm takes actions toward achieving strategic competitiveness and above-average returns. Effective strategic actions that take place in the context of carefully integrated strategy formulation and implementation actions result in desired strategic outcomes. It is a dynamic process, as ever-changing markets and competitive structures are coordinated with a firm's continuously evolving strategic inputs.[8]

In the remaining chapters of this book, we use the strategic management process to explain what firms should do to achieve strategic competitiveness and earn above-average returns. These explanations demonstrate why some firms consistently achieve competitive success while others fail to do so.[9] As you will see, the reality of global competition is a critical part of the strategic management process and significantly influences firms' performances.[10] Indeed, learning how to successfully compete in the globalized world is one of the most significant challenges for firms competing in the current century.[11]

Several topics are discussed in this chapter. First, we describe the current competitive landscape. This challenging landscape is being created primarily by the emergence of a global economy, globalization resulting from that economy, and rapid technological changes. Next, we examine two models that firms use to gather the information and knowledge required to choose their strategies and decide how to implement them. The insights gained from these models also serve as the foundation for forming the firm's vision and mission. The first model (industrial organization, or I/O) suggests that the external environment is the primary determinant of a firm's strategic actions. The key to this model is identifying and competing successfully in an attractive (i.e., profitable) industry.[12] The second model (resource-based) suggests that a firm's unique resources and capabilities are the critical link to strategic competitiveness.[13] Thus, the first model is concerned with the firm's external environment while the second model focuses on the firm's internal environment. After discussing vision and mission, direction-setting statements that influence the choice and use of organizational strategies, we describe the stakeholders that organizations serve. The degree to which stakeholders' needs can be met directly increases when firms achieve strategic competitiveness and earn above-average returns. Closing the chapter are introductions to strategic leaders and the elements of the strategic management process.

The Competitive Landscape

The fundamental nature of competition in many of the world's industries is changing.[14] The pace of this change is relentless and is increasing. Even determining the boundaries of an industry has become challenging. Consider, for example, how advances in interactive computer networks and telecommunications have blurred the boundaries of the entertainment industry. Today, not only do cable companies and satellite networks compete for entertainment revenue from television, but also telecommunication companies are moving into the entertainment business through significant improvements in fiber-optic lines with speeds "up to 50 times faster" than traditional broadband cable and DSL download speeds.[15] Partnerships among firms in different segments of the entertainment industry further blur industry boundaries. For example, MSNBC is co-owned by NBC Universal (which itself is owned by General Electric) and Microsoft.[16] Many firms are looking for the most profitable and interesting way to deliver video on demand (VOD) online besides cable and satellite companies. Raketu, a voice over the Internet protocol (VoIP) phone service in the United Kingdom, is seeking to provide a social experience while watching the same entertainment on a VOD using a chat feature on its phone service.[17] As the strategic focus later in the chapter suggests, Apple iPod has the current lead in offering VOD content; but others such as Netflix are vying to compete in this space because it would mean the probable death of their online DVD rental service. Blockbuster and Amazon are among others seeking a piece of this competitive pie.[18]

Other characteristics of the current competitive landscape are noteworthy. Conventional sources of competitive advantage such as economies of scale and huge advertising budgets are not as effective as they once were. Moreover, the traditional managerial mind-set is unlikely to lead a firm to strategic competitiveness. Managers must adopt a new mind-set that values flexibility, speed, innovation, integration, and the challenges that evolve from constantly changing conditions. The conditions of the competitive landscape result in a perilous business world, one where the investments required to compete on a global scale are enormous and the consequences of failure are severe.[19] Developing and implementing strategy remains an important element of success in this environment. It allows for strategic actions to be planned and to emerge when the environmental conditions are appropriate. It also helps to coordinate the strategies developed by business units in which the responsibility to compete in specific markets is decentralized.[20]

Hypercompetition is a term often used to capture the realities of the competitive landscape. Under conditions of hypercompetition, assumptions of market stability are replaced by notions of inherent instability and change.[21] Hypercompetition results from the dynamics of strategic maneuvering among global and innovative combatants. It is a condition of rapidly escalating competition based on price-quality positioning, competition to create new know-how and establish first-mover advantage, and competition to protect or invade established product or geographic markets.[22] In a hypercompetitive market, firms often aggressively challenge their competitors in the hopes of improving their competitive position and ultimately their performance.[23]

Several factors create hypercompetitive environments and influence the nature of the current competitive landscape. The tw o primary drivers are the emergence of a global economy and technology, specifically rapid technological change.

Lenovo, a Chinese company, recently purchased the PC assets of IBM. While IBM once held a competitive advantage in the area of personal computers, no competitive advantage is permanent.

The Global Economy

A **global economy** is one in which goods, services, people, skills, and ideas move freely across geographic borders. Relatively unfettered by artificial constraints, such as tariffs, the global economy significantly expands and complicates a firm's competitive environment.[24]

A **global economy** is one in which goods, services, people, skills, and ideas move freely across geographic borders.

Interesting opportunities and challenges are associated with the emergence of the global economy.[25] For example, Europe, instead of the United States, is now the world's largest single market, with 700 million potential customers. The European Union and the other Western European countries also have a gross domestic product that is more than

35 percent higher than the GDP of the United States.[26] "In the past, China was generally seen as a low-competition market and a low-cost land. Today, China is an extremely competitive market in which local market-seeking MNCs [multinational corporations] must fiercely compete against other MNCs and against those local companies that are more cost effective and faster in product development. While it is true that China has been viewed as a country from which to source low-cost goods, lately, many MNCs, such as P&G [Proctor and Gamble], are actually net exporters of local management talent; they have been dispatching more Chinese abroad than bringing foreign expatriates to China."[27] India, the world's largest democracy, has an economy that also is growing rapidly and now ranks as the world's fourth largest.[28] Many large multinational companies are also emerging as significant global competitors from these emerging economies.[29]

The statistics detailing the nature of the global economy reflect the realities of a hypercompetitive business environment, and challenge individual firms to think seriously about the markets in which they will compete. Consider the case of General Electric (GE). Although headquartered in the United States, GE expects that as much as 60 percent of its revenue growth between 2005 and 2015 will be generated by competing in rapidly developing economies (e.g., China and India). The decision to count on revenue growth in developing countries instead of in developed countries such as the United States and European nations, seems quite reasonable in the global economy. In fact, according to an analyst, what GE is doing is not by choice but by necessity: "Developing countries are where the fastest growth is occurring and more sustainable growth."[30] Based on its analyses of world markets and their potential, GE estimates that by 2024, China will be the world's largest consumer of electricity and will be the world's largest consumer and consumer-finance market (business areas in which GE competes). GE is making strategic decisions today, such as investing significantly in China and India, in order to improve its competitive position in what the firm believes are becoming vital sources of revenue and profitability.

The March of Globalization

Globalization is the increasing economic interdependence among countries and their organizations as reflected in the flow of goods and services, financial capital, and knowledge across country borders.[31] Globalization is a product of a large number of firms competing against one another in an increasing number of global economies.

In globalized markets and industries, financial capital might be obtained in one national market and used to buy raw materials in another one. Manufacturing equipment bought from a third national market can then be used to produce products that are sold in yet a fourth market. Thus, globalization increases the range of opportunities for companies competing in the current competitive landscape.[32]

The globalization of business has led Wal-Mart to open stores all over the world.

Wal-Mart, for instance, is trying to achieve boundary-less retailing with global pricing, sourcing, and logistics. Through boundary-less retailing, the firm seeks to make the movement of goods and the use of pricing strategies as seamless among all of its international operations as has historically been the case among its domestic stores. The firm is pursuing this type of retailing on an evolutionary basis. For example, most of Wal-Mart's original international investments were in Canada and Mexico, because it was easier for the firm to rehearse or apply its global practices in countries that are geographically close to its home base, the United States. Based on what it has learned, the firm has now expanded into Europe, South America, and Asia. In 2007, Wal-Mart was the world's largest retailer (with 3,443 units in and 2,760 units outside of the United States). Globalization makes it increasingly difficult to think of firms headquartered in various economies throughout the world as domestic-only companies. Consider the following facts about two U.S.-based organizations: On an annual basis, Wal-Mart continues to increase the percent of its total revenue that is coming from its international operations. GE expects more than 60 percent of its growth in sales revenue in the foreseeable future to come from operations in emerging markets. The challenge to companies experiencing globalization to the degree of these three firms is to understand the need for culturally sensitive decisions when using the strategic management process, and to anticipate ever-increasing complexity in their operations as goods, services, people, and so forth move freely across geographic borders and throughout different economic markets.

Globalization also affects the design, production, distribution, and servicing of goods and services. In many instances, for example, globalization results in higher-quality goods and services. Global competitor Toyota Motor Company provides an example of how this happens. Because Toyota initially emphasized product reliability and superior customer service, the company's products are in high demand across the globe. Because of the demand for its products, Toyota's competitive actions have forced its global competitors to make reliability and service improvements in their operations. Toyota has done this also by building plants in foreign markets in the United States, Brazil, and Mexico, while maintaining quality.[33] Indeed, almost any car or truck purchased today from virtually any manufacturer is of higher quality and is supported by better service than was the case before Toyota began successfully competing throughout the global economy. In particular, Ford, GM, and Chrysler are "trying to hammer home the message that consumers' perception of Detroit-built vehicles as bland and unreliable has not kept pace with significant improvements in recent years."[34]

Overall, it is important for firms to understand that globalization has led to higher levels of performance standards in many competitive dimensions, including those of quality, cost, productivity, product introduction time, and operational efficiency. In addition to firms competing in the global economy, these standards affect firms competing on a domestic-only basis. The reason is that customers will purchase from a global competitor rather than a domestic firm when the global company's good or service is superior. Because workers now flow rather freely among global economies, and because employees are a key source of competitive advantage, firms must understand that increasingly, "the best people will come from . . . anywhere."[35] Overall, firms must learn how to deal with the reality that in the competitive landscape of the twenty-first century, only companies capable of meeting, if not exceeding, global standards typically have the capability to earn above-average returns.[36]

As we have explained, globalization creates opportunities (such as those being pursued by Toyota and Wal-Mart, among many other firms). However, globalization is not risk free. Collectively, the risks of participating outside of a firm's domestic country in the global economy are labeled a "liability of foreignness."[37]

One risk of entering the global market is the amount of time typically required for firms to learn how to compete in markets that are new to them. A firm's performance can suffer until this knowledge is either developed locally or transferred from the home market to the newly established global location.[38] Additionally, a firm's performance may suffer with substantial amounts of globalization. In this instance, firms may overdiversify internationally beyond their ability to manage these extended operations.[39] The result of overdiversification can have strong negative effects on a firm's overall performance.[40]

Thus, entry into international markets, even for firms with substantial experience in the global economy, such as Toyota and GE, requires proper use of the strategic management process. It is also important to note that even though global markets are an attractive strategic option for some companies, they are not the only source of strategic competitiveness. In fact, for most companies, even for those capable of competing successfully in global markets, it is critical to remain committed to and strategically competitive in the both domestic and international markets through staying attuned to technological opportunities and potential competitive disruptions due to innovation.[41]

Technology and Technological Changes

Trends and conditions can be placed into three categories: technology diffusion and disruptive technologies, the information age, and increasing knowledge intensity. Through these categories, technology is significantly altering the nature of competition and contributing to unstable competitive environments as a result of doing so.

Technology Diffusion and Disruptive Technologies

The rate of technology diffusion—the speed at which new technologies become available and are used—has increased substantially over the past 15 to 20 years. Consider the following rates of technology diffusion:

It took the telephone 35 years to get into 25 percent of all homes in the United States. It took TV 26 years. It took radio 22 years. It took PCs 16 years. It took the Internet 7 years.[42]

Perpetual innovation is a term used to describe how rapidly and consistently new, information-intensive technologies replace older ones. The shorter product life cycles resulting from these rapid diffusions of new technologies place a competitive premium on being able to quickly introduce new, innovative goods and services into the marketplace.[43] For example, "In the computer industry during the early 1980s, hard disk drives would typically ship for four to six years, after which a new and better product became available. By the late 1980s, the expected shipping life had fallen to two to three years. By the 1990s, it was just six to nine months."[44]

In fact, when products become somewhat indistinguishable because of the widespread and rapid diffusion of technologies, speed to market with innovative products may be the primary source of competitive advantage (see Chapter 5).[45] Indeed, some argue that increasingly, the global economy is driven by or revolves around constant innovations. Not surprisingly, such innovations must be derived from an understanding of global standards and global expectations in terms of product functionality.[46]

Another indicator of rapid technology diffusion is that it now may take only 12 to 18 months for firms to gather information about their competitors' research and development and product decisions.[47] In the global economy, competitors can sometimes imitate a firm's successful competitive actions within a few days. Once a source of competitive advantage, the protection firms previously possessed through their patents has been stifled by the current rate of technological diffusion. Today, patents may be an effective way of protecting proprietary technology in a small number of industries such as pharmaceuticals. Indeed, many firms competing in the electronics industry often do not apply for patents to prevent competitors from gaining access to the technological knowledge included in the patent application.

Disruptive technologies—technologies that destroy the value of an existing technology and create new markets[48]—surface frequently in today's competitive markets. Think of the new markets created by the technologies underlying the development of products such as iPods, PDAs, WiFi, and the browser.[49] These types of products are thought by some to represent radical or breakthrough innovations.[50] (We talk more about radical innovations in Chapter 13.) A disruptive or radical technology can create what is essentially a new industry or can harm industry incumbents. Some incumbents, though, are able to adapt based on their superior resources, experience, and ability to gain access to the new technology through multiple sources (e.g., alliances, acquisitions, and ongoing internal research).[51] When a disruptive technology creates a new industry, competitors follow. As explained in the Strategic Focus, Apple has sought to create disruptive trends in the industry through its new products strategy.

In addition to making innovative use of new product designs, Steve Jobs, CEO of Apple, developed a great sense of timing that has allowed for great marketing of its innovative designs. As such, Apple shows a strong competency in studying information about its customers as well as potential consumers of the new product. These efforts result in opportunities to understand individual customers' needs and then target goods and services to satisfy those needs. Clearly, Apple understands the importance of information

Strategic Focus Strategic Focus Strategic Focus

Apple: Using Innovation to Create Technology Trends and Maintain Competitive Advantage

In partnership with *BusinessWeek*, the Boston Consulting Group conducts an annual survey of top executives of the "1,500 largest global corporations." In May of 2007 as a result of this survey, Apple was named by *BusinessWeek* as the most innovative company—for the third year in a row.

Apple started its regeneration in 2001 with its unveiling of the iPod, a portable digital music device; and then followed up with its complementary iTunes online music store, a service for downloading songs and other digital music and video clips. Even before iPod and iTunes, Apple had a strong foundation of innovation. Apple intends to continue its success in the future with the iPhone and Apple TV devices. Not only has it done well in producing simply designed products, such as the iPod and its other recent devices, but it also excels in marketing its aesthetic or elegant designs, which seem to please the customer and create a "market buzz" for Apple products.

Apple uses innovative product design and ease of use for its products as a competitive advantage.

While Apple focused on new product innovation, many other firms in the industry focused on cost control. Dell was successful with this strategy by being first to offer direct PC purchasing over the Internet. Through its efficient supply chain operations, Dell was able to manage powerful supplier firms such as Microsoft and Intel. However, more recently because of Apple's prowess in technology design and marketing, as well as excellent timing, it seems to surpass most other consumer electronics companies, including Dell and other traditionally strong manufacturers such as Sony.

Even at its stores, Apple has outpaced Sony and others who have failed, such as Gateway, and has forced Dell to enter into a recent alliance with Wal-Mart in order to have direct retail sales. Although HP has been able to manage the retail and direct sales approach, and has gained a lead over Dell in regard to PCs, it does not seem to have the same elegance and appeal for its products as Apple does.

In 2007, with more than 100 million products sold, the closest competitor to Apple's iPod has only 8 percent of the market share, leaving Apple with the vast majority. Although others are seeking to simply duplicate the complementary and innovative relationships between iPod and iTunes, Apple continues to innovate with products such as the iPhone and Apple TV. Apple's focus on innovation has helped it maintain a competitive advantage and marketing prowess over other industry players, who have historically been much stronger than Apple.

Apple seeks to "change the way people behave" versus just competing in the marketplace for traditional products. In doing so, it has been able to establish first mover advantages through radical concepts using elegant design, and relatively perfect market timing recently to establish its advantage. Others seem to compete in commodity businesses with incremental innovations, while Apple creates a new concept in the consumer's mind. It is most likely for this reason that other executives see Apple as a strong innovator in consumer electronics.

Sources: D. C. Chmielewski & M. Quinn, 2007, Movie studios fear the sequel to iPod: They see risk that new Apple TV signals effort to control distribution, *Los Angeles Times*, June 11, C1; J. McGregor, 2007, The world's most innovative companies: The leaders in nurturing cultures of creativity, *BusinessWeek*, http://www.businessweek.com, May 4; B. Schlender, 2007, The trouble with Apple TV, *Fortune*, June 11, 56; R. Stross, 2007, Apple's lesson for Sony's stores: Just connect, *New York Times*, http://www.nytimes.com, May 27; N. Wingfield, 2007, A new wireless player hopes to challenge iPod, *Wall Street Journal*, April 9, B1; 2007, Apple's "magical" iPhone unveiled, *BBC*, http://www.bbc.co.uk, January 9; R. Furchgott, 2006, Cell phones for the music fan, *The New York Times*, http://www.nytimes.com, December 28.

and knowledge (topics we discuss next) as competitive weapons for use in the current competitive landscape.

The Information Age

Dramatic changes in information technology occurred in recent years. Personal computers, cellular phones, artificial intelligence, virtual reality, and massive databases (e.g., LexisNexis) are a few examples of how information is used differently as a result of technological developments. An important outcome of these changes is that the ability to effectively and efficiently access and use information has become an important source of competitive advantage in virtually all industries. Information technology advances have given small firms more flexibility in competing with large firms, if that technology can be used with efficiency.[52]

Both the pace of change in information technology and its diffusion will continue to increase. For instance, the number of personal computers in use in the United States is expected to reach 278 million by 2010. The declining costs of information technologies and the increased accessibility to them are also evident in the current competitive landscape. The global proliferation of relatively inexpensive computing power and its linkage on a global scale via computer networks combine to increase the speed and diffusion of information technologies. Thus, the competitive potential of information technologies is now available to companies of all sizes throughout the world, not only to large firms in Europe, Japan, and North America.

The Internet is another technological innovation contributing to hypercompetition. Available to an increasing number of people throughout the world, the Internet provides an infrastructure that allows the delivery of information to computers in any location. Virtually all retailers, such as Abercrombie & Fitch, The Gap, and Benetton, use the Internet to provide abundant shopping privileges to customers in multiple locations. However, access to the Internet on smaller devices such as cell phones is having an ever-growing impact on competition in a number of industries. For example, Internet radio is projected to compete with satellite radio firms SIRIUS and XM, as small receiver devices are developed to receive radio transmissions over the Internet but on devices other than the personal computer. SanDisk's new Sansa Connect digital music player allows users to listen to online radio stations from Yahoo! Inc. when within range of WiFi connections.[53]

Increasing Knowledge Intensity

Knowledge (information, intelligence, and expertise) is the basis of technology and its application. In the competitive landscape of the twenty-first century, knowledge is a critical organizational resource and an increasingly valuable source of competitive advantage.[54] Indeed, starting in the 1980s, the basis of competition shifted from hard assets to intangible resources. For example, "Wal-Mart transformed retailing through its proprietary approach to supply chain management and its information-rich relationships with customers and suppliers."[55] Relationships, for instance with suppliers, are an example of an intangible resource.

Knowledge is gained through experience, observation, and inference and is an intangible resource (tangible and intangible resources are fully described in Chapter 3). The value of intangible resources, including knowledge, is growing as a proportion of total shareholder value.[56] The probability of achieving strategic competitiveness in the competitive landscape is enhanced for the firm that realizes that its survival depends on the ability to capture intelligence, transform it into usable knowledge, and diffuse it rapidly throughout the company.[57] Therefore, firms must develop (e.g., through training programs) and acquire (e.g., by hiring educated and experienced employees) knowledge, integrate it into the organization to create capabilities, and then apply it to gain a competitive advantage.[58] In addition, firms must build routines that facilitate the diffusion of local knowledge throughout the organization for use everywhere that it has value.[59] Firms are better able to do these things when they have strategic flexibility.

Strategic flexibility is a set of capabilities used to respond to various demands and opportunities existing in a dynamic and uncertain competitive environment.

Strategic flexibility is a set of capabilities used to respond to various demands and opportunities existing in a dynamic and uncertain competitive environment. Thus, strategic flexibility involves coping with uncertainty and its accompanying risks.[60] Firms should try to develop strategic flexibility in all areas of their operations. However, those working within firms to develop strategic flexibility should understand that the task is not an easy one, largely because of inertia that can build up over time. A firm's focus and past core competencies may actually slow change and strategic flexibility.[61]

To be strategically flexible on a continuing basis and to gain the competitive benefits of such flexibility, a firm has to develop the capacity to learn. In the words of John Browne, CEO of British Petroleum: "In order to generate extraordinary value for shareholders, a company has to learn better than its competitors and apply that knowledge throughout its businesses faster and more widely than they do."[62] Continuous learning provides the firm with new and up-to-date sets of skills, which allow it to adapt to its environment as it encounters changes.[63] Firms capable of rapidly and broadly applying what they have learned exhibit the strategic flexibility and the capacity to change in ways that will increase the probability of successfully dealing with uncertain, hypercompetitive environments. Often having a strong ability to manage information systems is associated with better strategic flexibility[64] because such systems create an advantage over competitors, as is illustrated in the Strategic Focus on Netflix.

The I/O Model of Above-Average Returns

From the 1960s through the 1980s, the external environment was thought to be the primary determinant of strategies that firms selected to be successful.[65] The industrial organization (I/O) model of above-average returns explains the external environment's dominant influence on a firm's strategic actions. The model specifies that the industry in which a company chooses to compete has a stronger influence on performance than do the choices managers make inside their organizations.[66] The firm's performance is believed to be determined primarily by a range of industry properties, including economies of scale, barriers to market entry, diversification, product differentiation, and the degree of concentration of firms in the industry.[67] These industry characteristics are examined in Chapter 2.

Grounded in economics, the I/O model has four underlying assumptions. First, the external environment is assumed to impose pressures and constraints that determine the strategies that would result in above-average returns. Second, most firms competing within an industry or within a certain segment of that industry are assumed to control similar strategically relevant resources and to pursue similar strategies in light of those resources. Third, resources used to implement strategies are assumed to be highly mobile across firms, so any resource differences that might develop between firms will be short-lived. Fourth, organizational decision makers are assumed to be rational and committed to acting in the firm's best interests, as shown by their profit-maximizing behaviors.[68] The I/O model challenges firms to locate the most attractive industry in which to compete. Because most firms are assumed to have similar valuable resources that are mobile across companies, their performance generally can be increased only when they operate in the industry with the highest profit potential and learn how to use their resources to implement the strategy required by the industry's structural characteristics.[69]

The five forces model of competition is an analytical tool used to help firms with this task. The model (explained in Chapter 2) encompasses several variables and tries to capture the complexity of competition. The five forces model suggests that an industry's profitability (i.e., its rate of return on invested capital relative to its cost of capital) is a function of interactions among five forces: suppliers, buyers, competitive rivalry among firms currently in the industry, product substitutes, and potential entrants to the industry.[70] The Strategic Focus on Netflix provides an illustration of how some of these threats have affected competition in the online DVD (movie) rental business with many new entrants, powerful suppliers (movie makers), substitute products (e.g., video on demand [VOD]), and intense rivalry.

Strategic Focus Strategic Focus Strategic Focus

Netflix Confronts a Turbulent Competitive Environment

Founded by CEO Reed Hastings in 1998, Netflix revolutionized the movie rental business through its online service. In its brief history, Netflix has gained close to 7 million subscribers with a library of more than 80,000 movies, television, and other entertainment shows available on DVD. Hastings indicated in a recent interview that his only regret was that he went public too soon and, therefore, revealed to competitors that the online model used by Netflix was profitable.

Reed Hastings, founder of Netflix, used an information technology innovation to start his company. Now that Netflix operates in a very competitive environment, its commitment to technological innovation and tracking customer preferences allows it to remain competitive.

This move, from his point of view, made Blockbuster aware of the threat that the online rental business presented relative to its brick-and-mortar business. Subsequently in 2004, Blockbuster entered into the online rental business through its introduction of Blockbuster Online. In late 2006, Blockbuster renamed its service Blockbuster Total Access and gave its customers the option of returning videos through the mail or dropping them off at the local Blockbuster store. In mid 2007, Blockbuster introduced a new plan named "Blockbuster by Mail." With this mail-only option, the rates start as low $4.99, and three-at-a-time limited rental plans cost $16.99 per month. These packages undercut Netflix's comparable plans by $1. Interestingly, Blockbuster introduced these plans even as it continued to lose money on its Total Access plan. Although Netflix cut its fee for its one-movie-at-home-at-a-time plan by $1 to $4.99 in January 2007 to counter the initial introduction of Total Access, Netflix does not have free in-store video exchange, and subscribers cannot return online rentals by dropping them off at a store. Netflix customers have to wait for Netflix to receive the movie in the mail before the next DVD shipment is initiated. Accordingly, customers can save time by utilizing Blockbuster's service.

A number of other small and large competitors such as Amazon.com are in the online rental service, in addition to Blockbuster and other brick-and-mortar stores. However, thwarting competitors is not the only threat on the horizon for Netflix. Netflix's current service is based on DVD rental and shipping. The biggest threat on the horizon is Video on Demand (VOD). In this market, a number of competitors are racing to be the dominant player to deliver videos directly to the computer, or ultimately the television. In August of 2007, Blockbuster completed an acquisition of Movielink, LLC, which provides streaming video over the Internet and has access to large movie producers' content, in an effort to capture some of the VOD market. Of course, this service has been available from cable and satellite companies but not over the Internet. Among others, Apple, Amazon.com, CinemaNow, Wal-Mart, and Hewlett-Packard are seeking to establish a download business in this market. In 2007, Apple's iTunes accounted for about "76 percent of the market" of the current available video content, albeit small at this point. Also, Apple TV—a device that gets movies from the Internet to the television and works primarily with video purchased through Apple's iTunes store—could potentially increase iTunes lead. Although the market is relatively small, it has the potential to be a $35 billion market as more content is digitized. Besides the significant number of potential strong competitors seeking VOD, Netflix must also deal with powerful suppliers in the movie industry.

Because many of the traditional movie industry players, such as Warner Brothers and Disney, experienced a loss of a significant amount of revenues and other difficult circumstances in regard to online audio piracy, as they work to digitize the content in their vast vaults of movies and television they want to make sure that they can take advantage of this potential with as little piracy as possible. Accordingly, they are cautious with whom they will contract for selling their digitized content. Coming up with the right solution to use these digitized videos will be a key issue in getting contracts with the movie industry. For instance, one Wall Street analyst observed that these suppliers fear Apple "will come to dominate online distribution of movies as it now controls more than 70 percent of the digital-music market in the United States."

Reed Hastings recognizes that VOD will ultimately create a total substitute for current Netflix video rental service. Whether this transition happens right away, within the next 2–3 years, or in 5–10 years will determine whether Netflix's current business model will continue to be successful. Although Netflix has a significant amount of turbulence in its environment, it also has some strong, well-developed competencies that allowed it to be successful thus far. These competencies include a cost structure that helped it make money relative to its brick-and-mortar competitors, a well-developed technology base, and an internal infrastructure for creating new technology with which it can develop its supply chain, for distributing DVDs, and manage customer satisfaction in a way that creates customer loyalty. Netflix hopes to be able to use this customer loyalty and technological base to launch a successful service in the VOD market as movie producers digitize their content.

Sources: 2007, Blockbuster acquires Movielink, *New York Times*, http://www.nyt, August 8; M. Boyle, 2007, Reed Hastings, *Fortune*, May 28, 30–32; T. Calburn & A. Gonsalves, 2007, Big dreams for online video rentals, *Information Week*, January 22, 22; J. Fortt, 2007, HP reels in Hollywood, *Business 2.0*, May, 42; P. Gogoi, 2007, Wal-Mart enters the movie download wars, *BusinessWeek*, http://www.businessweek.com, February 6; M. Kirdahy, 2007, Blockbuster takes on Netflix, *Forbes*, http://www.forbes.com, January 3; A. Pruitt, 2007, Blockbuster's online plan undercuts Netflix's rates, *Wall Street Journal*, June 13, B4; J. Rose, 2007, Amazon, Netflix volume rise on takeover rumor, *Wall Street Journal*, June 7, C4; J Schuman, 2007, The morning brief: Apple rental ambitions target pay-per-view; *Wall Street Journal Online*, http://www.wsj.com, June 11; N. Wingfield, 2007, Boss Talk: Netflix versus naysayers: CEO Hastings keeps growth strong: Plans for the future after the death of DVDs, *Wall Street Journal*, March 28, B1; 2006, What's next for Netflix, *Financial Times*, http://www.ft.com, November 2.

Firms can use this tool to understand an industry's profit potential and the strategy necessary to establish a defensible competitive position, given the industry's structural characteristics.[71] Typically, the model suggests that firms can earn above-average returns by manufacturing standardized products, or producing standardized services at costs below those of competitors (a cost leadership strategy), or by manufacturing differentiated products for which customers are willing to pay a price premium (a differentiation strategy). (The cost leadership and product differentiation strategies are fully described in Chapter 4.) Although Netflix is in a rather unattractive industry, given the industry forces that threaten its dominant business, the cost leadership strategy has helped to sustain Netflix performance in the face of these threats.

As shown in Figure 1.2, the I/O model suggests that above-average returns are earned when firms implement the strategy dictated by the characteristics of the general, industry, and competitor environments (environments that are discussed in Chapter 2). Companies that develop or acquire the internal skills needed to implement strategies required by the external environment are likely to succeed, while those that do not are likely to fail. Hence, this model suggests that returns are determined primarily by external characteristics rather than by the firm's unique internal resources and capabilities.

Research findings support the I/O model, in that approximately 20 percent of a firm's profitability can be explained by the industry in which it chooses to compete. This research also shows, however, that 36 percent of the variance in profitability could be attributed to the firm's characteristics and actions.[72] These findings suggest that both the environment and the firm's characteristics play a role in determining the firm's specific level of profitability. Thus, a reciprocal relationship is likely between the environment and the firm's strategy, thereby affecting the firm's performance.[73]

Figure 1.2 The I/O Model of Above-Average Returns

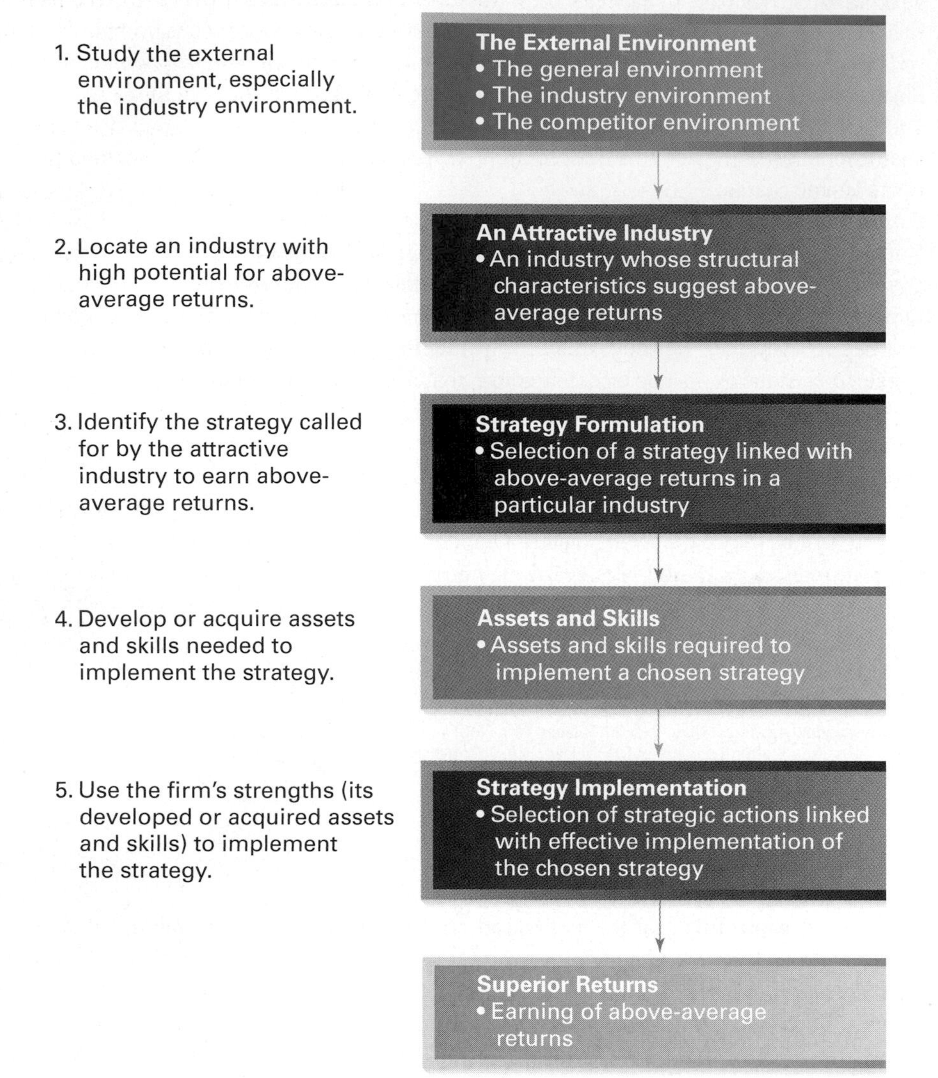

1. Study the external environment, especially the industry environment.
The External Environment
• The general environment
• The industry environment
• The competitor environment
2. Locate an industry with high potential for above-average returns.
An Attractive Industry
• An industry whose structural characteristics suggest above-average returns
3. Identify the strategy called for by the attractive industry to earn above-average returns.
Strategy Formulation
• Selection of a strategy linked with above-average returns in a particular industry
4. Develop or acquire assets and skills needed to implement the strategy.
Assets and Skills
• Assets and skills required to implement a chosen strategy
5. Use the firm's strengths (its developed or acquired assets and skills) to implement the strategy.
Strategy Implementation
• Selection of strategic actions linked with effective implementation of the chosen strategy
Superior Returns
• Earning of above-average returns

As you can see, the I/O model considers a firm's strategy to be a set of commitments, actions, and decisions that are formed in response to the characteristics of the industry in which the firm has decided to compete. The resource-based model, discussed next, takes a different view of the major influences on strategy formulation and implementation.

The Resource-Based Model of Above-Average Returns

Resources are inputs into a firm's production process, such as capital equipment, the skills of individual employees, patents, finances, and talented managers.

A **capability** is the capacity for a set of resources to perform a task or an activity in an integrative manner.

The resource-based model assumes that each organization is a collection of unique resources and capabilities. The *uniqueness* of its resources and capabilities is the basis for a firm's strategy and its ability to earn above-average returns.[74]

Resources are inputs into a firm's production process, such as capital equipment, the skills of individual employees, patents, finances, and talented managers. In general, a firm's resources are classified into three categories: physical, human, and organizational capital. Described fully in Chapter 3, resources are either tangible or intangible in nature.

Individual resources alone may not yield a competitive advantage.[75] In fact, resources have a greater likelihood of being a source of competitive advantage when they are formed into a capability. A **capability** is the capacity for a set of resources to perform a task or an activity in an integrative manner. Capabilities evolve over time and must be managed dynamically in pursuit of above-average returns.[76] **Core competencies** are resources and capabilities that serve as a source of competitive advantage for a firm over its rivals. Core competencies are often visible in the form of organizational functions. For example, the preceding Strategic Focus suggests that even though Netflix operates in a turbulent competitive environment, its strong capabilities in technology and tracking customer preferences for movies allow it to remain competitive, while others such as Blockbuster continue to lose money in the online movie rental business—even though they are gaining market share.

Core competencies are capabilities that serve as a source of competitive advantage for a firm over its rivals.

According to the resource-based model, differences in firms' performances across time are due primarily to their unique resources and capabilities rather than to the industry's structural characteristics. This model also assumes that firms acquire different resources and develop unique capabilities based on how they combine and use the resources; that resources and certainly capabilities are not highly mobile across firms; and that the differences in resources and capabilities are the basis of competitive advantage.[77] Through continued use, capabilities become stronger and more difficult for competitors to understand and imitate. As a source of competitive advantage, a capability "should be neither so simple that it is highly imitable, nor so complex that it defies internal steering and control."[78]

The resource-based model of superior returns is shown in Figure 1.3. As you will see, the resource-based model suggests that the strategy the firm chooses should allow it to

Figure 1.3 The Resource-Based Model of Above-Average Returns

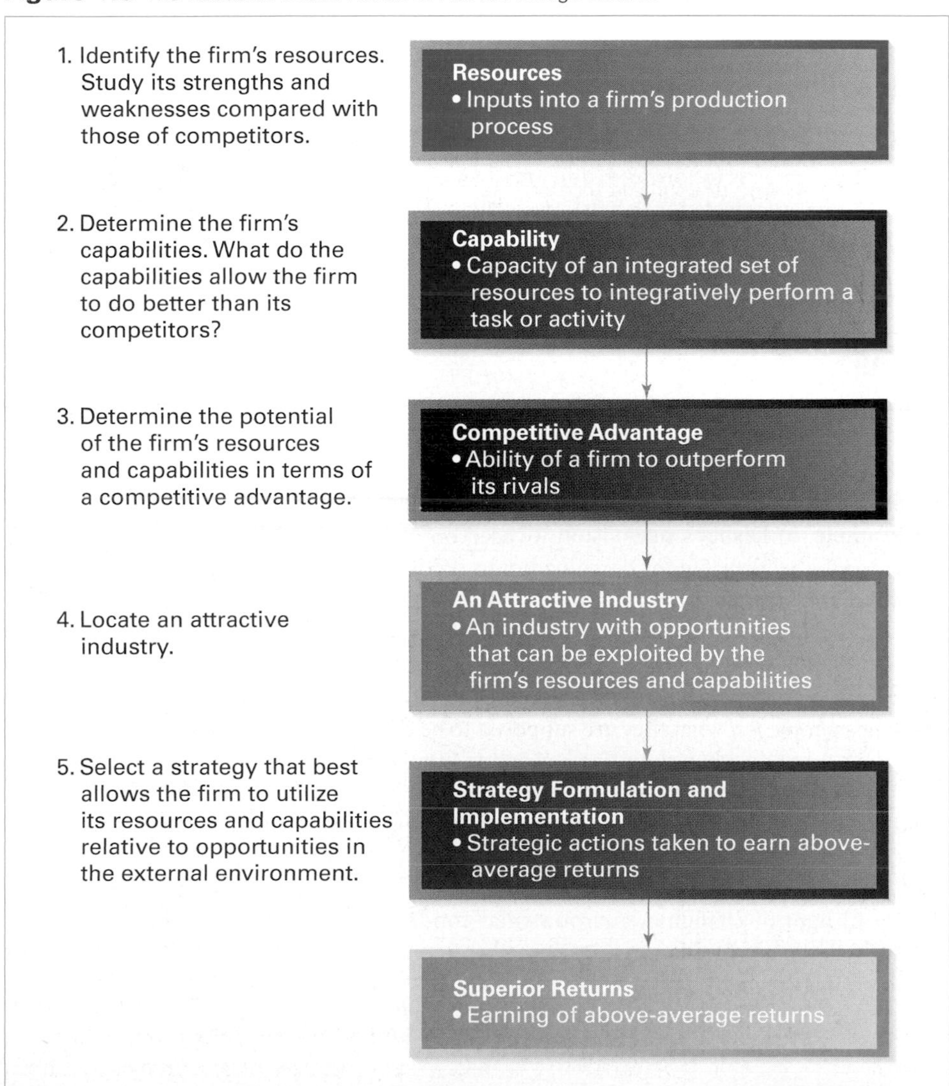
1. Identify the firm's resources. Study its strengths and weaknesses compared with those of competitors.
Resources
• Inputs into a firm's production process
2. Determine the firm's capabilities. What do the capabilities allow the firm to do better than its competitors?
Capability
• Capacity of an integrated set of resources to integratively perform a task or activity
3. Determine the potential of the firm's resources and capabilities in terms of a competitive advantage.
Competitive Advantage
• Ability of a firm to outperform its rivals
4. Locate an attractive industry.
An Attractive Industry
• An industry with opportunities that can be exploited by the firm's resources and capabilities
5. Select a strategy that best allows the firm to utilize its resources and capabilities relative to opportunities in the external environment.
Strategy Formulation and Implementation
• Strategic actions taken to earn above-average returns
Superior Returns
• Earning of above-average returns

use its competitive advantages in an attractive industry (the I/O model is used to identify an attractive industry).

Not all of a firm's resources and capabilities have the potential to be the basis for competitive advantage. This potential is realized when resources and capabilities are valuable, rare, costly to imitate, and nonsubstitutable.[79] Resources are *valuable* when they allow a firm to take advantage of opportunities or neutralize threats in its external environment. They are *rare* when possessed by few, if any, current and potential competitors. Resources are *costly to imitate* when other firms either cannot obtain them or are at a cost disadvantage in obtaining them compared with the firm that already possesses them. And they are *nonsubstitutable* when they have no structural equivalents. Many resources can either be imitated or substituted over time. Therefore, it is difficult to achieve and sustain a competitive advantage based on resources alone.[80] When these four criteria are met, however, resources and capabilities become core competencies.

As noted previously, research shows that both the industry environment and a firm's internal assets affect that firm's performance over time.[81] Thus, to form a vision and mission, and subsequently to select one or more strategies and to determine how to implement them, firms use both the I/O and the resource-based models.[82] In fact, these models complement each other in that one (I/O) focuses outside the firm while the other (resource-based) focuses inside the firm. Next, we discuss the forming of the firm's vision and mission—actions taken after the firm understands the realities of its external (Chapter 2) and internal (Chapter 3) environments.

Vision and Mission

After studying the external environment and the internal environment, the firm has the information it needs to form a vision and a mission (see Figure 1.1). Stakeholders (those who affect or are affected by a firm's performance, as discussed later in the chapter) learn a great deal about a firm by studying its vision and mission. Indeed, a key purpose of vision and mission statements is to inform stakeholders of what the firm is, what it seeks to accomplish, and who it seeks to serve.

Vision

Vision is a picture of what the firm wants to be and, in broad terms, what it wants to ultimately achieve.

Vision is a picture of what the firm wants to be and, in broad terms, what it wants to ultimately achieve.[83] Thus, a vision statement articulates the ideal description of an organization and gives shape to its intended future. In other words, a vision statement points the firm in the direction of where it would eventually like to be in the years to come.[84] For example, in Disney's new vision focused on multimedia, hit movies and associated music would be available for download onto iPods. Cell phones would be provided with ringtones from movie lines or tunes. Online video on Disney.com would include cast interviews and interpretation of scenes. Portable multimedia players would have games developed to let fans, for instance, outwit a crew of rogues from a familiar seen of *Pirates of the Caribbean* to find buried treasure.[85] Vision is "big picture" thinking with passion that helps people *feel* what they are supposed to be doing in the organization.[86] People feel what they are to do when their firm's vision is simple, positive, and emotional, but a good vision stretches and challenges people as well.

It is also important to note that vision statements reflect a firm's values and aspirations and are intended to capture the heart and mind of each employee and, hopefully, many of its other stakeholders. A firm's vision tends to be enduring while its mission can change in light of changing environmental conditions. A vision statement tends to be relatively short and concise, making it easily remembered. Examples of vision statements include the following:

Our vision is to be the world's best quick service restaurant. (McDonald's)

To make the automobile accessible to every American. (Ford Motor Company's vision when established by Henry Ford)

As a firm's most important and prominent strategic leader, the CEO is responsible for working with others to form the firm's vision. Experience shows that the most effective vision statement results when the CEO involves a host of people (e.g., other top-level managers, employees working in different parts of the organization, suppliers, and customers) to develop it. In addition, to help the firm reach its desired future state, a vision statement should be clearly tied to the conditions in the firm's external and internal environments as is evidenced in the multimedia vision already mentioned for Disney. Moreover, the decisions and actions of those involved with developing the vision, especially the CEO and the other top-level managers, must be consistent with that vision. At McDonald's, for example, a failure to openly provide employees with what they need to quickly and effectively serve customers would be a recipe for disaster.

Mission

The vision is the foundation for the firm's mission. A **mission** specifies the business or businesses in which the firm intends to compete and the customers it intends to serve.[87] The firm's mission is more concrete than its vision. However, like the vision, a mission should establish a firm's individuality and should be inspiring and relevant to all stakeholders.[88] Together, vision and mission provide the foundation the firm needs to choose and implement one or more strategies. The probability of forming an effective mission increases when employees have a strong sense of the ethical standards that will guide their behaviors as they work to help the firm reach its vision.[89] Thus, business ethics are a vital part of the firm's discussions to decide what it wants to become (its vision) as well as who it intends to serve and how it desires to serve those individuals and groups (its mission).[90]

A **mission** specifies the business or businesses in which the firm intends to compete and the customers it intends to serve.

Even though the final responsibility for forming the firm's mission rests with the CEO, the CEO and other top-level managers tend to involve a larger number of people in forming the mission. The main reason is that mission deals more directly with product markets and customers, and middle- and first-level managers and other employees have more direct contact with customers and the markets in which they are served. Examples of mission statements include the following:

Be the best employer for our people in each community around the world and deliver operational excellence to our customers in each of our restaurants. (McDonald's)

Our mission is to be recognized by our customers as the leader in applications engineering. We always focus on the activities customers desire; we are highly motivated and strive to advance our technical knowledge in the areas of material, part design and fabrication technology. (LNP, a GE Plastics Company)

Notice how the McDonald's mission statement flows from its vision of being the world's best quick service restaurant. LNP's mission statement describes the business areas (material, part design, and fabrication technology) in which the firm intends to compete.

While reading the vision and mission statements presented here, you likely recognized that the earning of above-average returns (sometimes called profit maximization) was not mentioned in any of them. All firms want to earn above-average returns (meaning that this intention does not differentiate the firm from its rivals), and that desired financial outcome results from properly serving certain customers while trying to achieving the firm's intended future. In other words, above-average returns are the fruits of the firm's efforts to achieve its vision and mission. In fact, research has shown that having an effectively formed vision and mission has a positive effect on performance as measured by growth in sales, profits, employment, and net worth.[91] In turn, positive firm performance increases the firm's ability to satisfy the interests of its stakeholders (whom we discuss next). The flip side of the coin also seems to be true—namely, the firm without an appropriately formed vision and mission is more likely to fail than the firm that has properly formed vision and mission statements.[92]

Stakeholders

Stakeholders are the individuals and groups who can affect, and are affected by, the strategic outcomes achieved and who have enforceable claims on a firm's performance.

Every organization involves a system of primary stakeholder groups with whom it establishes and manages relationships.[93] **Stakeholders** are the individuals and groups who can affect the vision and mission of the firm, are affected by the strategic outcomes achieved, and have enforceable claims on a firm's performance.[94] Claims on a firm's performance are enforced through the stakeholders' ability to withhold participation essential to the organization's survival, competitiveness, and profitability.[95] Stakeholders continue to support an organization when its performance meets or exceeds their expectations.[96] Also, recent research suggests that firms that effectively manage stakeholder relationships outperform those that do not. Stakeholder relationships can therefore be managed to be a source of competitive advantage.[97]

Although organizations have dependency relationships with their stakeholders, they are not equally dependent on all stakeholders at all times;[98] as a consequence, not every stakeholder has the same level of influence.[99] The more critical and valued a stakeholder's participation, the greater a firm's dependency on it. Greater dependence, in turn, gives the stakeholder more potential influence over a firm's commitments, decisions, and actions. Managers must find ways to either accommodate or insulate the organization from the demands of stakeholders controlling critical resources.[100]

Classifications of Stakeholders

The parties involved with a firm's operations can be separated into at least three groups.[101] As shown in Figure 1.4, these groups are the capital market stakeholders (shareholders and the major suppliers of a firm's capital), the product market stakeholders (the firm's primary customers, suppliers, host communities, and unions representing the workforce), and the organizational stakeholders (all of a firm's employees, including both nonmanagerial and managerial personnel).

Each stakeholder group expects those making strategic decisions in a firm to provide the leadership through which its valued objectives will be reached.[102] The objectives of the various stakeholder groups often differ from one another, sometimes placing those involved with the strategic management process in situations where trade-offs have to be made. The most obvious stakeholders, at least in United State's organizations, are *shareholders*—individuals and groups who have invested capital in a firm in the expectation of earning a positive return on their investments. These stakeholders' rights are grounded in laws governing private property and private enterprise.

In contrast to shareholders, another group of stakeholders—the firm's customers—prefers that investors receive a minimum return on their investments. Customers could have their interests maximized when the quality and reliability of a firm's products are improved, but without a price increase. High returns to customers might come at the expense of lower returns negotiated with capital market shareholders.

Because of potential conflicts, each firm is challenged to manage its stakeholders. First, a firm must carefully identify all important stakeholders. Second, it must prioritize them, in case it cannot satisfy all of them. Power is the most critical criterion in prioritizing stakeholders. Other criteria might include the urgency of satisfying each particular stakeholder group and the degree of importance of each to the firm.[103]

Figure 1.4 The Three Stakeholder Groups

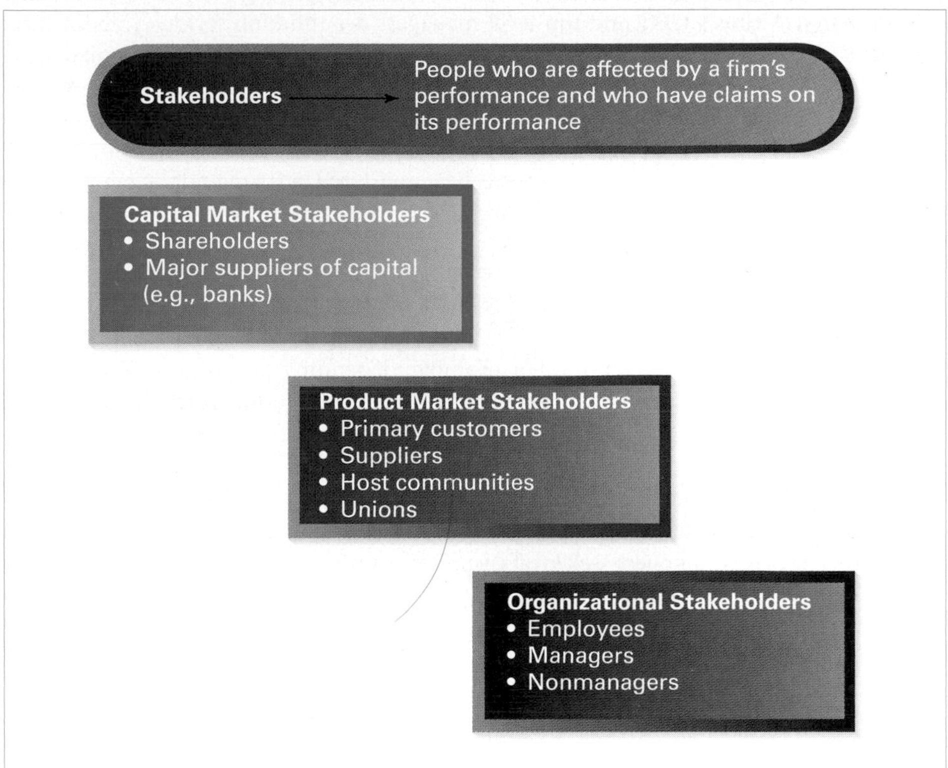

When the firm earns above-average returns, the challenge of effectively managing stakeholder relationships is lessened substantially. With the capability and flexibility provided by above-average returns, a firm can more easily satisfy multiple stakeholders simultaneously. When the firm is earning only average returns, it is unable to maximize the interests of all stakeholders. The objective then becomes one of at least minimally satisfying each stakeholder. Trade-off decisions are made in light of how important the support of each stakeholder group is to the firm. For example, environmental groups may be very important to firms in the energy industry but less important to professional service firms.[104] A firm earning below-average returns does not have the capacity to minimally satisfy all stakeholders. The managerial challenge in this case is to make trade-offs that minimize the amount of support lost from stakeholders. Societal values also influence the general weightings allocated among the three stakeholder groups shown in Figure 1.4. Although all three groups are served by firms in the major industrialized nations, the priorities in their service vary because of cultural differences. Next, we provide more details about each of the three major stakeholder groups.

Capital Market Stakeholders

Shareholders and lenders both expect a firm to preserve and enhance the wealth they have entrusted to it. The returns they expect are commensurate with the degree of risk accepted with those investments (i.e., lower returns are expected with low-risk investments, and higher returns are expected with high-risk investments). Dissatisfied lenders may impose stricter covenants on subsequent borrowing of capital. Dissatisfied shareholders may reflect their concerns through several means, including selling their stock.

When a firm is aware of potential or actual dissatisfactions among capital market stakeholders, it may respond to their concerns. The firm's response to stakeholders who are dissatisfied is affected by the nature of its dependency relationship with them (which, as noted earlier, is also influenced by a society's values). The greater and more significant the dependency relationship is, the more direct and significant the firm's response becomes. Given Airbus's situation, as explained in the Opening Case, it is reasonable to expect that Airbus's CEO and top-level managers are thinking seriously about what should be done to improve the firm's performance in order to satisfy its capital market stakeholders. In fact, Airbus attempted to lay off a number of employees as well as outsource some operations to lower its costs and to make itself more competitive relative to Boeing given Airbus's cost overruns for key planes such as the super jumbo A-380. However, in Europe where Airbus is headquartered, a strong public emphasis on employee stakeholders provides support to union protests over the cuts.[105]

Product Market Stakeholders

Some might think that product market stakeholders (customers, suppliers, host communities, and unions) share few common interests. However, all four groups can benefit as firms engage in competitive battles. For example, depending on product and industry characteristics, marketplace competition may result in lower product prices being charged to a firm's customers and higher prices being paid to its suppliers (the firm might be willing to pay higher supplier prices to ensure delivery of the types of goods and services that are linked with its competitive success).[106]

As is noted in Chapter 4, customers, as stakeholders, demand reliable products at the lowest possible prices. Suppliers seek loyal customers who are willing to pay the highest sustainable prices for the goods and services they receive. Host communities want companies willing to be long-term employers and providers of tax revenue without placing excessive demands on public support services. Union officials are interested in secure jobs, under highly desirable working conditions, for employees they represent. Thus, product market stakeholders are generally satisfied when a firm's profit margin reflects at least a balance between the returns to capital market stakeholders (i.e., the returns lenders and shareholders will accept and still retain their interests in the firm) and the returns in which they share.

Organizational Stakeholders

Employees—the firm's organizational stakeholders—expect the firm to provide a dynamic, stimulating, and rewarding work environment. As employees, we are usually satisfied working for a company that is growing and actively developing our skills, especially those skills required to be effective team members and to meet or exceed global work standards. Workers who learn how to use new knowledge productively are critical to organizational success. In a collective sense, the education and skills of a firm's workforce are competitive weapons affecting strategy implementation and firm performance.[107] As suggested by the following statement, strategic leaders are ultimately responsible for serving the needs of organizational stakeholders on a day-to-day basis: "[T]he job of [strategic] leadership is to fully utilize human potential, to create organizations in which people can grow and learn while still achieving a common objective, to nurture the human spirit."[108] Interestingly, research suggests that outside directors are more likely to propose layoffs compared to inside strategic leaders, while such insiders are likely to use preventative cost-cutting measures and seek to protect incumbent employees.[109]

Strategic Leaders

Strategic leaders are people located in different parts of the firm using the strategic management process to help the firm reach its vision and mission.

Strategic leaders are people located in different parts of the firm using the strategic management process to help the firm reach its vision and mission. Regardless of their location in the firm, successful strategic leaders are decisive and committed to nurturing those around them[110] and are committed to helping the firm create value for customers and returns for shareholders and other stakeholders.[111]

When identifying strategic leaders, most of us tend to think of chief executive officers (CEOs) and other top-level managers. Clearly, these people are strategic leaders. And, in the final analysis, CEOs are responsible for making certain their firm effectively uses the strategic management process. Indeed, the pressure on CEOs to manage strategically is stronger than ever.[112] However, many other people in today's organizations help choose a firm's strategy and then determine the actions for successfully implementing them.[113] The main reason is that the realities of twenty-first-century competition that we discussed earlier in this chapter (e.g., the global economy, globalization, rapid technological change, and the increasing importance of knowledge and people as sources of competitive advantage) are creating a need for those "closest to the action" to be the ones making decisions and determining the actions to be taken.[114] In fact, the most effective CEOs and top-level managers understand how to delegate strategic responsibilities to people throughout the firm who influence the use of organizational resources.[115]

Organizational culture also affects strategic leaders and their work. In turn, strategic leaders' decisions and actions shape a firm's culture. **Organizational culture** refers to the complex set of ideologies, symbols, and core values that are shared throughout the firm and that influence how the firm conducts business. It is the social energy that drives—or fails to drive—the organization.[116] For example, highly successful Southwest Airlines is known for having a unique and valuable culture. Its culture encourages employees to work hard but also to have fun while doing so. Moreover, its culture entails respect for others—employees and customers alike. The firm also places a premium on service, as suggested by its commitment to provide POS (Positively Outrageous Service) to each customer. Wal-Mart claims that its continuing success is largely attributable to its culture.[117]

Organizational culture refers to the complex set of ideologies, symbols, and core values that are shared throughout the firm and that influence how the firm conducts business.

Some organizational cultures are a source of disadvantage. It is important for strategic leaders to understand, however, that whether the firm's culture is functional or dysfunctional, their work takes place within the context of that culture. The relationship between organizational culture and strategic leaders' work continues to be reciprocal in that the culture shapes how they work while their work helps shape an ever-evolving organizational culture.

The Work of Effective Strategic Leaders

Perhaps not surprisingly, hard work, thorough analyses, a willingness to be brutally honest, a penchant for wanting the firm and its people to accomplish more, and common sense are prerequisites to an individual's success as a strategic leader.[118] In addition, strategic leaders must be able to "think seriously and deeply . . . about the purposes of the organizations they head or functions they perform, about the strategies, tactics, technologies, systems, and people necessary to attain these purposes and about the important questions that always need to be asked."[119] Additionally, effective strategic leaders work to set an ethical tone in their firms. For example, Kevin Thompson, IBM's Manager of Corporate Citizenship suggests, "We don't think you can survive without integrating business and societal values." This approach to ethical behavior helped to place IBM at the sixth place on the 2007 list of 100 Best Corporate Citizens published by *CRO Magazine*.[120]

IBM's organizational culture holds that there is indeed a corporate responsibility to bettering society at large.

Strategic leaders, regardless of their location in the organization, often work long hours, and the work is filled with ambiguous decision situations for which effective solutions are not easily determined.[121] However, the opportunities afforded by this work are appealing and offer exciting chances to dream and to act.[122] The following words, given as advice to the late Time Warner chair and co-CEO Steven J. Ross by his father, describe the opportunities in a strategic leader's work:

There are three categories of people—the person who goes into the office, puts his feet up on his desk, and dreams for 12 hours; the person who arrives at 5 A.M. and works for 16 hours, never once stopping to dream; and the person who puts his feet up, dreams for one hour, then does something about those dreams.[123]

The organizational term used for a dream that challenges and energizes a company is vision (discussed earlier in this chapter). Strategic leaders have opportunities to dream and to act, and the most effective ones provide a vision as the foundation for the firm's mission and subsequent choice and use of one or more strategies.

Predicting Outcomes of Strategic Decisions: Profit Pools

Strategic leaders attempt to predict the outcomes of their decisions before taking efforts to implement them, which is difficult to do. Many decisions that are a part of the strategic management process are concerned with an uncertain future and the firm's place in that future.[124]

A **profit pool** entails the total profits earned in an industry at all points along the value chain.

Mapping an industry's profit pool is something strategic leaders can do to anticipate the possible outcomes of different decisions and to focus on growth in profits rather than strictly growth in revenues. A **profit pool** entails the total profits earned in an industry at all points along the value chain.[125] (Value chain is explained in Chapter 3 and further discussed in Chapter 4.) Analyzing the profit pool in the industry may help a firm see something others are unable to see by helping it understand the primary sources of profits in an industry. There are four steps to identifying profit pools: (1) define the pool's boundaries, (2) estimate the pool's overall size, (3) estimate the size of the value-chain activity in the pool, and (4) reconcile the calculations.[126]

Let's think about how Airbus might map the commercial aerospace industry's profit pools. First, Airbus would need to define the industry's boundaries and, second, estimate its size. As discussed in the Opening Case, these boundaries would include markets across the globe, and the size of many of these markets, especially markets in emerging economies, continues to expand rapidly. Airbus would then be prepared to estimate the amount of profit potential in each part of the value chain (step 3). In this industry, product design and product features are likely more important sources of potential profits than marketing campaigns to sell the new designs. These types of issues are to be considered with the third step of actions used to map an industry's profit pool. Airbus would then have the information and insights needed to identify the strategies to use to be successful where the largest profit pools are located in the value chain.[127] As this brief discussion shows, profit pools are a tool the firm's strategic leaders can use to help recognize the actions to take to increase the likelihood of increasing profits.

The Strategic Management Process

As suggested by Figure 1.1, the strategic management process is a rational approach firms use to achieve strategic competitiveness and earn above-average returns. Figure 1.1 also outlines the topics we examine in this book to present the strategic management process to you.

This book is divided into three parts. In Part 1, we describe what firms do to analyze their external environment (Chapter 2) and internal organization (Chapter 3). These analyses are completed to identify marketplace opportunities and threats in the external environment (Chapter 2) and to decide how to use the resources, capabilities, and core competencies in the firm's internal organization to pursue opportunities and overcome threats (Chapter 3). With knowledge about its external environment and internal organization, the firm forms its vision and mission.

The firm's strategic inputs (see Figure 1.1) provide the foundation for choosing one or more strategies and deciding how to implement them. As suggested in Figure 1.1 by the horizontal arrow linking the two types of strategic actions, formulation and implementation must be simultaneously integrated if the firm is to successfully use the strategic management process. Integration happens as decision makers think about implementation issues when choosing strategies and as they think about possible changes to the firm's strategies while implementing a currently chosen strategy.

In Part 2 of this book, we discuss the different strategies firms may choose to use. First, we examine business-level strategies (Chapter 4). A business-level strategy describes a firm's actions designed to exploit its competitive advantage over rivals. A company competing in a single product market (e.g., a locally owned grocery store operating in only one location) has but one business-level strategy. As you will learn though, a diversified firm competing in multiple product markets (e.g., General Electric) forms a business-level strategy for each of its businesses. In Chapter 5, we describe the actions and reactions that occur among firms while using their strategies in marketplace competitions. As we will see, competitors respond to and try to anticipate each other's actions. The dynamics of competition affect the strategies firms choose to use as well as how they try to implement the chosen strategies.[128]

For the diversified firm, corporate-level strategy (Chapter 6) is concerned with determining the businesses in which the company intends to compete as well as how resources, capabilities, and core competencies are to be allocated among the different businesses. Other topics vital to strategy formulation, particularly in the diversified corporation, include acquiring other companies and, as appropriate, restructuring the firm's portfolio of businesses (Chapter 7) and selecting an international strategy (Chapter 8). With cooperative strategies (Chapter 9), firms form a partnership to share their resources and capabilities in order to develop a competitive advantage. Cooperative strategies are becoming increasingly important as firms try to find ways to compete in the global economy's array of different markets.[129] For example, Marriott International Inc. and Ian Schrager Company, which focuses on designing luxury boutique hotels, are teaming to jointly produce hotels to compete with successful brands such as the W offered by Starwood Hotels and Resorts Worldwide.[130]

To examine actions taken to implement strategies, we consider several topics in Part 3 of the book. First, we examine the different mechanisms used to govern firms (Chapter 10). With demands for improved corporate governance being voiced today by many stakeholders,[131] organizations are challenged to learn how to simultaneously satisfy their stakeholders' different interests.[132] Finally, the organizational structure and actions needed to control a firm's operations (Chapter 11), the patterns of strategic leadership appropriate for today's firms and competitive environments (Chapter 12), and strategic entrepreneurship (Chapter 13) as a path to continuous innovation are addressed.

Before closing this introductory chapter, it is important to emphasize that primarily because they are related to how a firm interacts with its stakeholders, almost all strategic management process decisions have ethical dimensions.[133] Organizational ethics are revealed by an organization's culture; that is to say, a firm's decisions are a product of the core values that are shared by most or all of a company's managers and employees. Especially in the turbulent and often ambiguous competitive landscape of the twenty-first century, those making decisions that are part of the strategic management process are challenged to recognize that their decisions affect capital market, product market, and organizational stakeholders differently and to evaluate the ethical implications of their decisions on a daily basis.[134] Decision makers failing to recognize these realities accept the risk of putting their firm at a competitive disadvantage when it comes to consistently engaging in ethical business practices.[135]

As you will discover, the strategic management process examined in this book calls for disciplined approaches to the development of competitive advantage. These approaches provide the pathway through which firms will be able to achieve strategic competitiveness and earn above-average returns. Mastery of this strategic management process will effectively serve you, our readers, and the organizations for which you will choose to work.

Summary

- Firms use the strategic management process to achieve strategic competitiveness and earn above-average returns. Strategic competitiveness is achieved when a firm has developed and learned how to implement a value-creating strategy. Above-average returns (in excess of what investors expect to earn from other investments with similar levels of risk) provide the foundation a firm needs to simultaneously satisfy all of its stakeholders.
- The fundamental nature of competition is different in the current competitive landscape. As a result, those making strategic decisions must adopt a different mind-set, one that allows them to learn how to compete in highly turbulent and chaotic environments that produce disorder and a great deal of uncertainty. The globalization of industries and their markets and rapid and significant technological changes are the two primary factors contributing to the turbulence of the competitive landscape.
- Firms use two major models to help them form their vision and mission and then choose one or more strategies to use in the pursuit of strategic competitiveness and above-average returns. The core assumption of the I/O model is that the firm's external environment has more of an influence on the choice of strategies than do the firm's internal resources, capabilities, and core competencies. Thus, the I/O model is used to understand the effects an industry's characteristics can have on a firm when deciding what strategy or strategies to use to compete against rivals. The logic supporting the I/O model suggests that above-average returns are earned when the firm locates an attractive industry and successfully implements the strategy dictated by that industry's characteristics. The core assumption of the resource-based model is that the firm's unique resources, capabilities, and core competencies have more of an influence on selecting and using strategies than does the firm's external environment. Above-average returns are earned when the firm uses its valuable, rare, costly-to-imitate, and nonsubstitutable resources and capabilities to compete against its rivals in one or more industries. Evidence indicates that both models yield insights that are linked to successfully selecting and using strategies. Thus, firms want to use their unique resources, capabilities, and core competencies as the foundation for one or more strategies that will allow them to compete in industries they understand.
- Vision and mission are formed in light of the information and insights gained from studying a firm's internal and external environments. Vision is a picture of what the firm wants to be and, in broad terms, what it wants to ultimately achieve. Flowing from the vision, the mission specifies the business or businesses in which the firm intends to compete and the customers it intends to serve. Vision and mission provide direction to the firm and signal important descriptive information to stakeholders.
- Stakeholders are those who can affect, and are affected by, a firm's strategic outcomes. Because a firm is dependent on the continuing support of stakeholders (shareholders, customers, suppliers, employees, host communities, etc.), they have enforceable claims on the company's performance. When earning above-average returns, a firm has the resources it needs to at minimum simultaneously satisfy the interests of all stakeholders. However, when the firm earns only average returns, different stakeholder groups must be carefully managed in order to retain their support. A firm earning below-average returns must minimize the amount of support it loses from dissatisfied stakeholders.
- Strategic leaders are people located in different parts of the firm using the strategic management process to help the firm reach its vision and mission. In the final analysis, though, CEOs are responsible for making certain that their firms properly use the strategic management process. Today, the effectiveness of the strategic management process increases when it is grounded in ethical intentions and behaviors. The strategic leader's work demands decision trade-offs, often among attractive alternatives. It is important for all strategic leaders, and especially the CEO and other members of the top-management team, to work hard, conduct thorough analyses of situations, be brutally and consistently honest, and ask the right questions of the right people at the right time.
- Strategic leaders must predict the potential outcomes of their strategic decisions. To do so, they must first calculate profit pools in their industry that are linked to value chain activities. In so doing, they are less likely to formulate and implement ineffective strategies.

Review Questions

1. What are strategic competitiveness, strategy, competitive advantage, above-average returns, and the strategic management process?
2. What are the characteristics of the current competitive landscape? What two factors are the primary drivers of this landscape?
3. According to the I/O model, what should a firm do to earn above-average returns?
4. What does the resource-based model suggest a firm should do to earn above-average returns?
5. What are vision and mission? What is their value for the strategic management process?
6. What are stakeholders? How do the three primary stakeholder groups influence organizations?
7. How would you describe the work of strategic leaders?
8. What are the elements of the strategic management process? How are they interrelated?

Experiential Exercises

Exercise 1: Business and Blogs

One element of industry structure analysis is the leverage that buyers can exert on firms. Is technology changing the balance of power between customers and companies? If so, how should business respond?

Blogs offer a mechanism for consumers to share their experiences—good or bad—regarding different companies. Bloggers first emerged in the late 1990s, and today the Technorati search engine currently monitors roughly 100 million blogs. With the wealth of this "citizen media" available, what are the implications for consumer power? One of the most famous cases of a blogger drawing attention to a company was Jeff Jarvis of the Web site http://www.buzzmachine.com. Jarvis, who writes on media topics, was having problems with his Dell computer, and shared his experiences on the Web. Literally thousands of other people recounted similar experiences, and the phenomena became known as "Dell hell." Eventually, Dell created its own corporate blog in an effort to deflect this wave of consumer criticism. What are the implications of the rapid growth in blogs? Work in a group on the following exercise.

Part One

Visit a corporate blog. Only a small percentage of large firms maintain a blog presence on the Internet. *Hint:* Multiple wikis online provide lists of such companies. A Web search using the term *fortune 500 blogs* will turn up several options. Review the content of the firm's blog. Was it updated regularly or not? Multiple contributors or just one? What was the writing style? Did it read like a marketing brochure, or something more informal? Did the blog allow viewer comments, or post replies to consumer questions?

Part Two

Based on the information you collected in the blog review, answer the following questions:

- Have you ever used blogs to help make decisions about something that you are considering purchasing? If so, how did the blog material affect your decision? What factors would make you more (or less) likely to rely on a blog in making your decision?
- How did the content of corporate blog affect your perception of that company and its good and services? Did it make you more or less likely to view the company favorably, or have no effect at all?
- Why do so few large companies maintain blogs?

Exercise 2: Creating a Shared Vision

Drawing on an analysis of internal and external constraints, firms create a mission and vision as a cornerstone of their strategy. This exercise will look at some of the challenges associated with creating a shared direction for the firm.

Part One

The instructor will break the class into a set of small teams. Half of the teams will be given an "A" designation, and the other half assigned as "B." Each individual team will need to plan a time outside class to complete Part 2; the exercise should take about half an hour.

Teams given the A designation will meet in a face-to-face setting. Each team member will need paper and a pen or pencil. Your meeting location should be free from distraction. The location should have enough space so that no person can see another's notepad.

Teams given the B designation will meet electronically. You may choose to meet through text messaging or IM. Be sure to confirm everyone's contact information and meeting time beforehand.

Part Two

Each team member prepares a drawing of a real structure. It can be a famous building, a monument, museum, or even your dorm. Do not tell other team members what you drew.

Randomly select one team member. The goal is for everyone else to prepare a drawing as similar to the selected team member as possible. That person is not allowed to show his or her drawing to the rest of the team. The rest of the group can ask questions about the drawing, but only ones that can be answered "yes" or "no."

After 10 minutes, have everyone compare their drawings. If you are meeting electronically, describe your drawings, and save them for the next time your team meets face to face.

Next, select a second team member and repeat this process again.

Part Three

In class, discuss the following questions:

- How easy (or hard) was it for you to figure out the "vision" of your team members?
- Did you learn anything in the first iteration that made the second drawing more successful?
- What similarities might you find between this exercise and the challenge of sharing a vision among company employees?
- How did the communication structure affect your process and outcomes?

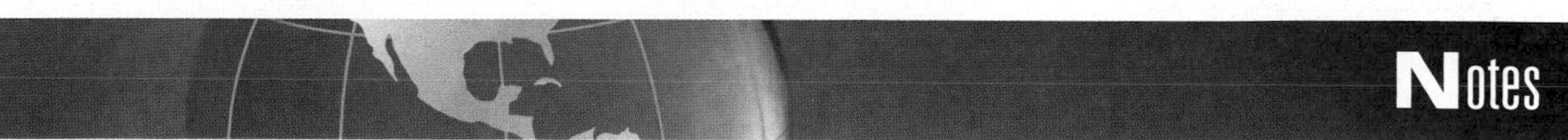

1. J. B. Barney & D. N. Clark, 2007, Resource-based theory: Creating and sustaining competitive advantage, New York: Oxford University Press; D. G. Sirmon, M. A. Hitt & R. D. Ireland, 2007, Managing firm resources in dynamic environments to create value: Looking inside the black box, *Academy of Management Review*, 32: 273–292.

2. D. Lei & J. W. Slocum, 2005, Strategic and organizational requirements for competitive advantage, *Academy of Management Executive*, 19(1): 31–45.

3. G. Pacheco-de-Almeida & P. Zemsky, 2007, The timing of resource development and sustainable competitive advantage, *Management Science*, 53: 651–666; D. J. Teece, G. Pisano & A. Shuen, 1997, Dynamic capabilities and strategic management, *Strategic Management Journal*, 18: 509–533.
4. P. Shrivastava, 1995, Ecocentric management for a risk society, *Academy of Management Review*, 20: 119.
5. F. Delmar, P. Davidsson & W. B. Gartner, 2003, Arriving at a high-growth firm, *Journal of Business Venturing*, 18: 189–216.
6. T. Bates, 2005, Analysis of young, small firms that have closed: Delineating successful from unsuccessful closures, *Journal of Business Venturing*, 20: 343–358.
7. A. M. McGahan & M. E. Porter, 2003, The emergence and sustainability of abnormal profits, *Strategic Organization*, 1: 79–108; T. C. Powell, 2001, Competitive advantage: Logical and philosophical considerations, *Strategic Management Journal*, 22: 875–888.
8. J. T. Mahoney & A. M. McGahan, 2007, The field of strategic management within the evolving science of strategic organization, *Strategic Organization*, 5: 79–99; R. D. Ireland & C. C. Miller, 2004, Decision-making and firm success, *Academy of Management Executive*, 18(4): 8–12.
9. P. Nutt, 2004, Expanding the search for alternatives during strategic decision-making, *Academy of Management Executive*, 18(4): 13–28; S. Dutta, M. J. Zbaracki & M. Bergen, 2003, Pricing process as a capability: A resource-based perspective, *Strategic Management Journal*, 24: 615–630.
10. S. Tallman & K. Fladmoe-Lindquist, 2002, Internationalization, globalization, and capability-based strategy, *California Management Review*, 45(1): 116–135; M. A. Hitt, R. D. Ireland, S. M. Camp & D. L. Sexton, 2001, Strategic entrepreneurship: Entrepreneurial strategies for wealth creation, *Strategic Management Journal*, 22 (Special Issue): 479–491; S. A. Zahra, R. D. Ireland & M. A. Hitt, 2000, International expansion by new venture firms: International diversity, mode of market entry, technological learning and performance, *Academy of Management Journal*, 43: 925–950.
11. R. Kirkland, 2005, Will the U.S. be flattened by a flatter world? *Fortune*, June 27, 47–48.
12. A. Nair & S. Kotha, 2001, Does group membership matter? Evidence from the Japanese steel industry, *Strategic Management Journal*, 22: 221–235; A. M. McGahan & M. E. Porter, 1997, How much does industry matter, really? *Strategic Management Journal*, 18 (Special Issue): 15–30.
13. F. J. Acedo, C. Barroso & J. L. Galan, 2006, The resource-based theory: Dissemination and main trends, *Strategic Management Journal*, 27: 621–636; D. G. Sirmon & M. A. Hitt, 2003, Managing resources: Linking unique resources, management and wealth creation in family firms, *Entrepreneurship Theory and Practice*, 27(4): 339–358; J. B. Barney, 2001, Is the resource-based "view" a useful perspective for strategic management research? Yes, *Academy of Management Review*, 26: 41–56.
14. T. Friedman, 2005, *The World Is Flat: A Brief History of the 21st Century*, New York, NY: Farrar, Strauss and Giroux; M. A. Hitt, B. W. Keats & S. M. DeMarie, 1998, Navigating in the new competitive landscape: Building competitive advantage and strategic flexibility in the 21st century, *Academy of Management Executive*, 12(4): 22–42; R. A. Bettis & M. A. Hitt, 1995, The new competitive landscape, *Strategic Management Journal*, 16 (Special Issue): 7–19.
15. D. Searcey, 2006, Beyond cable. Beyond DSL. *Wall Street Journal*, July 24, R9.
16. 2005, NBC could combine network and cable news-NY Post, http://www.reuters.com, June 30.
17. P. Taylor, 2007, Tools to bridge the divide: Raketu aims to outperform Skype in Internet telephony while throwing in a range of information and entertainment services, *Financial Times*, May 11, 16.
18. W. Swarts , 2006, Get reel (Netflix, Blockbuster, Apple Computer, Amazon.com), *SmartMoney.com*, http://www.smartmoney.com, October 24.
19. G. Probst & S. Raisch, 2005, Organizational crisis: The logic of failure, *Academy of Management Executive*, 19(1): 90–105; M. A. Hitt & V. Pisano, 2003, The cross-border merger and acquisition strategy, *Management Research*, 1: 133–144.
20. R. M. Grant, 2003, Strategic planning in a turbulent environment: Evidence from the oil majors, *Strategic Management Journal*, 24: 491–517.
21. J. W. Selsky, J. Goes & O. N. Babüroglu, 2007, Contrasting perspectives of strategy making: Applications in "Hyper" environments, *Organization Studies*, 28(1): 71–94; G. McNamara, P. M. Vaaler & C. Devers, 2003, Same as it ever was: The search for evidence of increasing hypercompetition, *Strategic Management Journal*, 24: 261–278.
22. R. A. D'Aveni, 1995, Coping with hypercompetition: Utilizing the new 7S's framework, *Academy of Management Executive*, 9(3): 46.
23. D. J. Bryce & J. H. Dyer, 2007, Strategies to crack well-guarded markets, *Harvard Business Review* 85(5): 84–92; R. A. D'Aveni, 2004, Corporate spheres of influence, *MIT Sloan Management Review*, 45(4): 38–46; W. J. Ferrier, 2001, Navigating the competitive landscape: The drivers and consequences of competitive aggressiveness, *Academy of Management Journal*, 44: 858-877.
24. S.-J. Chang & S. Park, 2005, Types of firms generating network externalities and MNCs' co-location decisions, *Strategic Management Journal*, 26: 595–615; S. C. Voelpel, M. Dous & T. H. Davenport, 2005, Five steps to creating a global knowledge-sharing systems: Siemens/ShareNet, *Academy of Management Executive*, 19(2): 9–23.
25. R. Belderbos & L. Sleuwaegen, 2005, Competitive drivers and international plant configuration strategies: A product-level test, *Strategic Management Journal*, 26: 577–593.
26. 2005, Organisation for Economic Co-operation and Development, OCED Statistical Profile of the United States—2005, http://www.oced.org; S. Koudsi & L. A. Costa, 1998, America vs. the new Europe: By the numbers, *Fortune*, December 21, 149–156.
27. Y. Luo, 2007, From foreign investors to strategic insiders: Shifting parameters, prescriptions and paradigms for MNCs in China, *Journal of World Business*, 42(1): 14–34.
28. A. Virmani, 2005, India a giant economy? Yes, by 2035! *Rediff.com*, http://www.rediff.com, January 21.
29. T. Khanna & K. G. Palepu, 2006, Emerging giants: Building world-class companies in developing countries, *Harvard Business Review*, 84(10): 60–69.
30. K. Kranhold, 2005, GE pins hopes on emerging markets, *Wall Street Journal Online*, http://www.wsj.com, March 2.
31. G. D. Bruton, G. G. Dess & J. J. Janney, 2007, Knowledge management in technology-focused firms in emerging economies: Caveats on capabilities, networks, and real options, *Asia Pacific Journal of Management*, 24(2): 115–130; P. Williamson & M. Zeng, 2004, Strategies for competing in a changed China, *MIT Sloan Management Review*, 45(4): 85–91; V. Govindarajan & A. K. Gupta, 2001, *The Quest for Global Dominance*, San Francisco: Jossey-Bass.
32. T. Khanna, K. G. Palepu & J. Sinha, 2005, Strategies that fit emerging markets, *Harvard Business Review*, 83(6): 63–76.
33. N. Shirouzu, 2007, Toyota's new U.S. plan: Stop building factories, *Wall Street Journal*, June 20, A1, A14.
34. B. Simon, 2007, Ford brands improve on vehicle quality, *Financial Times*, June 7, 20.
35. M. A. Prospero, 2005, The march of war, *Fast Company*, May, 14.
36. G. Fink & N. Holden, 2005, The global transfer of management knowledge, *Academy of Management Executive*, 19(2): 5–8; M. Subramaniam & N. Venkataraman, 2001, Determinants of transnational new product development capability: Testing the influence of transferring and deploying tacit overseas knowledge, *Strategic Management Journal*, 22: 359–378.
37. S. Zaheer & E. Mosakowski, 1997, The dynamics of the liability of foreignness: A global study of survival in financial services, *Strategic Management Journal*, 18: 439–464.
38. Bruton, Dess & Janney, Knowledge management in technology-focused firms in emerging economies; R. C. May, S. M. Puffer, & D. J. McCarthy, 2005, Transferring management knowledge

to Russia: A culturally based approach, *Academy of Management Executive,* 19(2): 24–35.
39. M. A. Hitt, R. E. Hoskisson & H. Kim, 1997, International diversification: Effects on innovation and firm performance in product-diversified firms, *Academy of Management Journal,* 40: 767–798.
40. D'Aveni, Coping with hypercompetition, 46.
41. R. D. Ireland & J. W. Webb, 2007, Strategic entrepreneurship: Creating competitive advantage through streams of innovation, *Business Horizons,* 50(1): 49–59; G. Hamel, 2001, Revolution vs. evolution: You need both, *Harvard Business Review,* 79(5): 150–156.
42. K. H. Hammonds, 2001, What is the state of the new economy? *Fast Company,* September, 101–104.
43. L. Yu, 2005, Does knowledge sharing pay off? *MIT Sloan Management Review,* 46(3): 5.
44. H. W. Chesbrough, 2007, Why companies should have open business models, *MIT Sloan Management Review,* 48(2): 22–28.
45. T. Talaulicar, J. Grundei1 & A. V. Werder, 2005, Strategic decision making in start-ups: The effect of top management team organization and processes on speed and comprehensiveness, *Journal of Business Venturing,* 20: 519–541; K. M. Eisenhardt, 1999, Strategy as strategic decision making, *Sloan Management Review,* 40(3): 65–72.
46. J. Santos, Y. Doz & P. Williamson, 2004, Is your innovation process global? *MIT Sloan Management Review,* 45(4): 31–37.
47. C. W. L. Hill, 1997, Establishing a standard: Competitive strategy and technological standards in winner-take-all industries, *Academy of Management Executive,* 11(2): 7–25.
48. C. Gilbert, 2003, The disruptive opportunity, *MIT Sloan Management Review,* 44(4): 27–32; C. M. Christensen, 1997, *The Innovator's Dilemma,* Boston: Harvard Business School Press.
49. P. Magnusson, 2005, Globalization is great—sort of, *BusinessWeek,* April 25, 25.
50. C. M. Christensen, 2006. The ongoing process of building a theory of disruption, *Journal of Product Innovation Management,* 23(1): 39–55; R. Adner, 2002, When are technologies disruptive? A demand-based view of the emergence of competition, *Strategic Management Journal,* 23: 667–688; G. Ahuja & C. M. Lampert, 2001, Entrepreneurship in the large corporation: A longitudinal study of how established firms create breakthrough inventions, *Strategic Management Journal,* 22 (Special Issue): 521–543.
51. C. L. Nichols-Nixon & C. Y. Woo, 2003, Technology sourcing and output of established firms in a regime of encompassing technological change, *Strategic Management Journal,* 24: 651–666; C. W. L. Hill & F. T. Rothaermel, 2003, The performance of incumbent firms in the face of radical technological innovation, *Academy of Management Review,* 28: 257–274.
52. K. Celuch, G. B. Murphy & S. K. Callaway, 2007, More bang for your buck: Small firms and the importance of aligned information technology capabilities and strategic flexibility, *Journal of High Technology Management Research,* 17: 187–197; G. Ferguson, S. Mathur & B. Shah, 2005, Evolving from information to insight, *MIT Sloan Management Review,* 46(2): 51–58.
53. S. McBride, 2007, Internet radio races to break free of the PC, *Wall Street Journal,* June 18, A1, A11.
54. A. C. Inkpen & E. W. K. Tsang, 2005, Social capital, networks, and knowledge transfer, *Academy of Management Review,* 30: 146–165; A. S. DeNisi, M. A. Hitt & S. E. Jackson, 2003, The knowledge-based approach to sustainable competitive advantage, in S. E. Jackson, M. A. Hitt & A. S. DeNisi (eds.), *Managing Knowledge for Sustained Competitive Advantage,* San Francisco: Jossey-Bass, 3–33.
55. M. Gottfredson, R. Puryear & S. Phillips, 2005, Strategic sourcing: From periphery to the core, *Harvard Business Review,* 83(2): 132–139.
56. K. G. Smith, C. J. Collins & K. D. Clark, 2005, Existing knowledge, knowledge creation capability, and the rate of new product introduction in high-technology firms, *Academy of Management Journal,* 48: 346–357; S. K. McEvily & B. Chakravarthy, 2002, The persistence of knowledge-based advantage: An empirical test for product performance and technological knowledge, *Strategic Management Journal,* 23: 285–305.
57. A. Capaldo, 2007, Network structure and innovation: The leveraging of a dual network as a distinctive relational capability, *Strategic Management Journal,* 28: 585–608; S. K. Ethirau, P. Kale, M. S. Krishnan & J. V. Singh, 2005, Where do capabilities come from and how do they matter? *Strategic Management Journal,* 26: 25–45; L. Rosenkopf & A. Nerkar, 2001, Beyond local search: Boundary-spanning, exploration, and impact on the optical disk industry, *Strategic Management Journal,* 22: 287–306.
58. Sirmon, Hitt & Ireland, Managing firm resources.
59. P. L. Robertson & P. R. Patel, 2007, New wine in old bottles: Technological diffusion in developed economies, *Research Policy,* 36(5): 708–721; K. Asakawa & M. Lehrer, 2003, Managing local knowledge assets globally: The role of regional innovation relays, *Journal of World Business,* 38: 31–42.
60. R. E. Hoskisson, M. A. Hitt & R. D. Ireland, 2008, *Competing for Advantage,* 2nd ed., Cincinnati: Thomson South-Western; K. R. Harrigan, 2001, Strategic flexibility in old and new economies, in M. A. Hitt, R. E. Freeman & J. S. Harrison (eds.), *Handbook of Strategic Management,* Oxford, UK: Blackwell Publishers, 97–123.
61. S. Nadkarni & V. K. Narayanan, 2007, Strategic schemas, strategic flexibility, and firm performance: The moderating role of industry clockspeed, *Strategic Management Journal,* 28: 243–270.
62. L. Gratton & S. Ghoshal, 2005, Beyond best practice, *MIT Sloan Management Review,* 46(3): 49–55.
63. K. Shimizu & M. A. Hitt, 2004, Strategic flexibility: Organizational preparedness to reverse ineffective strategic decisions, *Academy of Management Executive,* 18(4): 44–59; K. Uhlenbruck, K. E. Meyer & M. A. Hitt, 2003, Organizational transformation in transition economies: Resource-based and organizational learning perspectives, *Journal of Management Studies,* 40: 257–282.
64. M. J. Zhang, 2006, IS support for strategic flexibility, environmental dynamism, and firm performance, *Journal of Managerial Issues,* 18: 84–103; Celuch, Murphy & Callaway, More bang for your buck.
65. R. E. Hoskisson, M. A. Hitt, W. P. Wan & D. Yiu, 1999, Swings of a pendulum: Theory and research in strategic management, *Journal of Management,* 25: 417–456.
66. E. H. Bowman & C. E. Helfat, 2001, Does corporate strategy matter? *Strategic Management Journal,* 22: 1–23.
67. J. Shamsie, 2003, The context of dominance: An industry-driven framework for exploiting reputation, *Strategic Management Journal,* 24: 199–215; A. Seth & H. Thomas, 1994, Theories of the firm: Implications for strategy research, *Journal of Management Studies,* 31: 165–191.
68. Seth & Thomas, 169–173.
69. M. B. Lieberman & S. Asaba, 2006, Why do firms imitate each other? *Academy of Management Journal,* 31: 366–385; L. F. Feldman, C. G. Brush & T. Manolova, 2005, Co-alignment in the resource-performance relationship: Strategy as mediator, *Journal of Business Venturing,* 20: 359–383.
70. M. E. Porter, 1985, *Competitive Advantage,* New York: Free Press; M. E. Porter, 1980, *Competitive Strategy,* New York: Free Press.
71. J. C. Short, D. J. Ketchen, Jr., T. B. Palmer & G. T. M. Hult, 2007, Firm, strategic group, and industry influences on performance, *Strategic Management Journal,* 28: 147–167.
72. A. M. McGahan, 1999, Competition, strategy and business performance, *California Management Review,* 41(3): 74–101; McGahan & Porter, How much does industry matter, really?
73. R. Henderson & W. Mitchell, 1997, The interactions of organizational and competitive influences on strategy and performance, *Strategic Management Journal 18* (Special Issue): 5–14; C. Oliver, 1997, Sustainable competitive advantage: Combining institutional and resource-based views, *Strategic Management Journal,* 18: 697–713; J. L. Stimpert & I. M. Duhaime, 1997, Seeing the big picture: The influence of industry, diversification, and business strategy on performance, *Academy of Management Journal,* 40: 560–583.

74. F. J. Acedo, C. Barroso & J. L. Galan, 2006, The resource-based theory: Dissemination and main trends, *Strategic Management Journal,* 27: 621–636.
75. B.-S. Teng & J. L. Cummings, 2002, Trade-offs in managing resources and capabilities, *Academy of Management Executive,* 16(2): 81–91; R. L. Priem & J. E. Butler, 2001, Is the resource-based "view" a useful perspective for strategic management research? *Academy of Management Review,* 26: 22–40.
76. S. A. Zahra, H. Sapienza & P. Davidsson, 2006, Entrepreneurship and dynamic capabilities: A review, model and research agenda, *Journal of Management studies,* 43(4): 927–955; M. Blyler & R. W. Coff, 2003, Dynamic capabilities, social capital, and rent appropriation: Ties that split pies, *Strategic Management Journal,* 24: 677–686.
77. S. L. Newbert, 2007, Empirical research on the resource-based view of the firm: An assessment and suggestions for future research, *Strategic Management Journal,* 28: 121–146; P. Bansal, 2005, Evolving sustainability: A longitudinal study of corporate sustainable development, *Strategic Management Journal,* 26: 197–218.
78. P. J. H. Schoemaker & R. Amit, 1994, Investment in strategic assets: Industry and firm-level perspectives, in P. Shrivastava, A. Huff, & J. Dutton (eds.), *Advances in Strategic Management,* Greenwich, CT: JAI Press, 9.
79. A. A. Lado, N. G. Boyd, P. Wright & M. Kroll, 2006, Paradox and theorizing within the resource-based view, *Academy of Management Review,* 31: 115–131; D. M. DeCarolis, 2003, Competencies and imitability in the pharmaceutical industry: An analysis of their relationship with firm performance, *Journal of Management,* 29: 27–50; Barney, Is the resource-based "view" a useful perspective for strategic management research? Yes.
80. C. Zott, 2003, Dynamic capabilities and the emergence of intraindustry differential firm performance: Insights from a simulation study, *Strategic Management Journal,* 24: 97–125.
81. E. Levitas & H. A. Ndofor, 2006, What to do with the resource-based view: A few suggestions for what ails the RBV that supporters and opponents might accept, *Journal of Management Inquiry,* 15(2): 135–144; G. Hawawini, V. Subramanian & P. Verdin, 2003, Is performance driven by industry- or firm-specific factors? A new look at the evidence, *Strategic Management Journal,* 24: 1–16.
82. M. Makhija, 2003, Comparing the resource-based and market-based views of the firm: Empirical evidence from Czech privatization, *Strategic Management Journal,* 24: 433-451; T. J. Douglas & J. A. Ryman, 2003, Understanding competitive advantage in the general hospital industry: Evaluating strategic competencies, *Strategic Management Journal,* 24: 333–347.
83. R. D. Ireland, R. E. Hoskisson & M. A. Hitt. 2006, *Understanding Business Strategy,* Cincinnati: Thomson South-Western, 32–34.
84. R. Zolli, 2006, Recognizing tomorrow's hot ideas today, *BusinessWeek,* September 25: 12.
85. S. Steptoe, 2007, Building a better mouse, *Time,* June 25, 1.
86. 2005, The CEO's secret handbook, *Business 2.0,* July, 69–76.
87. R. D. Ireland & M. A. Hitt, 1992, Mission statements: Importance, challenge, and recommendations for development, *Business Horizons,* 35(3): 34–42.
88. W. J. Duncan, 1999, *Management: Ideas and Actions,* New York: Oxford University Press, 122–125.
89. J. H. Davis, J. A. Ruhe, M. Lee & U. Rajadhyaksha, 2007, Mission possible: Do school mission statements work? *Journal of Business Ethics,* 70: 99–110.
90. A. J. Ward, M. J. Lankau, A. C. Amason, J. A. Sonnenfeld & B. A. Agle, 2007, Improving the performance of top management teams, *MIT Sloan Management Review,* 48(3): 85–90; J. A. Pearce & J. P. Doh, 2005, The high impact of collaborative social initiatives, *MIT Sloan Management Review,* 46(3): 30–39.
91. J. R. Baum, E. A. Locke & S. A. Kirkpatrick, 1998, A longitudinal study of the relation of vision and vision communication to venture growth in entrepreneurial firms, *Journal of Applied Psychology,* 83: 43–54.
92. R. Kaufman, 2006, *Change, Choices, and Consequences: A Guide to Mega Thinking and Planning,* Amherst, MA: HRD Press; J. Humphreys, 2004, The vision thing, *MIT Sloan Management Review,* 45(4): 96.
93. P. A. Argenti, R. A. Howell & K. A. Beck, 2005, The strategic communication imperative, *MIT Sloan Management Review,* 46(3): 83–89; J. Frooman, 1999, Stakeholder influence strategies, *Academy of Management Review,* 24: 191–205.
94. J. P. Walsh & W. R. Nord, 2005, Taking stock of stakeholder management, *Academy of Management Review,* 30: 426–438; T. M. Jones & A. C. Wicks, 1999, Convergent stakeholder theory, *Academy of Management Review,* 24: 206–221; R. E. Freeman, 1984, Strategic Management: A Stakeholder Approach, Boston: Pitman, 53–54.
95. G. Donaldson & J. W. Lorsch, 1983, *Decision Making at the Top: The Shaping of Strategic Direction,* New York: Basic Books, 37–40.
96. S. Sharma & I. Henriques, 2005, Stakeholder influences on sustainability practices in the Canadian Forest products industry, *Strategic Management Journal,* 26: 159–180.
97. A. Mackey, T. B. Mackey & J. B. Barney, 2007, Corporate social responsibility and firm performance: Investor preferences and corporate strategies, *Academy of Management Review,* 32: 817–835; A. J. Hillman & G. D. Keim, 2001, Shareholder value, stakeholder management, and social issues: What's the bottom line? *Strategic Management Journal,* 22: 125–139.
98. J. M. Stevens, H. K. Steensma, D. A. Harrison & P. L. Cochran, 2005, Symbolic or substantive document? The influence of ethics codes on financial executives' decisions, *Strategic Management Journal,* 26: 181–195.
99. M. L. Barnett & R. M. Salomon, 2006, Beyond dichotomy: The curvilinear relationship between social responsibility and financial performance, *Strategic Management Journal,* 27: 1101–1122.
100. L.Vilanova, 2007, Neither shareholder nor stakeholder management: What happens when firms are run for their short-term salient stakeholder? *European Management Journal,* 25(2): 146–162.
101. R. E. Freeman & J. McVea, 2001, A stakeholder approach to strategic management, in M. A. Hitt, R. E. Freeman & J. S. Harrison (eds.), *Handbook of Strategic Management,* Oxford, UK: Blackwell Publishers, 189–207.
102. C. Caldwell & R. Karri, 2005, Organizational governance and ethical systems: A convenantal approach to building trust, *Journal of Business Ethics,* 58: 249–267; A. McWilliams & D. Siegel, 2001, Corporate social responsibility: A theory of the firm perspective, *Academy of Management Review,* 26: 117–127.
103. C. Hardy, T. B. Lawrence & D. Grant, 2005, Discourse and collaboration: The role of conversations and collective identity, *Academy of Management Review,* 30: 58–77; R. K. Mitchell, B. R. Agle & D. J. Wood, 1997, Toward a theory of stakeholder identification and salience: Defining the principle of who and what really count, *Academy of Management Review,* 22: 853–886.
104. S. Maitlis, 2005, The social process of organizational sensemaking, *Academy of Management Journal,* 48: 21–49.
105. D. Michaels, 2007, Airbus seeks union support; justifying job cuts may prove critical to allaying anger, *Wall Street Journal,* March 1, A11.
106. B. A. Neville & B. Menguc, 2006, Stakeholder multiplicity: Toward an understanding of the interactions between stakeholders, *Journal of Business Ethics,* 66: 377–391.
107. T. M. Gardner, 2005, Interfirm competition for human resources: Evidence from the software industry, *Academy of Management Journal,* 48: 237–256.
108. J. A. Byrne, 2005, Working for the boss from hell, *Fast Company,* July, 14.
109. N. Abe & S. Shimizutani, 2007, Employment policy and corporate governance—An empirical comparison of the stakeholder and the profit-maximization model, *Journal of Comparative Economics,* 35: 346–368.
110. D. Brady & D. Kiley, 2005, Short on sizzle, and losing steam, *BusinessWeek,* April 25, 44.
111. E. T. Prince, 2005, The fiscal behavior of CEOs, *MIT Sloan Management Review,* 46(3): 23–26.
112. D. C. Hambrick, 2007, Upper echelons theory: An update, *Academy of Management Review,* 32: 334–339.

113. A. Priestland & T. R. Hanig, 2005, Developing first-level managers, *Harvard Business Review,* 83(6): 113–120.
114. R. T. Pascale & J. Sternin, 2005, Your company's secret change agent, *Harvard Business Review,* 83(5): 72–81.
115. Y. L. Doz, M. Kosonen, 2007, The new deal at the top, *Harvard Business Review,* 85(6): 98–104.
116. D. Lavie, 2006, The competitive advantage of interconnected firms: An extension of the resource-based view, *Academy of Management Review,* 31: 638–658.
117. 2005, About Wal-Mart, www.walmart .com, July 3.
118. D. Rooke & W. R. Tolbert, 2005, Seven transformations of leadership, *Harvard Business Review,* 83(4): 66–76.
119. T. Leavitt, 1991, *Thinking about Management,* New York: Free Press, 9.
120. 2007, 100 Best Corporate citizens for 2007, *CRO Magazine,* www.thecro.com, June 19.
121. D. C. Hambrick, S. Finkelstein & A. C. Mooney, 2005, Executive job demands: New insights for explaining strategic decisions and leader behaviors, *Academy of Management Review,* 30: 472–491; J. Brett & L. K. Stroh, 2003, Working 61 plus hours a week: Why do managers do it? *Journal of Applied Psychology,* 88: 67–78.
122. J. A. Byrne, 2005, Great work if you can get it, *Fast Company,* April, 14.
123. M. Loeb, 1993, Steven J. Ross, 1927–1992, *Fortune,* January 25, 4.
124. Collins, Jim Collins on tough calls.
125. O. Gadiesh & J. L. Gilbert, 1998, Profit pools: A fresh look at strategy, *Harvard Business Review,* 76(3): 139–147.
126. O. Gadiesh & J. L. Gilbert, 1998, How to map your industry's profit pool, *Harvard Business Review,* 76(3): 149–162.
127. C. Zook, 2007, Finding your next CORE business, *Harvard Business Review,* 85(4): 66–75; M. J. Epstein & R. A. Westbrook, 2001, Linking actions to profits in strategic decision making, *Sloan Management Review,* 42(3): 39–49.
128. D. J. Ketchen, C. C. Snow & V. L. Street, 2004, Improving firm performance by matching strategic decision-making processes to competitive dynamics, *Academy of Management Executive,* 18(4): 29–43.
129. P. Evans & B. Wolf, 2005, Collaboration rules, *Harvard Business Review,* 83(7): 96–104.
130. P. Sanders, 2007, Strange bedfellows: Marriott, Schrager, *Wall Street Journal,* June 14: B1, B5.
131. M. Useem, 2006, How well-run board make decisions, *Harvard Business Review,* 84(11): 130–138; I. Le Breton-Miller & D. Miller, 2006, Why do some family businesses out-compete? Governance, long-term orientations, and sustainable capability, *Entrepreneurship Theory and Practice,* 30: 731–746.
132. C. Eesley & M. J. Lenox, 2006, Firm responses to secondary stakeholder action, *Strategic Management Journal,* 27: 765–781.
133. S. J. Reynolds, F. C. Schultz & D. R. Hekman, 2006, Stakeholder theory and managerial decision-making: Constraints and implications of balancing stakeholder interests, *Journal of Business Ethics,* 64: 285–301; L. K. Trevino & G. R. Weaver, 2003, *Managing Ethics in Business Organizations,* Stanford, CA: Stanford University Press.
134. J. R. Ehrenfeld, 2005, The roots of sustainability, *MIT Sloan Management Review,* 46(2): 23–25.
135. B. W. Heineman Jr., 2007, Avoiding integrity land minds, *Harvard Business Review,* 85(4): 100–108; 2005, Corporate citizenship on the rise, *BusinessWeek,* May 9, S1–S7.

The External Environment: Opportunities, Threats, Industry Competition, and Competitor Analysis

Studying this chapter should provide you with the strategic management knowledge needed to:

1. Explain the importance of analyzing and understanding the firm's external environment.
2. Define and describe the general environment and the industry environment.
3. Discuss the four activities of the external environmental analysis process.
4. Name and describe the general environment's six segments.
5. Identify the five competitive forces and explain how they determine an industry's profit potential.
6. Define strategic groups and describe their influence on the firm.
7. Describe what firms need to know about their competitors and different methods (including ethical standards) used to collect intelligence about them.

Environmental Pressures on Wal-Mart

© Justin Sullivan/Staff/Getty Images

Are key rivals outrunning Wal-Mart? Is the company receiving pressure because of its poor public image, environmental concerns, and accusations regarding the treatment of its associates? A recent article in *BusinessWeek* reported that Wal-Mart had the smallest percentage increase in sales for new stores opening in 2006, compared to competitors such as CVS, Target, and Kroger. In fact, same-store sales growth turned negative in November 2006 before rebounding to increase 1.6 percent in December. In the same time period, Costco and Target sales were up 9 percent and 4.1 percent, respectively. Additionally, Wal-Mart's stock (about $48 a share in the middle of 2007) was flat in an otherwise strong year for stocks. Because Wal-Mart is the nation's largest employer and the second-largest company by revenue, its every move is scrutinized. And, 2006 and 2007 proved to be tough years for the retail giant. Between legal troubles, public relations problems, and labor issues, Wal-Mart is beginning to experience problems with rivals' competitive actions.

Wal-Mart emerged from a small town in Arkansas to dominate the retail business market for nearly five decades. Its signature of "everyday low prices" is based on its cost leadership strategy on which its business model is built. But over the past two years, its growth formula has not worked as effectively as in the past, allowing opportunities for competitors. In 2006, its U.S. division only produced a 1.9 percent gain in same-store sales, which was its worst performance ever. By this key measure, competitors such as Target, Costco, Kroger, Safeway, Walgreens, CVS, and Best Buy now are all growing two-to-five times faster than Wal-Mart. Wal-Mart's growth in recent years has come primarily from opening new stores rather than from existing stores. For example, in 2005 Wal-Mart achieved an increase in U.S. revenues of 7.2 percent by opening new stores at the rate of nearly one a day. However, Wall Street is concerned about market saturation and Wal-Mart's stock price has stagnated. Many analysts also feel that Wal-Mart is relying too heavily on building new stores to compensate for sagging same-store sales.

Wal-Mart has been plagued by many other problems that likely are affecting its ability to attract new customers and increase sales. Some of the problems are political. For example, several cities erected legal obstacles to the location of Wal-Mart stores in specific areas. Wal-Mart has been criticized for the low pay and poor benefit packages provided to many of its associates. In response and to improve its image in communities, Lee Scott, Wal-Mart's CEO, pledged to raise wages 6 percent in a third of its stores. Critics are still not satisfied with his response because most of those funds will be offset by pay caps for longtime employees. Wal-Mart has also promised to reduce the cost of healt[illegible] care benefits to associates to as little as $23 a mo[illegible]

Environmentalists are also applying pressure on Wal-Mart. Because of its position as one of the world's largest companies, with more than 3,000 stores in the United States, the firm's efforts to go "green" could have a major impact. To address this pressure, Wal-Mart is revamping its overall environmental strategy with the assistance of Conservation International, a nonprofit environmental group that works closely with companies in creating environmental policies and initiatives. Lee Scott told associates in a recent speech that Wal-Mart was establishing ambitious goals such as increasing the efficiency of its vehicle fleet by 25 percent within three years and doubling the efficiency in ten years. The firm has targeted reducing energy use in stores by 30 percent and reducing solid wastes in the stores by 25 percent over a three-year period. Wal-Mart has agreed to invest $500 million annually in environmental technologies to be used in its stores. The new green initiatives include working toward a goal of producing no waste, providing fuel from renewable resources, and working closely with its suppliers to promote good environmental practices.

Wal-Mart committed to issue an initial environmental sustainability report in 2007, and provide data on its Web site that can be used to track its reduction of waste and greenhouse gas production. Even with the $500 million pledge for greening the stories, it is still less than one-fifth of one percentage point of Wal-Mart's total sales in 2006.

The entities with which Wal-Mart must deal have grown in number and complexity as it has entered additional international markets over the last decade. For example, Wal-Mart has significant operations in 15 foreign countries, including China, several Latin American countries, and the United Kingdom. Wal-Mart obtains many products sold in its stores from Chinese manufacturers, but it also has 73 stores in China to serve Chinese customers. It recently signed an agreement to enter the Indian market in a joint venture (JV) with the Indian company, Bharti Enterprises. This JV allows it to avoid Indian laws prohibiting foreign retailers. Still, the Indian government is receiving pressure to investigate from those who dislike Wal-Mart because of its market power and reputation.

Sources: A. Bianco, 2007, Wal-Mart's Midlife Crisis, *BusinessWeek*, http://www.businessweek.com, April 30; 2007, Key rivals outrun Wal-Mart, *BusinessWeek*, http://www.businessweek.com, April 30; G. Weiss, 2007, Wal-Mart comes to India, *Forbes*, http://www.forbes.com, March 26; J. Carey, 2007, Wal-Mart: Big strides to become the Jolly Green Giant, *BusinessWeek*, http://www.businessweek.com, January 29; M. Guenther, 2006, Wal-Mart sees green, CNNMoney, http://www.cnnmoney.com, July 27; J. Birchall, 2006, Wal-Mart picks a shade of green, *Financial Times*, http://www.ft.com, February 6; J. Birchall, 2005, Wal-Mart sets out stall for a greener future, *Financial Times*, http://www.ft.com, October 25; J. Birger, 2007, The unending woes of Lee Scott, *CNN Money*, http://www.money.cnn.com, January 9; F. Harvey and E. Rigby, 2006, Supermarkets' green credentials attacked, *Financial Times*, http://www.ft.com, September 14.

As described in the Opening Case and suggested by research, the external environment affects firm growth and profitability.[1] Wal-Mart's growth has been slowed and its profitability affected most directly by its competitors. In addition, Wal-Mart must deal with other important external parties such as local, state, and national government bodies (foreign governments as well); unions; and even special-purpose organizations including groups interested in promoting green environmental practices. Major political events such as the war in Iraq, the strength of separate nations' economies at different times, and the emergence of new technologies are a few examples of conditions in the external environment that affect firms throughout the world. These and other external environmental conditions create threats to and opportunities for firms that, in turn, have major effects on their strategic actions.[2]

Regardless of the industry, the external environment is critical to a firm's survival and success. This chapter focuses on how firms analyze and understand the external environment. The firm's understanding of the external environment is matched with knowledge about its internal environment (discussed in the next chapter) to form its vision, to develop its mission, and to identify and implement actions that result in strategic competitiveness and above-average returns (see Figure 1.1, on page 5).

As noted in Chapter 1, the environmental conditions in the current global economy differ from those previously faced by firms. Technological changes and the continuing growth of information gathering and processing capabilities demand more timely and effective competitive actions and responses.[3] The rapid sociological changes occurring in many countries affect labor practices and the nature of products demanded by increasingly diverse consumers. Governmental policies and laws also affect where and how firms may choose to compete.[4] For example, deregulation of utility firms in the United States has had a major effect on the strategies employed by utility firms in recent years.[5] To achieve strategic competitiveness and thrive, firms must be aware of and understand the different dimensions of the external environment.

Firms understand the external environment by acquiring information about competitors, customers, and other stakeholders to build their own base of knowledge and capabilities.[6] On the basis of the new information, firms may take actions to build new capabilities and buffer themselves against environmental effects or to build relationships with stakeholders in their environment.[7] In order to take successful action, they must effectively analyze the external environment.

The General, Industry, and Competitor Environments

An integrated understanding of the external and internal environments is essential for firms to understand the present and predict the future.[8] As shown in Figure 2.1, a firm's external environment is divided into three major areas: the general, industry, and competitor environments.

The **general environment** is composed of dimensions in the broader society that influence an industry and the firms within it.[9] We group these dimensions into six environmental *segments:* demographic, economic, political/legal, sociocultural, technological, and global. Examples of *elements* analyzed in each of these segments are shown in Table 2.1.

The **general environment** is composed of dimensions in the broader society that influence an industry and the firms within it.

Firms cannot directly control the general environment's segments and elements. Accordingly, successful companies gather the information required to understand each segment and its implications for the selection and implementation of the appropriate

Figure 2.1 The External Environment

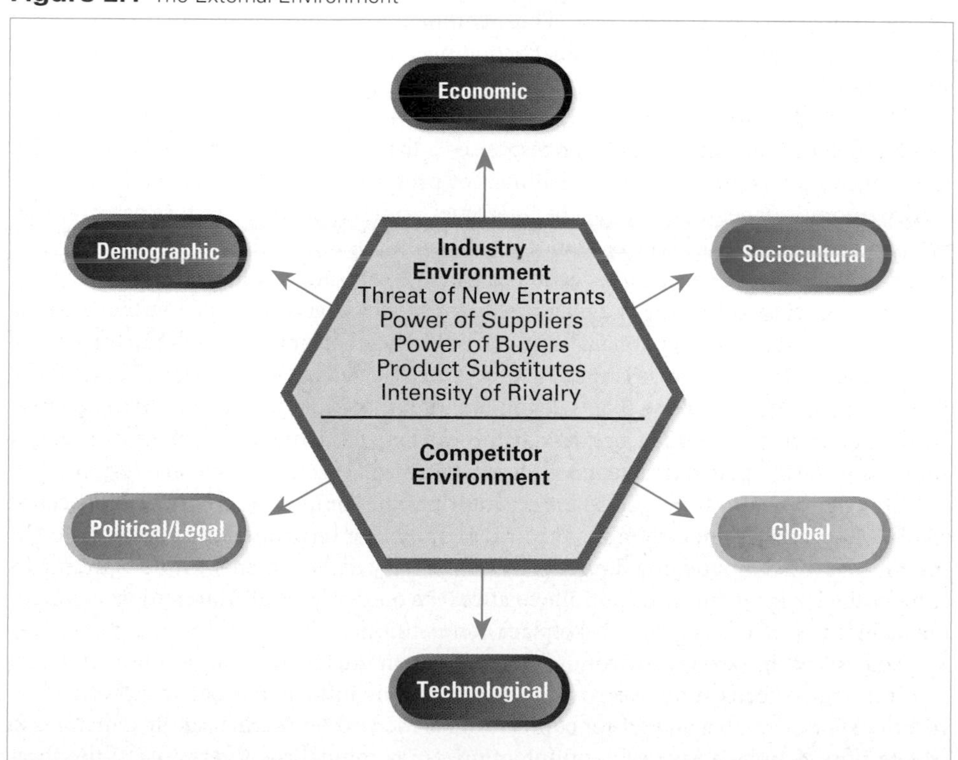

Table 2.1 The General Environment: Segments and Elements

Demographic Segment	• Population size • Age structure • Geographic distribution	• Ethnic mix • Income distribution
Economic Segment	• Inflation rates • Interest rates • Trade deficits or surpluses • Budget deficits or surpluses	• Personal savings rate • Business savings rates • Gross domestic product
Political/Legal Segment	• Antitrust laws • Taxation laws • Deregulation philosophies	• Labor training laws • Educational philosophies and policies
Sociocultural Segment	• Women in the workforce • Workforce diversity • Attitudes about the quality of work life	• Concerns about the environment • Shifts in work and career preferences • Shifts in preferences regarding product and service characteristics
Technological Segment	• Product innovations • Applications of knowledge	• Focus of private and government-supported R&D expenditures • New communication technologies
Global Segment	• Important political events • Critical global markets	• Newly industrialized countries • Different cultural and institutional attributes

strategies. For example, most firms have little individual effect on the economy or economies in which they compete, although each economy has a major effect on each firm's ability to operate and even survive. Thus, companies around the globe are challenged to understand the effects of individual economies' decline on their current and future strategies when it occurs.

The **industry environment** is the set of factors that directly influences a firm and its competitive actions and competitive responses: the threat of new entrants, the power of suppliers, the power of buyers, the threat of product substitutes, and the intensity of rivalry among competitors.

The **industry environment** is the set of factors that directly influences a firm and its competitive actions and competitive responses[10]: the threat of new entrants, the power of suppliers, the power of buyers, the threat of product substitutes, and the intensity of rivalry among competitors. In total, the interactions among these five factors determine an industry's profit potential. The challenge is to locate a position within an industry where a firm can favorably influence those factors or where it can successfully defend against their influence. In fact, positioning is a major issue for retailers, as is suggested in the Opening Case. Even though it is exceptionally large and powerful in the market, Wal-Mart faces substantial competitive rivalry as Target, Costco, Kroger, Safeway, Walgreens, CVS, and Best Buy are beginning to increase their sales and market shares. However, Wal-Mart's market power cannot be ignored. The greater a firm's capacity to favorably influence its industry environment, the greater the likelihood that the firm will earn above-average returns.

How companies gather and interpret information about their competitors is called *competitor analysis.* Understanding the firm's competitor environment complements the insights provided by studying the general and industry environments. Understanding its competitor environment will continue to affect the outcomes Wal-Mart and its competitors achieve as they engage in marketplace competition.

Analysis of the general environment is focused on the future; analysis of the industry environment is focused on the factors and conditions influencing a firm's profitability within its industry; and analysis of competitors is focused on predicting the dynamics of competitors' actions, responses, and intentions. In combination, the results of the three analyses the firm uses to understand its external environment influence its vision, mission, and strategic actions. Although we discuss each analysis separately, performance improves when the firm integrates the insights provided by analyses of the general environment, the industry environment, and the competitor environment.

External Environmental Analysis

Most firms face external environments that are highly turbulent, complex, and global—conditions that make interpreting those environments increasingly difficult.[11] To cope with often ambiguous and incomplete environmental data and to increase understanding of the general environment, firms engage in external environmental analysis. The continuous process includes four activities: scanning, monitoring, forecasting, and assessing (see Table 2.2). Analyzing the external environment is a difficult, yet significant, activity.[12]

An important objective of studying the general environment is identifying opportunities and threats. An **opportunity** is a condition in the general environment that, if exploited, helps a company achieve strategic competitiveness. For example, the number of people 65 and older is predicted to be slightly less than 20 million in 2014. This number represents a growth of almost 35 percent from the number 65 and older in 2004.[13] Retailers can target this market with goods and services designed to meet the needs of people in the age group and stage of their lives (e.g., leisure activities, medical supplies). In so doing, they can take advantage of the significant growth in the number of people in this market segment.

An **opportunity** is a condition in the general environment that, if exploited, helps a company achieve strategic competitiveness.

A **threat** is a condition in the general environment that may hinder a company's efforts to achieve strategic competitiveness.[14] The once-revered firm Polaroid can attest to the seriousness of external threats. Polaroid was a leader in its industry and considered one of the top 50 firms in the United States. When its competitors developed photographic equipment using digital technology, Polaroid was unprepared and never responded effectively. It filed for bankruptcy in 2001. In 2002, the former Polaroid Corp. was sold to Bank One's OEP Imaging unit, which promptly changed its own name to Polaroid Corp. Jacques Nasser, a former CEO at Ford, took over as CEO at Polaroid and found that the brand had continued life. Nasser used the brand in a partnership with Petters Group to put the Polaroid name on "TVs and DVDs made in Asian factories and sell them through Wal-Mart and Target."[15] Even though Polaroid went public again and was later sold to Petters Group in 2005, it was still a much smaller version of its original business. As these examples indicate, opportunities suggest competitive *possibilities,* while threats are potential *constraints.*

A **threat** is a condition in the general environment that may hinder a company's efforts to achieve strategic competitiveness.

Several sources can be used to analyze the general environment, including a wide variety of printed materials (such as trade publications, newspapers, business publications, and the results of academic research and public polls), trade shows and suppliers, customers, and employees of public-sector organizations. People in *boundary-spanning*

Table 2.2 Components of the External Environmental Analysis

Scanning	• Identifying early signals of environmental changes and trends
Monitoring	• Detecting meaning through ongoing observations of environmental changes and trends
Forecasting	• Developing projections of anticipated outcomes based on monitored changes and trends
Assessing	• Determining the timing and importance of environmental changes and trends for firms' strategies and their management

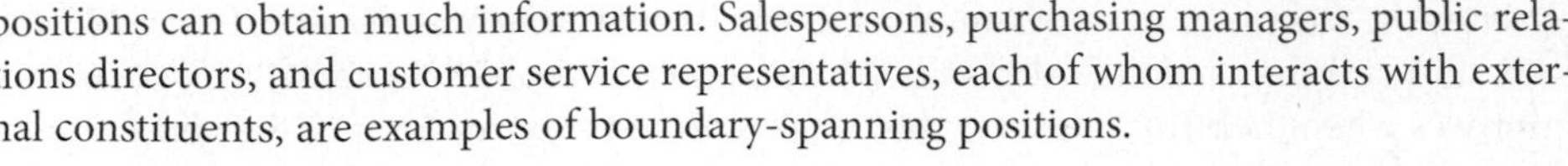

positions can obtain much information. Salespersons, purchasing managers, public relations directors, and customer service representatives, each of whom interacts with external constituents, are examples of boundary-spanning positions.

Scanning

Scanning entails the study of all segments in the general environment. Through scanning, firms identify early signals of potential changes in the general environment and detect changes that are already underway.[16] Scanning often reveals ambiguous, incomplete, or unconnected data and information. Thus, environmental scanning is challenging but critically important for firms competing in highly volatile environments.[17] In addition, scanning activities must be aligned with the organizational context; a scanning system designed for a volatile environment is inappropriate for a firm in a stable environment.[18]

Amazon.com uses special software to help with organizational scanning of its customers.

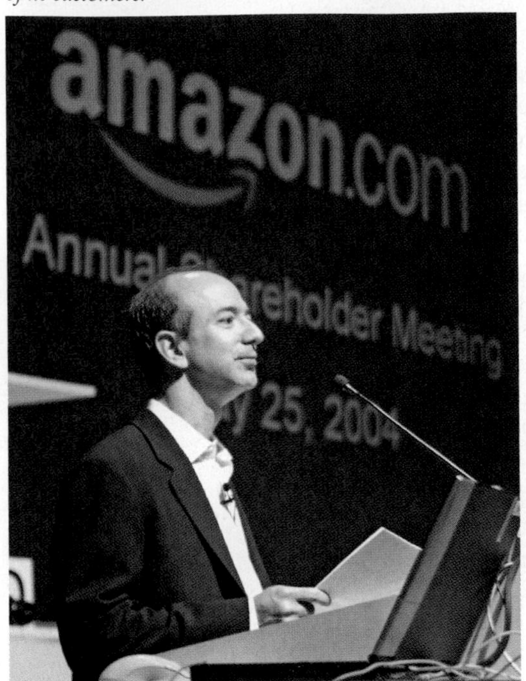

© AP Photo/Jim Bryant

Many firms use special software to help them identify events that are taking place in the environment and that are announced in public sources. For example, news event detection uses information-based systems to categorize text and reduce the trade-off between an important missed event and false alarm rates.[19] The Internet provides significant opportunities for scanning. For example, Amazon.com, similar to many Internet companies, records significant information about individuals visiting its Web site, particularly if a purchase is made. Amazon then welcomes these customers by name when they visit the Web site again. The firm even sends messages to them about specials and new products similar to those purchased in previous visits.

Additionally, many Web sites and advertisers on the Internet use "cookies" to obtain information from those who visit their sites. These files are saved to the visitors' hard drives, allowing customers to connect more quickly to a firm's Web site, but also allowing the firm to solicit a variety of information about them. Because cookies are often placed without customers' knowledge, their use can be a questionable practice. Although computer cookies have been a boon to online advertisers, they have brought a significant threat of computer viruses, hacking ability, spyware, spam, and other difficulties to computer users. The U.S. government and several states have passed legislation regarding spyware. In fact, the Federal Trade Commission (FTC) has recently taken action against major spyware organizations levying fines as large as $1.5 million. However, the FTC believes that stronger legislation is needed and has asked the U.S. Congress for a larger budget to pursue spyware organizations.[20]

Monitoring

When *monitoring,* analysts observe environmental changes to see if an important trend is emerging from among those spotted by scanning.[21] Critical to successful monitoring is the firm's ability to detect meaning in different environmental events and trends. For example, the size of the middle class of African Americans continues to grow in the United States. With increasing wealth, this group of citizens is more aggressively pursuing investment options.[22] Companies in the financial planning sector could monitor this change in the economic segment to determine the degree to which a competitively important trend is emerging. By monitoring trends, firms can be prepared to introduce new goods and services at the appropriate time to take advantage of the opportunities identified trends provide.[23]

Effective monitoring requires the firm to identify important stakeholders. Because the importance of different stakeholders can vary over a firm's life cycle, careful attention must be given to the firm's needs and its stakeholder groups across time.[24] Scanning and monitoring are particularly important when a firm competes in an industry with high technological uncertainty.[25] Scanning and monitoring not only can provide the firm with information, they also serve as a means of importing new knowledge about markets and about how to successfully commercialize new technologies that the firm has developed.[26]

Forecasting

Scanning and monitoring are concerned with events and trends in the general environment at a point in time. When *forecasting*, analysts develop feasible projections of what might happen, and how quickly, as a result of the changes and trends detected through scanning and monitoring.[27] For example, analysts might forecast the time that will be required for a new technology to reach the marketplace, the length of time before different corporate training procedures are required to deal with anticipated changes in the composition of the workforce, or how much time will elapse before changes in governmental taxation policies affect consumers' purchasing patterns.

Forecasting events and outcomes accurately is challenging. Alcas Corporation is a direct marketing company that features Cutco Cutlery, a well-known brand that produces an assortment of knives and cutting utensils. Cutco Cutlery has an alliance with Vector Marketing, which is also closely held by Alcas, and one of its specialties is sales forecasting. However, it recently experienced a difficult forecasting problem. The company had forecasted a 25 percent increase in sales, but sales actually increased 47 percent. Although generally positive, this increase created a shortage, and Cutco Cutlery did not have the capacity to fill orders in its usual timely fashion. Normal delivery of two to three weeks eventually was pushed to five or six weeks. This problem was critical because the company had built its reputation on quick delivery as a way to differentiate the value it provides to consumers.[28] Forecasting is important in order to adjust sales appropriately to meet demand.

Assessing

The objective of *assessing* is to determine the timing and significance of the effects of environmental changes and trends on the strategic management of the firm.[29] Through scanning, monitoring, and forecasting, analysts are able to understand the general environment. Going a step further, the intent of assessment is to specify the implications of that understanding for the organization. Without assessment, the firm is left with data that may be interesting but are of unknown competitive relevance. Even if formal assessment is inadequate, the appropriate interpretation of that information is important: "Research found that how accurate senior executives are about their competitive environments is indeed less important for strategy and corresponding organizational changes than the way in which they interpret information about their environments."[30] Thus, although gathering and organizing information is important, investing resources in the appropriate interpretation of that intelligence may be equally important. Accordingly, after information has been gathered, assessing whether a trend in the environment represents an opportunity or a threat is extremely important.

Segments of the General Environment

The general environment is composed of segments that are external to the firm (see Table 2.1, on page 36). Although the degree of impact varies, these environmental segments affect each industry and its firms. The challenge to the firm is to scan, monitor, forecast, and assess those elements in each segment that are of the greatest importance. These efforts should result in recognition of environmental changes, trends, opportunities, and threats. Opportunities are then matched with a firm's core competencies (the matching process is discussed further in Chapter 3).

The Demographic Segment

The **demographic segment** is concerned with a population's size, age structure, geographic distribution, ethnic mix, and income distribution.

The **demographic segment** is concerned with a population's size, age structure, geographic distribution, ethnic mix, and income distribution.[31] Often demographic segments are analyzed on a global basis because of their potential effects across countries' borders and because many firms compete in global markets.

Population Size

By the end of 2007, the world's population was slightly over 6.6 billion, up from 6.1 billion in 2000. Combined, China and India accounted for one-third of the 6.6 billion. Given the declining birth rate, experts speculate that the world population will reach about 9.2 billion by 2050. India (with more than 1.65 billion people projected) and China (with about 1.4 billion people projected) are expected to remain the most populous countries.[32] Interestingly, only slightly over 1 billion people live in developed countries whereas more than 5 billion live in developing countries.

Despite a declining birth rate, China is expected to remain one of the most populous countries in the world for years to come.

© Bill Bachmann/PhotoEdit

Observing demographic changes in populations highlights the importance of this environmental segment. For example, in 2006, 20 percent of Japan's citizens were 65 or older, while the United States and China will not reach this level until 2036.[33] Aging populations are a significant problem for countries because of the need for workers and the burden of funding retirement programs. In Japan and other countries, employees are urged to work longer to overcome these problems. Interestingly, the United States has a higher birthrate and significant immigration, placing it in a better position than Japan and other European nations.

Age Structure

As noted earlier, in Japan and other countries, the world's population is rapidly aging. In North America and Europe, millions of baby boomers are approaching retirement. However, even in developing countries with large numbers of people under the age of 35, birth rates have been declining sharply. In China, for example, by 2040 there will be more than 400 million people over the age of 60. The 90 million baby boomers in North America are fueling the current economy because they seem to continue to spend as they age. They are also thus expected to fuel growth in the financial planning sector as they inherit $1 trillion over the next 15 years and rush to save more before retirement. However, the future surrounding baby boomers is clouded in at least two areas. One problem is the significant increase in health care costs. For instance, Canadian health care, which has strong government subsidies, is predicted to consume 40 percent of all government tax revenues by 2040. The other problem is that as the number of retired baby boomers swells, the number of workers paying Social Security and other taxes will decrease significantly, leaving governments in North America and Europe to face significant choices. It seems that governments will have to increase the retirement age, cut benefits, raise taxes, and/or run significant budget deficits.[34]

Although emerging economy populations are aging as well, they still have a significantly younger large labor force. The consumer products being produced so cheaply in China and exported to the United States are helping North American consumers to contain inflation. However, the basic prices of commodities such as copper, oil, and gas have been rising as China increases its productivity and seeks to maintain employment levels of its large population. As the workforce in the West ages and education levels rise in emerging economies, the United States and Canada will likely have to accept larger numbers of immigrant workers. At the same time, Western firms are outsourcing work to such countries as India, which has a growing high-tech sector. As can be seen, changes in the age structure have significant effects on firms in an economy.

Geographic Distribution

For decades, the U.S. population has been shifting from the north and east to the west and south. Similarly, the trend of relocating from metropolitan to nonmetropolitan areas continues. These trends are changing local and state governments' tax bases. In turn, business firms' decisions regarding location are influenced by the degree of support that different taxing agencies offer as well as the rates at which these agencies tax businesses.

The geographic distribution of populations throughout the world is also affected by the capabilities resulting from advances in communications technology. Through computer technologies, for example, people can remain in their homes, communicating with others in remote locations to complete their work.

Ethnic Mix

The ethnic mix of countries' populations continues to change. Within the United States, the ethnicity of states and their cities varies significantly. For firms, the Hispanic market in the United States has been changing significantly. CSI TV, the 24-hour cable channel for young Latinos, was launched in February 2004 and now has 10 million viewers. Its motto is "Speak English. Live Latin." Firms need to focus on marketing not only to the broader Hispanic market but also to those who want to be integrated and "don't want to be segregated."[35] This latter market segment wants to see their own lives being portrayed on television, rather than those of Anglos. They want to shop at the same stores and have a similar lifestyle. Men's Wearhouse learned this by the failure of its Eddie Rodriguez clothing stores, which targeted Latino men; all six stores were closed in 2005. Consumers simply said "no" to the concept because they wanted to be integrated. Hispanic Americans between the ages of 14 and 34 want to be spoken to in English but stay true to their Latino identity. The Latino spending power is important for large consumer sectors such as grocery stores, movie studios, financial services, and clothing stores among others. Overall, the Hispanic market is approximately $1 trillion in size.[36] Through careful study, companies can develop and market products that satisfy the unique needs of different ethnic groups.

Changes in the ethnic mix also affect a workforce's composition and cooperation.[37] In the United States, for example, the population and labor force will continue to diversify, as immigration accounts for a sizable part of growth. Projections are that the combined Latino and Asian population shares will increase to more than 20 percent of the total U.S. population by 2014.[38] Interestingly, much of this immigrant workforce is bypassing high-cost coastal cities and settling in smaller rural towns. Many of these workers are in low-wage, labor-intensive industries such as construction, food service, lodging, and landscaping.[39] For this reason, if border security is tightened, these industries will likely face labor shortages.

Income Distribution

Understanding how income is distributed within and across populations informs firms of different groups' purchasing power and discretionary income. Studies of income distributions suggest that although living standards have improved over time, variations exist within and between nations.[40] Of interest to firms are the average incomes of households and individuals. For instance, the increase in dual-career couples has had a notable effect on average incomes. Although real income has been declining in general, the household income of dual-career couples has increased. These figures yield strategically relevant information for firms. For instance, research indicates that whether an employee is part of a dual-career couple can strongly influence the willingness of the employee to accept an international assignment.[41]

The Economic Segment

The health of a nation's economy affects individual firms and industries. For this reason, companies study the economic environment to identify changes, trends, and their strategic implications.

The **economic environment** refers to the nature and direction of the economy in which a firm competes or may compete.

The **economic environment** refers to the nature and direction of the economy in which a firm competes or may compete.[42] Because nations are interconnected as a result of the global economy, firms must scan, monitor, forecast, and assess the health of economies outside their host nation. For example, many nations throughout the world are affected by the U.S. economy.

The U.S. economy declined into a recession in 2001 that extended into 2002. In order to stimulate the economy, interest rates in the United States were cut to near record lows in 2003, equaling the rates in 1958.[43] Largely due to the low interest rates, the economy grew substantially in 2004 and 2005. Global trade was likewise stimulated. However, high oil prices have dampened global economic growth. Additionally, economic growth slowed in 2006 with the U.S. GDP growth slowing from more than 4 percent in 2005 to approximately 3.2 percent in 2006. This slowing growth is predicted to continue with a projected GDP growth of 2.3 percent in 2007.[44] Although bilateral trade can enrich the economies of the countries involved, it also makes each country more vulnerable to negative events in any one country. As our discussion of the economic segment suggests, economic issues are intertwined closely with the realities of the external environment's political/legal segment.

The Political/Legal Segment

The **political/legal segment** is the arena in which organizations and interest groups compete for attention, resources, and a voice in overseeing the body of laws and regulations guiding the interactions among nations.

The **political/legal segment** is the arena in which organizations and interest groups compete for attention, resources, and a voice in overseeing the body of laws and regulations guiding the interactions among nations.[45] Essentially, this segment represents how organizations try to influence government and how governments influence them. As the politics of regulations change, this segment influences the nature of competition through changing the rules (for other examples of political/legal elements, see Table 2.1, on page 36).

For example, when new regulations are adopted based on new laws (e.g., the Sarbanes-Oxley Act dealing with corporate governance—see Chapter 10 for more information), they often affect the competitive actions taken by firms (their actions are regulated). An example is the recent global trend toward privatization of government-owned or -regulated firms. The transformation from state-owned to private firms has substantial implications for the competitive landscapes in countries and industries.[46]

Firms must carefully analyze a new political administration's business-related policies and philosophies. Antitrust laws, taxation laws, industries chosen for deregulation, labor training laws, and the degree of commitment to educational institutions are areas in which an administration's policies can affect the operations and profitability of industries and individual firms. Often, firms develop a political strategy to influence governmental policies and actions that might affect them. The effects of global governmental policies on a firm's competitive position increase the importance of forming an effective political strategy.[47]

Business firms across the globe today confront an interesting array of political/legal questions and issues. For example, the debate continues over trade policies. Some believe that a nation should erect trade barriers to protect its companies' products. However, as countries continue to join the World Trade Organization (WTO), more countries seem to believe that free trade across nations serves the best interests of individual countries and their citizens. A Geneva-based organization, the WTO establishes rules for global trade. For instance, after joining the World Trade Organization, China ended a 40-year-old global textile-quota system regulating its exports. Earlier, to ease the problems created for other countries China had voluntarily enacted transition tariffs. When the quota system expired in early 2005, Chinese textiles flooded global markets, threatening domestic textile industries. Several countries responded by imposing even higher tariffs to level the playing field.[48]

The regulations related to pharmaceuticals and telecommunications, along with the approval or disapproval of major acquisitions, shows the power of government entities. This power also suggests how important it is for firms to have a political strategy. Countries tend to take different approaches to similar problems. For example, different policies have been applied by the United States' government and the leadership of the European Union (EU) with regard to genetically modified foods and on climate change. The U.S. government has taken a looser approach to genetically modified foods while the EU has been much more restrictive. As such, U.S. firms involved in genetically modified foods have experienced problems with their goods in the EU.[49] The regulations are too few for some and too many for others. Regardless, regulations tend to vary across countries and across central government administrations, and firms must cope with these variances.

The Sociocultural Segment

The **sociocultural segment** is concerned with a society's attitudes and cultural values. Because attitudes and values form the cornerstone of a society, they often drive demographic, economic, political/legal, and technological conditions and changes.

The **sociocultural segment** is concerned with a society's attitudes and cultural values.

Sociocultural segments differ across countries. For example, in the United States, the per capita amount spent on health care is $5,711, almost 50 percent more than the second highest per capita health care expenditures in Norway. The per capita health care expenditures are $3,809 in Norway, $3,776 in Switzerland, $3,110 in Iceland, and $3,001 in Germany. Interestingly, the U.S. rate of citizens' access to health care is below that of these and other countries.[50]

The reverse is true for retirement planning. A study in 15 countries indicated that retirement planning in the United States starts earlier than in other countries. "Americans are involved in retirement issues to a greater extent than other countries, particularly in western Europe where the Social Security and pensions systems provide a much higher percentage of income in retirement."[51] U.S. residents start planning for retirement in their 30s, while those in Portugal, Spain, Italy, and Japan start in their 40s and 50s. Attitudes regarding saving for retirement also affect a nation's economic and political/legal segments.

As the labor force has increased, it has also become more diverse as significantly more women and minorities from a variety of cultures entered the labor force. In 1993, the total U.S. workforce was slightly less than 130 million, but in 2005, it was slightly greater than 148 million. It is predicted to grow to more than 162 million by 2014. In 2014, the workforce is forecasted to be composed of 47 percent female workers, 5 percent Asian American workers, 12 percent African American workers and 16 percent Hispanic workers.[52] The growing gender, ethnic, and cultural diversity in the workforce creates challenges and opportunities, including combining the best of both men's and women's traditional leadership styles. Although diversity in the workforce has the potential to add improved performance, research indicates that important conditions require management of diversity initiatives in order to reap these organizational benefits. Human resource practitioners are trained to successfully manage diversity issues to enhance positive outcomes.[53]

Another manifestation of changing attitudes toward work is the continuing growth of contingency workers (part-time, temporary, and contract employees) throughout the global economy. This trend is significant in several parts of the world, including Canada, Japan, Latin America, Western Europe, and the United States. The fastest growing group of contingency workers is in the technical and professional area. Contributing to this growth are corporate restructurings and downsizings that occur in poor economic conditions along with a breakdown of lifetime employment practices (e.g., in Japan).

The continued growth of suburban communities in the United States and abroad is another major sociocultural trend. The increasing number of people living in the suburbs has a number of effects. For example, longer commute times to urban businesses increase pressure for better transportation systems and superhighway systems (e.g., outer beltways to serve the suburban communities). Suburban growth also has an effect on the number of electronic telecommuters, which is expected to increase rapidly in the twenty-first century. Beyond suburbs lie what the U.S. Census Bureau calls "micropolitan" areas. These areas are often 100 or more miles from a large city and have 10,000 to 49,999 people. They offer rural-like living with many of the larger city amenities such as strip malls and chain restaurants like Starbucks, Chili's, Long John Silver's, and Arby's, but housing and labor costs are much cheaper.[54] Following this growth, some businesses are locating in the suburbs closer to their employees. This work-style option is feasible because of changes in the technological segment, including the Internet's rapid growth and evolution.[55]

Although the lifestyle and workforce changes referenced previously reflect the values of the U.S. population, each country and culture has unique values and trends. As suggested earlier, national cultural values affect behavior in organizations and thus also influence organizational outcomes.[56] For example, the importance of collectivism and social relations in Chinese and Russian cultures lead to the open sharing of information and knowledge among members of an organization.[57] Knowledge sharing is important for defusing new knowledge in organizations increasing the speed in implementing innovations. Personal relationships are especially important in China as guanxi (personal connections) has become a way of doing business within the country.[58] Understanding the importance of guanxi is critical for foreign firms doing business in China.

The Technological Segment

The **technological segment** includes the institutions and activities involved with creating new knowledge and translating that knowledge into new outputs, products, processes, and materials.

Pervasive and diversified in scope, technological changes affect many parts of societies. These effects occur primarily through new products, processes, and materials. The **technological segment** includes the institutions and activities involved with creating new knowledge and translating that knowledge into new outputs, products, processes, and materials.

Given the rapid pace of technological change, it is vital for firms to thoroughly study the technological segment.[59] The importance of these efforts is suggested by the finding that early adopters of new technology often achieve higher market shares and earn higher returns. Thus, firms should continuously scan the external environment to identify potential substitutes for technologies that are in current use, as well as to identify newly emerging technologies from which their firm could derive competitive advantage.[60]

However, not only is forecasting more difficult today, but a company that misses its forecast is often disciplined by the market with a reduction in stock price. For example, DreamWorks Animation, a division of DreamWorks SKG, based its forecast of *Shrek 2* DVD sales in part on the historically long sales life of animated DVDs. But because of increased competition (more firms are releasing an increasing number of DVDs) and limited shelf space, DVD titles now have a much shorter retail life. When retailers started returning millions of unsold copies, DreamWorks' earnings fell short of analysts' forecasts by 25 percent and its stock price tumbled. Misjudging how much a title will sell can have a substantial effect on the bottom line of small studios such as DreamWorks Animation, which releases only two films a year.[61] In contrast, studios that produce many films each year are shielded from the effects of a short life in one film.

Even though the Internet was a significant technological advance and provided substantial power to companies utilizing its potential, wireless communication technology is predicted to be the next critical technological opportunity. Handheld devices and other wireless communications equipment are used to access a variety of network-based services. The use of handheld computers with wireless network connectivity, Web-enabled mobile phone handsets, and other emerging platforms (e.g., consumer Internet-access devices) is expected to increase substantially, soon becoming the dominant form of communication and commerce.[62]

Clearly, the Internet and wireless forms of communications are important technological developments for many reasons. One reason for their importance, however, is that they facilitate the diffusion of other technology and knowledge critical for achieving and maintaining a competitive advantage.[63] Companies must stay current with technologies as they evolve, but also must be prepared to act quickly to embrace important new disruptive technologies shortly after they are introduced.[64] Certainly on a global scale, the technological opportunities and threats in the general environment have an effect on whether firms obtain new technology from external sources (such as by licensing and acquisition) or develop it internally.

The Global Segment

The **global segment** includes relevant new global markets, existing markets that are changing, important international political events, and critical cultural and institutional characteristics of global markets.[65] Globalization of business markets creates both opportunities and challenges for firms.[66] For example, firms can identify and enter valuable new global markets.[67] In addition to contemplating opportunities, firms should recognize potential competitive threats in these markets. China presents many opportunities and some threats for international firms.[68] China's 2001 admission to the World Trade Organization creates additional opportunities. As mentioned earlier, the low cost of Chinese products threatens many firms in the textile industry. For instance, buyers of textile products such as Marks & Spencer in the United Kingdom and others throughout the world cannot ignore China's comparative advantages, even with tariffs in place. China's average labor costs are 90 percent lower than those in the United States and Italy. Furthermore, Chinese manufacturers are more efficient than garment manufacturers in other low-cost countries such as India or Vietnam. The WTO member countries can restrict Chinese imports until 2008 if they can show that local markets are disrupted. However, even with quotas a number of firms such as Wal-Mart and hotel chains such as Hilton and Radisson are increasing their sourcing from Chinese firms because of the significant cost advantage.[69]

The **global segment** includes relevant new global markets, existing markets that are changing, important international political events, and critical cultural and institutional characteristics of global markets.

Exemplifying the globalization trend is the increasing amount of global outsourcing. However, recent research suggests that organizations incur a trade-off between flexibility and efficiency if all work in a particular function or product is outsourced. Custom work to fill special orders, for example, is more efficiently done through domestic manufacturing; outsourcing standard products to an offshore facility needs to save at least 15 percent to be justified. Even in the textile industry, where much outsourcing is done for efficiency reasons, many order adjustments or special orders require flexibility and cannot be readily handled by low-cost offshore producers.[70] Thus, the research shows that the most effective approach is to integrate some outsourcing with other tasks done internally. In this way, only specialized tasks rather than a complete function are outsourced and the outsourcing alliance is more effectively managed.[71]

Moving into international markets extends a firm's reach and potential. Toyota receives almost 50 percent of its total sales revenue from outside Japan, its home country. More than 60 percent of McDonald's sales revenues and almost 98 percent of Nokia's sales revenues are from outside their home countries.[72] Firms can also increase the opportunity to sell innovations by entering international markets. The larger total market increases the probability that the firm will earn a return on its innovations. Certainly, firms entering new markets can diffuse new knowledge they have created and learn from the new markets as well.[73]

Firms should recognize the different sociocultural and institutional attributes of global markets. Companies competing in South Korea, for example, must understand the value placed on hierarchical order, formality, and self-control, as well as on duty rather than rights. Furthermore, Korean ideology emphasizes communitarianism, a characteristic of many Asian countries. Korea's approach differs from those of Japan and China, however,

Strategic Focus

Does Google Have the Market Power to Ignore External Pressures?

Google's continued growth and expansion of its services puts fear in the hearts of its rivals. Currently, Google is the most widely used Internet search engine and as such, it dominates online advertising. In 2004 Google was worth $23 billion. By mid-2007, the firm's market capitalization hit $169 billion, making Google worth more than IBM. The company is known for its loose corporate culture, with informal principles, and appears to have the goodwill of its customers. But as Google's fortunes continue to extend its reach, it is also experiencing more pressures from the external environment.

Google's strategy of bringing to the market 'search with content' by acquiring YouTube, upset the global media industry. The industry felt that a search engine that can show films and other copyrighted content for free is the act of piracy. Viacom filed a $1 billion lawsuit against Google and YouTube alleging that they are airing clips of its hit programs without permission. The lawsuit cited "massive intentional copyright infringement." Viacom accused YouTube of violating copyright law. In February 2007, Viacom demanded that YouTube remove more than 100,000 clips, and YouTube agreed. Viacom stated that more than 160,000 clips available on YouTube are being used without Viacom's permission.

Google's continued growth and domination–including its acquisition of YouTube–have caused more pressure from the external environment.

In addition, Google is involved in other lawsuits focused around copyright violations and trademark infringements. In 2006, a Belgium court ruled that Google should refrain from posting news articles from French and German language newspapers on the Google News services. In the United States, the Authors Guild and some additional publishers, supported by the Association of American Publishers, sued Google for making digital copies of copyrighted books from libraries. Microsoft has also accused Google of "systematically violating copyright" by scanning millions of books and journals from libraries around the world and making them available online. Google disputes these accusations, suggesting that all of their products comply with copyright law. Google argues that because only a small extract of a copyrighted work is shown in its search process, it is not in violation of the copyright law. For books that have been digitized in U.S. libraries and under copyright, Google only reports that the book exists.

Google's acquisition of DoubleClick represents another critical building block in its strategy. But this move is being scrutinized by companies such as Microsoft and AT&T, in this case suggesting that Google is violating antitrust laws. Basically they argue that Google's share of the search advertisements placed on third-party Web sites, combined with the recent purchase of DoubleClick (online advertising company), will create a dominant position in the overall online advertising business. Central to this complaint is the question of whether the search and display advertising businesses, until now separate, should be treated as a single market for regulatory purposes. According to AT&T, this acquisition would make any Web company that depends on online advertising dependent on a single supplier and, in effect, Google would be able to influence the revenue lifeline of other rival Internet companies.

A combination of these external pressures has affected Google's standing on Wall Street. Google is no longer considered the hot company. In fact, its stock price has underperformed the broader market index in recent times because investors fear that retaliation from competitors could limit the company's growth (recent statistics show Google's growth

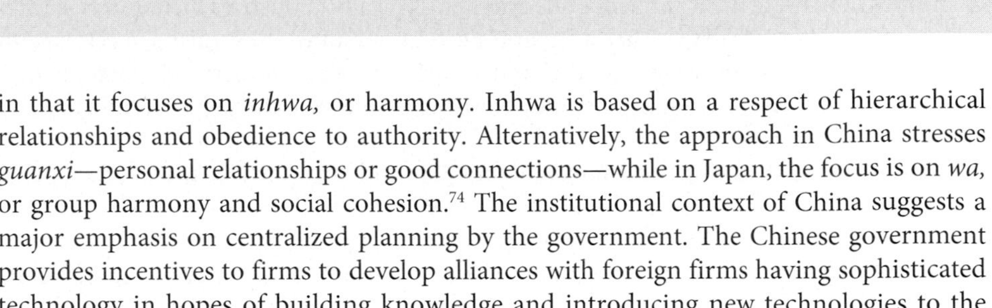

is slowing). As a result, Google's stock price has fallen. Google is now facing a number of rivals and drawing more attention of government officials as well. Still the market power of Google draws advertisers to guide traffic to their sites.

Sources: R. Waters, 2007, All eyes on Google advertising, *Financial Times*, http://www.ft.com, April 16; R. Wachman, 2007, Google's expansion is coming at a price: It's losing its popularity, *The Observer*, http://www.observer.co.uk, March 25; R. Hof, 2006, Ganging up on Google, *BusinessWeek*, http://www.businessweek.com, April 24; M. Devichand, 2007, Is Google really flouting copyright law? *BBC Law in Action*, http://www.news.bbc.co.uk, March 9; 2007, Viacom sues Google and YouTube, *International Herald Tribune*, http://www.IHT.com, March 13.

in that it focuses on *inhwa,* or harmony. Inhwa is based on a respect of hierarchical relationships and obedience to authority. Alternatively, the approach in China stresses *guanxi*—personal relationships or good connections—while in Japan, the focus is on *wa,* or group harmony and social cohesion.[74] The institutional context of China suggests a major emphasis on centralized planning by the government. The Chinese government provides incentives to firms to develop alliances with foreign firms having sophisticated technology in hopes of building knowledge and introducing new technologies to the Chinese markets over time.[75]

Firms based in other countries, particularly from some emerging markets have become quite active in global markets. Global markets offer firms more opportunities to obtain the resources needed for success. For example, the "dragon" (multinational firms from Asia Pacific countries) are growing in market power. Examples of dragon multinationals include Acer, Ispat International, Li & Fung, and the Hong Leong Group. These firms are entering international markets at a rapid pace, using new strategic approaches, and developing innovation. They are becoming a force in global markets with which firms from developed markets such as the United States and Western Europe must learn how to compete effectively.[76]

Additionally, global markets involve risk. As such some firms take a more reasoned approach to competing in international markets. These firms participate in what some refer to as *globalfocusing*. Globalfocusing often is used by firms with moderate levels of international operations who increase their internationalization by focusing on global niche markets.[77] In this way, they build on and use their special competencies and resources while limiting their risks with the niche market. Another way in which firms limit their risks in international markets is to focus their operations and sales in one region of the world.[78] In this way, they can build stronger relationships in and knowledge of their markets. As they build these strengths, rivals find it more difficult to enter their markets and compete successfully.

As explained in the Strategic Focus, Google's charmed life is being challenged with pressure from its external environment. These pressures have come from the global segment with court rulings in Europe and in the political-legal segment of the general environment with arguments that it is violating copyright laws in the United States. Its size provides market power and slack financial resources, but it also makes it more visible and vulnerable to attacks by rivals. Google has entered related industries (e.g., with the acquisition of YouTube) and faces such rivals as Viacom, Microsoft, and AT&T. Thus, it must deal with competitors' actions and responses in the industries in which it operates. Although the Strategic Focus discussion makes clear that the general environment is important to it (e.g., political legal—potential antitrust actions; global—Belgium court disallowing the posting of French and German news articles), most of the actions are the result of rivals' complaints or lawsuits. Thus, industry rivalry has a significant influence on Google.

A key objective of analyzing the general environment is identifying anticipated changes and trends among external elements. With a focus on the future, the analysis of the general environment allows firms to identify opportunities and threats. As a result, it is necessary to have a top management team with the experience, knowledge, and sensitivity required to effectively analyze this segment of the environment.[79] Also critical to a firm's future operations is an understanding of its industry environment and its competitors; these issues are considered next.

Industry Environment Analysis

An **industry** is a group of firms producing products that are close substitutes.

An **industry** is a group of firms producing products that are close substitutes. In the course of competition, these firms influence one another. Typically, industries include a rich mixture of competitive strategies that companies use in pursuing above-average returns. In part, these strategies are chosen because of the influence of an industry's characteristics.[80] The Strategic Focus on Google illustrates how the competitive forces in an industry can affect firms' behaviors.

Compared with the general environment, the industry environment often has a more direct effect on the firm's strategic competitiveness and above-average returns.[81] The intensity of industry competition and an industry's profit potential are functions of five forces of competition: the threats posed by new entrants, the power of suppliers, the power of buyers, product substitutes, and the intensity of rivalry among competitors (see Figure 2.2).

The five forces model of competition expands the arena for competitive analysis. Historically, when studying the competitive environment, firms concentrated on companies with which they competed directly. However, firms must search more broadly to recognize current and potential competitors by identifying potential customers as well as the firms serving them. Competing for the same customers and thus being influenced by how customers value location and firm capabilities in their decisions is referred to as the market microstructure.[82] Understanding this area is particularly important, because in recent years industry boundaries have become blurred. For example, telecommunications companies now compete with cable broadcasters, software manufacturers provide personal financial services, airlines sell mutual funds, and automakers sell insurance and provide financing.[83] In addition to the focus on customers rather than on specific

Figure 2.2 The Five Forces of Competition Model

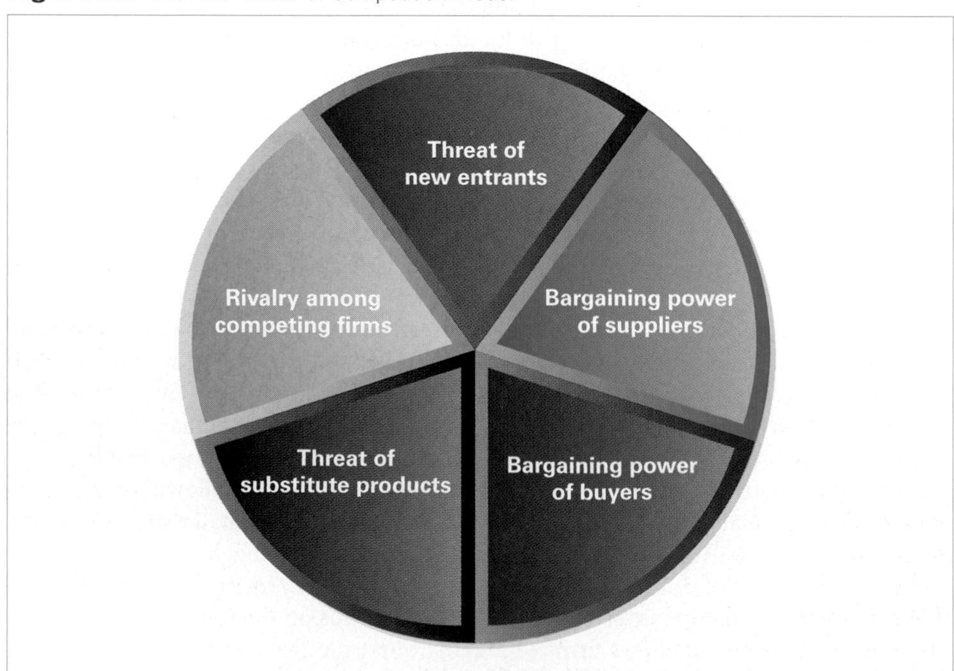

industry boundaries to define markets, geographic boundaries are also relevant. Research suggests that different geographic markets for the same product can have considerably different competitive conditions.[84]

Firms must also recognize that suppliers can become a firm's competitors (by integrating forward), as can buyers (by integrating backward). Several firms have integrated forward in the pharmaceutical industry by acquiring distributors or wholesalers. In addition, firms choosing to enter a new market and those producing products that are adequate substitutes for existing products can become a company's competitors.

Threat of New Entrants

Identifying new entrants is important because they can threaten the market share of existing competitors.[85] One reason new entrants pose such a threat is that they bring additional production capacity. Unless the demand for a good or service is increasing, additional capacity holds consumers' costs down, resulting in less revenue and lower returns for competing firms. Often, new entrants have a keen interest in gaining a large market share. As a result, new competitors may force existing firms to be more efficient and to learn how to compete on new dimensions (e.g., using an Internet-based distribution channel).

Gerald Grinstein, Delta Air Lines CEO, announces Delta's emergence from bankruptcy on May 3, 2007.

© AP Photo/Gene Blythe

The likelihood that firms will enter an industry is a function of two factors: barriers to entry and the retaliation expected from current industry participants. Entry barriers make it difficult for new firms to enter an industry and often place them at a competitive disadvantage even when they are able to enter. As such, high entry barriers increase the returns for existing firms in the industry and may allow some firms to dominate the industry.[86] Interestingly, though the airline industry has high entry barriers (e.g., substantial capital costs), new firms entered the industry in the late 1990s, among them AirTran Airways (ATA) and JetBlue. Both entrants created competitive challenges for the major airlines, especially with the economic problems in the early twenty-first century. Both firms compete in the low-cost segments, where consumer demand has increased, making the major high-cost legacy airlines less competitive. In fact, they, along with Southwest Airlines, were partly responsible for the bankruptcy of several large legacy airlines such as Delta. In September 2005, Delta announced it was going into bankruptcy, and in May 2007, it announced coming out of bankruptcy after completing a $3 billion restructuring program. The Delta CEO stated that his airline will be a fierce competitor but acknowledged it is a tough industry.[87]

Barriers to Entry

Existing competitors try to develop barriers to entry. For example, cable firms are entering the phone service business. Accordingly, local firm services such as AT&T are bundling services (e.g., high-speed Internet services, satellite television, and wireless services) in a single package and low price to prevent customer turnover. Potential entrants such as the cable firms seek markets in which the entry barriers are relatively insignificant. An absence of entry barriers increases the probability that a new entrant can operate profitably. Several kinds of potentially significant entry barriers may discourage competitors.

Economies of Scale *Economies of scale* are derived from incremental efficiency improvements through experience as a firm grows larger. Therefore, as the quantity of a product produced during a given period increases, the cost of manufacturing each unit declines. Economies of scale can be developed in most business functions, such as marketing, manufacturing, research and development, and purchasing.[88] Increasing economies of scale enhances a firm's flexibility. For example, a firm may choose to reduce its price and capture a greater share of the market. Alternatively, it may keep its price constant to increase profits. In so doing, it likely will increase its free cash flow, which is helpful in times of recession.

New entrants face a dilemma when confronting current competitors' scale economies. Small-scale entry places them at a cost disadvantage. Alternatively, large-scale entry, in which the new entrant manufactures large volumes of a product to gain economies of scale, risks strong competitive retaliation.

Some competitive conditions reduce the ability of economies of scale to create an entry barrier. Many companies now customize their products for large numbers of small customer groups. Customized products are not manufactured in the volumes necessary to achieve economies of scale. Customization is made possible by new flexible manufacturing systems (this point is discussed further in Chapter 4). In fact, the new manufacturing technology facilitated by advanced information systems has allowed the development of mass customization in an increasing number of industries. Although customization is not appropriate for all products, mass customization has become increasingly common in manufacturing products.[89] In fact, online ordering has enhanced the ability of customers to obtain customized products. They are often referred to as "markets of one."[90] Companies manufacturing customized products learn how to respond quickly to customers' desires rather than develop scale economies.

Product Differentiation Over time, customers may come to believe that a firm's product is unique. This belief can result from the firm's service to the customer, effective advertising campaigns, or being the first to market a good or service. Companies such as Coca-Cola, PepsiCo, and the world's automobile manufacturers spend a great deal of money on advertising to convince potential customers of their products' distinctiveness. Customers valuing a product's uniqueness tend to become loyal to both the product and the company producing it. Companies may also offer a series of different but highly related products to serve as an entry barrier (e.g., offering customers a variety of products from which to choose such as a series of different automobiles).[91] Typically, new entrants must allocate many resources over time to overcome existing customer loyalties. To combat the perception of uniqueness, new entrants frequently offer products at lower prices. This decision, however, may result in lower profits or even losses.

Capital Requirements Competing in a new industry requires a firm to have resources to invest. In addition to physical facilities, capital is needed for inventories, marketing activities, and other critical business functions. Even when a new industry is attractive, the capital required for successful market entry may not be available to pursue the market opportunity. For example, defense industries are difficult to enter because of the substantial resource investments required to be competitive. In addition, because of the high knowledge requirements of the defense industry, a firm might enter the defense industry through the acquisition of an existing firm. But it must have access to the capital necessary to do it.

Switching Costs Switching costs are the one-time costs customers incur when they buy from a different supplier. The costs of buying new ancillary equipment and of retraining employees, and even the psychic costs of ending a relationship, may be incurred in switching to a new supplier. In some cases, switching costs are low, such as when the consumer switches to a different soft drink. Switching costs can vary as a function of time. For example, in terms of credit hours toward graduation, the cost to a student to transfer from one university to another as a freshman is much lower than it is when the student is entering the senior year. Occasionally, a decision made by manufacturers to produce a new, innovative product creates high switching costs for the final consumer. Customer loyalty programs, such as airlines' frequent flyer miles, are intended to increase the customer's switching costs.

If switching costs are high, a new entrant must offer either a substantially lower price or a much better product to attract buyers. Usually, the more established the relationship between parties, the greater is the cost incurred to switch to an alternative offering.

Access to Distribution Channels Over time, industry participants typically develop effective means of distributing products. Once a relationship with its distributors has been built, a firm will nurture it thus creating switching costs for the distributors. Access to distribution channels can be a strong entry barrier for new entrants, particularly in consumer nondurable goods industries (e.g., in grocery stores where shelf space is limited) and in international markets. New entrants have to persuade distributors to carry their products, either in addition to or in place of those currently distributed. Price breaks and cooperative advertising allowances may be used for this purpose; however, those practices reduce the new entrant's profit potential.

Cost Disadvantages Independent of Scale Sometimes, established competitors have cost advantages that new entrants cannot duplicate. Proprietary product technology, favorable access to raw materials, desirable locations, and government subsidies are examples. Successful competition requires new entrants to reduce the strategic relevance of these factors. Delivering purchases directly to the buyer can counter the advantage of a desirable location; new food establishments in an undesirable location often follow this practice. Similarly, automobile dealerships located in unattractive areas (perhaps in a city's downtown area) can provide superior service (such as picking up the car to be serviced and delivering it to the customer thereafter) to overcome a competitor's location advantage.

Government Policy Through licensing and permit requirements, governments can also control entry into an industry. Liquor retailing, radio and TV broadcasting, banking, and trucking are examples of industries in which government decisions and actions affect entry possibilities. Also, governments often restrict entry into some industries because of the need to provide quality service or the need to protect jobs. Alternatively, deregulation of industries, exemplified by the airline industry and utilities in the United States, allows more firms to enter.[92] Some of the most publicized government actions are those involving antitrust. For example, the U.S. and European Union governments pursued an antitrust case against Microsoft. The final settlement in the United States involved a relatively small penalty for the company. However, the EU judgments were more severe.[93] As noted in the earlier Strategic Focus, Google has been accused of violating antitrust laws but the government has not shown significant concern as yet.

Expected Retaliation

Firms seeking to enter an industry also anticipate the reactions of firms in the industry. An expectation of swift and vigorous competitive responses reduces the likelihood of entry. Vigorous retaliation can be expected when the existing firm has a major stake in the industry (e.g., it has fixed assets with few, if any, alternative uses), when it has substantial resources, and when industry growth is slow or constrained. For example, any firm attempting to enter the airline industry at the current time can expect significant retaliation from existing competitors due to overcapacity.

Locating market niches not being served by incumbents allows the new entrant to avoid entry barriers. Small entrepreneurial firms are generally best suited for identifying and serving neglected market segments. When Honda first entered the U.S. motorcycle market, it concentrated on small-engine motorcycles, a market that firms such as Harley-Davidson ignored. By targeting this neglected niche, Honda avoided competition. After consolidating its position, Honda used its strength to attack rivals by introducing larger motorcycles and competing in the broader market. Competitive actions and competitive responses between firms such as Honda and Harley-Davidson are discussed more fully in Chapter 5.

Bargaining Power of Suppliers

Increasing prices and reducing the quality of their products are potential means used by suppliers to exert power over firms competing within an industry. If a firm is unable to recover cost increases by its suppliers through its own pricing structure, its profitability is reduced by its suppliers' actions. A supplier group is powerful when

- It is dominated by a few large companies and is more concentrated than the industry to which it sells.
- Satisfactory substitute products are not available to industry firms.
- Industry firms are not a significant customer for the supplier group.
- Suppliers' goods are critical to buyers' marketplace success.
- The effectiveness of suppliers' products has created high switching costs for industry firms.
- It poses a credible threat to integrate forward into the buyers' industry. Credibility is enhanced when suppliers have substantial resources and provide a highly differentiated product.

The airline industry is one in which suppliers' bargaining power is changing. Though the number of suppliers is low, the demand for major aircraft is also relatively low. Boeing and Airbus strongly compete for most orders of major aircraft. However, China recently announced plans to build a large commercial aircraft that will compete with the aircraft sold by Boeing and Airbus. This competitive action could be highly significant because China is projected to buy 2,230 new commercial aircraft between 2007 and 2025.[94]

Bargaining Power of Buyers

Firms seek to maximize the return on their invested capital. Alternatively, buyers (customers of an industry or a firm) want to buy products at the lowest possible price—the point at which the industry earns the lowest acceptable rate of return on its invested capital. To reduce their costs, buyers bargain for higher quality, greater levels of service, and lower prices. These outcomes are achieved by encouraging competitive battles among the industry's firms. Customers (buyer groups) are powerful when

- They purchase a large portion of an industry's total output.
- The sales of the product being purchased account for a significant portion of the seller's annual revenues.
- They could switch to another product at little, if any, cost.
- The industry's products are undifferentiated or standardized, and the buyers pose a credible threat if they were to integrate backward into the sellers' industry.

Armed with greater amounts of information about the manufacturer's costs and the power of the Internet as a shopping and distribution alternative have increased consumers' bargaining power in many industries. One reason for this shift is that individual buyers incur virtually zero switching costs when they decide to purchase from one manufacturer rather than another or from one dealer as opposed to a second or third one.

Threat of Substitute Products

Substitute products are goods or services from outside a given industry that perform similar or the same functions as a product that the industry produces. For example, as a sugar substitute, NutraSweet (and other sugar substitutes) places an upper limit on sugar manufacturers' prices—NutraSweet and sugar perform the same function, though with different characteristics. Other product substitutes include e-mail and fax machines instead of overnight deliveries, plastic containers rather than glass jars, and tea instead of coffee. Newspaper firms have experienced significant circulation declines over the past 10 years. The declines are due to substitute outlets for news including Internet sources, cable television news channels, and e-mail and cell phone alerts. These products are increasingly popular, especially among younger people, and as product substitutes they have significant potential to continue to reduce overall newspaper circulation sales.

In general, product substitutes present a strong threat to a firm when customers face few, if any, switching costs and when the substitute product's price is lower or its quality and performance capabilities are equal to or greater than those of the competing product. Differentiating a product along dimensions that customers value (such as price, quality, service after the sale, and location) reduces a substitute's attractiveness. As the Strategic Focus illustrates, Google has market power because it is the largest and most often used search engine. As a result, advertisers clearly prefer Google over most of its competitors because it gives them access to the largest possible audience.

Intensity of Rivalry Among Competitors

Because an industry's firms are mutually dependent, actions taken by one company usually invite competitive responses. In many industries, firms actively compete against one another. Competitive rivalry intensifies when a firm is challenged by a competitor's actions or when a company recognizes an opportunity to improve its market position.

Firms within industries are rarely homogeneous; they differ in resources and capabilities and seek to differentiate themselves from competitors.[95] Typically, firms seek to differentiate their products from competitors' offerings in ways that customers value and in which the firms have a competitive advantage. Common dimensions on which rivalry is based include price, service after the sale, and innovation. As explained in the Opening Case, the rivalry between Wal-Mart and many of its competitors is intense. In fact, competitors have been making inroads into Wal-Mart's market share. Same-store sales by many of its competitors—Target, Costco, Kroger, Safeway, Walgreen's, CVS, and Best Buy—are growing two to five times faster than sales at existing Wal-Mart stores.

Next, we discuss the most prominent factors that experience shows to affect the intensity of firms' rivalries.

Numerous or Equally Balanced Competitors

Intense rivalries are common in industries with many companies. With multiple competitors, it is common for a few firms to believe that they can act without eliciting a response. However, evidence suggests that other firms generally are aware of competitors' actions, often choosing to respond to them. At the other extreme, industries with only a few firms of equivalent size and power also tend to have strong rivalries. The large and often similar-sized resource bases of these firms permit vigorous actions and responses. The competitive battles between Airbus and Boeing exemplify intense rivalry between relatively equivalent competitors, although Boeing's position relative to Airbus grew stronger in 2007.

Slow Industry Growth

When a market is growing, firms try to effectively use resources to serve an expanding customer base. Growing markets reduce the pressure to take customers from competitors. However, rivalry in no-growth or slow-growth markets (slow change) becomes more intense as firms battle to increase their market shares by attracting competitors' customers.[96]

Typically, battles to protect market share are fierce. Certainly, this has been the case in the airline industry. The instability in the market that results from these competitive engagements reduces profitability for all airlines throughout the industry.

High Fixed Costs or High Storage Costs

When fixed costs account for a large part of total costs, companies try to maximize the use of their productive capacity. Doing so allows the firm to spread costs across a larger volume of output. However, when many firms attempt to maximize their productive capacity, excess capacity is created on an industry-wide basis. To then reduce inventories, individual companies typically cut the price of their product and offer rebates and other special discounts to customers. However, these practices, common in the automobile manufacturing industry, often intensify competition. The pattern of excess capacity at the industry level followed by intense rivalry at the firm level is observed frequently in industries with high storage costs. Perishable products, for example, lose their value rapidly with the passage of time. As their inventories grow, producers of perishable goods often use pricing strategies to sell products quickly.

Lack of Differentiation or Low Switching Costs

When buyers find a differentiated product that satisfies their needs, they frequently purchase the product loyally over time. Industries with many companies that have successfully differentiated their products have less rivalry, resulting in lower competition for individual firms. Firms that develop and sustain a differentiated product that cannot be easily imitated by competitors often earn higher returns.[97] However, when buyers view products as commodities (i.e., as products with few differentiated features or capabilities), rivalry intensifies. In these instances, buyers' purchasing decisions are based primarily on price and, to a lesser degree, service. Personal computers have become a commodity product. Thus, the rivalry among Dell, HP, and other computer manufacturers is strong.

The effect of switching costs is similar to the effect of differentiated products. The lower the buyers' switching costs, the easier it is for competitors to attract buyers through pricing and service offerings. High switching costs partially insulate the firm from rivals' efforts to attract customers. Even though the switching costs—such as pilot and mechanic training—are high in aircraft purchases, the rivalry between Boeing and Airbus remains intense because the stakes for both are extremely high.

High Strategic Stakes

Competitive rivalry is likely to be high when it is important for several of the competitors to perform well in the market. For example, although it is diversified and is a market leader in other businesses, Samsung has targeted market leadership in the consumer electronics market and is doing quite well. This market is quite important to Sony and other major competitors, such as Hitachi, Matsushita, NEC, and Mitsubishi. The substantial rivalry in this market is likely to continue over the next few years.

High strategic stakes can also exist in terms of geographic locations. For example, Japanese automobile manufacturers are committed to a significant presence in the U.S. marketplace because it is the world's largest single market for automobiles and trucks. Because of the stakes involved in this country for Japanese and U.S. manufacturers, rivalry among firms in the U.S. and the global automobile industry is intense. It should be noted that while proximity tends to promote greater rivalry, physically proximate competition has potentially positive benefits as well. For example, when competitors are located near each other, it is easier for suppliers to serve them, and competitors can develop economies of scale that lead to lower production costs. Additionally, communications with key industry stakeholders such as suppliers are more efficient when they are close to the firm.[98]

High Exit Barriers

Sometimes companies continue competing in an industry even though the returns on their invested capital are low or negative. Firms making this choice likely face high exit barriers, which include economic, strategic, and emotional factors causing them to remain in an industry when the profitability of doing so is questionable. Exit barriers are especially high in the airline industry. Common exit barriers include the following:

- Specialized assets (assets with values linked to a particular business or location)
- Fixed costs of exit (such as labor agreements)
- Strategic interrelationships (relationships of mutual dependence, such as those between one business and other parts of a company's operations, including shared facilities and access to financial markets)
- Emotional barriers (aversion to economically justified business decisions because of fear for one's own career, loyalty to employees, and so forth)
- Government and social restrictions (often based on government concerns for job losses and regional economic effects; are more common outside the United States)

Interpreting Industry Analyses

Effective industry analyses are products of careful study and interpretation of data and information from multiple sources. A wealth of industry-specific data is available to be analyzed. Because of globalization, international markets and rivalries must be included in the firm's analyses. In fact, research shows that in some industries, international variables are more important than domestic ones as determinants of strategic competitiveness. Furthermore, because of the development of global markets, a country's borders no longer restrict industry structures. In fact, movement into international markets enhances the chances of success for new ventures as well as more established firms.[99]

Analysis of the five forces in the industry allows the firm to determine the industry's attractiveness in terms of the potential to earn adequate or superior returns. In general, the stronger competitive forces are, the lower the profit potential for an industry's firms. An unattractive industry has low entry barriers, suppliers and buyers with strong bargaining positions, strong competitive threats from product substitutes, and intense rivalry among competitors. These industry characteristics make it difficult for firms to achieve strategic competitiveness and earn above-average returns. Alternatively, an attractive industry has high entry barriers, suppliers and buyers with little bargaining power, few competitive threats from product substitutes, and relatively moderate rivalry.[100] Next, we turn to strategic groups operating within industries.

Strategic Groups

A set of firms that emphasize similar strategic dimensions and use a similar strategy is called a **strategic group**.[101] The competition between firms within a strategic group is greater than the competition between a member of a strategic group and companies outside that strategic group. Therefore, intrastrategic group competition is more intense than is interstrategic group competition. In fact, more heterogeneity is evident in the performance of firms within strategic groups than across the groups. The performance leaders within groups are able to follow strategies similar to those of other firms in the group and yet maintain strategic distinctiveness to gain and sustain a competitive advantage.[102]

A **strategic group** is a set of firms emphasizing similar strategic dimensions to use a similar strategy.

The extent of technological leadership, product quality, pricing policies, distribution channels, and customer service are examples of strategic dimensions that firms in a strategic group may treat similarly. Thus, membership in a particular strategic group defines the essential characteristics of the firm's strategy.[103]

The notion of strategic groups can be useful for analyzing an industry's competitive structure. Such analyses can be helpful in diagnosing competition, positioning, and the profitability of firms within an industry.[104] High mobility barriers, high rivalry, and low resources among the firms within an industry will limit the formation of strategic groups.[105] However, research suggests that after strategic groups are formed, their membership remains relatively stable over time, making analysis easier and more useful.[106]

Using strategic groups to understand an industry's competitive structure requires the firm to plot companies' competitive actions and competitive responses along strategic dimensions such as pricing decisions, product quality, distribution channels, and so forth. This type of analysis shows the firm how certain companies are competing similarly in terms of how they use similar strategic dimensions. For example, companies may use unique radio markets because consumers prefer different music formats and programming (news radio, talk radio, etc.). Typically, a radio format is created through choices made regarding music or nonmusic style, scheduling, and announcer style. It is estimated that approximately 30 different radio formats exist, suggesting the presence of many strategic groups in this industry. The strategies within each of the 30 groups are similar, while the strategies across the total set of strategic groups are dissimilar. As a result, Clear Channel Communications often owns several stations in a large city, but each uses a different format. Therefore, Clear Channel likely has stations operating in most or all of the 30 strategic groups in this industry. Additionally, a new strategic group has been added as the satellite radio companies XM and SIRIUS have formed an intense rivalry in trying to attract corporate customers such as auto manufacturers and rental car companies as well as individual subscribers.[107] Satellite radio could be considered a substitute because it is technologically different from terrestrial radio, but the satellite companies, each with more than 100 different channels, offer the same types of music formats and programming that traditional stations do. Although satellite companies obtain most of their revenue from subscriptions, they are similar to terrestrial radio in that some advertising is done on talk, news, and sports channels. Firms can increase their understanding of competition in the commercial radio industry by plotting companies' actions and responses in terms of important strategic dimensions mentioned previously. With the addition of satellite radio, the competition among different strategic groups has increased.

Strategic groups have several implications. First, because firms within a group offer similar products to the same customers, the competitive rivalry among them can be intense. The more intense the rivalry, the greater the threat to each firm's profitability. Second, the strengths of the five industry forces (the threats posed by new entrants, the power of suppliers, the power of buyers, product substitutes, and the intensity of rivalry among competitors) differ across strategic groups. Third, the closer the strategic groups are in terms of their strategies, the greater is the likelihood of rivalry between the groups.

Having a thorough understanding of primary competitors helps a firm formulate and implement an appropriate strategy. Clearly XM and SIRIUS are in a strategic group and compete directly against each other. XM has been successful in its focus on new technology, while SIRIUS has focused on signing innovative and exclusive content. Volkswagen tried to break out of its strategic group of companies selling mid-priced autos. But it was unsuccessful in entering the strategic group of firms with similar strategies selling premium autos (e.g., Mercedes-Benz, BMW). Because of these efforts, VW lost market share in its primary markets.[108]

IBM has been a pioneer in the introduction of new technology but also more recently in analyzing its industry and major competitors. As explained in the Strategic Focus, IBM carefully analyzes its major competitors and formulates a new strategy or adjusts its existing strategy to maintain is competitive advantage. The knowledge gained from its team's analysis of Hewlett-Packard and Sun Microsystems helped it

IBM Closely Watches Its Competitors to Stay at the Top of Its Game

It is critical for companies to study their major rivals to help them shape and implement their strategies to counter competitors' strengths and to exploit their weaknesses. Armed with effective analyses of competitors, companies can enhance their market position and increase returns on their investments. International Business Machines (IBM) is the world's top provider of computer products and services. IBM makes mainframes and servers, storage systems, and peripherals, but also has the largest computer service unit in the world; it accounts for more than half of IBM's total revenue. To remain competitive in its various markets, IBM established a competitive analysis team with the sole purpose of observing and analyzing competitors such as Hewlett-Packard (HP) and Sun Microsystems. IBM uses the data from these analyses to adjust its strategies and business plans accordingly to ensure that the firm effectively competes with its major rivals.

IBM's competitive analysis team found that Sun's direct sales team focuses on the top 1,500 accounts in its installed base, and that its remaining customers are being serviced by business partners. The IBM team also found that Sun's sales reps primarily emphasize selling hardware instead of solutions, a definitive weakness that provided opportunities for IBM to take away customers from Sun. In addition, IBM's team carefully analyzed a large number of HP announcements for its e-business weak points in its high availability campaign. IBM said that the 5Minutes campaign is only a vision that has little business value for its customers, but the campaign has strong marketing value for HP. The analysis showed that HP has low software and services revenues and thus is primarily a hardware company. HP lost approximately 15 percent of its potential customers because it lacked its own support and consulting services and is too reliant on EDS, Accenture, Cisco, and HP resellers.

IBM's competitive analysis teams observe and analyze competitors such as Hewlett-Packard and Sun Microsystems.

IBM was a pioneer of the multinational business model. It created mini-IBMs in each country each with its own administration, manufacturing, and service operations. Based on the analyses of rival Indian technology companies, IBM identified that a flatter structure and leaner organization was needed to compete effectively. Likewise the competitor analyses discovered that Chinese competitors provided high-quality goods and services for a much lower price. These competitor analyses led IBM to develop global integrated operations. IBM's global shift makes it possible to use lower-cost talent in India to manage machines and software in data centers. In addition, the data centers are interchangeable, so if India has problems, IBM can reroute computing jobs and calls to other locations. Eventually, international competitors will build global delivery hubs, but they will be unlikely to compete with IBM's scientific research capabilities. IBM's integrated global services and research organizations enable it to design innovative services. The cost savings achieved through its global integration efforts lead to a higher earnings growth. The overall goal of this global integration plan is to lower costs while simultaneously providing superior services to customers. In doing so, IBM can enhance its competitiveness, increase its market share, and drive revenue and profit growth.

Based on the information obtained from recent competitor analyses, IBM decided only a few adjustments were needed. For example, IBM decided to emphasize its higher-margin business consulting services, which help companies change the way they operate,

and to focus less on technology integration. IBM also changed the strategy of its software division. Because software is the fastest-growing and most profitable segment of the company, IBM has made several acquisitions of software companies, including FileNet, MRO Software, and Webify Solutions. These acquisitions fill holes in IBM's product portfolio and increase its ability to compete effectively with Sun Microsystems and similar rivals.

IBM's strategic actions are creating positive results. Total revenues for the first quarter of 2007 reached $22.0 billion, an increase of 7 percent from the first quarter of 2006. First-quarter 2007 income increased 8 percent over 2006 to $1.8 billion. And, its first-quarter 2007 earnings of $1.21 per share represented an increase of 12 percent over the first quarter of 2006.

Sources: S. Hamm, 2006, Big Blue shift, *BusinessWeek*, http://www.businessweek.com, June 6; T. P. Morgan, 1999, IBM's competitive analysis on Sun, HP, *Computergram International*, http://www.findarticles.com, Oct. 4; LEX: IBM, 2005, *Financial Times*, http://www.ft.com, May 5; S. Hamm, 2006, IBM's revved-up software engine, *BusinessWeek*, http://www.businessweek.com, Aug. 15; J. Krippel, 2007, International Business Machines Corporation, *Hoovers*, http://www.hoovers.com; 2007, http://www.ibm.com/news, May 5.

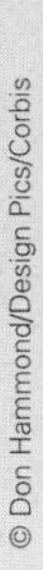

adjust its strategy and particularly remain at the forefront of its industry in computer and support services. To maintain that competitive advantage, IBM not only continues to improve its internal service capabilities but also adds to its portfolio by acquiring other high-quality, special-purpose service firms. It could not effectively design a strategy to maintain its competitive advantage without the knowledge gained from the analysis of its competitors.

Competitor Analysis

The competitor environment is the final part of the external environment requiring study. Competitor analysis focuses on each company against which a firm directly competes. For example, XM and SIRIUS satellite radio, Home Depot and Lowe's, and Boeing and Airbus should be keenly interested in understanding each other's objectives, strategies, assumptions, and capabilities. Furthermore, intense rivalry creates a strong need to understand competitors.[109] In a competitor analysis, the firm seeks to understand the following:

- What drives the competitor, as shown by its *future objectives*
- What the competitor is doing and can do, as revealed by its *current strategy*
- What the competitor believes about the industry, as shown by its *assumptions*
- What the competitor's capabilities are, as shown by its *strengths* and *weaknesses*[110]

Information about these four dimensions helps the firm prepare an anticipated response profile for each competitor (see Figure 2.3). The results of an effective competitor analysis help a firm understand, interpret, and predict its competitors' actions and responses. Understanding the actions of competitors clearly contributes to the firm's ability to compete successfully within the industry.[111] Interestingly, research suggests that analyzing possible reactions to competitive moves is not often carried out by executives.[112] This evidence suggests that those firms conducting such analyses can obtain a competitive advantage over firms that do not.

Competitor intelligence is the set of data and information the firm gathers to better understand and better anticipate competitors' objectives, strategies, assumptions, and capabilities.

Critical to an effective competitor analysis is gathering data and information that can help the firm understand its competitors' intentions and the strategic implications resulting from them.[113] Useful data and information combine to form **competitor intelligence:** the set of data and information the firm gathers to better understand and better

Figure 2.3 Competitor Analysis Components

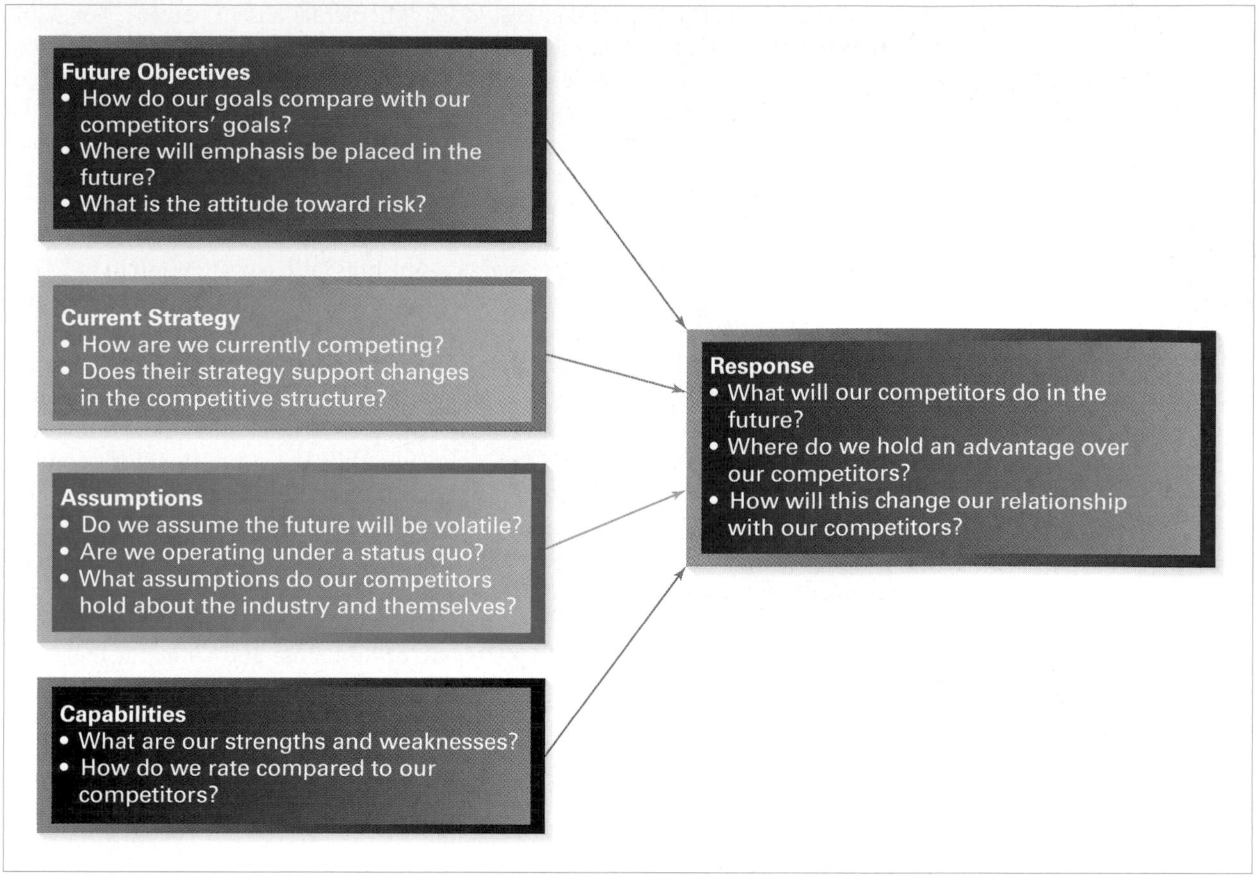

Future Objectives
- How do our goals compare with our competitors' goals?
- Where will emphasis be placed in the future?
- What is the attitude toward risk?

Current Strategy
- How are we currently competing?
- Does their strategy support changes in the competitive structure?

Assumptions
- Do we assume the future will be volatile?
- Are we operating under a status quo?
- What assumptions do our competitors hold about the industry and themselves?

Capabilities
- What are our strengths and weaknesses?
- How do we rate compared to our competitors?

Response
- What will our competitors do in the future?
- Where do we hold an advantage over our competitors?
- How will this change our relationship with our competitors?

anticipate competitors' objectives, strategies, assumptions, and capabilities. In competitor analysis, the firm should gather intelligence not only about its competitors, but also regarding public policies in countries around the world. Such intelligence facilitates an understanding of the strategic posture of foreign competitors.

Through effective competitive and public policy intelligence, the firm gains the insights needed to make effective strategic decisions about how to compete against its rivals. Microsoft continues to analyze its competitor Google for ways to overcome and dominate the search engine business as it did in the browser contest with Netscape. *Fortune* magazine reported that Bill Gates, Microsoft's founder, was doing his own competitive intelligence on Google by browsing Google's Web site when he came across a help-wanted page: "Why, he wondered, were the qualifications for so many of them identical to Microsoft job specs? Google was a Web search business, yet here on the screen were postings for engineers with backgrounds that had nothing to do with search and everything to do with Microsoft's core businesspeople trained in things like operating-system design, compiler optimization, and distributed-systems architecture. Gates wondered whether Microsoft might be facing much more than a war in search. An e-mail he sent to a handful of execs that day said, in effect, 'We have to watch these guys. It looks like they are building something to compete with us.'"[114]

Microsoft has found Google to be a formidable competitor. As such, Microsoft has again explored a merger with Yahoo! Inc. in an effort to compete more effectively with Google. However, this announcement had no notable effect on Google's stock, suggesting that investors do not see such a merger as a competitive threat to Google. In 2007,

Google has approximately 54 percent of the market for Internet searches, whereas Yahoo! has 22 percent of the market and MSN (Microsoft) has 10 percent. For 2007, it is projected that Google will garner almost 76 percent of the paid search advertising with Yahoo! garnering slightly over 16 percent and all others slightly over 8 percent combined. Some believe that a merger of Microsoft and Yahoo! would add value by integrating their respective strengths. Yet, most analysts do not agree. One Internet analyst suggested that "Instead of getting bigger, these companies need to think about getting smarter. I don't think that a partnership is necessarily going to achieve that goal."[115]

Complementors are the network of companies that sell complementary goods or services or are compatible with the focal firm's own product or service.

As the preceding analysis of Google suggests, one must also pay attention to the complementors of a firm's products and strategy.[116] **Complementors** are the network of companies that sell complementary goods or services or are compatible with the focal firm's own product or service. These firms might also include suppliers and buyers who have a strong "network" relationship with the focal firm. A strong network of complementors can solidify a competitive advantage, as it has in Google's case because of the number of Internet access products with which it functions smoothly. If a complementor's good or service adds value to the sale of the focal firm's good or service it is likely to create value for the focal firm. For example, a range of complements are necessary to sell automobiles, including financial services to arrange credit, luxury options including stereo equipment, and extended warranties. For this reason, analyzing competitors requires that its alliance network also be analyzed (see Chapter 9 for a complete examination of firm network and alliance strategies).[117] For example, a strength of Lufthansa and United is their participation in the STAR Alliance, an international network of commercial airlines. Firms must also be careful to identify the actions of firms that are performing poorly. Research suggests that some of these firms may find ways to create value and regain a competitive advantage or at least achieve competitive parity with specially designed strategic actions to turn around their performance.[118] Overlooking such firms in competitor analyses could be an error.

Ethical Considerations

Firms should follow generally accepted ethical practices in gathering competitor intelligence. Industry associations often develop lists of these practices that firms can adopt. Practices considered both legal and ethical include (1) obtaining publicly available information (e.g., court records, competitors' help-wanted advertisements, annual reports, financial reports of publicly held corporations, and Uniform Commercial Code filings), and (2) attending trade fairs and shows to obtain competitors' brochures, view their exhibits, and listen to discussions about their products.

In contrast, certain practices (including blackmail, trespassing, eavesdropping, and stealing drawings, samples, or documents) are widely viewed as unethical and often are illegal. To protect themselves from digital fraud or theft by competitors that break into their employees' PCs, some companies buy insurance to protect against PC hacking.[119]

Some competitor intelligence practices may be legal, but a firm must decide whether they are also ethical, given the image it desires as a corporate citizen. Especially with electronic transmissions, the line between legal and ethical practices can be difficult to determine. For example, a firm may develop Web site addresses that are similar to those of its competitors and thus occasionally receive e-mail transmissions that were intended for those competitors. The practice is an example of the challenges companies face in deciding how to gather intelligence about competitors while simultaneously determining how to prevent competitors from learning too much about them.

Open discussions of intelligence-gathering techniques can help a firm ensure that employees, customers, suppliers, and even potential competitors understand its convictions to follow ethical practices for gathering competitor intelligence. An appropriate guideline for competitor intelligence practices is to respect the principles of common morality and the right of competitors not to reveal certain information about their products, operations, and strategic intentions.[120]

Summary

- The firm's external environment is challenging and complex. Because of the external environment's effect on performance, the firm must develop the skills required to identify opportunities and threats existing in that environment.
- The external environment has three major parts: (1) the general environment (elements in the broader society that affect industries and their firms), (2) the industry environment (factors that influence a firm, its competitive actions and responses, and the industry's profit potential), and (3) the competitor environment (in which the firm analyzes each major competitor's future objectives, current strategies, assumptions, and capabilities).
- The external environmental analysis process has four steps: scanning, monitoring, forecasting, and assessing. Through environmental analyses, the firm identifies opportunities and threats.
- The general environment has six segments: demographic, economic, political/legal, sociocultural, technological, and global. For each segment, the firm wants to determine the strategic relevance of environmental changes and trends.
- Compared with the general environment, the industry environment has a more direct effect on the firm's strategic actions. The five forces model of competition includes the threat of entry, the power of suppliers, the power of buyers, product substitutes, and the intensity of rivalry among competitors. By studying these forces, the firm finds a position in an industry where it can influence the forces in its favor or where it can buffer itself from the power of the forces in order to earn above-average returns.
- Industries are populated with different strategic groups. A strategic group is a collection of firms that follow similar strategies along similar dimensions. Competitive rivalry is greater within a strategic group than it is between strategic groups.
- Competitor analysis informs the firm about the future objectives, current strategies, assumptions, and capabilities of the companies with which it competes directly. A thorough analysis examines complementors that sustain a competitor's strategy and major networks or alliances in which competitors participate. They should also attempt to identify and carefully monitor major actions taken by firms with performance below the industry norm.
- Different techniques are used to create competitor intelligence: the set of data, information, and knowledge that allows the firm to better understand its competitors and thereby predict their likely strategic and tactical actions. Firms should use only legal and ethical practices to gather intelligence. The Internet enhances firms' capabilities to gather insights about competitors and their strategic intentions.

Review Questions

1. Why is it important for a firm to study and understand the external environment?
2. What are the differences between the general environment and the industry environment? Why are these differences important?
3. What is the external environmental analysis process (four steps)? What does the firm want to learn when using this process?
4. What are the six segments of the general environment? Explain the differences among them.
5. How do the five forces of competition in an industry affect its profit potential? Explain.
6. What is a strategic group? Of what value is knowledge of the firm's strategic group in formulating that firm's strategy?
7. What is the importance of collecting and interpreting data and information about competitors? What practices should a firm use to gather competitor intelligence and why?

Experiential Exercises

Exercise 1: Airline Competitor Analysis

The International Air Transport Association (IATA) reports statistics on the number of passengers carried each year by major airlines. Passenger data for 2006 are reported for the top 10 fliers in three categories:

- Domestic flights
- International flights
- Combined traffic, domestic and international flights

The following table lists both passenger data and rankings for each category.

Airline	Int'l Ranking	Int'l Passengers	Domestic Ranking	Domestic Passengers	Combined Ranking	Combined Passengers
Air France	3	30,417			7	49,411
All Nippon Airlines			6	45,328	8	49,226
American Airlines	7	21,228	2	78,607	1	99,835
British Airways	4	29,498				
Cathay Pacific	10	16667				
China Southern Airlines			7	45,249	10	48,512
Continental Airlines			9	35,852		
Delta Airlines			3	63,446	3	73,584
Easyjet	6	21,917				
Emirates	9	16,748				
Japan Airlines Int'l			8	37,154	9	48,911
KLM	5	22,322				
Lufthansa	2	38,236			6	51,213
Northwest Airlines			5	45,743	5	55,925
Ryanair	1	40,532				
Singapore Airlines	8	18,022				
Southwest Airlines			1	96,277	2	96,277
United Airlines			4	58,801	4	69,265
US Airways			10	32,094		

For this exercise, you will develop competitor profiles of selected air carriers.

Part One

Working in groups of 5–7 people, each team member selects one airline from the table. The pool of selected airlines should contain a roughly even balance of three regions: North America, Europe/Middle East, and Asia. Using outside resources, answer the following questions:

- What drives this competitor (i.e., what are its objectives)?
- What is its current strategy?
- What does this competitor believe about its industry?
- What are its strengths and weaknesses?

When researching your companies, you should use multiple resources. The company's Web site is a good starting point. Public firms headquartered in the United States will also have annual reports and 10-K reports filed with the Securities and Exchange Commission.

Part Two

As a group, summarize the results of each competitor profile into a single table. Then, discuss the following topics:

- Which airlines in your group had the most similar strategies? The most different? Would you consider any of the firms you studied to be in the same strategic group (i.e., a group of firms that follow similar strategies along similar dimensions)?
- Create a composite 5 forces model based on the firms you reviewed. How might these elements of industry structure (e.g., substitutes, or bargaining power of buyers) differ from the perspective of individual airlines?
- How well do the strategies of these airlines fit with their industry and general environments? Which airlines do you expect to advance in passenger rankings, and which will lose ground?

Exercise 2: The Oracle at Delphi

In ancient Greece, people traveled to the temple at Delphi when they had important questions about the future. A priestess, who was ostensibly a direct connection to the god Apollo, would answer these questions in the form of a riddle. Today, executives are still faced with significant challenges in predicting the future, albeit with different processes.

Many strategies rely in part on qualitative forecasts and untested assumptions, simply because hard data may not exist, or because the data may be of poor quality. Such problems are particularly common in new product segments (e.g., early stages of the Internet) or in emerging economies (e.g., when Western firms first started selling in China). When making a subjective forecast, it is often helpful to rely on multiple opinions and perspectives. However, group discussions can often be skewed if some participants are more vocal than others, or if group members differ by status. The Delphi method provides a process for helping a group to reach consensus while minimizing individual biases.

The decision process starts with the selection of a question, or set of questions. A facilitator is designated to manage the process, and a group of experts is selected to provide input. The facilitator polls each expert, and creates a summary of the responses. The summary is then sent back to the expert pool, and each person is given the opportunity to revise his or her estimates. This process repeats until the summary scores have stabilized.

Part One

Select one group member to serve as facilitator. The facilitator's role is to select an issue currently in the news that has implications for a specific industry. Once a topic has been selected, the facilitator should prepare a couple of survey questions that can be numerically ranked by the expert panel (i.e., the rest of the team). For example, assume that the topic was an upcoming election, and how the results of that election might affect the attractiveness of an industry. If the election was to be among three candidates, the sample questions might look like the following:

> What is your assessment of the likelihood of Candidate Smith being elected?
>
> What is your assessment of the likelihood of Candidate Jones being elected?
>
> What is your assessment of the likelihood of Candidate Doe being elected?
> (Scale 1 = extremely unlikely   3 = moderately likely
> 5 = extremely likely)
>
> If Candidate Smith is elected, what is the likely effect on industry growth and profitability?
>
> If Candidate Jones is elected, what is the likely effect on industry growth and profitability?
>
> If Candidate Doe is elected, what is the likely effect on industry growth and profitability?
> (Scale 1 = worsened substantially   3 = unchanged
> 5 = improved substantially)

Part Two

The facilitator should administer the survey to each group member. Prepare a summary that includes the average score and range for each item. Repeat the survey, using the same questions, two more times following this process.

Part Three

As a group, discuss the following questions:

- How much did the feedback of composite scores affect your assessment?
- In your opinion, were the final scores an improvement over the initial scores? Why or why not?
- How might a Delphi process lead to low-quality results? What steps could you take to help ensure a more accurate forecast?
- Bonus question: How is the logic of the Delphi method similar to that of the book *Wisdom of Crowds,* by James Surowiecki?

Notes

1. S. R. Miller & L. Eden, 2006, Local density and foreign subsidiary performance, *Academy of Management Journal*, 49: 341–355; C. Williams & W. Mitchell, 2004, Focusing firm evolution: The impact of information infrastructure on market entry by U.S. telecommunications companies, 1984–1998, *Management Science*, 5: 1561–1575;.
2. J. Weiser, 2007, Untapped: Strategies for success in underserved markets, *Journal of Business Strategy*, 28(2): 30–37; J. Tan, 2005, Venturing in turbulent water: A historical perspective of economic reform and entrepreneurial transformation, *Journal of Business Venturing*, 20: 689–704; P. Chattopadhyay, W. H. Glick, & G. P. Huber, 2001, Organizational actions in response to threats and opportunities, *Academy of Management Journal*, 44: 937–955.
3. J. Gimeno, R. E. Hoskisson, B. D. Beal, & W. P. Wan, 2005, Explaining the clustering of international expansion moves: A critical test in the U.S. telecommunications industry, *Academy of Management Journal*, 48: 297–319; C. M. Grimm, H. Lee, & K. G. Smith, 2005, *Strategy as Action: Competitive Dynamics and Competitive Advantages*, New York: Oxford University Press.
4. J.-P. Bonardi, G. I. F. Holburn, & R. G. Vanden Bergh, 2006, Nonmarket strategy performance: Evidence from U.S. electric utilities, *Academy of Management Journal*, 49: 1209–1228; S. Rangan & A. Drummond, 2004, Explaining outcomes in competition among foreign multinationals in a focal host market, *Strategic Management Journal*, 25: 285–293;
5. M. Delmas, M.V. Russo, & M. J. Montes-Sancho, 2007, Deregulation and environmental differentiation in the electric utility industry, *Strategic Management Journal*, 28: 189–209.
6. G. Szulanski & R. J. Jensen, 2006, Presumptive adaptation and the effectiveness of knowledge transfer, *Strategic Management Journal*, 27: 937–957; K. G. Smith, C. J. Collins, & K. D. Clark, 2005, Existing knowledge, knowledge creation capability, and the rate of new product introduction in high-technology firms, *Academy of Management Journal*, 48: 346–357.
7. C. Eesley & M. J. Lenox, 2006, Firm responses to secondary stakeholder action, *Strategic Management Journal*, 27: 765–781; R. M. Grant, 2003, Strategic planning in a turbulent environment: Evidence from the oil majors, *Strategic Management Journal*, 24: 491–517.
8. M. T. Dacin, C. Oliver, & J.-P. Roy, 2007, The legitimacy of strategic alliances: An institutional perspective, *Strategic Management Journal*, 28: 169–187; M. Song, C. Droge, S. Hanvanich, & R. Calantone, 2005, Marketing and technology resource complementarity: An analysis of their interaction effect in two environmental contexts, *Strategic Management Journal*, 26: 259–276;
9. L. Fahey, 1999, *Competitors*, New York: John Wiley & Sons; B. A. Walters & R. L. Priem, 1999, Business strategy and CEO intelligence acquisition, *Competitive Intelligence Review*, 10(2): 15–22.
10. J. C. Short, D. J. Ketchen, Jr., T. B. Palmer, & G. T. Hult, 2007, Firm, strategic group, and industry influences on performance, *Strategic Management Journal*, 28: 147–167.
11. R. D. Ireland & M. A. Hitt, 1999, Achieving and maintaining strategic competitiveness in the 21st century: The role of strategic leadership, *Academy of Management Executive*, 13(1): 43–57; M. A. Hitt, B. W. Keats, & S. M. DeMarie, 1998, Navigating in the new competitive landscape: Building strategic flexibility and competitive advantage in the 21st century, *Academy of Management Executive*, 12(4): 22–42.
12. L. Välikangas & M. Gibbert, 2005, Boundary-setting strategies for escaping innovation traps, *MIT Sloan Management Review*, 46(3): 58–65.
13. Characteristics of the civilian labor force, 2004 and 2014, 2007. *Infoplease*, http://www.infoplease.com, May 2.
14. G. Panagiotou, 2003, Bring SWOT into focus, *Business Strategy Review*, 14(2): 8–10.
15. P. Lattman, 2005, Rebound, *Forbes*, March 28, 58.
16. K. M. Patton & T. M. McKenna, 2005, Scanning for competitive intelligence, *Competitive Intelligence Magazine*, 8(2): 24–26; D. F. Kuratko, R. D. Ireland, & J. S. Hornsby, 2001, Improving firm performance through entrepreneurial actions: Acordia's corporate entrepreneurship strategy, *Academy of Management Executive*, 15(4): 60–71.
17. K. M. Eisenhardt, 2002, Has strategy changed? *MIT Sloan Management Review*, 43(2): 88–91; I. Goll & A. M. A. Rasheed, 1997, Rational decision-making and firm performance: The moderating role of environment, *Strategic Management Journal*, 18: 583–591.
18. J. R. Hough & M. A. White, 2004, Scanning actions and environmental dynamism: Gathering information for strategic decision making, *Management Decision*, 42: 781–793; V. K. Garg, B. A. Walters, & R. L. Priem, 2003, Chief executive scanning emphases, environmental dynamism, and manufacturing firm performance, *Strategic Management Journal*, 24: 725–744.
19. C.-P. Wei & Y.-H. Lee, 2004, Event detection from online news documents for supporting environmental scanning, *Decision Support Systems*, 36: 385–401.
20. N. Anderson, 2007, FTC to Congress: Spyware purveyors need to do hard time, *Ars Technica*, http://www.arstechnica.com, April 11.
21. Fahey, *Competitors*, 71–73.
22. Characteristics of the civilian labor force, 2004 and 2014, *Infoplease;* P. Yip, 1999, The road to wealth, *Dallas Morning News*, August 2, D1, D3.
23. F. Dahlsten, 2003, Avoiding the customer satisfaction rut, *MIT Sloan Management Review*, 44(4): 73–77; Y. Luo & S. H. Park, 2001, Strategic alignment and performance of market-seeking MNCs in China, *Strategic Management Journal*, 22: 141–155.
24. K. Buysse & A. Verbke, 2003, Proactive strategies: A stakeholder management perspective, *Strategic Management Journal*, 24: 453–470; I. M. Jawahar & G. L. McLaughlin, 2001, Toward a prescriptive stakeholder theory: An organizational life cycle approach, *Academy of Management Review*, 26: 397–414.
25. M. L. Perry, S. Sengupta, & R. Krapfel, 2004, Effectiveness of horizontal strategic alliances in technologically uncertain environments: Are trust and commitment enough, *Journal of Business Research*, 9: 951–956; M. Song & M. M. Montoya-Weiss, 2001, The effect of perceived technological uncertainty on Japanese new product development, *Academy of Management Journal*, 44: 61–80.
26. F. Sanna-Randaccio & R. Veugelers, 2007, Multinational knowledge spillovers with decentralized R&D: A game theoretic approach, *Journal of International Business Studies*, 38: 47–63.
27. Fahey, *Competitors*.
28. Alcas corporation, 2007, http://www.alcas.com, May 5; K. Schelfhaudt & V. Crittenden, 2005, Growing pains for Alcas Corporation, *Journal of Business Research*, 58: 999–1002.
29. Fahey, *Competitors*, 75–77.
30. K. M. Sutcliffe & K. Weber, 2003, The high cost of accurate knowledge, *Harvard Business Review*, 81(5): 74–82.
31. J. M. Pappas & B. Wooldridge, 2007, Middle managers' divergent strategic activity: an investigation of multiple measures of network centrality, *Journal of Management Studies*, 44: 323–341; L. Fahey & V. K. Narayanan, 1986, *Macroenvironmental Analysis for Strategic Management*, St. Paul, MN: West Publishing Company, 58.
32. 2006, World Population Prospects: 2006, http://www.esa.un.org. May 5, 2007.
33 Ibid.; S. Moffett, 2005, Fast-aging Japan keeps its elders on the job longer, *Wall Street Journal*, June 15, A1, A8.

34. Ibid.; 2006, Per capita health expenditures, by country, *Infoplease*, http://www.infoplease.com, May 4, 2007; T. Fennell, 2005, The next 50 years, http://www.camagazine.com, April.
35. J. Ordonez, 2005, 'Speak English. Live Latin,' *Newsweek*, May 30, 30.
36. The growing Hispanic market in the United States, 2007, *Strictly Spanish Communications*, http://www.strictlyspanish.com, May 5.
37. J. A. Chatman & S. E. Spataro, 2005, Using self-categorization theory to understand relational demography-based variations in people's responsiveness to organizational culture, *Academy of Management Journal*, 48: 321–331.
38. Characteristics of the civilian labor force, 2004 and 2014, *Infoplease*.
39. J. Millman, 2005, Low-wage U.S. jobs get "Mexicanized," but there's a price, *Wall Street Journal*, May 2, A2.
40. A. McKeown, 2007, Periodizing globalization, *History Workshop Journal*, 63(1): 218–230.
41. R. Konopaske, C. Robie, & J. M. Ivancevich, 2005, A preliminary model of spouse influence on managerial global assignment willingness, *International Journal of Human Resource Management*, 16: 405–426.
42. A. Jones & N. Ennis, 2007, Bringing the environment into economic development, *Local Economy*, 22(1): 1–5; Fahey & Narayanan, *Macroenvironmental Analysis*, 105.
43. G. Ip, 2003, Federal Reserve maintains interest-rate target at 1%, *Wall Street Journal Online*, http://www.wsj.com, August 13.
44. GDP Picture, 2007, Economic Policy Institute, http://www.epi.org, April 27; Economists cut GDP forecast for 2007, 2007, Yahoo! News, news.yahoo.com, April 10.
45. J.-P. Bonardi, A. J. Hillman, & G. D. Keim, 2005, The attractiveness of political markets: Implications for firm strategy, *Academy of Management Review*, 30: 397–413; G. Keim, 2001, Business and public policy: Competing in the political marketplace, in M. A. Hitt, R. E. Freeman, and J. S. Harrison (eds.), *Handbook of Strategic Management*, Oxford, UK: Blackwell Publishers, 583–601.
46. W. Chen, 2007, Does the colour of the cat matter? The red hat strategy in China's private enterprises, *Management and Organizational Review*, 3: 55–80; I. P. Mahmood & C. Rufin, 2005, Governments' dilemma: The role of government in imitation and innovation, *Academy of Management Review*, 30: 338–360
47. M. A. Hitt, L. Bierman, K. Uhlenbruck, & K. Shimizu, 2006, The importance of resources in the internationalization of professional service firms: The good, the bad, and the ugly, *Academy of Management Journal*, 49: 1137–1157; D. A. Schuler, K. Rehbein, & R. D. Cramer, 2003, Pursuing strategic advantage through political means: A multivariate approach, *Academy of Management Journal*, 45: 659–672.
48. C. Hutzler, 2005, Beijing rescinds textile duties, slams U.S., EU on import limits, *Wall Street Journal*, May 31, A3.
49. J. P. Doh & T. R. Guay, 2006, Corporate social responsibility, public policy and NGO activism in Europe and the United States: An institutional-stakeholder perspective, *Journal of Management Studies*, 43: 48–73.
50. Per capita health expenditures, by country, 2006. *Infoplease*, http://www.infoplease.com, May 6, 2007; 2003, U.S. spends the most on healthcare but dollars do not equal health, *Medica Portal*, http://www.medica.de.
51. C. Debaise, 2005, U. S. workers start early on retirement savings, *Wall Street Journal*, January 20, D2.
52. Characteristics of the civilian labor force, 2004 and 2014, *Infoplease;* 2005, U.S. Department of Labor, Bureau of Labor Statistics data, http://www.bls.gov, April.
53. M. E. A. Jayne & R. L. Dipboye, 2004, Leveraging diversity to improve business performance: Research findings and recommendations for organizations, *Human Resource Management*, 43: 409–425.
54. M. J. McCarthy, 2004, New outposts: Granbury, Texas, isn't a rural town: It's a 'micropolis'; Census Bureau adopts term for main street America, and marketers take note; beans, ribs and Starbucks, *Wall Street Journal*, June 3, A1.
55. T. Fleming, 2003, Benefits of taking the superhighway to work, *Canadian HR Reporter*, 16(11): G7.
56. B. L. Kirkman, K. B. Lowe, & C. B. Gibson, 2006, A quarter of a century of culture's consequences: A review old empirical research incorporating Hofstede's cultural values framework, *Journal of International Business Studies*, 37: 285–320.
57. S. Michailova & K. Hutchings, 2006, National cultural influences on knowledge sharing: A comparison of China and Russia, *Journal of Management Studies*, 43: 384–405.
58. P. J. Buckley, J. Clegg, & H. Tan, 2006, Cultural awareness in knowledge transfer to China—The role of guanxi and mianzi, *Journal of World Business*, 41: 275–288.
59. A. L. Porter & S. W. Cunningham, 2004, Tech mining: Exploiting new technologies for competitive advantage, Hoboken, NJ: Wiley.
60. D. Lavie, 2006, Capability reconfiguration: An analysis of incumbent responses to technological change, *Academy of Management Review*, 31: 153–174; C. W. L. Hill & F. T. Rothaermel, 2003, The performance of incumbent firms in the face of radical technological innovation, *Academy of Management Review*, 28: 257–274;
61. M. Marr, 2005, How DreamWorks misjudged DVD sales of its monster hit, *Wall Street Journal*, May 31, A1, A9.
62. N. Wingfield, 2003, Anytime, anywhere: The number of Wi-Fi spots is set to explode, bringing the wireless technology to the rest of us, *Wall Street Journal*, March 31, R6, R12.
63. R. Sampson, 2007, R&D alliances and firm performance: The impact of technological diversity and alliance organization on innovation, *Academy of Management Journal*, 50: 364–386; A. Andal-Ancion, P. A. Cartwright, & G. S. Yip, 2003, The digital transformation of traditional businesses, *MIT Sloan Management Review*, 44(4): 34–41.
64. Y. Y. Kor & J. T. Mahoney, 2005, How dynamics, management, and governance of resource deployments influence firm-level performance, *Strategic Management Journal*, 26: 489–497; C. Nichols-Nixon & C. Y. Woo, 2003, Technology sourcing and output of established firms in a regime of encompassing technological change, *Strategic Management Journal*, 24: 651–666.
65. W. P. Wan, 2005, Country resource environments, firm capabilities, and corporate diversification strategies, *Journal of Management Studies*, 42: 161–182; M. Wright, I. Filatotchev, R. E. Hoskisson, & M. W. Peng, 2005, Strategy research in emerging economies: Challenging the conventional wisdom, *Journal of Management Studies*, 42: 1–30.
66. F. Vermeulen & H. Barkema, 2002, Pace, rhythm, and scope: Process dependence in building a multinational corporation, *Strategic Management Journal*, 23: 637–653.
67. M. A. Hitt, L. Tihanyi, T. Miller, & B. Connelly, 2006, International diversification: Antecedents, outcomes, and moderators, *Journal of Management*, 32: 831–867; F. T. Rothaermel, S. Kotha, & H. K. Steensma, 2006, International market entry by U.S. Internet firms: An empirical analysis of country risk, national culture, and market size, *Journal of Management*, 32: 56–82;
68. V. Nee, S. Opper, & S. Wong, 2007, Developmental state and corporate governance in China, *Managemement and Organization Review*, 3: 19–53; G. D. Bruton & D. Ahlstrom, 2002, An institutional view of China's venture capital industry: Explaining the differences between China and the West, *Journal of Business Venturing*, 18: 233–259.
69. M. Fong, 2005, Unphased by barriers, retailers flock to China for clothes, *Wall Street Journal*, May 27, B1, B2.
70. K. Cattani, E. Dahan, & G. Schmidt, 2005, Offshoring versus "Spackling," *MIT Sloan Management Review*, 46(3): 6–7.
71. F. T. Rothaermel, M. A. Hitt, & L. Jobe, 2006, Balancing vertical integration and strategic outsourcing: Effects on product portfolio, product success, and firm performance, *Journal of Management*, 27: 1033–1056.
72. R. D. Ireland, M. A. Hitt, S. M. Camp, & D. L. Sexton, 2001, Integrating entrepreneurship and strategic management actions to create firm wealth, *Academy of Management Executive*, 15(1): 49–63.

73. S. Li & H. Scullion, 2006, Bridging the distance: Managing cross-border knowledge holders, *Asia Pacific Journal of Management,* 23: 71–92; Z. Emden, A. Yaprak, & S. T. Cavusgil, 2005, Learning from experience in international alliances: Antecedents and firm performance implications, *Journal of Business Research,* 58: 883–892.
74. G. D. Bruton, D. Ahlstrom, & J. C. Wan, 2003, Turnaround in East Asian firms: Evidence from ethnic overseas Chinese communities, *Strategic Management Journal,* 24: 519–540; S. H. Park & Y. Luo, 2001, Guanxi and organizational dynamics: Organizational networking in Chinese firms, *Strategic Management Journal,* 22: 455–477; M. A. Hitt, M. T. Dacin, B. B. Tyler, & D. Park, 1997, Understanding the differences in Korean and U.S. executives' strategic orientations, *Strategic Management Journal,* 18: 159–167.
75. M. A. Hitt, D. Ahlstrom, M. T. Dacin, E. Levitas, & L. Svobodina, 2004, The institutional effects on strategic alliance partner selection: China versus Russia, *Organization Science,* 15: 173–185.
76. J. A. Mathews, 2006, Dragon multinationals: New players in 21st century globalization, *Asia Pacific Journal of Management,* 23: 5–27.
77. K. E. Meyer, 2006, Globalfocusing: From domestic conglomerates to global specialists, *Journal of Management Studies,* 43: 1110–1144.
78. C. H. Oh & A.M. Rugman, 2007, Regional multinationals and the Korean cosmetics industry, *Asia Pacific Journal of Management,* 24: 27–42.
79. C. A. Bartlett & S. Ghoshal, 2003, What is a global manager? *Harvard Business Review,* 81(8): 101–108; M. A. Carpenter & J. W. Fredrickson, 2001, Top management teams, global strategic posture and the moderating role of uncertainty, *Academy of Management Journal,* 44: 533–545.
80. V. K. Narayanan & L. Fahey, 2005, The relevance of the institutional underpinnings of Porter's five forces framework to emerging economies: An epistemological analysis, *Journal of Management Studies,* 42: 207–223; N. Argyres & A. M. McGahan, 2002, An interview with Michael Porter, *Academy of Management Executive,* 16(2): 43–52.
81. V. F. Misangyl, H. Elms, T. Greckhamer, & J. A. Lepine, 2006, A new perspective on a fundamental debate: A multilevel approach to industry, corporate, and business unit effects, *Strategic Management Journal,* 27: 571–590; G. Hawawini, V. Subramanian, & P. Verdin, 2003, Is performance driven by industry or firm-specific factors? A new look at the evidence, *Strategic Management Journal,* 24: 1–16.
82. S. Zaheer & A. Zaheer, 2001, Market microstructure in a global b2b network, *Strategic Management Journal,* 22: 859–873.
83. M. A. Hitt, J. E. Ricart, & R. D. Nixon, 1998, The new frontier, in M. A. Hitt, J. E. Ricart, & R. D. Nixon (eds.), *Managing Strategically in an Interconnected World,* Chichester: John Wiley & Sons, 3–12.
84. Gimeno, Hoskisson, Beal, & Wan, Explaining the clustering of international expansion moves; C. Garcia-Pont & N. Nohria, 2002, Local versus global mimetism: The dynamics of alliance formation in the automobile industry, *Strategic Management Journal,* 23: 307–321.
85. E. D. Jaffe, I. D. Nebenzahl, & I. Schorr, 2005, Strategic options of home country firms faced with MNC entry, *Long Range Planning,* 38(2): 183–196.
86. A. V. Mainkar, M. Lubatkin, & W. S. Schulze, 2006, Toward a product-proliferation theory of entry barriers, *Academy of management Review,* 31: 1062–1075; J. Shamsie, 2003, The context of dominance: An industry-driven framework for exploiting reputation, *Strategic Management Journal,* 24: 199–215.
87. Delta Airlines exits bankruptcy, 2007, *USA Today,* http://www.usatoday.com, May 1.
88. R. Makadok, 1999, Interfirm differences in scale economies and the evolution of market shares, *Strategic Management Journal,* 20: 935–952.
89. F. Salvador & C. Forza, 2007, Principles for efficient and effective sales configuration design, *International Journal of Mass Customisation,* 2(1,2): 114–127; B. J. Pine II, 2004, Mass customization: The new imperative, *Strategic Direction,* January, 2–3.
90. F. Keenan, S. Holmes, J. Greene, & R. O. Crockett, 2002, A mass market of one, *BusinessWeek,* December 2, 68–72.
91. Mainkar, Lubatkin, & Schulze, Toward a product-proliferation theory of entry barriers.
92. M. A. Hitt, R. M. Holmes, T. Miller, and M. P. Salmador, 2006, Modeling country institutional profiles: The dimensions and dynamics of institutional environments, presented at the Strategic Management Society Conference, October; G. Walker, T. L. Madsen, & G. Carini, 2002, How does institutional change affect heterogeneity among firms? *Strategic Management Journal,* 23: 89–104.
93. A. Reinhardt, 2005, The man who said no to Microsoft, *BusinessWeek,* May 31, 49; 2002, The long shadow of big blue, *The Economist,* November 9, 63–64.
94. China approves plan to build large commercial aircraft, 2007, Associated Press, http://www.ocregister.com, May 7.
95. S. Dutta, O. Narasimhan, & S. Rajiv, 2005, Conceptualizing and measuring capabilities: Methodology and empirical application, *Strategic Management Journal,* 26: 277–285; A. M. Knott, 2003, Persistent heterogeneity and sustainable innovation, *Strategic Management Journal,* 24: 687–705;.
96. S. Nadkarni & V. K. Narayanan, 2007, Strategic schemas, strategic flexibility, and firm performance: The moderating role of industry clockspeed, *Strategic Management Journal,* 28: 243–270.
97. D. M. De Carolis, 2003, Competencies and imitability in the pharmaceutical industry: An analysis of their relationship with firm performance, *Journal of Management,* 29: 27–50; D. L. Deephouse, 1999, To be different, or to be the same? It's a question (and theory) of strategic balance, *Strategic Management Journal,* 20: 147–166.
98. L. Canina, C. A. Enz, & J. S. Harrison, 2005, Agglomeration effects and strategic orientations: Evidence from the U.S. lodging industry, *Academy of Management Journal,* 48: 565–581; W. Chung & A. Kalnins, 2001, Agglomeration effects and performance: Test of the Texas lodging industry, *Strategic Management Journal,* 22: 969–988.
99. A. S. Cui, D. A. Griffith, S. T. Cavusgil, & M. Dabic, 2006, The influence of market and cultural environmental factors on technology transfer between foreign MNCs and local subsidiaries: A Croatian illustration, *Journal of World Business,* 41: 100–111; K. D. Brouthers, L. E. Brouthers, & S. Werner, 2003, Transaction cost-enhanced entry mode choices and firm performance, *Strategic Management Journal,* 24: 1239–1248.
100. M. E. Porter, 1980, *Competitive Strategy,* New York: Free Press.
101. M. S. Hunt, 1972, Competition in the major home appliance industry, 1960–1970 (doctoral dissertation, Harvard University); Porter, *Competitive Strategy,* 129.
102. G. McNamara, D. L. Deephouse, & R. A. Luce, 2003, Competitive positioning within and across a strategic group structure: The performance of core, secondary, and solitary firms, *Strategic Management Journal,* 24: 161–181.
103. M. W. Peng, J. Tan, & T. W. Tong, 2004, Ownership types and strategic groups in an emerging economy, *Journal of Management Studies,* 41: 1105–1129; R. K. Reger & A. S. Huff, 1993, Strategic groups: A cognitive perspective, *Strategic Management Journal,* 14: 103–123.
104. M. Peteraf & M. Shanley, 1997, Getting to know you: A theory of strategic group identity, *Strategic Management Journal,* 18 (Special Issue): 165–186.
105. J. Lee, K. Lee, & S. Rho, 2002, An evolutionary perspective on strategic group emergence: A genetic algorithm-based model, *Strategic Management Journal,* 23: 727–746.
106. J. A. Zuniga-Vicente, J. M. de la Fuente Sabate, & I. S. Gonzalez. 2004, Dynamics of the strategic group membership-performance linkage in rapidly changing environments, *Journal of Business Research,* 57: 1378–1390.
107. S. McBride, 2005, Battle stations: Two upstarts vie for dominance in satellite radio, *Wall Street Journal,* March 30, A1, A9.
108. V. J. Racanelli, 2005, Turnaround ahead at VW, *Barron's,* May 16, 26–27.

109. Gimeno, Hoskisson, Beal, & Wan, Explaining the clustering of international expansion moves.
110. Porter, *Competitive Strategy*, 49.
111. M. B. Lieberman & S. Asaba, 2006, Why do firms imitate each other? *Academy of Management Journal*, 31: 366–385; G. McNamara, R. A. Luce, & G. H. Tompson, 2002, Examining the effect of complexity in strategic group knowledge structures on firm performance, *Strategic Management Journal*, 23: 153–170.
112. D. B. Montgomery, M. C. Moore, & J. E. Urbany, 2005, Reasoning about competitive reactions: Evidence from executives, *Marketing Science*, 24: 138–149.
113. P. M. Norman, R. D. Ireland, K. W. Artz, & M. A. Hitt, 2000, Acquiring and using competitive intelligence in entrepreneurial teams, paper presented at the Academy of Management, Toronto, Canada.
114. F. Vogelstein & P. Lewis, 2005, Search and destroy, *Fortune*, May 2, 73–79.
115. J. Menn, 2007, Google shrugs at possible rival deal, *Los Angeles Times*, http://www.latimes.com, May 5; R. A. Guth & K. J. Delaney, 2007, Microsoft, Yahoo! discussed deal, *Wall Street Journal*, online.wsj.com, May 5.
116. A. Afuah, 2000, How much do your co-opetitors' capabilities matter in the face of technological change? *Strategic Management Journal*, 21: 387A; Brandenburger & B. Nalebuff, 1996, *Co-opetition*, New York: Currency Doubleday.
117. S. G. Lazzarini, 2007, The impact of membership in competing alliance constellations: Evidence on the operational performance of global airlines, *Strategic Management Journal*, 28: 345–367.
118. J. L. Morrow, D. G. Sirmon, M. A. Hitt & T. R. Holcomb, 2007, Creating value in the face of declining performance: Firm strategies and organizational recovery, *Strategic Management Journal*, 28: 271–283.
119. R. D'Ovidio, 2007, The evolution of computers and crime: Complicating security practice, *Security Journal*, 20: 45-49.
120. A. Crane, 2005, In the company of spies: When competitive intelligence gathering becomes industrial espionage, *Business Horizons*, 48(3): 233–240.

The Internal Organization: Resources, Capabilities, Core Competencies, and Competitive Advantages

Studying this chapter should provide you with the strategic management knowledge needed to:

1. Explain why firms need to study and understand their internal organization.
2. Define value and discuss its importance.
3. Describe the differences between tangible and intangible resources.
4. Define capabilities and discuss their development.
5. Describe four criteria used to determine whether resources and capabilities are core competencies.
6. Explain how value chain analysis is used to identify and evaluate resources and capabilities.
7. Define outsourcing and discuss reasons for its use.
8. Discuss the importance of identifying internal strengths and weaknesses.

Managing the Tension Between Innovation and Efficiency

© Karen Bleier/AFP/Getty Images

As we discussed in Chapter 1, being able to wisely use a firm's assets to continuously innovate in ways that create value for customers is an important source of competitive advantage. For decades, 3M, the widely diversified technology company with six business segments, was a model of successful corporate innovation. The firm's commitment to innovation, and the importance innovation had to its competitive actions, is suggested by its slogan: "The Spirit of Innovation. That's 3M." In a practical, everyday sense, innovation's importance is signaled by 3M's famous intention of generating at least one-third of its annual sales from products introduced to the marketplace in the most recent five years.

For decades, 3M was indeed recognized for its innovation-related abilities and resulting product successes. Relying on the skills of its scientists and engineers, the firm developed 30-plus core technologies that were the basis for more than 55,000 products it produced and sold to customers throughout the world. But times have changed. In mid-2007, only 25 percent of 3M's sales were earned from products introduced over the previous five-year period. Less money was being allocated to research and development (R&D), which typically is the wellspring of product innovations. A number of financial analysts criticized the reduction in R&D spending. Full-year (2006) profits were below expectations, an outcome that did little to convince investors and potentially other stakeholders (e.g., suppliers, customers, and perhaps even employees) that new CEO George Buckley was putting a strategy into place that would return 3M to its glory years.

What contributed to the change in 3M's outputs of innovations? Some believe that the introduction of a Six Sigma program under the tutelage of former CEO James McNerney (who served immediately prior to Buckley) helped to shape the recent form of 3M. Six Sigma is a widely used "series of management techniques designed to decrease production defects and increase efficiency." Focusing on work processes, Six Sigma techniques are used to spot problems and use rigorous measurements to reduce production variations and eliminate defects. McNerney became intimately familiar with Six Sigma as an upper-level executive at General Electric (GE) where the techniques were used extensively during Jack Welch's tenure as that firm's CEO.

Using techniques such as Six Sigma is completely appropriate in that reducing waste and increasing efficiency contribute to a firm's profitability. The issue is that innovation-generating and efficiency-generating actions can sometimes be at odds with each other. In an analyst's words: "When (Six Sigma) types of initiatives become ingrained in a company's culture, as they did at 3M, creativity (and innovation that result from it) can easily get squelched." Indeed,

Six Sigma focuses on actions to define, measure, analyze, improve, and control. Some argue that focusing on these actions creates *sameness* rather than *innovation*. One 3M employee internalized the tension between efficiency and innovation as "Six Sigma Control" versus "Innovative Freedom." Because 3M had been about innovation for so long, other employees concluded that what they believed was an overemphasis on the discipline generated by Six Sigma caused 3M to lose its *soul*.

Recently, CEO Buckley said that 3M's stakeholders can expect a reenergization of R&D. Buckley believes it is the way to refocus 3M on growth and innovation. However, the necessity of using highly efficient work processes will remain a priority at 3M.

Sources: D. DePass, 2007, 3M earnings disappoint Wall Street, *The Star Tribune*, January 31, D1, D3; B. Hindo, 2007, At 3M, a struggle between efficiency and creativity, *BusinessWeek*, June 3, 8–14; J. Rae, 2007, Have it both ways, *BusinessWeek*, June 3, 16; Scrutinize Six Sigma, 2007, *BusinessWeek*, July 2, 90–91.

As discussed in the first two chapters, several factors in the global economy, including the rapid development of the Internet's capabilities[1] and of globalization in general have made it increasingly difficult for firms to find ways to develop a competitive advantage that can be sustained for any period of time.[2] As is suggested by 3M's experiences, innovation may be a vital path to efforts to develop sustainable competitive advantages.[3] Sometimes, product innovation serves simultaneously as the foundation on which a firm is started as well as the source of its competitive advantages. Artemis Pet Food Co., for example, emphasizes quality as it manufactures pet food. Using natural ingredients that are suitable for humans, the firm has grown rapidly and has a cadre of loyal customers even though some of its products are more than twice the price of competitors' offerings.[4] (In the Opening Case for Chapter 4, you will learn about the innovations of another firm—PetSmart—competing in the pet industry.)

Competitive advantages and the differences they create in firm performance are often strongly related to the resources firms hold and how they are managed.[5] "Resources are the foundation for strategy, and unique bundles of resources generate competitive advantages that lead to wealth creation."[6] As 3M's experience shows, resources must be managed to simultaneously allow production efficiency and an ability to form competitive advantages such as the consistent development of innovative products.

To identify and successfully use resources over time, those leading firms need to think constantly about how to manage them to increase the value for customers who "are arbiters of value"[7] as they compare firms' goods and services against each other before making a purchase decision. As this chapter shows, firms achieve strategic competitiveness and earn above-average returns when their unique core competencies are effectively acquired, bundled, and leveraged to take advantage of opportunities in the external environment in ways that create value for customers.[8]

People are an especially critical resource for helping organizations learn how to continuously innovate as a means of achieving successful growth.[9] In other words, "smart growth" happens when the firm manages its need to grow with its ability to successfully manage growth.[10] People are a critical resource to efforts to grow successfully at 3M, where the director of global compensation says that harnessing the innovative powers of the firm's employees is the means for rekindling growth.[11] And, people at 3M as well as virtually all other firms who know how to effectively manage resources to help organizations learn how to continuously innovate are themselves a source of competitive advantage.[12] In fact, a global labor market now exists as firms seek talented individuals to add to their fold. As Richard Florida argues, "[W]herever talent goes, innovation, creativity, and economic growth are sure to follow."[13]

The fact that over time the benefits of any firm's value-creating strategy can be duplicated by its competitors is a key reason for having employees who know how to manage resources. These employees are critical to firms' efforts to perform well. Because all competitive advantages have a limited life,[14] the question of duplication is not *if* it will happen, but *when*. In general, the sustainability of a competitive advantage is a function of three factors: (1) the rate of core competence obsolescence because of environmental changes, (2) the availability of substitutes for the core competence, and (3) the imitability of the core competence.[15] The challenge for all firms, then, is to effectively manage current core competencies while simultaneously developing new ones.[16] Only when firms develop a continuous stream of capabilities that contribute to competitive advantages do they achieve strategic competitiveness, earn above-average returns, and remain ahead of competitors (see Chapter 5).

In Chapter 2, we examined general, industry, and competitor environments. Armed with this knowledge about the realities and conditions of their external environment, firms have a better understanding of marketplace opportunities and the characteristics of the competitive environment in which those opportunities exist. In this chapter, we focus on the firm itself. By analyzing its internal organization, a firm determines what it *can do*. Matching what a firm *can do* (a function of its resources, capabilities, core competencies, and competitive advantages) with what it *might do* (a function of opportunities and threats in the external environment) allows the firm to develop vision, pursue its mission, and select and implement its strategies.

We begin this chapter by briefly discussing conditions associated with analyzing the firm's internal organization. We then discuss the roles of resources and capabilities in developing core competencies, which are the sources of the firm's competitive advantages. Included in this discussion are the techniques firms use to identify and evaluate resources and capabilities and the criteria for selecting core competencies from among them. Resources and capabilities are not inherently valuable, but they create value when the firm can use them to perform certain activities that result in a competitive advantage. Accordingly, we also discuss the value chain concept and examine four criteria to evaluate core competencies that establish competitive advantage.[17] The chapter closes with cautionary comments about the need for firms to prevent their core competencies from becoming core rigidities. The existence of core rigidities indicates that the firm is too anchored to its past, which prevents it from continuously developing new competitive advantages.

Using a global mind-set, Volkswagen's leaders decided that the firm should open facilities in Slovakia. Opening these facilities long before their competitors has led to a distinct competitive advantage for VW in Slovakia and surrounding countries.

Analyzing the Internal Organization

The Context of Internal Analysis

In the global economy, traditional factors such as labor costs, access to financial resources and raw materials, and protected or regulated markets remain sources of competitive advantage, but to a lesser degree.[18] One important reason is that competitors can apply their resources to successfully use an international strategy (discussed in Chapter 8) as a means of overcoming the advantages created by these more traditional sources. For example, Volkswagen began establishing production facilities in Slovakia "shortly after the Russians moved out" as part of its international strategy. With a total investment exceeding $1.6 billion, Volkswagen is thought to have a competitive advantage over rivals such as France's Peugeot Citroen and South Korea's Kia Motors, firms that are now investing in Slovakia in an effort to duplicate the competitive advantage that has accrued to Volkswagen.[19]

Increasingly, those who analyze their firm's internal organization should use a global mind-set to do so. A **global mind-set** is the ability to study an internal organization in ways that are not dependent on the assumptions of a single country, culture,

A **global mind-set** is the ability to study an internal organization in ways that are not dependent on the assumptions of a single country, culture, or context.

or context.[20] Because they are able to span artificial boundaries,[21] those with a global mind-set recognize that their firms must possess resources and capabilities that allow understanding of and appropriate responses to competitive situations that are influenced by country-specific factors and unique societal cultures. Firms populated with people having a global mind-set have a "key source of long-term competitive advantage in the global marketplace."[22]

Finally, analysis of the firm's internal organization requires that evaluators examine the firm's portfolio of resources and the *bundles* of heterogeneous resources and capabilities managers have created.[23] This perspective suggests that individual firms possess at least some resources and capabilities that other companies do not—at least not in the same combination. Resources are the source of capabilities, some of which lead to the development of a firm's core competencies or its competitive advantages.[24] Understanding how to *leverage* the firm's unique bundle of resources and capabilities is a key outcome decision makers seek when analyzing the internal organization.[25] Figure 3.1 illustrates the relationships among resources, capabilities, and core competencies and shows how firms use them to create strategic competitiveness. Before examining these topics in depth, we describe value and its creation.

Creating Value

Value is measured by a product's performance characteristics and by its attributes for which customers are willing to pay.

By exploiting their core competencies or competitive advantages to at least meet if not exceed the demanding standards of global competition, firms create value for customers.[26] **Value** is measured by a product's performance characteristics and by its attributes for which customers are willing to pay. Customers of Luby Cafeterias, for example, pay for meals that are value-priced, generally healthy, and served quickly in a causal setting.[27]

Firms with a competitive advantage offer value to customers that is superior to the value competitors provide.[28] Firms create value by innovatively bundling and leveraging their resources and capabilities.[29] Firms unable to creatively bundle and leverage their

Figure 3.1 Components of Internal Analysis Leading to Competitive Advantage and Strategic Competitiveness

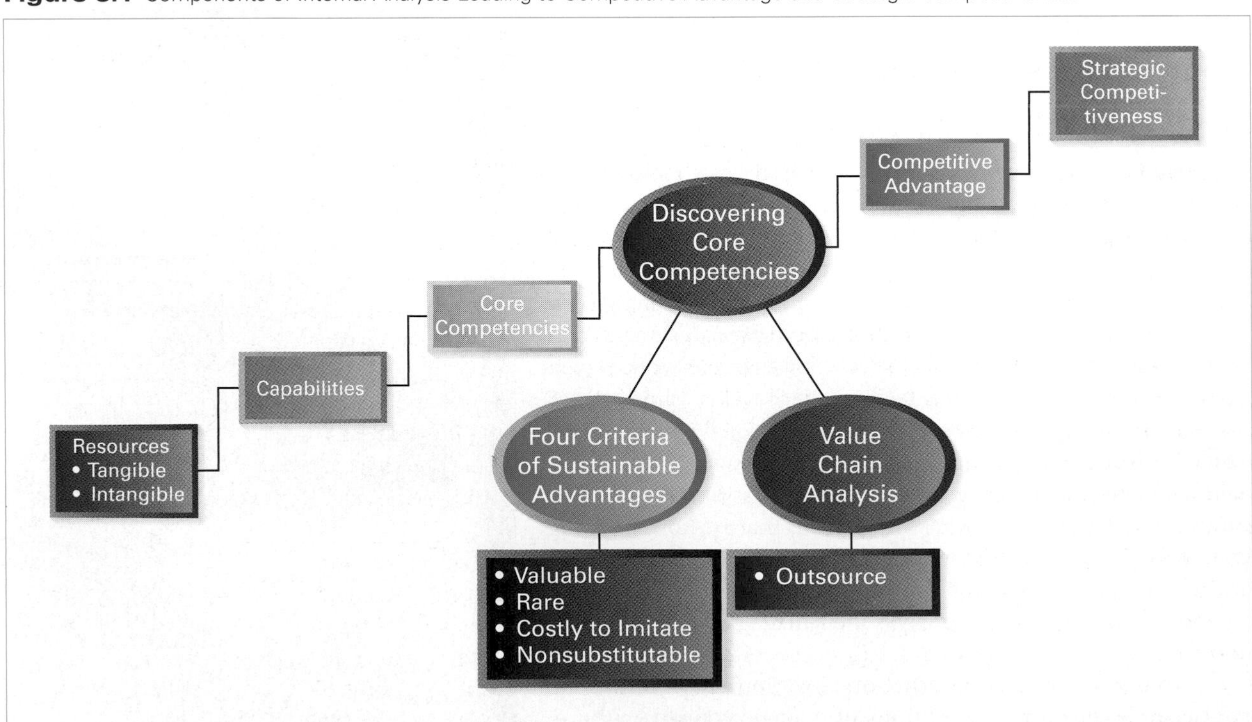

resources and capabilities in ways that create value for customers suffer performance declines. Sometimes, it seems that these declines may happen because firms fail to understand what customers value. For example, after learning that General Motors (GM) intended to focus on visual design to create value for buyers, one former GM customer said that in his view, people buying cars and trucks valued durability, reliability, good fuel economy, and a low cost of operation more than visual design.[30]

Ultimately, creating value for customers is the source of above-average returns for a firm. What the firm intends regarding value creation affects its choice of business-level strategy (see Chapter 4) and its organizational structure (see Chapter 11).[31] In Chapter 4's discussion of business-level strategies, we note that value is created by a product's low cost, by its highly differentiated features, or by a combination of low cost and high differentiation, compared with competitors' offerings. A business-level strategy is effective only when it is grounded in exploiting the firm's core competencies and competitive advantages. Thus, successful firms continuously examine the effectiveness of current and future core competencies and advantages.[32]

At one time, the strategic management process was concerned largely with understanding the characteristics of the industry in which the firm competed and, in light of those characteristics, determining how the firm should position itself relative to competitors. This emphasis on industry characteristics and competitive strategy underestimated the role of the firm's resources and capabilities in developing competitive advantage. In fact, core competencies, in combination with product-market positions, are the firm's most important sources of competitive advantage.[33] The core competencies of a firm, in addition to results of analyses of its general, industry, and competitor environments, should drive its selection of strategies. The resources held by the firm and their context are important when formulating strategy.[34] As Clayton Christensen noted, "Successful strategists need to cultivate a deep understanding of the processes of competition and progress and of the factors that undergird each advantage. Only thus will they be able to see when old advantages are poised to disappear and how new advantages can be built in their stead."[35] By emphasizing core competencies when formulating strategies, companies learn to compete primarily on the basis of firm-specific differences, but they must be very aware of how things are changing in the external environment as well.[36]

The Challenge of Analyzing the Internal Organization

The strategic decisions managers make about the components of their firm's internal organization are nonroutine,[37] have ethical implications,[38] and significantly influence the firm's ability to earn above-average returns.[39] These decisions involve choices about the assets the firm needs to collect and how to best use those assets. "Managers make choices precisely because they believe these contribute substantially to the performance and survival of their organizations."[40]

Making decisions involving the firm's assets—identifying, developing, deploying, and protecting resources, capabilities, and core competencies—may appear to be relatively easy. However, this task is as challenging and difficult as any other with which managers are involved; moreover, it is increasingly internationalized.[41] Some believe that the pressure on managers to pursue only decisions that help the firm meet the quarterly earnings expected by market analysts makes it difficult to accurately examine the firm's internal organization.[42]

The challenge and difficulty of making effective decisions are implied by preliminary evidence suggesting that one-half of organizational decisions fail.[43] Sometimes, mistakes are made as the firm analyzes conditions in its internal organization.[44] Managers might, for example, identify capabilities as core competencies that do not create a competitive advantage. This misidentification may have been the case at Polaroid Corporation as decision makers continued to believe that the skills it used to build its instant film cameras were highly relevant at the time its competitors were developing and using the skills required to introduce digital cameras.[45] When a mistake occurs, such as was the case at Polaroid, decision makers must have the confidence to admit it and take corrective actions.[46] A firm can still grow through well-intended errors; the learning generated by making and correcting mistakes can be important to the creation of new competitive advantages.[47] Moreover, firms and those managing them can learn from the failure resulting from a mistake—that is, what *not* to do when seeking competitive advantage.[48]

To facilitate developing and using core competencies, managers must have courage, self-confidence, integrity, the capacity to deal with uncertainty and complexity, and a willingness to hold people accountable for their work and to be held accountable themselves.[49] Thus, difficult managerial decisions concerning resources, capabilities, and core competencies are characterized by three conditions: uncertainty, complexity, and intraorganizational conflicts (see Figure 3.2).[50]

Managers face *uncertainty* in terms of new proprietary technologies, rapidly changing economic and political trends, transformations in societal values, and shifts in customer demands.[51] Environmental uncertainty increases the *complexity* and range of issues to examine when studying the internal environment.[52] Consider the complexity associated with the decisions Gregory H. Boyce is encountering as CEO of Peabody Energy Corp. Peabody is the world's largest coal company. But coal is thought of as a "dirty fuel," meaning that some think its future prospects are dim in light of global warming issues. What decisions should Boyce make given global warming and the nature of his company's core product? Obviously, the complexity of these decisions is quite significant.[53] Biases about how to cope with uncertainty affect decisions about the resources and capabilities that will become the foundation of the firm's competitive advantage.[54] For example, Boyce strongly believes in coal's future, suggesting that automobiles capable of burning coal should be built. Finally, *intraorganizational conflict* surfaces when decisions are made about the core competencies to nurture as well as how to nurture them.

In making decisions affected by these three conditions, judgment is required. *Judgment* is the capability of making successful decisions when no obviously correct model or rule is available or when relevant data are unreliable or incomplete. In this type of situation, decision makers must be aware of possible cognitive biases. Overconfidence, for example, can often lower value when a correct decision is not obvious, such as making a judgment as to whether an internal resource is a strength or a weakness.[55]

Figure 3.2 Conditions Affecting Managerial Decisions About Resources, Capabilities, and Core Competencies

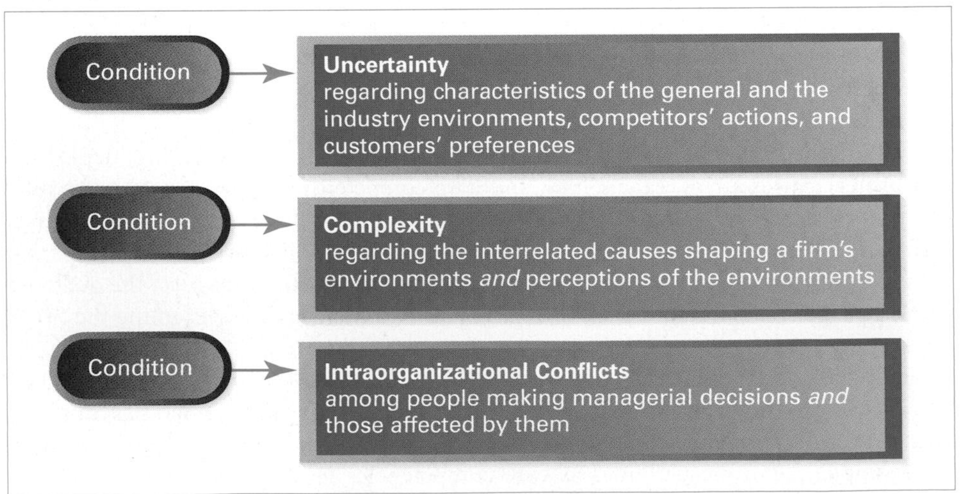

Source: Adapted from R. Amit & P. J. H. Schoemaker, 1993, Strategic assets and organizational rent, *Strategic Management Journal*, 14: 33.

Strategic Focus Strategic Focus Strategic Focus

Hyundai Cars: The Quality Is There, So Why Aren't the Cars Selling?

Once known as a producer of cheap, entry-level cars that suffered from multiple manufacturing defects, Hyundai Motor Company has reversed its performance from the perspective of product quality. In fact, according to Strategic Vision, a well-known market research company and consultant to automakers, Hyundai had leadership positions in five categories (including large car, minivan, and small sport utility vehicle) in the firm's 2007 vehicle quality study. This performance caused one analyst to suggest that "when it comes to car quality, (consumers should) think Korean." This recommendation is consistent with the perspective of the firm's CEO who says that "At present, the Hyundai brand stands for high quality." Evidence from J.D. Power's Initial Quality Study appears to support these views in that Hyundai's quality is actually rated ahead of Toyota, trailing only Lexus and Porsche.

Surprisingly, at least to Hyundai officials, the significant improvements in product quality are not translating into sales growth in the key European and U.S. markets. In Europe, the firm's new car registrations in 2006 declined 5.7 percent from its registrations in 2005, resulting in a total European market share of 1.9 percent. (Leader Volkswagen had 20.3 percent of the European market in 2006.) In the United States, the firm's unsold inventory was swelling in 2007. As the fastest-growing carmaker in the U.S. market during 2000–2005, this inventory increase was unexpected. Based on its success in the early twenty-first century, Hyundai established a target of selling 1 million units in the United States in 2010. That goal has now been reduced to 700,000 units with a desire to sell 900,000 units in this particular market by 2012. In turn, sales declines, as represented by swelling inventories, had a significantly negative effect on the firm's earnings.

Hyundai's sales-related problems meant that the firm faced an uncertain and complex future and that judgment had to be used to make decisions. As a first step, executives needed to identify the cause of the firm's problems. According to Hyundai's vice president for sales, the firm needs a new story. In his words: "When we don't have a price story, we have no story." In consultation with others, the firm's new chief operating officer (COO) decided that Hyundai "needed a new 'big idea' to redefine its brand and move it away from an association with cheap, tin-pot vehicles." What is the new big idea? Essentially, the firm is being repositioned as an "overachieving, underappreciated brand that smart people are discovering." Decisions made to support this repositioning include those of allocating additional resources to R&D to focus the design image of its cars and establishing production facilities in Europe (Czech Republic) and India with the intention of better understanding local consumers needs while reducing manufacturing costs and making additional gains with product quality.

Sources: Hyundai Motor Company, 2007, *Hyundai Motor World,* 15(55): 1–15; D. Goodman, 2007, Hyundai takes lead in 2007 auto quality study, *The Salt Lake Tribune Online,* June 4, http://www.sltrib.com; D. Kiley, Hyundai still gets no respect; Marketing guru Steve Wilhite has to sell drivers a new story, *BusinessWeek Online,* May 21, http://businessweek.com; L. Rousek, 2007, Hyundai Motor breaks ground on its first European car plant, *Wall Street Journal Online,* http://wsj.com; C. A. Sawyer, 2007, Joe Piaskowski & Hyundai's exploratory approach, *Automotive Design & Production,* 119(4): 22.

When exercising judgment, decision makers often take intelligent risks. In the current competitive landscape, executive judgment can be a particularly important source of competitive advantage. One reason is that, over time, effective judgment allows a firm to build a strong reputation and retain the loyalty of stakeholders whose support is linked to above-average returns.[56]

As explained in the Strategic Focus, Hyundai's executives use their judgment to make decisions as their firm faces an uncertain and complex future. Of course, the firm's

Some business analysts feel that Hermes's cautious entry into new international markets is too slow and ineffective.

executives hope that their decisions are the product of effective judgment. Decision makers at Hermes hope the same thing is true for them. This luxury retailer has been slow to enter international markets, opening its first store in India in 2008 "several years after competitors such as Louis Vuitton and Chanel."[57] Some believe that entering international markets slowly and cautiously is proving to be an ineffective decision for Hermes. A comprehensive decision-making process (a process in which a great deal of information is collected and analyzed)[58] may be what Hyundai and Hermes executives should use given the uncertainty and complexity of the conditions facing their firms.

Resources, Capabilities, and Core Competencies

Resources, capabilities, and core competencies are the foundation of competitive advantage. Resources are bundled to create organizational capabilities. In turn, capabilities are the source of a firm's core competencies, which are the basis of competitive advantages.[59] Figure 3.1, on page 72, depicts these relationships. Here, we define and provide examples of these building blocks of competitive advantage.

Resources

Broad in scope, resources cover a spectrum of individual, social, and organizational phenomena.[60] Typically, resources alone do not yield a competitive advantage.[61] In fact, a competitive advantage is generally based on the *unique bundling of several resources.*[62] For example, Amazon.com combined service and distribution resources to develop its competitive advantages. The firm started as an online bookseller, directly shipping orders to customers. It quickly grew large and established a distribution network through which it could ship "millions of different items to millions of different customers." Lacking Amazon's combination of resources, traditional bricks-and-mortar companies, such as Borders, found it difficult to establish an effective online presence. These difficulties led some of them to develop partnerships with Amazon. Through these arrangements, Amazon now handles the online presence and the shipping of goods for several firms, including Borders—which now can focus on sales in its stores.[63] These types of arrangements are useful to the bricks-and-mortar companies because they are not accustomed to shipping so much diverse merchandise directly to individuals.

Tangible resources are assets that can be seen and quantified.

Intangible resources include assets that are rooted deeply in the firm's history and have accumulated over time.

Some of a firm's resources (defined in Chapter 1 as inputs to the firm's production process) are tangible while others are intangible. **Tangible resources** are assets that can be seen and quantified. Production equipment, manufacturing facilities, distribution centers, and formal reporting structures are examples of tangible resources. **Intangible resources** are assets that are rooted deeply in the firm's history and have accumulated over time. Because they are embedded in unique patterns of routines, intangible resources are relatively difficult for competitors to analyze and imitate. Knowledge, trust between managers and employees, managerial capabilities, organizational routines (the unique ways people work together), scientific capabilities, the capacity for innovation, brand name, and the firm's reputation for its goods or services and how it interacts with people (such as employees, customers, and suppliers) are intangible resources.[64]

The four types of tangible resources are financial, organizational, physical, and technological (see Table 3.1). The three types of intangible resources are human, innovation, and reputational (see Table 3.2).

Table 3.1 Tangible Resources

Financial Resources	• The firm's borrowing capacity • The firm's ability to generate internal funds
Organizational Resources	• The firm's formal reporting structure and its formal planning, controlling, and coordinating systems
Physical Resources	• Sophistication and location of a firm's plant and equipment • Access to raw materials
Technological Resources	• Stock of technology, such as patents, trademarks, copyrights, and trade secrets

Sources: Adapted from J. B. Barney, 1991, Firm resources and sustained competitive advantage, *Journal of Management,* 17: 101; R. M. Grant, 1991, *Contemporary Strategy Analysis,* Cambridge, U.K.: Blackwell Business, 100–102.

Table 3.2 Intangible Resources

Human Resources	• Knowledge • Trust • Managerial capabilities • Organizational routines
Innovation Resources	• Ideas • Scientific capabilities • Capacity to innovate
Reputational Resources	• Reputation with customers • Brand name • Perceptions of product quality, durability, and reliability • Reputation with suppliers • For efficient, effective, supportive, and mutually beneficial interactions and relationships

Sources: Adapted from R. Hall, 1992, The strategic analysis of intangible resources, *Strategic Management Journal,* 13: 136–139; R. M. Grant, 1991, *Contemporary Strategy Analysis,* Cambridge, U.K.: Blackwell Business, 101–104.

Tangible Resources

As tangible resources, a firm's borrowing capacity and the status of its physical facilities are visible. The value of many tangible resources can be established through financial statements; but these statements do not account for the value of all the firm's assets, because they disregard some intangible resources.[65] The value of tangible resources is also constrained because they are hard to leverage—it is difficult to derive additional business or value from a tangible resource. For example, an airplane is a tangible resource or asset, but "You can't use the same airplane on five different routes at the same time. You can't put the same crew on five different routes at the same time. And the same goes for the financial investment you've made in the airplane."[66]

Although production assets are tangible, many of the processes to use these assets are intangible. Thus, the learning and potential proprietary processes associated with a tangible resource, such as manufacturing facilities, can have unique intangible attributes, such as quality control processes, unique manufacturing processes, and technology that develop over time and create competitive advantage.[67]

Intangible Resources

Compared to tangible resources, intangible resources are a superior source of core competencies.[68] In fact, in the global economy, "the success of a corporation lies more in its intellectual and systems capabilities than in its physical assets. [Moreover], the capacity to manage human intellect—and to convert it into useful products and services—is fast becoming the critical executive skill of the age."[69]

Because intangible resources are less visible and more difficult for competitors to understand, purchase, imitate, or substitute for, firms prefer to rely on them rather than on tangible resources as the foundation for their capabilities and core competencies. In fact, the more unobservable (i.e., intangible) a resource is, the more sustainable will be the competitive advantage that is based on it.[70] Another benefit of intangible resources is that, unlike most tangible resources, their use can be leveraged. For instance, sharing knowledge among employees does not diminish its value for any one person. To the contrary, two people sharing their individualized knowledge sets often can be leveraged to create additional knowledge that, although new to each of them, contributes to performance improvements for the firm.[71] With intangible resources, the larger is the network of users, the greater the benefit to each party.

As shown in Table 3.2, the intangible resource of reputation is an important source of competitive advantage. Indeed, some argue that "a firm's reputation is widely considered to be a valuable resource associated with sustained competitive advantage."[72] Earned through the firm's actions as well as its words, a value-creating reputation is a product of years of superior marketplace competence as perceived by stakeholders.[73] A reputation indicates the level of awareness a firm has been able to develop among stakeholders and the degree to which they hold the firm in high esteem.[74]

Harley-Davidson's reputation, an intangible resource, has led to associations with other companies and an expansion of its own product lines.

A well-known and highly valued brand name is an application of reputation as a source of competitive advantage.[75] A continuing commitment to innovation and aggressive advertising facilitate firms' efforts to take advantage of the reputation associated with their brands.[76] Because of the desirability of its reputation, the Harley-Davidson brand name, for example, has such status that it adorns a limited edition Barbie doll, a popular restaurant in New York City, and a line of L'Oréal cologne. Additionally, the firm offers a broad range of clothing items, from black leather jackets to fashions for tots through Harley-Davidson MotorClothes.[77] Other firms are trying to build their reputations. For example, Li-Ning, a manufacturer and marketer of athletic shoes, competes in the Chinese market against Nike and Adidas, firms with well-known brands. To prepare for the 2008 Olympic Games in Beijing, Li-Ning hired a veteran with experience at Procter & Gamble as vice president of marketing to build its image. The hired executive's first initiative was to partner with the National Basketball Association to use its logo on Li-Ning shoes.[78]

Because of their ability to influence performance, companies do everything possible to nurture and protect their brand name. When something happens to tarnish a brand, firms respond aggressively. For example, PepsiCo's brand name and reputation have been tarnished in India as explained in the Strategic Focus. But the firm is dealing directly with the matter. The interest, of course, is to restore the luster of the brand name in a market the firm considers "strategic" to its future success. While doing so, it seems that PepsiCo also seeks to contribute to the welfare of India's citizenry.

Strategic Focus Strategic Focus Strategic Focus

Seeking to Repair a Tarnished Brand Name

"For somebody to think that Pepsi would jeopardize its brand—its global brand—by doing something stupid in one country is crazy." These words, spoken by PepsiCo's CEO Indra K. Nooyi, demonstrate the intensity of the situation the firm (as well as its main rival, Coca-Cola Company) faces in India. A native of India, Nooyi believes that her home country is a top "strategic priority" for the growth of the firm she heads. (The fact that PepsiCo has 35 plants in India is one indication of the market's importance to the firm.) Taking actions that are consistent with the concept of "performance with purpose," Nooyi seeks to "make PepsiCo a groundbreaker in areas like selling healthy food and diversifying its workforce." Perhaps these intentions, and the underlying values they suggest, account for some of Nooyi's disappointment and surprise about the allegations being leveled against PepsiCo in India.

The foundation for the situation concerning Nooyi and her firm was laid in 2003 when tests conducted by the India-based Center for Science and Environment (CSE) suggested that the amount of pesticide residues in 12 soft drinks (including Pepsi products) ranged from 11 to 70 times the European-established limit. Because CSE is a private research and advocacy group, its announcement caused quite an uproar among consumers. Almost immediately, consumer rage was felt by Pepsi and other soft drink manufacturers in the form of a sales decline in the range of 30–40 percent for their products. Pepsi officials responded by saying that the water used in their soft drinks met local norms as well as those established in Europe and the United States. Also affecting the controversy were the results of tests conducted by a government agency. Seeking to verify CSE's assertions, the agency's results actually showed "pesticide residues in [the companies'] soft drinks to be far lower" than CSE contended. Pepsi officials also took action to contextualize the allegations, saying that drinking a single cup of tea made with the water available to many Indian citizens yields as much pesticide as 394 cups of soda.

Spring forward to 2007. PepsiCo (along with Coca-Cola again) is also being charged with consuming an excessive amount of Indian groundwater (water that is purified in the process of making soft drinks). Part of the issue here is the "meaning water holds for Indians." In response, Nooyi says that she is aware of the delicacy of issues related to water in her native land, but she also "points out that soft drinks and bottled water account for less than .04 percent of industrial water usage in India."

Wanting to be a good corporate citizen and desiring for its brand name to be respected and valued, Pepsi is taking various actions in India including digging wells in villages for local residents, harvesting rainwater, and teaching better techniques for growing rice and tomatoes. Nooyi and others throughout PepsiCo are committed to recapturing the value of its brand name in India and helping the citizenry while doing so. In Nooyi's words: "We have to invest in educating communities in how to farm better, collect water, and then work with industry to retrofit plants and recycle."

Sources: D. Brady, 2007, Pepsi: Repairing a poisoned reputation in India, *BusinessWeek*, June 11, 46–54; B. Bremner & N. Lakshman, 2006, India: Behind the scare over pesticides in Pepsi and Coke, *BusinessWeek Online*, September 4, http://www.businessweek.com; F. Hills, 2006, Coca-Cola: Lab tests prove Cokes sold in India are safe, *Financial Wire*, August 14, http://www.financialwire.com; J. Johnson, 2006, Giving the goliaths a good kicking, *Financial Times*, August 12, http://www.financialtimes.com.

Capabilities

Capabilities exist when resources have been purposely integrated to achieve a specific task or set of tasks. These tasks range from human resource selection to product marketing and research and development activities.[79] Critical to the building of competitive advantages, capabilities are often based on developing, carrying, and exchanging information and knowledge through the firm's human capital.[80] Client-specific capabilities often develop from repeated interactions with clients and the learning about their needs that occurs.[81] As a result, capabilities often evolve and develop over time.[82] The foundation of many capabilities lies in the unique skills and knowledge of a firm's employees[83] and, often, their functional expertise. Hence, the value of human capital in developing and using capabilities and, ultimately, core competencies cannot be overstated.[84]

While global business leaders increasingly support the view that the knowledge possessed by human capital is among the most significant of an organization's capabilities and may ultimately be at the root of all competitive advantages,[85] firms must also be able to utilize the knowledge they have and transfer it among their business units.[86] Given this reality, the firm's challenge is to create an environment that allows people to integrate their individual knowledge with that held by others in the firm so that, collectively, the firm has significant organizational knowledge.[87]

As illustrated in Table 3.3, capabilities are often developed in specific functional areas (such as manufacturing, R&D, and marketing) or in a part of a functional area (e.g., advertising). Table 3.3 shows a grouping of organizational functions and the capabilities that some companies are thought to possess in terms of all or parts of those functions.

Table 3.3 Examples of Firms' Capabilities

Functional Areas	Capabilities	Examples of Firms
Distribution	Effective use of logistics management techniques	Wal-Mart
Human resources	Motivating, empowering, and retaining employees	Microsoft
Management information systems	Effective and efficient control of inventories through point-of-purchase data collection methods	Wal-Mart
Marketing	Effective promotion of brand-name products	Procter & Gamble Polo Ralph Lauren Corp. McKinsey & Co.
	Effective customer service	Nordstrom Inc. Norrell Corporation
	Innovative merchandising	Crate & Barrel
Management	Ability to envision the future of clothing	Hugo Boss
	Effective organizational structure	PepsiCo
Manufacturing	Design and production skills yielding reliable products	Komatsu
	Product and design quality	Witt Gas Technology
	Miniaturization of components and products	Sony
Research & development	Innovative technology	Caterpillar
	Development of sophisticated elevator control solutions	Otis Elevator Co.
	Rapid transformation of technology into new products and processes	Chaparral Steel
	Digital technology	Thomson Consumer Electronics

Core Competencies

Defined in Chapter 1, *core competencies* are capabilities that serve as a source of competitive advantage for a firm over its rivals. Core competencies distinguish a company competitively and reflect its personality. Core competencies emerge over time through an organizational process of accumulating and learning how to deploy different resources and capabilities.[88] As the capacity to take action, core competencies are "crown jewels of a company," the activities the company performs especially well compared with competitors and through which the firm adds unique value to its goods or services over a long period of time.[89]

Innovation is thought to be a core competence at Xerox today. In ways, it is not surprising because this firm was built on a world-changing innovation—xerography. And even though Xerox was the first firm to integrate the mouse with the graphical user interface of a PC, it was Apple Computer that initially recognized the incredible value of this innovation and derived value from it. In 2000, then CEO Paul Allaire admitted that Xerox's business model no longer worked and that the firm had lost its innovative ability. Some seven-plus years later, things have changed for the better at Xerox. Using the capabilities of its scientists, engineers, and researchers, Xerox has reconstituted innovation as a core competence. In the main, these innovations are oriented to helping customers deal with their document-intensive processes. For example, the firm now produces new technologies that read, understand, route, and protect documents. Reconstituting innovation as a core competence has yielded financial payoffs as is shown by the three-fold increase in Xerox's profit margins since 2003.[90]

How many core competencies are required for the firm to have a sustained competitive advantage? Responses to this question vary. McKinsey & Co. recommends that its clients identify no more than three or four competencies around which their strategic actions can be framed. Supporting and nurturing more than four core competencies may prevent a firm from developing the focus it needs to fully exploit its competencies in the marketplace. At Xerox, services expertise, employee talent, and technological skills are thought to be core competencies along with innovation.[91]

Building Core Competencies

Two tools help firms identify and build their core competencies. The first consists of four specific criteria of sustainable competitive advantage that firms can use to determine those capabilities that are core competencies. Because the capabilities shown in Table 3.3 have satisfied these four criteria, they are core competencies. The second tool is the value chain analysis. Firms use this tool to select the value-creating competencies that should be maintained, upgraded, or developed and those that should be outsourced.

Four Criteria of Sustainable Competitive Advantage

As shown in Table 3.4, capabilities that are valuable, rare, costly to imitate, and nonsubstitutable are core competencies. In turn, core competencies are sources of competitive advantage for the firm over its rivals. Capabilities failing to satisfy the four criteria of sustainable competitive advantage are not core competencies, meaning that although every core competence is a capability, not every capability is a core competence. In slightly different words, for a capability to be a core competence, it must be valuable and unique from a customer's point of view. For a competitive advantage to be sustainable, the core competence must be inimitable and nonsubstitutable from a competitor's point of view.

A sustained competitive advantage is achieved only when competitors cannot duplicate the benefits of a firm's strategy or when they lack the resources to attempt imitation. For some period of time, the firm may earn a competitive advantage by using capabilities that are, for example, valuable and rare, but imitable. Take, for example, Artemis Pet

Table 3.4 The Four Criteria of Sustainable Competitive Advantage

Valuable Capabilities	• Help a firm neutralize threats or exploit opportunities
Rare Capabilities	• Are not possessed by many others
Costly-to-Imitate Capabilities	• Historical: A unique and a valuable organizational culture or brand name • Ambiguous cause: The causes and uses of a competence are unclear • Social complexity: Interpersonal relationships, trust, and friendship among managers, suppliers, and customers
Nonsubstitutable Capabilities	• No strategic equivalent

Food Co., the firm mentioned earlier in this chapter. Recall that Artemis uses natural ingredients in its foods for pets. However, competitors such as Natural Balance can and do use the same or similar ingredients,[92] suggesting that Artemis's competitive advantage is likely imitable. The length of time a firm can expect to retain its competitive advantage is a function of how quickly competitors can successfully imitate a good, service, or process. Sustainable competitive advantage results only when all four criteria are satisfied.

Valuable

Valuable capabilities allow the firm to exploit opportunities or neutralize threats in its external environment.

Valuable capabilities allow the firm to exploit opportunities or neutralize threats in its external environment. By effectively using capabilities to exploit opportunities, a firm creates value for customers. Under former CEO Jack Welch's leadership, GE built a valuable competence in financial services. It built this powerful competence largely through acquisitions and its core competence in integrating newly acquired businesses. In addition, making such competencies as financial services highly successful required placing the right people in the right jobs. As Welch emphasized, human capital is important in creating value for customers.[93]

Rare

Rare capabilities are capabilities that few, if any, competitors possess.

Rare capabilities are capabilities that few, if any, competitors possess. A key question to be answered when evaluating this criterion is, "How many rival firms possess these valuable capabilities?" Capabilities possessed by many rivals are unlikely to be sources of competitive advantage for any one of them. Instead, valuable but common (i.e., not rare) resources and capabilities are sources of competitive parity.[94] Competitive advantage results only when firms develop and exploit valuable capabilities that differ from those shared with competitors.

Costly to Imitate

Costly-to-imitate capabilities are capabilities that other firms cannot easily develop.

Costly-to-imitate capabilities are capabilities that other firms cannot easily develop. Capabilities that are costly to imitate are created because of one reason or a combination of three reasons (see Table 3.4). First, a firm sometimes is able to develop capabilities because of *unique historical conditions.* "As firms evolve, they pick up skills, abilities and resources that are unique to them, reflecting their particular path through history."[95]

A firm with a unique and valuable *organizational culture* that emerged in the early stages of the company's history "may have an imperfectly imitable advantage over firms founded in another historical period"[96]—one in which less valuable or less competitively useful values and beliefs strongly influenced the development of the firm's culture. Briefly discussed in Chapter 1, *organizational culture* is a set of values that are shared by members in the organization, as we explain in Chapter 12. An organizational culture is a source of advantage when employees are held together tightly by their belief in it.[97]

UPS has been the prototype in many areas of the parcel delivery business because of its excellence in products, systems, marketing, and other operational business capabilities. "Its fundamental competitive strength, however, derives from the organization's unique culture, which has spanned almost a century, growing deeper all along. This culture provides solid, consistent roots for everything the company does, from skills training to technological innovation."[98] Culture may also be a competitive advantage at Mustang Engineering (an engineering and project management firm based in Houston, Texas). Established as a place where people are expected to take care of people, Mustang offers "a company culture that we believe is unique in the industry. Mustang is a work place with a family feel. A client once described Mustang as a world-class company with a mom-and-pop culture."[99]

Mustang Engineering's culture makes it a business that is costly to imitate.

A second condition of being costly to imitate occurs when the link between the firm's capabilities and its competitive advantage is *causally ambiguous.*[100] In these instances, competitors can't clearly understand how a firm uses its capabilities as the foundation for competitive advantage. As a result, firms are uncertain about the capabilities they should develop to duplicate the benefits of a competitor's value-creating strategy. For years, firms tried to imitate Southwest Airlines' low-cost strategy but most have been unable to do so, primarily because they can't duplicate Southwest's unique culture. Of all Southwest imitators, Ryanair, an Irish airline headquartered in Dublin, is the most successful. However, "Ryanair is also one of Europe's most controversial companies, praised by some, criticized by others."[101] As such, the firm's long-term future does not appear to be as certain as Southwest's.

Social complexity is the third reason that capabilities can be costly to imitate. Social complexity means that at least some, and frequently many, of the firm's capabilities are the product of complex social phenomena. Interpersonal relationships, trust, friendships among managers and between managers and employees, and a firm's reputation with suppliers and customers are examples of socially complex capabilities. Southwest Airlines is careful to hire people that fit with its culture. This complex interrelationship between the culture and human capital adds value in ways that other airlines cannot such as jokes by the flight attendants or the cooperation between gate personnel and pilots.

Nonsubstitutable

Nonsubstitutable capabilities are capabilities that do not have strategic equivalents. This final criterion for a capability to be a source of competitive advantage "is that there must be no strategically equivalent valuable resources that are themselves either not rare or imitable. Two valuable firm resources (or two bundles of firm resources) are strategically equivalent when they each can be separately exploited to implement the same strategies."[102] In general, the strategic value of capabilities increases as they become more difficult to substitute. The more invisible capabilities are, the more difficult it is for firms to find substitutes and the greater the challenge is to competitors trying to imitate a firm's value-creating strategy. Firm-specific knowledge and trust-based working relationships between managers and nonmanagerial personnel, such as existed for years at Southwest Airlines, are examples of capabilities that are difficult to identify and for which finding a substitute is challenging. However, causal ambiguity may make it difficult for the firm to learn as well and may stifle progress, because the firm may not know how to improve processes that are not easily codified and thus are ambiguous.[103]

Nonsubstitutable capabilities are capabilities that do not have strategic equivalents.

Table 3.5 Outcomes from Combinations of the Criteria for Sustainable Competitive Advantage

Is the Resource or Capability Valuable?	Is the Resource or Capability Rare?	Is the Resource or Capability Costly to Imitate?	Is the Resource or Capability Nonsubstitutable?	Competitive Consequences	Performance Implications
No	No	No	No	Competitive disadvantage	Below-average returns
Yes	No	No	Yes/no	Competitive parity	Average returns
Yes	Yes	No	Yes/no	Temporary competitive advantage	Average returns to above-average returns
Yes	Yes	Yes	Yes	Sustainable competitive advantage	Above-average returns

In summary, only using valuable, rare, costly-to-imitate, and nonsubstitutable capabilities creates sustainable competitive advantage. Table 3.5 shows the competitive consequences and performance implications resulting from combinations of the four criteria of sustainability. The analysis suggested by the table helps managers determine the strategic value of a firm's capabilities. The firm should not emphasize capabilities that fit the criteria described in the first row in the table (i.e., resources and capabilities that are neither valuable nor rare and that are imitable and for which strategic substitutes exist). Capabilities yielding competitive parity and either temporary or sustainable competitive advantage, however, will be supported. Some competitors such as Coca-Cola and PepsiCo may have capabilities that result in competitive parity. In such cases, the firms will nurture these capabilities while simultaneously trying to develop capabilities that can yield either a temporary or sustainable competitive advantage.

Value Chain Analysis

Value chain analysis allows the firm to understand the parts of its operations that create value and those that do not.[104] Understanding these issues is important because the firm earns above-average returns only when the value it creates is greater than the costs incurred to create that value.[105]

The value chain is a template that firms use to understand their cost position and to identify the multiple means that might be used to facilitate implementation of a chosen business-level strategy.[106] Today's competitive landscape demands that firms examine their value chains in a global, rather than a domestic-only context.[107] In particular, activities associated with supply chains should be studied within a global context.[108]

Primary activities are involved with a product's physical creation, its sale and distribution to buyers, and its service after the sale.

Support activities provide the assistance necessary for the primary activities to take place.

As shown in Figure 3.3, a firm's value chain is segmented into primary and support activities. **Primary activities** are involved with a product's physical creation, its sale and distribution to buyers, and its service after the sale. **Support activities** provide the assistance necessary for the primary activities to take place.

The value chain shows how a product moves from the raw-material stage to the final customer. For individual firms, the essential idea of the value chain is to create additional value without incurring significant costs while doing so and to capture the value that has been created. In a globally competitive economy, the most valuable links on the chain are people who have knowledge about customers. This locus of value-creating possibilities applies just as strongly to retail and service firms as to manufacturers. Moreover, for organizations in all sectors, the effects of e-commerce make it increasingly necessary for companies to develop value-adding knowledge processes to compensate for the value and margin that the Internet strips from physical processes.[109]

Figure 3.3 The Basic Value Chain

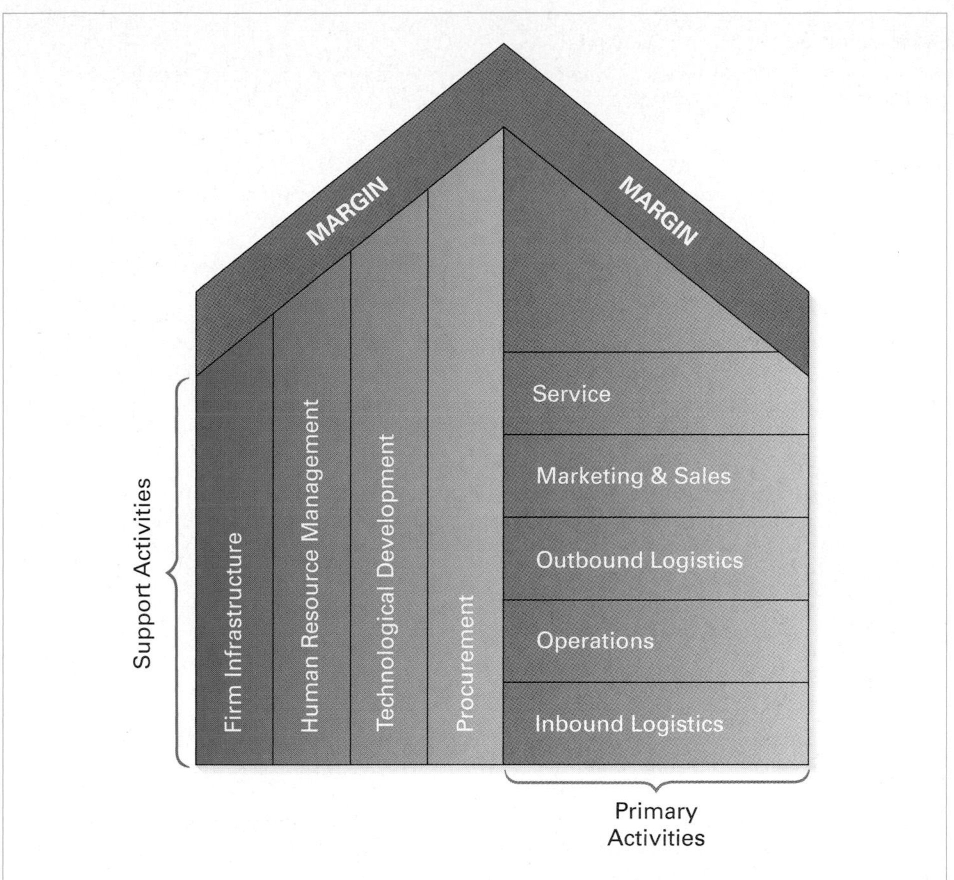

Table 3.6 lists the items that can be evaluated to determine the value-creating potential of primary activities. In Table 3.7, the items for evaluating support activities are shown. All items in both tables should be evaluated relative to competitors' capabilities. To be a source of competitive advantage, a resource or capability must allow the firm (1) to perform an activity in a manner that provides value superior to that provided by competitors, or (2) to perform a value-creating activity that competitors cannot perform. Only under these conditions does a firm create value for customers and have opportunities to capture that value.

Sometimes start-up firms create value by uniquely reconfiguring or recombining parts of the value chain. FedEx changed the nature of the delivery business by reconfiguring outbound logistics (a primary activity) and human resource management (a support activity) to provide overnight deliveries, creating value in the process. As shown in Figure 3.4, on page 87, the Internet has changed many aspects of the value chain for a broad range of firms. A key reason is because the Internet affects how people communicate, locate information, and buy goods and services.

Rating a firm's capability to execute its primary and support activities is challenging. Earlier in the chapter, we noted that identifying and assessing the value of a firm's resources and capabilities requires judgment. Judgment is equally necessary when using value chain analysis, because no obviously correct model or rule is universally available to help in the process.

What should a firm do about primary and support activities in which its resources and capabilities are not a source of core competence and, hence, of competitive advantage? Outsourcing is one solution to consider.

Table 3.6 Examining the Value-Creating Potential of Primary Activities

Inbound Logistics

Activities, such as materials handling, warehousing, and inventory control, used to receive, store, and disseminate inputs to a product.

Operations

Activities necessary to convert the inputs provided by inbound logistics into final product form. Machining, packaging, assembly, and equipment maintenance are examples of operations activities.

Outbound Logistics

Activities involved with collecting, storing, and physically distributing the final product to customers. Examples of these activities include finished-goods warehousing, materials handling, and order processing.

Marketing and Sales

Activities completed to provide means through which customers can purchase products and to induce them to do so. To effectively market and sell products, firms develop advertising and promotional campaigns, select appropriate distribution channels, and select, develop, and support their sales force.

Service

Activities designed to enhance or maintain a product's value. Firms engage in a range of service-related activities, including installation, repair, training, and adjustment.

Each activity should be examined relative to competitors' abilities. Accordingly, firms rate each activity as *superior, equivalent,* or *inferior.*

Source: Adapted with the permission of The Free Press, an imprint of Simon & Schuster Adult Publishing Group, from *Competitive Advantage: Creating and Sustaining Superior Performance,* by Michael E. Porter, pp. 39–40, Copyright © 1985, 1998 by Michael E. Porter.

Table 3.7 Examining the Value-Creating Potential of Support Activities

Procurement

Activities completed to purchase the inputs needed to produce a firm's products. Purchased inputs include items fully consumed during the manufacture of products (e.g., raw materials and supplies, as well as fixed assets—machinery, laboratory equipment, office equipment, and buildings).

Technological Development

Activities completed to improve a firm's product and the processes used to manufacture it. Technological development takes many forms, such as process equipment, basic research and product design, and servicing procedures.

Human Resource Management

Activities involved with recruiting, hiring, training, developing, and compensating all personnel.

Firm Infrastructure

Firm infrastructure includes activities such as general management, planning, finance, accounting, legal support, and governmental relations that are required to support the work of the entire value chain. Through its infrastructure, the firm strives to effectively and consistently identify external opportunities and threats, identify resources and capabilities, and support core competencies.

Each activity should be examined relative to competitors' abilities. Accordingly, firms rate each activity as *superior, equivalent,* or *inferior.*

Source: Adapted with the permission of The Free Press, an imprint of Simon & Schuster Adult Publishing Group, from *Competitive Advantage: Creating and Sustaining Superior Performance,* by Michael E. Porter, pp. 40–43, Copyright © 1985, 1998 by Michael E. Porter.

Figure 3.4 Prominent Applications of the Internet in the Value Chain

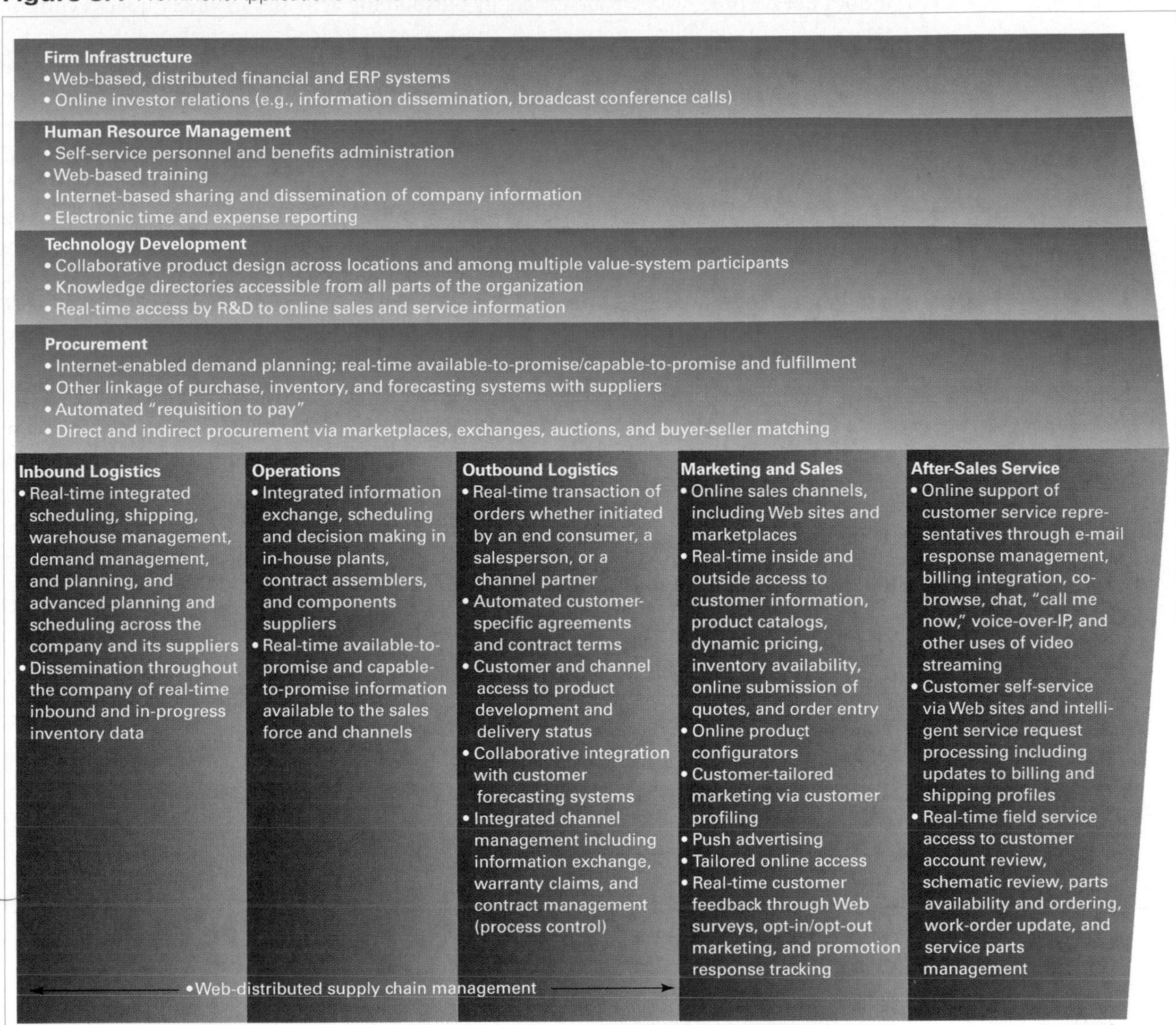

Firm Infrastructure
• Web-based, distributed financial and ERP systems
• Online investor relations (e.g., information dissemination, broadcast conference calls)
Human Resource Management
• Self-service personnel and benefits administration
• Web-based training
• Internet-based sharing and dissemination of company information
• Electronic time and expense reporting
Technology Development
• Collaborative product design across locations and among multiple value-system participants
• Knowledge directories accessible from all parts of the organization
• Real-time access by R&D to online sales and service information
Procurement
• Internet-enabled demand planning; real-time available-to-promise/capable-to-promise and fulfillment
• Other linkage of purchase, inventory, and forecasting systems with suppliers
• Automated "requisition to pay"
• Direct and indirect procurement via marketplaces, exchanges, auctions, and buyer-seller matching
Inbound Logistics
• Real-time integrated scheduling, shipping, warehouse management, demand management, and planning, and advanced planning and scheduling across the company and its suppliers
• Dissemination throughout the company of real-time inbound and in-progress inventory data
Operations
• Integrated information exchange, scheduling and decision making in in-house plants, contract assemblers, and components suppliers
• Real-time available-to-promise and capable-to-promise information available to the sales force and channels
Outbound Logistics
• Real-time transaction of orders whether initiated by an end consumer, a salesperson, or a channel partner
• Automated customer-specific agreements and contract terms
• Customer and channel access to product development and delivery status
• Collaborative integration with customer forecasting systems
• Integrated channel management including information exchange, warranty claims, and contract management (process control)
Marketing and Sales
• Online sales channels, including Web sites and marketplaces
• Real-time inside and outside access to customer information, product catalogs, dynamic pricing, inventory availability, online submission of quotes, and order entry
• Online product configurators
• Customer-tailored marketing via customer profiling
• Push advertising
• Tailored online access
• Real-time customer feedback through Web surveys, opt-in/opt-out marketing, and promotion response tracking
After-Sales Service
• Online support of customer service representatives through e-mail response management, billing integration, co-browse, chat, "call me now," voice-over-IP, and other uses of video streaming
• Customer self-service via Web sites and intelligent service request processing including updates to billing and shipping profiles
• Real-time field service access to customer account review, schematic review, parts availability and ordering, work-order update, and service parts management
• Web-distributed supply chain management

Source: Reprinted by permission of *Harvard Business Review* from "Strategy and the Internet" by Michael E. Porter, March 2001, p. 75.

Outsourcing

Outsourcing is the purchase of a value-creating activity from an external supplier.

Concerned with how components, finished goods, or services will be obtained, **outsourcing** is the purchase of a value-creating activity from an external supplier.[110] Not-for-profit agencies as well as for-profit organizations actively engage in outsourcing.[111] Firms engaging in effective outsourcing increase their flexibility, mitigate risks, and reduce their capital investments.[112] In multiple global industries, the trend toward outsourcing continues at a rapid pace.[113] Moreover, in some industries virtually all firms seek the value that can be captured through effective outsourcing. The auto manufacturing industry and, more recently, the electronics industry are two such examples. As with other strategic management process decisions, careful analysis is required before the firm decides to engage in outsourcing.[114]

Outsourcing can be effective because few, if any, organizations possess the resources and capabilities required to achieve competitive superiority in all primary and support activities. For example, research suggests that few companies can afford to develop internally all the technologies that might lead to competitive advantage.[115] By nurturing a smaller number of capabilities, a firm increases the probability of developing a competitive advantage because it does not become overextended. Too, by outsourcing activities in which it lacks competence, the firm can fully concentrate on those areas in which it can create value.

Firms must outsource only activities where they cannot create value or where they are at a substantial disadvantage compared to competitors.[116] To verify that the appropriate primary and support activities are outsourced, managers should have four skills: strategic thinking, deal making, partnership governance, and change management.[117] Managers need to understand whether and how outsourcing creates competitive advantage within their company—they need to be able to think strategically.[118] To complete effective outsourcing transactions, these managers must also be deal makers, able to secure rights from external providers that can be fully used by internal managers. They must be able to oversee and govern appropriately the relationship with the company to which the services were outsourced. Because outsourcing can significantly change how an organization operates, managers administering these programs must also be able to manage that change, including resolving employee resistance that accompanies any significant change effort.[119]

The consequences of outsourcing cause additional concerns.[120] For the most part, these concerns revolve around the potential loss in firms' innovative ability and the loss of jobs within companies that decide to outsource some of their work activities to others. Thus, innovation and technological uncertainty are two important issues to consider in making outsourcing decisions.[121] Companies must be aware of these issues and be prepared to fully consider the concerns about outsourcing when different stakeholders (e.g., employees) express them.

As is true with all strategic management tools and techniques, criteria should be established to guide outsourcing decisions. Outsourcing is big business (U.S. firms spent more than $68 billion on outsourcing in 2006 alone), but not every outsourcing decision is successful. For example, amid delays and cost overruns, Electronic Data Systems abandoned a $1 billion opportunity to run Dow Chemical Co.'s phone-and-computer networks. Stemming from customer complaints, Dell and Lehman Brothers Holdings decided not to move some of the customer call center operations to locations outside the United States.[122] These less-than-desirable outcomes indicate that firms should carefully study outsourcing possibilities to verify that engaging in them will indeed create value that exceeds the cost incurred to generate that value.

Competencies, Strengths, Weaknesses, and Strategic Decisions

At the conclusion of the internal analysis, firms must identify their strengths and weaknesses in resources, capabilities, and core competencies. For example, if they have weak capabilities or do not have core competencies in areas required to achieve a competitive advantage, they must acquire those resources and build the capabilities and competencies needed. Alternatively, they could decide to outsource a function or activity where they are weak in order to improve the value that they provide to customers.[123]

Therefore, firms need to have the appropriate resources and capabilities to develop the desired strategy and create value for customers and other stakeholders such as shareholders.[124] Managers should understand that having a significant quantity of resources is not the same as having the "right" resources. Moreover, decision makers sometimes become more focused and productive when their organization's resources are constrained.[125] In the final analysis, those with decision-making responsibilities must help the firm obtain and use resources, capabilities, and core competencies in ways that will generate value-creating competitive advantages. Top-level managers are responsible for verifying that these tasks happen.[126]

Tools such as outsourcing help the firm focus on its core competencies as the source of its competitive advantages. However, evidence shows that the value-creating ability of core competencies should never be taken for granted. Moreover, the ability of a core competence to be a permanent competitive advantage can't be assumed. The reason for these cautions is that all core competencies have the potential to become *core rigidities.* Leslie Wexner, CEO of Limited Brands, describes this possibility: "Success doesn't beget success. Success begets failure because the more that you know a thing works, the less likely you are to think that it won't work. When you've had a long string of victories, it's harder to foresee your own vulnerabilities."[127] Thus, a core competence is usually a strength because it is the source of competitive advantage. If emphasized when it is no longer competitively relevant, it can become a weakness, a seed of organizational inertia.

Inertia around organizational culture may be a problem at Ford Motor Company where some argue that in essence, the firm's culture has become a core rigidity that is constraining efforts to improve performance. In one writer's words: "One way or another, the company will have to figure out how to produce more vehicles that consumers actually want. And doing that will require addressing the most fundamental problem of all: Ford's dysfunctional, often defeatist culture."[128] In contrast, Toyota, which earned record profits of

What is the "Toyota Code of Conduct"?

Our daily business operations are built on and supported by the corporate philosophy and its values and methods that have developed through years of diligent effort and passed down from generation to generation throughout TOYOTA MOTOR CORPORATION and its subsidiaries ("**TOYOTA**").

The "Guiding Principles at Toyota" (originally issued in 1992, revised in 1997) summarize the corporate philosophy and reflects TOYOTA's vision of what kind of company TOYOTA would like to be. The "Guiding Principles at Toyota" were created with the expectation that we would understand and share our fundamental management principles, and that we would contribute to society by referring to these principles.

The "Toyota Way" and the "Toyota Code of Conduct" serve as important guiding tools when implementing our daily business operations to realize the "Guiding Principles at Toyota". "Toyota Way" (issued in 2001) describes the values and methods to be shared for the people of the global TOYOTA organization.

The present "Toyota Code of Conduct" (originally issued in 1998, revised in 2006) seeks to provide a basic code of conduct and to serve as a model and compass. It also provides detailed explanations and examples of the actions and issues that we must be aware of when carrying out actual business activities (including in our jobs and daily business operations) and living in our global society.

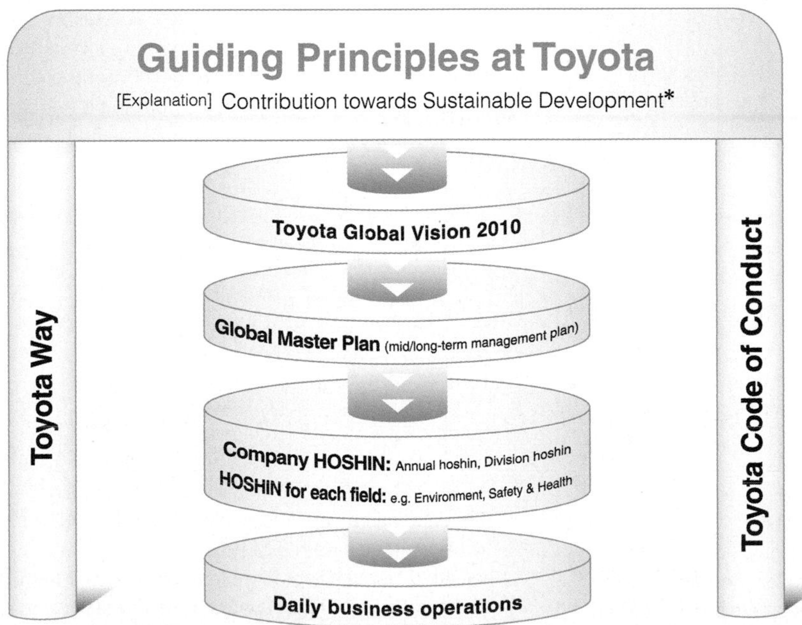

*Interprets the "Guiding Principles at Toyota" from the standpoint of how TOYOTA can work towards sustainable development in its interactions with its stakeholders (Issued in January 2005).

Toyota's Code of Conduct clearly outlines, for its employees, the firm's competencies and methods for continuous improvement. This code has been revised twice and is based on Toyota's Guiding Principles.

$15 billion in 2006, is carefully reexamining product planning, customer service, sales and marketing, and employee training practices to prevent "being spoiled by success."[129]

Events occurring in the firm's external environment create conditions through which core competencies can become core rigidities, generate inertia, and stifle innovation. "Often the flip side, the dark side, of core capabilities is revealed due to external events when new competitors figure out a better way to serve the firm's customers, when new technologies emerge, or when political or social events shift the ground underneath."[130] However, in the final analysis, changes in the external environment do not cause core competencies to become core rigidities; rather, strategic myopia and inflexibility on the part of managers are the cause.

After studying its external environment to determine what it *might choose to do* (as explained in Chapter 2) and its internal organization to understand what it *can do* (as explained in this chapter), the firm has the information required to select a business-level strategy that will help it reach its vision and mission. We describe different business-level strategies in the next chapter.

Summary

- In the global business environment, traditional factors (e.g., labor costs and superior access to financial resources and raw materials) can still create a competitive advantage. However, these factors are less and less often a source of competitive advantage. In the new landscape, the resources, capabilities, and core competencies in the firm's internal organization may have a relatively stronger influence on its performance than do conditions in the external environment. The most effective organizations recognize that strategic competitiveness and above-average returns result only when core competencies (identified by studying the firm's internal organization) are matched with opportunities (determined by studying the firm's external environment).
- No competitive advantage lasts forever. Over time, rivals use their own unique resources, capabilities, and core competencies to form different value-creating propositions that duplicate the value-creating ability of the firm's competitive advantages. In general, the Internet's capabilities are reducing the sustainability of many competitive advantages. Because competitive advantages are not permanently sustainable, firms must exploit their current advantages while simultaneously using their resources and capabilities to form new advantages that can lead to future competitive success.
- Effectively managing core competencies requires careful analysis of the firm's resources (inputs to the production process) and capabilities (resources that have been purposely integrated to achieve a specific task or set of tasks). The knowledge possessed by human capital is among the most significant of an organization's capabilities and may ultimately be at the root of all competitive advantages. The firm must create an environment that allows people to integrate their individual knowledge with that held by others so that, collectively, the firm has significant organizational knowledge.
- Individual resources are usually not a source of competitive advantage. Capabilities are a more likely source of competitive advantages, especially relatively sustainable ones. The firm's nurturing and support of core competencies that are based on capabilities is less visible to rivals and, as such, harder to understand and imitate.
- Only when a capability is valuable, rare, costly to imitate, and nonsubstitutable is it a core competence and a source of competitive advantage. Over time, core competencies must be supported, but they cannot be allowed to become core rigidities. Core competencies are a source of competitive advantage only when they allow the firm to create value by exploiting opportunities in its external environment. When it can no longer do so, the company shifts its attention to selecting or forming other capabilities that do satisfy the four criteria of sustainable competitive advantage.
- Value chain analysis is used to identify and evaluate the competitive potential of resources and capabilities. By studying their skills relative to those associated with primary and support activities, firms can understand their cost structure and identify the activities through which they can create value.
- When the firm cannot create value in either a primary or support activity, outsourcing is considered. Used commonly in the global economy, outsourcing is the purchase of a value-creating activity from an external supplier. The firm must outsource only to companies possessing a competitive advantage in terms of the particular primary or support activity under consideration. In addition, the firm must continuously verify that it is not outsourcing activities from which it could create value.

Review Questions

1. Why is it important for a firm to study and understand its internal organization?
2. What is value? Why is it critical for the firm to create value? How does it do so?
3. What are the differences between tangible and intangible resources? Why is it important for decision makers to understand these differences? Are tangible resources linked more closely to the creation of competitive advantages than are intangible resources, or is the reverse true? Why?
4. What are capabilities? What must firms do to create capabilities?
5. What are the four criteria used to determine which of a firm's capabilities are core competencies? Why is it important for these criteria to be used?
6. What is value chain analysis? What does the firm gain when it successfully uses this tool?
7. What is outsourcing? Why do firms outsource? Will outsourcing's importance grow in the twenty-first century? If so, why?
8. How do firms identify internal strengths and weaknesses? Why is it vital that managers have a clear understanding of their firm's strengths and weaknesses?

Experiential Exercises

Exercise 1: Dot.Com Boom and Bust

The focus of this chapter is on understanding how firm resources and capabilities serve as the cornerstone for competencies, and, ultimately, a competitive advantage. Strategists have long understood the importance of internal analysis: For example, Porter's value chain model was introduced in 1985, more than 20 years ago. How, then, can a large number of prominent firms create strategies while apparently disregarding the importance of internal analysis?

The late 1990s saw the launch of thousands of Internet start-ups, often supported by venture capital. These new businesses were heralded as part of the "new economy" and were characterized as having a superior business model compared to the models being used by traditional bricks-and-mortar firms. The collapse of the dot.com bubble had global economic ramifications. Some of the more prominent e-business failures included:

Webvan.com	Pets.com
Kosmo.com	Zap.com
Cyberrebate.com	Flooz.com
Go.com	Digiscents.com
Boo.com	eToys.com
Kibu.com	Yadayada.com

As a group, select a failed dot.com business. You may choose one of the companies from the preceding list, or another dot.com that you identify on your own. Using library and Internet resources, prepare a brief PowerPoint presentation that covers these questions:

- How did the company describe its value proposition (i.e., how did the firm plan to create value for its customers)?
- Describe the resources, capabilities, and competencies that supported this value proposition.
- Why do you think the firm failed? Was it a poor concept, or a sound concept that was not well executed? Apply the concepts of value, rarity, imitation, and sustainability when preparing your answer.
- Are any other firms presently using a similar approach to create value for their customers? If so, what makes them different from the failed company that you studied?

Exercise 2: Competitive Advantage and Pro Sports

What makes one team successful while another team struggles? At first glance, a National Football League franchise or women's National Basketball Association team may not seem like a typical business. However, professional sports have been around for a long time: Pro hockey in the United Stated emerged around World War I, and pro basketball shortly after World War II; both could be considered newcomers relative to the founding of baseball leagues. Pro sports are big business as well, as evidenced by David Beckham's 2007 multimillion-dollar contract with Major League Soccer.

With this exercise, we will use tools and concepts from the chapter to analyze factors underlying the success or failure of different sports teams. Working as a group, pick two teams that play in the same league. For each team, address the following questions:

- How successful are the two teams you selected? How stable has their performance been over time?
- Make an inventory of the characteristics of the two teams. Characteristics you might choose to identify include reputation, coaching, fan base, playing style and tactics, individual players, and so on. For each characteristic you describe:
    - Decide whether it is best characterized as a tangible, intangible, or capability.
    - Apply the concepts of value, rarity, imitation, and sustainability to analyze its value-creating ability.
- Does any evidence show bundling in this situation (i.e., the combination of different resources and capabilities)?
- What would it take for these two teams to substantially change their competitive position over time? For example, if a team is a leader, what types of changes in resources and capabilities might affect it negatively? If a team is below average, what changes would you recommend to its portfolio of resources and capabilities?

Notes

1. M. E. Mangelsdorf, 2007, Beyond enterprise 2.0, *MIT Sloan Management Review,* 48(3): 50–55.
2. J. G. Covin & M. P. Miles, 2007, Strategic use of corporate venturing, *Entrepreneurship Theory and Practice,* 31, 183–207; R. R. Wiggins & T. W. Ruefli, 2002, Sustained competitive advantage: Temporal dynamics and the incidence of persistence of superior economic performance, *Organization Science,* 13: 82–105.
3. W. M. Becker & V. M. Freeman, 2006, Going from global trends to corporate strategy, *McKinsey Quarterly,* Number 3: 17–27; S. K. McEvily, K. M. Eisenhardt, & J. E. Prescott, 2004, The global acquisition, leverage, and protection of technological competencies, *Strategic Management Journal,* 25: 713–722.
4. J. Quittner, 2007, Selling pet owners peace of mind, *Business Week,* May 8, 48.
5. N. T. Sheehan & N. J. Foss, 2007, Enhancing the prescriptiveness of the resource-based view through Porterian activity analysis, *Management Decision,* 45: 450–461; S. Dutta, M. J. Zbaracki, & M. Bergen, 2003, Pricing process as a capability: A resource-based perspective, *Strategic Management Journal,* 24: 615–630; A. M. Knott, 2003, Persistent heterogeneity and sustainable innovation, *Strategic Management Journal,* 24: 687–705.
6. C. G. Brush, P. G. Greene, & M. M. Hart, 2001, From initial idea to unique advantage: The entrepreneurial challenge of constructing a resource base, *Academy of Management Executive,* 15(1): 64–78.
7. R. L. Priem, 2007, A consumer perspective on value creation, *Academy of Management Review,* 32: 219–235.
8. D. G. Sirmon, M. A. Hitt, & R. D. Ireland, 2007, Managing firm resources in dynamic markets to create value: Looking inside the black box, *Academy of Management Review,* 32: 273–292.
9. S. C. Kang, S. S. Morris, & S. A. Snell, 2007, Relational archetypes, organizational learning, and value creation: Extending the human resource architecture, *Academy of Management Review,* 32: 236–256.
10. S. Raisch & G. von Krog, 2007, Navigating a path to smart growth, *MIT Sloan Management Review,* 48(3): 65–72.
11. D. DePass, 2006, Cuts in incentives upset 3M supervisors, *Star Tribune,* December 16.
12. C. D. Zatzick & R. D. Iverson, 2007, High-involvement management and workforce reduction: Competitive advantage or disadvantage? *Academy of Management Journal,* 49: 999–1015.
13. R. Florida, 2005, *The Flight of the Creative Class,* New York: HarperBusiness.
14. A. W. King, 2007, Disentangling interfirm and intrafirm causal ambiguity: A conceptual model of causal ambiguity and sustainable competitive advantage, *Academy of Management Review,* 32: 156–178; J. Shamsie, 2003, The context of dominance: An industry-driven framework for exploiting reputation, *Strategic Management Journal,* 24: 199–215.
15. U. Ljungquist, 2007, Core competency beyond identification: Presentation of a model, *Management Decision,* 45: 393–402; M. Makhija, 2003, Comparing the resource-based and market-based view of the firm: Empirical evidence from Czech privatization, *Strategic Management Journal,* 24: 433–451.
16. R. D. Ireland & J. W. Webb, 2007, Strategic entrepreneurship: Creating competitive advantage through streams of innovation, *Business Horizons,* 50: 49–59.
17. M. A. Peteraf & J. B. Barney, 2003, Unraveling the resource-based tangle, *Managerial and Decision Economics,* 24: 309–323; J. B. Barney, 2001, Is the resource-based "view" a useful perspective for strategic management research? Yes, *Academy of Management Review,* 26: 41–56.
18. D. P. Lepak, K. G. Smith, & M. Susan Taylor, 2007, Value creation and value capture: A multilevel perspective, *Academy of Management Review,* 32: 180–194.
19. G. Katz, 2007, Assembling a future, *Houston Chronicle,* July 5, D1, D4.
20. T. M. Begley & D. P. Boyd, 2003, The need for a corporate global mind-set, *MIT Sloan Management Review,* 44(2): 25–32.
21. L. Gratton, 2007, Handling hot spots, *Business Strategy Review,* 18(2): 9–14.
22. O. Levy, S. Beechler, S. Taylor, & N. A. Boyacigiller, 2007, What we talk about when we talk about "global mindset": Managerial cognition in multinational corporations, *Journal of International Business Studies,* 38: 231–258.
23. Sirmon, Hitt, & Ireland, Managing resources in a dynamic environment.
24. D. A. Chmielewski & A. Paladino, 2007, Driving a resource orientation: Reviewing the role of resource and capability characteristics, *Managerial Decision,* 45: 462–483; Barney, Is the resource-based "view" a useful perspective for strategic management research? Yes.
25. K. J. Mayer & R. M. Salomon, 2006, Capabilities, contractual hazards, and governance: Integrating resource-based and transaction cost perspectives, *Academy of Management Journal,* 49: 942–959.
26. S. K. McEvily & B. Chakravarthy, 2002, The persistence of knowledge-based advantage: An empirical test for product performance and technological knowledge, *Strategic Management Journal,* 23: 285–305.
27. D. Kaplan, 2007, A new look for Luby's, *Houston Chronicle,* July 4, D1, D5.
28. J. L. Morrow, Jr., D. G. Sirmon, M. A. Hitt, & T. R. Holcomb, 2007, Creating value in the face of declining performance: Firm strategies and organizational recovery, *Strategic Management Journal,* 28: 271–283.
29. E. Danneels, 2007, The process of technological competence leveraging, *Strategic Management Journal,* 28: 511–533; S. Nambisan, 2002, Designing virtual customer environments for new product development: Toward a theory, *Academy of Management Review,* 27: 392–413.
30. J. J. Neff, 2007, What drives consumers not to buy cars, *BusinessWeek,* July 9, 16.
31. K. Chaharbaghi, 2007, The problematic of strategy: A way of seeing is also a way of not seeing, *Management Decision,* 45: 327–339.
32. V. Shankar & B. L. Bayus, 2003, Network effects and competition: An empirical analysis of the home video game industry, *Strategic Management Journal,* 24: 375–384.
33. Morrow, Sirmon, Hitt, & Holcomb, Creating value in the face of declining performance; G. Hawawini, V. Subramanian, & P. Verdin, 2003, Is performance driven by industry- or firm-specific factors? A new look at the evidence, *Strategic Management Journal,* 24: 1–16.
34. M. R. Haas & M. T. Hansen, 2005, When using knowledge can hurt performance: The value of organizational capabilities in a management consulting company, *Strategic Management Journal,* 26: 1–24.
35. C. M. Christensen, 2001, The past and future of competitive advantage, *Sloan Management Review,* 42(2): 105–109.
36. O. Gottschalg & M. Zollo, 2007, Interest alignment and competitive advantage, *Academy of Management Review,* 32: 418–437.
37. D. P. Forbes, 2007, Reconsidering the strategic implications of decision comprehensiveness, *Academy of Management Review,* 32: 361–376; J. R. Hough & M. A. White, 2003, Environmental dynamism and strategic decision-making rationality: An examination at the decision level, *Strategic Management Journal,* 24: 481–489.
38. T. M. Jones, W. Felps, & G. A. Bigley, 2007, Ethical theory and stakeholder-related decisions: The role of stakeholder culture, *Academy of Management Review,* 32: 137–155; D. C. Kayes, D. Stirling, & T. M. Nielsen, 2007, Building organizational integrity, *Business Horizons,* 50: 61–70.
39. Y. Deutsch, T. Keil, & T. Laamanen, 2007, Decision making in acquisitions: The effect of outside directors' compensation on acquisition patterns, *Journal of Management,* 33: 30–56.
40. M. De Rond & R. A. Thietart, 2007, Choice, chance, and inevitability in strategy, *Strategic Management Journal,* 28: 535–551.
41. C. C. Miller & R. D. Ireland, 2005, Intuition in strategic decision making:

Friend or foe in the fast-paced 21st century? *Academy of Management Executive,* 19(1): 19–30; P. Westhead, M. Wright, & D. Ucbasaran, 2001, The internationalization of new and small firms: A resource-based view, *Journal of Business Venturing,* 16: 333–358.

42. L. M. Lodish & C. F. Mela, 2007, If brands are built over years, why are they managed over quarters? *Harvard Business Review,* 85(7/8): 104–112; H. J. Smith, 2003, The shareholders vs. stakeholders debate, *MIT Sloan Management Review,* 44(4): 85–90.
43. P. C. Nutt, 2002, *Why Decisions Fail,* San Francisco: Berrett-Koehler Publishers.
44. R. Martin, 2007, How successful leaders think, 85(6): *Harvard Business Review,* 61–67.
45. Polaroid Corporation, 2007, Wikipedia, http://en.wikipedia.org/wiki/Polaroid_Corporation, July 5.
46. J. M. Mezias & W. H. Starbuck, 2003, What do managers know, anyway? *Harvard Business Review,* 81(5): 16–17.
47. P. G. Audia, E. Locke, & K. G. Smith, 2000, The paradox of success: An archival and a laboratory study of strategic persistence following radical environmental change, *Academy of Management Journal,* 43: 837–853; R. G. McGrath, 1999, Falling forward: Real options reasoning and entrepreneurial failure, *Academy of Management Review,* 24: 13–30.
48. C. O. Longenecker, M. J. Neubert, & L. S. Fink, 2007, Causes and consequences of managerial failure in rapidly changing organizations, *Business Horizons,* 50: 145–155; G. P. West III & J. DeCastro, 2001, The Achilles' heel of firm strategy: Resource weaknesses and distinctive inadequacies, *Journal of Management Studies,* 38: 417–442; G. Gavetti & D. Levinthal, 2000, Looking forward and looking backward: Cognitive and experimental search, *Administrative Science Quarterly,* 45: 113–137.
49. K. K. Reardon, 2007, Courage as a skill, *Harvard Business Review,* 85(1): 58–64.
50. R. Amit & P. J. H. Schoemaker, 1993, Strategic assets and organizational rent, *Strategic Management Journal,* 14: 33–46.
51. S. J. Carson, A. Madhok, & T. Wu, 2006, Uncertainty, opportunism, and governance: The effects of volatility and ambiguity on formal and relational contracting, *Academy of Management Journal,* 49: 1058–1077; R. E. Hoskisson & L. W. Busenitz, 2001, Market uncertainty and learning distance in corporate entrepreneurship entry mode choice, in M. A. Hitt, R. D. Ireland, S. M. Camp, & D. L. Sexton (eds.), *Strategic Entrepreneurship: Creating a New Integrated Mindset,* Oxford, UK: Blackwell Publishers, 151–172.
52. C. M. Fiol & E. J. O'Connor, 2003, Waking up! Mindfulness in the face of bandwagons, *Academy of Management Review,* 28: 54–70.
53. N. Byrnes & A. Aston, 2007, Coal? Yes, coal, *Business Week,* May 7, 60–63.
54. G. P. West, III, 2007, Collective cognition: When entrepreneurial teams, not individuals, make decisions, *Entrepreneurship Theory and Practice,* 31: 77–102.
55. N. J. Hiller & D. C. Hambrick, 2005, Conceptualizing executive hubris: The role of (hyper-) core self-evaluations in strategic decision making, *Strategic Management Journal,* 26: 297–319.
56. C. Stadler, 2007, The four principles of enduring success, *Harvard Business Review,* 85(7/8): 62–72.
57. C. Pasariello, 2007, Is Hermes out of fashion? *Wall Street Journal Online,* June 7, http://online.wsj.com.
58. Forbes, Reconsidering the strategic implications.
59. Mayer & Salomon, Capabilities, contractual hazards, and governance; D. M. De Carolis, 2003, Competencies and imitability in the pharmaceutical industry: An analysis of their relationship with firm performance, *Journal of Management,* 29: 27–50.
60. G. Ahuja & R. Katila, 2004, Where do resources come from? The role of idiosyncratic situations, *Strategic Management Journal,* 25: 887–907.
61. J. McGree & H. Thomas, 2007, Knowledge as a lens on the jigsaw puzzle of strategy, *Management Decision,* 45: 539–563.
62. Sirmon, Hitt, & Ireland, Managing firm resources in dynamic environments; S. Berman, J. Down, & C. Hill, 2002, Tacit knowledge as a source of competitive advantage in the National Basketball Association, *Academy of Management Journal,* 45: 13–31.
63. 2007, Borders. Teamed with Amazon.com, July 7, http://www.amazon.com.
64. K. G. Smith, C. J. Collins, & K. D. Clark, 2005, Existing knowledge, knowledge creation capability, and the rate of new product introduction in high-technology firms, *Academy of Management Journal,* 48: 346–357; S. G. Winter, 2005, Developing evolutionary theory for economics and management, in K. G. Smith and M. A. Hitt (eds.), *Great Minds in Management: The Process of Theory Development.* Oxford, UK: Oxford University Press, 509–546.
65. J. A. Dubin, 2007, Valuing intangible assets with a nested logit market share model, *Journal of Econometrics,* 139: 285–302.
66. A. M. Webber, 2000, New math for a new economy, *Fast Company,* January/February, 214–224.
67. M. Song, C. Droge, S. Hanvanich, & R. Calantone, 2005, Marketing and technology resource complementarity: An analysis of their interaction effect in two environmental contexts, *Strategic Management Journal,* 26: 259–276; R. G. Schroeder, K. A. Bates, & M. A. Junttila, 2002, A resource-based view of manufacturing strategy and the relationship to manufacturing performance, *Strategic Management Journal,* 23: 105–117.
68. M. A. Hitt & R. D. Ireland, 2002, The essence of strategic leadership: Managing human and social capital, *Journal of Leadership and Organization Studies,* 9(1): 3–14.
69. J. B. Quinn, P. Anderson, & S. Finkelstein, 1996, Making the most of the best, *Harvard Business Review,* 74(2): 71–80.
70. N. Stieglitz & K. Heine, 2007, Innovations and the role of complementarities in a strategic theory of the firm, *Strategic Management Journal,* 28: 1–15.
71. R. D. Ireland, M. A. Hitt, & D. Vaidyanath, 2002, Managing strategic alliances to achieve a competitive advantage, *Journal of Management,* 28: 416–446.
72. E. Fischer & R. Reuber, 2007, The good, the bad, and the unfamiliar: The challenges of reputation formation facing new firms, *Entrepreneurship Theory and Practice,* 31: 53–75.
73. D. L. Deephouse, 2000, Media reputation as a strategic resource: An integration of mass communication and resource-based theories, *Journal of Management,* 26: 1091–1112.
74. P. Engardio & M. Arndt, 2007, What price reputation? *BusinessWeek,* July 9, 70–79.
75. P. Berthon, M. B. Holbrook, & J. M. Hulbert, 2003, Understanding and managing the brand space, *MIT Sloan Management Review,* 44(2): 49–54; D. B. Holt, 2003, What becomes an icon most? *Harvard Business Review,* 81(3): 43–49.
76. J. Blasberg & V. Vishwanath, 2003, Making cool brands hot, *Harvard Business Review,* 81(6): 20–22.
77. 2007, Harley-Davidson MotorClothes Merchandise, July 7, http://www.harley-davidson.com.
78. D. Roberts & S. Holmes, 2005, China's real sports contest, *BusinessWeek Online,* http://www.businessweek.com, March 14.
79. S. Dutta, O. Narasimhan, & S. Rajiv, 2005, Conceptualizing and measuring capabilities: Methodology and empirical application, *Strategic Management Journal,* 26: 277–285.
80. J. Bitar & T. Hafsi, 2007, Strategizing through the capability lens: Sources and outcomes of integration, *Management Decision,* 45: 403–419; M. A. Hitt, R. D. Ireland, & H. Lee, 2000, Technological learning, knowledge management, firm growth and performance: An introductory essay, *Journal of Engineering and Technology Management,* 17: 231–246.
81. S. K. Ethiraj, P. Kale, M. S. Krishnan, & J. V. Singh, 2005, Where do capabilities come from and do they matter? A study in the software services industry, *Strategic Management Journal,* 26: 25–45.
82. M. G. Jacobides & S. G. Winter, 2005, The co-evolution of capabilities and transaction costs: Explaining the institutional structure of production, *Strategic Management Journal,* 26: 395–413.
83. R. W. Coff & P. M. Lee, 2003, Insider trading as a vehicle to appropriate rent from R&D, *Strategic Management Journal,* 24: 183–190.
84. T. A. Stewart & A. P. Raman, 2007, Lessons from Toyota's long drive, *Harvard Business Review,* 85(7/8): 74–83.
85. Y. Liu, J. G. Combs, D. J. Ketchen, Jr., & R. D. Ireland, 2007, The value of human resource management for organizational performance, *Business Horizons,* in press;

D. L. Deeds, 2003, Alternative strategies for acquiring knowledge, in S. E. Jackson, M. A. Hitt, & A. S. DeNisi (eds.), *Managing Knowledge for Sustained Competitive Advantage,* San Francisco: Jossey-Bass, 37–63.

86. B. Connelly, M. A. Hitt, A. S. DeNisi, & R. D. Ireland, 2007, Expatriates and corporate-level international strategy: Governing with the knowledge contract, *Management Decision,* 45: 564–581.
87. M. J. Tippins & R. S. Sohi, 2003, IT competency and firm performance: Is organizational learning a missing link? *Strategic Management Journal,* 24: 745–761.
88. C. Zott, 2003, Dynamic capabilities and the emergence of intraindustry differential firm performance: Insights from a simulation study, *Strategic Management Journal,* 24: 97–125.
89. K. Hafeez, Y. B. Zhang, & N. Malak, 2002, Core competence for sustainable competitive advantage: A structured methodology for identifying core competence, *IEEE Transactions on Engineering Management,* 49(1): 28–35; C. K. Prahalad & G. Hamel, 1990, The core competence of the corporation, *Harvard Business Review,* 68(3): 79–93.
90. G. Colvin, 2007, Xerox's inventor-in-chief, *Fortune,* July 9, 65–72.
91. 2006, Xerox Annual Report, December, http://www.zerox.com.
92. Quittner, Selling pet owners peace of mind.
93. 2005, Jack Welch: It's all in the sauce, *Fortune Online,* April 4, http://www.fortune.com.
94. J. B. Barney, 1995, Looking inside for competitive advantage, *Academy of Management Executive,* 9(4): 49–60.
95. Ibid., 53.
96. J. B. Barney, 1991, Firm resources and sustained competitive advantage, *Journal of Management,* 17: 99–120.
97. L. E. Tetrick & N. Da Silva, 2003, Assessing the culture and climate for organizational learning, in S. E. Jackson, M. A. Hitt, & A. S. DeNisi (eds.), *Managing Knowledge for Sustained Competitive Advantage,* San Francisco: Jossey-Bass, 333–359.
98. L. Soupata, 2001, Managing culture for competitive advantage at United Parcel Service, *Journal of Organizational Excellence,* 20(3): 19–26.
99. K. Stinebaker, 2007, Global company puts focus on people, *Houston Chronicle Online,* February 18, http://www.chron.com.
100. A. W. King & C. P. Zeithaml, 2001, Competencies and firm performance: Examining the causal ambiguity paradox, *Strategic Management Journal,* 22: 75–99.
101. 2007, Ryanair, Wikipedia, July 7, http://en.wikipedia.org/wiki/ryanair.
102. Barney, Firm resources, 111.
103. M. J. Benner & M. L. Tushman, 2003, Exploitation, exploration, and process management: The productivity dilemma revisited, *Academy of Management Review,* 28: 238–256; S. K. McEvily, S. Das, & K. McCabe, 2000, Avoiding competence substitution through knowledge sharing, *Academy of Management Review,* 25: 294–311.
104. D. J. Ketchen, Jr., & G. T. M. Hult, 2007, Bridging organization theory and supply chain management: The case of best value supply chains, *Journal of Operations Management,* 25: 573–580.
105. M. E. Porter, 1985, *Competitive Advantage,* New York: Free Press, 33–61.
106. J. Alcacer, 2006, Location choices across the value chain: How activity and capability influence co-location, *Management Science,* 52: 1457–1471.
107. 2007, Riding the global value chain, *Chief Executive Online,* January/February, http://www.chiefexecutive.net.
108. R. Locke & M. Romis, 2007, Global supply chain, *MIT Sloan Management Review,* 48(2): 54–62.
109. R. Amit & C. Zott, 2001, Value creation in e-business, *Strategic Management Journal,* 22 (Special Issue): 493–520; M. E. Porter, 2001, Strategy and the Internet, *Harvard Business Review,* 79(3): 62–78.
110. M. J. Power, K. C. DeSouze, & C. Bonifazi, 2006, *The Outsourcing Handbook: How to Implement a Successful Outsourcing Process,* Philadelphia: Kogan Page.
111. P.-W. Tam, 2007, Business technology: Outsourcing finds new niche, *Wall Street Journal,* April 17, B5.
112. S. Nambisan & M. Sawhney, 2007, A buyer's guide to the innovation bazaar, *Harvard Business Review,* 85(6): 109–118.
113. Y. Shi, 2007, Today's solution and tomorrow's problem: The business process outsourcing risk management puzzle, *California Management Review,* 49(3): 27–44.
114. A. Tiwana & M. Keil, 2007, Does peripheral knowledge complement control? An empirical test in technology outsourcing alliances, *Strategic Management Journal,* 28: 623–634; M. J. Leiblein, J. J. Reuer, & F. Dalsace, 2002, Do make or buy decisions matter? The influence of organizational governance on technological performance, *Strategic Management Journal,* 23: 817–833.
115. J. C. Linder, S. Jarvenpaa, & T. H. Davenport, 2003, Toward an innovation sourcing strategy, *MIT Sloan Management Review,* 44(4): 43–49.
116. S. Lohr, 2007, At IBM, a smarter way to outsource, *New York Times Online,* July 5, http://nytimes.com.
117. M. Useem & J. Harder, 2000, Leading laterally in company outsourcing, *Sloan Management Review,* 41(2): 25–36.
118. R. C. Insinga & M. J. Werle, 2000, Linking outsourcing to business strategy, *Academy of Management Executive,* 14(4): 58–70.
119. B. Arrunada & X. H. Vazquez, 2006, When your contract manufacturer becomes your competitor, *Harvard Business Review,* 84(9): 135–144.
120. E. Perez & J. Karp, 2007, U.S. to probe outsourcing after ITT case, *Wall Street Journal* (Eastern Edition), March 28, A3, A6.
121. M. J. Mol, P. Pauwels, P. Matthyssens, & L. Quintens, 2004, A technological contingency perspective on the depth and scope of international outsourcing, *Journal of International Management,* 10: 287–305.
122. S. Thurm, 2007, Beyond outsourcing: Promise and pitfalls, *Wall Street Journal* (Eastern Edition), February 26, B3, B6.
123. M. A. Hitt, D. Ahlstrom, M. T. Dacin, E. Levitas, & L. Svobodina, 2004, The institutional effects on strategic alliance partner selection in transition economies: China versus Russia, *Organization Science,* 15: 173–185.
124. T. Felin & W. S. Hesterly, 2007, The knowledge-based view, nested heterogeneity, and new value creation: Philosophical considerations on the locus of knowledge, *Academy of Management Review,* 32: 195–218; Y. Mishina, T. G. Pollock, & J. F. Porac, 2004, Are more resources always better for growth? Resource stickiness in market and product expansion, *Strategic Management Journal,* 25: 1179–1197.
125. M. Gibbert, M. Hoegl, & L. Valikangas, 2007, In praise of resource constraints, *MIT Sloan Management Review,* 48(3): 15–17.
126. D. S. Elenkov & I. M. Manev, 2005, Top management leadership and influence in innovation: The role of sociocultural context, *Journal of Management,* 31: 381–402.
127. M. Katz, 2001, Planning ahead for manufacturing facility changes: A case study in outsourcing, *Pharmaceutical Technology,* March: 160–164.
128. D. Kiley, 2007, The new heat on Ford, *BusinessWeek,* June 4, 32–37.
129. D. Welch, 2007, Staying paranoid at Toyota, *BusinessWeek,* July 2, 80–82.
130. Leonard-Barton, *Wellsprings of Knowledge,* 30–31.

Part 2 Strategic Actions: Strategy Formulation

Business-Level Strategy

Studying this chapter should provide you with the strategic management knowledge needed to:

1. Define business-level strategy.
2. Discuss the relationship between customers and business-level strategies in terms of *who, what,* and *how.*
3. Explain the differences among business-level strategies.
4. Use the five forces of competition model to explain how above-average returns can be earned through each business-level strategy.
5. Describe the risks of using each of the business-level strategies.

From Pet Food to PetSmart

From Pet Food to PetSmart, this company has remained on top of the pet care industry in spite of fierce competition from PETCO (number 2), and major retailers Wal-Mart and Target by focusing on customer service. Although PetSmart began with a warehouse format and strategy, the company changed when research indicated that the average dog owner could spend more than $15,000 over the lifetime of the pet, if all available services were purchased. Thus, the "Engaging the Enthusiast" strategy emerged, along with a new vision: "to provide Total Lifetime Care for every pet, every parent, every time."

PetSmart first opened its doors in 1987, with two stores that operated under the name of PetFood Warehouse. Over the next two years the company changed its warehouse strategy to become a "MART for PETs that's SMART about PETs." The name and logo also changed to "PetsMart." The main focus was providing the best selection of products at the best prices. In 1993 PetsMart went public, and by 1994 had changed its slogan to "Where pets are family." By 2000 the company realized the importance of its services to pet owners (referred to as "pet parents") and developed a new vision statement: To provide Total Lifetime Care for every pet, every parent, every time. In 2001 PetsMart began an extensive customer training program for its associates (the company's name for employees). Associates were trained to identify customers' needs and how to provide solutions. By 2005 top executives decided to leave behind the "mart" concept and move to a new focus on providing "Smart" solutions and information. The name was changed to PetSmart and a new logo was created.

Specialized services and dedication to the community distinguish PetSmart from its competitors. Services available at most PetSmart stores include pet training classes where the customer is allowed to retake the class if not 100% satisfied, grooming facilities with certified pet groomers, PetsHotels that provide daycare and extended stay facilities with 24-hour caregivers on duty, full-service pet hospitals, pet adoption centers, and new pet centers. More than 2.9 million pets have been adopted through the adoption service. In addition to services, PetSmart has implemented a universal return policy, which means that it will accept returned merchandise even if it was purchased from a competitor. Through its PetPerks customer loyalty program, customers use a card such as the ones used in many grocery stores to track customer purchases and to help develop effective marketing strategies. In return customers receive special discount offers and communications to help them become more knowledgeable about caring for their pets. PetSmart Charities, an independent nonprofit animal welfare association, was started in 1994 and has donated more than $52 million to animal welfare programs.

In addition to its traditional brick-and-mortar stores, PetSmart offers products and services through both catalog sales and on the Internet at www.petsmart.com. At PetSmart.com, customer service is taken a step further. Customers can order merchandise, learn about the company, and donate to PetSmart Charities. PetSmart is the largest online retailer of pet products and services.

PetSmart continues to increase its focus on customer service and continues to grow. Currently the firm has about 39,000 trained associates, most of them pet owners, and more than 13,000 different products are available for purchase, all at low prices, at more than 900 stores in 45 states. The market for pets and pet services continues to grow in the United States as the baby boomers and empty nesters acquire pets to fill the void left by children who have moved away, and younger Americans are choosing to wait longer to have children. PetSmart offers "Total Lifetime Care" for their new family members.

Sources: V. L. Facenda, 2000, Pet-opia, *Retail Merchandiser*, 40(7): 11; 2000, Calling all returns, *Chain Store Age*, 76(4): 41; J. Covert, 2005, PetSmart focuses on big returns by coming up with new services, *Wall Street Journal*, June 1, A1; 2007, PetSmart Fact Sheet, http://www.petsmart.com, May; 2007, PetSmart pet experts, http://www.petsmart.com/global/customerservice; T. Sullivan, 2006, Fido's at the front desk, as PetSmart adds "hotels," *Wall Street Journal Online*, http://online.wsj.com, October 8.

Increasingly important to firm success,[1] strategy is concerned with making choices among two or more alternatives.[2] As we noted in Chapter 1, when choosing a strategy, the firm decides to pursue one course of action instead of others. The choices are influenced by opportunities and threats in the firm's external environment[3] (see Chapter 2) as well as the nature and quality of its internal resources, capabilities, and core competencies[4] (see Chapter 3). PetSmart identified a large potential market that was being underserved. It developed the capabilities to offer a portfolio of goods and services that provided pet owners one-stop shopping for all of their pet needs. The full service offerings of the firm provide differentiation from and an advantage over competitors.

The fundamental objective of using any type of strategy (see Figure 1.1) is to gain strategic competitiveness and earn above-average returns.[5] Strategies are purposeful, precede the taking of actions to which they apply, and demonstrate a shared understanding of the firm's vision and mission.[6] An effectively formulated strategy marshals, integrates, and allocates the firm's resources, capabilities, and competencies so that it will be properly aligned with its external environment.[7] A properly developed strategy also rationalizes the firm's vision and mission along with the actions taken to achieve them.[8] Information about a host of variables including markets, customers, technology, worldwide finance, and the changing world economy must be collected and analyzed to properly form and use strategies. In the final analysis, sound strategic choices that reduce uncertainty regarding outcomes[9] are the foundation on which successful strategies are built.[10]

A **business-level strategy** is an integrated and coordinated set of commitments and actions the firm uses to gain a competitive advantage by exploiting core competencies in specific product markets.

Business-level strategy, this chapter's focus, is an integrated and coordinated set of commitments and actions the firm uses to gain a competitive advantage by exploiting core competencies in specific product markets.[11] Business-level strategy indicates the choices the firm has made about how it intends to compete in individual product markets. The choices are important because long-term performance is linked to a firm's strategies.[12] Given the complexity of successfully competing in the global economy, these choices are often quite difficult to make.[13] For example, to increase the effectiveness of its differentiation business-level strategy (we define and discuss this strategy later in the chapter), Kimberly-Clark executives decided to close some manufacturing facilities and to reduce its labor force. Describing these decisions, the firm's CEO said: "These are tough decisions, and these are ones that we don't take lightly. But I believe they are absolutely necessary to improve our competitive position."[14] Decisions made at Frederick Cooper, such as the closing of the manufacturing facility, were also difficult.

Every firm must form and use a business-level strategy.[15] However, every firm may not use all the strategies—corporate-level, acquisition and restructuring, international, and cooperative—that we examine in Chapters 6 through 9. A firm competing in a single-product market area in a single geographic location does not need a corporate-level strategy to deal with product diversity or an international strategy to deal with geographic diversity. In contrast, a diversified firm will use one of the corporate-level strategies as well as choose a separate business-level strategy for each product market area in which it competes. Every firm—from the local dry cleaner to the multinational corporation—chooses at least one business-level strategy. Thus business-level strategy is the *core* strategy—the strategy that the firm forms to describe how it intends to compete in a product market.[16]

We discuss several topics as we examine business-level strategies. Because customers are the foundation of successful business-level strategies and should never be taken for granted,[17] we present information about customers relevant to business-level strategies. In terms of customers, when selecting a business-level strategy the firm determines (1) *who* will be served, (2) *what* needs those target customers have that it will satisfy, and (3) *how* those needs will be satisfied. Selecting customers and deciding which of their needs the firm will try to satisfy, as well as how it will do so, are challenging tasks. Global competition has created many attractive options for customers thus making it difficult to determine the strategy to best serve them. Effective global competitors have become adept at identifying the needs of customers in different cultures and geographic regions as well as learning how to quickly and successfully adapt the functionality of the firms' good or service to meet those needs.

Descriptions of the purpose of business-level strategies—and of the five business-level strategies—follows the discussion of customers. The five strategies we examine are called *generic* because they can be used in any organization competing in any industry.[18] Our analysis describes how effective use of each strategy allows the firm to favorably position itself relative to the five competitive forces in the industry (see Chapter 2). In addition, we use the value chain (see Chapter 3) to show examples of the primary and support activities necessary to implement specific business-level strategies. Because no strategy is risk-free,[19] we also describe the different risks the firm may encounter when using these strategies.

In Chapter 11, we explain the organizational structures and controls linked with the successful use of each business-level strategy.

Customers: Their Relationship with Business-Level Strategies

Strategic competitiveness results only when the firm is able to satisfy a group of customers by using its competitive advantages as the basis for competing in individual product markets.[20] A key reason firms must satisfy customers with their business-level strategy is that returns earned from relationships with customers are the lifeblood of all organizations.[21]

The most successful companies try to find new ways to satisfy current customers and/or to meet the needs of new customers. Dell captured a significant market share in the personal computer market during the 1990s by using a low-cost strategy while simultaneously satisfying customer needs. It became the largest seller of PCs. However, it lost much of its customer focus by overemphasizing cost reduction through its supply chain. In so doing, Hewlett-Packard (HP) began to capture greater market share. HP learned how to manage its supply chain to lower costs, thereby gaining competitive parity with Dell. But it also provided a broader portfolio of goods and services that better satisfied customer needs and thereby captured customers from Dell.[22] Many

Recently, Hewlett-Packard overtook Dell in total number of sales of PCs.

firms attempt to imitate the capabilities of their competitors, as HP did in building capabilities to manage its supply chain activities similar to Dell, in order to gain competitive parity.[23] Yet firms can continue to build and leverage their tacit knowledge to avoid imitation.[24] Dell became too inward-focused and did not take actions to avoid the imitation of the capabilities that had provided it a competitive advantage. Thus, it lost that advantage and significant market share with it.

Effectively Managing Relationships with Customers

The firm's relationships with its customers are strengthened when it delivers superior value to them. Strong interactive relationships with customers often provide the foundation for the firm's efforts to profitably serve customers' unique needs.

Harrah's Entertainment believes that it provides superior value to customers by "being the most service-oriented, geographically diversified company in gaming."[25] Importantly, delivering superior value often results in increased customer loyalty. In turn, customer loyalty has a positive relationship with profitability. However, more choices and easily accessible information about the functionality of firms' products are creating increasingly sophisticated and knowledgeable customers, making it difficult to earn their loyalty.[26]

STRATEGY RIGHT NOW

A number of companies have become skilled at the art of *managing* all aspects of their relationship with their customers.[27] For example, Amazon.com is an Internet-based venture widely recognized for the quality of information it maintains about its customers, the services it renders, and its ability to anticipate customers' needs.[28] Using the information it has, Amazon tries to serve what it believes are the unique needs of each customer. Based in Mexico, CEMEX SA is the "leading building-solutions company in the world." It is a global producer and marketer of quality cement and ready-mix concrete.[29] CEMEX uses the Internet to link its customers, cement plants, and main control room, allowing the firm to automate orders and optimize truck deliveries in highly congested Mexico City. Analysts believe that CEMEX's integration of Web technology with its cost leadership strategy differentiates it from competitors. As a result, CEMEX has become the largest cement producer in North America and one of the largest in the world.[30]

As we discuss next, firms' relationships with customers are characterized by three dimensions. Companies such as Amazon.com and CEMEX understand these dimensions and manage their relationships with customers in light of them.

Reach, Richness, and Affiliation

The *reach* dimension of relationships with customers is concerned with the firm's access and connection to customers. For instance, the largest physical retailer in bookstores, Barnes & Noble, carries 200,000-plus titles in 793 stores that average 25,000 square feet.[31] By contrast, Amazon.com offers more than 4.5 million titles and is located on tens of millions of computer screens with additional customer connections being established across the globe. Indeed, Amazon "has virtually unlimited online shelf space and can offer customers a vast selection of products through an efficient search and retrieval interface."[32] Even though Barnes & Noble also has an Internet presence (barnesandnoble.com), Amazon.com's reach is significantly greater. In general, firms seek to extend their reach, adding customers in the process of doing so.

Richness, the second dimension, is concerned with the depth and detail of the two-way flow of information between the firm and the customer. The potential of the richness dimension to help the firm establish a competitive advantage in its relationship with customers led many firms to offer online services in order to better manage information exchanges with their customers. Broader and deeper information-based exchanges allow firms to better understand their customers and their needs. Such exchanges also enable customers to become more knowledgeable about how the firm can satisfy them. Internet technology and e-commerce transactions have substantially reduced the costs of meaningful information exchanges with current and potential customers. Amazon.com is the leader in using the Internet to build relationships with customers. In fact, it bills itself as the most "customer-centric company" on earth. Executives at Amazon.com suggest that the company starts with the customer and works backwards.[33]

Affiliation, the third dimension, is concerned with facilitating useful interactions with customers. Internet navigators such as Microsoft's MSN Autos helps online clients find and sort information. MSN Autos provides data and software to prospective car buyers that enable them to compare car models along multiple objective specifications. The program can supply this information at no charge to the consumer because Internet technology allows a great deal of information to be collected from a variety of sources at a low cost. A prospective buyer who has selected a specific car based on comparisons of different models can then be linked to dealers that meet the customer's needs and purchasing requirements. Because its revenues come not from the final customer or end user but from other sources (such as advertisements on its Web site, hyperlinks, and associated products and services), MSN Autos represents the customer's interests, a service that fosters affiliation.[34] Viewing the world through the customer's eyes and constantly seeking ways to create more value for the customer have positive effects in terms of affiliation.

As we discuss next, effective management of customer relationships (along the dimensions of reach, richness, and affiliation) helps the firm answer questions related to the issues of *who, what,* and *how.*

Who: Determining the Customers to Serve

Deciding *who* the target customer is that the firm intends to serve with its business-level strategy is an important decision.[35] Companies divide customers into groups based on differences in the customers' needs (needs are discussed further in the next section) to make this decision. Dividing customers into groups based on their needs is called **market segmentation,** which is a process that clusters people with similar needs into individual and identifiable groups.[36] In the animal health business, for example, the needs for food products of owners of companion pets (e.g., dogs and cats) differ from the needs for food products of those owning production animals (e.g., livestock).[37] PetSmart serves the market segment for companion pets and not for the livestock segment. As part of its business-level strategy, the firm develops a marketing program to effectively sell products to its particular target customer group.[38]

Market segmentation is a process used to cluster people with similar needs into individual and identifiable groups.

Almost any identifiable human or organizational characteristic can be used to subdivide a market into segments that differ from one another on a given characteristic. Common characteristics on which customers' needs vary are illustrated in Table 4.1. Based on their internal core competencies and opportunities in the external environment, companies choose a business-level strategy to deliver value to target customers and satisfy their specific needs.

Customer characteristics are often combined to segment markets into specific groups that have unique needs. In the consumer clothing market, for example, Gap learned that its female and male customers want different shopping experiences. In a company official's words, "Research showed that men want to come and go easily, while women want an exploration."[39] In light of these research results, women's sections in Gap stores are organized by occasion (e.g., work, entertainment) with accessories for those occasions scattered throughout the section to facilitate browsing. The men's sections of Gap stores are more straightforward, with signs directing male customers to clothing items that are commonly stacked by size. Thus, Gap is using its understanding of some of the psychological factors (see Table 4.1) influencing its customers' purchasing intentions to better serve unique groups' needs.

Demographic factors (see Table 4.1 and the discussion in Chapter 2) can also be used to segment markets into generations with unique interests and needs. Evidence suggests, for example, that direct mail is an effective communication medium for the World War II generation (those born before 1932). The Swing generation (those born between 1933 and 1945) values taking cruises and purchasing second homes. Once financially conservative but now willing to spend money, members of this generation seek product information

Table 4.1 Basis for Customer Segmentation

Consumer Markets

1. Demographic factors (age, income, sex, etc.)
2. Socioeconomic factors (social class, stage in the family life cycle)
3. Geographic factors (cultural, regional, and national differences)
4. Psychological factors (lifestyle, personality traits)
5. Consumption patterns (heavy, moderate, and light users)
6. Perceptual factors (benefit segmentation, perceptual mapping)

Industrial Markets

1. End-use segments (identified by SIC code)
2. Product segments (based on technological differences or production economics)
3. Geographic segments (defined by boundaries between countries or by regional differences within them)
4. Common buying factor segments (cut across product market and geographic segments)
5. Customer size segments

Source: Adapted from S. C. Jain, 2000, *Marketing Planning and Strategy*, Cincinnati: South-Western College Publishing, 120.

from knowledgeable sources. The Baby Boom generation (born between 1946 and 1964) desires products that reduce the stress generated by trying to balance career demands and the needs of older parents with those of their own children. Ellen Tracy clothes, known for their consistency of fit and color, are targeted to Baby Boomer women. More conscious of hype, the 60-million-plus people in Generation X (born between 1965 and 1976) want products that deliver as promised. The Xers use the Internet as a primary shopping tool and expect visually compelling marketing. Members of this group are the fastest-growing segment of mutual-fund shareholders, with their holdings overwhelmingly invested in stock funds. As employees, the top priorities of Xers are to work in a creative learning environment, to receive constant feedback from managers, and to be rewarded for using their technical skills.[40] Different marketing campaigns and distribution channels (e.g., the Internet for Generation X customers, direct mail for the World War II generation) affect the implementation of strategies for those companies interested in serving the needs of different generations.

What: Determining Which Customer Needs to Satisfy

After the firm decides *who* it will serve, it must identify the targeted customer group's needs that its goods or services can satisfy. Successful firms learn how to deliver to customers what they want and when they want it.[41] In a general sense, *needs (what)* are related to a product's benefits and features.[42] Having close and frequent interactions with both current and potential customers helps the firm identify those individuals' and groups' current and future needs.[43] From a strategic perspective, a basic need of all customers is to buy products that create value for them. The generalized forms of value that goods or services provide are either low cost with acceptable features or highly differentiated features with acceptable cost. The most effective firms continuously strive to anticipate changes in customers' needs. Failure to anticipate results in the loss of customers to competitors who are offering greater value in terms of product features and functionalities. For example, some analysts believe that discounters, department stores, and other home furnishing chains are taking customers away from Pier 1 Imports Inc., which suggests that Pier 1 has not anticipated changes in its customers' needs in as timely a manner as should be the case.

In any given industry, consumers' needs often vary a great deal.[44] The need some consumers have for high-quality, fresh sandwiches is what Jason's Deli seeks to satisfy with its menu items. In contrast, many large fast-food companies satisfy customer needs for lower-cost food items with acceptable quality that are delivered quickly. Diversified food and soft-drink producer PepsiCo believes that "any one consumer has different needs at different times of the day." Through its soft drinks (Pepsi products), snacks (Frito-Lay), juices (Tropicana), and cereals (Quaker), PepsiCo is developing new products from breakfast bars to healthier potato chips "to make certain that it covers all those needs."[45] In general, and across multiple product groups (e.g., automobiles, clothing, food), evidence suggests that middle-market consumers in the United States want to trade up to higher levels of quality and taste. These customers are willing to pay large premiums for well-designed, well-engineered, and well-crafted goods.[46] These needs represent opportunities for some firms to pursue through their business-level strategies.

To ensure success, a firm must be able to fully understand the needs of the customers in the target group it has selected to serve. The company translates these needs into features and performance capabilities of their products designed to serve those customers. The most effective firms are committed to understanding the customers' current as well as future needs.

How: Determining Core Competencies Necessary to Satisfy Customer Needs

As explained in Chapters 1 and 3, *core competencies* are resources and capabilities that serve as a source of competitive advantage for the firm over its rivals. Firms use core competencies (*how*) to implement value-creating strategies and thereby satisfy customers' needs. Only those firms with the capacity to continuously improve, innovate, and upgrade their competencies can expect to meet and hopefully exceed customers' expectations across time.[47]

Companies draw from a wide range of core competencies to produce goods or services that can satisfy customers' needs. SAS Institute is the world's largest privately owned software company and is the leader in business intelligence and analytics. Customers use SAS's programs for data warehousing, data mining, and decision support purposes. Allocating more than 30 percent of revenues to research and development (R&D), SAS relies on its core competence in R&D to satisfy the data-related needs of such customers as the U.S. Census Bureau and a host of consumer goods firms (e.g., hotels, banks, and catalog companies).[48] Vans Inc. relies on its core competencies in innovation and marketing to design and sell skateboards and other products. The firm also pioneered thick-soled, slip-on sneakers that can absorb the shock of five-foot leaps on wheels. The company uses an unusual marketing mix to capitalize on its pioneering products. In lieu of mass media ads, the firm sponsors skateboarding events, and is building skateboard parks at malls around the country. In 2007, the company sponsored Vans Warped Tour in a variety of cities across North America to promote skateboarding and its related product lines.[49]

All organizations, including SAS and Vans Inc., must use their core competencies (the *how*) to satisfy the needs (the *what*) of the target group of customers (the *who*) the firm has chosen to serve by using its business-level strategy. Recent research suggests that firms should carefully identify clues from customers regarding the quality of their service provided and use simple as well as sophisticated means of assessing customer satisfaction.[50]

Next, we describe the formal purpose of a business-level strategy and then the five business-level strategies available to all firms.

The Purpose of a Business-Level Strategy

The purpose of a business-level strategy is to create differences between the firm's position and those of its competitors.[51] To position itself differently from competitors, a firm must decide whether it intends to *perform activities differently* or to *perform different activities*. In fact, "choosing to perform activities differently or to perform different activities than

Figure 4.1 Southwest Airlines' Activity System

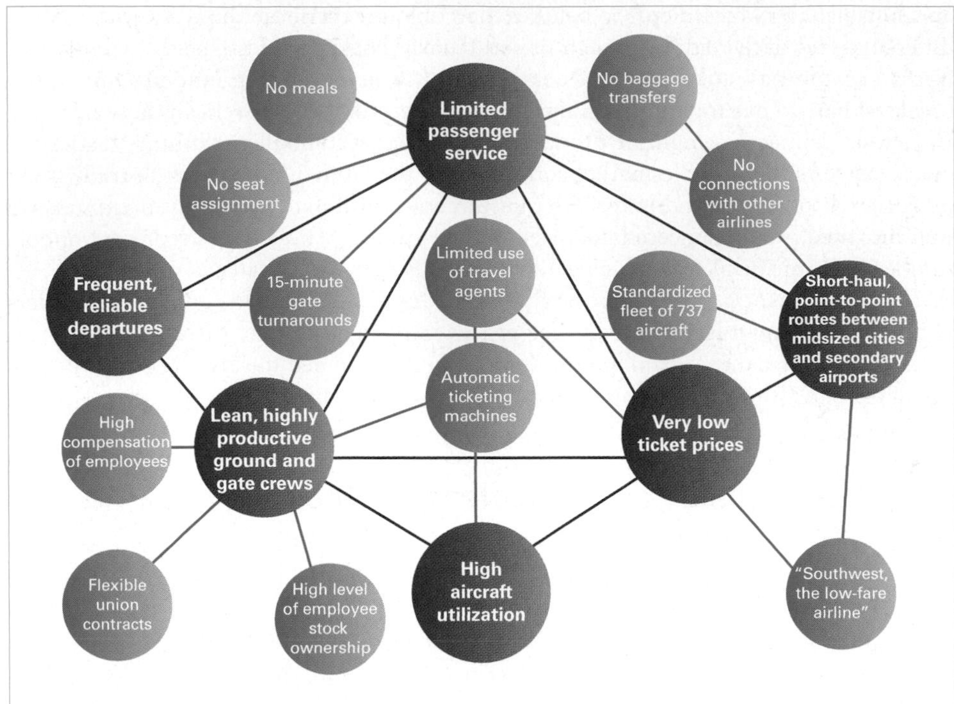

rivals" is the essence of business-level strategy.[52] Thus, the firm's business-level strategy is a deliberate choice about how it will perform the value chain's primary and support activities to create unique value. Indeed, in the complex twenty-first–century competitive landscape, successful use of a business-level strategy results only when the firm learns how to integrate the activities it performs in ways that create superior value for customers and thus contribute to competitive advantages.

Firms develop an activity map to show how they integrate the activities they perform. We show Southwest Airlines' activity map in Figure 4.1. The manner in which Southwest has integrated its activities is the foundation for the successful use of its integrated cost leadership/differentiation strategy (this strategy is discussed later in the chapter).[53] The tight integration among Southwest's activities is a key source of the firm's ability to operate more profitably than its competitors. In fact, in 2007, Southwest announced its sixty-fourth consecutive quarter of profitability, unprecedented in the industry.[54]

As shown in Figure 4.1, Southwest Airlines has configured the activities it performs into six strategic themes—limited passenger service; frequent, reliable departures; lean, highly productive ground and gate crews; high aircraft utilization; very low ticket prices; and short-haul, point-to-point routes between midsized cities and secondary airports. Individual clusters of tightly linked activities make it possible for the outcome of a strategic theme to be achieved. For example, no meals, no seat assignments, and no baggage transfers form a cluster of individual activities that support the strategic theme of limited passenger service (see Figure 4.1).

Southwest's tightly integrated activities make it difficult for competitors to imitate the firm's integrated cost leadership/differentiation strategy. The firm's culture influences these activities and their integration and contributes to the firm's ability to continuously identify additional ways to differentiate Southwest's service from its competitors' as well as to lower its costs. In fact, the firm's unique culture and customer service, both of which are sources of competitive advantages, are features that rivals have been unable to imitate, although some have tried. US Airways' MetroJet subsidiary, United Airlines' United Shuttle, Delta's Song and Continental Airlines' Continental Lite all failed in attempts to imitate Southwest's strategy. Hindsight shows that these competitors offered low prices to customers, but weren't able to operate at costs close to those of Southwest or to provide customers with any notable sources of differentiation, such as a unique experience while in the air.

Fit among activities is a key to the sustainability of competitive advantage for all firms, including Southwest Airlines. As Michael Porter comments, "Strategic fit among many activities is fundamental not only to competitive advantage but also to the sustainability of that advantage. It is harder for a rival to match an array of interlocked activities than it is merely to imitate a particular sales-force approach, match a process technology, or replicate a set of product features. Positions built on systems of activities are far more sustainable than those built on individual activities."[55]

Types of Business-Level Strategies

Firms choose from among five business-level strategies to establish and defend their desired strategic position against competitors: *cost leadership, differentiation, focused cost leadership, focused differentiation,* and *integrated cost leadership/differentiation* (see Figure 4.2). Each business-level strategy helps the firm to establish and exploit a particular *competitive advantage* within a particular *competitive scope.* How firms integrate the activities they perform within each different business-level strategy demonstrates how they differ from one another.[56] For example, firms have different activity maps, and thus, a Southwest Airlines' activity map differs from those of competitors JetBlue, Continental, American Airlines, and so forth. Superior integration of activities increases the likelihood of being able to gain an advantage over competitors and to earn above-average returns.

When selecting a business-level strategy, firms evaluate two types of potential competitive advantage: "lower cost than rivals, or the ability to differentiate and command a premium price that exceeds the extra cost of doing so."[57] Having lower cost derives from

Figure 4.2 Five Business-Level Strategies

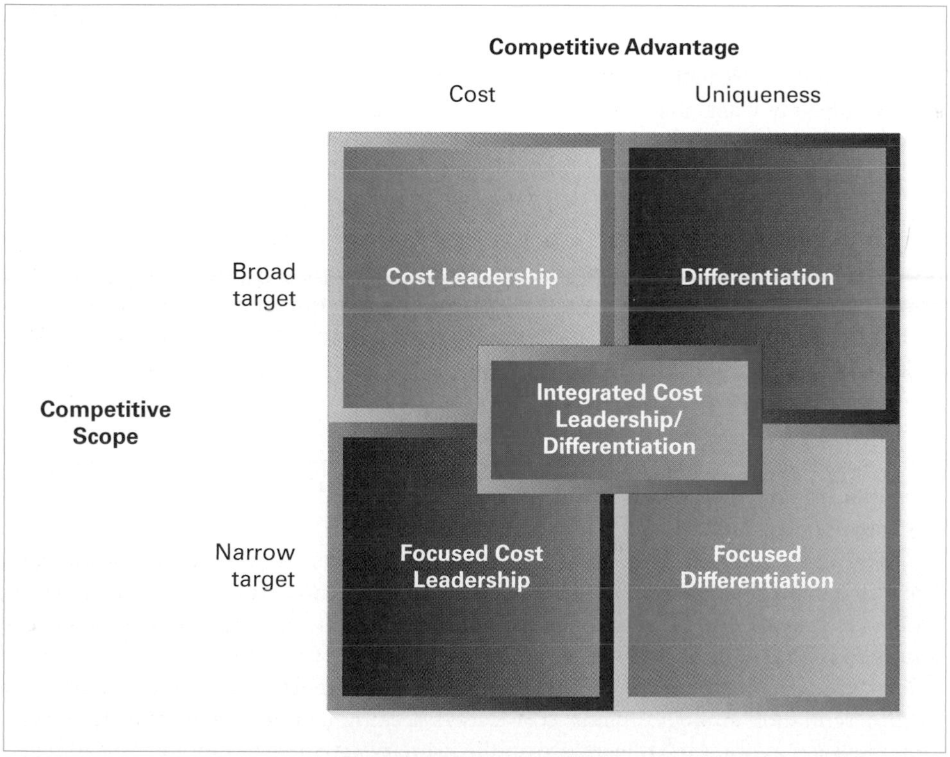

Source: Adapted with the permission of The Free Press, an imprint of Simon & Schuster Adult Publishing Group, from *Competitive Advantage: Creating and Sustaining Superior Performance,* by Michael E. Porter, 12. Copyright © 1985, 1998 by Michael E. Porter.

the firm's ability to perform activities differently than rivals; being able to differentiate indicates the firm's capacity to perform different (and valuable) activities.[58] Thus, based on the nature and quality of its internal resources, capabilities, and core competencies, a firm seeks to form either a cost competitive advantage or a uniqueness competitive advantage as the basis for implementing its business-level strategy.

Two types of competitive scope are broad target and narrow target (see Figure 4.2). Firms serving a broad target market seek to use their competitive advantage on an industry-wide basis. A narrow competitive scope means that the firm intends to serve the needs of a narrow target customer group. With focus strategies, the firm "selects a segment or group of segments in the industry and tailors its strategy to serving them to the exclusion of others."[59] Buyers with special needs and buyers located in specific geographic regions are examples of narrow target customer groups. As shown in Figure 4.2, a firm could also strive to develop a combined cost/uniqueness competitive advantage as the foundation for serving a target customer group that is larger than a narrow segment but not as comprehensive as a broad (or industry-wide) customer group. In this instance, the firm uses the integrated cost leadership/differentiation strategy. None of the five business-level strategies shown in Figure 4.2 is inherently or universally superior to the others.[60] The effectiveness of each strategy is contingent both on the opportunities and threats in a firm's external environment and on the strengths and weaknesses derived from the firm's resource portfolio. It is critical, therefore, for the firm to select a business-level strategy that is based on a match between the opportunities and threats in its external environment and the strengths of its internal environment as shown by its core competencies.

Cost Leadership Strategy

The **cost leadership strategy** is an integrated set of actions taken to produce goods or services with features that are acceptable to customers at the lowest cost, relative to that of competitors.

The **cost leadership strategy** is an integrated set of actions taken to produce goods or services with features that are acceptable to customers at the lowest cost, relative to that of competitors.[61] Firms using the cost leadership strategy commonly sell standardized goods or services (but with competitive levels of quality) to the industry's most typical customers. Cost leaders' goods and services must have competitive levels of quality (and often differentiation in terms of features) that create value for customers. At the extreme, concentrating only on reducing costs could result in the firm efficiently producing products that no customer wants to purchase. In fact, such extremes could lead to limited potential for innovation, employment of lower-skilled workers, poor conditions on the production line, accidents, and a poor quality of work-life for employees.[62]

As shown in Figure 4.2, the firm using the cost leadership strategy targets a broad customer segment or group. Cost leaders concentrate on finding ways to lower their costs relative to those of their competitors by constantly rethinking how to complete their primary and support activities to reduce costs still further while maintaining competitive levels of differentiation.[63] Cost leader Greyhound Lines Inc., for example, continuously seeks ways to reduce the costs it incurs to provide bus service while offering customers an acceptable experience. Recently Greyhound sought to improve the quality of the experience customers have when paying the firm's low prices for its services by "refurbishing buses, updating terminals, adding greeters and improving customer service training." Greyhound enjoys economies of scale by serving more than 20 million passengers annually with about 1,700 destinations in the United States and operating 1,500 buses.[64]

As primary activities, inbound logistics (e.g., materials handling, warehousing, and inventory control) and outbound logistics (e.g., collecting, storing, and distributing products to customers) often account for significant portions of the total cost to produce some goods and services. Research suggests that having a competitive advantage in terms of logistics creates more value when using the cost leadership strategy than when using the differentiation strategy.[65] Thus, cost leaders seeking competitively valuable ways to reduce costs may want to concentrate on the primary activities of inbound logistics and outbound logistics. In so doing many now outsource the operations (often manufacturing) to low-cost firms with low-wage employees (e.g., China).[66]

Cost leaders also carefully examine all support activities to find additional sources of potential cost reductions. Developing new systems for finding the optimal combination of low cost and acceptable quality in the raw materials required to produce the firm's goods or services is an example of how the procurement support activity can facilitate successful use of the cost leadership strategy.

Big Lots uses a cost leadership strategy by selling name brand merchandise at a lower cost.

Big Lots Inc. uses the cost leadership strategy. With its vision of being "The World's Best Bargain Place," Big Lots is the largest closeout discount chain in the United States. The firm strives constantly to drive its costs lower by relying on what some analysts see as a highly disciplined merchandise cost and inventory management system.[67] The firm's stores sell name-brand products at prices that are 20 to 40 percent below those of discount retailers and roughly 70 percent below those of traditional retailers.[68] Big Lots' buyers search for manufacturer overruns and discontinued styles to find goods priced well below wholesale prices. In addition, the firm buys from overseas suppliers. Big Lots satisfies the customers' need to access the differentiated features and capabilities of brand-name products, but at a fraction of their initial cost. The tight integration of purchasing and inventory management activities across its full set of stores (slightly under 1,400 stores) is the main core competence Big Lots uses to satisfy its customers' needs.

As described in Chapter 3, firms use value-chain analysis to determine the parts of the company's operations that create value and those that do not. Figure 4.3 demonstrates the primary and support activities that allow a firm to create value through the cost leadership strategy. Companies unable to link the activities shown in this figure through the activity map they form typically lack the core competencies needed to successfully use the cost leadership strategy.

Effective use of the cost leadership strategy allows a firm to earn above-average returns in spite of the presence of strong competitive forces (see Chapter 2). The next sections (one for each of the five forces) explain how firms implement a cost leadership strategy.

Rivalry with Existing Competitors

Having the low-cost position is valuable to deal with rivals. Because of the cost leader's advantageous position, rivals hesitate to compete on the basis of price, especially before evaluating the potential outcomes of such competition.[69] Wal-Mart is known for its ability to both control and reduce costs, making it difficult for firms to compete against it on the basis of costs. The discount retailer achieves strict cost control in several ways: "Wal-Mart's 660,000-square-foot main headquarters, with its drab gray interiors and frayed carpets, looks more like a government building than the home of one of the world's largest corporations. Business often is done in the no-frills cafeteria, and suppliers meet with managers in stark, cramped rooms. Employees have to throw out their own garbage at the end of the day and double up in hotel rooms on business trips."[70] The former Kmart's decision to compete against Wal-Mart on the basis of cost contributed to the firm's failure and subsequent bankruptcy filing. Its competitively inferior distribution system—an inefficient and high-cost system compared to Wal-Mart's—is one of the factors that prevented Kmart from having a competitive cost structure.

Bargaining Power of Buyers (Customers)

Powerful customers can force a cost leader to reduce its prices, but not below the level at which the cost leader's next-most-efficient industry competitor can earn average returns. Although powerful customers might be able to force the cost leader to reduce prices even below this level, they probably would not choose to do so. Prices that are low enough to

Figure 4.3 Examples of Value-Creating Activities Associated with the Cost Leadership Strategy

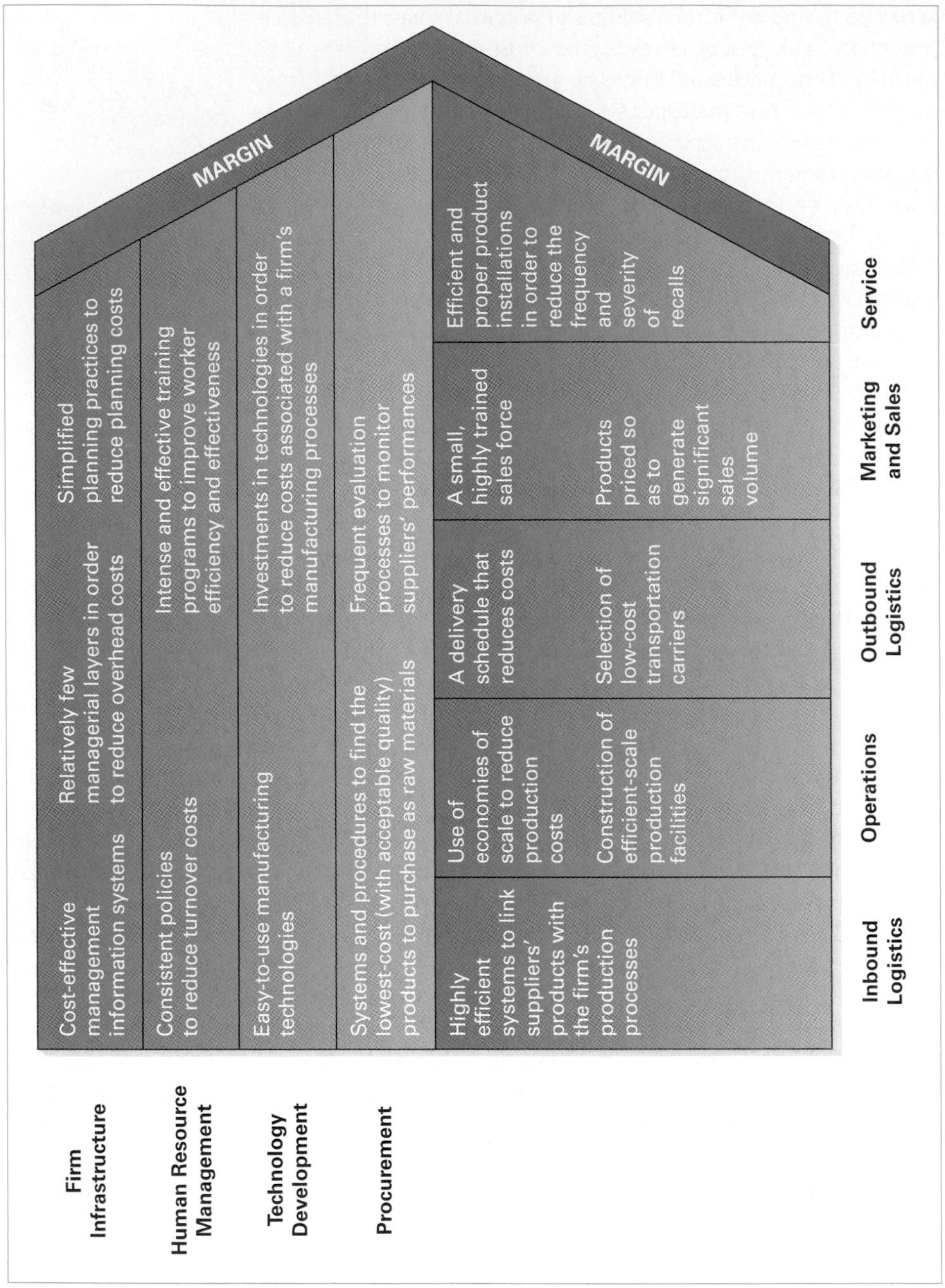

Source: Adapted with the permission of The Free Press, an imprint of Simon & Schuster Adult Publishing Group, from *Competitive Advantage: Creating and Sustaining Superior Performance,* by Michael E. Porter, 47. Copyright © 1985, 1998 by Michael E. Porter.

prevent the next-most-efficient competitor from earning average returns would force that firm to exit the market, leaving the cost leader with less competition and in an even stronger position. Customers would thus lose their power and pay higher prices if they were forced to purchase from a single firm operating in an industry without rivals. Consider Wal-Mart in this regard. Part of the reason this firm's prices continue to be the lowest available is that Wal-Mart continuously searches for ways to reduce its costs relative to competitors who try to implement a cost leadership strategy (such as Costco). Thus, customers benefit by Wal-Mart having to compete against others trying to use the cost leadership strategy and lowering its prices to engage in competitive battles.

Bargaining Power of Suppliers

The cost leader operates with margins greater than those of competitors. Among other benefits, higher margins relative to those of competitors make it possible for the cost leader to absorb its suppliers' price increases. When an industry faces substantial increases in the cost of its supplies, only the cost leader may be able to pay the higher prices and continue to earn either average or above-average returns. Alternatively, a powerful cost leader may be able to force its suppliers to hold down their prices, which would reduce the suppliers' margins in the process. Wal-Mart uses its power with suppliers (gained because it buys such large quantities from many suppliers) to extract lower prices from them. These savings are then passed on to customers in the form of lower prices, which further strengthens Wal-Mart's position relative to competitors lacking the power to extract lower prices from suppliers. Wal-Mart has significant market power. It controls 29 percent of the nonfood grocery sales, 30 percent of the health and beauty aids sales, and 45 percent of the general merchandise sales in the total U.S. retail market.[71] Of course, other firms may use alliances with suppliers to gain access to complementary resources that help them keep their overall costs low. In other words, they can share the costs with others helping them to maintain a low-cost structure.[72]

Potential Entrants

Through continuous efforts to reduce costs to levels that are lower than competitors', a cost leader becomes highly efficient. Because ever-improving levels of efficiency (e.g., economies of scale) enhance profit margins, they serve as a significant entry barrier to potential competitors.[73] New entrants must be willing and able to accept no-better-than-average returns until they gain the experience required to approach the cost leader's efficiency. To earn even average returns, new entrants must have the competencies required to match the cost levels of competitors other than the cost leader. The low profit margins (relative to margins earned by firms implementing the differentiation strategy) make it necessary for the cost leader to sell large volumes of its product to earn above-average returns. However, firms striving to be the cost leader must avoid pricing their products so low that their ability to operate profitably is reduced, even though volume increases.

Product Substitutes

Compared with its industry rivals, the cost leader also holds an attractive position in terms of product substitutes. A product substitute becomes an issue for the cost leader when its features and characteristics, in terms of cost and differentiated features, are potentially attractive to the firm's customers. When faced with possible substitutes, the cost leader has more flexibility than its competitors. To retain customers, it can reduce the price of its good or service. With still lower prices and competitive levels of differentiation, the cost leader increases the probability that customers will prefer its product rather than a substitute.

Competitive Risks of the Cost Leadership Strategy

The cost leadership strategy is not risk free. One risk is that the processes used by the cost leader to produce and distribute its good or service could become obsolete because of competitors' innovations. These innovations may allow rivals to produce at costs lower than those of the original cost leader, or to provide additional differentiated features without increasing the product's price to customers.

A second risk is that too much focus by the cost leader on cost reductions may occur at the expense of trying to understand customers' perceptions of "competitive levels of differentiation." However, Wal-Mart has begun to experience problems exemplified by Costco's ability to out-compete Wal-Mart's Sam's Club. Costco does it with an appropriate combination of low cost and quality—differentiated products.[74] A final risk of the cost leadership strategy concerns imitation. Using their own core competencies, competitors sometimes learn how to successfully imitate the cost leader's strategy. When this imitation occurs, the cost leader must increase the value that its good or service provides to customers. Commonly, value is increased by selling the current product at an even lower price or by adding differentiated features that customers value while maintaining price.

Differentiation Strategy

The **differentiation strategy** is an integrated set of actions taken to produce goods or services (at an acceptable cost) that customers perceive as being different in ways that are important to them.

The **differentiation strategy** is an integrated set of actions taken to produce goods or services (at an acceptable cost) that customers perceive as being different in ways that are important to them.[75] While cost leaders serve a typical customer in an industry, differentiators target customers for whom value is created by the manner in which the firm's products differ from those produced and marketed by competitors.

Firms must be able to produce differentiated products at competitive costs to reduce upward pressure on the price that customers pay. When a product's differentiated features are produced at noncompetitive costs, the price for the product can exceed what the firm's target customers are willing to pay. When the firm has a thorough understanding of what its target customers value, the relative importance they attach to the satisfaction of different needs, and for what they are willing to pay a premium, the differentiation strategy can be successful.

Through the differentiation strategy, the firm produces nonstandardized products for customers who value differentiated features more than they value low cost. For example, superior product reliability and durability and high-performance sound systems are among the differentiated features of Toyota Motor Corporation's Lexus products. The Lexus promotional statement—"We pursue perfection, so you can pursue living"—suggests a strong commitment to overall product quality as a source of differentiation. However, Lexus offers its vehicles to customers at a competitive purchase price. As with Lexus products, a good's or service's unique attributes, rather than its purchase price, provide the value for which customers are willing to pay.

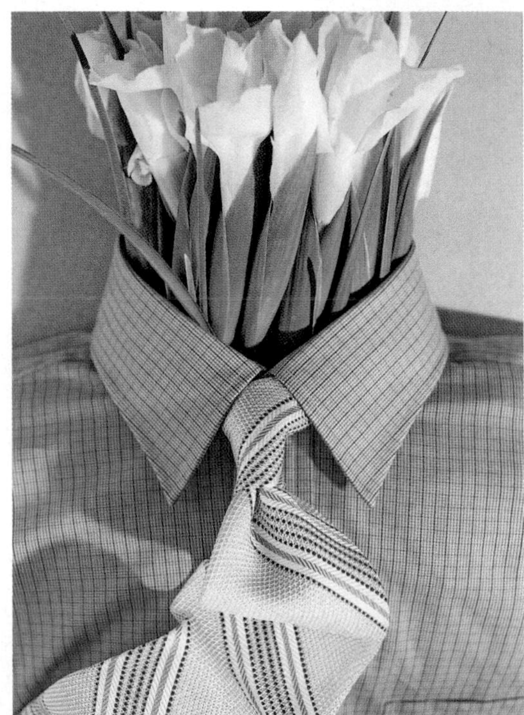

A Robert Talbott shirt and tie is differentiated from the market by its quality, craftsmanship, and attention to detail.

Continuous success with the differentiation strategy results when the firm consistently upgrades differentiated features that customers value and/or creates new ones (innovates) without significant cost increases.[76] This approach requires firms to constantly change their product lines.[77] Such firms may also offer a portfolio of products that complement each other, thereby enriching the differentiation for the customer and perhaps satisfying a portfolio of consumer needs.[78] Because a differentiated product satisfies customers' unique needs, firms following the differentiation strategy are able to charge premium prices. For customers to be willing to pay a premium price, however, a "firm must truly be unique at something or be perceived as unique."[79] The ability to sell a good or service at a price that substantially exceeds the cost of creating its differentiated features allows the firm to outperform rivals and earn above-average returns. For example, shirt and neckwear manufacturer Robert Talbott follows stringent standards of craftsmanship and pays meticulous attention to every detail of production. The firm imports exclusive fabrics from the world's finest mills to make men's dress shirts and neckwear. Single-needle tailoring is used, and precise collar cuts are made to produce shirts. According to the company, customers purchasing one of its products can be assured that they are being provided with the finest fabrics available.[80] Thus, Robert Talbott's success rests on the firm's ability to produce and sell its differentiated products at a price significantly higher than the costs of imported fabrics and its unique manufacturing processes.

Rather than costs, a firm using the differentiation strategy always concentrates on investing in and developing features that differentiate a good or service in ways that customers value. Robert Talbott, for example, uses the finest silks from Europe and Asia to produce its "Best of Class" collection of ties. Overall, a firm using the differentiation strategy seeks to be different from its competitors on as many dimensions as possible. The less similarity between a firm's goods or services and those of competitors, the more buffered it is from rivals' actions. Commonly recognized differentiated goods include Toyota's Lexus, Ralph Lauren's wide array of product lines, and Caterpillar's heavy-duty earth-moving equipment. Thought by some to be the world's most expensive and prestigious consulting firm, McKinsey & Co. is a well-known example of a firm that offers differentiated services.

A good or service can be differentiated in many ways. Unusual features, responsive customer service, rapid product innovations and technological leadership, perceived prestige and status, different tastes, and engineering design and performance are examples of approaches to differentiation.[81] The number of ways to reduce costs may be limited (as demonstrated by successful use of the cost leadership strategy). In contrast, virtually anything a firm can do to create real or perceived value is a basis for differentiation. Consider product design as a case in point. Because it can create a positive experience for customers, design is becoming an increasingly important source of differentiation and hopefully for firms emphasizing it, of competitive advantage.[82] Apple is often cited as the firm that sets the standard in design (see the Strategic Focus in Chapter 1). The iPod is a good case in point, and the iPhone, introduced in 2007, provides another example of Apple's creativity and design capabilities.[83]

A firm's value chain can be analyzed to determine whether the firm is able to link the activities required to create value by using the differentiation strategy. Examples of primary and support activities that are commonly used to differentiate a good or service are shown in Figure 4.4. Companies without the skills needed to link these activities cannot expect to successfully use the differentiation strategy. Next, we explain how firms using the differentiation strategy can successfully position themselves in terms of the five forces of competition (see Chapter 2) to earn above-average returns.

Rivalry with Existing Competitors

Customers tend to be loyal purchasers of products differentiated in ways that are meaningful to them. As their loyalty to a brand increases, customers' sensitivity to price increases is reduced. The relationship between brand loyalty and price sensitivity insulates a firm from competitive rivalry. Thus, Robert Talbott's "Best of Class" neckwear line is insulated from competition, even on the basis of price, as long as the company continues to satisfy the differentiated needs of its target customer group. Likewise, Bose is insulated from intense rivalry as long as customers continue to perceive that its stereo equipment offers superior sound quality at a competitive purchase price. Both Robert Talbot and Bose have strong positive reputations for the high quality and unique products that they provide. Thus, reputations can sustain the competitive advantage of firms following a differentiation strategy.[84]

Bargaining Power of Buyers (Customers)

The uniqueness of differentiated goods or services reduces customers' sensitivity to price increases. Customers are willing to accept a price increase when a product still satisfies their perceived unique needs better than a competitor's offering can. Thus, the golfer whose needs are uniquely satisfied by Callaway golf clubs will likely continue buying those products even if their cost increases. Similarly, the customer who has been highly satisfied with a 10-year-old Louis Vuitton wallet will probably replace that wallet with another one made by the same company even though the purchase price is higher than the original one. Purchasers of brand-name food items (e.g., Heinz ketchup and Kleenex tissues) will accept price increases in those products as long as they continue to perceive that the product satisfies their unique needs at an acceptable cost. In all of these instances, the customers are relatively insensitive to price increases because they do not think that an acceptable product alternative exists.

Figure 4.4 Examples of Value-Creating Activities Associated with the Differentiation Strategy

Support Activities	Examples		
Firm Infrastructure	Highly developed information systems to better understand customers' purchasing preferences	A company-wide emphasis on the importance of producing high-quality products	
Human Resource Management	Compensation programs intended to encourage worker creativity and productivity	Somewhat extensive use of subjective rather than objective performance measures	Superior personnel training
Technology Development	Strong capability in basic research	Investments in technologies that will allow the firm to produce highly differentiated products	
Procurement	Systems and procedures used to find the highest-quality raw materials	Purchase of highest-quality replacement parts	

Inbound Logistics	**Operations**	**Outbound Logistics**	**Marketing and Sales**	**Service**
Superior handling of incoming raw materials so as to minimize damage and to improve the quality of the final product	Consistent manufacturing of attractive products	Accurate and responsive order-processing procedures	Extensive granting of credit buying arrangements for customers	Extensive buyer training to assure high-quality product installations
	Rapid responses to customers' unique manufacturing specifications	Rapid and timely product deliveries to customers	Extensive personal relationships with buyers and suppliers	Complete field stocking of replacement parts

MARGIN

MARGIN

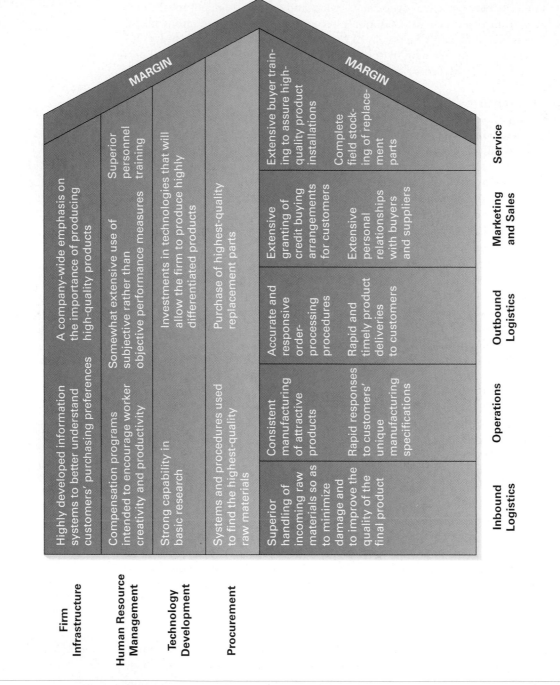

Source: Adapted with the permission of The Free Press, an imprint of Simon & Schuster Adult Publishing Group, from *Competitive Advantage: Creating and Sustaining Superior Performance,* by Michael E. Porter, 47. Copyright © 1985, 1998 by Michael E. Porter.

Bargaining Power of Suppliers

Because the firm using the differentiation strategy charges a premium price for its products, suppliers must provide high-quality components, driving up the firm's costs. However, the high margins the firm earns in these cases partially insulate it from the influence of suppliers in that higher supplier costs can be paid through these margins. Alternatively, because of buyers' relative insensitivity to price increases, the differentiated firm might choose to pass the additional cost of supplies on to the customer by increasing the price of its unique product.

Potential Entrants

Customer loyalty and the need to overcome the uniqueness of a differentiated product present substantial barriers to potential entrants. Entering an industry under these conditions typically demands significant investments of resources and patience while seeking customers' loyalty.

Product Substitutes

Firms selling brand-name goods and services to loyal customers are positioned effectively against product substitutes. In contrast, companies without brand loyalty face a higher probability of their customers switching either to products that offer differentiated features that serve the same function (particularly if the substitute has a lower price) or to products that offer more features and perform more attractive functions.

Competitive Risks of the Differentiation Strategy

As with the other business-level strategies, the differentiation strategy is not risk free. One risk is that customers might decide that the price differential between the differentiator's product and the cost leader's product is too large. In this instance, a firm may be offering differentiated features that exceed target customers' needs. The firm then becomes vulnerable to competitors that are able to offer customers a combination of features and price that is more consistent with their needs.

Another risk of the differentiation strategy is that a firm's means of differentiation may cease to provide value for which customers are willing to pay. A differentiated product becomes less valuable if imitation by rivals causes customers to perceive that competitors offer essentially the same good or service, but at a lower price.[85] For example, Walt Disney Company operates different theme parks, including The Magic Kingdom, Epcot Center, and the newly developed Animal Kingdom. Each park offers entertainment and educational opportunities. However, Disney's competitors, such as Six Flags Corporation, also offer entertainment and educational experiences similar to those available at Disney's locations. To ensure that its facilities create value for which customers will be willing to pay, Disney continuously reinvests in its operations to more crisply differentiate them from those of its rivals.[86]

A third risk of the differentiation strategy is that experience can narrow customers' perceptions of the value of a product's differentiated features. For example, customers having positive experiences with generic tissues may decide that the differentiated features of the Kleenex product are not worth the extra cost. Similarly, while a customer may be impressed with the quality of a Robert Talbott "Best of Class" tie, positive experiences with less expensive ties may lead to a conclusion that the price of the "Best of Class" tie exceeds the benefit. To counter this risk, firms must continue to meaningfully differentiate their product for customers at a price they are willing to pay.

Counterfeiting is the differentiation strategy's fourth risk. Makers of counterfeit goods—products that attempt to convey a firm's differentiated features to customers at significantly reduced prices—represent a concern for many firms using the differentiation strategy.

Caribou Coffee has taken several actions to differentiate its goods and services from Starbucks and other competitors. As explained in the Strategic Focus, Caribou has been innovative in the type of coffee offered (environmentally friendly) and in the services extended to customers. Innovation is important for differentiation strategies, particularly in the development of complementary goods and services (e.g., free WiFi).[87]

Focus Strategies

Firms choose a focus strategy when they intend to use their core competencies to serve the needs of a particular industry segment or niche to the exclusion of others. Examples

Strategic Focus Strategic Focus Strategic Focus

Caribou Coffee: When You Are Number Two, You Try Harder

If you're number 2, how do you compete with number 1? Caribou Coffee, has tried to differentiate as much as possible from number 1, Starbucks.

The concept for Caribou Coffee began with an idea in 1990, when engaged Dartmouth graduates Kim Whitehead and John Puckett were on vacation in Denali National Park in Alaska. The vast beauty of the environment so impressed them that as they looked down upon a herd of caribou running through a valley, they decided to start a business that would make a difference in the world.

Caribou Coffee has several differentiation strategies including free WiFi and a family-friendly atmosphere.

Caribou Coffee Company, Inc., founded in 1992 in Minneapolis, Minnesota, is the second largest specialty coffee company and coffeehouse operator in the United States. Caribou Coffee went public in 2005 and currently owns more than 430 stores, including more than 20 franchises, in 18 states plus the District of Columbia. Its coffeehouses are located predominantly in the central and eastern United States, and it employs more than 5,000 people. The company's mission is "to provide an experience that makes the day better."

Even though both Caribou Coffee and Starbucks are dedicated to providing the highest quality products and customer service, their methods of delivering them are quite different. Starbucks provides a comfortable setting for urban customers who prefer references to sizes such as "venti" and "grande." Caribou has chosen to use the more common names of "small," "medium," and "large" that are familiar to most customers. Caribou's coffeehouses are designed with a focus on customer comfort and are modeled after mountain ski lodges and Alaskan cabins. Décor includes fireplaces, wooden ceiling beams, and comfortable furniture such as large chairs and sofas. They also provide a children's play area with toys and games, contributing to a family-friendly atmosphere.

In 2006 Caribou formed an alliance with Wandering WiFi to become the first coffee company to offer free WiFi service and the latest security technology to its customers. Wandering WiFi president, John Marshall believes that Caribou Coffee is committed to providing the most customer convenience, excellent coffee, and a comfortable atmosphere.

Caribou also formed an alliance with Apple Computer to offer a podcast version of an instant win game from Caribou's CEO Michael Coles, called "Wake Up and Smell the Music." In this game customers can win iTunes, iPods, and coffee. Michael Coles emphasizes the synergies between Apple and Caribou, calling them both "challenger brands" that offer desirable products and compete through innovation to provide a unique customer experience. In March 2006, Caribou provided free live music for customers in celebration of the first day of spring. Caribou has alliances with a number of other firms such as Frontier Airlines, USA Today, General Mills (Caribou Coffee Bars), Lifetime Fitness, Kemps (Caribou Coffee Ice Cream), and Mall of America. Finally, in January 2007 Caribou entered a partnership with Keurig, Inc., a leading manufacturer of single-cup coffee makers for home and office use. In the summer of 2007, Caribou Coffee and Coca-Cola launched new Caribou Coffee ready-to-drink products.

Caribou Coffee is dedicated to the environment. For example, in 1996 Caribou supported the Wilderness Society in its efforts to persuade Congress to protect the Arctic National

Wildlife Refuge by displaying petitions in the coffeehouses. More than 100,000 caribou travel to the refuge each spring to give birth to their young. Caribou Coffee also supported preservation efforts for the Boundary Waters Canoe Area and similar areas in U.S. national parks. In May 2007 the Rainforest Alliance awarded the Corporate Green Globe Award to Caribou Coffee for its efforts in utilizing "sustainably grown" coffee beans from Rainforest Alliance Certified farms. Caribou made the further commitment that half of its coffee will come from such farms in 2008 and beyond.

Because of its differentiation efforts Caribou Coffee continues to enjoy its success as the number 2 specialty coffee company in the United States, a position it intends to further solidify in the future. The company has positioned itself for expansion across multiple business channels as a base for profitable growth in the future.

Sources: S. Reeves, 2005, Caribou Coffee's robust IPO, *Forbes*, http://www.forbes.com/strategies, September 23; G. Hayes, 2006, Caribou Coffee offers free WiFi service for customers, Caribou Coffee, http://www.cariboucoffee.com, August 28; G. Hayes, 2006, Coffee CEO podcast relays power of branding and music, Caribou Coffee, http://www.cariboucoffee.com, March 16; 2007, Caribou Coffee Company plans for continued business expansion, 2006 operating highlights and 2007 guidance, *Business Wire*, January 8; 2000, A different kind of bottom line, *Wilderness*, May 23; 2007, Rainforest alliance bestows corporate green globe award on Caribou Coffee, *PR Newswire US*, May 22.

of specific market segments that can be targeted by a focus strategy include (1) a particular buyer group (e.g., youths or senior citizens), (2) a different segment of a product line (e.g., products for professional painters or the do-it-yourself group), or (3) a different geographic market (e.g., the East or the West in the United States).[88] Thus, the **focus strategy** is an integrated set of actions taken to produce goods or services that serve the needs of a particular competitive segment.

The **focus strategy** is an integrated set of actions taken to produce goods or services that serve the needs of a particular competitive segment.

To satisfy the needs of a certain size of company competing in a particular geographic market, firms often specialize, such as an investment bank.[89] Los Angeles–based investment banking firm Greif & Company positions itself as "The Entrepreneur's Investment Bank." Greif & Company is a leader in providing merger and acquisition advice to medium-sized businesses located in the western United States.[90] Goya Foods is the largest U.S.-based Hispanic-owned food company in the United States. Segmenting the Hispanic market into unique groups, Goya offers more than 1,500 products to consumers. The firm seeks "to be the be-all for the Latin community."[91] By successfully using a focus strategy, firms such as Greif & Company and Goya Foods gain a competitive advantage in specific market niches or segments, even though they do not possess an industry-wide competitive advantage.

Although the breadth of a target is clearly a matter of degree, the essence of the focus strategy "is the exploitation of a narrow target's differences from the balance of the industry."[92] Firms using the focus strategy intend to serve a particular segment of an industry more effectively than can industry-wide competitors. They succeed when they effectively serve a segment whose unique needs are so specialized that broad-based competitors choose not to serve that segment or when they satisfy the needs of a segment being served poorly by industry-wide competitors.[93]

Firms can create value for customers in specific and unique market segments by using the focused cost leadership strategy or the focused differentiation strategy.

Focused Cost Leadership Strategy

Based in Sweden, IKEA, a global furniture retailer with locations in 44 countries and sales revenue of $23.5 billion in 2006, follows the focused cost leadership strategy. The firm's vision is "Good design and function at low prices."[94] Young buyers desiring style at a low cost are IKEA's target customers.[95] For these customers, the firm offers home furnishings that combine good design, function, and acceptable quality with low prices. According to the firm, "Low cost is always in focus. This applies to every phase of our activities."[96]

IKEA emphasizes several activities to keep its costs low.[97] For example, instead of relying primarily on third-party manufacturers, the firm's engineers design low-cost,

IKEA, known for its low-priced home furnishings, has continued to distinguish itself using focused cost leadership strategies.

modular furniture ready for assembly by customers. To eliminate the need for sales associates or decorators, IKEA positions the products in its stores so that customers can view different living combinations (complete with sofas, chairs, tables, etc.) in a single room-like setting, which helps the customer imagine how a grouping of furniture will look in the home. A third practice that helps keep IKEA's costs low is requiring customers to transport their own purchases rather than providing delivery service.

Although it is a cost leader, IKEA also offers some differentiated features that appeal to its target customers, including its unique furniture designs, in-store playrooms for children, wheelchairs for customer use, and extended hours. IKEA believes that these services and products "are uniquely aligned with the needs of [its] customers, who are young, are not wealthy, are likely to have children (but no nanny), and, because they work, have a need to shop at odd hours."[98] Thus, IKEA's focused cost leadership strategy also includes some differentiated features with its low-cost products.

Focused Differentiation Strategy

Other firms implement the focused differentiation strategy. As noted earlier, firms can differentiate their products in many ways. The Internet furniture venture Casketfurniture.com, for example, targets Gen-Xers who are interested in using the Internet as a shopping vehicle and who want to buy items with multiple purposes. The company considers itself to be "The Internet's Leading Provider of Top Quality Furniture Products." Casketfurniture.com offers a collection of products, including display cabinets, coffee tables, and entertainment centers, that can be easily converted into coffins if desired. The firm also makes custom casket products for customers.[99]

An example of a specialty firm is a Chinese food restaurant. Interestingly, most Chinese food restaurants offer similar fare and thus end up competing largely on price. At least, these competitive conditions exist for Chinese restaurants in the San Gabriel Valley in California. It is so competitive that some restaurants send "spies" into their competitors' kitchens to gain information on their recipes and cooking practices. David Gong, owner of Alhambra's Kitchen believes that the "cutthroat" competition and price wars have reduced the quality of food served in many Chinese food restaurants (he is president of the American Chinese Restaurant Association). Gong's goal is to elevate the status of Chinese food. He hired a chef from Sydney, Australia, to be his food director for the restaurant. His focus is on preparing and serving the finest Chinese food possible. And his food has been rated by food critics as the finest in the San Gabriel Valley.[100]

With a focus strategy, firms must be able to complete various primary and support activities in a competitively superior manner to develop and sustain a competitive advantage and earn above-average returns. The activities required to use the focused cost leadership strategy are virtually identical to those of the industry-wide cost leadership strategy (Figure 4.3), and activities required to use the focused differentiation strategy are largely identical to those of the industry-wide differentiation strategy (Figure 4.4). Similarly, the manner in which each of the two focus strategies allows a firm to deal successfully with the five competitive forces parallels those of the two broad strategies. The only difference is in the firm's competitive scope; the firm focuses on a narrow industry segment. Thus, Figures 4.3 and 4.4 and the text regarding the five competitive forces also describe the relationship between each of the two focus strategies and competitive advantage.

Competitive Risks of Focus Strategies

With either focus strategy, the firm faces the same general risks as does the company using the cost leadership or the differentiation strategy, respectively, on an industry-wide basis. However, focus strategies have three additional risks.

First, a competitor may be able to focus on a more narrowly defined competitive segment and "outfocus" the focuser. For example, Confederate Motor Co. is producing a highly differentiated motorcycle that might appeal to some of Harley-Davidson's customers. Obsessed with making a "fiercely American motorcycle" (one that is even more American than Harley's products), Confederate's motorcycles are produced solely by hand labor. In fact, a full week is required to make a single bike. Digital technology is used to design Confederate's products, which have a radical appearance. At a price of $62,000 or above, the firm's products likely will appeal only to customers wanting to buy a truly differentiated product such as the new B120 Wraith introduced in 2007 (which is receiving "rave reviews in the motorcycling press").[101]

Confederate Motor Company's new B120 Wraith motorcycle is hand-manufactured and much different than its competitors' offerings.

Second, a company competing on an industry-wide basis may decide that the market segment served by the focus strategy firm is attractive and worthy of competitive pursuit. Consider the possibility that other manufacturers and marketers of women's clothing might determine that the profit potential in the narrow segment being served by Anne Fontaine is attractive. Companies such as Gap Inc., for example, have tried to design and market products that would compete with Anne Fontaine's product lines.

The third risk involved with a focus strategy is that the needs of customers within a narrow competitive segment may become more similar to those of industry-wide customers as a whole over time. As a result, the advantages of a focus strategy are either reduced or eliminated. At some point, for example, the needs of IKEA's customers for stylish furniture may dissipate, although their desire to buy relatively inexpensive furnishings may not. If this change in needs occurred, IKEA's customers might buy from large chain stores that sell more standardized furniture at low costs.

Integrated Cost Leadership/Differentiation Strategy

As stated earlier, many consumers have high expectations when purchasing a good or service. In a strategic context, these customers want to purchase low-priced, differentiated products. Because of these customer expectations, a number of firms engage in primary and support activities that allow them to simultaneously pursue low cost and differentiation. Firm's with this type of activity map use the **integrated cost leadership/differentiation strategy**. The objective of using this strategy is to efficiently produce products with differentiated attributes. Efficient production is the source of maintaining low costs while differentiation is the source of unique value. Firms that successfully use the integrated cost leadership/differentiation strategy usually adapt quickly to new technologies and rapid changes in their external environments. Simultaneously concentrating on developing two sources of competitive advantage (cost and differentiation) increases the number of primary and support activities in which the firm must become competent. Such firms often have strong networks with external parties that perform some of the primary and support activities.[102] In turn, having skills in a larger number of activities makes a firm more flexible.

The **integrated cost leadership/differentiation strategy** involves engaging in primary and support activities that allow a firm to simultaneously pursue low cost and differentiation.

Concentrating on the needs of its core customer group (higher-income, fashion-conscious discount shoppers), Target Stores uses an integrated cost leadership/differentiation strategy. The company's annual report describes this strategy: "Through careful nurturing and an intense focus on consistency and coordination throughout our organization, Target has built a strong, distinctive brand. At the core of our brand is our

Strategic Focus Strategic Focus Strategic Focus

Zara: Integrating Both Sides of the Coin

Zara is one of seven chains owned by Europe's largest specialty clothing company, Inditex SA of Spain. Early in 2007, Inditex received the Global Retailer of the Year award from the World Retail Congress. The first Zara store opened in 1975. It moved overseas about 1990. Currently Zara operates more than 1,000 stores located in 64 countries, including China and Russia.

Zara follows an integrated cost leadership differentiation strategy with its low-cost fashion goods.

Zara sells what has been referred to as "fast" fashion, or "disposable" fashion, fashion "on demand" and "fashion that you wear 10 times." It copies runway fashions and produces quality goods and sells them at affordable prices. The actual prices are market based. Zara determines the existing market price for a product, and then establishes a price below the lowest competitor's price for a similar product.

Zara is vertically integrated and controls its products from the design decision to the point of sale. This level of control allows Zara to keep the costs low. Designers closely monitor popular fashions, styles that celebrities are seen wearing, clothes worn on MTV, and so on. A just-in-time manufacturing system was implemented, and its most fashion sensitive items are produced internally. Zara has the ability to develop and begin manufacturing a new product line in three weeks compared to an industry average of nine months. Approximately 10,000 separate items are produced annually, all shipped directly from a central distribution center twice each week. Thus, no warehouses are needed because inventories are minimal. Only a limited number of products are shipped to its stores, to maintain the perception of scarcity. The most fashionable items are considered riskier and are produced in smaller quantities. The rapid product turnover also keeps customers coming back to the stores more frequently.

Zara locates attractive storefronts in prime locations in major shopping districts and designs them with the comfort of customers in mind. An emphasis on an attractive decor motivates customers to return frequently. Salespeople frequently change the location of items in the stores, which also contributes to the perception of scarcity. Information downloaded on a daily basis from each store enables designers to better monitor customer preferences.

Zara spends a relatively small amount on advertising—usually only for its end-of-season sales—compared to its major competitors such as Benetton, The Gap, and H&M of Sweden.

Sources: 2007, Zara, http://www.zara.com, July 5; 2007, Inditex, http://www.inditex.com, July 5; 2006, Inditex SA: Net climbs 22% amid cuts in costs, store openings, *Wall Street Journal*, December 14, B10; C. Rohwedder, 2006, Can Inditex stock stay as hip as its "fast fashion" clothes? *Wall Street Journal*, September 21, C14; L. Yaeger, 2003, Fete accompli, *Village Voice*, December 17, 12; 2003, Zara creates a ready to wear business: Leading fashion label designs its whole operation to fit the customer, *Strategic Direction*, November/December, 19(11): 24; L. Yaeger, 2002, Spring breaks, *Village Voice*, April 23, 14; B. Jones, 2001, Madrid: Zara pioneers fashion on demand, *Europe*, September, 43; 2001, Business: Floating on air, *Economist*, May 19, 56; C. Vitzthum, 2001, Just-in-time fashion—Spanish retailer Zara makes low-cost lines in weeks by running its own show, *Wall Street Journal*, May 18, B1.

commitment to deliver the right balance of differentiation and value through our 'Expect More. Pay Less' brand promise."[103] Target relies on its relationships with, among others, Sonia Kashuk in cosmetics, Mossimo in apparel, Eddie Bauer in camping and outdoor gear, and Michael Graves in home, garden, and electronics products to offer differentiated products at discounted prices. Committed to presenting a consistent upscale image, the firm has 1,500 stores in 47 states, including more than 175 SuperTarget stores that provide upscale grocery items. In addition most Target stores provide customers photo processing, a pharmacy, and Food Avenue restaurants.[104]

Evidence suggests a relationship between successful use of the integrated strategy and above-average returns.[105] Thus, firms able to produce relatively differentiated products at relatively low costs can expect to perform well.[106] Researchers have discovered that "businesses which combined multiple forms of competitive advantage outperformed businesses that only were identified with a single form."[107] Firms using this strategy must search for the appropriate balance between the two strategies. Because of trade-offs between the strategies, firms rarely can optimize both of them.[108]

Zara follows an integrated cost leadership/differentiation strategy. It offers current and desirable fashions goods at relatively low prices. To implement this strategy effectively requires sophisticated designers and effective means of managing costs, which well fits Zara's capabilities. Zara can design and begin manufacturing a new fashion in three weeks, which suggests a highly flexible organization that can adapt easily to changes in the market or with competitors.

Flexibility is required for firms to complete primary and support activities in ways that allow them to produce somewhat differentiated products at relatively low costs. Flexible manufacturing systems, information networks, and total quality management systems are three sources of flexibility that are particularly useful for firms trying to balance the objectives of continuous cost reductions and continuous enhancements to sources of differentiation as called for by the integrated strategy.

Flexible Manufacturing Systems

A flexible manufacturing system (FMS) increases the "flexibilities of human, physical, and information resources"[109] that the firm integrates to create relatively differentiated products at relatively low costs. A significant technological advance, FMS is a computer-controlled process used to produce a variety of products in moderate, flexible quantities with a minimum of manual intervention.[110] Often the flexibility is derived from modularization of the manufacturing process (and sometimes other value chain activities as well).[111]

The goal of an FMS is to eliminate the "low cost versus product variety" trade-off that is inherent in traditional manufacturing technologies. Firms use an FMS to change quickly and easily from making one product to making another.[112] Used properly, an FMS allows the firm to respond more effectively to changes in its customers' needs, while retaining low-cost advantages and consistent product quality.[113] Because an FMS also enables the firm to reduce the lot size needed to manufacture a product efficiently, the firm's capacity to serve the unique needs of a narrow competitive scope is higher. In industries of all types, effective mixes of the firm's tangible assets (e.g., machines) and intangible assets (e.g., people's skills) facilitate implementation of complex competitive strategies, especially the integrated cost leadership/differentiation strategy.[114]

Information Networks

By linking companies with their suppliers, distributors, and customers, information networks provide another source of flexibility. These networks, when used effectively, help the firm to satisfy customer expectations in terms of product quality and delivery speed.[115] International subsidiaries also must draw on their parent firm's knowledge to effectively serve their customers (integrating the parent's knowledge with understanding of the local market and environment).[116]

Earlier, we discussed the importance of managing the firm's relationships with its customers in order to understand their needs. Customer relationship management (CRM) is one form of an information-based network process that firms use for this purpose.[117] An effective CRM system provides a 360-degree view of the company's relationship with customers, encompassing all contact points, business processes, and communication media and sales channels.[118] The firm can then use this information to determine the trade-offs its customers are willing to make between differentiated features and low cost—an assessment that is vital for companies using the integrated cost leadership/differentiation strategy.

Thus, to make comprehensive strategic decisions with effective knowledge of the organization's context, good information flow is essential. Better quality managerial decisions require accurate information on the firm's environment.[119]

Total Quality Management Systems

Total quality management (TQM) is a managerial innovation that emphasizes an organization's total commitment to the customer and to continuous improvement of every process through the use of data-driven, problem-solving approaches based on empowerment of employee groups and teams.

Total quality management (TQM) is a "managerial innovation that emphasizes an organization's total commitment to the customer and to continuous improvement of every process through the use of data-driven, problem-solving approaches based on empowerment of employee groups and teams."[120] Firms develop and use TQM systems in order to (1) increase customer satisfaction, (2) cut costs, and (3) reduce the amount of time required to introduce innovative products to the marketplace.[121] Most firms use TQM to improve product and service quality.[122] U.S. auto manufacturers have made progress using TQM in this way, but they "still lag behind some foreign competitors, primarily the Japanese, by most quality measures."[123]

Firms able to simultaneously reduce costs while enhancing their ability to develop innovative products increase their flexibility, an outcome that is particularly helpful to firms implementing the integrated cost leadership/differentiation strategy. Exceeding customers' expectations regarding quality is a differentiating feature, and eliminating process inefficiencies to cut costs allows the firm to offer that quality to customers at a relatively low price. Thus, an effective TQM system helps the firm develop the flexibility needed to spot opportunities to simultaneously increase differentiation and reduce costs. Yet, TQM systems are available to all competitors. So they may help firms maintain competitive parity, but rarely alone will they lead to a competitive advantage.[124]

Competitive Risks of the Integrated Cost Leadership/ Differentiation Strategy

The potential to earn above-average returns by successfully using the integrated cost leadership/differentiation strategy is appealing. However, it is a risky strategy, because firms find it difficult to perform primary and support activities in ways that allow them to produce relatively inexpensive products with levels of differentiation that create value for the target customer. Moreover, to properly use this strategy across time, firms must be able to simultaneously reduce costs incurred to produce products (as required by the cost leadership strategy) while increasing products' differentiation (as required by the differentiation strategy).

Firms that fail to perform the primary and support activities in an optimum manner become "stuck in the middle."[125] Being stuck in the middle means that the firm's cost structure is not low enough to allow it to attractively price its products and that its products are not sufficiently differentiated to create value for the target customer. These firms will not earn above-average returns and will earn average returns only when the structure of the industry in which it competes is highly favorable.[126] Thus, companies implementing the integrated cost leadership/differentiation strategy must be able to perform the primary and support activities in ways that allow them to produce products that offer the target customer some differentiated features at a relatively low cost/price. As explained earlier, Southwest Airlines follows this strategy and has avoided becoming stuck in the middle.

Firms can also become stuck in the middle when they fail to successfully implement *either* the cost leadership *or* the differentiation strategy. In other words, industry-wide competitors too can become stuck in the middle. Trying to use the integrated strategy is costly in that firms must pursue both low costs and differentiation. Firms may need to form alliances with other firms to achieve differentiation, yet alliance partners may extract prices for the use of their resources that make it difficult to be a cost leader.[127] Firms may be motivated to make acquisitions to maintain their differentiation through innovation or to add products to their portfolio not offered by competitors.[128] Recent research suggests that firms using "pure strategies," either cost leadership or differentiation, often outperform firms attempting to use a "hybrid strategy" (i.e., integrated cost leadership/differentiation strategy). But sometimes firms using integrated strategies also performed equally well as those using pure strategies. This research suggests the risky nature of using an integrated strategy.[129] However, the integrated strategy is becoming more common and perhaps necessary in many industries due to technological advances and global competition.

Summary

- A business-level strategy is an integrated and coordinated set of commitments and actions the firm uses to gain a competitive advantage by exploiting core competencies in specific product markets. Five business-level strategies (cost leadership, differentiation, focused cost leadership, focused differentiation, and integrated cost leadership/differentiation) are examined in the chapter.
- Customers are the foundation of successful business-level strategies. When considering customers, a firm simultaneously examines three issues: *who, what,* and *how.* These issues, respectively, refer to the customer groups to be served, the needs those customers have that the firm seeks to satisfy, and the core competencies the firm will use to satisfy customers' needs. Increasing segmentation of markets throughout the global economy creates opportunities for firms to identify more unique customer needs they can serve with one of the business-level strategies.
- Firms seeking competitive advantage through the cost leadership strategy produce no-frills, standardized products for an industry's typical customer. However, these low-cost products must be offered with competitive levels of differentiation. Above-average returns are earned when firms continuously emphasize efficiency such that their costs are lower than those of their competitors, while providing customers with products that have acceptable levels of differentiated features.
- Competitive risks associated with the cost leadership strategy include (1) a loss of competitive advantage to newer technologies, (2) a failure to detect changes in customers' needs, and (3) the ability of competitors to imitate the cost leader's competitive advantage through their own unique strategic actions.
- Through the differentiation strategy, firms provide customers with products that have different (and valued) features. Differentiated products must be sold at a cost that customers believe is competitive relative to the product's features as compared to the cost/feature combinations available from competitors' goods. Because of their uniqueness, differentiated goods or services are sold at a premium price. Products can be differentiated along any dimension that some customer group values. Firms using this strategy seek to differentiate their products from competitors' goods or services along as many dimensions as possible. The less similarity to competitors' products, the more buffered a firm is from competition with its rivals.
- Risks associated with the differentiation strategy include (1) a customer group's decision that the differences between the differentiated product and the cost leader's goods or services are no longer worth a premium price, (2) the inability of a differentiated product to create the type of value for which customers are willing to pay a premium price, (3) the ability of competitors to provide customers with products that have features similar to those of the differentiated product, but at a lower cost, and (4) the threat of counterfeiting, whereby firms produce a cheap "knockoff" of a differentiated good or service.
- Through the cost leadership and the differentiated focus strategies, firms serve the needs of a narrow competitive segment (e.g., a buyer group, product segment, or geographic area). This strategy is successful when firms have the core competencies required to provide value to a specialized market segment that exceeds the value available from firms serving customers on an industry-wide basis.
- The competitive risks of focus strategies include (1) a competitor's ability to use its core competencies to "outfocus" the focuser by serving an even more narrowly defined market segment, (2) decisions by industry-wide competitors to focus on a customer group's specialized needs, and (3) a reduction in differences of the needs between customers in a narrow market segment and the industry-wide market.
- Firms using the integrated cost leadership/differentiation strategy strive to provide customers with relatively low-cost products that also have valued differentiated features. Flexibility is required for the firm to learn how to use primary and support activities in ways that allow them to produce differentiated products at relatively low costs. The primary risk of this strategy is that a firm might produce products that do not offer sufficient value in terms of either low cost or differentiation. In such cases, the company is "stuck in the middle." Firms stuck in the middle compete at a disadvantage and are unable to earn more than average returns.

Review Questions

1. What is a business-level strategy?
2. What is the relationship between a firm's customers and its business-level strategy in terms of *who, what,* and *how*? Why is this relationship important?
3. What are the differences among the cost leadership, differentiation, focused cost leadership, focused differentiation, and integrated cost leadership/differentiation business-level strategies?
4. How can each one of the business-level strategies be used to position the firm relative to the five forces of competition in a way that helps the firm earn above-average returns?
5. What are the specific risks associated with using each business-level strategy?

Experiential Exercises

Exercise 1: Customer Needs and Stock Trading

Nearly 100 million Americans have investments in the stock market through shares of individual companies or positions in mutual funds. At its peak volume, the New York Stock Exchange trades more than 3.5 billion shares in a single day. Stock brokerage firms are the conduit to help individuals plan their portfolios and manage transactions. Given the scope of this industry, no single definition describes what customers consider to be "superior value" from a brokerage operation.

Part One

After forming small teams, the instructor will ask the teams to count off by threes. The teams will study three different brokerage firms, with team 1 examining Edward Jones (Web site: http://www.edwardjones.com), team 2 E*TRADE (ticker: ETFC), and team 3, Charles Schwab (ticker: SCHW).

Part Two

Each team should research its target company to answer the following questions:

- Describe the "who, what, and how" for your firm. How stable is this focus? How much have these elements changed in the past five years?
- Describe your firm's strategy.
- How does your firm's strategy offer protection against each of the five forces?

Part Three

In class, the instructor will ask two teams for each firm to summarize their results.

Then, the whole class will discuss which firm is most effective at meeting the needs of its customer base.

Exercise 2: Attribute Maps

How can companies better understand what customers really need? One helpful tool is the attribute map, described by McGrath and MacMillan in their 2000 book *The Entrepreneurial Mindset*. The map is a grid of product attributes and customer attitudes. On the vertical axis are different types of customer attitudes toward a specific product; these attitudes can be positive or negative. On the horizontal axis are product attributes that will affect the intensity of a customer's attitude. A simplified attribute map is shown here.

Product Attributes

Customer Attitude	Basic	Discriminator	Energizer
Positive	**Nonnegotiable.** Performs at least as well as competition.	**Differentiator.** Performs better than the competition where it really counts.	**Exciter.** Performs better than the competition.
Negative	**Tolerable.** Performs no worse than the competition.	**Dissatisfier.** Performs below competition.	**Enrager.** Must be corrected at any cost.

A *nonnegotiable* is a positive feature that is also expected as a 'given' by your customers.

A *differentiator* is a product attribute that is valued by customers and is not readily available from competitors.

An *exciter* is essentially a turbo-charged differentiator. Typically, this feature or attribute is so desirable that it often serves as a deal-closer in purchasing decisions.

A *tolerable* attribute is something that customers dislike but are willing to put up with.

A *dissatisfier* is a negative feature or attribute that is more intense than a tolerable. These attributes will gradually drive away customers.

Finally, an *enrager* is an attribute that leads to strong negative feelings about a product. Enragers will drive off customers quickly and have the potential to cripple or kill off demand for a specific product.

Part One

The instructor will ask for suggestions of commonly used products; shampoos, cell phone providers, and college bookstores are possible examples. After selecting a product category, the instructor will break the class into six teams: one team for every cell in the attribute map.

Part Two

Each team will brainstorm for 10 minutes in order to develop a list of product attributes for its cell in the attribute map. The instructor will ask for one person from each team to summarize its findings.

Part Three

Based on the completed attribute map, discuss the following questions:

- Do any products/companies seem to be competing solely on a basis of nonnegotiables? Is this strategy viable, or not?
- Has anyone had exciter or enrager experiences in this product category? How did these experiences affect future purchases in this area?
- If you were going to build a customer's "dream product" based on this map, what would it be? What steps can a company take to prevent a competitor from rolling out a duplicate good?

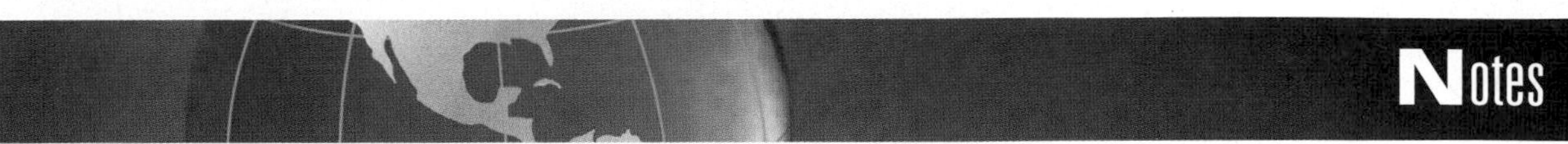

Notes

1. V. F. Misangyi, H. Elms, T. Greckhamer, & J. A. LePine, 2006, A new perspective on a fundamental debate: A multilevel approach to industry, corporate, and business unit effects, *Strategic Management Journal,* 27: 571–590; G. Gavetti & J. W. Rivkin, 2005, How strategists really think, *Harvard Business Review,* 83(4): 54–63.
2. G. Gavetti, D. A. Levinthal, & J. W. Rivkin, 2005, Strategy making in novel and complex worlds: The power of analogy, *Strategic Management Journal,* 26: 691–712.
3. S. Elbanna & J. Child, 2007, The influence of decision, environmental and firm characteristics on the rationality of strategic decision-making, *Journal of Management Studies,* 44: 561–591; T. Yu & A. A. Cannella, Jr., 2007, Rivalry between multinational enterprises: An event history approach, *Academy of Management Journal,* 50: 665–686.
4. J. Tan & D. Tan, 2005, Environment-strategy co-evolution and co-alignment: A staged model of Chinese SOEs under transition, *Strategic Management Journal,* 26: 141–157.
5. P. Megicks, 2007, Levels of strategy and performance in UK small retail businesses, *Management Decision,* 45: 484–502; G. George, J. Wiklund, & S. A. Zahra, 2005, Ownership and the internationalization of small firms, *Journal of Management,* 31: 210–233.
6. E. Kim, D. Nam, & J. L. Stimpert, 2004, The applicability of Porter's generic strategies in the digital age: Assumptions, conjectures, and suggestions, *Journal of Management,* 30: 569–589; R. D. Ireland, M. A. Hitt, S. M. Camp, & D. L. Sexton, 2001, Integrating entrepreneurship and strategic management actions to create firm wealth, *Academy of Management Executive,* 15(1): 49–63.
7. K. Shimizu & M. A. Hitt, 2004, Strategic flexibility: Organizational preparedness to reverse ineffective strategic decisions, *Academy of Management Executive,* 18(4): 44–59.
8. D. J. Ketchen Jr., C. C. Snow, & V. L. Street, 2004, Improving firm performance by matching strategic decision-making processes to competitive dynamics, *Academy of Management Executive,* 18(4): 29–43.
9. Elbanna & Child, The influence of decision, environmental and firm characteristics on the rationality of strategic decision-making; J. J. Janney & G. G. Dess, 2004, Can real-options analysis improve decision-making? Promises and pitfalls, *Academy of Management Executive,* 18(4): 60–75.
10. R. D. Ireland & C. C. Miller, 2005, Decision-making and firm success, *Academy of Management Executive,* 18(4): 8–12.
11. J.R. Hough, 2006, Business segment performance redux: A multilevel approach, *Strategic Management Journal,* 27: 45-61; N. Park, J. M. Mezias, & J. Song, 2004, Increasing returns, strategic alliances, and the values of E-commerce firms, *Journal of Management,* 30: 7–27.
12. M. C. Mankins & R. Steele, 2005, Turning great strategy into great performance, *Harvard Business Review,* 83(7): 65–72; T. J. Douglas & J. A. Ryman, 2003, Understanding competitive advantage in the general hospital industry: Evaluating strategic competencies, *Strategic Management Journal,* 24: 333–347.
13. D. Lei & J. W. Slocum, 2005, Strategic and organizational requirements for competitive advantage, *Academy of Management Executive,* 19(1): 31–45.
14. B. M. Case, 2005, Irving firm to cut jobs, *Dallas Morning News,* July 23, D1, D9.
15. J. B. Barney & T. B. Mackey, 2005, Testing resource-based theory, in D. J. Ketchen Jr. & D. D. Bergh (eds.), *Research Methodology in Strategy and Management,* 2nd ed., London: Elsevier, 1–13.
16. C. B. Dobni & G. Luffman, 2003, Determining the scope and impact of market orientation profiles on strategy implementation and performance, *Strategic Management Journal,* 24: 577–585.
17. R. Priem, 2007, A consumer perspective on value creation, *Academy of Management Review,* 32: 219–235; R. Gulati & J. B. Oldroyd, 2005, The quest for customer focus, *Harvard Business Review,* 83(4): 92–101.
18. M. E. Porter, 1980, *Competitive Strategy,* New York: Free Press.
19. A. J. Slywotzky & J. Drzik, 2005, Countering the biggest risk of all, *Harvard Business Review,* 83(4): 78–88.
20. D. G. Sirmon, M. A. Hitt, & R. D. Ireland, 2007, Managing firm resources in dynamic environments to create value: Inside the black box, *Academy of Management Review,* 32: 273–292.
21. F. E. Webster Jr., A. J. Malter, & S. Ganesan, 2005, The decline and dispersion of marketing competence, *MIT Sloan Management Review,* 6(4): 35–43.
22. K. Allison & R. Waters, 2007, Hewlett-Packard comes back fighting, *Financial Times,* http://www.ft.com, April 29.
23. M. B. Lieberman & S. Asaba, 2006, Why do firms imitate each other? *Academy of Management Review,* 31: 366–385.
24. R. W. Coff, D. C. Coff, & R. Eastvold, 2006, The knowledge-leveraging paradox: How to achieve scale without making knowledge imitable, *Academy of Management Review,* 31: 452–465.
25. 2007, About us, Harrah's Entertainment, http://www.harrahs.com, July 1.
26. P. R. Berthon, L. F. Pitt, I. McCarthy, & S. M. Kates, 2007, When customers get clever: Managerial approaches to dealing with creative customers, *Business Horizons,* 50(1): 39–47; J. E. Blose, W. B. Tankersley, & L. R. Flynn, 2005, Managing service quality using data envelopment analysis, http://www.asq.org, June.
27. R. Dhar & R. Glazer, 2003, Hedging customers, *Harvard Business Review,* 81(5): 86–92.
28. 2005, Amazon.com, *Standard & Poor's Stock Report,* http://www.standardandpoors.com, June 25.
29. 2007, This is CEMEX, CEMEX, http://www.cemex.com, July 1.
30. 2003, Fitch Mexico assigns AA qualifications to certificates of CEMEX, *Emerging Markets Economy,* April 8, 3; L. Walker, 2001, Plugged in for maximum efficiency, *Washington Post,* June 20, G1, G4.
31. 2007, Our company, Barnes & Noble, Inc., http://www.barnesandnobleinc.com, July 1.
32. 2005, Amazon.com, *Standard & Poor's Stock Reports,* http://www.standardandpoors.com, July 16.

33. 2007, Amazon.com annual shareholders meeting, http://library.corporate-ir.net/library/97/976/97664/items/249939/2007_Shareholder.pdf June 14.
34. 2007, http://www.autos.msn.com, July 1.
35. G. Dowell, 2006, Product-line strategies of new entrants in an established industry: Evidence from the U.S. bicycle industry, *Strategic Management Journal,* 27: 959–979; A. Reed II & L. E. Bolton, 2005, The complexity of identity, *MIT Sloan Management Review,* 46(3): 18–22.
36. C. W. Lamb Jr., J. F. Hair Jr., & C. McDaniel, 2006, *Marketing,* 8th ed., Mason, OH: Thomson South-Western, 224; A. Dutra, J. Frary, & R. Wise, 2004, Higher-order needs drive new growth in mature consumer markets, *Journal of Business Strategy,* 25(5): 26–34.
37. A. Baur, S. P. Hehner, & G. Nederegger, 2003, Pharma for Fido, *The McKinsey Quarterly,* Number 2, 7–10.
38. S. S. Hassan & S. H. Craft, 2005, Linking global market segmentation decisions with strategic positioning options, *Journal of Consumer Marketing,* 22(2/3): 81–88.
39. S. Hamner, 2005, Filling the Gap, *Business 2.0,* July, 30.
40. 2003, Unions and Gen-X: What does the future hold? *HR Focus,* March, 3; F. Marshall, 2003, Storehouse wakes up to Gen-X employees, *Furniture Today,* February 10, 2–3; J. Pereira, 2003, Best on the street, *Wall Street Journal,* May 12, R7; C. Burritt, 2001, Aging boomers reshape resort segment, *Lodging Hospitality,* 57(3): 31–32; J. D. Zbar, 2001, On a segmented dial, digital cuts wire finer, *Advertising Age,* 72(16): S12.
41. P. D. Ellis, 2006, Market orientation and performance: A meta-analysis and cross-national comparisons, *Journal of Management Studies,* 43: 1089–1107; J. P. Womack, 2005, Lean consumption, *Harvard Business Review,* 83(3): 58–68.
42. A. Panjwani, 2005, Open source vs. proprietary software: The pluses and minuses, *The Financial Express online,* http://www.financialexpress.com, May 2.
43. M. E. Raynor & H. S. Weinberg, 2004, Beyond segmentation, *Marketing Management,* 13(6): 22–29.
44. W. Reinartz, J. S. Thomas, & V. Kumar, 2005, Balancing acquisition and retention resources to maximize customer profitability, *Journal of Marketing,* 69: 63–85.
45. D. Foust, F. F. Jespersen, F. Katzenberg, A. Barrett, & R. O. Crockett, 2003, The best performers, *BusinessWeek Online,* http://www.businessweek.com, March 24.
46. M. J. Silverstein & N. Fiske, 2003, Luxury for the masses, *Harvard Business Review,* 81(4): 48–57.
47. C. W. L. Hill & F. T. Rothaermel, 2003, The performance of incumbent firms in the face of radical technological innovation, *Academy of Management Review,* 28: 257–274; A. W. King, S. W. Fowler, & C. P. Zeithaml, 2001, Managing organizational competencies for competitive advantage: The middle-management edge, *Academy of Management Executive,* 15(2): 95–106.
48. 2007, SAS Institute, http://www.sas.com, July 2.
49. 2007, Vans warped tour, http://www.vans.com; A. Weintraub & G. Khermouch, 2001, Chairman of the board, *BusinessWeek,* May 28, 94.
50. P. B. Barger & A. A. Grandry, 2006, Service with a smile and encounter satisfaction: Emotional contagion and appraisal mechanisms, *Academy of Management Journal,* 49: 1229–1238; L. L. Berry, E. A. Wall, & L. P. Carbone, 2006, Service clues and customer assessment of the service experience, *Academy of Management Perspective,* 20(2): 43–57.
51. M. E. Porter, 1985, *Competitive Advantage,* New York: Free Press, 26.
52. M. E. Porter, 1996, What is strategy? *Harvard Business Review,* 74(6): 61–78.
53. S. Warren & E. Perez, 2005, Southwest's net rises by 41%; Delta lifts cap on some fares, *Wall Street Journal Online,* http://www.wsj.com, July 15.
54. D. Cameron, 2007, Southwest seeks new sources of revenue, *Financial Times,* http://www.ft.com, April 19.
55. Porter, What is strategy?
56. C. Zott, 2003, Dynamic capabilities and the emergence of intraindustry differential firm performance: Insights from a simulation study, *Strategic Management Journal,* 24: 97–125.
57. M. E. Porter, 1994, Toward a dynamic theory of strategy, in R. P. Rumelt, D. E. Schendel, & D. J. Teece (eds.), *Fundamental Issues in Strategy,* Boston: Harvard Business School Press, 423–461.
58. Porter, What is strategy?, 62.
59. Porter, *Competitive Advantage,* 15.
60. G. G. Dess, G. T. Lumpkin, & J. E. McGee, 1999, Linking corporate entrepreneurship to strategy, structure, and process: Suggested research directions, *Entrepreneurship: Theory & Practice,* 23(3): 85–102; P. M. Wright, D. L. Smart, & G. C. McMahan, 1995, Matches between human resources and strategy among NCAA basketball teams, *Academy of Management Journal,* 38: 1052–1074.
61. Porter, *Competitive Strategy,* 35–40.
62. D. Mehri, 2006, The dark side of lean: An insider's perspective on the realities of the Toyota production system, *Academy of Management Perspectives,* 20(2): 21–42.
63. D. F. Spulber, 2004, *Management Strategy,* New York: McGrawHill/Irwin, 175.
64. 2007, Greyhound Lines, Inc. fact sheet, Hoovers, http://www.hoovers.com/greyhound, July 3; K. Yung, 2005, Greyhound taking new direction, *Dallas Morning News,* http://www.dallasnews.com, June 26.
65. D. F. Lynch, S. B. Keller, & J. Ozment, 2000, The effects of logistics capabilities and strategy on firm performance, *Journal of Business Logistics,* 21(2): 47–68.
66. P. Edwards & M. Ram, 2006, Surviving on the margins of the economy: Working relationships in small, low-wage firms, *Journal of Management Studies,* 43: 895–916.
67. 2005, Big Lots, *Standard & Poor's Stock Reports,* http://www.standardandpoors.com, July 16.
68. 2007, Big Lots, Inc, Hoovers profile, http://www.answers.com, July 3; 2005, Big Lots Inc. names Steve Fishman chairman, chief executive officer, and president, *Reuters,* http://www.reuters.com, June 10.
69. L. K. Johnson, 2003, Dueling pricing strategies, *The McKinsey Quarterly,* 44(3): 10–11.
70. A. D'Innocenzio, 2001, We are paranoid, *Richmond Times-Dispatch,* June 10, E1, E2.
71. A. Bianco, 2007, Wal-Mart's midlife crisis, *BusinessWeek,* April 30: 46-56; M. Maier, 2005, How to beat Wal-Mart, *Business 2.0,* May, 108–114.
72. D. Lavie, 2006, The competitive advantage of interconnected firms: An extension of the resource-based view, *Academy of Management Review,* 31: 638–658.
73. J. Bercovitz & W. Mitchell, 2007, When is more better? The impact of business scale and scope on long-term business survival, while controlling for profitability, *Strategic Management Journal,* 28: 61–79.
74. Bianco, Wal-Mart's midlife crisis.
75. Porter, *Competitive Strategy,* 35–40.
76. D. Ashmos Plowman, L. T. Baker, T. E. Beck, M. Kulkarni, S. Thomas-Solansky, & D. V. Travis, 2007, Radical change accidentally: The emergence and amplification of small change, *Academy of Management Journal,* 50: 515–543; A. Wadhwa & S. Kotha, 2006, Knowledge creation through external venturing: Evidence from the telecommunications equipment manufacturing industry, *Academy of Management Journal,* 49: 819–835.
77. M. J. Benner, 2007, The incumbent discount: Stock market categories and response to radical technological change, *Academy of Management Review,* 32:703–720.
78. F. T. Rothaermel, M. A. Hitt, & L. A. Jobe, 2006, Balancing vertical integration and strategic outsourcing: Effects on product portfolio, product success and firm performance, *Strategic Management Journal,* 27: 1033–1056; A. V. Mainkar, M. Lubatkin, & W. S. Schulze, 2006, Toward a product-proliferation theory of entry barriers, *Academy of Management Review,* 31: 1062–1075.
79. Porter, *Competitive Advantage,* 14.
80. 2007, History, http://www.roberttalbott.com, July 3.
81. W. C. Bogner & P. Bansal, 2007, Knowledge management as a basis for sustained high performance, *Journal of Management Studies,* 44:165–188; M. Semadeni, 2006, Minding your distance: How management consulting firms use service marks to position competitively, *Strategic Management Journal,* 27: 169–187.
82. J. A. Byrne, 2005, The power of great design, *Fast Company,* June, 14.
83. W. Mossberg, 2007, iPod, iPhone, iTunes, Apple tv: Where Steve Jobs sees them all

heading, *Wall Street Journal,* http://www.online.wsj.com, June 18; J. Scanlon, 2007, Apple sets the design standard, *BusinessWeek,* http://www.businessweek.com, January 8.

84. V. P. Rindova, T. G. Pollock, & M. A. Hayward, 2006, Celebrity firms: The social construction of market popularity, *Academy of Management Review,* 31: 50–71.
85. F. K. Pil & S. K. Cohen, 2006, Modularity: Implications for imitation, innovation, and sustained advantage, *Academy of Management Review,* 31: 995–1011.
86. Barney, *Gaining and Sustaining Competitive Advantage,* 268.
87. N. Stieglitz & K. Heine, 2007, Innovations and the role of complementarities in a strategic theory of the firm, *Strategic Management Journal,* 28: 1–15; S. K. Ethiraj, 2007, Allocation of inventive effort in complex product systems, *Strategic Management Journal,* 28: 563–584.
88. Porter, *Competitive Strategy,* 98.
89. A. V. Shipilov, 2006, Network strategies and performance of Canadian investment banks, *Academy of Management Journal,* 49: 590–604.
90. 2007, Greif & Co., http://www.greifco.com, July 4.
91. 2007, About Goya foods, http://www.goyafoods.com, July 4; D. Kaplan, 2005, Lots of food for diverse culture, *Houston Chronicle,* July 19, D2.
92. Porter, *Competitive Advantage,* 15.
93. Ibid., 15–16.
94. 2007, About IKEA, http://www.ikeagroup.ikea.com/corporate, July 4.
95. K. Kling & I. Goteman, 2003, IKEA CEO Andres Dahlvig on international growth and IKEA's unique corporate culture and brand identity, *Academy of Management Executive,* 17(1): 31–37.
96. About IKEA, http://www.ikeagroup.ikea.com/corporate.
97. P. Szuchman, 2005, Can this kitchen be saved? *Wall Street Journal Online,* http://www.wsj.com, April 29.
98. G. Evans, 2003, Why some stores strike me as special, *Furniture Today,* 27(24): 91; Porter, What is strategy?, 65.
99. 2007, About Casket Furniture, http://www.casketfurniture.com, July 4.
100. D. Pierson, 2007, An experiment in Alhambra's Kitchen, *Los Angeles Times,* http://www.latimes.com, April 22.
101. 2007, The art of rebellion, http://www.confederate.com, July 4; 2006, Paparazzi magnet, *Los Angeles Times,* December 20, G1–G2; B. Breen, 2005, Rebel yell, *Fast Company,* August, 60–61.
102. J. H. Dyer & N. W. Hatch, 2006, Relation-specific capabilities and barriers to knowledge transfers: Creating advantage through network relationships, *Strategic Management Journal,* 27: 701–719.
103. 2006, Annual Report, Target Corporation, http://www.target.com, July 5.
104. 2007, Target, http://www.target.com, July 5; 2001, The engine that drives differentiation, *DSN Retailing Today,* April 2, 52.
105. Dess, Lumpkin, & McGee, Linking corporate entrepreneurship to strategy, 89.
106. P. Ghemawat, 2001, *Strategy and the Business Landscape,* Upper Saddle River, NJ: Prentice Hall, 56.
107. Dess, Gupta, Hennart, & Hill, Conducting and integrating strategy research, 377.
108. M. L. Barnett, 2006, Finding a working balance between competitive and communal strategies, *Journal of Management Studies,* 43: 1753–1773.
109. R. Sanchez, 1995, Strategic flexibility in product competition, *Strategic Management Journal,* 16 (Special Issue): 140.
110. A. Faria, P. Fenn, & A. Bruce, 2005, Production technologies and technical efficiency: Evidence from Portuguese manufacturing industry, *Applied Economics,* 37: 1037–1046.
111. M. Kotabe, R. Parente, & J. Y. Murray, 2007, Antecedents and outcomes of modular production in the Brazilian automobile industry: A grounded theory approach, *Journal of International Business Studies,* 38: 84–106.
112. J. Baljko, 2003, Built for speed—When putting the reams of supply chain data they've amassed to use, companies are discovering that agility counts, *EBN,* 1352: 25–28.
113. E. K. Bish, A. Muriel, & S. Biller, 2005, Managing flexible capacity in a make-to-order environment, *Management Science,* 51: 167–180.
114. S. M. Iravani, M. P. van Oyen, & K. T. Sims, 2005, Structural flexibility: A new perspective on the design of manufacturing and service operations, *Management Science,* 51: 151–166.
115. F. Mattern, S. Schonwalder, & W. Stein, 2003, Fighting complexity in IT, *The McKinsey Quarterly,* no. 1, 57–65.
116. M. A. Lyles & J. E. Salk, 2007, Knowledge acquisition from foreign parents in international joint ventures: An empirical examination in the Hungarian context, *Journal of International Business Studies,* 38: 3–18.
117. S. W. Brown, 2003, The employee experience, *Marketing Management,* 12(2): 12–13.
118. S. Isaac & R. N. Tooker, 2001, The many faces of CRM, *LIMRA's MarketFacts Quarterly,* 20(1): 84–89.
119. D. P. Forbes, 2007, Reconsidering the strategic implications of decision comprehensiveness, *Academy of Management Review,* 32: 361–376.
120. J. D. Westphal, R. Gulati, & S. M. Shortell, 1997, Customization or conformity: An institutional and network perspective on the content and consequences of TQM adoption, *Administrative Science Quarterly,* 42: 366–394.
121. V. W. S. Yeung & R. W. Armstrong, 2003, A key to TQM benefits: Manager involvement in customer processes, *International Journal of Services Technology and Management,* 4(1): 14–29.
122. D. Welch, K. Kerwin, & C. Tierney, 2003, Way to go, Detroit—Now go a lot farther, *BusinessWeek,* May 26, 44.
123. N. Ganguli, T. V. Kumaresh, & A. Satpathy, 2003, Detroit's new quality gap, *The McKinsey Quarterly,* no. 1, 148–151.
124. R. J. David & S. Strang, 2006, When fashion is fleeting: Transitory collective beliefs and the dynamics of TQM consulting, *Academy of Management Journal,* 49: 215–233.
125. Porter, *Competitive Advantage,* 16.
126. Ibid., 17.
127. M. A. Hitt, L. Bierman, K. Uhlenbruck, & K. Shimizu, 2006, The importance of resources in the internationalization of professional service firms: The good, the bad, and the ugly, *Academy of Management Journal,* 49: 1137–1157.
128. P. Puranam, H. Singh, & M. Zollo, 2006, Organizing for innovation: Managing the coordination-autonomy dilemma in technology acquisitions, *Academy of Management Journal,* 49: 263–280.
129. S. Thornhill & R. E. White, 2007, Strategic purity: A multi-industry evaluation of pure vs. hybrid business strategies, *Strategic Management Journal,* 28: 553–561.

Competitive Rivalry and Competitive Dynamics

Studying this chapter should provide you with the strategic management knowledge needed to:

1. Define competitors, competitive rivalry, competitive behavior, and competitive dynamics.
2. Describe market commonality and resource similarity as the building blocks of a competitor analysis.
3. Explain awareness, motivation, and ability as drivers of competitive behavior.
4. Discuss factors affecting the likelihood a competitor will take competitive actions.
5. Discuss factors affecting the likelihood a competitor will respond to actions taken against it.
6. Explain competitive dynamics in slow-cycle, fast-cycle, and standard-cycle markets.

Competition Between Hewlett-Packard and Dell: The Battle Rages On

© AP Photo/Matt Slocum

"I'm going to be the CEO for the next several years. We're going to fix this business." Michael Dell's words suggest that Dell Inc.'s founder and newly reinstalled CEO intends to do everything he can to correct the problems that led to the loss of the position as the top seller of personal computers (PCs) on a global basis. Indeed, at the close of 2006, Hewlett-Packard (HP) commanded 18.1 percent of the global PC market while Dell's share slipped to 14.7 percent. The market share loss seemingly contributed to the 32 percent total decline in the value of Dell Inc.'s stock during 2005 and 2006. (HP's stock doubled in value over the same time period.)

The performance declines were a new experience for Dell, which grew from an initial $1,000 investment in 1984 to a $56 billion dollar business in 2007. Dell's growth was founded on a "stroke of genius—to bypass the middle-man and sell custom-built computers directly to the consumer." Some analysts consider this approach, which became known as the "Dell Way," to be "one of the revolutionary business models of the late 20th century." But this approach no longer creates value to the degree that has been the case historically. The reasons for the change flow out of a tale of competitive actions and competitive reactions.

Over time, Dell and its competitive actions focused on finding ways to use its business model to continuously lower its costs and hence the prices of its products. Concentrating on a single business model can lead to quick growth when demand for a firm's products continues to expand. Across time though, innovation and reinvention are the foundation for continued success.

Over the past several years, HP found ways to innovate and reinvent itself. After examining its business model, Todd Bradely, the executive who now heads HP's PC operations, concluded that "HP was fighting on the wrong battlefield. HP was concentrating its resources to fight Dell where Dell was strong, in direct sales over the Internet and phone. Instead (Bradely) decided, HP should focus on its strength, retail stores, where Dell had no presence at all." To successfully change its focus, HP developed close relationships with retailers, even trying to "personalize" PCs. Consistent with a "The Computer Is Personal Again" campaign, HP features celebrities (e.g., fashion designer Vera Wang and hip-hop mogul Jay-Z) in its advertisements and is producing unique products for different retailers. For example, HP worked with Best Buy to design and produce a white-and-silver notebook computer. Aimed at attracting female customers, this machine was priced at $1,100 and was one of Best Buy's top-selling notebooks during the 2006 holiday season.

Dell's decision to venture into retail selling is a competitive reaction to HP's actions. Dell is now partnering with a Japanese retailer (Bic Camera Inc.) to sell notebooks and desktops throughout Japan. Additionally, Dell is experimenting with its own retail stores, opening its first one in Dallas, Texas, in July 2007. (Other Dell retail outlets are in the planning stages.) Dell is also committing additional monies to research and development (to find product innovations) and is restructuring some of its advertising campaigns "to remind consumers of the benefits of customizing computers."

Sources: M. Bartiromo, 2007, Will Dell be a comeback kid? *BusinessWeek*, February 26, 128; N. Byrnes & P. Burrows, 2007, Where Dell went wrong, *BusinessWeek*, February 19, 62–66; C. Lawton, 2007, How H-P reclaimed its PC lead over Dell, *Wall Street Journal Online*, http://online.wsj.com/article, June 5; L. Lee & P. Burrows, 2007, Is Dell too big for Michael Dell? *BusinessWeek*, February 12, 33; R. Mullins, 2007, Dell goes retail in Japan, *PCWorld*, http://www.pcworld.com, July 28.

Competitors are firms operating in the same market, offering similar products, and targeting similar customers.

Firms operating in the same market, offering similar products, and targeting similar customers are **competitors.**[1] Southwest Airlines, Delta, United, Continental, and JetBlue are competitors, as are PepsiCo and Coca-Cola Company. As described in the Opening Case, Dell Inc. and Hewlett-Packard (HP) are competitors who are actively engaging each other in competitive battles. Even though Dell's "build-to-order" business model served it well for many years, it seems that adjustments to this model are necessary because of the recent success of competitors such as HP. At a minimum, Dell's CEO, Michael Dell, says that his firm is "looking to expand services (and is) likely to do more internationally"[2] in order to improve its competitive position.

Firms interact with their competitors as part of the broad context within which they operate while attempting to earn above-average returns.[3] The decisions firms make about their interactions with their competitors significantly affect their ability to earn above-average returns.[4] Because 80 to 90 percent of new firms fail, learning how to select the markets in which to compete and how to best compete within them is highly important.[5]

Competitive rivalry is the ongoing set of competitive actions and competitive responses that occur among firms as they maneuver for an advantageous market position.

Competitive rivalry is the ongoing set of competitive actions and competitive responses that occur among firms as they maneuver for an advantageous market position.[6] Especially in highly competitive industries, firms constantly jockey for advantage as they launch strategic actions and respond or react to rivals' moves.[7] It is important for those leading organizations to understand competitive rivalry, in that "the central, brute empirical fact in strategy is that some firms outperform others,"[8] meaning that competitive rivalry influences an individual firm's ability to gain and sustain competitive advantages.[9]

Competitive behavior is the set of competitive actions and competitive responses the firm takes to build or defend its competitive advantages and to improve its market position.

Multimarket competition occurs when firms compete against each other in several product or geographic markets.

Competitive dynamics refer to all competitive behaviors—that is, the total set of actions and responses taken by all firms competing within a market.

A sequence of firm-level moves, rivalry results from firms initiating their own competitive actions and then responding to actions taken by competitors. **Competitive behavior** is the set of competitive actions and competitive responses the firm takes to build or defend its competitive advantages and to improve its market position.[10] Through competitive behavior, the firm tries to successfully position itself relative to the five forces of competition (see Chapter 2) and to defend current competitive advantages while building advantages for the future (see Chapter 3). Increasingly, competitors engage in competitive actions and responses in more than one market.[11] Firms competing against each other in several product or geographic markets are engaged in **multimarket competition.**[12] All competitive behavior—that is, the total set of actions and responses taken by all firms competing within a market—is called **competitive dynamics**. The relationships among these key concepts are shown in Figure 5.1.

This chapter focuses on competitive rivalry and competitive dynamics. The essence of these important topics is that a firm's strategies are dynamic in nature. Actions taken by one firm elicit responses from competitors that, in turn, typically result in responses from the firm that took the initial action.[13] As explained in the Opening Case, this sequence of action and reaction is occurring between Dell and HP. To change how it competes with Dell, HP developed highly personalized relationships with retailers selling its PCs. Noting that customers were responding favorably to the opportunity to personally "touch" and

Figure 5.1 From Competitors to Competitive Dynamics

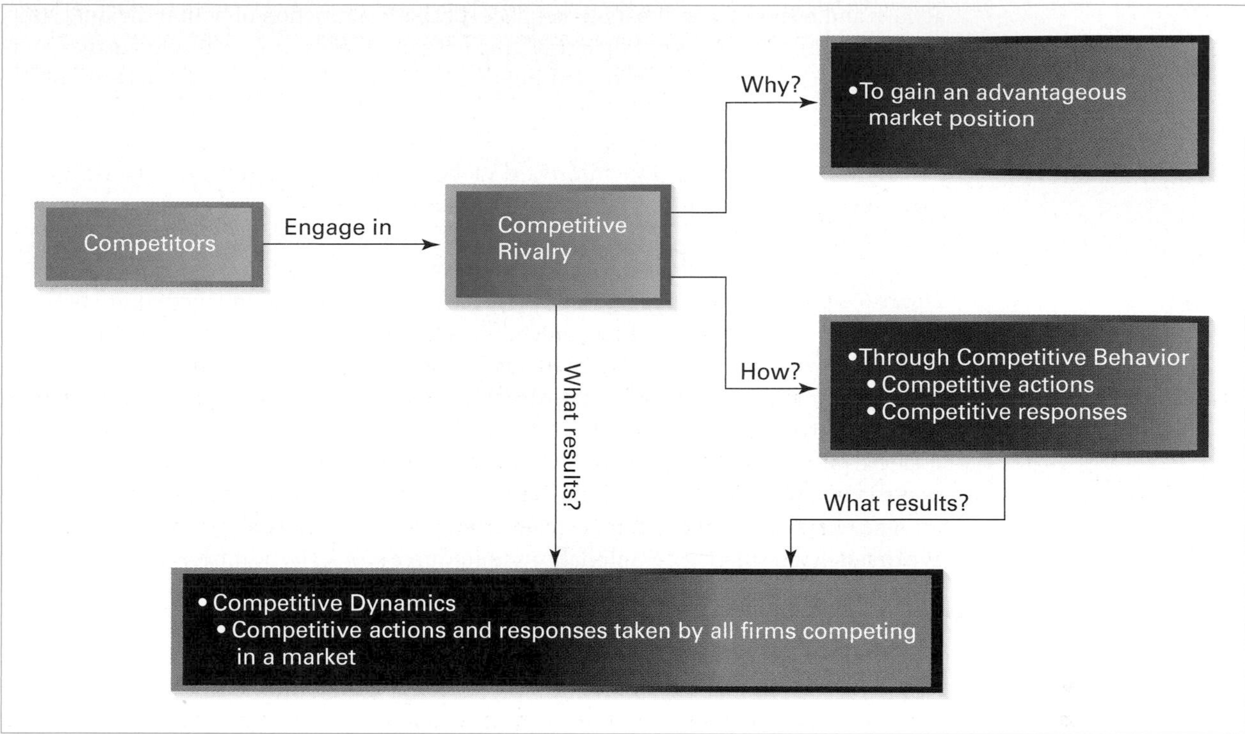

Source: Adapted from M. J. Chen, 1996, Competitor analysis and interfirm rivalry: Toward a theoretical integration, *Academy of Management Review*, 21: 100–134.

"interact" with a PC prior to making a purchase decision, Dell starting experimenting with its own retail outlets and decided to sell its PCs through retailers including 3,500 Wal-Mart stores located in Canada and the United States.[14]

Another way of highlighting competitive rivalry's effect on the firm's strategies is to say that a strategy's success is determined not only by the firm's initial competitive actions but also by how well it anticipates competitors' responses to them *and* by how well the firm anticipates and responds to its competitors' initial actions (also called attacks).[15] Although competitive rivalry affects all types of strategies (e.g., corporate-level, acquisition, and international), its most dominant influence is on the firm's business-level strategy or strategies. Indeed, firms' actions and responses to those of their rivals are the basic building block of business-level strategies.[16] Recall from Chapter 4 that business-level strategy is concerned with what the firm does to successfully use its competitive advantages in specific product markets. In the global economy, competitive rivalry is intensifying,[17] meaning that the significance of its effect on firms' business-level strategies is increasing. Rivalry is intensifying in the flat panel television market, for example. One reason is the price competition created by the price cuts of up to 40 percent below the leading brands' products by firms such as Westinghouse and Maxent.[18] However, firms that develop and use effective business-level strategies tend to outperform competitors in individual product markets, even when experiencing intense competitive rivalry that price cuts bring about.[19]

A Model of Competitive Rivalry

Over time, firms take many competitive actions and responses. As noted earlier, competitive rivalry evolves from this pattern of actions and responses as one firm's competitive actions have noticeable effects on competitors, eliciting competitive responses from them.[20]

This pattern shows that firms are mutually interdependent, that they feel each other's actions and responses, and that marketplace success is a function of both individual strategies and the consequences of their use.[21] Increasingly, too, executives recognize that competitive rivalry can have a major and direct effect on the firm's financial performance:[22] Research shows that intensified rivalry within an industry results in decreased average profitability for the competing firms.[23]

Figure 5.2 presents a straightforward model of competitive rivalry at the firm level; this type of rivalry is usually dynamic and complex.[24] The competitive actions and responses the firm takes are the foundation for successfully building and using its capabilities and core competencies to gain an advantageous market position.[25] The model in Figure 5.2 presents the sequence of activities commonly involved in competition between a particular firm and each of its competitors. Companies can use the model to understand how to be able to predict competitors' behavior (actions and responses) and reduce the uncertainty associated with competitors' actions.[26] Being able to predict competitors' actions and responses has a positive effect on the firm's market position and its subsequent financial performance.[27] The sum of all the individual rivalries modeled in Figure 5.2 that occur in a particular market reflects the competitive dynamics in that market.

The remainder of the chapter explains components of the model shown in Figure 5.2. We first describe market commonality and resource similarity as the building blocks of a competitor analysis. Next, we discuss the effects of three organizational characteristics—awareness, motivation, and ability—on the firm's competitive behavior. We then examine competitive rivalry between firms, or interfirm rivalry, in detail by describing the factors that affect the likelihood a firm will take a competitive action and the factors that affect the likelihood a firm will respond to a competitor's action. In the chapter's final section, we turn our attention to competitive dynamics to describe how market characteristics affect competitive rivalry in slow-cycle, fast-cycle, and standard-cycle markets.

Competitor Analysis

As previously noted, a competitor analysis is the first step the firm takes to be able to predict the extent and nature of its rivalry with each competitor. Recall that a competitor is a firm operating in the same market, offering similar products, and targeting similar customers. The number of markets in which firms compete against each other (called market commonality, defined on the following pages) and the similarity in their resources (called

Figure 5.2 A Model of Competitive Rivalry

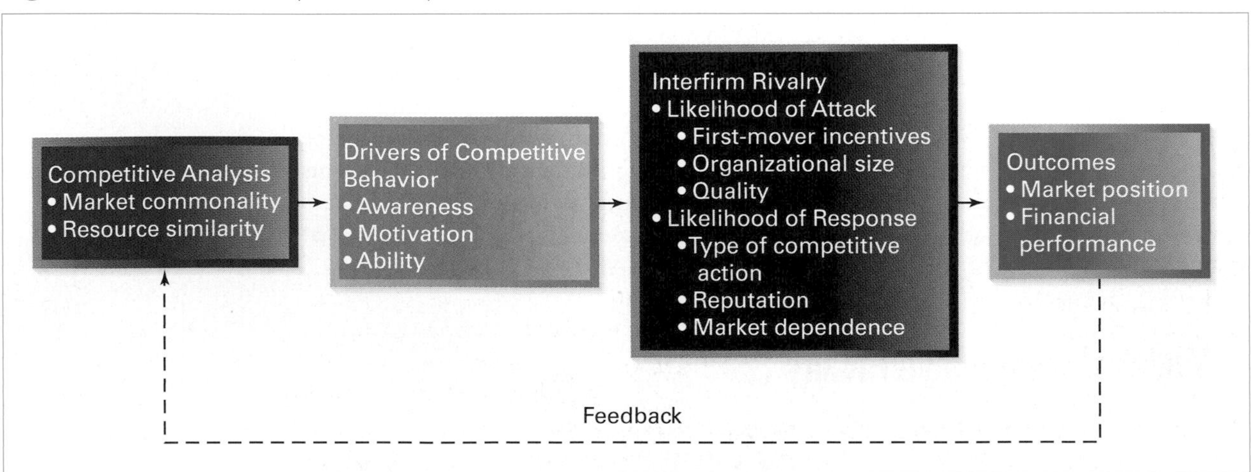

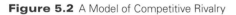

Source: Adapted from M. J. Chen, 1996, Competitor analysis and interfirm rivalry: Toward a theoretical integration, *Academy of Management Review*, 21: 100–134.

resource similarity, also defined in the following section) determine the extent to which the firms are competitors. Firms with high market commonality and highly similar resources are "clearly direct and mutually acknowledged competitors."[28] As is suggested in the Opening Case, Dell and HP are direct competitors as are Acer and Lenovo. The direct competition between Acer and Lenovo to claim the third largest share of the global PC market is quite intense with "Acer gaining ground thanks to low-cost machines and unconventional distribution" practices.[29] However, being direct competitors does not necessarily mean that the rivalry between the firms will be intense as is the case between Dell and HP and between Acer and Lenovo. The drivers of competitive behavior—as well as factors influencing the likelihood that a competitor will initiate competitive actions and will respond to its competitor's actions—influence the intensity of rivalry, even for direct competitors.[30]

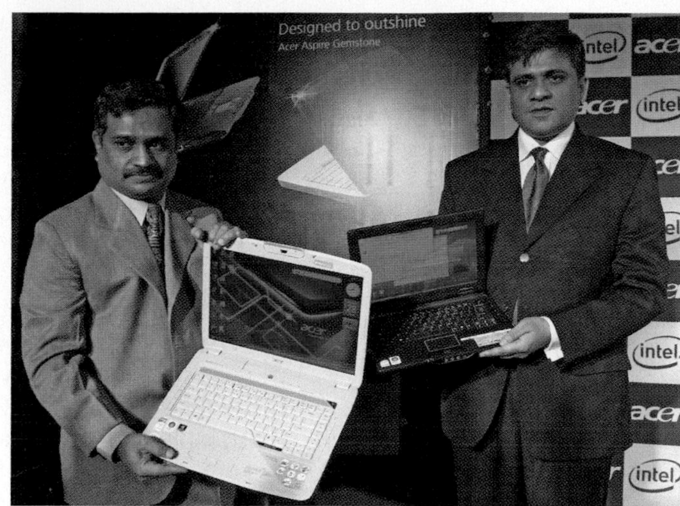

Lenova and Acer are intense competitors for the global market share of personal computers.

In Chapter 2, we discussed competitor analysis as a technique firms use to understand their competitive environment. Together, the general, industry, and competitive environments comprise the firm's external environment. We also described how competitor analysis is used to help the firm *understand* its competitors. This understanding results from studying competitors' future objectives, current strategies, assumptions, and capabilities (see Figure 2.3, on page 59). In this chapter, the discussion of competitor analysis is extended to describe what firms study to be able to *predict* competitors' behavior in the form of their competitive actions and responses. The discussions of competitor analysis in Chapter 2 and in this chapter are complementary in that firms must first *understand* competitors (Chapter 2) before their competitive actions and competitive responses can be *predicted* (this chapter).

Market Commonality

Each industry is composed of various markets. The financial services industry has markets for insurance, brokerage services, banks, and so forth. To concentrate on the needs of different, unique customer groups, markets can be further subdivided. The insurance market, for example, could be broken into market segments (such as commercial and consumer), product segments (such as health insurance and life insurance), and geographic markets (such as Western Europe and Southeast Asia). In general, the capabilities the Internet's technologies generate help to shape the nature of industries' markets along with the competition among firms operating in them.[31] For example, widely available electronic news sources affect how traditional print news distributors such as newspapers conduct their business.

Competitors tend to agree about the different characteristics of individual markets that form an industry.[32] For example, in the transportation industry, the understanding is that the commercial air travel market differs from the ground transportation market, which is served by such firms as YRC Worldwide (one of the largest transportation service providers in the world)[33] and major YRC competitors Arkansas Best, Con-way Inc., and FedEx Freight.[34] Although differences exist, most industries' markets are somewhat related in terms of technologies used or core competencies needed to develop a competitive advantage. For example, different types of transportation companies need to provide reliable and timely service. Commercial air carriers such as Southwest, Continental, and JetBlue must therefore develop service competencies to satisfy their passengers, while YRC and its major competitors must develop such competencies to serve the needs of those using their fleets to ship goods.

Market commonality is concerned with the number of markets with which the firm and a competitor are jointly involved and the degree of importance of the individual markets to each.

Firms sometimes compete against each other in several markets that are in different industries. This situation finds competitors coming into contact with each other several times, a condition called market commonality. More formally, **market commonality** is concerned with the number of markets with which the firm and a competitor are jointly involved and the degree of importance of the individual markets to each.[35] Firms competing against one another in several or many markets engage in multimarket competition.[36] McDonald's and Burger King compete against each other in multiple geographic markets across the world,[37] Prudential Insurance and Cigna Insurance Corporation compete against each other in several market segments (such as institutional and retail) as well as product markets (such as life insurance and health insurance),[38] and Anheuser-Busch Cos. and Dutch brewer Heineken compete in multiple global and product (i.e., premium and light beer) markets.[39] Airlines, chemicals, pharmaceuticals, and consumer foods are examples of other industries in which firms often simultaneously compete against each other in multiple markets.

Heineken faces market commonality on many fronts with its competitor Anheuser-Busch.

Firms competing in several markets have the potential to respond to a competitor's actions not only within the market in which the actions are taken, but also in other markets where they compete with the rival. This potential creates a complicated competitive mosaic in which "the moves an organization makes in one market are designed to achieve goals in another market in ways that aren't immediately apparent to its rivals."[40] This potential complicates the rivalry between competitors. In fact, research suggests that "a firm with greater multimarket contact is less likely to initiate an attack, but more likely to move (respond) aggressively when attacked."[41] Thus, in general, multimarket competition reduces competitive rivalry.[42]

Resource Similarity

Resource similarity is the extent to which the firm's tangible and intangible resources are comparable to a competitor's in terms of both type and amount.

Resource similarity is the extent to which the firm's tangible and intangible resources are comparable to a competitor's in terms of both type and amount.[43] Firms with similar types and amounts of resources are likely to have similar strengths and weaknesses and use similar strategies.[44] The competition between FedEx and United Parcel Service (UPS) to find the most effective ways to use information technology to improve the efficiency of their operations and to reduce costs demonstrates these expectations. Pursuing similar strategies that are supported by similar resource profiles, personnel in these firms work at a feverish pace to receive, sort, and ship packages. At a UPS hub, for example, "workers have less than four hours (on a peak night) to process more than a million packages from at least 100 planes and probably 160 trucks."[45] (FedEx employees face the same receiving, sorting, and shipping challenges.) FedEx and UPS are both spending more than $1 billion annually on research and development (R&D) to find ways to improve efficiency and reduce costs. According to an analyst, these firms engage in such R&D because "when you handle millions of packages, a minute's delay can cost a fortune."[46]

When performing a competitor analysis, a firm analyzes each of its competitors in terms of market commonality and resource similarity. The results of these analyses can be mapped for visual comparisons. In Figure 5.3, we show different hypothetical intersections between the firm and individual competitors in terms of market commonality and resource similarity. These intersections indicate the extent to which the firm and those with which it is compared are competitors. For example, the firm and its competitor displayed in quadrant I of Figure 5.3 have similar types and amounts of resources (i.e., the two firms have a similar portfolio of resources). The firm and its competitor in quadrant I would use their similar resource portfolios

Figure 5.3 A Framework of Competitor Analysis

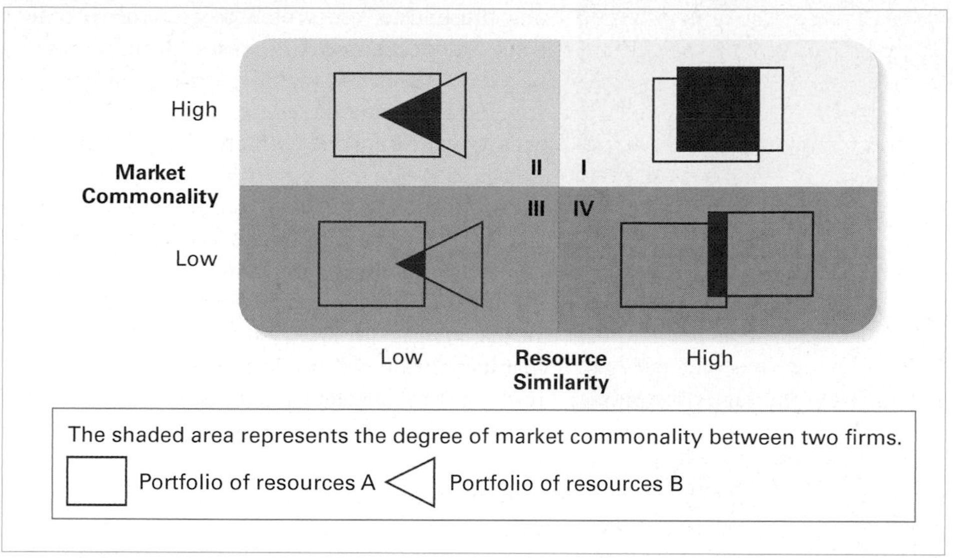

Source: Adapted from M. J. Chen, 1996, Competitor analysis and interfirm rivalry: Toward a theoretical integration, *Academy of Management Review*, 21: 100–134.

to compete against each other in many markets that are important to each. These conditions lead to the conclusion that the firms modeled in quadrant I are direct and mutually acknowledged competitors (e.g., FedEx and UPS). In contrast, the firm and its competitor shown in quadrant III share few markets and have little similarity in their resources, indicating that they aren't direct and mutually acknowledged competitors. Thus, a small local, family-owned Italian restaurant does not compete directly against Olive Garden nor does it have resources that are similar to those of Darden Restaurants, Inc. (Olive Garden's owner). The firm's mapping of its competitive relationship with rivals is fluid as firms enter and exit markets and as companies' resources change in type and amount. Thus, the companies with which the firm is a direct competitor change across time.

Drivers of Competitive Actions and Responses

As shown in Figure 5.2 (on page 130) market commonality and resource similarity influence the drivers (awareness, motivation, and ability) of competitive behavior. In turn, the drivers influence the firm's competitive behavior, as shown by the actions and responses it takes while engaged in competitive rivalry.[47]

Awareness, which is a prerequisite to any competitive action or response taken by a firm, refers to the extent to which competitors recognize the degree of their mutual interdependence that results from market commonality and resource similarity.[48] Awareness tends to be greatest when firms have highly similar resources (in terms of types and amounts) to use while competing against each other in multiple markets. Komatsu Ltd., Japan's top construction machinery maker and U.S.-based Caterpillar Inc. have similar resources and are certainly aware of each other's actions.[49] The same is true for Wal-Mart and France's Carrefour, the two largest supermarket groups in the world. The last two firms' joint awareness has increased as they use similar resources to compete against each other for dominant positions in multiple European and South American markets.[50] Awareness affects the extent to which the firm understands the consequences of its competitive actions and responses. A lack of awareness can lead to excessive competition, resulting in a negative effect on all competitors' performance.[51]

Komatsu Ltd., Japan's top construction machinery maker, and U.S.-based Caterpillar Inc. have similar resources and compete against each other in multiple markets.

As explained in the Strategic Focus, rivals Netflix and Blockbuster are acutely aware of each other's competitive actions and responses. Indeed, the rivalry between these firms is quite intense. As you will see from reading about these firms and their competitive actions and responses, both are highly motivated to engage each other in competitive battles.

Motivation, which concerns the firm's incentive to take action or to respond to a competitor's attack, relates to perceived gains and losses. Thus, a firm may be aware of competitors but may not be motivated to engage in rivalry with them if it perceives that its position will not improve or that its market position won't be damaged if it doesn't respond.[52]

Market commonality affects the firm's perceptions and resulting motivation. For example, all else being equal, the firm is more likely to attack the rival with whom it has low market commonality than the one with whom it competes in multiple markets. The primary reason is the high stakes involved in trying to gain a more advantageous position over a rival with whom the firm shares many markets. As we mentioned earlier, multimarket competition can find a competitor responding to the firm's action in a market different from the one in which the initial action was taken. Actions and responses of this type can cause both firms to lose focus on core markets and to battle each other with resources that had been allocated for other purposes. Because of the high stakes of competition under the condition of market commonality, the probability is high that the attacked firm will respond to its competitor's action in an effort to protect its position in one or more markets.[53]

In some instances, the firm may be aware of the large number of markets it shares with a competitor and may be motivated to respond to an attack by that competitor, but it lacks the ability to do so. *Ability* relates to each firm's resources and the flexibility they provide. Without available resources (such as financial capital and people), the firm lacks the ability to attack a competitor or respond to its actions. However, similar resources suggest similar abilities to attack and respond. When a firm faces a competitor with similar resources, careful study of a possible attack before initiating it is essential because the similarly resourced competitor is likely to respond to that action.[54]

Resource *dissimilarity* also influences competitive actions and responses between firms, in that "the greater is the resource imbalance between the acting firm and competitors or potential responders, the greater will be the delay in response"[55] by the firm with a resource disadvantage. For example, Wal-Mart initially used a focused cost leadership strategy to compete only in small communities (those with a population of 25,000 or less). Using sophisticated logistics systems and extremely efficient purchasing practices as advantages, among others, Wal-Mart created what was at that time a new type of value (primarily in the form of wide selections of products at the lowest competitive prices) for customers in small retail markets. Local competitors lacked the ability to marshal needed resources at the pace required to respond quickly and effectively. However, even when facing competitors with greater resources (greater ability) or more attractive market positions, firms should eventually respond, no matter how daunting the task seems. Choosing not to respond can ultimately result in failure, as happened with at least some local retailers who didn't respond to Wal-Mart's competitive actions.

Strategic Focus Strategic Focus Strategic Focus

Who Will Win the Competitive Battles Between Netflix and Blockbuster?

Netflix pioneered the online movie rental business. Offering customers different plans, one of which allows them to rent up to three movies at a time with no time limit on each title's return, the firm grew rapidly during its first eight years.

From the beginning, Netflix's growth was fueled by adding subscribers. In late 2004, Netflix founder and CEO Reed Hastings decided to reduce the prices of his firm's plans in order to continue adding subscribers. The pricing strategy worked. Moreover, because the firm's margins were attractive at the plans' 2004 price levels (levels that were essentially unchanged in early 2007), Netflix's profits grew from $6.5 million in 2003 to $49 million in 2006. But Blockbuster, Netflix's major rival, is aware of every competitive action its chief competitor takes. Moreover, Blockbuster is now responding aggressively to Netflix's marketplace actions. In the eyes of some, the competition between these firms has become "ugly." Even worse, it may be that the firms are now "locked into (a) mutually destructive competitive situation."

Evidence suggests that Netflix's momentum tapped out somewhat dramatically when Blockbuster launched a new option in its online rental service in 2006. Called "Total Access," subscribers pay an additional $1 per month for the ability to return and check out rentals in Blockbuster's physical stores as well as handle these transactions online. This convenience is one that Netflix cannot offer customers because its products are delivered only through the mail. Fully aware of this competitive action, Netflix responded in mid-2007 with still lower prices for its plans. The disadvantage in this response is that the lower prices cut into the firm's profits. However, Netflix also started its "Watch Now" movie downloading service in 2007. This service uses high-speed Internet connections to allow customers to download movies and watch them on their television sets or PCs.

In the continuing saga of competition between competitors who are keenly aware of each other and their actions and responses, one might wonder how Blockbuster will react to Netflix's "Watch Now" service. It seems that Blockbuster could easily imitate this service, meaning that it will be difficult for Netflix to gain a competitive advantage by using it. And both firms will have to decide how long they are willing to engage in competitive battles that are severely damaging their ability to earn profits. The window for this level of destructive competition may soon close. In mid-2007, Blockbuster stated in a Securities and Exchange Commission filing that the firm would modify its online service "to strike the appropriate balance between continued subscriber growth and enhanced profitability."

Sources: 2007, Netflix to cut rental fees in battle with Blockbuster, *USA Today Online*, http://usatoday.com, July 31; D. King, 2007, Netflix trims forecast amid war with Blockbuster, *Houston Chronicle Online*, http://www.chron.com, July 23; M. Liedtke, 2007, Netflix gives up profit to gain business, *Houston Chronicle Online*, http://www.chron.com, July 23; B. Steverman, 2007, Netflix battle with Blockbuster gets ugly, *BusinessWeek Online*, http://businessweek.com, July 24.

Competitive Rivalry

The ongoing competitive action/response sequence between a firm and a competitor affects the performance of both firms;[56] thus it is important for companies to carefully study competitive rivalry to select and implement successful strategies. Understanding a competitor's awareness, motivation, and ability helps the firm to predict the likelihood of an attack by that competitor and the probability that a competitor will respond to actions taken against it.

As we described earlier, the predictions drawn from studying competitors in terms of awareness, motivation, and ability are grounded in market commonality and resource similarity. These predictions are fairly general. The value of the final set of predictions

A **competitive action** is a strategic or tactical action the firm takes to build or defend its competitive advantages or improve its market position.

A **competitive response** is a strategic or tactical action the firm takes to counter the effects of a competitor's competitive action.

A **strategic action or a strategic response** is a market-based move that involves a significant commitment of organizational resources and is difficult to implement and reverse.

A **tactical action or a tactical response** is a market-based move that is taken to fine-tune a strategy; it involves fewer resources and is relatively easy to implement and reverse.

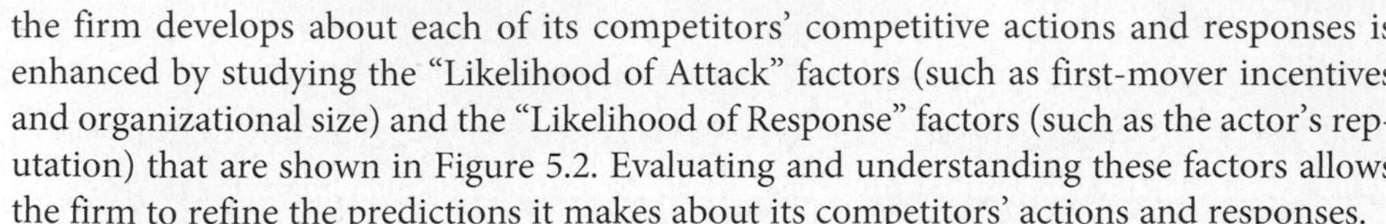

the firm develops about each of its competitors' competitive actions and responses is enhanced by studying the "Likelihood of Attack" factors (such as first-mover incentives and organizational size) and the "Likelihood of Response" factors (such as the actor's reputation) that are shown in Figure 5.2. Evaluating and understanding these factors allows the firm to refine the predictions it makes about its competitors' actions and responses.

Strategic and Tactical Actions

Firms use both strategic and tactical actions when forming their competitive actions and competitive responses in the course of engaging in competitive rivalry.[57] A **competitive action** is a strategic or tactical action the firm takes to build or defend its competitive advantages or improve its market position. A **competitive response** is a strategic or tactical action the firm takes to counter the effects of a competitor's competitive action. A **strategic action or a strategic response** is a market-based move that involves a significant commitment of organizational resources and is difficult to implement and reverse. A **tactical action or a tactical response** is a market-based move that is taken to fine-tune a strategy; it involves fewer resources and is relatively easy to implement and reverse.

The decision a few years ago by newly installed leaders at Guess Inc. to take their firm's brand of denims and related products upscale rather than dilute the brand more by lowering prices when Guess was losing market share is an example of a strategic response.[58] And Boeing's decision to commit the resources required to build the super-efficient 787 midsized jetliner for delivery in 2008[59] demonstrates a strategic action. Changes in airfares are somewhat frequently announced by airlines. As tactical actions that are easily reversed, pricing decisions are often taken by these firms to increase demand in certain markets during certain periods.

Jamba Juice has recently begun changing the texture of some of its smoothies. This change may not require a strategic response from its competitors.

As discussed in the Strategic Focus, Wal-Mart prices aggressively as a means of increasing revenues and gaining market share at the expense of competitors. But discounted prices and higher expenses (which the firm is incurring in order to upgrade its stores) weigh on margins and slow profit growth. Although pricing aggressively is at the core of what Wal-Mart is and how it competes, can the tactical action of aggressive pricing continue to lead to the competitive success the firm has enjoyed historically? Is Wal-Mart achieving the type of balance between strategic and tactical competitive actions and competitive responses that is a foundation for all firms' success in marketplace competitions?

When engaging rivals in competition, firms must recognize the differences between strategic and tactical actions and responses and should develop an effective balance between the two types of competitive actions and responses. Airbus, Boeing's major competitor in terms of commercial airliners, should note that its competitor is strongly committed to taking actions it believes are necessary to successfully launch the 787 jetliner, because deciding to design, build, and launch the 787 is a major strategic action. On the other hand, Jamba Juice's recent attempts to develop different textures for its smoothie drinks is a tactical action that may not demand a strategic response from competitors such as Zuka Juice.[60]

Likelihood of Attack

In addition to market commonality, resource similarity, and the drivers of awareness, motivation, and ability, other factors affect the likelihood a competitor will use strategic

Strategic Focus Strategic Focus Strategic Focus

Using Aggressive Pricing as a Tactical Action at Wal-Mart

"Every Day Low Prices." People throughout the world are familiar with Wal-Mart's famous slogan—a slogan on which the firm's business model is built. This model has led to remarkable success. In mid-2007, Wal-Mart had 6,775 stores and was on track to exceed $350 billion in sales for the year. With roughly 40 percent of its sales revenue being earned outside the United States, Wal-Mart continues to expand internationally and is the number one retailer in Canada and Mexico. Some analysts believe that Wal-Mart's business model will prove compelling in a number of emerging markets although the firm is struggling to operate profitably in some developed markets such as Japan and Germany. Europe's Carrefour, Costco Wholesale, and Target are Wal-Mart's major competitors, although a number of other companies (including Kohl's, J.C. Penney, and BJ's Wholesale Club) also compete against the retailing giant.

As a tactical action, Wal-Mart prices some products to increase overall sales revenue and to attract customers to its stores in hopes that they will purchase other items as well. Aggressive pricing works (for Wal-Mart and others such as Costco Wholesale using the practice) when reduced prices generate sales revenues in excess of revenues that would have been generated without the price cuts and when customers buy other higher-margin items while shopping. Recently, both Wal-Mart and Costco added gasoline to their operations as another means of attracting customers to their stores. Both stores are pricing gasoline attractively in hopes of enticing customers to buy other items located in their stores.

As a tactical action, aggressive pricing is used with virtually all products that Wal-Mart sells. (Some analysts describe Wal-Mart's price cuts as "taking a knife to prices.") Toys and electronics (i.e., flat panel televisions, PCs, and telephones) are priced aggressively during holiday seasons. More recently, Wal-Mart aggressively priced appliances in order to compete against Best Buy, Home Depot, and Lowe's in this product category. For the back-to-school season, Wal-Mart often cuts prices (anywhere from 10 percent to 50 percent) on as many as 16,000 school-related items.

Firms must carefully evaluate the effectiveness of all of their competitive actions and competitive responses. Some feel that Wal-Mart's emphasis on low prices is preventing the firm from allocating sufficient resources to remodel aging stores and to upgrade the quality of its merchandising mix. Competitors Kohl's and Costco appear to be attracting some of Wal-Mart's customers by offering more appealing mixes of merchandise and a marginally more pleasant shopping experience that modernized facilities provide. Thus, Wal-Mart must carefully assess the degree to which its tactical action of aggressive pricing is allowing it to successfully engage competitors in marketplace competitions.

Sources: M. Barbaro, 2007, Wal-Mart and Studios in film deal, *New York Times Online*, http://www.nytimes.com, February 6; A. D'Innocenzio, 2007, Wal-Mart sets in motion a price-cutting campaign, *Houston Chronicle Online*, http://www.chron.com, July 23; A. Feldman, 2007, The tiger in Costco's tank, *Fast Company*, July/August, 38–40; R. Fuhrmann, 2007, Wal-Mart vs. AT&T: Wal-Mart, *Motley Fool Stock Advisor*, http://www.fool.com, March, 15; 2007, Wal-Mart Stores, Inc., *Hoovers*, http://www.hovers.com, July 31.

actions and tactical actions to attack its competitors. Three of these factors—first-mover incentives, organizational size, and quality—are discussed next.

First-Mover Incentives

A **first mover** is a firm that takes an initial competitive action in order to build or defend its competitive advantages or to improve its market position. The first-mover concept has been influenced by the work of the famous economist Joseph Schumpeter, who argued that firms achieve competitive advantage by taking innovative actions[61] (innovation is

A **first mover** is a firm that takes an initial competitive action in order to build or defend its competitive advantages or to improve its market position.

defined and described in detail in Chapter 13). In general, first movers "allocate funds for product innovation and development, aggressive advertising, and advanced research and development."[62]

The benefits of being a successful first mover can be substantial.[63] Especially in fast-cycle markets (discussed later in the chapter), where changes occur rapidly and where it is virtually impossible to sustain a competitive advantage for any length of time, "a first mover may experience five to ten times the valuation and revenue of a second mover."[64] This evidence suggests that although first-mover benefits are never absolute, they are often critical to a firm's success in industries experiencing rapid technological developments and relatively short product life cycles.[65] In addition to earning above-average returns until its competitors respond to its successful competitive action, the first mover can gain (1) the loyalty of customers who may become committed to the goods or services of the firm that first made them available, and (2) market share that can be difficult for competitors to take during future competitive rivalry.[66] The general evidence that first movers have greater survival rates than later market entrants[67] is perhaps the culmination of first-mover benefits.

The firm trying to predict its competitors' competitive actions might conclude that they will take aggressive strategic actions to gain first movers' benefits. However, even though a firm's competitors might be motivated to be first movers, they may lack the ability to do so. First movers tend to be aggressive and willing to experiment with innovation and take higher, yet reasonable, levels of risk.[68] To be a first mover, the firm must have readily available the resources to significantly invest in R&D as well as to rapidly and successfully produce and market a stream of innovative products.[69]

Organizational slack makes it possible for firms to have the ability (as measured by available resources) to be first movers. *Slack* is the buffer or cushion provided by actual or obtainable resources that aren't currently in use and are in excess of the minimum resources needed to produce a given level of organizational output.[70] As a liquid resource, slack can quickly be allocated to support competitive actions, such as R&D investments and aggressive marketing campaigns that lead to first-mover advantages. This relationship between slack and the ability to be a first mover allows the firm to predict that a competitor who is a first mover likely has available slack and will probably take aggressive competitive actions to continuously introduce innovative products. Furthermore, the firm can predict that as a first mover, a competitor will try to rapidly gain market share and customer loyalty in order to earn above-average returns until its competitors are able to effectively respond to its first move.

Firms evaluating their competitors should realize that being a first mover carries risk. For example, it is difficult to accurately estimate the returns that will be earned from introducing product innovations to the marketplace.[71] Additionally, the first mover's cost to develop a product innovation can be substantial, reducing the slack available to support further innovation. Thus, the firm should carefully study the results a competitor achieves as a first mover. Continuous success by the competitor suggests additional product innovations, while lack of product acceptance over the course of the competitor's innovations may indicate less willingness in the future to accept the risks of being a first mover.

A **second mover** is a firm that responds to the first mover's competitive action, typically through imitation.

A **second mover** is a firm that responds to the first mover's competitive action, typically through imitation. More cautious than the first mover, the second mover studies customers' reactions to product innovations. In the course of doing so, the second mover also tries to find any mistakes the first mover made so that it can avoid them and the problems they created. Often, successful imitation of the first mover's innovations allows the second mover "to avoid both the mistakes and the huge spending of the pioneers [first movers]."[72]

Second movers also have the time to develop processes and technologies that are more efficient than those used by the first mover or that create additional value for consumers.[73] Through a project with a code name of Goya, Kodak is developing a consumer inkjet printer. The product is based on "droplets of a new ink Kodak scientists produced (that) yield photo prints with vivid colors lasting a lifetime."[74] Commenting about the daunting task Kodak faces as a new entrant to the $50 billion printer business that HP dominants, Kodak's CEO took the following position: "We're very proud that we're coming to market 20 years late. We think it will give us an opportunity to disrupt the industry's business model and address consumers' key dissatisfaction: the high cost of ink."[75] Overall, the outcomes of the first mover's competitive actions may provide an effective blueprint for second and even late movers as they determine the nature and timing of their competitive responses.[76] Kodak may experience the benefits of this effectiveness as it enters the inkjet printer business after carefully studying HP's actions as a first mover in this competitive arena.

Kodak is trying to use a second-mover strategy with the introduction of its new ink jet printer.

Determining whether a competitor is an effective second mover (based on its past actions) allows a first-mover firm to predict that the competitor will respond quickly to successful, innovation-based market entries. The first mover can expect a successful second-mover competitor to study its market entries and to respond with its own new entry into the market within a short time period. As a second mover, the competitor will try to respond with a product that provides greater customer value than does the first mover's product. The most successful second movers are able to rapidly and meaningfully interpret market feedback to respond quickly, yet successfully, to the first mover's successful innovations.

A **late mover** is a firm that responds to a competitive action a significant amount of time after the first mover's action and the second mover's response. Typically, a late response is better than no response at all, although any success achieved from the late competitive response tends to be considerably less than that achieved by first and second movers. With an anticipated price of under $10,000, it is possible that the Chevy Trax, Beat, and Groove are late as entries to the small, super-efficient segment of automobiles. These cars are competitors for Honda's Fit, Toyota's Yaris, and Nissan's Versa, among others.[77]

A **late mover** is a firm that responds to a competitive action a significant amount of time after the first mover's action and the second mover's response.

The firm competing against a late mover can predict that the competitor will likely enter a particular market only after both the first and second movers have achieved success in that market. Moreover, on a relative basis, the firm can predict that the late mover's competitive action will allow it to earn average returns only after the considerable time required for it to understand how to create at least as much customer value as that offered by the first and second movers' products. Although exceptions exist, most of the late mover's competitive actions will be ineffective relative to those initiated by first and second movers.

Organizational Size

An organization's size affects the likelihood it will take competitive actions as well as the types and timing of those actions.[78] In general, small firms are more likely than large companies to launch competitive actions and tend to do it more quickly. Smaller firms are thus perceived as nimble and flexible competitors who rely on speed and surprise to defend their competitive advantages or develop new ones while engaged in competitive rivalry, especially with large companies, to gain an advantageous market position.[79] Small firms' flexibility and nimbleness allow them to develop variety in their competitive actions; large firms tend to limit the types of competitive actions used.[80]

Large firms, however, are likely to initiate more competitive actions along with more strategic actions during a given period.[81] Thus, when studying its competitors in terms of organizational size, the firm should use a measurement such as total sales revenue or total number of employees. The competitive actions the firm likely will encounter from competitors larger than it is will be different from the competitive actions it will encounter from smaller competitors.

The organizational size factor adds another layer of complexity. When engaging in competitive rivalry, the firm often prefers a large number of unique competitive actions. Ideally, the organization has the amount of slack resources held by a large firm to launch a greater *number* of competitive actions and a small firm's flexibility to launch a greater *variety* of competitive actions. Herb Kelleher, cofounder and former CEO of Southwest Airlines, addressed this matter: "Think and act big and we'll get smaller. Think and act small and we'll get bigger."[82]

In the context of competitive rivalry, Kelleher's statement can be interpreted to mean that relying on a limited number or types of competitive actions (which is the large firm's tendency) can lead to reduced competitive success across time, partly because competitors learn how to effectively respond to the predictable. In contrast, remaining flexible and nimble (which is the small firm's tendency) in order to develop and use a wide variety of competitive actions contributes to success against rivals.

As explained in the Strategic Focus, Wal-Mart is a huge firm and generates annual sales revenue that makes it the world's largest company. Partly because of its size, Wal-Mart has the flexibility required to take many types of competitive actions. In the 2007 back-to-school selling season, for example, Wal-Mart hired a new advertising agency to help it "emphasize its product selection while striking a chord with customers." This message was seen as a sharp departure from the firm's typical "price-centric pitches." This campaign was undertaken partly in response to a disappointing spring sales season in 2007. Demonstrating its flexibility, the firm decided that, at least for the back-to-school season, it wanted customers to see that Wal-Mart had "the brands you want at the price you want" to pay.[83] Demonstrating this type of flexibility in terms of competitive actions may prove critical to Wal-Mart's battles with competitors such as Costco, Kohl's, and Target among others.

Quality

Quality has many definitions, including well-established ones relating it to the production of goods or services with zero defects[84] and seeing it as a never-ending cycle of continuous improvement.[85] From a strategic perspective, we consider quality to be an outcome of how the firm completes primary and support activities (see Chapter 3). Thus, **quality** exists when the firm's goods or services meet or exceed customers' expectations. Some evidence suggests that quality may be the most critical component in satisfying the firm's customers.[86]

Quality exists when the firm's goods or services meet or exceed customers' expectations.

In the eyes of customers, quality is about doing the right things relative to performance measures that are important to them.[87] Customers may be interested in measuring the quality of a firm's goods and services against a broad range of dimensions. Sample quality dimensions in which customers commonly express an interest are shown in Table 5.1. Quality is possible only when top-level managers support it and when its importance is institutionalized throughout the entire organization.[88] When quality is institutionalized and valued by all, employees and managers alike become vigilant about continuously finding ways to improve quality.[89]

Quality is a universal theme in the global economy and is a necessary but not sufficient condition for competitive success.[90] Without quality, a firm's products lack credibility, meaning that customers don't think of them as viable options. Indeed, customers won't consider buying a product until they believe that it can satisfy at least their base-level expectations in terms of quality dimensions that are important to them. Thus, Great Wall Motor Company, a Chinese manufacturer of low-cost automobiles, can anticipate difficulty in its efforts to sell cars in Europe until customers believe that the firm's cars have at least acceptable levels of quality.[91]

Quality affects competitive rivalry. The firm evaluating a competitor whose products suffer from poor quality can predict declines in the competitor's sales revenue until the quality issues are resolved. In addition, the firm can predict that the competitor likely won't be aggressive in its competitive actions until the quality problems are corrected in order to gain credibility with customers. However, after the problems are corrected, that competitor is likely to take more aggressive competitive actions. Additionally, a firm

Table 5.1 Quality Dimensions of Goods and Services

Product Quality Dimensions

1. *Performance*—Operating characteristics
2. *Features*—Important special characteristics
3. *Flexibility*—Meeting operating specifications over some period of time
4. *Durability*—Amount of use before performance deteriorates
5. *Conformance*—Match with preestablished standards
6. *Serviceability*—Ease and speed of repair
7. *Aesthetics*—How a product looks and feels
8. *Perceived quality*—Subjective assessment of characteristics (product image)

Service Quality Dimensions

1. *Timeliness*—Performed in the promised period of time
2. *Courtesy*—Performed cheerfully
3. *Consistency*—Giving all customers similar experiences each time
4. *Convenience*—Accessibility to customers
5. *Completeness*—Fully serviced, as required
6. *Accuracy*—Performed correctly each time

Source: Adapted from J. Evans, 2008, *Managing for Quality and Performance,* 7th ed., Mason, OH: Thomson Publishing.

can predict that a competitor for whom quality has always been important will act to regain its ability to produce products recognized for their quality, as may be the case for Mercedes-Benz automobiles.

Historically, Mercedes-Benz automobiles were known for their quality and engineering. Indeed, product quality was a competitive advantage for DaimlerBenz. However, it seems that acquiring Chrysler Corporation and becoming DaimlerChrysler negatively affected the quality of Mercedes-Benz cars. In fact, between 2003 and early 2006, company officials admitted that Mercedes' products were on a "downward spiral" in terms of quality. In 2004 and 2005, for example, difficulties with cars' electronics led to widespread recalls. A failure to recognize the rather urgent need to modernize the firm's facilities and manufacturing techniques contributed to the decline in product quality. It is possible that the attention being devoted to integrating the two formerly independent companies contributed to the relative inattention paid to Mercedes' needs. However, the decision to sell the Chrysler unit immediately resulted in changes for Mercedes' cars. Thousands of stress tests are now being made during manufacturing processes to catch problems before the cars are distributed, facilities have been upgraded, and efforts are underway to fully engage suppliers with Mercedes' personnel to increase quality and manufacturing efficiency.[92] Given these developments, competitors such as BMW and Lexus can expect that Mercedes will again promote the quality of its products as it competes with them.

Likelihood of Response

The success of a firm's competitive action is affected by the likelihood that a competitor will respond to it as well as by the type (strategic or tactical) and effectiveness of that response. As noted earlier, a competitive response is a strategic or tactical action the firm takes to counter the effects of a competitor's competitive action. In general, a firm is likely to respond to a competitor's action when (1) the action leads to better use of the competitor's capabilities to gain or produce stronger competitive advantages or an improvement in its market position, (2) the action damages the firm's ability to use its capabilities to create or maintain an advantage, or (3) the firm's market position becomes less defensible.[93]

In addition to market commonality and resource similarity and awareness, motivation, and ability, firms evaluate three other factors—type of competitive action, reputation, and market dependence—to predict how a competitor is likely to respond to competitive actions (see Figure 5.2, on page 130).

Type of Competitive Action

Competitive responses to strategic actions differ from responses to tactical actions. These differences allow the firm to predict a competitor's likely response to a competitive action that has been launched against it. In general, strategic actions receive strategic responses and tactical actions receive tactical responses.

In general, strategic actions elicit fewer total competitive responses because strategic responses, such as market-based moves, involve a significant commitment of resources and are difficult to implement and reverse.[94] Palm Inc.'s decision to sell 25 percent of itself to Elevation Partners, a private equity firm, is a strategic action that will be difficult to reverse. However, the infusion of $325 million provided the capability Palm required to grow in the highly competitive smartphone market.[95]

Another reason that strategic actions elicit fewer responses than do tactical actions is that the time needed to implement a strategic action and to assess its effectiveness can delay the competitor's response to that action.[96] In contrast, a competitor likely will respond quickly to a tactical action, such as when an airline company almost immediately matches a competitor's tactical action of reducing prices in certain markets. Either strategic actions or tactical actions that target a large number of a rival's customers are likely to elicit strong responses.[97] In fact, if the effects of a competitor's strategic action on the focal firm are significant (e.g., loss of market share, loss of major resources such as critical employees), a response is likely to be swift and strong.[98]

Actor's Reputation

In the context of competitive rivalry, an *actor* is the firm taking an action or a response while *reputation* is "the positive or negative attribute ascribed by one rival to another based on past competitive behavior."[99] A positive reputation may be a source of above-average returns, especially for consumer goods producers.[100] Thus, a positive corporate reputation is of strategic value[101] and affects competitive rivalry. To predict the likelihood of a competitor's response to a current or planned action, firms evaluate the responses that the competitor has taken previously when attacked—past behavior is assumed to be a predictor of future behavior.

Competitors are more likely to respond to strategic or tactical actions when they are taken by a market leader.[102] In particular, evidence suggests that commonly successful actions, especially strategic actions, will be quickly imitated. For example, although a second mover, IBM committed significant resources to enter the PC market. When IBM was immediately successful in this endeavor, competitors such as Dell, Compaq, HP, and Gateway responded with strategic actions to enter the market. IBM's reputation as well as its successful strategic action strongly influenced entry by these competitors. However, the competitive landscape has changed dramatically over time. As explained in the Opening Case, HP now holds the largest share of the global PC market. Dell is seeking to regain its edge in the marketplace; Compaq merged with HP some years ago; Gateway is struggling to survive; and Lenovo, a Chinese firm, paid $1.75 billion in 2005 to buy IBM's PC division.

In contrast to a firm with a strong reputation such as IBM, competitors are less likely to take responses against a company with a reputation for competitive behavior that is risky, complex, and unpredictable. The firm with a reputation as a price predator (an actor that frequently reduces prices to gain or maintain market share) generates few responses to its pricing tactical actions because price predators, which typically increase prices once their market share objective is reached, lack credibility with their competitors.[103]

Dependence on the Market

Market dependence denotes the extent to which a firm's revenues or profits are derived from a particular market.[104] In general, firms can predict that competitors with high market dependence are likely to respond strongly to attacks threatening their market position.[105] Interestingly, the threatened firm in these instances may not always respond quickly, even though an effective response to an attack on the firm's position in a critical market is important.

Sargento Foods is a family-owned company based in Wisconsin. The firm is a leading packager and marketer of "shredded, snack and specialty cheeses (that are) sold under the Sargento brand, cheese and non-cheese snack food items and ethnic sauces." With sales exceeding $600 million annually, Sargento's business is founded on a passion for cheese. Because Sargento's business operations revolve strictly around cheese products, it is totally dependent on the market for cheese. As such, any competitor that chooses to attack Sargento and its market positions can anticipate a strong response to its competitive actions.

Competitive Dynamics

Whereas competitive rivalry concerns the ongoing actions and responses between a firm and its competitors for an advantageous market position, competitive dynamics concern the ongoing actions and responses taking place among *all* firms competing within a market for advantageous positions.

To explain competitive rivalry, we described (1) factors that determine the degree to which firms are competitors (market commonality and resource similarity), (2) the drivers of competitive behavior for individual firms (awareness, motivation, and ability) and (3) factors affecting the likelihood that a competitor will act or attack (first-mover incentives, organizational size, and quality) and respond (type of competitive action, reputation, and market dependence). Building and sustaining competitive advantages are at the core of competitive rivalry, in that advantages are the key to creating value for shareholders.[106]

To explain competitive dynamics, we discuss the effects of varying rates of competitive speed in different markets (called slow-cycle, fast-cycle, and standard-cycle markets) on the behavior (actions and responses) of all competitors within a given market. Competitive behaviors as well as the reasons or logic for taking them are similar within each market type, but differ across market types.[107] Thus, competitive dynamics differ in slow-cycle, fast-cycle, and standard-cycle markets. The sustainability of the firm's competitive advantages differs across the three market types.

As noted in Chapter 1, firms want to sustain their competitive advantages for as long as possible, although no advantage is permanently sustainable. The degree of sustainability is affected by how quickly competitive advantages can be imitated and how costly it is to do so.

Slow-Cycle Markets

Slow-cycle markets are those in which the firm's competitive advantages are shielded from imitation commonly for long periods of time and where imitation is costly.[108] Thus, competitive advantages are sustainable in slow-cycle markets.

Slow-cycle markets are those in which the firm's competitive advantages are shielded from imitation commonly for long periods of time and where imitation is costly.

Building a unique and proprietary capability produces a competitive advantage and success in a slow-cycle market. This type of advantage is difficult for competitors to understand. As discussed in Chapter 3, a difficult-to-understand and costly-to-imitate resource or capability usually results from unique historical conditions, causal ambiguity, and/or social complexity. Copyrights, geography, patents, and ownership of an information resource are examples of resources.[109] After a proprietary advantage is developed, the firm's competitive behavior in a slow-cycle market is oriented to protecting, maintaining, and extending that advantage. Thus, the competitive dynamics in slow-cycle markets usually concentrate on competitive actions and responses that enable firms to protect, maintain, and extend their competitive advantage. Major strategic actions in these markets, such acquisitions, usually carry less risk than in faster cycle markets.[110]

Walt Disney Co. continues to extend its proprietary characters, such as Mickey Mouse, Minnie Mouse, and Goofy. These characters have a unique historical development as a result of Walt and Roy Disney's creativity and vision for entertaining people. Products based on the characters seen in Disney's animated films are sold through Disney's theme park shops as well as freestanding retail outlets called Disney Stores. Because copyrights shield it, the proprietary nature of Disney's advantage in terms of animated character trademarks protects the firm from imitation by competitors.

Consistent with another attribute of competition in a slow-cycle market, Disney protects its exclusive rights to its characters and their use as shown by the fact that "the company once sued a day-care center, forcing it to remove the likeness of Mickey Mouse from a wall of the facility."[111] As with all firms competing in slow-cycle markets, Disney's competitive actions (such as building theme parks in France, Japan, and China) and responses (such as lawsuits to protect its right to fully control use of its animated characters) maintain and extend its proprietary competitive advantage while protecting it.

Patent laws and regulatory requirements such as those in the United States requiring FDA (Food and Drug Administration) approval to launch new products shield pharmaceutical companies' positions. Competitors in this market try to extend patents on their drugs to maintain advantageous positions that the patents provide. However, after a patent expires, the firm is no longer shielded from competition, allowing generic imitations and usually leading to a loss of sales.

The competitive dynamics generated by firms competing in slow-cycle markets are shown in Figure 5.4. In slow-cycle markets, firms launch a product (e.g., a new drug) that has been developed through a proprietary advantage (e.g., R&D) and then exploit it for as long as possible while the product is shielded from competition. Eventually, competitors respond to the action with a counterattack. In markets for drugs, this counterattack commonly occurs as patents expire or are broken through legal means, creating the need for another product launch by the firm seeking a protected market position.

Fast-Cycle Markets

Fast-cycle markets are markets in which the firm's capabilities that contribute to competitive advantages aren't shielded from imitation and where imitation is often rapid and inexpensive.

Fast-cycle markets are markets in which the firm's capabilities that contribute to competitive advantages aren't shielded from imitation and where imitation is often rapid and inexpensive. Thus, competitive advantages aren't sustainable in fast-cycle markets. Firms

Figure 5.4 Gradual Erosion of a Sustained Competitive Advantage

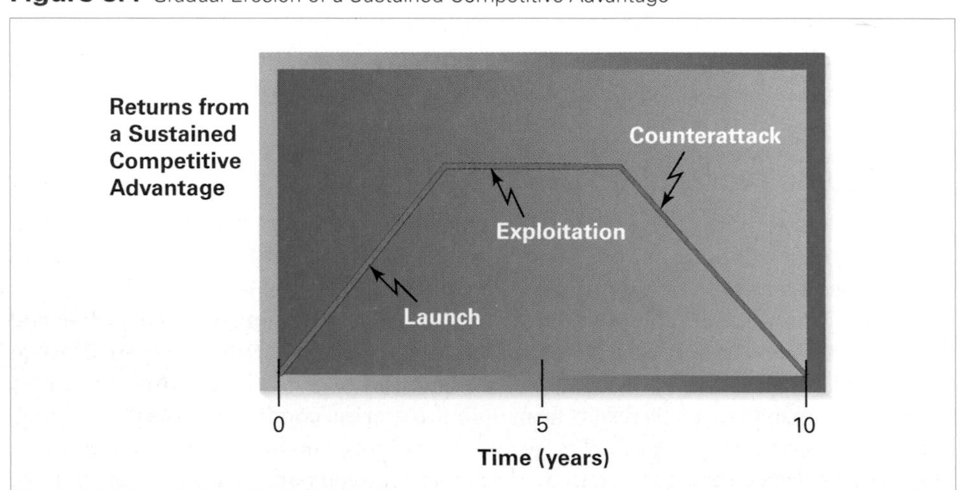

Source: Adapted from I. C. MacMillan, 1988, Controlling competitive dynamics by taking strategic initiative, *Academy of Management Executive*, II(2): 111–118.

competing in fast-cycle markets recognize the importance of speed; these companies appreciate that "time is as precious a business resource as money or head count—and that the costs of hesitation and delay are just as steep as going over budget or missing a financial forecast."[112] Such high-velocity environments place considerable pressures on top managers to quickly make strategic decisions that are also effective.[113] The often substantial competition and technology-based strategic focus make the strategic decision complex, increasing the need for a comprehensive approach integrated with decision speed, two often-conflicting characteristics of the strategic decision process.[114]

Reverse engineering and the rate of technology diffusion in fast-cycle markets facilitate rapid imitation. A competitor uses reverse engineering to quickly gain the knowledge required to imitate or improve the firm's products. Technology is diffused rapidly in fast-cycle markets, making it available to competitors in a short period. The technology often used by fast-cycle competitors isn't proprietary, nor is it protected by patents as is the technology used by firms competing in slow-cycle markets. For example, only a few hundred parts, which are readily available on the open market, are required to build a PC. Patents protect only a few of these parts, such as microprocessor chips.[115]

Fast-cycle markets are more volatile than slow-cycle and standard-cycle markets. Indeed, the pace of competition in fast-cycle markets is almost frenzied, as companies rely on innovations as the engines of their growth. Because prices fall quickly in these markets, companies need to profit quickly from their product innovations. Imitation of many fast-cycle products is relatively easy, as demonstrated by Dell and HP, along with a host of local PC vendors, that have partly or largely imitated the original PC design to create their products. Continuous declines in the costs of parts, as well as the fact that the information required to assemble a PC isn't especially complicated and is readily available, make it possible for additional competitors to enter this market without significant difficulty.[116]

The fast-cycle market characteristics just described make it virtually impossible for companies in this type of market to develop sustainable competitive advantages. Recognizing this reality, firms avoid "loyalty" to any of their products, preferring to cannibalize their own before competitors learn how to do so through successful imitation. This emphasis creates competitive dynamics that differ substantially from those found in slow-cycle markets. Instead of concentrating on protecting, maintaining, and extending competitive advantages, as in slow-cycle markets, companies competing in fast-cycle markets focus on learning how to rapidly and continuously develop new competitive advantages that are superior to those they replace. Commonly, they search for fast and effective means of developing new products. For example, it is common in some industries for firms to use strategic alliances to gain access to new technologies and thereby develop and introduce more new products into the market.[117]

The competitive behavior of firms competing in fast-cycle markets is shown in Figure 5.5. As suggested by the figure, competitive dynamics in this market type entail taking actions and responses that are oriented to rapid and continuous product introductions and the development of a stream of ever-changing competitive advantages. The firm launches a product to achieve a competitive action and then exploits the advantage for as long as possible. However, the firm also tries to develop another temporary competitive advantage before competitors can respond to the first one (see Figure 5.5). Thus, competitive dynamics in fast-cycle markets often result in rapid product upgrades as well as quick product innovations.[118]

As our discussion suggests, innovation plays a dominant role in the competitive dynamics in fast-cycle markets. For individual firms, then, innovation is a key source of competitive advantage. Through innovation, the firm can cannibalize its own products before competitors successfully imitate them.

Standard-cycle markets are markets in which the firm's competitive advantages are moderately shielded from imitation and where imitation is moderately costly.

Standard-Cycle Markets

Standard-cycle markets are markets in which the firm's competitive advantages are moderately shielded from imitation and where imitation is moderately costly. Competitive advantages are partially sustainable in standard-cycle markets, but only when the firm is

Figure 5.5 Developing Temporary Advantages to Create Sustained Advantage

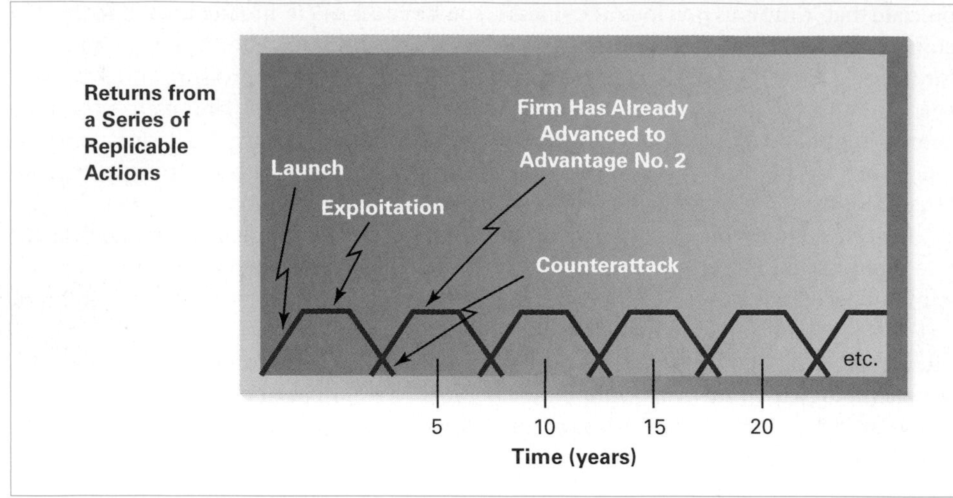

Source: Adapted from I. C. MacMillan, 1988, Controlling competitive dynamics by taking strategic initiative, *Academy of Management Executive,* II(2): 111–118.

able to continuously upgrade the quality of its capabilities, making the competitive advantages dynamic. The competitive actions and responses that form a standard-cycle market's competitive dynamics are designed to seek large market shares, to gain customer loyalty through brand names, and to carefully control a firm's operations in order to consistently provide the same positive experience for customers.[119]

Standard-cycle companies serve many customers in competitive markets. Because the capabilities and core competencies on which their competitive advantages are based are less specialized, imitation is faster and less costly for standard-cycle firms than for those competing in slow-cycle markets. However, imitation is slower and more expensive in these markets than in fast-cycle markets. Thus, competitive dynamics in standard-cycle markets rest midway between the characteristics of dynamics in slow-cycle and fast-cycle markets. Imitation comes less quickly and is more expensive for standard-cycle competitors when a firm is able to develop economies of scale by combining coordinated and integrated design and manufacturing processes with a large sales volume for its products.

Because of large volumes, the size of mass markets, and the need to develop scale economies, the competition for market share is intense in standard-cycle markets. This form of competition is readily evident in the battles among consumer foods' producers. Recently, companies such as Frito-Lay, Pepperidge Farm, Nabisco, and Hershey started "placing bigger bets on smaller packages."[120] Essentially, these firms are offering products that they already offer to consumers in smaller packages. Beef Jerky (Frito-Lay), Goldfish (Pepperidge Farm), Animals Choco Crackers (Nabisco), and Twizzlers (Hershey) are examples of food items being offered in 100-calorie per package servings. For the firms, this rapidly developing market is attractive in that they can take an existing product, put smaller amounts of it into single-serving bags, and then "sell several of the bags for about the same or more as a regular-sized package."[121] Package design and ease of availability are examples of the competitive dimensions on which these firms are now competing in efforts to outperform their rivals in this attractive market segment.

Innovation can also drive competitive actions and responses in standard-cycle markets, especially when rivalry is intense. Some innovations in standard-cycle markets are incremental rather than radical in nature (incremental and radical innovations are discussed in Chapter 13). For example, consumer foods' producers are innovating in terms of healthy products. Believing that "brown is better," Kraft Foods recently introduced the DiGiorno Harvest Wheat Crust frozen pizza under its "Sensible Solution" banner. General Mills' bakery division is using white whole wheat flour to make products such as cinnamon rolls, puff pastries, and croissants. Finally, Kellogg introduced a new Tiger

Power brand of whole-grain wheat cereal for kids featuring Tony the Tiger on the box.[122] Overall, these firms are relying on innovation as a means of competing in standard-cycle markets and to earn above-average returns.

In the final analysis, innovation has a substantial influence on competitive dynamics as it affects the actions and responses of all companies competing within a slow-cycle, fast-cycle, or standard-cycle market. We have emphasized the importance of innovation to the firm's strategic competitiveness in earlier chapters and do so again in Chapter 13. Our discussion of innovation in terms of competitive dynamics extends the earlier discussions by showing its importance in all types of markets in which firms compete.

Summary

- Competitors are firms competing in the same market, offering similar products, and targeting similar customers. Competitive rivalry is the ongoing set of competitive actions and competitive responses occurring between competitors as they compete against each other for an advantageous market position. The outcomes of competitive rivalry influence the firm's ability to sustain its competitive advantages as well as the level (average, below average, or above average) of its financial returns.
- For the individual firm, the set of competitive actions and responses it takes while engaged in competitive rivalry is called competitive behavior. Competitive dynamics is the set of actions and responses taken by all firms that are competitors within a particular market.
- Firms study competitive rivalry in order to be able to predict the competitive actions and responses that each of their competitors likely will take. Competitive actions are either strategic or tactical in nature. The firm takes competitive actions to defend or build its competitive advantages or to improve its market position. Competitive responses are taken to counter the effects of a competitor's competitive action. A strategic action or a strategic response requires a significant commitment of organizational resources, is difficult to successfully implement, and is difficult to reverse. In contrast, a tactical action or a tactical response requires fewer organizational resources and is easier to implement and reverse. For an airline company, for example, entering major new markets is an example of a strategic action or a strategic response; changing its prices in a particular market is an example of a tactical action or a tactical response.
- A competitor analysis is the first step the firm takes to be able to predict its competitors' actions and responses. In Chapter 2, we discussed what firms do to *understand* competitors. This discussion was extended in this chapter as we described what the firm does to *predict* competitors' market-based actions. Thus, understanding precedes prediction. Market commonality (the number of markets with which competitors are jointly involved and their importance to each) and resource similarity (how comparable competitors' resources are in terms of type and amount) are studied to complete a competitor analysis. In general, the greater the market commonality and resource similarity, the more firms acknowledge that they are direct competitors.
- Market commonality and resource similarity shape the firm's awareness (the degree to which it and its competitor understand their mutual interdependence), motivation (the firm's incentive to attack or respond), and ability (the quality of the resources available to the firm to attack and respond). Having knowledge of a competitor in terms of these characteristics increases the quality of the firm's predictions about that competitor's actions and responses.
- In addition to market commonality and resource similarity and awareness, motivation, and ability, three more specific factors affect the likelihood a competitor will take competitive actions. The first of these concerns first-mover incentives. First movers, those taking an initial competitive action, often earn above-average returns until competitors can successfully respond to their action and gain loyal customers. Not all firms can be first movers in that they may lack the awareness, motivation, or ability required to engage in this type of competitive behavior. Moreover, some firms prefer to be a second mover (the firm responding to the first mover's action). One reason for this is that second movers, especially those acting quickly, can successfully compete against the first mover. By evaluating the first mover's product, customers' reactions to it, and the responses of other competitors to the first mover, the second mover can avoid the early entrant's mistakes and find ways to improve upon the value created for customers by the first mover's good or service. Late movers (those that respond a long time after the original action was taken) commonly are lower performers and are much less competitive.
- Organizational size, the second factor, tends to reduce the variety of competitive actions that large firms launch while it increases the variety of actions undertaken by smaller competitors. Ideally, the firm would like to initiate a large number of diverse actions when engaged in competitive rivalry. The third factor, quality, is a base denominator to successful competition in the global economy. It is a necessary prerequisite to achieve competitive parity. It is a necessary but insufficient condition for gaining an advantage.

- The type of action (strategic or tactical) the firm took, the competitor's reputation for the nature of its competitor behavior, and that competitor's dependence on the market in which the action was taken are studied to predict a competitor's response to the firm's action. In general, the number of tactical responses taken exceeds the number of strategic responses. Competitors respond more frequently to the actions taken by the firm with a reputation for predictable and understandable competitive behavior, especially if that firm is a market leader. In general, the firm can predict that when its competitor is highly dependent for its revenue and profitability in the market in which the firm took a competitive action, that competitor is likely to launch a strong response. However, firms that are more diversified across markets are less likely to respond to a particular action that affects only one of the markets in which they compete.
- Competitive dynamics concerns the ongoing competitive behavior occurring among all firms competing in a market for advantageous positions. Market characteristics affect the set of actions and responses firms take while competing in a given market as well as the sustainability of firms' competitive advantages. In slow-cycle markets, where competitive advantages can be maintained, competitive dynamics finds firms taking actions and responses that are intended to protect, maintain, and extend their proprietary advantages. In fast-cycle markets, competition is almost frenzied as firms concentrate on developing a series of temporary competitive advantages. This emphasis is necessary because firms' advantages in fast-cycle markets aren't proprietary and, as such, are subject to rapid and relatively inexpensive imitation. Standard-cycle markets experience competition between slow-cycle and fast-cycle markets; firms are moderately shielded from competition in these markets as they use capabilities that produce competitive advantages that are moderately sustainable. Competitors in standard-cycle markets serve mass markets and try to develop economies of scale to enhance their profitability. Innovation is vital to competitive success in each of the three types of markets. Companies should recognize that the set of competitive actions and responses taken by all firms differs by type of market.

Review Questions

1. Who are competitors? How are competitive rivalry, competitive behavior, and competitive dynamics defined in the chapter?
2. What is market commonality? What is resource similarity? What does it mean to say that these concepts are the building blocks for a competitor analysis?
3. How do awareness, motivation, and ability affect the firm's competitive behavior?
4. What factors affect the likelihood a firm will take a competitive action?
5. What factors affect the likelihood a firm will initiate a competitive response to the action taken by a competitor?
6. What competitive dynamics can be expected among firms competing in slow-cycle markets? In fast-cycle markets? In standard-cycle markets?

Experiential Exercises

Exercise 1: Win-Win, Win-Lose, or Lose-Lose?

A key aspect of company strategy concerns the interactions between two or more firms. When a new market segment emerges, should a firm strive for a first-mover advantage, or wait to see how the market takes shape? Diversified firms compete against one another in multiple market segments and must often consider how actions in one market might be subject to retaliation by a competitor in another segment. Similarly, when a competitor initiates a price war, a firm must decide whether it should respond in kind.

Game theory is helpful for understanding the strategic interaction between firms. Game theory uses assumptions about the behavior of rivals to help a company choose a specific strategy that maximizes its return. In this exercise, you will use game theory to help analyze business decisions.

Individual

One of the classic illustrations of game theory can be found in the prisoner's dilemma. Two criminals have been apprehended by the police for suspicion of a robbery. The police separate the thieves and offer them the same deal: Inform on your peer and receive a lesser sentence. Let your peer inform on you and receive a harsher sentence. What should you tell the police?

Visit http://www.gametheory.net where you can play the prisoner's dilemma against a computer. Play the dilemma using different parameters, and make notes of your experience.

Groups

Many examples of game theory can be found in popular culture, from the reality show *Survivor* to episodes of *The Simpsons*. Revisit http://www.gametheory.net and select either a TV or movie illustration. Discuss the applications of game theory with your team.

As a group, prepare a one-page summary of how game theory can be applied to competitive interactions between firms.

Exercise 2: Strategy as Warfare

It is common to see military analogies and phrasing used to describe strategy topics, particularly in regard to competitive dynamics and interfirm rivalry. For example, executives often speak about guerilla marketing, launching preemptive strikes on rivals, or battles for market share. Al Dunlap, a former CEO of Sunbeam, was once known as "Rambo in pinstripes" and even posed for a business magazine photo shoot wearing machine guns.

Military texts are often used to help understand how firms should act in relation to their competitors. Von Clauswitz's book *On War* draws on his experience in the Napoleonic Wars. Sun Tzu's *Art of War* is a much earlier—circa 500 B.C.E.—and more influential text, however. Sun Tzu was a Chinese general who, according to legend, was hired by the king after a demonstration of training using the king's concubines.

Part One

Break into teams of 4–6 persons. Each member should select a different chapter of *Art of War* (which has 13 chapters in total). Numerous sources on the Internet offer free downloads of the book, including an audiobook version at Project Gutenberg. (http://www.gutenberg.org). After reading your chapter, prepare a bullet-point summary for your team members on the chapter's relevance to corporate strategy.

Part Two

Have the team meet and ask each member to explain her/his summary of what was read. Then, answer the following questions:

- Which of Sun Tzu's ideas offered the most insightful analogies for interfirm rivalry?
- Which of Sun Tzu's ideas seemed to be the *least* relevant for understanding competitive dynamics among firms?
- What ideas from *Art of War* can you apply to an example used earlier in this chapter?

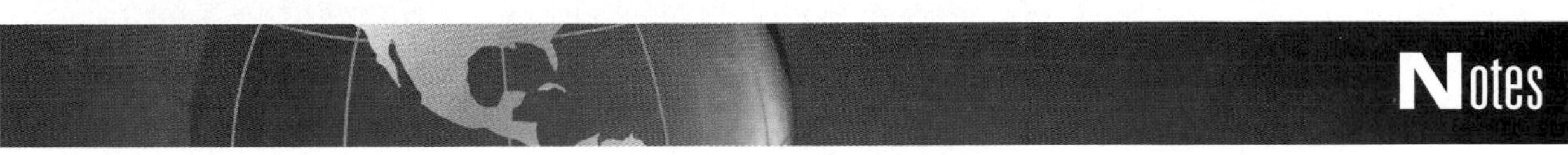

Notes

1. D. F. Spulber, 2004, *Management Strategy,* Boston: McGraw-Hill/Irwin, 87–88; M.-J. Chen, 1996, Competitor analysis and interfirm rivalry: Toward a theoretical integration, *Academy of Management Review,* 21: 100–134.
2. M. Bartiromo, 2007, Will Dell be a come-back kid? *BusinessWeek*, February 26, 128.
3. M. Schrage, 2007, The myth of commoditization, *MIT Sloan Management Review,* 48(2): 10–14; T. Galvin, 2002, Examining institutional change: Evidence from the founding dynamics of U.S. health care interest associations, *Academy of Management Journal,* 45: 673–696.
4. R. D. Ireland & J. W. Webb, 2007, Strategic entrepreneurship: Creating competitive advantage through streams of innovation, *Business Horizons,* 50: 49–59.
5. B. R. Barringer & R. D. Ireland, 2008, *Entrepreneurship: Successfully Launching New Ventures,* 2nd ed., Upper Saddle River, NJ: Prentice Hall; A. M. Knott & H. E. Posen, 2005, Is failure good? *Strategic Management Journal,* 26: 617–641.
6. C. M. Grimm, H. Lee, & K. G. Smith, 2006, *Strategy as Action: Competitive Dynamics and Competitive Advantage,* New York: Oxford University Press.
7. J. W. Selsky, J. Goes, & O. N. Baburoglu, 2007, Contrasting perspectives of strategy making: Applications in "hyper" environments, *Organization Studies,* 28(1): 71–94; A. Nair & L. Filer, 2003, Cointegration of firm strategies within groups: A long-run analysis of firm behavior in the Japanese steel industry, *Strategic Management Journal,* 24: 145–159.
8. T. C. Powell, 2003, Varieties of competitive parity, *Strategic Management Journal,* 24: 61–86.
9. J. Rodriguez-Pinto, J. Gutierrez-Cillan, & A. I. Rodriguez-Escudero, 2007, Order and scale market entry, firm resources, and performance, *European Journal of Marketing,* 41: 590–607; S. Jayachandran, J. Gimeno, & P. R. Varadarajan, 1999, Theory of multimarket competition: A synthesis and implications for marketing strategy, *Journal of Marketing,* 63: 49–66.
10. Grimm, Lee & Smith, *Strategy as Action*; G. Young, K. G. Smith, C. M. Grimm, & D. Simon, 2000, Multimarket contact and resource dissimilarity: A competitive dynamics perspective, *Journal of Management,* 26: 1217–1236.
11. T. L. Sorenson, 2007, Credible collusion in multimarket oligopoly, *Managerial and Decision Economics,* 28(2): 115-128; H. A. Haveman & L. Nonnemaker, 2000, Competition in multiple geographic markets: The impact on growth and market entry, *Administrative Science Quarterly,* 45: 232–267.
12. K. G. Smith, W. J. Ferrier, & H. Ndofor, 2001, Competitive dynamics research: Critique and future directions, in M. A. Hitt, R. E. Freeman, & J. S. Harrison (eds.), *Handbook of Strategic Management,* Oxford, UK: Blackwell Publishers, 326.
13. G. Young, K. G. Smith, & C. M. Grimm, 1996, "Austrian" and industrial organization perspectives on firm-level competitive activity and performance, *Organization Science,* 73: 243–254.
14. 2007, Dell to sell PCs at Wal-Mart in retail drive, http://www.reuters.com, May 24.
15. H. D. Hopkins, 2003, The response strategies of dominant U.S. firms to Japanese challengers, *Journal of Management,* 29: 5–25; G. S. Day & D. J. Reibstein, 1997, The dynamic challenges for theory and practice, in G. S. Day & D. J. Reibstein (eds.), *Wharton on Competitive Strategy,* New York: John Wiley & Sons, 2.
16. M.-J. Chen & D. C. Hambrick, 1995, Speed, stealth, and selective attack: How small firms differ from large firms in competitive behavior, *Academy of Management Journal,* 38: 453–482.
17. T. Dewett & S. David, 2007, Innovators and imitators in novelty-intensive markets: A research agenda, *Creativity and Innovation Management,* 16(1): 80–92.
18. P. Engardio, 2007, Flat panels, thin margins, *BusinessWeek,* February 26, 50–51.
19. A. Sahay, 2007, How to reap higher profits with dynamic pricing, *MIT Sloan Management Review,* 48(4): 53–60; T. J. Douglas & J. A. Ryman, 2003, Understanding competitive advantage in the general hospital industry: Evaluating strategic competencies, *Strategic Management Journal,* 24: 333–347.
20. T. Yu & A. A. Cannella, Jr., 2007, Rivalry between multinational enterprises: An event history approach, *Academy of Management Journal,* 50: 665–686; W. J. Ferrier, 2001, Navigating the competitive landscape: The drivers and consequences of competitive aggressiveness, *Academy of Management Journal,* 44: 858–877.
21. Smith, Ferrier, & Ndofor, Competitive dynamics research, 319.
22. J. Shamsie, 2003, The context of dominance: An industry-driven framework for exploiting reputation, *Strategic Management Journal,* 24: 199–215; K. Ramaswamy, 2001, Organizational ownership, competitive intensity, and firm

performance: An empirical study of the Indian manufacturing sector, *Strategic Management Journal,* 22: 989–998.

23. K. Cool, L. H. Roller, & B. Leleux, 1999, The relative impact of actual and potential rivalry on firm profitability in the pharmaceutical industry, *Strategic Management Journal,* 20: 1–14.
24. G. Leask & D. Parker, 2007, Strategic groups, competitive groups and performance within the U.K. pharmaceutical industry: Improving our understanding of the competitive process, *Strategic Management Journal,* 28: 723–745; D. R. Gnyawali & R. Madhavan, 2001, Cooperative networks and competitive dynamics: A structural embeddedness perspective, *Academy of Management Review,* 26: 431–445.
25. Y. Y. Kor & J. T. Mahoney, 2005, How dynamics, management, and governance of resource deployments influence firm-level performance, *Strategic Management Journal,* 26: 489–496.
26. R. L. Priem, L. G. Love, & M. A. Shaffer, 2002, Executives' perceptions of uncertainty scores: A numerical taxonomy and underlying dimensions, *Journal of Management,* 28: 725–746.
27. J. C. Bou & A. Satorra, 2007, The persistence of abnormal returns at industry and firm levels: Evidence from Spain, *Strategic Management Journal,* 28: 707–722.
28. Chen, Competitor analysis, 108.
29. B. Einhorn, 2007, A racer called Acer, *BusinessWeek,* February 26, 72.
30. Chen, Competitor analysis, 109.
31. K. Uhlenbruck, M. A. Hitt, & M. Semadeni, 2005, Market value effects of acquisitions of Internet firms: A resource-based analysis, working paper, University of Montana; A. Afuah, 2003, Redefining firm boundaries in the face of the Internet: Are firms really shrinking? *Academy of Management Review,* 28: 34–53.
32. H. Gebauer, 2007, Entering low-end markets: A new strategy for Swiss companies, *Journal of Business Strategy,* 27(5): 23–31.
33. 2007, YRC Worldwide, http://www.yrcw.com, July 30.
34. 2007, YRC Worldwide Inc., *Hoovers,* http://www.hoovers.com/yrc-worldwide, July 30.
35. Chen, Competitor analysis, 106.
36. M. J. Chen , K.-H. Su, & W. Tsai, 2007, Competitive tension: The awareness-motivation-capability perspective, *Academy of Management Journal,* 50: 101–118; J. Gimeno & C. Y. Woo, 1999, Multimarket contact, economies of scope, and firm performance, *Academy of Management Journal,* 42: 239–259.
37. M. Arndt, 2007, McDonald's, *BusinessWeek,* February 5, 64–72.
38. 2007, Prudential Financial Inc., *Standard & Poor's Stock Reports,* http://www.standardandpoors.com, July 12.
39. A. Carter, 2007, A shining light for Heineken, *BusinessWeek,* January 15, 46.
40. I. C. MacMillan, A. B. van Putten, & R. S. McGrath, 2003, Global gamesmanship, *Harvard Business Review,* 81(5): 62–71.
41. Young, Smith, Grimm, & Simon, Multimarket contact, 1230.
42. J. Gimeno, 1999, Reciprocal threats in multimarket rivalry: Staking out "spheres of influence" in the U.S. airline industry, *Strategic Management Journal,* 20: 101–128; N. Fernandez & P. L. Marin, 1998, Market power and multimarket contact: Some evidence from the Spanish hotel industry, *Journal of Industrial Economics,* 46: 301–315.
43. Jayachandran, Gimeno, & Varadarajan, Theory of multimarket competition, 59; Chen, Competitor analysis, 107.
44. J. Gimeno & C. Y. Woo, 1996, Hypercompetition in a multimarket environment: The role of strategic similarity and multimarket contact on competitive de-escalation, *Organization Science,* 7: 322–341.
45. C. H. Deutsch, 2007, UPS embraces high-tech delivery methods, *New York Times Online,* http://www.nytimes.com, July 12.
46. Ibid.
47. Chen, Su & Tsai, Competitive tension; Chen, Competitor analysis, 110.
48. Ibid.; W. Ocasio, 1997, Towards an attention-based view of the firm, *Strategic Management Journal,* 18 (Special Issue): 187–206; Smith, Ferrier, & Ndofor, Competitive dynamics research, 320.
49. 2007, Komatsu lifts outlook, outdoes rival Caterpillar, *New York Times Online,* http://www.nytimes.com, July 30.
50. 2007, Carrefour battles Wal-Mart in South America, Elsevier Food International, http://www.foodinternational.net, July 31.
51. S. Tallman, M. Jenkins, N. Henry, & S. Pinch, 2004, Knowledge, clusters and competitive advantage, *Academy of Management Review,* 29: 258–271; J. F. Porac & H. Thomas, 1994, Cognitive categorization and subjective rivalry among retailers in a small city, *Journal of Applied Psychology,* 79: 54–66.
52. S. H. Park & D. Zhou, 2005, Firm heterogeneity and competitive dynamics in alliance formation, *Academy of Management Review,* 30: 531–554.
53. Chen, Competitor analysis, 113.
54. R. Belderbos & L. Sleuwaegen, 2005, Competitive drivers and international plant configuration strategies: A product-level test, *Strategic Management Journal,* 26: 577–593.
55. C. M. Grimm & K. G. Smith, 1997, *Strategy as Action: Industry Rivalry and Coordination,* Cincinnati: South-Western Publishing Co., 125.
56. B. Webber, 2007, Volatile markets, *Business Strategy Review,* 18(2): 60–67; K. G. Smith, W. J. Ferrier, & C. M. Grimm, 2001, King of the hill: Dethroning the industry leader, *Academy of Management Executive,* 15(2): 59–70.
57. W. J. Ferrier & H. Lee, 2003, Strategic aggressiveness, variation, and surprise: How the sequential pattern of competitive rivalry influences stock market returns, *Journal of Managerial Issues,* 14: 162–180.
58. C. Palmeri, 2007, How Guess got its groove back, *BusinessWeek,* July 23, 126.
59. S. Holmes, 2007, Better living at 30,000 feet, *BusinessWeek,* August 6, 76–77.
60. L. Lee, 2007, A smoothie you can chew on, *BusinessWeek,* June 11, 64–65.
61. J. Schumpeter, 1934, *The Theory of Economic Development,* Cambridge, MA: Harvard University Press.
62. J. L. C. Cheng & I. F. Kesner, 1997, Organizational slack and response to environmental shifts: The impact of resource allocation patterns, *Journal of Management,* 23: 1–18.
63. F. F. Suarez & G. Lanzolla, 2007, The role of environmental dynamics in building a first mover advantage theory, *Academy of Management Review,* 32: 377–392.
64. F. Wang, 2000, Too appealing to overlook, *America's Network,* December, 10–12.
65. D. P. Forbes, 2005, Managerial determinants of decision speed in new ventures, *Strategic Management Journal,* 26: 355–366.
66. W. T. Robinson & S. Min, 2002, Is the first to market the first to fail? Empirical evidence for industrial goods businesses, *Journal of Marketing Research,* 39: 120–128.
67. T. Cottrell & B. R. Nault, 2004, *Strategic Management Journal,* 25: 1005–1025; R. Agarwal, M. B. Sarkar, & R. Echambadi, 2002, The conditioning effect of time on firm survival: An industry life cycle approach, *Academy of Management Journal,* 45: 971–994.
68. A. Srivastava & H. Lee, 2005, Predicting order and timing of new product moves: The role of top management in corporate entrepreneurship, *Journal of Business Venturing,* 20: 459–481; A. Nerer & P. W. Roberts, 2004, Technological and product-market experience and the success of new product introductions in the pharmaceutical industry, *Strategic Management Journal,* 25: 779–799.
69. M. S. Giarratana & A. Fosfuri, 2007, Product strategies and survival in Schumpeterian environments: Evidence from the U.S. security software industry, *Organization Studies,* 28(6): 909–929; J. W. Spencer & T. P. Murtha, 2005, How do governments matter to new industry creation? *Academy of Management Review,* 30: 321–337.
70. Z. Simsek, J. F. Veiga, & M. H. Lubatkin, 2007, The impact of managerial environmental perceptions on corporate entrepreneurship: Toward understanding discretionary slack's pivotal role, *Journal of Management Studies,* in press; S. W. Geiger & L. H. Cashen, 2002, A multidimensional examination of slack and its impact on innovation, *Journal of Managerial Issues,* 14: 68–84.
71. B.-S. Teng, 2007, Corporate entrepreneurship activities through strategic alliances: A resource-based approach toward competitive advantage, *Journal of Management Studies,* 44: 119–142; M. B. Lieberman & D. B. Montgomery, 1988, First-mover advantages, *Strategic Management Journal,* 9: 41–58.
72. 2001, Older, wiser, webbier, *The Economist,* June 30, 10.

73. M. Shank, 2002, Executive strategy report, IBM business strategy consulting, http://www.ibm.com, March 14; W. Boulding & M. Christen, 2001, First-mover disadvantage, *Harvard Business Review,* 79(9): 20–21.
74. S. Hamm, 2007, Kodak's moment of truth, *BusinessWeek*, February 19, 42–49.
75. Ibid., 42.
76. J. Gimeno, R. E. Hoskisson, B. B. Beal, & W. P. Wan, 2005, Explaining the clustering of international expansion moves: A critical test in the U.S. telecommunications industry, *Academy of Management Journal,* 48: 297–319; K. G. Smith, C. M. Grimm, & M. J. Gannon, 1992, *Dynamics of Competitive Strategy,* Newberry Park, CA.: Sage Publications.
77. E. Schine, 2007, GM's big move to small Chevrolets, *BusinessWeek*, April 9, 9.
78. S. D. Dobrev & G. R. Carroll, 2003, Size (and competition) among organizations: Modeling scale-based selection among automobile producers in four major countries, 1885–1981, *Strategic Management Journal,* 24: 541–558.
79. F. K. Pil & M. Hoiweg, 2003, Exploring scale: The advantage of thinking small, *The McKinsey Quarterly,* 44(2): 33–39; Chen & Hambrick, Speed, stealth, and selective attack.
80. M. A. Hitt, L. Bierman & J. D. Collins, 2007, The strategic evolution of U.S. law firms, *Business Horizons*, 50: 17–28; D. Miller & M. J. Chen, 1996, The simplicity of competitive repertoires: An empirical analysis, *Strategic Management Journal,* 17: 419–440.
81. Young, Smith, & Grimm, "Austrian" and industrial organization perspectives.
82. B. A. Melcher, 1993, How Goliaths can act like Davids, *BusinessWeek,* Special Issue, 193.
83. G. McWilliams & S. Vranica, 2007, Wal-Mart raises its emotional pitch, *Wall Street Journal Online*, http://online.wsj.com, July 20.
84. P. B. Crosby, 1980, *Quality Is Free*, New York: Penguin.
84. W. E. Deming, 1986, *Out of the Crisis,* Cambridge, MA: MIT Press.
86. D. A. Mollenkopf, E. Rabinovich, T. M. Laseter, & K. K. Boyer, 2007, Managing Internet product returns: A focus on effective service operations, *Decision Sciences*, 38: 215–250; L. B. Crosby, R. DeVito, & J. M. Pearson, 2003, Manage your customers' perception of quality, *Review of Business,* 24(1): 18–24.
87. K. Watanabe, 2007, Lessons from Toyota's long drive, *Harvard Business Review,* 85(7/8): 74–83; R. S. Kaplan & D. P. Norton, 2001, *The Strategy-Focused Organization,* Boston: Harvard Business School Press.
88. O. Bayazit & B. Karpak, 2007, An analytical network process-based framework for successful total quality management (TQM): An assessment of Turkish manufacturing industry readiness, *International Journal of Production Economics*, 105(1): 79–96.
89. K. E. Weick & K. M. Sutcliffe, 2001, *Managing the Unexpected,* San Francisco: Jossey-Bass, 81–82.
90. G. Macintosh, 2007, Customer orientation, relationship quality, and relational benefits to the firm, *Journal of Services Marketing,* 21(3): 150–159; G. Yeung & V. Mok, 2005, What are the impacts of implementing ISOs on the competitiveness of manufacturing industry in China, *Journal of World Business,* 40: 139–157.
91. J. Tagliabue, 2007, Low-cost Chinese cars making restrained entry to European market, *New York Times Online,* http://www.nytimes.com, July 13.
92. G. Edmondson, 2006, Mercedes gets back up to speed, *BusinessWeek*, November 13, 46–47.
93. J. Schumpeter, 1950, *Capitalism, Socialism and Democracy*, New York: Harper; Smith, Ferrier, & Ndofor, Competitive dynamics research, 323.
94. M. J. Chen & I. C. MacMillan, 1992, Nonresponse and delayed response to competitive moves, *Academy of Management Journal,* 35: 539–570; Smith, Ferrier, & Ndofor, Competitive dynamics research, 335.
95. M. Wong, 2007, Battling rivals, Palm sells 25% to Elevation, *The Salt Lake Tribune Online*, http://www.sltrib.com, June 4.
96. M. J. Chen, K. G. Smith, & C. M. Grimm, 1992, Action characteristics as predictors of competitive responses, *Management Science*, 38: 439–455.
97. M. J. Chen & D. Miller, 1994, Competitive attack, retaliation and performance: An expectancy-valence framework, *Strategic Management Journal,* 15: 85–102.
98. T. Gardner, 2005, Interfirm competition for human resources: Evidence from the software industry, *Academy of Management Journal*, 48: 237–258; N. Huyghebaert & L. M. van de Gucht, 2004, Incumbent strategic behavior in financial markets and the exit of entrepreneurial start-ups, *Strategic Management Journal*, 25: 669–688.
99. Smith, Ferrier, & Ndofor, Competitive dynamics research, 333.
100. V. P. Rindova, A. P. Petkova, & S. Kotha, 2007, Standing out: How firms in emerging markets build reputation, *Strategic Organization*, 5: 31–70; J. Shamsie, 2003, The context of dominance: An industry-driven framework for exploiting reputation, *Strategic Management Journal*, 24: 199–215.
101. A. D. Smith, 2007, Making the case for the competitive advantage of corporate social responsibility, *Business Strategy Series*, 8(3): 186–195; P. W. Roberts & G. R. Dowling, 2003, Corporate reputation and sustained superior financial performance, *Strategic Management Journal*, 24: 1077–1093.
102. W. J. Ferrier, K. G. Smith, & C. M. Grimm, 1999, The role of competitive actions in market share erosion and industry dethronement: A study of industry leaders and challengers, *Academy of Management Journal*, 42: 372–388.
103. Smith, Grimm, & Gannon, *Dynamics of Competitive Strategy.*
104. A. Karnani & B. Wernerfelt, 1985, Multiple point competition, *Strategic Management Journal*, 6: 87–97.
105. Smith, Ferrier, & Ndofor, Competitive dynamics research, 330.
106. S. L. Newbert, 2007, Empirical research on the resource-based view of the firm: An assessment and suggestions for future research, *Strategic Management Journal,* 28: 121–146; G. McNamara, P. M. Vaaler, & C. Devers, 2003, Same as it ever was: The search for evidence of increasing hypercompetition, *Strategic Management Journal,* 24: 261–278.
107. A. Kalnins & W. Chung, 2004, Resource-seeking agglomeration: A study of market entry in the lodging industry, *Strategic Management Journal,* 25: 689–699.
108. J. R. Williams, 1992, How sustainable is your competitive advantage? *California Management Review,* 34(3): 29–51.
109. D. A. Chmielewski & A. Paladino, 2007, Driving a resource orientation: Reviewing the role of resources and capability characteristics, *Management Decision*, 45: 462–483.
110. N. Pangarkar & J. R. Lie, 2004, The impact of market cycle on the performance of Singapore acquirers, *Strategic Management Journal,* 25: 1209–1216.
111. Ibid., 57.
112. 2003, How fast is your company? *Fast Company,* June, 18.
113. D. P. Forbes, 2007, Reconsidering the strategic implications of decision comprehensiveness, *Academy of Management Review,* 32: 361–376; T. Talaulicar, J. Grundei, & A. V. Werder, 2005, Strategic decision making in start-ups: The effect of top management team organization and processes on speed and comprehensiveness, *Journal of Business Venturing,* 20: 519–541.
114. M. Song, C. Droge, S. Hanvanich, & R. Calantone, 2005, Marketing and technology resource complementarity: An analysis of their interaction effect in two environmental contexts, *Strategic Management Journal,* 26: 259–276.
115. R. Williams, 1999, Renewable advantage: Crafting strategy through economic time, New York: Free Press, 8.
116. Ibid.
117. D. Li, L. E. Eden, M. A. Hitt, & R. D. Ireland, 2008, Friends, acquaintances or strangers? Partner selection in R&D alliances, *Academy of Management Journal*, in press; D. Gerwin, 2004, Coordinating new product development in strategic alliances, *Academy of Management Review,* 29: 241–257.
118. P. Carbonell & A. I. Rodriguez, 2006, The impact of market characteristics and innovation speed on perceptions of positional advantage and new product performance, *International Journal of Research in Marketing*, 23(1): 1–12; R. Sanchez, 1995, Strategic flexibility in production competition, *Strategic Management Journal,* 16 (Special Issue): 9–26.
119. Williams, *Renewable Advantage*, 7.
120. J. W. Peters, 2007, In small packages, fewer calories and more profit, *New York Times Online*, http://www.nytimes.com, July 7.
121. Ibid.
122. P. Bhatnagar, 2006, What's for dinner in 2006? *CNNMoney*, http://cnnmoney.com, January 11.

Corporate-Level Strategy

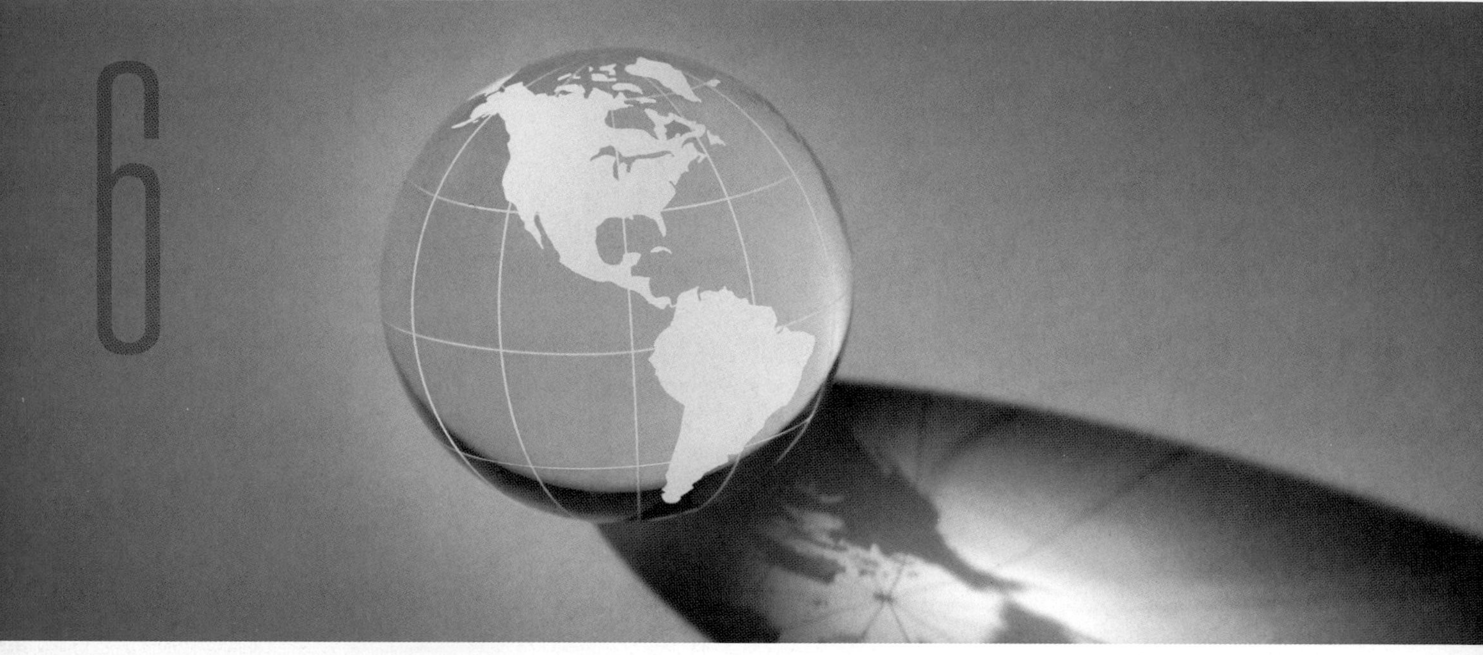

Studying this chapter should provide you with the strategic management knowledge needed to:

1. Define corporate-level strategy and discuss its purpose.
2. Describe different levels of diversification with different corporate-level strategies.
3. Explain three primary reasons firms diversify.
4. Describe how firms can create value by using a related diversification strategy.
5. Explain the two ways value can be created with an unrelated diversification strategy.
6. Discuss the incentives and resources that encourage diversification.
7. Describe motives that can encourage managers to overdiversify a firm.

Procter and Gamble's Diversification Strategy

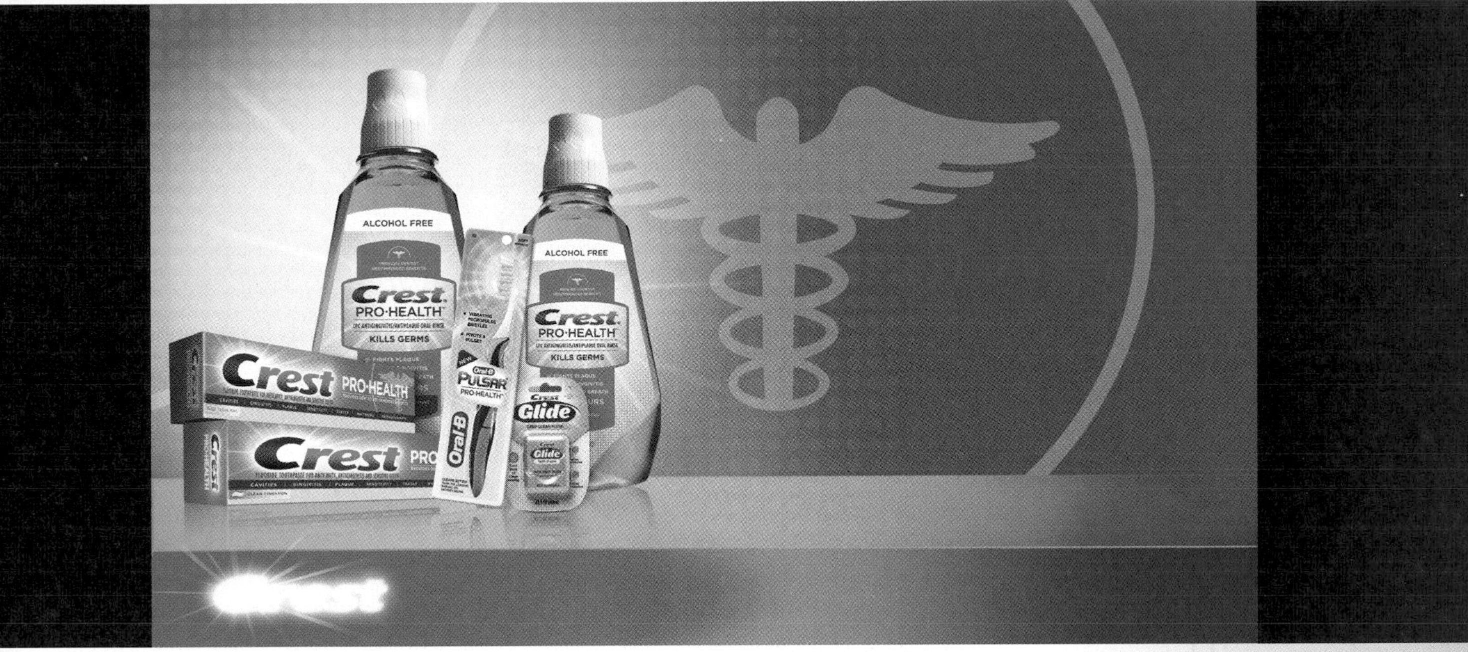

As firms grow they often seek to use the expertise and knowledge that they have gained in one business by diversifying into a business where this knowledge can be used in a related way. Economists call it "economizing on the scope of the firm," or more succinctly economies of scope (this concept will be defined more formally in the chapter). Once a firm is able to diversify using its previous expertise in other businesses, it applies a concept known as synergy, where the value added by the corporate office adds up to more than the value would be if the different businesses in the corporate portfolio were separate and independent. However, creating synergistic relationships between businesses is often more difficult than it appears. Procter & Gamble (P&G) has been seeking to create relatedness between various consumer product businesses for many years.

In 2005, Procter & Gamble Companies acquired the Gillette Company with high expectations to create synergies between these businesses. Because Gillette's consumer health care products—including products marketed under Gillette, Braun, Duracell and Oral-B brands, among others—were focused mainly on more masculine market areas and P&G had more focus on beauty products for women and baby care products, management saw complementary opportunities between these two corporations. To complete the merger, however, both businesses needed to sell off other product lines to meet antitrust requirements. For example, Gillette had to sell off its Rembrandt toothpaste brand and P&G had to sell off its Spin Brush toothbrush brand.

One area in which they sought to create the potential synergy was combining the toothbrush and toothpaste businesses. Colgate had recently surpassed P&G's previously leading brand—Crest toothpaste. In a strategy designed to regain the lead, P&G sought to combine the Crest Toothpaste brand with the Oral-B Toothbrush using the "Pro-Health" label in seeking to sell both these complementary products. Previously the oral care retail shelves were fragmented with toothbrushes in one area and toothpaste in another. This arrangement is different from hair care or skin care products where the brands usually can be located together. As such, the combined approach may provide P&G an advantage that allows retailers to save precious shelf space and makes it easier for customers to find the separate products. However, because they had to sell off some of the other leading brands in the oral health segment, they lost some prospective market power.

Although this strategy appeared to have potential, it was much more difficult to create actual operational relatedness between the products (operational relatedness will be defined more clearly later in the chapter) than either P&G or Gillette had expected. First, Bruce Cleverly (from Gillette) and Charlie Pierce (from P&G), decided that they needed to commingle the employees in one place. Accordingly, they moved the essence of the operations to Cincinnati, Ohio, near P&G's headquarters. In the process, however, many of the Boston-area Gillette employees decided not to move, leading to an exit of talent. Second, P&G and Gillette had different ways of making business decisions. Although Cleverly was in charge, he was used to having freedom to make decisions, whereas the culture of P&G was more of a consensus-seeking process in making major decisions. Ultimately, Cleverly retired and turned the decision making over to Pierce. The business cultures never truly united, even after the combination of employees in Cincinnati, because these firms had previously been competitors.

The combination of the research unit in charge of providing new products for the Pro-Health project proceeded much better than the combination of the production and marketing personnel in Ohio. The most likely reason is that the research unit employees were able to stay in their general locations and collaborate through conferences and electronic means. Despite the difficulties, in 2007 the combined P&G brands overtook Colgate in market share with 35 percent to Colgate's 32 percent. As this case illustrates, merging two diverse firms to create operational relatedness or synergy between products can be more difficult to achieve than is apparent in the design phase.

Sources: 2007, P&G to be divided into three global units, Gillette will no longer be a separate unit, *FireWire,* May 15,1; E. Byron, 2007, Colgate's changing of the guard, *Wall Street Journal,* July 2, B7; E. Byron, 2007, Merger challenge: Unite toothbrush, toothpaste: P&G and Gillette find creating synergy can be harder than it looks, *Wall Street Journal,* April 24, A1, A17; J. Chang, 2007, Design to sell, *Sales and Working Management,* May; J. Neff, 2007, P&G struggles to hang on to top Gillette talent, *Advertising Age,* May 28, 28–29; J. Neff, 2007, Who wins? *Advertising Age,* June 18, 36–37; S. Brangen & C. Huxham, 2006, Achieving a collaborative advantage: Understanding the challenge and making it happen, *Strategic Direction,* 22(2): 3–5.

Our discussions of business-level strategies (Chapter 4) and the competitive rivalry and competitive dynamics associated with them (Chapter 5) concentrate on firms competing in a single industry or product market.[1] In this chapter, we introduce you to corporate-level strategies, which are strategies firms use to *diversify* their operations from a single business competing in a single market into several product markets and, most commonly, into several businesses. Thus, a **corporate-level strategy** specifies actions a firm takes to gain a competitive advantage by selecting and managing a group of different businesses competing in different product markets. Corporate-level strategies help companies select new strategic positions—positions that are expected to increase the firm's value.[2] As explained in the Opening Case, Procter & Gamble (P&G) competes in a number of different consumer product markets and often uses related diversification as illustrated through combining two of its brands, Crest toothpaste and Oral-B toothbrushes (part of the Gillette acquisition in 2005), into the Crest Pro-Health label to jointly market its products.

A **corporate-level strategy** specifies actions a firm takes to gain a competitive advantage by selecting and managing a group of different businesses competing in different product markets.

As is the case with P&G, firms use corporate-level strategies as a means to grow revenues and profits. But the decision to take actions to pursue growth is never a risk-free choice for firms to make. Indeed, as the Opening Case illustrated, P&G experienced difficulty in integrating the Crest and Oral-B brand operations to produce the Pro-Health products. Effective firms carefully evaluate their growth options (including the different corporate-level strategies) before committing firm resources to any of them.[3]

Because the diversified firm operates in several different and unique product markets and likely in several businesses, it forms two types of strategies: corporate level (or company-wide) and business level (or competitive).[4] Corporate-level strategy is concerned with two key issues: in what product markets and businesses the firm should compete and how corporate headquarters should manage those businesses.[5] For the diversified corporation, a business-level strategy (see Chapter 4) must be selected for each of the businesses in which the firm has decided to compete. In this regard, each of P&G's products or businesses uses a differentiation business-level strategy.

As is the case with a business-level strategy, a corporate-level strategy is expected to help the firm earn above-average returns by creating value.[6] Some suggest that few corporate-level strategies actually create value.[7] As the Opening Case indicates, realizing value through a corporate strategy can be difficult to achieve. In fact, the degree to which corporate-level strategies create value beyond the sum of the value created by all of a firm's business units remains an important research question.[8]

Evidence suggests that a corporate-level strategy's value is ultimately determined by the degree to which "the businesses in the portfolio are worth more under the management of the company than they would be under any other ownership."[9] Thus, an effective corporate-level strategy creates, across all of a firm's businesses, aggregate returns that exceed what those returns would be without the strategy[10] and contributes to the firm's strategic competitiveness and its ability to earn above-average returns.[11]

Product diversification, a primary form of corporate-level strategies, concerns the scope of the markets and industries in which the firm competes as well as "how managers buy, create and sell different businesses to match skills and strengths with opportunities presented to the firm."[12] Successful diversification is expected to reduce variability in the firm's profitability as earnings are generated from different businesses.[13] Because firms incur development and monitoring costs when diversifying, the ideal portfolio of businesses balances diversification's costs and benefits. CEOs and their top-management teams are responsible for determining the ideal portfolio for their company.[14]

We begin this chapter by examining different levels of diversification (from low to high). After describing the different reasons firms diversify their operations, we focus on two types of related diversification (related diversification signifies a moderate to a high level of diversification for the firm). When properly used, these strategies help create value in the diversified firm, either through the sharing of resources (the related constrained strategy) or the transferring of core competencies across the firm's different businesses (the related linked strategy). We then discuss unrelated diversification, which is another corporate-level strategy that can create value. The chapter then shifts to the topic of incentives and resources that may stimulate diversification which is value neutral. However, managerial motives to diversify, the final topic in the chapter, can actually destroy some of the firm's value.

Levels of Diversification

Diversified firms vary according to their level of diversification and the connections between and among their businesses. Figure 6.1 lists and defines five categories of businesses according to increasing levels of diversification. The single- and dominant-business categories denote relatively low levels of diversification; more fully diversified firms are classified into related and unrelated categories. A firm is related through its diversification when its businesses share several links; for example, businesses may share products (goods or services), technologies, or distribution channels. The more links among businesses, the more "constrained" is the relatedness of diversification. Unrelatedness refers to the absence of direct links between businesses.

Low Levels of Diversification

A firm pursing a low level of diversification uses either a single- or a dominant-business, corporate-level diversification strategy. A *single-business diversification strategy* is a corporate-level strategy wherein the firm generates 95 percent or more of its sales revenue from its core business area.[15] For example, Wm. Wrigley Jr. Company, the world's largest producer of chewing and bubble gums, historically used a single-business strategy while operating in relatively few product markets. Wrigley's trademark chewing gum brands include Spearmint, Doublemint, and Juicy Fruit, although the firm produces other products as well. Sugar-free Extra, which currently holds the largest share of the U.S. chewing gum market, was introduced in 1984.

Wrigley is beginning to diversify its product portfolio to become an important player in the confectionery market. In 2005, Wrigley acquired certain confectionary assets from

Figure 6.1 Levels and Types of Diversification

Low Levels of Diversification		
Single business:	95% or more of revenue comes from a single business.	 A
Dominant business:	Between 70% and 95% of revenue comes from a single business.	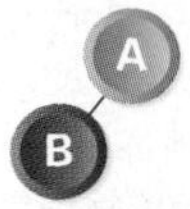 A–B
Moderate to High Levels of Diversification		
Related constrained:	Less than 70% of revenue comes from the dominant business, and all businesses share product, technological, and distribution linkages.	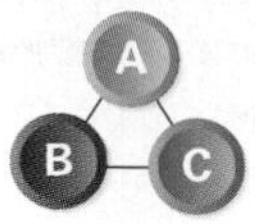 A–B–C (all linked)
Related linked (mixed related and unrelated):	Less than 70% of revenue comes from the dominant business, and there are only limited links between businesses.	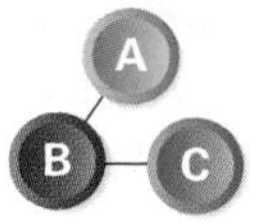 A–B–C (limited links)
Very High Levels of Diversification		
Unrelated:	Less than 70% of revenue comes from the dominant business, and there are no common links between businesses.	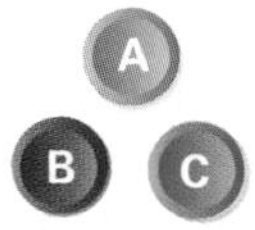 A B C

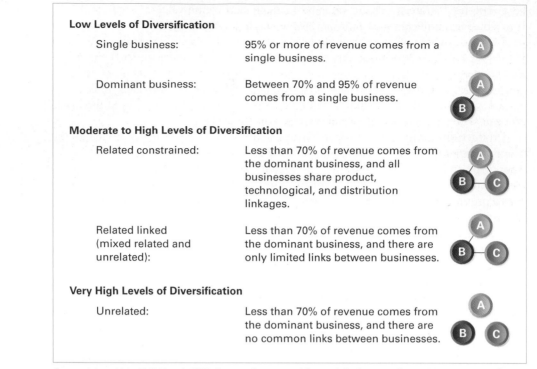

Source: Adapted from R. P. Rumelt, 1974, *Strategy, Structure and Economic Performance,* Boston: Harvard Business School.

Kraft Foods Inc., including the well-known brands Life Savers and Altoids. Apparently, Wrigley management has had a difficult time integrating this acquisition because Wrigley's share price has since decreased in value. Hershey recently offered to merge with Cadbury Schweppe's gum brands. If in response Wrigley tried to buy Hershey, it would probably have to pay a high premium for the Hershey assets. Alternatively, it may be in an even more "sticky" situation if Cadbury is able to acquire Hershey's assets. Thus, diversification strategies can be risky whether a company or its rival buys the assets of a firm.[16] With increasing diversification of its product lines, Wrigley may soon begin using the dominant-business corporate-level strategy.

With the *dominant-business diversification strategy,* the firm generates between 70 and 95 percent of its total revenue within a single business area. United Parcel Service (UPS) uses this strategy. Recently UPS generated 74 percent of its revenue from its U.S. package delivery business and 17 percent from its international package business, with the remaining 9 percent coming from the firm's non-package business.[17] Though the U.S. package delivery business currently generates the largest percentage of UPS's sales revenue, the firm anticipates that in the future its other two businesses will account for the majority of revenue growth. This expectation suggests that UPS may become more diversified, both in terms of its goods and services and in the number of countries in which those goods and services are offered.

Moderate and High Levels of Diversification

A firm generating more than 30 percent of its revenue outside a dominant business and whose businesses are related to each other in some manner uses a related diversification corporate-level strategy. When the links between the diversified firm's businesses are rather direct, a *related constrained diversification strategy* is being used. Campbell Soup, Procter & Gamble, Kodak, and Merck & Company all use a related constrained strategy, as do some large cable companies. With a related constrained strategy, a firm shares resources and activities between its businesses.

The diversified company with a portfolio of businesses that have only a few links between them is called a mixed related and unrelated firm and is using the *related linked diversification strategy* (see Figure 6.1). Johnson & Johnson, Procter & Gamble, and General Electric (GE) use this corporate-level diversification strategy. Compared with related constrained firms, related linked firms share fewer resources and assets between their businesses, concentrating instead on transferring knowledge and core competencies between the businesses. As with firms using each type of diversification strategy, companies implementing the related linked strategy constantly adjust the mix in their portfolio of businesses as well as make decisions about how to manage these businesses.

Li Ka-Shing (center), CEO of Hutchison Whampoa Limited (HWL), runs a conglomerate that follows an unrelated diversification strategy.

A highly diversified firm that has no relationships between its businesses follows an *unrelated diversification strategy*. United Technologies, Textron, Samsung, and Hutchison Whampoa Limited (HWL) are examples of firms using this type of corporate-level strategy. Commonly, firms using this strategy are called *conglomerates.*

HWL is a leading international corporation committed to innovation and technology with businesses spanning the globe.[18] Ports and related services, telecommunications, property and hotels, retail and manufacturing, and energy and infrastructure are HWL's five core businesses. These businesses are not related to each other, and the firm makes no efforts to share activities or to transfer core competencies between or among them. Each of these five businesses is quite large; for example, the retailing arm of the retail and manufacturing business has more than 6,200 stores in 31 countries. Groceries, cosmetics, electronics, wine, and airline tickets are some of the product categories featured in these stores. This firm's size and diversity suggest the challenge of successfully managing the unrelated diversification strategy. However, Hutchison's CEO Li Ka-shing, has been successful at not only making smart acquisitions, but also at divesting businesses at good prices.[19]

Reasons for Diversification

A firm uses a corporate-level diversification strategy for a variety of reasons (see Table 6.1). Typically, a diversification strategy is used to increase the firm's value by improving its overall performance. Value is created either through related diversification or through unrelated diversification when the strategy allows a company's businesses to increase revenues or reduce costs while implementing their business-level strategies.

Other reasons for using a diversification strategy may have nothing to do with increasing the firm's value; in fact, diversification can have neutral effects or even reduce a firm's value. Value-neutral reasons for diversification include those of a desire to match and thereby neutralize a competitor's market power (such as to neutralize another firm's advantage by acquiring a similar distribution outlet). Decisions to expand a firm's portfolio of businesses to reduce managerial risk can have a negative effect on the firm's value. Greater amounts of diversification reduce managerial risk in that if one of the businesses in a diversified firm fails, the top executive of that business does not risk total failure by the corporation. As such, this reduces the top executives' employment risk. In addition, because diversification can increase a firm's size and thus managerial compensation, managers have motives to diversify a firm to a level that reduces its value.[20] Diversification rationales that may have a neutral or negative effect on the firm's value are discussed later in the chapter.

Operational relatedness and corporate relatedness are two ways diversification strategies can create value (see Figure 6.2 on page 159). Studies of these independent relatedness

Table 6.1 Reasons for Diversification

Value-Creating Diversification

- Economies of scope (related diversification)
  - Sharing activities
  - Transferring core competencies
- Market power (related diversification)
  - Blocking competitors through multipoint competition
  - Vertical integration
- Financial economies (unrelated diversification)
  - Efficient internal capital allocation
  - Business restructuring

Value-Neutral Diversification

- Antitrust regulation
- Tax laws
- Low performance
- Uncertain future cash flows
- Risk reduction for firm
- Tangible resources
- Intangible resources

Value-Reducing Diversification

- Diversifying managerial employment risk
- Increasing managerial compensation

dimensions show the importance of resources and key competencies.[21] The figure's vertical dimension depicts opportunities to share operational activities between businesses (operational relatedness) while the horizontal dimension suggests opportunities for transferring corporate-level core competencies (corporate relatedness). The firm with a strong capability in managing operational synergy, especially in sharing assets between its businesses, falls in the upper left quadrant, which also represents vertical sharing of assets through vertical integration. The lower right quadrant represents a highly developed corporate capability for transferring one or more core competencies across businesses. This capability is located primarily in the corporate headquarters office. Unrelated diversification is also illustrated in Figure 6.2 in the lower left quadrant. Financial economies (discussed later), rather than either operational or corporate relatedness, are the source of value creation for firms using the unrelated diversification strategy.

Value-Creating Diversification: Related Constrained and Related Linked Diversification

Economies of scope are cost savings that the firm creates by successfully sharing some of its resources and capabilities or transferring one or more corporate-level core competencies that were developed in one of its businesses to another of its businesses.

With the related diversification corporate-level strategy, the firm builds upon or extends its resources and capabilities to create value.[22] The company using the related diversification strategy wants to develop and exploit economies of scope between its businesses.[23] Available to companies operating in multiple product markets or industries,[24] **economies of scope** are cost savings that the firm creates by successfully sharing some of its resources and capabilities or transferring one or more corporate-level core competencies that were developed in one of its businesses to another of its businesses.

Figure 6.2 Value-Creating Diversification Strategies: Operational and Corporate Relatedness

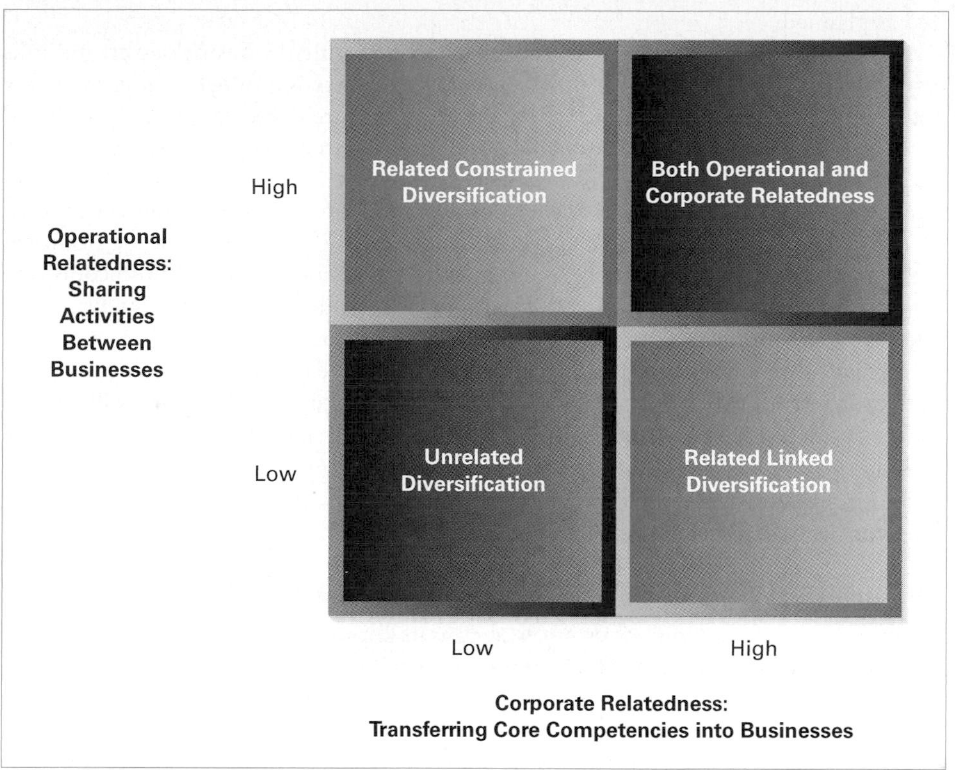

As illustrated in Figure 6.2, firms seek to create value from economies of scope through two basic kinds of operational economies: sharing activities (operational relatedness) and transferring corporate-level core competencies (corporate relatedness). The difference between sharing activities and transferring competencies is based on how separate resources are jointly used to create economies of scope. To create economies of scope tangible resources, such as plant and equipment or other business-unit physical assets, often must be shared. Less tangible resources, such as manufacturing know-how can also be shared. However, know-how transferred between separate activities with no physical or tangible resource involved is a transfer of a corporate-level core competence, not an operational sharing of activities.[25]

Operational Relatedness: Sharing Activities

Firms can create operational relatedness by sharing either a primary activity (such as inventory delivery systems) or a support activity (such as purchasing practices)—see Chapter 3's discussion of the value chain. Firms using the related constrained diversification strategy share activities in order to create value. Procter & Gamble (P&G) uses this corporate-level strategy. P&G's paper towel business and baby diaper business both use paper products as a primary input to the manufacturing process. The firm's paper production plant produces inputs for both businesses and is an example of a shared activity. In addition, because they both produce consumer products, these two businesses are likely to share distribution channels and sales networks.

As noted in the Opening Case, P&G acquired Gillette Co. Operational relatedness has been necessary in the research and marketing activities needed for the creation of Crest Pro-Health label through combining the Crest and Oral-B brands. To further foster operational relatedness, many of the people associated with the production operations of Oral-B toothbrush products were relocated to Cincinnati, near the Crest division operations as well P&G headquarters.[26] Firms expect activity sharing among units to result in increased strategic competitiveness and improved financial returns.[27] Through its shared product approach, P&G has improved its market share position. However, as previously mentioned, pursuing operational relatedness is not easy, and often synergies are not realized as planned.

Activity sharing is also risky because ties among a firm's businesses create links between outcomes. For instance, if demand for one business's product is reduced, it may not generate sufficient revenues to cover the fixed costs required to operate the shared facilities. These types of organizational difficulties can reduce activity-sharing success.[28]

Although activity sharing across businesses is not risk-free, research shows that it can create value. For example, studies that examined acquisitions of firms in the same industry (horizontal acquisitions), such as the banking industry, found that sharing resources and activities and thereby creating economies of scope contributed to postacquisition increases in performance and higher returns to shareholders.[29] Additionally, firms that sold off related units in which resource sharing was a possible source of economies of scope have been found to produce lower returns than those that sold off businesses unrelated to the firm's core business.[30] Still other research discovered that firms with closely related businesses have lower risk.[31] These results suggest that gaining economies of scope by sharing activities across a firm's businesses may be important in reducing risk and in creating value. Further, more attractive results are obtained through activity sharing when a strong corporate headquarters office facilitates it.[32]

Corporate Relatedness: Transferring of Core Competencies

Corporate-level core competencies are complex sets of resources and capabilities that link different businesses, primarily through managerial and technological knowledge, experience, and expertise.

Over time, the firm's intangible resources, such as its know-how, become the foundation of core competencies. **Corporate-level core competencies** are complex sets of resources and capabilities that link different businesses, primarily through managerial and technological knowledge, experience, and expertise.[33] The ability to successfully price new products in all of the firm's businesses is an example of what research has shown to be a value-creating, corporate-level competence.[34] Firms seeking to create value through corporate relatedness use the related linked diversification strategy.

In at least two ways, the related linked diversification strategy helps firms to create value.[35] First, because the expense of developing a core competence has been incurred in one of the firm's businesses, transferring it to a second business eliminates the need for that second business to allocate resources to develop it. Such is the case at Hewlett-Packard (HP), where the firm transferred its competence in ink printers to high-end copiers. Rather than the standard laser printing technology in most high-end copiers, HP is using ink-based technology. One manager liked the product because, as he noted, "We are able to do a lot better quality at less price."[36] This capability will also give HP the opportunity to sell more ink products, which is how it has been able to create higher profit margins.

Hewlett-Packard's high-end copiers are a result of the firm's transferring competence from ink printers to this new product.

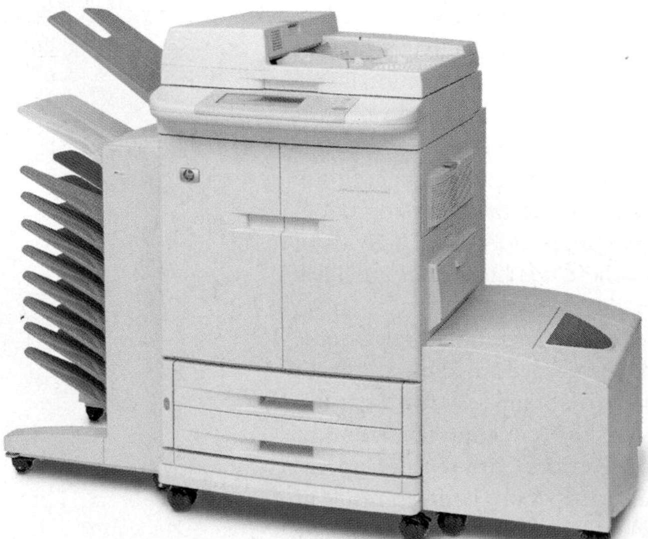

Resource intangibility is a second source of value creation through corporate relatedness. Intangible resources are difficult for competitors to understand and imitate. Because of this difficulty, the unit receiving a transferred corporate-level competence often gains an immediate competitive advantage over its rivals.[37]

A number of firms have successfully transferred one or more corporate-level core competencies across their businesses. Virgin Group Ltd. transfers its marketing core competence across travel, cosmetics, music, drinks, mobile phones, health clubs, and a number of other businesses.[38] Thermo Electron uses its entrepreneurial core competence to start new ventures and maintain a new-venture network.[39] Honda has developed and transferred its competence in engine design and manufacturing to its businesses making products such as motorcycles, lawnmowers, and cars and trucks. With respect to smaller engines, for example, the transfers of the corporate-level competence in terms of engine design and manufacturing have been successful; company officials indicate that "Honda is the world's largest manufacturer of engines and has earned its reputation for unsurpassed quality, performance and reliability."[40]

One way managers facilitate the transfer of corporate-level core competencies is by moving key people into new management positions.[41] However, the manager of an older business may be reluctant to transfer key people who have accumulated knowledge and experience critical to the business's success. Thus, managers with the ability to facilitate the transfer of a core competence may come at a premium, or the key people involved may not want to transfer. Additionally, the top-level managers from the transferring business may not want the competencies transferred to a new business to fulfill the firm's diversification objectives. As the Strategic Focus on Smith & Wesson indicates, corporate competencies were bolstered by hiring a number of managers from outside the firm to facilitate improvement in the transfer of desired corporate competencies. Moreover, it seems that businesses in which performance does improve often demonstrate a corporate-wide passion for pursuing skill transfer and appropriate coordination mechanisms for realizing economies of scope.

Market Power

Firms using a related diversification strategy may gain market power when successfully using their related constrained or related linked strategy. **Market power** exists when a firm is able to sell its products above the existing competitive level or to reduce the costs of its primary and support activities below the competitive level, or both.[42] Nestlé SA, a large food company, will increase its market share for its baby-food line through the acquisition of Gerber Products from Novartis AG. Although Nestlé has a large baby-food position in emerging economies such as Brazil and China, it lacks a presence in the United States. Gerber has nearly an 80 percent share of baby foods in the United States. This opportunity materialized for Nestlé because Novartis decided to focus on three main areas: new prescription medicine, low-cost generic medicine, and over-the-counter medicine. Due to market and governance pressures many firms are focusing on a narrower set of businesses (see the Strategic Focus later in the chapter on the Revival of the Unrelated Strategy). This trend among pharmaceutical firms such as Novartis created an opportunity for Nestlé to buy the divested business. Certainly through this move, Nestlé will substantially increase its market power worldwide.[43]

Market power exists when a firm is able to sell its products above the existing competitive level or to reduce the costs of its primary and support activities below the competitive level, or both.

In addition to efforts to gain scale as a means of increasing market power, as Nestlé is attempting to do by acquiring Gerber Products, firms can create market power through multipoint competition[44] and vertical integration. **Multipoint competition** exists when two or more diversified firms simultaneously compete in the same product areas or geographic markets.[45] The actions taken by United Parcel Service (UPS) and FedEx in two markets, overnight delivery and ground shipping, illustrate multipoint competition. UPS has moved into overnight delivery, FedEx's stronghold; FedEx has been buying trucking and ground shipping assets to move into ground shipping, UPS's stronghold. Moreover, geographic competition for markets increases as DHL, the strongest shipping company in Europe, tries to move into the U.S. market. All three competitors (UPS, FedEx, and DHL) are trying to move into large foreign markets to either gain a stake in a market or to expand their existing share of a market. For instance, because China was allowed into the World Trade Organization (WTO) and government officials have declared the market more open to foreign competition, the battle for global market share among these three top shippers is raging in China and other countries throughout the world.[46] If one of these firms successfully gains strong positions in several markets while competing against its rivals, its market power may increase.

Multipoint competition exists when two or more diversified firms simultaneously compete in the same product areas or geographical markets.

Vertical integration exists when a company produces its own inputs (backward integration) or owns its own source of output distribution (forward integration).

Some firms using a related diversification strategy engage in vertical integration to gain market power. **Vertical integration** exists when a company produces its own inputs (backward integration) or owns its own source of output distribution (forward integration). In some instances, firms partially integrate their operations, producing and selling their products by using company businesses as well as outside sources.[47]

Vertical integration is commonly used in the firm's core business to gain market power over rivals. Market power is gained as the firm develops the ability to save on its operations, avoid market costs, improve product quality, and, possibly, protect its technology from imitation by rivals.[48] Market power also is created when firms have strong ties between their assets for which no market prices exist. Establishing a market price would result in high search and transaction costs, so firms seek to vertically integrate rather than remain separate businesses.[49]

Vertical integration has its limitations. For example, an outside supplier may produce the product at a lower cost. As a result, internal transactions from vertical integration may be expensive and reduce profitability relative to competitors. Also, bureaucratic costs may occur with vertical integration. And, because vertical integration can require substantial investments in specific technologies, it may reduce the firm's flexibility, especially when technology changes quickly. Finally, changes in demand create capacity balance and coordination problems. If one business is building a part for another internal business, but achieving economies of scale requires the first division to manufacture quantities that are beyond the capacity of the internal buyer to absorb, it would be necessary to sell the parts outside the firm as well as to the internal business. Thus, although vertical integration can create value, especially through market power over competitors, it is not without risks and costs.[50]

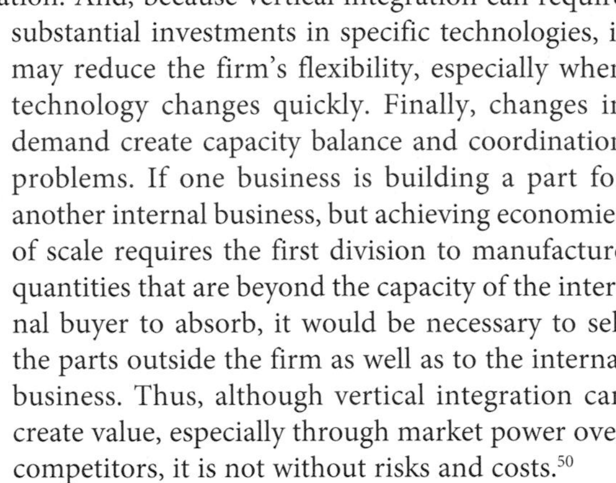

CVS, which recently merged with Caremark, demonstrates a vertical integration strategy for growth and competition.

For example, CVS, a drug store competitor to Walgreens, recently merged with Caremark, a large pharmaceutical benefits manager. For CVS this merger represents a forward vertical move broadening its business from retail into health care. However, Medco a competitor to Caremark indicates that competitor companies to CVS "are more comfortable with [their] neutral position than they are with the concept of a combination" between CVS and Caremark.[51] Thus, although CVS may gain some market power, it risks alienating rivals such as Walgreens who may choose to collaborate with other benefit managers such as Medco or Express Scripts.

Many manufacturing firms no longer pursue vertical integration as a means of gaining market power.[52] In fact, deintegration is the focus of most manufacturing firms, such as Intel and Dell, and even some large auto companies, such as Ford and General Motors, as they develop independent supplier networks.[53] Flextronics, an electronics contract manufacturer, represents a new breed of large contract manufacturers that is helping to foster this revolution in supply-chain management. Flextronics itself is diversifying with a proposed acquisition with Solectron Corp., another contract manufacturer with a complementary portfolio of businesses.[54] Such firms often manage their customers' entire product lines and offer services ranging from inventory management to delivery and after-sales service. Conducting business through e-commerce also allows vertical integration to be changed into "virtual integration."[55] Thus, closer relationships are possible with suppliers and customers through virtual integration or electronic means of integration, allowing firms to reduce the costs of processing transactions while improving their supply-chain management skills and tightening the control of their inventories. This evidence suggests that *virtual integration* rather than *vertical integration* may be a more common source of market power gains for today's firms.

Simultaneous Operational Relatedness and Corporate Relatedness

As Figure 6.2 suggests, some firms simultaneously seek operational and corporate relatedness to create economies of scope.[56] The ability to simultaneously create economies of scope by sharing activities (operational relatedness) and transferring core competencies (corporate relatedness) is difficult for competitors to understand and learn how to imitate. However, firms that fail in their efforts to simultaneously obtain operational and corporate relatedness may create the opposite of what they seek—namely, diseconomies of scope instead of economies of scope.[57]

As the Strategic Focus on Smith & Wesson and Luxottica suggests, both of these companies have used a strategy that combines operational and corporate relatedness with some success. Likewise, Walt Disney Co. uses a related diversification strategy to simultaneously create economies of scope through operational and corporate relatedness. Within the firm's Studio Entertainment business, for example, Disney can gain economies of scope by sharing activities among its different movie distribution companies such as Touchstone Pictures, Hollywood Pictures, and Dimension Films, among others. Broad and deep knowledge about its customers is a capability on which Disney relies to develop corporate-level core competencies in terms of advertising and marketing. With these competencies, Disney is able to create economies of scope through corporate relatedness as it cross-sells products that are highlighted in its movies through the distribution channels that are part of its Parks and Resorts and Consumer Products businesses. Thus, characters created in movies (think of those in *The Lion King*) become figures that are marketed through Disney's retail stores (which are part of the Consumer Products business). In addition, themes established in movies become the source of new rides in the firm's theme parks, which are part of the Parks and Resorts business.[58]

As we described, Smith & Wesson, Luxottica, and Walt Disney Co. have been able to successfully use related diversification as a corporate-level strategy through which they create economies of scope by sharing some activities and by transferring core competencies. However, it can be difficult for investors to actually observe the value created by a firm (such as Walt Disney Co.) as it shares activities and transfers core competencies. For this reason, the value of the assets of a firm using a diversification strategy to create economies of scope in this manner tends to be discounted by investors. For example, analysts have complained that both Citibank and UBS, two large multiplatform banks, have underperformed their more focused counterparts in regard to stock market appreciation. In fact, both banks have heard calls for breaking up their separate businesses in insurance, hedge funds, consumer lending, and investment banking.[59] One analyst speaking of Citigroup suggested that "creating real synergy between its divisions has been hard," implying that Citigroup's related diversification strategy suffered from some possible diseconomies of scale.[60]

Unrelated Diversification

Firms do not seek either operational relatedness or corporate relatedness when using the unrelated diversification corporate-level strategy. An unrelated diversification strategy (see Figure 6.2) can create value through two types of financial economies. **Financial economies** are cost savings realized through improved allocations of financial resources based on investments inside or outside the firm.[61]

Financial economies are cost savings realized through improved allocations of financial resources based on investments inside or outside the firm.

Efficient internal capital allocations can lead to financial economies. Efficient internal capital allocations reduce risk among the firm's businesses—for example, by leading to the development of a portfolio of businesses with different risk profiles. The second type of financial economy concerns the restructuring of acquired assets. Here, the diversified firm buys another company, restructures that company's assets in ways that allow it to

Strategic Focus Strategic Focus Strategic Focus

Operational and Corporate Relatedness: Smith & Wesson and Luxottica

Both Smith & Wesson Holding Company, a traditional handgun manufacturer, and Luxottica, a luxury sunglass producer, have been pursuing the combined operational and corporate relatedness strategy. Smith & Wesson Holding Company is one of the most recognized brands in the world, made famous partly because of the use of its .44 magnum in the movie *Dirty Harry.* Interestingly, until a short time ago Smith & Wesson did not have other weapon-related products besides handguns. But recently it moved beyond its traditional handgun market into producing shotguns and rifles, which are weekend and hunting products. These products are close to its roots in operational, technological, and marketing areas. Michael F. Golden who took over as CEO in 2004, initiated this operationally related diversification strategy by purchasing Thompson/Center Arms Company for $1.1 billion. Thompson's manufacturing expertise has helped accelerate Smith & Wesson's growth in longer barrel markets.

Golden, who did not know much about guns when he took over as CEO, had helped Black & Decker expand its tool business through improved marketing of its hardware products. Similarly in developing corporate relatedness areas for Smith & Wesson, Golden pushed into licensing agreements where the Smith & Wesson brand is now used for product advertisements such as men's cologne. "Marketing surveys showed gun buyers were interested in purchasing shotguns, hunting rifles, ammunition, even security alarm services from Smith & Wesson." To develop this strategy Golden hired executives with marketing backgrounds from Coca-Cola, Frito Lay, Stanley Works, and Harley-Davidson. Its licensing revenues rose 17 percent in the second quarter of 2007. With its dual diversification strategy (using both operational and corporate relatedness), Smith & Wesson expects sales gains of "40 percent or more for fiscal 2007 and 2008."

Luxotica used related diversification as a corporate-level strategy in acquiring Oakley, Inc., sports-brand sunglasses.

Additionally Smith & Wesson with a new .45 caliber–sized handgun expects to increase sales to the military for government contracts previously held by Beretta. This contract alone could be worth $500 million in sales. Also, through innovation of a high-tech, lightweight, yet high-strength plastic, it plans to manufacture a handgun that is likely to appeal to police departments and increase its sales to law enforcement agencies.

Similarly Luxottica moved from a focus on fashion to sports brand sunglasses. To make this shift, Luxottica acquired Oakley, Inc., which is primarily focused in the sports eyewear segment. Operationally, due to synergies between these two businesses, Luxottica expects to see proposed savings over three years equivalent to $932 million due to opportunities for operational relatedness, which is higher than the premium paid of $663 million for Oakley. The big question is whether it can manage the brand change from fashion to sports using a corporate relatedness strategy given its image as a fashion sunglass manufacturer. Another concern is that the acquisition will make Luxottica 80 percent focused on retail markets in the United States. It had signaled earlier that it would like to expand its retail outlets in more affluent markets. Thus it has risked being overly focused in the U.S. market. In summary, both Smith & Wesson and Luxottica are examples of firms that are pursuing both operational and corporate relatedness as they diversify to increase their opportunities for growth.

Sources: 2007, Cheap sunglasses? Not for Luxottica: The Italian optics giant snares performance eyewear maker Oakley in a $2.1 billion deal, *BusinessWeek,* http://www.businessweek.com, June 21; R. Owen, 2007, Oakley goes to Luxottica in $2 bn deal, *The Times,* http://www.business.timesonline.co.uk, June 22; A. Pressman, 2007, Smith & Wesson: A gun maker loaded with offshoots, *BusinessWeek,* June 4, 66; S. Walters & R. Stone, 2007, The trouble with rose-colored sunglasses, *Barron's,* 25, M10; C. Hajim, 2006, A stock with fire power: Smith & Wesson, *Fortune,* http://www.cnnMoney.com, October 9.

operate more profitably, and then sells the company for a profit in the external market.[62] Next, we discuss the two types of financial economies in greater detail.

Efficient Internal Capital Market Allocation

In a market economy, capital markets are thought to efficiently allocate capital. Efficiency results as investors take equity positions (ownership) with high expected future cash-flow values. Capital is also allocated through debt as shareholders and debtholders try to improve the value of their investments by taking stakes in businesses with high growth and profitability prospects.

In large diversified firms, the corporate headquarters office distributes capital to its businesses to create value for the overall corporation. The nature of these distributions may generate gains from internal capital market allocations that exceed the gains that would accrue to shareholders as a result of capital being allocated by the external capital market.[63] Because those in a firm's corporate headquarters generally have access to detailed and accurate information regarding the actual and prospective performance of the company's portfolio of businesses, they have the best information to make capital distribution decisions.

Compared with corporate office personnel, external investors have relatively limited access to internal information and can only estimate the performances of individual businesses as well as their future prospects. Moreover, although businesses seeking capital must provide information to potential suppliers (such as banks or insurance companies), firms with internal capital markets may have at least two informational advantages. First, information provided to capital markets through annual reports and other sources may not include negative information, instead emphasizing positive prospects and outcomes. External sources of capital have limited ability to understand the operational dynamics of large organizations. Even external shareholders who have access to information have no guarantee of full and complete disclosure.[64] Second, although a firm must disseminate information, that information also becomes simultaneously available to the firm's current and potential competitors. With insights gained by studying such information, competitors might attempt to duplicate a firm's value-creating strategy. Thus, an ability to efficiently allocate capital through an internal market may help the firm protect the competitive advantages it develops while using its corporate-level strategy as well as its various business-unit level strategies.

If intervention from outside the firm is required to make corrections to capital allocations, only significant changes are possible, such as forcing the firm into bankruptcy or changing the top management team. Alternatively, in an internal capital market, the corporate headquarters office can fine-tune its corrections, such as choosing to adjust managerial incentives or suggesting strategic changes in one of the firm's businesses. Thus, capital can be allocated according to more specific criteria than is possible with external market allocations. Because it has less accurate information, the external capital market may fail to allocate resources adequately to high-potential investments. The corporate headquarters office of a diversified company can more effectively perform such tasks as disciplining underperforming management teams through resource allocations.[65]

Large highly diversified businesses often face what is known as the "conglomerate discount." This discount results from analysts not knowing how to value a vast array of large businesses with complex financial reports. For instance, one analyst suggested in regard to figuring out GE's financial results in its quarterly report, "A rubik's cube may in fact be easier to figure out."[66] To overcome this discount many unrelated diversified or industrial conglomerates have sought to establish a brand for the parent company. For instance, recent advertisements by BASF AG, a diversified German chemical company, have included a campaign ad/slogan: "We don't make a lot of the products you buy. We make a lot of the products you buy better." General Electric and others, besides BASF AG, have been successful to varying degrees, in running such ad campaigns. More recently United Technologies initiated a brand development approach with the slogan

"United Technologies. You can see everything from here." United Technologies suggested that its earnings multiple (PE ratio) compared to its stock price is only average even though its performance has been better than other conglomerates in its group. It is hoping that the "umbrella" brand advertisement will raise its PE to a level comparable to its competitors.[67]

In spite of the challenges associated with it, a number of corporations continue to use the unrelated diversification strategy, especially in Europe and in emerging markets. Siemens, for example, is a large German conglomerate with a highly diversified approach. The former CEO argued that "When you are in an up-cycle and the capital markets have plenty of opportunities to invest in single-industry companies . . . investors savor those opportunities. But when things change pure plays go down faster than you can look."[68]

The Achilles' heel for firms using the unrelated diversification strategy in a developed economy is that competitors can imitate financial economies more easily than they can replicate the value gained from the economies of scope developed through operational relatedness and corporate relatedness. This issue is less of a problem in emerging economies, where the absence of a "soft infrastructure" (including effective financial intermediaries, sound regulations, and contract laws) supports and encourages use of the unrelated diversification strategy.[69] In fact, in emerging economies such as those in India and Chile, research has shown that diversification increases the performance of firms affiliated with large diversified business groups.[70]

Restructuring of Assets

Financial economies can also be created when firms learn how to create value by buying, restructuring, and then selling other companies' assets in the external market.[71] As in the real estate business, buying assets at low prices, restructuring them, and selling them at a price that exceeds their cost generates a positive return on the firm's invested capital.[72]

As the Strategic Focus on unrelated diversified companies who pursue this strategy suggests, creating financial economies by acquiring and restructuring other companies' assets requires an understanding of significant trade-offs. As in the ITW case, for example, success usually calls for a focus on mature, low-technology businesses because of the uncertainty of demand for high-technology products. In high-technology businesses, resource allocation decisions become too complex, creating information-processing overload on the small corporate headquarters offices that are common in unrelated diversified firms. High-technology businesses are often human-resource dependent; these people can leave or demand higher pay and thus appropriate or deplete the value of an acquired firm.[73]

Buying and then restructuring service-based assets so they can be profitably sold in the external market is also difficult. Here, sales often are a product of close personal relationships between a client and the representative of the firm being restructured. Thus, for both high-technology firms and service-based companies, relatively few tangible assets can be restructured to create value and profitably sold. It is difficult to restructure intangible assets such as human capital and effective relationships that have evolved over time between buyers (customers) and sellers (firm personnel).

Value-Neutral Diversification: Incentives and Resources

The objectives firms seek when using related diversification and unrelated diversification strategies all have the potential to help the firm create value by using a corporate-level strategy. However, these strategies, as well as single- and dominant-business diversification strategies, are sometimes used with value-neutral rather than value-creating objectives in mind. As we discuss next, different incentives to diversify sometimes surface, and the quality of the firm's resources may permit only diversification that is value neutral rather than value creating.

Strategic Focus Strategic Focus Strategic Focus

Revival of the Unrelated Strategy (Conglomerate): Small Firms Acquire Castoffs from Large Firms and Seek to Improve Their Value

Shareholders with significant ownership positions are exerting pressure on many large diversified firms to focus their portfolios and to divest previously high-selling brands, especially those associated with a vast array of products. As these restructuring castoffs have become available, a number of small unrelated firms, besides private equity firms, have been purchasing them. Jarden Corporation, for instance, acquired Coleman Camping Goods in 2005 after its previous owner had gone into bankruptcy. At that point, Jarden's CEO Martin Franklin was able to transact a low price in a friendly takeover of this firm that had otherwise been pressured by competitors. Franklin stated, "We look for brands that are market leaders but haven't been innovative." Similar acquisitions by Jarden include Ball Canning Jars, Bicycle Playing Cards, and Crock-Pot Cookers.

Jarden Corporation has acquired many recognizable brand labels that it feels have the potential for renewed success with a bit of innovation.

Prestige Brands Holdings, Inc., is also a regular player in buying these castoffs. Prestige has been buying castoffs from large consumer product companies, such as Procter & Gamble, Unilever, and Colgate-Palmolive, as they sell their underperforming brands such as Sure and Right Guard deodorants, Comet Cleaner, Aqua Net standard products, Pert Plus Shampoo, and Rit Dye. Prestige also sought to revive Cutex Nail Polish Remover and Spic-n-Span cleaner, among other brands. Henkel KGaA, a German firm, follows a similar strategy. Under its Dial platform, it acquired Right Guard, Soft-n-Dry, and Dry Idea from Procter & Gamble (which it was later forced by the Federal Trade Commission to divest when it acquired Gillette). To differentiate Right Guard in its new brand, RGX, it sought to establish a target market of older men whereas TAG and Unilever's Axe brands battle over younger adolescent males.

Innovative Brands, in partnership with promotional agent Ten United, bought and revived old brands such as Cloraseptic Sore Throat Treatment and Pert Shampoo. This restructuring strategy is attractive to these firms because less money is required to get their products out on the shelves by reviving old brands than starting from scratch. However, one of the risks associated with this strategy is that retailers are often limited to holding just a few leading brands, plus their own private label brands, in their inventory. This practice often squeezes companies that have acquired these brands because powerful retailers such as Wal-Mart present them with narrowing shelf space opportunity.

This diversification strategy is not only found in consumer product industries, but also in the clothing, hardware, and tool industries. For instance CEO Mackey J. McDonald transformed VF Corporation from a manufacturer of Lee and Wrangler Jeans and Vanity Fair underwear labels into the largest apparel maker in the world. VF Brands also include Reef, JanSport, Nautica, and John Varvatos. VF Corporation seeks to maintain an entrepreneurial approach by keeping the founders of the business and managers, if possible, and giving them lots of autonomy, but at the same time alerting them that they will be under the tight financial control systems of the corporation to make sure that the entrepreneurs know how things will operate after the acquisition.

Illinois Tool Works (ITW) started out as a tool maker and tripled its size in the past decade to 750 business units worldwide. Its acquisition and diversification strategy focuses on small, low-margin but mature industrial businesses. Examples of its products include screws, auto parts, deli-slicers, and the plastic rings that hold together soft drink cans. It seeks to restructure each business it acquires in order to increase the business unit's profit margins

by focusing on a narrowly defined product range and targeting the most lucrative products and customers using the 80/20 concept, where 80 percent of the revenues are derived by 20 percent of the customers. Most of its acquisitions are under $100 million, and the price is usually relatively cheap. The firms exampled in this strategic focus often seek to buy low, restructure, and operate, as well as selectively divest after the restructuring.

Sources: R. Brat, 2007, Turning managers into take over artists: How conglomerate ITW mints new deal makers to fuel its expansion, *Wall Street Journal,* April 6, A1, A8; E. Byron, 2007, How to turn trash into treasure, *Wall Street Journal,* April 13, B1, B2; A. Cordeiro, 2007, Jarden's bargain hunting wins fans on Wall Street, *Wall Street Journal,* May 23, B3; M. Kanellos, 2007, Corporate castoffs bring new light to VC, CNet News, http://www.news.com, April 11; R.A. Smith, 2007, Boss talk, A special report; VF's new man: (Strong entrepreneurs) + (Financial controls) = Growth, January 22, R4; 2007, Ten United to help revive Sure and Pert Plus: Agency to renew interest in two heritage brands, Press Release, http://www.tenunited.com, January 24; 2006, Henkel successfully concludes the acquisition of deodorant brands in the USA, Henkel Press Release Archive, http://www.henkel.com, May 2.

Incentives to Diversify

Incentives to diversify come from both the external environment and a firm's internal environment. External incentives include antitrust regulations and tax laws. Internal incentives include low performance, uncertain future cash flows, and the pursuit of synergy and reduction of risk for the firm.

Antitrust Regulation and Tax Laws

Government antitrust policies and tax laws provided incentives for U.S. firms to diversify in the 1960s and 1970s.[74] Antitrust laws prohibiting mergers that created increased market power (via either vertical or horizontal integration) were stringently enforced during that period.[75] Merger activity that produced conglomerate diversification was encouraged primarily by the Celler-Kefauver Antimerger Act (1950), which discouraged horizontal and vertical mergers. As a result, many of the mergers during the 1960s and 1970s were "conglomerate" in character, involving companies pursuing different lines of business. Between 1973 and 1977, 79.1 percent of all mergers were conglomerate.[76]

During the 1980s, antitrust enforcement lessened, resulting in more and larger horizontal mergers (acquisitions of target firms in the same line of business, such as a merger between two oil companies).[77] In addition, investment bankers became more open to the kinds of mergers facilitated by regulation changes; as a consequence, takeovers increased to unprecedented numbers.[78] The conglomerates, or highly diversified firms, of the 1960s and 1970s became more "focused" in the 1980s and early 1990s as merger constraints were relaxed and restructuring was implemented.[79]

In the late 1990s and early 2000s, antitrust concerns emerged again with the large volume of mergers and acquisitions (see Chapter 7).[80] Mergers are now receiving more scrutiny than they did in the 1980s and through the early 1990s.[81] For example, in the merger between P&G and Gillette (see the Opening Case), regulators required that each firm divest certain businesses before they were allowed to secure the deal.

The tax effects of diversification stem not only from corporate tax changes, but also from individual tax rates. Some companies (especially mature ones) generate more cash from their operations than they can reinvest profitably. Some argue that *free cash flows* (liquid financial assets for which investments in current businesses are no longer economically viable) should be redistributed to shareholders as dividends.[82] However, in the 1960s and 1970s, dividends were taxed more heavily than were capital gains. As a result, before 1980, shareholders preferred that firms use free cash flows to buy and build companies in high-performance industries. If the firm's stock value appreciated over the long term, shareholders might receive a better return on those funds than if the funds had been redistributed as dividends, because returns from stock sales would be taxed more lightly than dividends would.

Under the 1986 Tax Reform Act, however, the top individual ordinary income tax rate was reduced from 50 to 28 percent, and the special capital gains tax was changed to treat capital gains as ordinary income. These changes created an incentive for shareholders to stop encouraging firms to retain funds for purposes of diversification. These tax law changes also influenced an increase in divestitures of unrelated business units after 1984. Thus, while individual tax rates for capital gains and dividends created a shareholder incentive to increase diversification before 1986, they encouraged less diversification after 1986, unless it was funded by tax-deductible debt. The elimination of personal interest deductions, as well as the lower attractiveness of retained earnings to shareholders, might prompt the use of more leverage by firms, for which interest expense is tax deductible.

Corporate tax laws also affect diversification. Acquisitions typically increase a firm's depreciable asset allowances. Increased depreciation (a non-cash-flow expense) produces lower taxable income, thereby providing an additional incentive for acquisitions. Before 1986, acquisitions may have been the most attractive means for securing tax benefits,[83] but the 1986 Tax Reform Act diminished some of the corporate tax advantages of diversification.[84] The recent changes recommended by the Financial Accounting Standards Board—eliminating the "pooling of interests" method for accounting for the acquired firm's assets and eliminating the write-off for research and development in process—reduced some of the incentives to make acquisitions, especially acquisitions in related high-technology industries (these changes are discussed further in Chapter 7).[85]

Although federal regulations were loosened somewhat in the 1980s and then retightened in the late 1990s, a number of industries experienced increased merger activity due to industry-specific deregulation activity, including banking, telecommunications, oil and gas, and electric utilities. For instance, in banking the Garns–St. Germain Deposit Institutions Act of 1982 (GDIA) and the Competitive Equality Banking Act of 1987 (CEBA) reshaped the acquisition frequency in banking by relaxing the regulations that limited interstate bank acquisitions.[86] Regulations changes have also affected convergence between media and telecommunications industries, which has allowed a number of mergers, such as the successive Time Warner and AOL mergers. The Federal Communications Commission (FCC) made a highly contested ruling "allowing broadcasters to own TV stations that reach 45 percent of U.S. households, up from 35 percent, own three stations in the largest markets (up from two) and own a TV station and newspaper in the same town."[87] Thus, regulatory changes such as the ones we have described create incentives for diversification.

Low Performance

Some research shows that low returns are related to greater levels of diversification.[88] If "high performance eliminates the need for greater diversification,"[89] then low performance may provide an incentive for diversification. eBay looked to diversify beyond its auction business because its auction growth had slowed and it shut down its stand-alone Web sites in China and Japan. It then created a Web site for online shoppers called eBay Express. This site sells only fixed price items and appeals to online shoppers who are not comfortable bidding for items from a stranger. This business has not flourished as hoped and part of the problem may be eBay's image as an auction site and that some of the traditional customers prefer to have control over the purchase price. A large number of rivals, such as Amazon.com, which can offer low prices as well as free shipping, might also have reduced the success of the eBay Express diversification strategy.[90]

eBay's fixed-price site, eBay Express, hasn't flourished as its creators had hoped.

Research evidence and the experience of a number of firms suggest that an overall curvilinear relationship, as illustrated in Figure 6.3, may exist between diversification and performance.[91] Although low performance can be an incentive to

Figure 6.3 The Curvilinear Relationship between Diversification and Performance

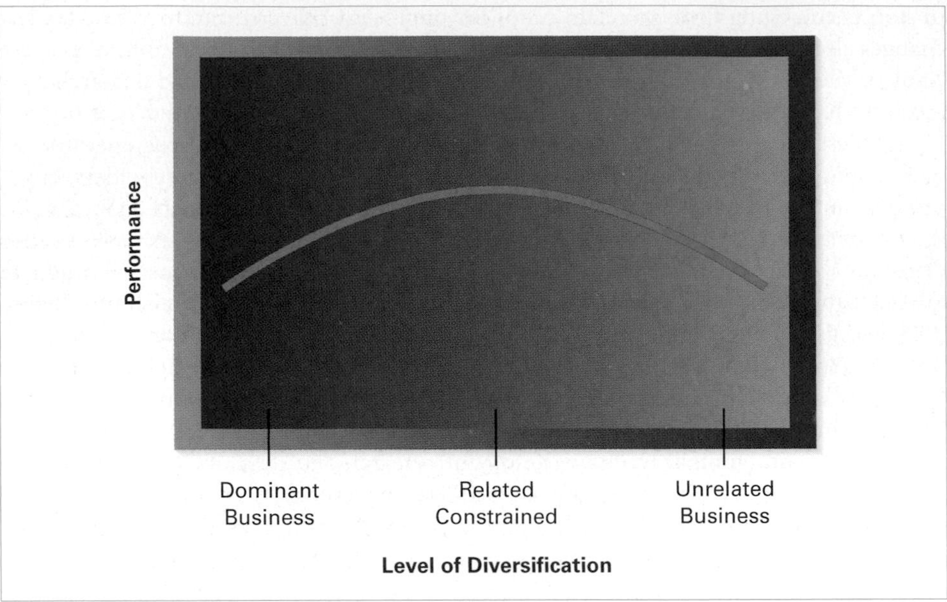

diversify, firms that are more broadly diversified compared to their competitors may have overall lower performance. Further, broadly based banks, such as Citigroup and UBS as noted earlier, have been under pressure to "break up" because they seem to underperform compared to their peer banks. Japanese firm Sanyo Electric felt the need to restructure because it had too many businesses to manage. Its portfolio ranged from Internet service providers, financial and recruiting services, a retirement home, and a golf course to semiconductors and batteries. Due to poor performance, Sanyo required a $2.6 billion restructuring loan from a consortium of lenders led by investment bank Goldman Sachs Group. Since 2004 when it began its restructuring, Sanyo has laid off 15 percent of its personnel, closed factories, and divested unprofitable businesses.[92]

Uncertain Future Cash Flows

As a firm's product line matures or is threatened, diversification may be taken as an important defensive strategy.[93] Small firms and companies in mature or maturing industries sometimes find it necessary to diversify for long-term survival.[94] For example, uncertainty was one of the dominant reasons for diversification among railroad firms during the 1960s and 1970s. Railroads diversified primarily because of the trucking industry's potential to substantially affect the rail business in a negative way. The trucking industry created uncertainty for railroad operators regarding the future levels of demand for their services.

Diversifying into other product markets or into other businesses can reduce the uncertainty about a firm's future cash flows. Thomson Corp., a large Canadian company, once owned 130 local newspapers across North America including Toronto's *Globe and Mail,* besides owning the *Times* of London in the United Kingdom. In 1997, the CEO saw two major threats: "the disappearance of its traditional small retailer advertisers across the United States, which were being gobbled up by large store chains, and the loss of classified-advertising revenue to the Internet."[95] Accordingly, the company embarked on a $30 billion acquisition strategy to move away from its dominant business. Thomson recently reached an agreement to purchase rival Reuters Group along with its other businesses, providing professionals with electronic data in finance, law, and health care.

Synergy and Firm Risk Reduction

Diversified firms pursuing economies of scope often have investments that are too inflexible to realize synergy between business units. As a result, a number of problems may

Synergy exists when the value created by business units working together exceeds the value that those same units create working independently.

arise. **Synergy** exists when the value created by business units working together exceeds the value that those same units create working independently. But as a firm increases its relatedness between business units, it also increases its risk of corporate failure, because synergy produces joint interdependence between businesses that constrains the firm's flexibility to respond. This threat may force two basic decisions.

First, the firm may reduce its level of technological change by operating in environments that are more certain. This behavior may make the firm risk averse and thus uninterested in pursuing new product lines that have potential, but are not proven. Alternatively, the firm may constrain its level of activity sharing and forgo synergy's potential benefits. Either or both decisions may lead to further diversification. The former would lead to related diversification into industries in which more certainty exists. The latter may produce additional, but unrelated, diversification.[96] Research suggests that a firm using a related diversification strategy is more careful in bidding for new businesses, whereas a firm pursuing an unrelated diversification strategy may be more likely to overprice its bid, because an unrelated bidder may not have full information about the acquired firm.[97] However, firms using either a related or an unrelated diversification strategy must understand the consequences of paying large premiums. For example, even though the P&G and Gillette transaction is being viewed positively, as noted in the Opening Case, the annual growth rate of Gillette's product lines in the newly created company will need to average 12.1 percent or more for P&G's shareholders to benefit financially from the additional diversification resulting from this merger.[98]

Resources and Diversification

As already discussed, firms may have several value-neutral incentives as well as value-creating incentives (such as the ability to create economies of scope) to diversify. However, even when incentives to diversify exist, a firm must have the types and levels of resources and capabilities needed to successfully use a corporate-level diversification strategy.[99] Although both tangible and intangible resources facilitate diversification, they vary in their ability to create value. Indeed, the degree to which resources are valuable, rare, difficult to imitate, and nonsubstitutable (see Chapter 3) influence a firm's ability to create value through diversification. For instance, free cash flows are a tangible, financial resource that may be used to diversify the firm. However, compared with diversification that is grounded in intangible resources, diversification based on financial resources only is more visible to competitors and thus more imitable and less likely to create value on a long-term basis.[100]

Tangible resources usually include the plant and equipment necessary to produce a product and tend to be less-flexible assets. Any excess capacity often can be used only for closely related products, especially those requiring highly similar manufacturing technologies. For example, some firms in the memory chip-making business examined the market and found that demand for standard memory products for DRAMs (Dynamic Random-Access Memory chips) used in personal computers was likely to decrease. Some firms such as Samsung Electronics and Hynix Semiconductors, both from South Korea, diversified their businesses into NAND flash memory chips used in MP3 players, digital cameras, and other products based on the their tangible assets in manufacturing chips. The chip makers who diversified into flash chips performed better than those who maintained their focus on DRAM chip output including U.S. firm Micron Technology, Germany's Infineon AG, and Japan's Elpida Memory. As such, Samsung and Hynix earnings were cushioned by the higher profit margins from the NAND product.[101]

Excess capacity of other tangible resources, such as a sales force, can be used to diversify more easily. Again, excess capacity in a sales force is more effective with related diversification, because it may be utilized to sell similar products. The sales force would be more knowledgeable about related-product characteristics, customers, and distribution channels.[102] Tangible resources may create resource interrelationships in production, marketing, procurement, and technology, defined earlier as activity sharing. Intangible resources are more flexible than tangible physical assets in facilitating diversification. Although the sharing of tangible resources may induce diversification, intangible resources such as tacit knowledge could encourage even more diversification.[103]

Sometimes, however, the benefits expected from using resources to diversify the firm for either value-creating or value-neutral reasons are not gained.[104] For example, as noted in the Opening Case, implementing operational relatedness has been difficult for P&G and Gillette in recasting the Crest Pro-Health brand, creating jointly marketed dental hygiene products (e.g., toothpaste and toothbrushes). Also, Sara Lee found that it could not realize synergy between its diversified portfolio and subsequently shed businesses accounting for 40 percent of is revenue to focus on food and food-related products to more readily achieve synergy.[105]

Value-Reducing Diversification: Managerial Motives to Diversify

Managerial motives to diversify can exist independently of value-neutral reasons (i.e., incentives and resources) and value-creating reasons (e.g., economies of scope). The desire for increased compensation and reduced managerial risk are two motives for top-level executives to diversify their firm beyond value-creating and value-neutral levels.[106] In slightly different words, top-level executives may diversify a firm in order to diversify their own employment risk, as long as profitability does not suffer excessively.[107]

Diversification provides additional benefits to top-level managers that shareholders do not enjoy. Research evidence shows that diversification and firm size are highly correlated, and as firm size increases, so does executive compensation.[108] Because large firms are complex, difficult-to-manage organizations, top-level managers commonly receive substantial levels of compensation to lead them.[109] Greater levels of diversification can increase a firm's complexity, resulting in still more compensation for executives to lead an increasingly diversified organization. Governance mechanisms, such as the board of directors, monitoring by owners, executive compensation practices, and the market for corporate control, may limit managerial tendencies to overdiversify. These mechanisms are discussed in more detail in Chapter 10.

In some instances, though, a firm's governance mechanisms may not be strong, resulting in a situation in which executives may diversify the firm to the point that it fails to earn even average returns.[110] The loss of adequate internal governance may result in poor relative performance, thereby triggering a threat of takeover. Although takeovers may improve efficiency by replacing ineffective managerial teams, managers may avoid takeovers through defensive tactics, such as "poison pills," or may reduce their own exposure with "golden parachute" agreements.[111] Therefore, an external governance threat, although restraining managers, does not flawlessly control managerial motives for diversification.[112]

Most large publicly held firms are profitable because the managers leading them are positive stewards of firm resources, and many of their strategic actions, including those related to selecting a corporate-level diversification strategy, contribute to the firm's success.[113] As mentioned, governance mechanisms should be designed to deal with exceptions to the managerial norms of making decisions and taking actions that will increase the firm's ability to earn above-average returns. Thus, it is overly pessimistic to assume that managers usually act in their own self-interest as opposed to their firm's interest.[114]

Top-level executives' diversification decisions may also be held in check by concerns for their reputation. If a positive reputation facilitates development and use of managerial power, a poor reputation may reduce it. Likewise, a strong external market for managerial talent may deter managers from pursuing inappropriate diversification.[115] In addition, a diversified firm may police other firms by acquiring those that are poorly managed in order to restructure its own asset base. Knowing that their firms could be acquired if they are not managed successfully encourages executives to use value-creating, diversification strategies.

As shown in Figure 6.4, the level of diversification that can be expected to have the greatest positive effect on performance is based partly on how the interaction of resources, managerial motives, and incentives affects the adoption of particular diversification strategies. As indicated earlier, the greater the incentives and the more flexible the resources, the higher the level of expected diversification. Financial resources (the most flexible) should have a stronger relationship to the extent of diversification than either tangible or intangible resources. Tangible resources (the most inflexible) are useful primarily for related diversification.

As discussed in this chapter, firms can create more value by effectively using diversification strategies. However, diversification must be kept in check by corporate governance (see Chapter 10). Appropriate strategy implementation tools, such as organizational structures, are also important (see Chapter 11).

We have described corporate-level strategies in this chapter. In the next one, we discuss mergers and acquisitions as prominent means for firms to diversify and to grow profitably while doing so.[116] These trends toward more diversification through acquisitions, which have been partially reversed due to restructuring (see Chapter 7), indicate that learning has taken place regarding corporate-level diversification strategies.[117] Accordingly, firms that diversify should do so cautiously, choosing to focus on relatively few, rather than many, businesses. In fact, research suggests that although unrelated diversification has decreased, related diversification has increased, possibly due to the

Figure 6.4 Summary Model of the Relationship between Diversification and Firm Performance

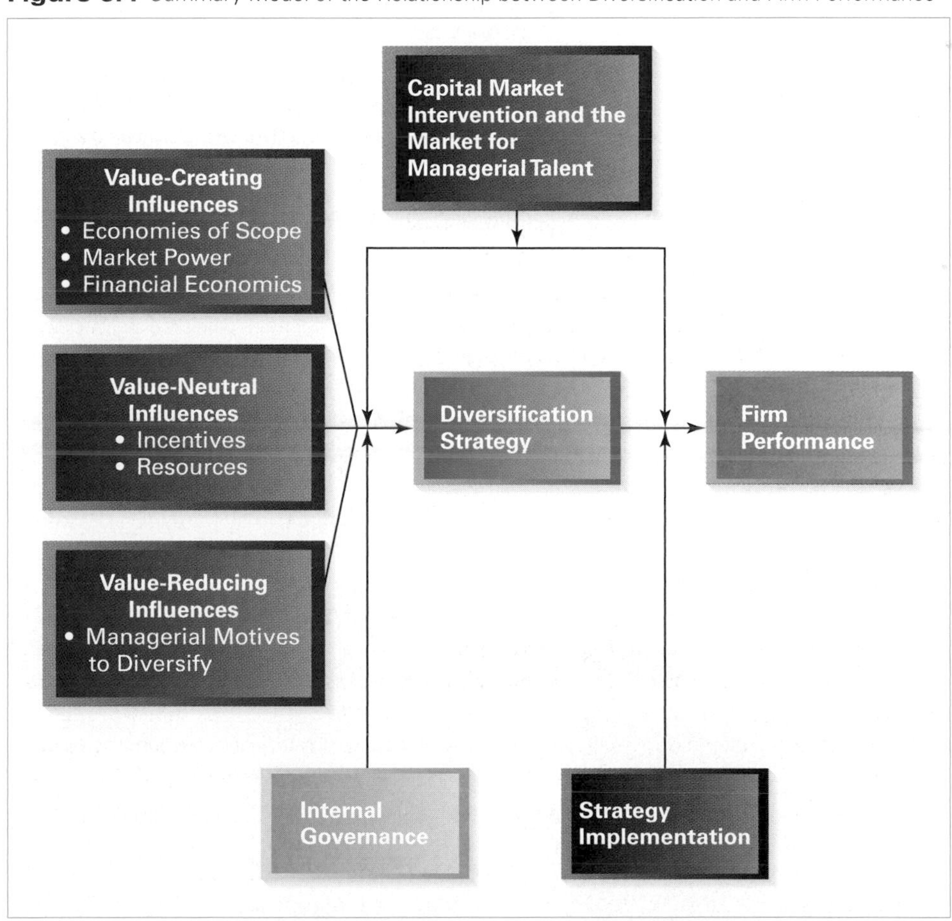

Source: Adapted from R. E. Hoskisson & M. A. Hitt, 1990, Antecedents and performance outcomes of diversification: A review and critique of theoretical perspectives, *Journal of Management,* 16: 498.

restructuring that continued into the 1990s and early twenty-first century. This sequence of diversification followed by restructuring is now taking place in Europe and other places such as Korea, mirroring actions of firms in the United States and the United Kingdom.[118] Firms can improve their strategic competitiveness when they pursue a level of diversification that is appropriate for their resources (especially financial resources) and core competencies and the opportunities and threats in their country's institutional and competitive environments.[119]

Summary

- The primary reason a firm uses a corporate-level strategy to become more diversified is to create additional value. Using a single- or dominant-business corporate-level strategy may be preferable to seeking a more diversified strategy, unless a corporation can develop economies of scope or financial economies between businesses, or unless it can obtain market power through additional levels of diversification. Economies of scope and market power are the main sources of value creation when the firm diversifies by using a corporate-level strategy with moderate to high levels of diversification.
- The corporate-level strategy of related diversification helps the firm to create value by sharing activities or transferring competencies between different businesses in the company's portfolio.
- Sharing activities usually involves sharing tangible resources between businesses. Transferring core competencies involves transferring core competencies developed in one business to another business. It also may involve transferring competencies between the corporate headquarter's office and a business unit.
- Sharing activities is usually associated with the related constrained diversification corporate-level strategy. Activity sharing is costly to implement and coordinate, may create unequal benefits for the divisions involved in the sharing, and may lead to fewer managerial risk-taking behaviors.
- Transferring core competencies is often associated with related linked (or mixed related and unrelated) diversification, although firms pursuing both sharing activities and transferring core competencies can also use the related linked strategy.
- Efficiently allocating resources or restructuring a target firm's assets and placing them under rigorous financial controls are two ways to accomplish successful unrelated diversification. Firms using the unrelated diversification strategy focus on creating financial economies to generate value.
- Diversification is sometimes pursued for value-neutral reasons. Incentives from tax and antitrust government policies, performance disappointments, or uncertainties about future cash flow are examples of value-neutral reasons that firms may choose to become more diversified.
- Managerial motives to diversify (including to increase compensation) can lead to overdiversification and a subsequent reduction in a firm's ability to create value. Evidence suggests, however, that certainly the majority of top-level executives seek to be good stewards of the firm's assets and to avoid diversifying the firm in ways and amounts that destroy value.
- Managers need to pay attention to their firm's internal organization and its external environment when making decisions about the optimum level of diversification for their company. Of course, internal resources are important determinants of the direction that diversification should take. However, conditions in the firm's external environment may facilitate additional levels of diversification, as might unexpected threats from competitors.

Review Questions

1. What is corporate-level strategy and why is it important?
2. What are the different levels of diversification firms can pursue by using different corporate-level strategies?
3. What are three reasons firms choose to diversify their operations?
4. How do firms create value when using a related diversification strategy?
5. What are the two ways to obtain financial economies when using an unrelated diversification strategy?
6. What incentives and resources encourage diversification?
7. What motives might encourage managers to overdiversify their firm?

Experiential Exercises

Exercise 1: Comparison of Diversification Strategies

The use of diversification varies both across and within industries. In some industries, most firms may follow a single- or dominant-product approach. Other industries are characterized by a mix of both single-product and heavily diversified firms. The purpose of this exercise is to learn how the use of diversification varies across firms in an industry, and the implications of such use.

Part One

Working in small teams of 4–7 persons, select an industry to research. You will then select two firms in that industry for further analysis. Many resources can aid in your identification of specific firms in an industry for analysis. One option is to visit the Web site of the New York Stock Exchange (http://www.nyse.com), which has an option to screen firms by industry group. A second option is http://www.hoovers.com, which offers similar listings. Identify two public firms based in the United States. (Note that Hoovers includes some private firms, and the NYSE includes some foreign firms. Data for the exercise are often unavailable for foreign or private companies.)

Once you have identified your target firms, you will need to collect business segment data for each company. Segment data break down the company's revenues and net income by major lines of business. These data are reported in the firm's SEC 10-K filing, and may also be reported in the annual report. Both the annual report and 10-K are usually found on the company's Web site; both the Hoovers and NYSE listings include company homepage information. For the most recent three-year period available, calculate the following:

- Percentage growth in segment sales
- Net profit margin by segment
- Bonus item: Compare profitability to industry averages (*Industry Norms and Key Business Ratios* publishes profit norms by major industry segment.)

Next, based on your reading of the company filings and these statistics, determine whether the firm is best classified as:

- Single product
- Dominant product
- Related diversified
- Unrelated diversified

Part Two

Prepare a brief PowerPoint presentation for use in class discussion. Address the following in your presentation:

- Describe the extent and nature of diversification used at each firm.
- Can you provide a motive for their diversification strategy, given the rationales for diversification put forth in the chapter?
- Which firm's diversification strategy appears to be more effective? Try to justify your answer by explaining why you think one firm's strategy is more effective than the other?

Exercise 2: Corporate Juggling

What are the implications for managers when their firm shifts from competing in a single product segment to multiple segments? Additionally, how is the manager's role affected by the similarity or dissimilarity of these segments?

This exercise will be completed in class. The instructor will assign students randomly to two different types of teams: Part of the class will be assigned to teams of 5–7 persons, and the remainder of the class will be assigned to teams of 10–14 persons. Each team will assign one person to serve as a facilitator.

The instructor will give each facilitator a bag of objects. The goal is for each team to juggle as many objects as possible. The team will start with one object, which should be tossed from person to person. When the group is ready, ask the facilitator for a second object. Continue to add objects up to your group's ability.

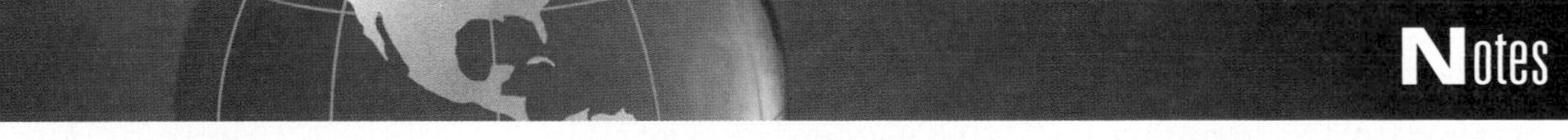

Notes

1. M. E. Porter, 1980, *Competitive Strategy,* New York: The Free Press, xvi.
2. A. Pehrsson, 2006, Business relatedness and performance: A study of managerial perceptions, *Strategic Management Journal,* 27: 265–282.
3. N. J. Moss, 2005, The relative value of growth, *Harvard Business Review,* 83(4): 102–112.
4. M. E. Porter, 1987, From competitive advantage to corporate strategy, *Harvard Business Review,* 65(3): 43–59.
5. Ibid.; C. A. Montgomery, 1994, Corporate diversification, *Journal of Economic Perspectives,* 8: 163–178.
6. J. R. Hough, 2006, Business segment performance redux: A multilevel approach, *Strategic Management Journal,* 27: 45–61; M. Kwak, 2002, Maximizing value through diversification, *MIT Sloan Management Review,* 43(2): 10.
7. M. Ammann & M. Verhofen, 2006, The conglomerate discount: A new explanation based on credit risk, 9(8): 1201–1214; S. A. Mansi & D. M. Reeb, 2002, Corporate diversification: What gets discounted? *Journal of Finance,* 57: 2167–2183; C. C. Markides & P. J. Williamson, 1996, Corporate diversification and organizational structure: A resource-based view, *Academy of Management Journal,* 39: 340–367.
8. C. E. Helfat & K. M. Eisenhardt, 2004, Intertemporal economies of scope organizational modularity, and the dynamics of diversification, *Strategic Management Journal,* 25: 1217–1232.

9. A. Campbell, M. Goold, & M. Alexander, 1995, Corporate strategy: The question for parenting advantage, *Harvard Business Review,* 73(2): 120–132.
10. D. Collis, D. Young, & M. Goold, 2007, The size, structure, and performance of corporate headquarters, *Strategic Management Journal,* 28: 283–405; M. Goold & A. Campbell, 2002, Parenting in complex structures, *Long Range Planning,* 35(3): 219–243; T. H. Brush, P. Bromiley, & M. Hendrickx, 1999, The relative influence of industry and corporation on business segment performance: An alternative estimate, *Strategic Management Journal,* 20: 519–547.
11. D. Miller, 2006, Technological diversity, related diversification, and firm performance, *Strategic Management Journal,* 27: 601–619; D. J. Miller, 2004, Firms' technological resources and the performance effects of diversification: A longitudinal study, *Strategic Management Journal,* 25: 1097–1119.
12. D. D. Bergh, 2001, Diversification strategy research at a crossroads: Established, emerging and anticipated paths, in M. A. Hitt, R. E. Freeman, & J. S. Harrison (eds.), *Handbook of Strategic Management,* Oxford, UK: Blackwell Publishers, 363–383.
13. H. C. Wang & J. B. Barney, 2006, Employee incentives to make firm-specific investments: Implications for resource-based theories of corporate diversification, *Academy of Management Journal,* 31: 466–476.
14. A. J. Ward, M. J. Lankau, A. C. Amason, J. A. Sonnenfeld, & B. R. Agle, 2007, Improving the performance of top management teams, *MIT Sloan Management Review,* 48(3): 85–90.
15. R. P. Rumelt, *Strategy, Structure, and Economic Performance,* Boston: Harvard Business School, 1974; L. Wrigley, 1970, *Divisional Autonomy and Diversification* (Ph.D. dissertation), Harvard Business School.
16. J. Christy, R. Cox, & A. Currie, 2007, Wrigley is in a sticky spot, *Wall Street Journal,* April 4, C12.
17. A. Ward, 2006, UPS tries to boost delivery to investors; parcels group has struggled to integrate acquisitions and justify its strategy since going public, *Financial Times,* November 28, 21.
18. J. Spencer, 2007, Hutchison's Li Looks to make well-timed exit; Indian wireless assets may yield a windfall; a bigger risk to buyers, *Wall Street Journal,* January 29, B4.
19. 2007, What has Superman got up his sleeve? *Euroweek,* February 23, 1.
20. S. W. Geiger & L. H. Cashen, 2007, Organizational size and CEO compensation: The moderating effect of diversification in downscoping organizations, *Journal of Managerial Issues,* 9(2): 233–252; R. K. Aggarwal & A. A. Samwick, 2003, Why do managers diversify their firms? Agency reconsidered, *Journal of Finance,* 58: 71–118.
21. D. J. Miller, M. J. Fern, & L. B. Cardinal, 2007, The use of knowledge for technological innovation within diversified firms, *Academy of Management Journal,* 50: 308–326.
22. M. S. Gary, 2005, Implementation strategy and performance outcomes in related diversification, *Strategic Management Journal,* 26: 643–664; H. Tanriverdi & N. Venkatraman, 2005, Knowledge relatedness and the performance of multibusiness firms, *Strategic Management Journal,* 26: 97–119.
23. H. Tanriverdi, 2006, Performance effects of information technology synergies in multibusiness firms, *MIS Quarterly,* 30(1): 57–78.
24. M. E. Porter, 1985, *Competitive Advantage,* New York: The Free Press, 328.
25. D. Miller, 2006, Technological diversity, related diversification, and firm performance, *Strategic Management Journal,* 27: 601–619.
26. E. Byron, 2007, Merger challenge: Unite toothbrush, toothpaste: P&G and Gillette find creating synergy can be harder than it looks, *Wall Street Journal,* April 24, A1, A17.
27. Tanriverdi, Performance effects of information technology synergies in multibusiness firms; D. Gupta & Y. Gerchak, 2002, Quantifying operational synergies in a merger/acquisition, *Management Science,* 48: 517–533.
28. M. L. Marks & P. H. Mirvis, 2000, Managing mergers, acquisitions, and alliances: Creating an effective transition structure, *Organizational Dynamics,* 28(3): 35–47.
29. P. Puranam & K Srikanth, 2007, What they know vs. what they do: How acquirers leverage technology acquisitions, *Strategic Management Journal,* 28: 805–825; C. Park, 2003, Prior performance characteristics of related and unrelated acquirers, *Strategic Management Journal,* 24: 471–480; G. Delong, 2001, Stockholder gains from focusing versus diversifying bank mergers, *Journal of Financial Economics,* 2: 221–252; T. H. Brush, 1996, Predicted change in operational synergy and post-acquisition performance of acquired businesses, *Strategic Management Journal,* 17.
30. D. D. Bergh, 1995, Size and relatedness of units sold: An agency theory and resource-based perspective, *Strategic Management Journal,* 16: 221–239.
31. M. Lubatkin & S. Chatterjee, 1994, Extending modern portfolio theory into the domain of corporate diversification: Does it apply? *Academy of Management Journal,* 37: 109–136.
32. A. Van Oijen, 2001, Product diversification, corporate management instruments, resource sharing, and performance, *Academy of Management Best Paper Proceedings* (on CD-ROM, Business Policy and Strategy Division); T. Kono, 1999, A strong head office makes a strong company, *Long Range Planning,* 32(2): 225.
33. Puranam & Srikanth, What they know vs. what they do; F. T. Rothaermel, M. A. Hitt, & L. A. Jobe, 2006, Balancing vertical integration and strategic outsourcing: effects on product portfolio, product success, and firm performance, *Strategic Management Journal,* 27: 1033–1056; L. Capron, P. Dussauge, & W. Mitchell, 1998, Resource redeployment following horizontal acquisitions in Europe and the United States, 1988–1992, *Strategic Management Journal,* 19: 631–661; S. Chatterjee & B. Wernerfelt, 1991, The link between resources and type of diversification: Theory and evidence, *Strategic Management Journal,* 12: 33–48.
34. S. Dutta, M. J. Zbaracki, & M. Bergen, 2003, Pricing process as a capability: A resource-based perspective, *Strategic Management Journal,* 24: 615–630.
35. A. Rodríguez-Duarte, F. D. Sandulli, B. Minguela-Rata, & J. I. López-Sánchez, 2007, The endogenous relationship between innovation and diversification, and the impact of technological resources on the form of diversification, *Research Policy,* 36: 652–664; L. Capron & N. Pistre, 2002, When do acquirers earn abnormal returns? *Strategic Management Journal,* 23: 781–794.
36. C. Lawton, 2007, H-P begins push into high-end copiers, *Wall Street Journal,* April 24, B3.
37. Miller, Fern, & Cardinal, The use of knowledge for technological innovation within diversified firms; J. W. Spencer, 2003, Firms' knowledge-sharing strategies in the global innovation system: Empirical evidence from the flat panel display industry, *Strategic Management Journal,* 24: 217–233.
38. 2007, Virgin Group Ltd., *Hoovers,* www.hoovers.com, July 6.
39. 2007, Thermo Fisher Scientific, Thermo Fisher Scientiific Home Page, www.thermofisher.com, July 6.
40. 2007, Honda engines, Honda Motor Company Home Page, http://www.honda.com, July 6.
41. L. C. Thang, C. Rowley, T. Quang, & M. Warner, 2007, To what extent can management practices be transferred between countries?: The case of human resource management in Vietnam, *Journal of World Business,* 42(1): 113–127; G. Stalk Jr., 2005, Rotate the core, *Harvard Business Review,* 83(3): 18–19.
42. S. Chatterjee & J. Singh, 1999, Are trade-offs inherent in diversification moves? A simultaneous model for type of diversification and mode of expansion decisions, *Management Science,* 45: 25–41.
43. J. Whalen, 2007, Nestle Bolsters baby-food line, *Wall Street Journal,* April 12, A3.
44. Bergh, Diversification strategy research at a crossroads, 369.
45. L. Fuentelsaz & J. Gomez, 2006, Multi-point competition, strategic similarity and

entry into geographic markets, *Strategic Management Journal,* 27: 477–499; J. Gimeno & C. Y. Woo, 1999, Multimarket contact, economies of scope, and firm performance, *Academy of Management Journal,* 42: 239–259.

46. R. Kwong, 2007, Big four hope expansion will deliver the goods, *Financial Times,* May 23, 15.
47. T. A. Shervani, G. Frazier, & G. Challagalla, 2007, The moderating influence of firm market power on the transaction cost economics model: An empirical test in a forward channel integration context, *Strategic Management Journal,* 28: 635–652; R. Gulati, P. R. Lawrence, & P. Puranam, 2005, Adaptation in vertical relationships: Beyond incentive conflict, *Strategic Management Journal,* 26: 415–440.
48. D. A. Griffin, A. Chandra, & T. Fealey, 2005, Strategically employing natural channels in an emerging market, *Thunderbird International Business Review,* 47(3): 287–311; A. Darr & I. Talmud, 2003, The structure of knowledge and seller-buyer networks in markets for emergent technologies, *Organization Studies,* 24: 443–461.
49. R. Carter & G. M. Hodgson, 2006, The impact of empirical tests of transaction cost economics on the debate on the nature of the firm, *Strategic Management Journal,* 27: 461–476; O. E. Williamson, 1996, Economics and organization: A primer, *California Management Review,* 38(2): 131–146.
50. Rothaermel, Hitt, & Jobe, Balancing vertical integration and strategic outsourcing; M. G. Jacobides, 2005, Industry change through vertical disintegration: How and why markets emerged in mortgage banking, *Academy of Management Journal,* 48: 465–498.
51. W. D. Brin, 2007, Earnings digest—Health care: As rivals tussle, Medco sees gains; drug-benefit manager cites competitive edge due to business model, *Wall Street Journal,* February 22, C6.
52. L. R. Kopczak & M. E. Johnson, 2003, The supply-chain management effect, *MIT Sloan Management Review,* 3: 27–34; K.R. Harrigan, 2001, Strategic flexibility in the old and new economies, in M. A. Hitt, R. E. Freeman, & J. S. Harrison (eds.), *Handbook of Strategic Management,* Oxford, UK: Blackwell Publishers, 97–123.
53. G. Smith, 2007, Factories go south. So does pay; Mexico's auto industry is booming, but parts outsourcing is keeping a lid on wages, *BusinessWeek,* April 9, 76.
54. D. Clark, 2007, Flextronics-Solectron deal unites assembling titans, *Wall Street Journal,* June 5, A3.
55. P. Kothandaraman & D. T. Wilson, 2001, The future of competition: Value-creating networks, *Industrial Marketing Management,* 30: 379–389.
56. K. M. Eisenhardt & D. C. Galunic, 2000, Coevolving: At last, a way to make synergies work, *Harvard Business Review,* 78(1): 91–111.
57. A. Willem, 2006, The role of inter-unit coordination mechanisms in knowledge sharing: A case study of a British MNC, *Journal of Information Scinece,* 32: 539–561; R. Schoenberg, 2001, Knowledge transfer and resource sharing as value creation mechanisms in inbound continental European acquisitions, *Journal of Euro-Marketing,* 10: 99–114.
58. M. Marr, 2007, The magic kingdom looks to hit the road, *Wall Street Journal,* http://www.wsj.com, February 8.
59. E. Taylor & J. Singer, 2007, New UBS chief keeps strategy intact, *Wall Street Journal,* July 7, A3.
60. 2007, Breakingviews.com: Citi to world: Drop "group," *Wall Street Journal,* January 17, C16.
61. D. D. Bergh, 1997, Predicting divestiture of unrelated acquisitions: An integrative model of ex ante conditions, *Strategic Management Journal,* 18: 715–731; C. W. L. Hill, 1994, Diversification and economic performance: Bringing structure and corporate management back into the picture, in R. P. Rumelt, D. E. Schendel, & D. J. Teece (eds.), *Fundamental Issues in Strategy,* Boston: Harvard Business School Press, 297–321.
62. Porter, *Competitive Advantage.*
63. D. Collis, D. Young, & M. Goold, 2007, The size, structure, and performance of corporate headquarters, *Strategic Management Journal,* 28: 283–405; O. E. Williamson, 1975, *Markets and Hierarchies: Analysis and Antitrust Implications,* New York: Macmillan Free Press.
64. R. J. Indjejikian, 2007, Discussion of accounting information, disclosure, and the cost of capital, *Journal of Accounting Research,* 45(2): 421–426.
65. D. Miller, R. Eisenstat, & N. Foote, 2002, Strategy from the inside out: Building capability-creating organizations, *California Management Review,* 44(3): 37–54; M. E. Raynor & J. L. Bower, 2001, Lead from the center: How to manage divisions dynamically, *Harvard Business Review,* 79(5): 92–100; P. Taylor & J. Lowe, 1995, A note on corporate strategy and capital structure, *Strategic Management Journal,* 16: 411–414.
66. K. Kranhold, 2007, GE report raises doubts, *Wall Street Journal,* January 20–21, A3.
67. J. Lunsford & B. Steinberg, 2006, Conglomerates' conundrum, *Wall Street Journal,* B1, B7.
68. F. Guerrera, Siemens chief makes the case for conglomerates, *Financial Times,* http://www.ft.com, February 5.
69. M. W. Peng & A. Delios, 2006, What determines the scope of the firm over time and around the world? An Asia Pacific perspective, *Asia Pacific Journal of Management,* 23: 385–405; T. Khanna, K. G. Palepu, & J. Sinha, 2005, Strategies that fit emerging markets, *Harvard Business Review,* 83(6): 63–76.
70. A. Chakrabarti, K. Singh, & I. Mahmood, 2006, Diversification and performance: Evidence from East Asian firms, *Strategic Management Journal,* 28: 101–120. T. Khanna & K. Palepu, 2000, Is group affiliation profitable in emerging markets? An analysis of diversified Indian business groups, *Journal of Finance,* 55: 867–892; T. Khanna & K. Palepu, 2000, The future of business groups in emerging markets: Long-run evidence from Chile, *Academy of Management Journal,* 43: 268–285.
71. C. Decker & M. Mellewigt, 2007, Thirty years after Michael E. Porter: What do we know about business exit? *Academy of Management Perspectives,* 2: 41–55; R. E. Hoskisson, R. A. Johnson, D. Yiu, & W. P. Wan, 2001, Restructuring strategies and diversified business groups: Differences associated with country institutional environments, in M. A. Hitt, R. E. Freeman, & J. S. Harrison (eds.), *Handbook of Strategic Management,* Oxford, UK: Blackwell Publishers, 433–463; S. J. Chang & H. Singh, 1999, The impact of entry and resource fit on modes of exit by multibusiness firms, *Strategic Management Journal,* 20: 1019–1035.
72. W. Ng & C. de Cock, 2002, Battle in the boardroom: A discursive perspective, *Journal of Management Studies,* 39: 23–49.
73. R. Coff, 2003, Bidding wars over R&D-intensive firms: Knowledge, opportunism, and the market for corporate control, *Academy of Management Journal,* 46: 74–85.
74. M. Lubatkin, H. Merchant, & M. Srinivasan, 1997, Merger strategies and shareholder value during times of relaxed antitrust enforcement: The case of large mergers during the 1980s, *Journal of Management,* 23: 61–81.
75. D. P. Champlin & J. T. Knoedler, 1999, Restructuring by design? Government's complicity in corporate restructuring, *Journal of Economic Issues,* 33(1): 41–57.
76. R. M. Scherer & D. Ross, 1990, *Industrial Market Structure and Economic Performance,* Boston: Houghton Mifflin.
77. A. Shleifer & R. W. Vishny, 1994, Takeovers in the 1960s and 1980s: Evidence and implications, in R. P. Rumelt, D. E. Schendel, & D. J. Teece (eds.), *Fundamental Issues in Strategy,* Boston: Harvard Business School Press, 403–422.
78. S. Chatterjee, J. S. Harrison, & D. D. Bergh, 2003, Failed takeover attempts, corporate governance and refocusing, *Strategic Management Journal,* 24: 87–96; Lubatkin, Merchant, & Srinivasan, Merger strategies and shareholder value; D. J. Ravenscraft & R. M. Scherer, 1987, *Mergers, Sell-Offs and Economic Efficiency,* Washington, DC: Brookings Institution, 22.
79. D. A. Zalewski, 2001, Corporate takeovers, fairness, and public policy, *Journal of Economic Issues,* 35: 431–437; P. L. Zweig, J. P. Kline, S. A. Forest, & K. Gudridge,

1995, The case against mergers, *BusinessWeek,* October 30, 122–130; J. R. Williams, B. L. Paez, & L. Sanders, 1988, Conglomerates revisited, *Strategic Management Journal,* 9: 403–414.

80. E. J. Lopez, 2001, New anti-merger theories: A critique, *Cato Journal,* 20: 359–378; 1998, The trustbusters' new tools, *The Economist,* May 2, 62–64.
81. R. Croyle & P. Kager, 2002, Giving mergers a head start, *Harvard Business Review,* 80(10): 20–21.
82. M. C. Jensen, 1986, Agency costs of free cash flow, corporate finance, and takeovers, *American Economic Review,* 76: 323–329.
83. R. Gilson, M. Scholes, & M. Wolfson, 1988, Taxation and the dynamics of corporate control: The uncertain case for tax motivated acquisitions, in J. C. Coffee, L. Lowenstein, & S. Rose-Ackerman (eds.), *Knights, Raiders, and Targets: The Impact of the Hostile Takeover,* New York: Oxford University Press, 271–299.
84. C. Steindel, 1986, Tax reform and the merger and acquisition market: The repeal of the general utilities, *Federal Reserve Bank of New York Quarterly Review,* 11(3): 31–35.
85. M. A. Hitt, J. S. Harrison, & R. D. Ireland, 2001, *Mergers and Acquisitions: A Guide to Creating Value for Stakeholders,* New York: Oxford University Press.
86. J. Haleblian; J.-Y. Kim, & N. Rajagopalan, 2006, The influence of acquisition experience and performance on acquisition behavior: Evidence from the U.S. commercial banking industry, *Academy of Management Journal,* 49: 357–370.
87. D. B. Wilkerson & R. Britt, 2003, It's showtime for media deals: Radio lessons fuel debate over control of TV, newspapers, *MarketWatch,* http://www.marketwatch.com, May 30.
88. J. M. Shaver, 2006, A paradox of synergy: Contagion and capacity effects in mergers and acquisitions, *Academy of Management Journal,* 31: 962–976; C. Park, 2002, The effects of prior performance on the choice between related and unrelated acquisitions: Implications for the performance consequences of diversification strategy, *Journal of Management Studies,* 39: 1003–1019.
89. Rumelt, *Strategy, Structure and Economic Performance,* 125.
90. V. Vara, 2006, eBay's bid to go beyond auctions isn't selling well, *Wall Street Journal,* December 20, B1.
91. L. E. Palich, L. B. Cardinal, & C. C. Miller, 2000, Curvilinearity in the diversification-performance linkage: An examination of over three decades of research, *Strategic Management Journal,* 21: 155–174.
92. Y. I. Kane, 2007, Sanyo ends era of family rule, *Wall Street Journal,* March 29, B4.
93. D. G. Sirmon, M. A. Hitt, & R. D. Ireland, 2007, Managing firm resources in dynamic environments to create value: Looking inside the black box, *Academy of Management Review,* 32: 273–292; A. E. Bernardo & B. Chowdhry, 2002, Resources, real options, and corporate strategy, *Journal of Financial Economics,* 63: 211–234.
94. N. W. C. Harper & S. P. Viguerie, 2002, Are you too focused? *McKinsey Quarterly,* Mid-Summer, 29–38; J. C. Sandvig & L. Coakley, 1998, Best practices in small firm diversification, *Business Horizons,* 41(3): 33–40; C. G. Smith & A. C. Cooper, 1988, Established companies diversifying into young industries: A comparison of firms with different levels of performance, *Strategic Management Journal,* 9: 111–121.
95. C. Bryan-Low, 2007, How old Thomson stayed fresh, *Wall Street Journal,* June 12, A10.
96. N. M. Kay & A. Diamantopoulos, 1987, Uncertainty and synergy: Towards a formal model of corporate strategy, *Managerial and Decision Economics,* 8: 121–130.
97. R. W. Coff, 1999, How buyers cope with uncertainty when acquiring firms in knowledge-intensive industries: Caveat emptor, *Organization Science,* 10: 144–161.
98. S. Tully, 2005, The urge to merge, *Fortune,* February 21, 21–22.
99. S. J. Chatterjee & B. Wernerfelt, 1991, The link between resources and type of diversification: Theory and evidence, *Strategic Management Journal,* 12: 33–48.
100. W. Keuslein, 2003, The Ebitda folly, *Forbes,* March 17, 165–167; Kochhar & Hitt, Linking corporate strategy to capital structure.
101. Y.-H. Kim, 2005, Chipmakers find diversity pays, *Wall Street Journal,* August 4, B4.
102. L. Capron & J. Hulland, 1999, Redeployment of brands, sales forces, and general marketing management expertise following horizontal acquisitions: A resource-based view, *Journal of Marketing,* 63(2): 41–54.
103. A. M. Knott, D. J. Bryce, & H. E. Posen, 2003, On the strategic accumulation of intangible assets, *Organization Science,* 14: 192–207; J. Castillo, 2002, A note on the concept of tacit knowledge, *Journal of Management Inquiry,* 11(1): 46–57; R. D. Smith, 2000, Intangible strategic assets and firm performance: A multi-industry study of the resource-based view, *Journal of Business Strategies,* 17(2): 91–117.
104. K. Shimizu & M. A. Hitt, 2005, What constrains or facilitates divestitures of formerly acquired firms? The effects of organizational inertia, *Journal of Management,* 31: 50–72.
105. J. Jargon & J. Vuocolo, 2007, Sara Lee CEO challenged on antitakeover defenses, *Wall Street Journal,* May 11, B4.
106. J. G. Combs & M. S. Skill, 2003, Managerialist and human capital explanation for key executive pay premiums: A contingency perspective, *Academy of Management Journal,* 46: 63–73; M. A. Geletkanycz, B. K. Boyd, & S. Finkelstein, 2001, The strategic value of CEO external directorate networks: Implications for CEO compensation, *Strategic Management Journal,* 9: 889–898; W. Grossman & R. E. Hoskisson, 1998, CEO pay at the crossroads of Wall Street and Main: Toward the strategic design of executive compensation, *Academy of Management Executive,* 12(1): 43–57.
107. W. Shen & A. A. Cannella Jr., 2002, Power dynamics within top management and their impacts on CEO dismissal followed by inside succession, *Academy of Management Journal,* 45: 1195–1206; P. J. Lane, A. A. Cannella Jr., & M. H. Lubatkin, 1998, Agency problems as antecedents to unrelated mergers and diversification: Amihud and Lev reconsidered, *Strategic Management Journal,* 19: 555–578; D. L. May, 1995, Do managerial motives influence firm risk reduction strategies? *Journal of Finance,* 50: 1291–1308.
108. Geiger & Cashen, Organizational size and CEO compensation; J. J. Cordeiro & R. Veliyath, 2003, Beyond pay for performance: A panel study of the determinants of CEO compensation, *American Business Review,* 21(1): 56–66; Wright, Kroll, & Elenkov, Acquisition returns, increase in firm size, and chief executive officer compensation; S. R. Gray & A. A. Cannella Jr., 1997, The role of risk in executive compensation, *Journal of Management,* 23: 517–540.
109. R. Bliss & R. Rosen, 2001, CEO compensation and bank mergers, *Journal of Financial Economics,* 1: 107–138; W. G. Sanders & M. A. Carpenter, 1998, Internationalization and firm governance: The roles of CEO compensation, top team composition, and board structure, *Academy of Management Journal,* 41: 158–178.
110. J. J. Janney, 2002, Eat or get eaten? How equity ownership and diversification shape CEO risk-taking, *Academy of Management Executive,* 14(4): 157–158; J. W. Lorsch, A. S. Zelleke, & K. Pick, 2001, Unbalanced boards, *Harvard Business Review,* 79(2): 28–30; R. E. Hoskisson & T. Turk, 1990, Corporate restructuring: Governance and control limits of the internal market, *Academy of Management Review,* 15: 459–477.
111. M. Kahan & E. B. Rock, 2002, How I learned to stop worrying and love the pill: Adaptive responses to takeover law, *University of Chicago Law Review,* 69(3): 871–915.

112. R. C. Anderson, T. W. Bates, J. M. Bizjak, & M. L. Lemmon, 2000, Corporate governance and firm diversification, *Financial Management,* 29(1): 5–22; J. D. Westphal, 1998, Board games: How CEOs adapt to increases in structural board independence from management, *Administrative Science Quarterly,* 43: 511–537; J. K. Seward & J. P. Walsh, 1996, The governance and control of voluntary corporate spin offs, *Strategic Management Journal,* 17: 25–39; J. P. Walsh & J. K. Seward, 1990, On the efficiency of internal and external corporate control mechanisms, *Academy of Management Review,* 15: 421–458.
113. M. Wiersema, 2002, Holes at the top: Why CEO firings backfire, *Harvard Business Review,* 80(12): 70–77.
114. N. Wasserman, 2006, Stewards, agents, and the founder discount: Executive compensation in new ventures, *Academy of Management Journal,* 49: 960–976; V. Kisfalvi & P. Pitcher, 2003, Doing what feels right: The influence of CEO character and emotions on top management team dynamics, *Journal of Management Inquiry,* 12(10): 42–66; W. G. Rowe, 2001, Creating wealth in organizations: The role of strategic leadership, *Academy of Management Executive,* 15(1): 81–94.
115. E. F. Fama, 1980, Agency problems and the theory of the firm, *Journal of Political Economy,* 88: 288–307.
116. R. Ettenson & J. Knowles, 2007, M&A blind spot; When negotiating a merger, leave a seat at the table for a marketing expert, *Wall Street Journal,* June 16, R4; F. Vermeulen, 2005, How acquisitions can revitalize companies, *MIT Sloan Management Review,* 46(4): 45–51.
117. M. L. A. Hayward, 2002, When do firms learn from their acquisition experience? Evidence from 1990–1995, *Strategic Management Journal,* 23: 21–39; L. Capron, W. Mitchell, & A. Swaminathan, 2001, Asset divestiture following horizontal acquisitions: A dynamic view, *Strategic Management Journal,* 22: 817–844.
118. R. E. Hoskisson, R. A. Johnson, L. Tihanyi, & R. E. White, 2005, Diversified business groups and corporate refocusing in emerging economies, *Journal of Management,* 31: 941–965.
119. Chakrabarti, Singh, & Mahmood, Diversification and performance: Evidence from East Asian firms; W. P. Wan & R. E. Hoskisson, 2003, Home country environments, corporate diversification strategies, and firm performance, *Academy of Management Journal,* 46: 27–45.

Acquisition and Restructuring Strategies

7

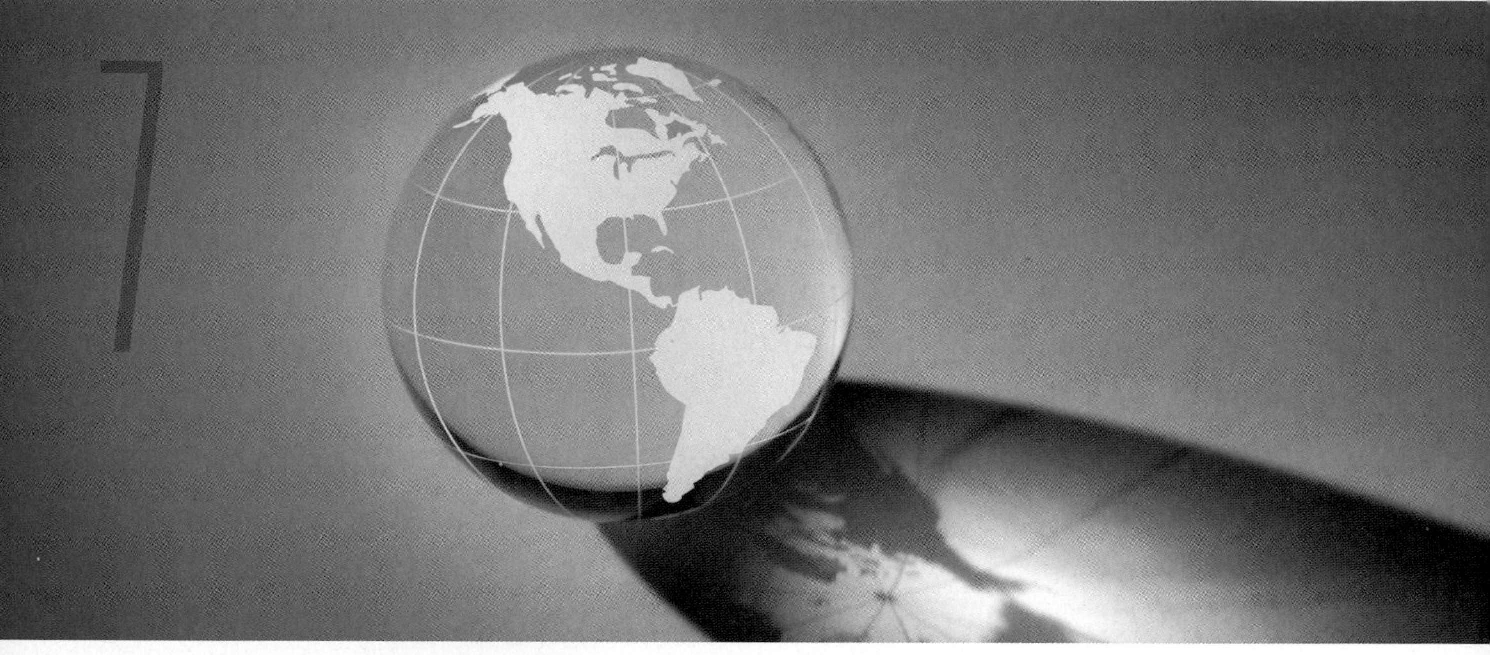

Studying this chapter should provide you with the strategic management knowledge needed to:

1. Explain the popularity of acquisition strategies in firms competing in the global economy.
2. Discuss reasons why firms use an acquisition strategy to achieve strategic competitiveness.
3. Describe seven problems that work against developing a competitive advantage using an acquisition strategy.
4. Name and describe attributes of effective acquisitions.
5. Define the restructuring strategy and distinguish among its common forms.
6. Explain the short- and long-term outcomes of the different types of restructuring strategies.

The Increased Trend Toward Cross-Border Acquisitions

© Keith Dannemiller/CORBIS

The number of cross-border acquisitions illustrates the increasingly globalized nature of conducting business affairs in globally competitive markets. The increase is especially apparent as one looks at the number of foreign acquisitions in large, developed markets such as in the United States and the United Kingdom. Foreign direct investments increased 76.7 percent to $161.5 billion in 2006 from $91.4 billion the previous year in the United States. This level was the highest since 2000 when totals reached $335.6 billion at the peak of the dot.com boom. Even though a protectionist mood characterizes the U.S. Congress, investments in the United States appear to remain attractive. Two thirds, or $147.8 billion, of total foreign investment is due to foreign acquisitions of U.S. affiliates.

The United Kingdom has also benefited enormously from having open borders and open markets that allow foreign capital to purchase domestic U.K assets and from the foreign managerial talent associated with managing such acquired assets. However, concerns have surfaced about whether or not foreign acquisitions will make it much harder for British employees to become top-level managers. Furthermore, some industry watchers wonder if foreign takeovers will reduce intellectual property, such that foreign firms will reduce the long-term viability of British industry firms with foreign firms spending their R&D investment in their home countries. The takeover boom affected even significant icons such as Manchester United, which was purchased by Malcolm Glazer, a U.S. sports tycoon.

Other European firms such as those from Spain have been purchasing a significant number of foreign firms. Spanish firms gained experience through an international push in Latin America decades ago. Particularly Telefonica, a large telecommunication firm, purchased a number of telecommunication companies that had been privatized in Latin America. Similarly Spanish banks grew in Latin America through a number of purchases. This experience has now been transferred across Europe not only in the merging of telecommunication firms and banks, but also in merging train and airport management services, and infrastructure management services. For instance Ferrobial sought to buy BAA, the largest train and airport manager in the United Kingdom, which was recently privatized. Furthermore Banco Santander was looking to purchase Abbey National in the United Kingdom, as well as a number of other banks. Recently Abertis sought to takeover Autostrade SpA, which will provide the Spanish firm control over the train routes in Italy and other countries in Europe.

Japanese firms have also become active in large overseas takeovers after being somewhat inactive for a number of years. For example, Japan Tobacco Inc. recently acquired Gallaher Group PLC for $14.7 billion. The acquisition of this British tobacco firm will greatly increase Japan Tobacco's overseas revenues. Interestingly, much of the acquisition activity by European and Japanese firms have been driven by currency valuations, especially relative to the United States, because the dollar is much lower in value than either the euro or the Japanese yen currencies compared to the 1990s.

Emerging economies, for example, from India have become quite aggressive in overseas transactions as well. India's Tata Group won the bid for British steel maker Corus Group PLC for $13.2 billion. Similarly, Hindalco Industries Ltd. purchased Novelis Inc., an aluminum producer that manufactures products such as beer cans and rolled automobile aluminum, for $5.73 billion. Novelis was spun off from Alcan, the second largest (in size) aluminum producer next to Alcoa, and is incorporated in Canada but headquartered in Atlanta. Although pursuing smaller acquisitions, Infosys Technologies Ltd., another India-based company which provides software services, increased its growth 9 percent a year by acquiring small software providers.

Similarly many Latin American firms have been buying U.S. firms. In fact, the largest producers of cement in the United States are all owned by foreign producers, including France's Lafarge SA, Switzerland's Holcim Ltd, and Mexico's Cemex SA. Besides these large global players, a number of medium-sized producers such as Brazil's Botoratin Cinentos SA and Colombia's Cementos Argos SA have been buying North American assets and fleets of mixing trucks to deliver the concrete. Similarly a regional Mexican producer, Grupo Cementos de Chihuahua SA, made additional acquisitions in Colorado and Oklahoma following purchases in Minnesota and South Dakota. Many of these purchases were driven by the high consumption rate for cement during the building boom when cement was in a seller's market. With a slowdown in housing, it is likely this acquisition activity will slow down as well.

In summary the number of cross-border deals continues to increase, leading many emerging-country firms to pursue acquisitions in developed countries, especially in the United States, the United Kingdom, and other places in Europe. These developed economies have more open policies that allow the emerging-country economies to make inroads, especially in mature globalizing businesses such as steel, aluminum, and cement, or basic services including managing airports and railroads, or infrastructure management services such as managing toll roads.

Sources: 2007, Marauding Maharajahs; India's acquisitive companies, *Economist*, March, 86; D. K. Berman, 2007, Mergers hit record, with few stop signs, *Wall Street Journal*, C11; S. Daneshkhu, 2007, FDI flow into richest countries set to rise 20% this year, *Financial Times*, June 22, 7; J. McCary, 2007, Foreign investments rise, *Wall Street Journal*, June 6, A5; J. Saigol, M&A activity gets off to a sprinting start, *Financial Times*, June 30, 18; L. R. McNeil, 2007, Foreign direct investment in the United States: New investment in 2006, *Survey of Current Business*, 87(6): 44–48; J. Singer, K. Johnson & V. O'Connell, 2007, Tobacco consolidation speeds, *Wall Street Journal*, March 16, A3; A. Thompson, 2007, Foreign acquisitions: Success at home has bred victory abroad, *Financial Times*, May 9, 6; P. Wonacott & P. Glader, 2007, Hindalco pact to buy Novelis underlines India's push overseas, *Wall Street Journal*, February 12, A11; A. Galloni, 2006, European acquisition creates toll-road giant, *Wall Street Journal*, April 24, A3; K. Johnson, 2006, Spain emerges as M&A powerhouse, *Wall Street Journal*, September 26, A6; J. Millman, 2006, Cement demand paves path to takeovers, *Wall Street Journal*, May 23, A8; P. Engardio, M. Arndt & G. Smith, 2006, Emerging giants, *BusinessWeek*, July 31, 40.

In Chapter 6 we studied corporate-level strategies, focusing on types and levels of product diversification strategies that are derived from core competencies and create competitive advantage. As noted in that chapter, diversification allows a firm to create value by productively using excess resources.[1] In this chapter, we explore mergers and acquisitions, often combined with a diversification strategy, as a prominent strategy employed by firms throughout the world. As described in the Opening Case many firms, not only from developed countries, but also from emerging economies are increasingly becoming involved in merger and acquisition activities.

In the latter half of the twentieth century, acquisition became a prominent strategy used by major corporations to achieve growth and meet competitive challenges. Even smaller and more focused firms began employing acquisition strategies to grow and to enter new markets.[2] However, acquisition strategies are not without problems; some acquisitions fail. Thus, we focus on how acquisitions can be used to produce value for a firm's stakeholders.[3] Before describing attributes associated with effective acquisitions, we examine the most prominent problems companies experience when using an acquisition strategy. For example, when acquisitions contribute to poor performance, a firm may deem it necessary to restructure its operations as explained in the Strategic Focus on the DaimlerChrysler divestiture of Chrysler. Closing the chapter are descriptions of three restructuring strategies, as well as the short- and long-term outcomes resulting from their use. Setting the stage for these topics is an examination of the popularity of mergers and acquisitions and a discussion of the differences among mergers, acquisitions, and takeovers.

The Popularity of Merger and Acquisition Strategies

The acquisition strategy has been a popular strategy among U.S. firms for many years. Some believe that this strategy played a central role in an effective restructuring of U.S. businesses during the 1980s and 1990s and into the twenty-first century.[4] Increasingly, as the Opening Case reveals, acquisition strategies are becoming more popular with firms in other nations and economic regions, including Europe and other emerging economies such as India, China, and Brazil. In fact, a large percentage of the acquisitions in recent years have been made across country borders (i.e., a firm headquartered in one country acquiring a firm headquartered in another country).

For instance, spending on global deals totaled $3.6 trillion in 2006, the best year on record.[5] However, by July 2007 the quantity of deals was ahead of the 2006 amount by nearly 25 percent. The Organization for Economic Co-operation and Development (OECD) reported, "If the months January through May are indicative of the year 2007 as a whole, then the total value of cross-border M&As in OECD countries will exceed $1 trillion."[6] Interestingly, 20 percent of the deals worldwide have been funded by private equity, largely through the use of debt. It is also worthy to note that this volume increased to 40 percent of the deal total when focused on deals originating in the United States alone.[7]

An acquisition strategy is sometimes used because of the uncertainty in the competitive landscape. A firm may make an acquisition to increase its market power because of a competitive threat, to enter a new market because of the opportunity available in that market, or to spread the risk due to the uncertain environment.[8] In addition, as volatility brings undesirable changes to its primary markets, a firm may acquire other companies to shift its core business into different markets. Such options may arise because of industry or regulatory changes. For instance, as mentioned in Chapter 6, Thomson, a large media conglomerate headquartered in Toronto, Canada, shifted it business model from a focus on newspapers to a focus on selling electronic data services, especially to provide support for firms needing legal and financial data and analysis.[9]

The strategic management process (see Figure 1.1, on page 5) calls for an acquisition strategy to increase a firm's strategic competitiveness as well as its returns to shareholders. Thus, an acquisition strategy should be used only when the acquiring firm will be able to increase its value through ownership of the acquired firm and the use of its assets.[10]

However, evidence suggests that, at least for the acquiring firms, acquisition strategies may not always result in these desirable outcomes.[11] Researchers have found that shareholders of acquired firms often earn above-average returns from an acquisition, while shareholders of acquiring firms typically earn returns from the transaction that are close to zero. These results may suggest that for large firms, it is now more difficult to create sustainable value by using an acquisition strategy to buy publicly traded companies.[12] In approximately two-thirds of all acquisitions, the acquiring firm's stock price falls immediately after the intended transaction is announced. This negative response is an indication of investors' skepticism about the likelihood that the acquirer will be able to achieve the synergies required to justify the premium.[13]

Mergers, Acquisitions, and Takeovers: What Are the Differences?

A **merger** is a strategy through which two firms agree to integrate their operations on a relatively coequal basis.

A **merger** is a strategy through which two firms agree to integrate their operations on a relatively coequal basis. Few true mergers actually occur, because one party is usually dominant in regard to market share or firm size. DaimlerChrysler AG was termed a "merger of equals" and, although Daimler-Benz was the dominant party in the automakers' transaction, Chrysler managers would not allow the business deal to be completed unless it was termed a *merger*. However, a merger of equals does not always last as Daimler of the former DaimlerChrysler is changing its name to Daimler AG as it sells off the Chrysler assets, as indicated in the Strategic Focus later in the chapter.[14]

An **acquisition** is a strategy through which one firm buys a controlling, or 100 percent, interest in another firm with the intent of making the acquired firm a subsidiary business within its portfolio.

An **acquisition** is a strategy through which one firm buys a controlling, or 100 percent, interest in another firm with the intent of making the acquired firm a subsidiary business within its portfolio. In this case, the management of the acquired firm reports to the management of the acquiring firm. Although most mergers are friendly transactions, acquisitions can be friendly or unfriendly.

A **takeover** is a special type of an acquisition strategy wherein the target firm does not solicit the acquiring firm's bid.

A **takeover** is a special type of an acquisition strategy wherein the target firm does not solicit the acquiring firm's bid. The number of unsolicited takeover bids increased in the economic downturn of 2001–2002, a common occurrence in economic recessions, because the poorly managed firms that are undervalued relative to their assets are more easily identified.[15] Many takeover attempts are not desired by the target firm's managers and are referred to as hostile. In a few cases, unsolicited offers may come from parties familiar and possibly friendly to the target firm. However, research has "found that hostile acquirers deliver significantly higher shareholder value than friendly acquirers" for the acquiring firm.[16]

On a comparative basis, acquisitions are more common than mergers and takeovers. Accordingly, this chapter focuses on acquisitions.

Reasons for Acquisitions

In this section, we discuss reasons that support the use of an acquisition strategy. Although each reason can provide a legitimate rationale for an acquisition, the acquisition may not necessarily lead to a competitive advantage.

Increased Market Power

A primary reason for acquisitions is to achieve greater market power.[17] Defined in Chapter 6, *market power* exists when a firm is able to sell its goods or services above competitive levels or when the costs of its primary or support activities are lower than those of its competitors. Market power usually is derived from the size of the firm and its resources and capabilities to compete in the marketplace.[18] It is also affected by the firm's share of the market. Therefore, most acquisitions that are designed to achieve greater market power entail buying a competitor, a supplier, a distributor, or a business in a highly related industry to allow the exercise of a core competence and to gain competitive advantage in the acquiring firm's primary market. One goal in achieving market power is to become a market leader. As noted in Chapter 6, Nestlé SA, will increase its market share for its baby-food line through the acquisition of Gerber Products from Novartis AG.[19] Gerber has nearly an 80 percent share of baby foods in the United States, and through this acquisition Nestlé will substantially increase its market power worldwide. Research in marketing suggests that performance of the merged firm increases if marketing-related issues are involved. The performance improvement of the merged firm subsequent to a horizontal acquisition is even more significant than the average potential cost savings if marketing of the combined firms improves economies of scope.[20] To increase their market power, firms often use horizontal, vertical, and related acquisitions.

Oracle Makes a Series of Horizontal Acquisitions While CVS Makes a Vertical Acquisition

Oracle, SAP, and Microsoft compete in the database management software area. Currently SAP is leading at approximately 22 percent market share, while Oracle and Microsoft have 10 percent and 5 percent, respectively. Rivalry between these firms has heated up as they compete for customer firms that have not yet integrated their firm's business units using database software. Once a database software configuration is in place, significant switching costs to move to another software platform exist. This point has led Oracle to pursue growth through horizontal acquisition strategy. Oracle's acquisition strategy facilitates growth because each new firm acquired has existing customers that will likely be retained, a sales force that can be integrated into Oracle's existing sales force to pursue new sales, and new software applications that can be applied in industries where Oracle may not yet be involved, but with which the target firm will already have a clientele.

Larry Ellison, CEO of Oracle, has been the architect of Oracle's acquisition strategy in the corporate-software industry.

In 2004 Oracle acquired PeopleSoft for $10.3 billion through a hostile takeover. This acquisition also gave it the rights to J.D. Edwards, another industry rival that PeopleSoft had previously acquired. Oracle's acquisition strategy began when Larry Ellison decided that the corporate-software industry had matured and needed consolidation. Since then Oracle has spent $24 billion to buy a number of companies, including the recent $3.3 billion takeover of Hyperion Solutions. This series of acquisitions led to Oracle's revenue increase of 50 percent to $17.7 billion in the fiscal year ending May 2007. The acquisitions also enabled Oracle to develop a refined set of industry focuses with applications in retail, financial services, utilities, communications, and government service.

As an example, Oracle acquired Retek Inc. as well as ProfitLogic and 360Commerce to put together a set of retail software applications. These acquisitions allowed Oracle to win 30 new retail customers in 2006 and 2007 such as Wal-Mart, Nordstrom, and Perry Ellis International. Perry Ellis's CIO indicated that the company expects to save more than $20 million a year in improved just-in-time inventory controls, improved merchandising efficiency, and software that helps to adapts its pricing by store and region efficiently through the application of the newly integrated Oracle software applications.

Comparatively, SAP is ahead in specific industry applications. It has applications in 26 industries compared to Oracle's five. Also, beyond large corporations in specific industries, both companies are pursuing growth in small- to medium-sized enterprises. The equalizer for Oracle has been its acquisition strategy. However, facilitating alignment and integrating the operations of these firms with Oracle is no easy task, but Oracle's increasing acquisition experience has made for improved acquisition integration processes.

In a vertical merger, CVS Corporation, a drugstore chain, purchased pharmacy-benefits manager (PBM) Caremark RX, Inc., for $21 billion in 2007. The combined company will have $75 billion in annual sales, far higher than any other competitor, including Walgreens and comparable PBMs such as Medco Health. In this vertical acquisition CVS is purchasing a powerful customer that negotiates on behalf of large companies and their health insurance providers. One of the incentives for this vertical merger is that PBMs have put pressure on drugstores by negotiating prices on behalf of their clients and forcing firms into mail-order plans for prescription drugs. The merger will help CVS obtain large deals with big companies by offering significant discounts to employees for CVS private-label products. When Wal-Mart began charging much lower prices for generic drugs in many of their stores, drugstores and

PBM firms felt additional pressure for mergers. Walgreens, a large competitor of CVS, also plans to increase its PMB business, but it has not signaled whether it will use an acquisition process.

These two examples represent horizontal and vertical mergers that seek to simultaneously gain market power and reduce costs due to potential synergy and/or complementarity.

Sources: S. Hamm, 2007, Oracle; Larry Ellison engineered a string of acquisitions that have given boost to the software giant's revenues, *BusinessWeek*, March 26, 64–65; G. Marcial, 2007, Hail to CVS/Caremark, 2007, *BusinessWeek*, April 9, 99; A. Ricadela, 2007, Oracle vs. SAP: Sound or fiery? *BusinessWeek*, April 9, 38; V. Vara, 2007, Oracle adds business-intelligence from Hyperion, *Wall Street Journal*, March 2, B3; V. Vara, 2007, Oracle's profit shows acquisition spree is paying off, *Wall Street Journal*, June 27, A3; K. Whitehouse, 2007, CVS/Caremark directors win election, *Wall Street Journal*, May 10, B6; D. Armstrong & B. Martinez, 2006, CVS, Caremark deal to create drug-sale giant, *Wall Street Journal*, November 2, B1, B2; D. K. Berman, W. M. Bulkeley, & S. Hensley, 2006, Higher bid lifts Caremark, for now, *Wall Street Journal*, December 19, A2; S. Pritchard, 2006, How Oracle and SAP are moving down "The Tail," *Financial Times*, October 18, 5.

Horizontal Acquisitions

The acquisition of a company competing in the same industry as the acquiring firm is referred to as a *horizontal acquisition*. Horizontal acquisitions increase a firm's market power by exploiting cost-based and revenue-based synergies.[21] Research suggests that horizontal acquisitions result in higher performance when the firms have similar characteristics.[22] Examples of important similar characteristics include strategy, managerial styles, and resource allocation patterns. Similarities in these characteristics make the integration of the two firms proceed more smoothly.[23] Horizontal acquisitions are often most effective when the acquiring firm integrates the acquired firm's assets with its own assets, but only after evaluating and divesting excess capacity and assets that do not complement the newly combined firm's core competencies.[24] As the Strategic Focus illustrates, Oracle has pursued a strategy of horizontal acquisitions of other software firms quite successfully in its competition with SAP and IBM.

Vertical Acquisitions

A *vertical acquisition* refers to a firm acquiring a supplier or distributor of one or more of its goods or services.[25] A firm becomes vertically integrated through this type of acquisition in that it controls additional parts of the value chain (see Chapters 3 and 6).[26] As the Strategic Focus indicates, the acquisition of Caremark, a pharmacy-benefits manager (PBM), will allow an increase in market power for drugstore chain CVS because it will have more power to negotiate deals with large companies who have been putting pricing pressure on drug store chains through their PBMs and insurance providers.

Google's acquisition of DoubleClick is a vertical acquisition designed to allow Google to provide better quality on-line advertising.

Vertical acquisitions also occur with online businesses. For instance, Google's acquisition of DoubleClick will allow it to provide better-quality online advertisements than it can produce on its own. DoubleClick specializes in providing online display advertisements, especially customer pop-ups and video, while Google specializes in online and text banner ads. As such, Google is buying one of its suppliers in an area where it has been weak on its own. Interestingly, Microsoft complained about the deal, suggesting that it would give Google excessive market power, even though Microsoft was outbid by Google for DoubleClick.[27]

Related Acquisitions

The acquisition of a firm in a highly related industry is referred to as a *related acquisition.* IBM's traditional core business has been selling computer hardware. More recently it moved into services that have become its dominant sales growth engine. However, to sell service solutions, it must have software applications. As such, IBM has been purchasing smaller server and software providers in order to stay competitive. Of course, the software providers are related to IBM's hardware and service businesses. "Since 2003, IBM has spent $11.8 billion on 54 acquisitions: 36 software and 18 services companies."[28] However, because of the difficulty in achieving synergy, related acquisitions are often difficult to value.[29]

Acquisitions intended to increase market power are subject to regulatory review as well as to analysis by financial markets.[30] For example, as noted in the Opening Case in Chapter 6, the successful takeover of Gillette by Procter & Gamble was subjected to a significant amount of government scrutiny as well as close examination by financial analysts. Ultimately, P&G had to sell off several businesses to gain the Federal Trade Commission's approval for the acquisition. Thus, firms seeking growth and market power through acquisitions must understand the political/legal segment of the general environment (see Chapter 2) in order to successfully use an acquisition strategy.

Overcoming Entry Barriers

Barriers to entry (introduced in Chapter 2) are factors associated with the market or with the firms currently operating in it, which increase the expense and difficulty faced by new ventures trying to enter that particular market. For example, well-established competitors may have substantial economies of scale in the manufacture or service of their products. In addition, enduring relationships with customers often create product loyalties that are difficult for new entrants to overcome. When facing differentiated products, new entrants typically must spend considerable resources to advertise their goods or services and may find it necessary to sell at prices below competitors' to entice new customers.

Facing the entry barriers created by economies of scale and differentiated products, a new entrant may find acquiring an established company to be more effective than entering the market as a competitor offering a good or service that is unfamiliar to current buyers. In fact, the higher the barriers to market entry, the greater the probability that a firm will acquire an existing firm to overcome them. Although an acquisition can be expensive, it does provide the new entrant with immediate market access.

For example, as the Opening Case illustrated, many of the cross-border acquisitions, especially of firms in developing countries, are utilized to overcome entry barriers. A notable example is the cement companies, including France's Lafarge SA, Switzerland's Holcim Ltd, and Mexico's Cemex SA, which are now the largest producers of cement in the United States.

In addition, acquisitions are a commonly used method to overcome barriers to enter international markets.[31] Large multinational corporations from developed economies seek to enter emerging economies such as Brazil, Russia, India, and China (BRIC) because they are among the fastest growing economies in the world.[32] As discussed next, purchasing a local target allows a firm to enter these fast-growing economies more rapidly than learning about the local institutional barriers on its own through a greenfield or internally derived venture.

Cross-Border Acquisitions

Acquisitions made between companies with headquarters in different countries are called *cross-border acquisitions.* As mentioned previously, these acquisitions are often made to overcome entry barriers. In Chapter 9, we examine cross-border alliances and the reasons for their use. Compared with a cross-border alliance, a cross-border acquisition gives a firm more control over its international operations.[33]

Historically, U.S. firms have been the most active acquirers of companies outside their domestic market.[34] However, in the global economy, companies throughout the world are choosing this strategic option with increasing frequency.[35] In recent years, cross-border acquisitions represented as much as 40 percent of the annual total number of acquisitions.[36] Because of relaxed regulations, the amount of cross-border activity among nations within the European community also continues to increase. Many large European corporations have approached the limits of growth within their domestic markets and thus seek growth in other markets, which is what some analysts believe accounts for the growth in the range of cross-border acquisitions.

Many European and U.S. firms participated in cross-border acquisitions across Asian countries that experienced a financial crisis due to significant currency devaluations in 1997. Research indicates that these acquisitions facilitated the survival and restructuring of many large Asian companies, which enabled these economies to recover more quickly than they would have without the cross-border acquisitions.[37]

Although cross-border acquisitions are taking place across a wide variety of industries to overcome entry barriers (see the Opening Case), such acquisitions can be difficult to negotiate and operate because of the differences in foreign cultures.[38]

Cost of New Product Development and Increased Speed to Market

Developing new products internally and successfully introducing them into the marketplace often requires significant investment of a firm's resources, including time, making it difficult to quickly earn a profitable return.[39] Because an estimated 88 percent of innovations fail to achieve adequate returns, firm managers are also concerned with achieving adequate returns from the capital invested to develop and commercialize new products. Perhaps contributing to these less-than-desirable rates of return is the successful imitation of approximately 60 percent of innovations within four years after the patents are obtained. These types of outcomes may lead managers to perceive internal product development as a high-risk activity.[40]

Acquisitions are another means a firm can use to gain access to new products and to current products that are new to the firm. Compared with internal product development processes, acquisitions provide more predictable returns as well as faster market entry. Returns are more predictable because the performance of the acquired firm's products can be assessed prior to completing the acquisition.[41] For these reasons, extensive bidding wars and acquisitions are more frequent in high-technology industries.[42]

Acquisition activity is also extensive throughout the pharmaceutical industry, where firms frequently use acquisitions to enter markets quickly, to overcome the high costs of developing products internally and to increase the predictability of returns on their investments. Usually it is larger biotech or pharmaceutical firms acquiring smaller biotech firms that have drug opportunities close to market entry. For example, Gilead Sciences emerged as a leader in drugs that treat AIDS, one of the world's leading causes of death. However, with its $2.5 billion acquisition of Myogen, Inc., a smaller biotech company and one other acquisition, the company has quickly been able to diversify its pipeline into hypertension (high blood pressure), as well as drugs that treat other respiratory and heart diseases, all lines of development with high potential demand and growth.[43]

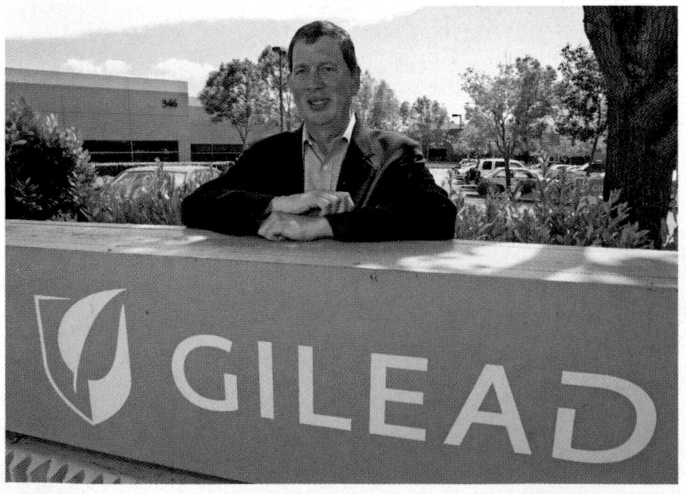

Gilead's recent acquisition of Myogen, Inc. was a strategy designed to allow for quick entry into the pharmaceutical hypertension market.

Besides quick entry into new product markets compared with internal product development, acquisitions often represent the fastest means to enter international markets and help firms overcome the liabilities associated with such strategic moves.[44] Acquisitions provide rapid access both to new markets and to new capabilities. Using new capabilities to pioneer new products and to enter markets quickly can create advantageous market positions.[45] Pharmaceutical firms, for example, access new products through acquisitions of other drug manufacturers. They also acquire biotechnology firms both for new products and for new technological capabilities. Pharmaceutical firms often provide the manufacturing and marketing capabilities to take the new products developed by biotechnology firms to the market.[46]

Lower Risk Compared to Developing New Products

Because the outcomes of an acquisition can be estimated more easily and accurately than the outcomes of an internal product development process, managers may view acquisitions as lowering risk.[47] The difference in risk between an internal product development process and an acquisition can be seen in the results of Gilead Sciences' strategy just described.

As with other strategic actions discussed in this book, the firm must exercise caution when using a strategy of acquiring new products rather than developing them internally. Even though research suggests that they have become a common means of avoiding risky internal ventures (and therefore risky R&D investments), acquisitions may also become a substitute for innovation.[48] Also, risks are associated with acquisitions where the target firm misrepresents its assets or capabilities.[49] Thus, acquisitions are not a risk-free alternative to entering new markets through internally developed products.

Increased Diversification

Acquisitions are also used to diversify firms. Based on experience and the insights resulting from it, firms typically find it easier to develop and introduce new products in markets currently served by the firm. In contrast, it is difficult for companies to develop products that differ from their current lines for markets in which they lack experience.[50] Thus, it is uncommon for a firm to develop new products internally to diversify its product lines.[51] Cisco Systems has historically pursued many acquisitions, several of which have helped build its network components business focused on producing hardware. Recently, however, Cisco purchased IronPort Systems Inc., a company focused on producing security software for networks. This acquisition will help Cisco expand beyond its original expertise in network hardware and basic software. Cisco previously acquired technology in the security area through its purchase of Riverhead Networks Inc., Protego Networks Inc., and Perfigo Inc. However, the IronPort deal provides software service in networks that can help guard against spam and viruses that travel through e-mail and Web-based traffic. Accordingly, Cisco could make other acquisitions in service-based offerings connected to its other products. Thus the IronPort Group acquisition represents a diversifying acquisition for Cisco.[52]

Both related diversification and unrelated diversification strategies can be implemented through acquisitions.[53] For example, United Technologies Corp. (UTC) has used acquisitions to build a conglomerate. Since the mid-1970s it has been building a portfolio of stable and noncyclical businesses, including Otis Elevator Co. and Carrier Corporation (air conditioners), in order to reduce its dependence on the volatile aerospace industry. Its main businesses have been Pratt & Whitney (jet engines), Sikorsky (helicopters), and Hamilton Sundstrand (aerospace parts). UTC has also acquired a hydrogen-fuel-cell business. Perceiving an opportunity in security caused by problems at airports and because security has become a top concern both for governments and for corporations, United Technologies in 2003 acquired Chubb PLC, a British electronic-security company, for $1 billion. With its acquisition of Kidde PLC in 2004 for $2.84 billion and the security unit of Rentokil Initial PLC for $1.6 billion in 2007, UTC will have obtained a significant portion of the world's market share in electronic security and become the leading firm in the Netherlands and second-largest electronic-security provider in both Britain and France.[54] All businesses UTC purchases are involved in manufacturing industrial and commercial products. However, many have a relatively low focus on technology (e.g., elevators, air conditioners, and security systems).[55]

Although acquisitions can be either related or unrelated, research has shown that the more related the acquired firm is to the acquiring firm, the greater the probability is that the acquisition will be successful.[56] Thus, horizontal acquisitions (through which a firm acquires a competitor) and related acquisitions tend to contribute more to the firm's strategic competitiveness than would the acquisition of a company that operates in product markets quite different from those in which the acquiring firm competes.[57]

Reshaping the Firm's Competitive Scope

As discussed in Chapter 2, the intensity of competitive rivalry is an industry characteristic that affects the firm's profitability.[58] To reduce the negative effect of an intense rivalry on their financial performance, firms may use acquisitions to lessen their dependence on one or more products or markets. Reducing a company's dependence on specific markets alters the firm's competitive scope.

As the Strategic Focus illustrated, Oracle's acquisition strategy helped it shift its scope through purchasing firms with application software in order to create industry service specializations in retail, financial services, utilities, communications, and government service. These capabilities are helping Oracle compete against other leading database management providers such as SAP. Similarly, GE reduced its emphasis in the electronics market many years ago by making acquisitions in the financial services industry. Today, GE is considered a service firm because a majority of its revenue now comes from services instead of from industrial products.[59] Furthermore, as the example of Thomson suggested, acquisitions helped the company shift from a focus primarily on newspapers (with classified ad revenues declining due to online competition from the likes of Craig's List) to having most of its revenues derived from selling electronic data services in finance and law.[60]

Learning and Developing New Capabilities

Some acquisitions are made to gain capabilities that the firm does not possess. For example, acquisitions may be used to acquire a special technological capability. Research has shown that firms can broaden their knowledge base and reduce inertia through acquisitions.[61] Therefore, acquiring a firm with skills and capabilities that differ from its own helps the acquiring firm to gain access to new knowledge and remain agile.[62] For example, research suggests that firms increase the potential of their capabilities when they acquire diverse talent through cross-border acquisitions. This greater value is created through the international expansion versus a simple acquisition without such diversity and resource creation potential.[63] Of course, firms are better able to learn these capabilities if they share some similar properties with the firm's current capabilities. Thus, firms should seek to acquire companies with different but related and complementary capabilities in order to build their own knowledge base.[64]

David Brennen, CEO of British drug maker AstraZeneca, orchestrated the acquisition of MedImmune, Inc. and Cambridge Antibody Technology in order to build up AstraZeneca's biological drug production process.

A number of large pharmaceutical firms are acquiring the ability to create "large molecule" drugs, also known as biological drugs, by buying biotechnology firms. Thus, these firms are not only seeking the pipeline of possible drugs, but also the capabilities that these firms have to produce such drugs. Such capabilities are important for large pharmaceutical firms because these biological drugs are more difficult to duplicate by chemistry alone (the historical basis on which most pharmaceutical firms have expertise). These capabilities will allow generic drug makers to be more successful after chemistry-based drug patents expire. To illustrate the difference between these types of drugs, David Brennen, CEO of British drug maker AstraZeneca, suggested, "Some of these [biological-based drugs] have demonstrated that they're not just symptomatic treatments but that they actually alter the course of the disease."[65] Furthermore, biological drugs must clear more regulatory barriers or hurdles, which, when accomplished, add more to a firm's advantage. For example, AstraZeneca bought biological-drug producer MedImmune Inc. for $15.6 billion in 2007 and a small biologic-centered firm, Cambridge Antibody Technology, for $1.6 billion in 2006 in order to build up its capabilities in biological-based drug production processes.

Problems in Achieving Acquisition Success

Acquisition strategies based on reasons described in this chapter can increase strategic competitiveness and help firms earn above-average returns. However, acquisition strategies are not risk-free. Reasons for the use of acquisition strategies and potential problems with such strategies are shown in Figure 7.1.

Figure 7.1 Reasons for Acquisitions and Problems in Achieving Success

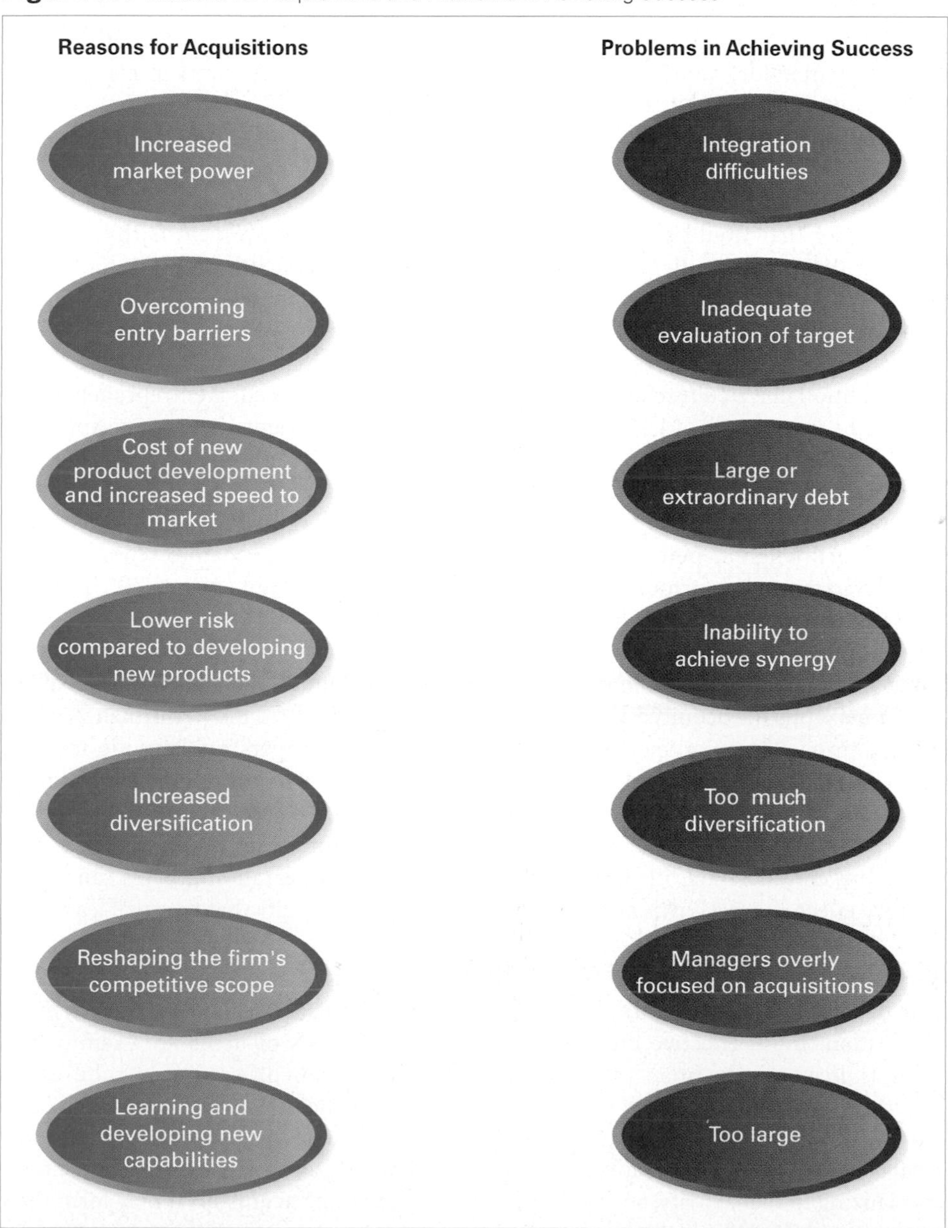

Research suggests that perhaps 20 percent of all mergers and acquisitions are successful, approximately 60 percent produce disappointing results, and the remaining 20 percent are clear failures.[66] Successful acquisitions generally involve having a well-conceived strategy for selecting the target, not paying too high a premium (doing appropriate due diligence), and employing an effective integration process.[67] As shown in Figure 7.1, several problems may prevent successful acquisitions.

Integration Difficulties

Integrating two companies following an acquisition can be quite difficult. Integration challenges include melding two disparate corporate cultures, linking different financial and control systems, building effective working relationships (particularly when management styles differ), and resolving problems regarding the status of the newly acquired firm's executives.[68]

The importance of a successful integration should not be underestimated.[69] Without it, an acquisition is unlikely to produce positive returns. Thus, as suggested by a researcher studying the process, "Managerial practice and academic writings show that the post-acquisition integration phase is probably the single most important determinant of shareholder value creation (and equally of value destruction) in mergers and acquisitions."[70]

Integration is complex and involves a large number of activities, which if overlooked can lead to significant difficulties. For example, when United Parcel Service (UPS) acquired Mail Boxes Etc., a large retail shipping chain, it appeared to be a complementary merger that would provide benefits to both firms. The problem is that most of the Mail Boxes Etc. outlets were owned by franchisees. Once the merger took place the franchisees lost the ability to deal with other shipping companies such as FedEx, which reduced their competitiveness. Furthermore, franchisees complained that UPS often built company-owned shipping stores close by franchisee outlets of Mail Boxes Etc. Additionally, a culture clash evolved between the free-wheeling entrepreneurs who owned the franchises of Mail Boxes Etc. and the efficiency-oriented corporate approach of the UPS operation, which focused on managing a large fleet of trucks and an information system to efficiently pick up and deliver packages. Also, Mail Boxes Etc. was focused on retail traffic, whereas UPS was focused more on the logistics of wholesale pickup and delivery. Although 87 percent of Mail Boxes Etc. franchisees decided to rebrand under the UPS name, many formed an owner's group and even filed suit against UPS in regard to the unfavorable nature of the franchisee contract.[71]

It is important to maintain the human capital of the target firm after the acquisition. Much of an organization's knowledge is contained in its human capital.[72] Turnover of key personnel from the acquired firm can have a negative effect on the performance of the merged firm.[73] The loss of key personnel, such as critical managers, weakens the acquired firm's capabilities and reduces its value. When a deal for an acquisition is being considered, completing due diligence on the human capital to make sure that key people—who are necessary to help run the company after the integration process—will not leave is an important consideration.[74] If implemented effectively, the integration process can have a positive effect on target firm managers and reduce the probability that they will leave.[75]

Inadequate Evaluation of Target

Due diligence is a process through which a potential acquirer evaluates a target firm for acquisition. In an effective due-diligence process, hundreds of items are examined in areas as diverse as the financing for the intended transaction, differences in cultures between the acquiring and target firm, tax consequences of the transaction, and actions that would be necessary to successfully meld the two workforces. Due diligence is commonly performed by investment bankers, accountants, lawyers, and management consultants specializing in that activity, although firms actively pursuing acquisitions may form their own internal due-diligence team.[76]

The failure to complete an effective due-diligence process may easily result in the acquiring firm paying an excessive premium for the target company. Interestingly, research shows that in times of high or increasing stock prices due diligence is relaxed; firms often overpay during these periods and long-run performance of the merged firm suffers.[77] Research also shows that without due diligence, "the purchase price is driven by the pricing of other 'comparable' acquisitions rather than by a rigorous assessment of where, when, and how management can drive real performance gains. [In these cases], the price paid may have little to do with achievable value."[78]

Many firms use investment banks to perform their due diligence, but in the post-Enron era the process is increasingly performed in-house. Although investment bankers such as Credit Suisse First Boston and Citibank still play a large role in due diligence for large mergers and acquisitions, their role in smaller mergers and acquisitions seems to be decreasing.[79] However, when it comes to financing the deal, investment banks are critical to the process, whether the firm remains public or is taken private by a private equity firm.

Large or Extraordinary Debt

To finance a number of acquisitions completed during the 1980s and 1990s, some companies significantly increased their levels of debt. A financial innovation called junk bonds helped make this increase possible. *Junk bonds* are a financing option through which risky acquisitions are financed with money (debt) that provides a large potential return to lenders (bondholders). Because junk bonds are unsecured obligations that are not tied to specific assets for collateral, interest rates for these high-risk debt instruments sometimes reached between 18 and 20 percent during the 1980s.[80] Some prominent financial economists viewed debt as a means to discipline managers, causing them to act in the shareholders' best interests.[81]

Junk bonds are now used less frequently to finance acquisitions, and the conviction that debt disciplines managers is less strong. Nonetheless, some firms still take on significant debt to acquire companies. For example, more debt is being used in cross-border acquisitions such as the deal between India's Tata Steel and Corus Group PLC of the United Kingdom mentioned in the Opening Case. First, the deal went through nine rounds of bidding with two main contenders Tata Steel and Brazil's Cia Siderurgica Nacional, or CSN, which increased the price 34 percent above Tata Steel's initial offer to $11.3 billion. However, Tata proposed financing the deal using a debt approach, and its shares fell 11 percent upon this announcement because, as one analyst suggested, "Tata was paying too much for Corus and that debt incurred to fund the acquisition could affect the company's earnings for years to come."[82]

High debt can have several negative effects on the firm. For example, because high debt increases the likelihood of bankruptcy, it can lead to a downgrade in the firm's credit rating by agencies such as Moody's and Standard & Poor's.[83] In fact, in the Tata-Corus deal just noted, the stock price drop was influenced by a warning from Standard & Poor's that it might downgrade Tata's debt rating, which would effectively raise its cost of debt. In addition, high debt may preclude needed investment in activities that contribute to the firm's long-term success, such as R&D, human resources training, and marketing.[84] Still, leverage can be a positive force in a firm's development, allowing it to take advantage of attractive expansion opportunities. However, too much leverage (such as extraordinary debt) can lead to negative outcomes, including postponing or eliminating investments, such as R&D expenditures, that are necessary to maintain strategic competitiveness over the long term.

Inability to Achieve Synergy

Derived from *synergos*, a Greek word that means "working together," *synergy* exists when the value created by units working together exceeds the value those units could create working independently (see Chapter 6). That is, synergy exists when assets are worth more when used in conjunction with each other than when they are used separately.[85] For shareholders, synergy generates gains in their wealth that they could not duplicate or exceed through their own portfolio diversification decisions.[86] Synergy is created by the efficiencies derived from economies of scale and economies of scope and by sharing resources (e.g., human capital and knowledge) across the businesses in the merged firm.[87]

A firm develops a competitive advantage through an acquisition strategy only when a transaction generates private synergy. *Private synergy* is created when the combination and integration of the acquiring and acquired firms' assets yield capabilities and core competencies that could not be developed by combining and integrating either firm's assets with another company. Private synergy is possible when firms' assets are complementary in unique ways; that is, the unique type of asset complementarity is not possible by combining either company's assets with another firm's assets.[88] Because of its uniqueness, private synergy is difficult for competitors to understand and imitate. However, private synergy is difficult to create.

A firm's ability to account for costs that are necessary to create anticipated revenue- and cost-based synergies affects the acquisition's success. Firms experience several expenses when trying to create private synergy through acquisitions. Called transaction costs, these expenses are incurred when firms use acquisition strategies to create synergy.[89] Transaction costs may be direct or indirect. Direct costs include legal fees and charges from investment bankers who complete due diligence for the acquiring firm. Indirect costs include managerial time to evaluate target firms and then to complete negotiations, as well as the loss of key managers and employees following an acquisition.[90] Firms tend to underestimate the sum of indirect costs when the value of the synergy that may be created by combining and integrating the acquired firm's assets with the acquiring firm's assets is calculated.

As the Strategic Focus later in the chapter on the sale of Chrysler by Daimler points out, synergies are often difficult to achieve. In this regard, Dieter Zetsche, Daimler's CEO and a former head of Chrysler, pointedly notes: "Obviously we overestimated the potential for synergies (between Mercedes and Chrysler). Given the very different nature of the markets we operate in, the gap between luxury and volume was too great."[91] One analyst noted as well, "What once seemed like a perfect fit now just seems like a mistaken vision."[92]

Too Much Diversification

As explained in Chapter 6, diversification strategies can lead to strategic competitiveness and above-average returns. In general, firms using related diversification strategies outperform those employing unrelated diversification strategies. However, conglomerates formed by using an unrelated diversification strategy also can be successful, as demonstrated by United Technologies Corp.

At some point, however, firms can become overdiversified. The level at which overdiversification occurs varies across companies because each firm has different capabilities to manage diversification. Recall from Chapter 6 that related diversification requires more information processing than does unrelated diversification. Because of this additional information processing, related diversified firms become overdiversified with a smaller number of business units than do firms using an unrelated diversification strategy.[93] Regardless of the type of diversification strategy implemented, however, overdiversification leads to a decline in performance, after which business units are often divested.[94] There seems to be a pattern of excessive diversification followed by divestments of underperforming business units previously acquired in the automobile industry. We discuss this issue later in a Strategic Focus on DaimlerChrysler. Not only is Daimler divesting assets (Chrysler), but Ford and other companies have been unwinding previous acquisitions. Ford acquired Volvo, beating out Fiat and Volkswagen in a bidding war at a cost of $6.5 billion. However, Ford is now seeking to sell the Volvo assets and has likewise considered selling its other luxury brands that it acquired (Jaguar, Aston Martin, and

Land Rover). General Motors has also reversed acquisitions by selling off stakes in foreign companies such as Fiat and Fuji Heavy Industries.[95] These cycles were also frequent among U.S. firms during the 1960s through the 1980s.[96]

Even when a firm is not overdiversified, a high level of diversification can have a negative effect on the firm's long-term performance. For example, the scope created by additional amounts of diversification often causes managers to rely on financial rather than strategic controls to evaluate business units' performance (financial and strategic controls are defined and explained in Chapters 11 and 12). Top-level executives often rely on financial controls to assess the performance of business units when they do not have a rich understanding of business units' objectives and strategies. Use of financial controls, such as return on investment (ROI), causes individual business-unit managers to focus on short-term outcomes at the expense of long-term investments. When long-term investments are reduced to increase short-term profits, a firm's overall strategic competitiveness may be harmed.[97]

Another problem resulting from too much diversification is the tendency for acquisitions to become substitutes for innovation. Typically, managers do not intend acquisitions to be used in that way. However, a reinforcing cycle evolves. Costs associated with acquisitions may result in fewer allocations to activities, such as R&D, that are linked to innovation. Without adequate support, a firm's innovation skills begin to atrophy. Without internal innovation skills, the only option available to a firm to gain access to innovation is to complete still more acquisitions. Evidence suggests that a firm using acquisitions as a substitute for internal innovations eventually encounters performance problems.[98]

Managers Overly Focused on Acquisitions

Typically, a considerable amount of managerial time and energy is required for acquisition strategies to contribute to the firm's strategic competitiveness. Activities with which managers become involved include (1) searching for viable acquisition candidates, (2) completing effective due-diligence processes, (3) preparing for negotiations, and (4) managing the integration process after the acquisition is completed.

Top-level managers do not personally gather all of the data and information required to make acquisitions. However, these executives do make critical decisions on the firms to be targeted, the nature of the negotiations, and so forth. Company experiences show that participating in and overseeing the activities required for making acquisitions can divert managerial attention from other matters that are necessary for long-term competitive success, such as identifying and taking advantage of other opportunities and interacting with important external stakeholders.[99]

Both theory and research suggest that managers can become overly involved in the process of making acquisitions.[100] One observer suggested, "Some executives can become preoccupied with making deals—and the thrill of selecting, chasing and seizing a target."[101] The overinvolvement can be surmounted by learning from mistakes and by not having too much agreement in the board room. Dissent is helpful to make sure that all sides of a question are considered (see Chapter 10).[102] When failure does occur, leaders may be tempted to blame the failure on others and on unforeseen circumstances rather than on their excessive involvement in the acquisition process.

An example of being overly focused on making acquisitions is Liz Claiborne Inc. Over a number of years Claiborne's leadership made a number of acquisitions in sportswear apparel and grew from

Liz Claiborne's CEO, William McComb, has indicated that the company will be shedding up to 16 brands due to being overly focused on making acquisitions.

16 to 36 brands; with sales beginning at $800 million and topping off at approximately $5 billion. However, while its managers were focused on making acquisitions, changes were taking place that created problems, given its number of brands. Most Claiborne sales were focused on traditional department stores, but consolidations through acquisitions in this sector left less room for as many brands, given the purchasing habits of the large department stores. Also, specialty stores, such as Coach, with their own brands were on the increase, leaving fewer sales available for established brands. As such, Claiborne's new CEO William McComb plans to divest up to 16 brands and emphasize brands with more potential.[103]

Too Large

Most acquisitions create a larger firm, which should help increase its economies of scale. These economies can then lead to more efficient operations—for example, two sales organizations can be integrated using fewer sales representative because such sales personnel can sell the products of both firms (particularly if the products of the acquiring and target firms are highly related).[104]

Many firms seek increases in size because of the potential economies of scale and enhanced market power (discussed earlier). At some level, the additional costs required to manage the larger firm will exceed the benefits of the economies of scale and additional market power. The complexities generated by the larger size often lead managers to implement more bureaucratic controls to manage the combined firm's operations. *Bureaucratic controls* are formalized supervisory and behavioral rules and policies designed to ensure consistency of decisions and actions across different units of a firm. However, through time, formalized controls often lead to relatively rigid and standardized managerial behavior. Certainly, in the long run, the diminished flexibility that accompanies rigid and standardized managerial behavior may produce less innovation. Because of innovation's importance to competitive success, the bureaucratic controls resulting from a large organization (i.e., built by acquisitions) can have a detrimental effect on performance. As one analyst noted, "Striving for size per se is not necessarily going to make a company more successful. In fact, a strategy in which acquisitions are undertaken as a substitute for organic growth has a bad track record in terms of adding value."[105]

Citigroup is the world's largest financial services company with $270 billion in market value. However, the company has been pressured to sell some of its assets to reduce the complexity associated with managing so many different financial service businesses because its stock price has not appreciated as much as other large but less complex bank organizations. The cross-selling between insurance and banking services has not created as much value as expected.[106]

Effective Acquisitions

Earlier in the chapter, we noted that acquisition strategies do not consistently produce above-average returns for the acquiring firm's shareholders.[107] Nonetheless, some companies are able to create value when using an acquisition strategy.[108] For example, few companies have grown as successfully by acquisition as Cisco. A number of other network companies pursued acquisitions to build up their ability to sell into the network equipment binge, but only Cisco retained much of its value in the post-bubble era. Many firms, such as Lucent, Nortel, and Ericsson, teetered on the edge of bankruptcy after the dot.com bubble burst. When it makes an acquisition, "Cisco has gone much further in its thinking about integration. Not only is retention important, but Cisco also works to minimize the distractions caused by an acquisition. This is important, because the speed of change is so great, that even if the target firm's product development teams are distracted, they will be slowed, contributing to acquisition failure. So, integration must be rapid and reassuring."[109]

Results from a research study shed light on the differences between unsuccessful and successful acquisition strategies and suggest that a pattern of actions can improve the probability of acquisition success.[110] The study shows that when the target firm's assets are complementary to the acquired firm's assets, an acquisition is more successful. With complementary assets, the integration of two firms' operations has a higher probability of creating synergy. In fact, integrating two firms with complementary assets frequently produces unique capabilities and core competencies.[111] With complementary assets, the acquiring firm can maintain its focus on core businesses and leverage the complementary assets and capabilities from the acquired firm. Often, targets were selected and "groomed" by establishing a working relationship prior to the acquisition.[112] As discussed in Chapter 9, strategic alliances are sometimes used to test the feasibility of a future merger or acquisition between the involved firms.[113]

The study's results also show that friendly acquisitions facilitate integration of the firms involved in an acquisition. Through friendly acquisitions, firms work together to find ways to integrate their operations to create synergy.[114] In hostile takeovers, animosity often results between the two top-management teams, a condition that in turn affects working relationships in the newly created firm. As a result, more key personnel in the acquired firm may be lost, and those who remain may resist the changes necessary to integrate the two firms.[115] With effort, cultural clashes can be overcome, and fewer key managers and employees will become discouraged and leave.[116]

Additionally, effective due-diligence processes involving the deliberate and careful selection of target firms and an evaluation of the relative health of those firms (financial health, cultural fit, and the value of human resources) contribute to successful acquisitions.[117] Financial slack in the form of debt equity or cash, in both the acquiring and acquired firms, also frequently contributes to success in acquisitions. Even though financial slack provides access to financing for the acquisition, it is still important to maintain a low or moderate level of debt after the acquisition to keep debt costs low. When substantial debt was used to finance the acquisition, companies with successful acquisitions reduced the debt quickly, partly by selling off assets from the acquired firm, especially noncomplementary or poorly performing assets. For these firms, debt costs do not prevent long-term investments such as R&D, and managerial discretion in the use of cash flow is relatively flexible.

Another attribute of successful acquisition strategies is an emphasis on innovation, as demonstrated by continuing investments in R&D activities. Significant R&D investments show a strong managerial commitment to innovation, a characteristic that is increasingly important to overall competitiveness, as well as acquisition success.

Flexibility and adaptability are the final two attributes of successful acquisitions. When executives of both the acquiring and the target firms have experience in managing change and learning from acquisitions, they will be more skilled at adapting their capabilities to new environments.[118] As a result, they will be more adept at integrating the two organizations, which is particularly important when firms have different organizational cultures.

Efficient and effective integration may quickly produce the desired synergy in the newly created firm. Effective integration allows the acquiring firm to keep valuable human resources in the acquired firm from leaving.[119]

The attributes and results of successful acquisitions are summarized in Table 7.1. Managers seeking acquisition success should emphasize the seven attributes that are listed. Berkshire Hathaway is a conglomerate holding company for Warren Buffett, one of the world's richest men. The company operates widely in the insurance industry and also has stakes in gems, candy, apparel, pilot training, and shoes. The company owns an interest in such well-known firms as Wal-Mart, American Express, Coca-Cola, The Washington Post Company, and Wells Fargo. Also, Buffett has bought an interest in: a U.S. utility firm, PacifiCorp.; Russell, a clothing manufacturer; Iscar, an Israeli tool manufacturer; and most recently invested $3 billion in Burlington Northern Santa Fe, a

Table 7.1 Attributes of Successful Acquisitions

Attributes	Results
1. Acquired firm has assets or resources that are complementary to the acquiring firm's core business	1. High probability of synergy and competitive advantage by maintaining strengths
2. Acquisition is friendly	2. Faster and more effective integration and possibly lower premiums
3. Acquiring firm conducts effective due diligence to select target firms and evaluate the target firm's health (financial, cultural, and human resources)	3. Firms with strongest complementarities are acquired and overpayment is avoided
4. Acquiring firm has financial slack (cash or a favorable debt position)	4. Financing (debt or equity) is easier and less costly to obtain
5. Merged firm maintains low to moderate debt position	5. Lower financing cost, lower risk (e.g., of bankruptcy), and avoidance of trade-offs that are associated with high debt
6. Acquiring firm has sustained and consistent emphasis on R&D and innovation	6. Maintain long-term competitive advantage in markets
7. Acquiring firm manages change well and is flexible and adaptable	7. Faster and more effective integration facilitates achievement of synergy

large Texas-based railroad and freight company.[120] His acquisition strategy in insurance and other business has been particularly successful because he has followed many of the suggestions in Table 7.1.

As we have learned, some acquisitions enhance strategic competitiveness. However, the majority of acquisitions that took place from the 1970s through the 1990s did not enhance firms' strategic competitiveness. In fact, "history shows that anywhere between one-third [and] more than half of all acquisitions are ultimately divested or spun-off."[121] Thus, firms often use restructuring strategies to correct the failure of a merger or an acquisition.

Restructuring

Restructuring is a strategy through which a firm changes its set of businesses or its financial structure.

Defined formally, **restructuring** is a strategy through which a firm changes its set of businesses or its financial structure.[122] From the 1970s into the 2000s, divesting businesses from company portfolios and downsizing accounted for a large percentage of firms' restructuring strategies. Restructuring is a global phenomenon.[123]

The failure of an acquisition strategy is often followed by a restructuring strategy. The Strategic Focus highlights the acquisition of Chrysler by Daimler and how an acquisition that looked like an excellent opportunity turned into a financial disaster for Daimler. Daimler subsequently sold the Chrysler assets to a private equity firm, Cerberus Capital Management LP, in order to cut its significant losses.

In other instances, however, firms use a restructuring strategy because of changes in their external and internal environments. For example, opportunities sometimes surface in the external environment that are particularly attractive to the diversified firm in light of its core competencies. In such cases, restructuring may be appropriate to position the firm to create more value for stakeholders, given the environmental changes.[124]

Strategic Focus Strategic Focus Strategic Focus

DaimlerChrysler Is Now Daimler AG: The Failed Merger with Chrysler Corporation

Daimler Benz acquired Chrysler in 1998 for $36 billion. In May 2007 DaimlerChrysler, the merged firm, sold the Chrysler business to a consortium of private equity investors led by Cerberus Capital Management LP for $7.4 billion. Through this deal, Daimler Chrysler changed its name to Daimler AG and retained only 20 percent of the ownership of Chrysler assets. Of the $7.4 billion provided by the private equity firm, $5 billion will be put into the operations of Chrysler and approximately $1 billion into Chrysler Financial Services with the rest going to pay miscellaneous expenses. Interestingly, DaimlerChrysler will only get $1.35 billion, but Daimler also expects to pay Chrysler $1.6 billion before the deal closes to subsidize its current negative cash flow. The bottom line is that Daimler will not get much out of its original $32 billion investment other than to unload $18 billion in pension and health care liabilities from its books. Many of the problems with the merger are derived from the labor and health care legacy cost differences, which have been estimated to be as high as $1,500 per vehicle on average, compared to an estimated $250 per vehicle for foreign firms such as Toyota.

This deal failure is reminiscent of the failed acquisition of Rover by BMW. BMW ultimately sold the Rover assets for little in return except that BMW was able to unload debt off its books. The Rover assets were similarly acquired by private equity firms with additional investment from a Chinese firm, Nanjing Automobile, which wished to gain entry into more developed markets such as those in Europe and the United States.

The former Daimler CEO, Jurgen Scrempp, the mastermind behind the acquisition of Chrysler had likewise made acquisitions in Asia by acquiring controlling interest in Japan's Mitsubishi Motors Corp. and with Korea's Hyundai Motors Corp. These investments also had problems, and Daimler divested the Mitsubishi assets in 2004 and likewise in the same year sold its 10 percent stake in Hyundai because of significant losses after the recession of 2000.

Dieter Zetsche, CEO of Daimler and former head of Chrysler, has admitted that perceived synergies between the two companies never came to fruition and the differences in markets for the companies was too much to overcome.

In many private equity deals, like the Chrysler deal, in recent years, private equity firms buy up a large array of businesses across a wide variety of industries in automobiles, steel, natural resources, and even electronics. (Phillips Electronics recently sold pieces of its firm to private equity operations.) The finance industry is able to facilitate the restructuring of these industrial assets due to the availability of debt, which is substituted for equity in publicly traded firms.

The hope in Detroit among the other auto firms is that the financial experts associated with private equity firms will help the Big Three auto firms (GM, Ford, and Chrysler) in the United States deal with their excessive cost structure associated with union pensions and health care costs, which make up the bulk of the cost differences between U.S. and foreign firms. If they are not able to restructure the cost situation, the next step will be bankruptcy, the method used by many other firms in the airline and steel industries to restructure these costs. Private equity firms were also involved with these deals, especially after they came out of bankruptcy.

One potential opportunity for Chrysler is the area of financing auto and other purchases. Previous to the Chrysler deal, Cerberus purchased 51 percent ownership in the GMAC assets from General Motors Corporation. GMAC is the financing line of General Motors. Likewise in the Chrysler deal, Cerberus gains control of the Chrysler finance operation. In combination with the GMAC assets, once the financial unit activities are extracted from the operations of Chrysler, Cerberus hopes to develop a strong financing business, not only in financing automobiles but also potentially in financing opportunities

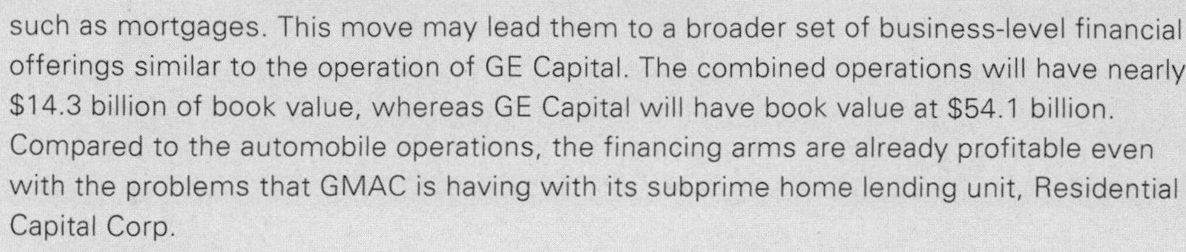

such as mortgages. This move may lead them to a broader set of business-level financial offerings similar to the operation of GE Capital. The combined operations will have nearly \$14.3 billion of book value, whereas GE Capital will have book value at \$54.1 billion. Compared to the automobile operations, the financing arms are already profitable even with the problems that GMAC is having with its subprime home lending unit, Residential Capital Corp.

The Chrysler example represents many important aspects of this chapter: the riskiness of acquisitions, the difficulty of integration, as well as what happens with failed acquisitions leading to divestiture and how private equity firms are involved in the process. Chrysler illustrates the potential for success as well as the risk of failure, and how firms deal with exit when an acquisition strategy fails.

Sources: J. Fox, 2007, Buying a used Chrysler, *Time,* May 28, 46; J. S. Gordon, 2007, Back to the future, Detroit-style *Barron's,* June 25, 45; S. Power, 2007, After pact to shed Chrysler, Daimler turns focus to other challenges, *Wall Street Journal,* May 15, A14; J. Reed, 2007, Nanjing Automobile begins UK production of MG cars, *Financial Times,* May 30, 20; B. Simon, 2007, "New" Chrysler ready to party, *Financial Times,* July 5, 26; A. Taylor III, 2007, America's best car company, *Fortune,* March 19, 98; D. Welch, N. Byrnes, & A. Bianco, 2007, A deal that could save Detroit: A Chrysler sale to Cerberus may spark a plan to eliminate most of the health care liabilities crushing carmakers, *BusinessWeek,* May 28, 30; B. White, 2007, Chrysler's coy guardian: The Cerberus head has an onerous task turning round the carmaker, says Ben White, *Financial Times,* May 19, 9; G. Zuckerman, S. Ng, & D. Cimilluca, 2007, Cerberus finds luster in Detroit, *Wall Street Journal,* May 15, C1–C2; A. Sloan, 2006, A tough race for GM against Toyota, *Newsweek,* http://www.msnbc.msn.com, March 6.

As discussed next, three restructuring strategies are used: downsizing, downscoping, and leveraged buyouts.

Downsizing

Once thought to be an indicator of organizational decline, downsizing is now recognized as a legitimate restructuring strategy.[125] *Downsizing* is a reduction in the number of a firm's employees and, sometimes, in the number of its operating units, but it may or may not change the composition of businesses in the company's portfolio. Thus, downsizing is an intentional proactive management strategy, whereas "decline is an environmental or organizational phenomenon that occurs involuntarily and results in erosion of an organization's resource base."[126] Downsizing has been shown to be associated with acquisitions, especially when excessive premiums are paid.[127]

In the late 1980s, early 1990s, and early 2000s, thousands of jobs were lost in private and public organizations within the United States. One study estimates that 85 percent of *Fortune* 1000 firms have used downsizing as a restructuring strategy.[128] Moreover, *Fortune* 500 firms laid off more than 1 million employees, or 4 percent of their collective workforce, in 2001 and into the first few weeks of 2002.[129] This trend continues in many industries. As noted earlier, Citigroup, and its CEO Charles Prince, has been under pressure to restructure its operations. To deal in part with this pressure, Citigroup signaled in 2007 that it would cut 15,000 jobs and possibly up to 5 percent of its 327,000 worldwide workforce (equivalent to more than 30,000 jobs) over time. In the process, it would take a \$1 billion charge.[130]

Downscoping

Downscoping has a more positive effect on firm performance than downsizing does.[131] *Downscoping* refers to divestiture, spin-off, or some other means of eliminating businesses that are unrelated to a firm's core businesses. Commonly, downscoping is described as a set of actions that causes a firm to strategically refocus on its core businesses.[132] American Standard Companies decided to refocus on its air-conditioning systems and services business through its flagship brand line, Trane. It will accomplish this by splitting into three businesses and spinning its vehicle control systems business into a publicly traded company to be named Wabco. Furthermore, it will sell off its original business focused on bath and kitchen fixtures. The breakup and refocus has become necessary because the bath and kitchen business has underperformed compared to the other two businesses, Trane and Wabco.[133]

A firm that downscopes often also downsizes simultaneously. However, it does not eliminate key employees from its primary businesses in the process, because such action could lead to a loss of one or more core competencies. Instead, a firm that is simultaneously downscoping and downsizing becomes smaller by reducing the diversity of businesses in its portfolio.[134]

By refocusing on its core businesses, the firm can be managed more effectively by the top management team. Managerial effectiveness increases because the firm has become less diversified, allowing the top management team to better understand and manage the remaining businesses.[135]

In general, U.S. firms use downscoping as a restructuring strategy more frequently than European companies do, while the trend in Europe, Latin America, and Asia has been to build conglomerates. In Latin America, these conglomerates are called *grupos.* Many Asian and Latin American conglomerates have begun to adopt Western corporate strategies in recent years and have been refocusing on their core businesses. This downscoping has occurred simultaneously with increasing globalization and with more open markets that have greatly enhanced the competition. By downscoping, these firms have been able to focus on their core businesses and improve their competitiveness.[136]

Downscoping has been practiced recently by many emerging market firms. For example, the Tata Group, founded by Jamsetji Nusserwanji Tata in 1868 as a private trading firm and now India's largest business group, includes 91 firms in a wide range of industries. The group covers chemicals, communications, consumer products, energy, engineering, information systems, materials, and services industries. The group's revenue in 2003–2004 was $14.25 billion, about 2.6 percent of India's GDP. Tata's member companies employ about 220,000 people and export their products to 140 countries. However, as India has changed, Tata executives have sought to restructure its member businesses to "build a more focused company without abandoning the best of Tata's manufacturing tradition."[137] Over a 10-year period Tata restructured to retain 91 businesses down from 250. However, with the Tata Steel acquisition of Corus mentioned earlier, it has begun to build global businesses as well.[138]

Leveraged Buyouts

Traditionally, leveraged buyouts were used as a restructuring strategy to correct for managerial mistakes or because the firm's managers were making decisions that primarily served their own interests rather than those of shareholders.[139] A *leveraged buyout* (LBO) is a restructuring strategy whereby a party buys all of a firm's assets in order to take the firm private. Once the transaction is completed, the company's stock is no longer traded publicly. Firms that facilitate or engage in taking public firms, or a business unit of a firm, private are called *private equity firms.* However, some firms are using buyouts to build firm resources and expand rather than simply restructure distressed assets as the Tata Steel acquisition of Corus illustrates.[140]

Usually, significant amounts of debt are incurred to finance a buyout; hence the term *leveraged* buyout. To support debt payments and to downscope the company to concentrate on the firm's core businesses, the new owners may immediately sell a number of assets.[141] It is not uncommon for those buying a firm through an LBO to restructure the firm to the point that it can be sold at a profit within a five- to eight-year period.

Management buyouts (MBOs), employee buyouts (EBOs), and whole-firm buyouts, in which one company or partnership purchases an entire company instead of a part of it, are the three types of LBOs. In part because of managerial incentives, MBOs, more so than EBOs and whole-firm buyouts, have been found to lead to downscoping, increased strategic focus, and improved performance.[142] Research has shown that management buyouts can also lead to greater entrepreneurial activity and growth.[143]

Among the different reasons for a buyout is protecting against a capricious financial market, and allowing the owners to focus on developing innovations and bringing them to the market.[144] As such, buyouts can represent a form of firm rebirth to facilitate entrepreneurial efforts and stimulate strategic growth.[145]

Restructuring Outcomes

The short-term and long-term outcomes resulting from the three restructuring strategies are shown in Figure 7.2. As indicated, downsizing does not commonly lead to higher firm performance.[146] Still, in free-market-based societies at large, downsizing has generated an incentive for individuals who have been laid off to start their own businesses.

Research has shown that downsizing contributed to lower returns for both U.S. and Japanese firms. The stock markets in the firms' respective nations evaluated downsizing negatively. Investors concluded that downsizing would have a negative effect on companies' ability to achieve strategic competitiveness in the long term. Investors also seem to assume that downsizing occurs as a consequence of other problems in a company.[147] This assumption may be caused by a firm's diminished corporate reputation when a major downsizing is announced.[148] These issues were clearly part of the Citigroup layoffs mentioned earlier.

An unintentional outcome of downsizing, however, is that laid-off employees often start new businesses in order to live through the disruption in their lives. Accordingly, downsizing has generated a host of new entrepreneurial ventures.

As shown in Figure 7.2, downsizing tends to result in a loss of human capital in the long term. Losing employees with many years of experience with the firm represents a major loss of knowledge. As noted in Chapter 3, knowledge is vital to competitive success in the global economy. Thus, in general, research evidence and corporate experience suggest that downsizing may be of more tactical (or short-term) value than strategic (or long-term) value.[149]

Downscoping generally leads to more positive outcomes in both the short- and the long-term than does downsizing or engaging in a leveraged buyout (see Figure 7.2). Downscoping's desirable long-term outcome of higher performance is a product of

Figure 7.2 Restructuring and Outcomes

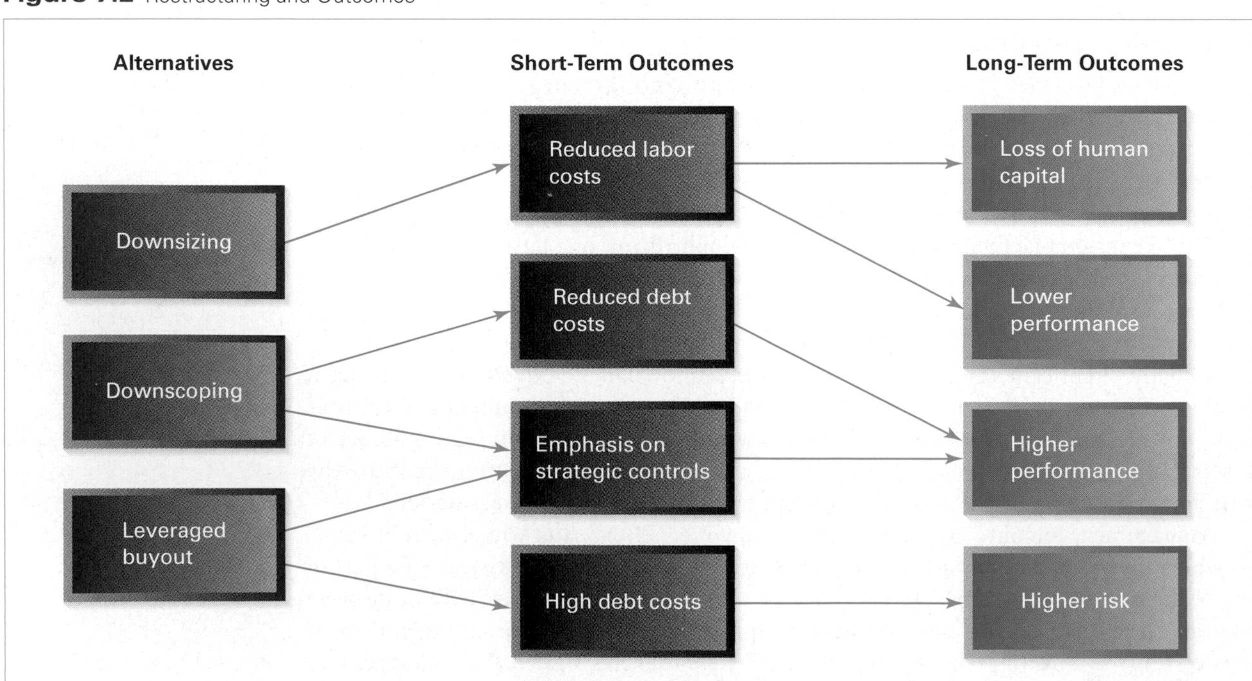

reduced debt costs and the emphasis on strategic controls derived from concentrating on the firm's core businesses. In so doing, the refocused firm should be able to increase its ability to compete.[150]

Although whole-firm LBOs have been hailed as a significant innovation in the financial restructuring of firms, they can involve negative trade-offs.[151] First, the resulting large debt increases the financial risk of the firm, as is evidenced by the number of companies that filed for bankruptcy in the 1990s after executing a whole-firm LBO. Sometimes, the intent of the owners to increase the efficiency of the bought-out firm and then sell it within five to eight years creates a short-term and risk-averse managerial focus.[152] As a result, these firms may fail to invest adequately in R&D or take other major actions designed to maintain or improve the company's core competence.[153] Research also suggests that in firms with an entrepreneurial mind-set, buyouts can lead to greater innovation, especially if the debt load is not too great.[154] However, because buyouts more often result in significant debt, most LBOs have taken place in mature industries where stable cash flows are possible. This situation enables the buyout firm to meet the recurring debt payments as exemplified by Tata Steel's buyout of Corus in the steel industry described in the Opening Case and expanded on later in the chapter.

Summary

- Acquisition strategies are increasingly popular. Because of globalization, deregulation of multiple industries in many different economies, and favorable legislation, the number and size of domestic and cross-border acquisitions continues to increase, especially from emerging economies.
- Firms use acquisition strategies to (1) increase market power, (2) overcome entry barriers to new markets or regions, (3) avoid the costs of developing new products and increase the speed of new market entries, (4) reduce the risk of entering a new business, (5) become more diversified, (6) reshape their competitive scope by developing a different portfolio of businesses, and (7) enhance their learning, thereby adding to their knowledge base.
- Among the problems associated with the use of an acquisition strategy are (1) the difficulty of effectively integrating the firms involved, (2) incorrectly evaluating the target firm's value, (3) creating debt loads that preclude adequate long-term investments (e.g., R&D), (4) overestimating the potential for synergy, (5) creating a firm that is too diversified, (6) creating an internal environment in which managers devote increasing amounts of their time and energy to analyzing and completing the acquisition, and (7) developing a combined firm that is too large, necessitating extensive use of bureaucratic, rather than strategic, controls.
- Effective acquisitions have the following characteristics: (1) the acquiring and target firms have complementary resources that can be the basis of core competencies in the newly created firm; (2) the acquisition is friendly, thereby facilitating integration of the two firms' resources; (3) the target firm is selected and purchased based on thorough due diligence; (4) the acquiring and target firms have considerable slack in the form of cash or debt capacity; (5) the merged firm maintains a low or moderate level of debt by selling off portions of the acquired firm or some of the acquiring firm's poorly performing units; (6) the acquiring and acquired firms have experience in terms of adapting to change; and (7) R&D and innovation are emphasized in the new firm.
- Restructuring is used to improve a firm's performance by correcting for problems created by ineffective management. Restructuring by downsizing involves reducing the number of employees and hierarchical levels in the firm. Although it can lead to short-term cost reductions, they may be realized at the expense of long-term success, because of the loss of valuable human resources (and knowledge) and overall corporate reputation.
- The goal of restructuring through downscoping is to reduce the firm's level of diversification. Often, the firm divests unrelated businesses to achieve this goal. Eliminating unrelated businesses makes it easier for the firm and its top-level managers to refocus on the core businesses.
- Leveraged buyouts (LBOs) represent an additional restructuring strategy by private equity firms such as KKR or Blackstone Group. Through an LBO, a firm is purchased so that it can become a private entity. LBOs usually are financed largely through debt. The three types of LBOs are management buyouts (MBOs), employee buyouts (EBOs), and whole-firm LBOs. Because they provide clear managerial incentives, MBOs have been the most successful of the three. Often, the intent of a buyout is to improve efficiency and performance to the point where the firm can be sold successfully within five to eight years.
- Commonly, restructuring's primary goal is gaining or reestablishing effective strategic control of the firm. Of the three restructuring strategies, downscoping is aligned most closely with establishing and using strategic controls and usually improves performance more on a comparative basis.

Review Questions

1. Why are acquisition strategies popular in many firms competing in the global economy?
2. What reasons account for firms' decisions to use acquisition strategies as a means to achieving strategic competitiveness?
3. What are the seven primary problems that affect a firm's efforts to successfully use an acquisition strategy?
4. What are the attributes associated with a successful acquisition strategy?
5. What is the restructuring strategy, and what are its common forms?
6. What are the short- and long-term outcomes associated with the different restructuring strategies?

Experiential Exercises

Exercise 1: The Gap

Gap Inc. opened with a single store in 1969. Located near San Francisco State University, Gap initially sold only Levi's blue jeans, along with tapes and records. The company soon expanded its product offerings to include clothing for men, women, and children. Gap went public in 1976 and was one of the largest selling apparel brands worldwide by the early 1990s. The firm has expanded horizontally by using both acquisition strategies and internal development.

Working in groups of 5–7 persons, answer the following questions. You should use corporate documents available on the firm's Web site (http://www.gapinc.com), supplemented as needed by news articles.

1. Describe Gap's emphasis on acquisition versus internal development.
2. Between 2006 and 2007, how well have the different divisions of Gap performed?
3. What restructuring has the company undertaken? Would you recommend additional restructuring? Why?

Exercise 2: Cadbury Schweppes: Too Much of a Sugar Rush?

Cadbury and Schweppes are two prominent and long-established companies. Cadbury was founded in 1824 and is the world's largest confectionary company. The bulk of Cadbury's sales come from Europe, with a substantially smaller presence in the Americas. Schweppes was founded in 1783, when its founder Jacob Schweppes invented a system to carbonate mineral water. Today, its brands include 7-Up, Dr. Pepper, Sunkist, Snapple, Schweppes, and Motts Juice. Cadbury and Schweppes merged in 1969. In 2007, the firm's market value was approximately £12–13 billion (British pounds). In March of 2007, CEO Todd Stitzer announced a plan to split the candy and beverage operations.

Working in teams, prepare a brief PowerPoint presentation to address the following questions. You will need to consult the company's Web site (http://www.cadburyschweppes.com/EN) as well as conduct an article search to collect the information and data required to answer the questions. Your presentation should include one page for each of the following questions:

1. What precipitated Stitzer's announcement to separate the beverage and candy operations?
2. What were the main factors hindering the success of the Cadbury Schweppes merger?
3. What are the pros and cons of divesting the beverage segment?
4. What are the different options Stitzer can pursue to divest Schweppes?

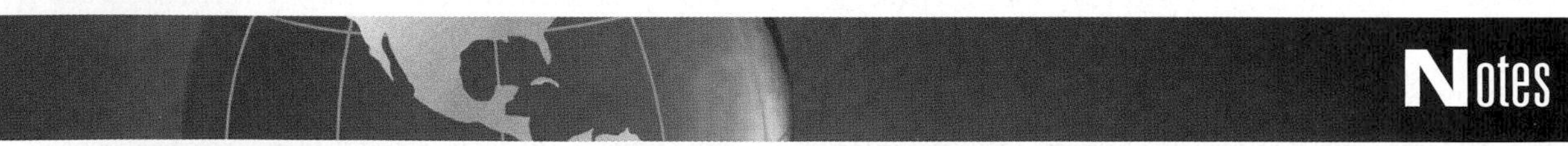

Notes

1. K. Uhlenbruck, M. A. Hitt, & M. Semadeni, 2006, Market value effects of acquisitions involving Internet firms: A resource-based analysis, *Strategic Management Journal,* 27: 899–913; J. Anand, 2004, Redeployment of corporate resources: A study of acquisition strategies in the U.S. defense industries, 1978–1996, *Managerial and Decision Economics,* 25: 383–400; L. Capron & N. Pistre, 2002, When do acquirers earn abnormal returns? *Strategic Management Journal,* 23: 781–794.
2. C.-C. Lu, 2006, Growth strategies and merger patterns among small and medium-sized enterprises: An empirical study, *International Journal of Management,* 23: 529–547.
3. J. Haleblian; J.-Y. Kim, & N. Rajagopalan, 2006, The influence of acquisition experience and performance on acquisition behavior: Evidence from the U.S. commercial banking industry, *Academy of Management Journal,* 49: 357–370; H. Shahrur, 2005, Industry structure and horizontal takeovers: Analysis of wealth effects on rivals, suppliers, and corporate customers, *Journal of Financial Economics,* 76: 61–98; M. A. Hitt, J. S. Harrison, & R. D. Ireland, 2001, *Mergers and Acquisitions: A Guide to Creating Value for Stakeholders,* New York: Oxford University Press.
4. R. Dobbs & V. Tortorici, 2007, Cool heads will bring in the best deals; Boardroom discipline is vital if the M&A boom is to benefit shareholders, *Financial Times,* February 28, 6.

5. D. Cimilluca, 2007, Buyout firms fuel a record; Pace of M&A pacts could start to slow amid tighter credit, *Wall Street Journal,* July 2, C8.
6. S. Daneshkhu, 2007, FDI flow into richest countries set to rise 20% this year, *Financial Times,* June 22, 7.
7. Cimilluca, Buyout firms fuel a record.
8. A. G. Warner, J. F. Fairbank, & H. K. Steensma, 2006, Managing uncertainty in a formal standards-based industry: A real options perspective on acquisition timing, *Journal of Management,* 32: 279–298; R. Coff, 2003, Bidding wars over R&D-intensive firms: Knowledge, opportunism, and the market for corporate control, *Academy of Management Journal,* 46: 74–85; P. Chattopadhyay, W. H. Glick, & G. P. Huber, 2001, Organizational actions in response to threats and opportunities, *Academy of Management Journal,* 44: 937–955.
9. C. Bryan-Low, 2007, Thomson evolution takes next step; Reuters deal, emphasis on data services mark latest efforts to adapt, *Wall Street Journal,* June 13, A10.
10. G. Cullinan, J.-M. Le Roux, & R.-M. Weddigen, 2004, When to walk away from a deal, *Harvard Business Review,* 82(4): 96–104; L. Selden & G. Colvin, 2003, M&A needn't be a loser's game, *Harvard Business Review,* 81(6): 70–73.
11. J. J. Reuer, 2005, Avoiding lemons in M&A deals, *MIT Sloan Management Review,* 46(3): 15–17; M. C. Jensen, 1988, Takeovers: Their causes and consequences, *Journal of Economic Perspectives,* 1(2): 21–48.
12. C. Tuch & N. O'Sullivan, 2007, The impact of acquisitions on firm performance: A review of the evidence, *International Journal of Management Review,* 9(2): 141–170.
13. K. Cool & M. Van de Laar, 2006, The performance of acquisitive companies in the U.S. In L. Renneboog, (ed.), *Advances in Corporate Finance and Asset Pricing,* Amsterdam, Netherlands: Elsevier Science, 77–105; D. K. Berman, 2005, Mergers horror II: The rhetoric, *Wall Street Journal,* May 24, C1; T. Wright, M. Kroll, A. Lado, & B. Van Ness, 2002, The structure of ownership and corporate acquisition strategies, *Strategic Management Journal,* 23: 41–53; A. Rappaport & M. L. Sirower, 1999, Stock or cash? *Harvard Business Review,* 77(6): 147–158.
14. 2007, Happily never after mergers, like marriages, fail without a meeting of minds, *Financial Times,* May 15, 14.
15. E. Thornton, F. Keenan, C. Palmeri, & L. Himelstein, 2002, It sure is getting hostile, *BusinessWeek,* January 14, 28–30.
16. S. Sudarsanam & A. A. Mahate, 2006, Are friendly acquisitions too bad for shareholders and managers? Long-term value creation and top management turnover in hostile and friendly acquirers, *British Journal of Management: Supplement,* 17(1): S7–S30.
17. A. M. Marino & J. Zábojník, 2006, Merger, ease of entry and entry deterrence in a dynamic model, *Journal of Industrial Economics,* 54: 397–423; P. Haspeslagh, 1999, Managing the mating dance in equal mergers, "Mastering Strategy" (Part Five), *Financial Times,* October 25, 14–15.
18. P. Wright, M. Kroll, & D. Elenkov, 2002, Acquisition returns, increase in firm size and chief executive officer compensation: The moderating role of monitoring, *Academy of Management Journal,* 45: 599–608.
19. J. Whalen, 2007, Nestle bolsters baby-food line, *Wall Street Journal,* April 12, A3.
20. R. W. Palmatier, C. F. Miao, & E. Fang, 2007, Sales channel integration after mergers and acquisitions: A methodological approach for avoiding common pitfalls, *Industrial Marketing Management,* 36(5): 589–603; C. Hamburg & M. Bucerius, 2005, A marketing perspective on mergers and acquisitions: How marketing integration affects post-merger performance, *Journal of Marketing,* 69: 95–113.
21. E. Gal-Or & A. Dukes, 2006, On the profitability of media mergers, *Journal of Business,* 79: 489–525; Capron & Pistre, When do acquirers earn abnormal returns?; L. Capron, 1999, Horizontal acquisitions: The benefits and risks to long-term performance, *Strategic Management Journal,* 20: 987–1018.
22. C. E. Fee & S. Thomas, 2004, Sources of gains in horizontal mergers: Evidence from customer, supplier, and rival firms, *Journal of Financial Economics,* 74: 423–460.
23. M. Lubatkin, W. S. Schulze, A. Mainkar, & R. W. Cotterill, 2001, Ecological investigation of firm effects in horizontal mergers, *Strategic Management Journal,* 22: 335–357; K. Ramaswamy, 1997, The performance impact of strategic similarity in horizontal mergers: Evidence from the U.S. banking industry, *Academy of Management Journal,* 40: 697–715.
24. L. Capron, W. Mitchell, & A. Swaminathan, 2001, Asset divestiture following horizontal acquisitions: A dynamic view, *Strategic Management Journal,* 22: 817–844.
25. J. P. H. Fan & V. K. Goyal, 2006, On the patterns and wealth effects of vertical mergers, *Journal of Business,* 79: 877–902; F. T. Rothaermel, M. A. Hitt, & L. A. Jobe, 2006, Balancing vertical integration and strategic outsourcing: Effects on product portfolio, product success, and firm performance, *Strategic Management Journal,* 27: 1033–1056.
26. A. Parmigiani, 2007, Why do firms both make and buy? An investigation of concurrent sourcing, *Strategic Management Journal,* 28: 285–311.
27. J. B. Stewart, 2007, Common sense: Google's DoubleClick play still makes it a good bet, *Wall Street Journal,* April 18, D3.
28. S. Lohr, 2007, I.B.M. showing that giants can be nimble, *New York Times,* http://www.nyt.com, July 18.
29. D. Gupta & Y. Gerchak, 2002, Quantifying operational synergies in a merger/acquisition, *Management Science,* 48: 517–533.
30. R. Sinha, 2006, Regulation: The market for corporate control and corporate governance, *Global Finance Journal,* 16(3): 264–282; D. E. M. Sappington, 2003, Regulating horizontal diversification, *International Journal of Industrial Organization,* 21: 291–315.
31. S.-F. S. Chen & M. Zeng, 2004, Japanese investors' choice of acquisitions vs. startups in the U.S.: The role of reputation barriers and advertising outlays, *International Journal of Research in Marketing,* 21(2): 123–136; S. J. Chang & P. M. Rosenzweig, 2001, The choice of entry mode in sequential foreign direct investment, *Strategic Management Journal,* 22: 747–776.
32. S. McGee, 2007, Seeking value in BRICs, *Barron's,* July 9, L10–L11.
33. B. Villalonga & A. M. Mcgahan, 2005, The choice among acquisitions, alliances, and divestitures, *Strategic Management Journal,* 26: 1183–1208; K. Shimizu, M. A. Hitt, D. Vaidyanath, & V. Pisano, 2004, Theoretical foundations of cross-border mergers and acquisitions: A review of current research and recommendations for the future, *Journal of International Management,* 10: 307–353; J. A. Doukas & L. H. P. Lang, 2003, Foreign direct investment, diversification and firm performance, *Journal of International Business Studies,* 34: 153–172; M. A. Hitt, J. S. Harrison, & R. D. Ireland, 2001, *Mergers and Acquisitions: A Guide to Creating Value for Stakeholders,* New York: Oxford University Press, Chapter 10.
34. A. Seth, K. P. Song, & R. R. Pettit, 2002, Value creation and destruction in cross-border acquisitions: An empirical analysis of foreign acquisitions of U.S. firms, *Strategic Management Journal,* 23: 921–940.
35. M. W. Peng & A. Delios, 2006, What determines the scope of the firm over time and around the world? An Asia Pacific perspective, *Asia Pacific Journal of Management,* 23: 385–405.
36. J. A. Schmidt, 2002, Business perspective on mergers and acquisitions, in J. A. Schmidt (ed.), *Making Mergers Work,* Alexandria, VA: Society for Human Resource Management, 23–46.
37. T. Clissold, 2006, The strange paradox of economic nationalism, *Financial Times,* August 10, 13; A. M. Agami, 2002, The role that foreign acquisitions of Asian companies played in the recovery of the Asian financial crisis, *Multinational Business Review,* 10(1): 11–20.
38. C. Firstbrook, 2007, Transnational mergers and acquisitions: How to beat the odds of disaster, *Journal of Business Strategy,* 28(1): 53–56; P. Quah & S. Young, 2005, Post-acquisition management: A phases approach for cross-border M&As, *European Management Journal,* 17(1), 65–75; J. K. Sebenius, 2002, The hidden challenge of cross-border negotiations, *Harvard Business Review,* 80(3): 76–85.

39. C. Homburg & M. Bucerius, 2006, Is speed of integration really a success factor of mergers and acquisitions? An analysis of the role of internal and external relatedness, *Strategic Management Journal,* 27: 347–367; V. Bannert & H. Tschirky, 2004, Integration planning for technology intensive acquisitions, *R&D Management,* 34(5): 481–494; W. Vanhaverbeke, G. Duysters, & N. Noorderhaven, 2002, External technology sourcing through alliances or acquisitions: An analysis of the application-specific integrated circuits industry, *Organization Science,* 6: 714–733.
40. S. Karim, 2006, Modularity in organizational structure: The reconfiguration of internally developed and acquired business units, *Strategic Management Journal,* 27: 799–823; H. Gatignon, M. L. Tushman, W. Smith, & P. Anderson, 2002, A structural approach to assessing innovation: Construct development of innovation locus, type, and characteristics, *Management Science,* 48: 1103–1122; Hitt, Harrison, & Ireland, *Mergers and Acquisitions.*
41. R. E. Hoskisson & L. W. Busenitz, 2002, Market uncertainty and learning distance in corporate entrepreneurship entry mode choice, in M. A. Hitt, R. D. Ireland, S. M. Camp, & D. L. Sexton (eds.), *Strategic Entrepreneurship: Creating a New Mindset,* Oxford, U.K.: Blackwell Publishers, 151–172; M. A. Hitt, R. E. Hoskisson, R. A. Johnson, & D. D. Moesel, 1996, The market for corporate control and firm innovation, *Academy of Management Journal,* 39: 1084–1119.
42. Coff, Bidding wars over R&D-intensive firms: Knowledge, opportunism, and the market for corporate control.
43. J. Palmer, 2007, Gilead's War on AIDS, *Barron's,* July 9, 25.
44. R. Mudambi & S. A. Zahra, 2007, The survival of international new ventures, *Journal of International Business Studies,* 38: 333–352; Y. Luo, O. Shenkar, & M.-K. Nyaw, 2002, Mitigating liabilities of foreignness: Defensive versus offensive approaches, *Journal of International Management,* 8: 283–300.
45. Uhlenbruck, Hitt, & Semadeni, Market value effects of acquisitions involving Internet firms: A resource-based analysis; C. W. L. Hill & F. T. Rothaermel, 2003, The performance of incumbent firms in the face of radical technological innovation, *Academy of Management Review,* 28: 257–274.
46. F. Rothaermel, 2001, Incumbent's advantage through exploiting complementary assets via interfirm cooperation, *Strategic Management Journal,* 22 (Special Issue): 687–699.
47. L.-F. Hsieh & Y.-T. Tsai, 2005, Technology investment mode of innovative technological corporations: M&A strategy intended to facilitate innovation, *Journal of American Academy of Business,* 6(1): 185–194; G. Ahuja & R. Katila, 2001, Technological acquisitions and the innovation performance of acquiring firms: A longitudinal study, *Strategic Management Journal,* 22: 197–220; M. A. Hitt, R. E. Hoskisson, & R. D. Ireland, 1990, Mergers and acquisitions and managerial commitment to innovation in M-form firms, *Strategic Management Journal,* 11 (Special Issue): 29–47.
48. Hitt, Hoskisson, Johnson, & Moesel, The market for corporate control.
49. P. Parvinen & H. Tikkanen, 2007, Incentive asymmetries in the mergers and acquisitions process, *Journal of Management Studies,* 44: 759–787; P. Strebel & A.-V. Ohlsson, 2006, The art of making smart big moves, *MIT Sloan Management Review,* 47(2): 79–83.
50. Hoskisson & Busenitz, Market uncertainty and learning distance in corporate entrepreneurship entry mode choice; Hill & Rothaermel, The performance of incumbent firms in the face of radical technological innovation.
51. F. Vermeulen, 2005, How acquisitions can revitalize companies, *MIT Sloan Management Review,* 46(4): 45–51; M. A. Hitt, R. E. Hoskisson, R. D. Ireland, & J. S. Harrison, 1991, Effects of acquisitions on R&D inputs and outputs, *Academy of Management Journal,* 34: 693–706.
52. B. White, 2007, Cisco to buy IronPort, a network-security firm, *Wall Street Journal,* January 4, A10.
53. C. E. Helfat & K. M. Eisenhardt, 2004, Inter-temporal economies of scope, organizational modularity, and the dynamics of diversification, *Strategic Management Journal,* 25: 1217–1232; C. Park, 2003, Prior performance characteristics of related and unrelated acquirers, *Strategic Management Journal,* 24: 471–480.
54. J. L. Lunsford, 2007, United Technologies reaches a deal to buy Rentokil's security division, *Wall Street Journal,* March 30, C3.
55. J. L. Lunsford, 2007, Boss talk: Transformer in transition; He turned UTC into giant; now, CEO George David carefully prepares successor, *Wall Street Journal,* May 17, B1.
56. D. J. Miller, M. J. Fern, & L. B. Cardinal, 2007, The use of knowledge for technological innovation within diversified firms, *Academy of Management Journal,* 50: 308–326; Krishnan, Hitt, & Park, Acquisition premiums, subsequent workforce reductions and post-acquisition performance; Hitt, Harrison, & Ireland, *Mergers and Acquisitions.*
57. J. Anand & H. Singh, 1997, Asset redeployment, acquisitions and corporate strategy in declining industries, *Strategic Management Journal,* 18 (Special Issue): 99–118.
58. Helfat & Eisenhardt, Inter-temporal economies of scope, organizational modularity, and the dynamics of diversification; W. J. Ferrier, 2001, Navigating the competitive landscape: The drivers and consequences of competitive aggressiveness, *Academy of Management Journal,* 44: 858–877.
59. F. Guerrera, 2007, M&A vision highlights change of focus at House that Jack Built, *Financial Times,* January 16, 19.
60. Bryan-Low, Thomson evolution takes next step.
61. P. Puranam & K. Srikanth, 2007, What they know vs. what they do: How acquirers leverage technology acquisitions, *Strategic Management Journal,* 28: 805–825; F. Vermeulen & H. Barkema, 2001, Learning through acquisitions, *Academy of Management Journal,* 44: 457–476.
62. Vermeulen, How acquisitions can revitalize firms; J. Gammelgaard, 2004, Access to competence: An emerging acquisition motive, *European Business Forum,* Spring, 44–48; M. L. A. Hayward, 2002, When do firms learn from their acquisition experience? Evidence from 1990–1995, *Strategic Management Journal,* 23: 21–39.
63. J. Anand, L. Capron, & W. Mitchell, 2005, Using acquisitions to access multinational diversity: Thinking beyond the domestic versus cross-border M&A comparison, *Industrial and Corporate Change,* 14(2): 191–224.
64. J. S. Harrison, M. A. Hitt, R. E. Hoskisson, & R. D. Ireland, 2001, Resource complementarity in business combinations: Extending the logic to organizational alliances, *Journal of Management,* 27: 679–690.
65. J. Whalen, 2007, AstraZeneca thinks bigger; new chief increases commitment to 'large molecule' biological drugs, *Wall Street Journal,* May 22, A7.
66. Schmidt, Business perspective on mergers and acquisitions.
67. M. Zollo & H. Singh, 2004, Deliberate learning in corporate acquisitions: Post-acquisition strategies and integration capability in U.S. bank mergers, *Strategic Management Journal,* 25: 1233–1256; P. Mallette, C. L. Fowler, & C. Hayes, 2003, The acquisition process map: Blueprint for a successful deal, *Southern Business Review,* 28(2): 1–13; Hitt, Harrison, & Ireland, *Mergers and Acquisitions.*
68. J. Harrison, 2007, Why integration success eludes many buyers, *Mergers and Acquisitions,* 42(3): 18–20; R. A. Weber & C. F. Camerer, 2003, Cultural conflict and merger failure: An experimental approach, *Management Science,* 49: 400–415; J. Vester, 2002, Lessons learned about integrating acquisitions, *Research Technology Management,* 45(3): 33–41; D. K. Datta, 1991, Organizational fit and acquisition performance: Effects of post-acquisition integration, *Strategic Management Journal,* 12: 281–297.
69. F. Vermeulen, 2007, Business insight (a special report); bad deals: Eight warning signs that an acquisition may not pay off, *Wall Street Journal,* April 28, R10; J. R. Carleton & C. S. Lineberry, 2004, *Achieving Post-Merger Success,* New York: John Wiley & Sons; Y. Weber &

E. Menipaz, 2003, Measuring cultural fit in mergers and acquisitions, *International Journal of Business Performance Management,* 5(1): 54–72.

70. M. Zollo, 1999, M&A—The challenge of learning to integrate, "Mastering Strategy" (Part Eleven), *Financial Times,* December 6, 14–15.
71. R. Gibson, 2006, Package deal; UPS's purchase of Mail Boxes Etc. looked great on paper. Then came the culture clash., *Wall Street Journal,* May 8, R13.
72. M. A. Hitt, L. Bierman, K. Shimizu, & R. Kochhar, 2001, Direct and moderating effects of human capital on strategy and performance in professional service firms, *Academy of Management Journal,* 44: 13–28.
73. J. A. Krug, 2003, Why do they keep leaving? *Harvard Business Review,* 81(2): 14–15; H. A. Krishnan & D. Park, 2002, The impact of workforce reduction on subsequent performance in major mergers and acquisitions: An exploratory study, *Journal of Business Research,* 55(4): 285–292; G. G. Dess & J. D. Shaw, 2001, Voluntary turnover, social capital and organizational performance, *Academy of Management Review,* 26: 446–456.
74. D. Harding & T. Rouse, 2007, Human due diligence, *Harvard Business Review,* 85(4): 124–131.
75. T. McIntyre, 2004, A model of levels of involvement and strategic roles of human resource development (HRD) professionals as facilitators of due diligence and the integration process, *Human Resource Development Review,* 3(2): 173–182; J. A. Krug & H. Hegarty, 2001, Predicting who stays and leaves after an acquisition: A study of top managers in multinational firms, *Strategic Management Journal,* 22: 185–196.
76. G. Cullinan, J.-M. Le Roux, & R.-M. Weddigen, 2004, When to walk away from a deal, *Harvard Business Review,* 82(4): 96–104.
77. R. J. Rosen, 2006, Merger momentum and investor sentiment: The stock market reaction to merger announcements, *Journal of Business,* 79: 987–1017.
78. Rappaport & Sirower, Stock or cash? 149.
79. E. Thornton, 2003, Bypassing the street, *BusinessWeek,* June 2, 79.
80. G. Yago, 1991, *Junk Bonds: How High Yield Securities Restructured Corporate America,* New York: Oxford University Press, 146–148.
81. M. C. Jensen, 1986, Agency costs of free cash flow, corporate finance, and takeovers, *American Economic Review,* 76: 323–329.
82. E. Bellman, 2007, Tata's Corus deal raises fears about likely heavy debt load, *Wall Street Journal,* February 1, C7.
83. T. H. Noe & M. J. Rebello, 2006, The role of debt purchases in takeovers: A tale of two retailers, *Journal of Economics & Management Strategy,* 15 (3): 609–648; M. A. Hitt & D. L. Smart, 1994, Debt: A disciplining force for managers or a debilitating force for organizations? *Journal of Management Inquiry,* 3: 144–152.
84. Hitt, Harrison, & Ireland, *Mergers and Acquisitions.*
85. T. N. Hubbard, 1999, Integration strategies and the scope of the company, "Mastering Strategy" (Part Eleven), *Financial Times,* December 6, 8–10.
86. Hitt, Harrison, & Ireland, *Mergers and Acquisitions.*
87. A. B. Sorescu, R. K. Chandy, & J. C. Prabhu, 2007, Why some acquisitions do better than others: Product capital as a driver of long-term stock returns, *Journal of Marketing Research,* 44(1): 57–72; T. Saxton & M. Dollinger, 2004, Target reputation and appropriability: Picking and deploying resources in acquisitions, *Journal of Management,* 30: 123–147.
88. Harrison, Hitt, Hoskisson & Ireland, Resource complementarity in business combinations; J. B. Barney, 1988, Returns to bidding firms in mergers and acquisitions: Reconsidering the relatedness hypothesis, *Strategic Management Journal,* 9 (Special Issue): 71–78.
89. O. E. Williamson, 1999, Strategy research: Governance and competence perspectives, *Strategic Management Journal,* 20: 1087–1108.
90. S. Chatterjee, 2007, Why is synergy so difficult in mergers of related businesses? *Strategy & Leadership,* 35(2): 46–52; Hitt, Hoskisson, Johnson, & Moesel, The market for corporate control.
91. 2007, Divorce puts paid to carmaking dream, *Financial Times,* May 15, 28.
92. Ibid.
93. C. W. L. Hill & R. E. Hoskisson, 1987, Strategy and structure in the multiproduct firm, *Academy of Management Review,* 12: 331–341.
94. M. L. A. Hayward & K. Shimizu, 2006, De-commitment to losing strategic action: Evidence from the divestiture of poorly performing acquisitions, *Strategic Management Journal,* 27: 541–557; R. A. Johnson, R. E. Hoskisson, & M. A. Hitt, 1993, Board of director involvement in restructuring: The effects of board versus managerial controls and characteristics, *Strategic Management Journal,* 14 (Special Issue): 33–50; C. C. Markides, 1992, Consequences of corporate refocusing: Ex ante evidence, *Academy of Management Journal,* 35: 398–412.
95. M. Maynard, 2007, Ford seeking a future by going backward, *New York Times,* http://www.nytimes.com, July 16.
96. M. Brauer, 2006, What have we acquired and what should we acquire in divestiture research? A review and research agenda, *Journal of Management,* 32: 751–785; D. Palmer & B. N. Barber, 2001, Challengers, elites and families: A social class theory of corporate acquisitions, *Administrative Science Quarterly,* 46: 87–120.
97. Hitt, Harrison, & Ireland, *Mergers and Acquisitions;* R. E. Hoskisson & R. A. Johnson, 1992, Corporate restructuring and strategic change: The effect on diversification strategy and R&D intensity, *Strategic Management Journal,* 13: 625–634.
98. Ibid.
99. Vermeulen, Business insight (a special report); bad deals: Eight warning signs that an acquisition may not pay off; Hughes, Lang, Mester, Moon, & Pagano, Do bankers sacrifice value to build empires? Managerial incentives, industry consolidation, and financial performance; Hitt, Hoskisson, Johnson, & Moesel, The market for corporate control; Hitt, Hoskisson, & Ireland, Mergers and acquisitions and managerial commitment to innovation in M-form firms.
100. M. L. A. Hayward & D. C. Hambrick, 1997, Explaining the premiums paid for large acquisitions: Evidence of CEO hubris, *Administrative Science Quarterly* 42: 103–127; R. Roll, 1986, The hubris hypothesis of corporate takeovers, *Journal of Business,* 59: 197–216.
101. Vermeulen, Business insight (a special report); bad deals: Eight warning signs that an acquisition may not pay off.
102. Haleblian, Kim, & Rajagopalan, The influence of acquisition experience and performance on acquisition behavior; Hayward, When do firms learn from their acquisition experience?
103. R. Dobbs, 2007, Claiborne seeks to shed 16 apparel brands, *Wall Street Journal,* July 11, B1, B2.
104. Palmatier, Miao, & Fang, Sales channel integration after mergers and acquisitions.
105. Vermeulen, Business insight (a special report); bad deals: Eight warning signs that an acquisition may not pay off.
106. D. Enrich, 2007, Moving the market: Will chorus grow at Citi?; Lampert may join calls for shake-up after buying stake, *Wall Street Journal,* May 17, C3.
107. Cool & Van de Laar, The performance of acquisitive companies in the U.S.
108. C. Duncan & M. Mtar, 2006, Determinants of international acquisition success: Lessons from FirstGroup in North America, *European Management Journal,* 24(6): 396-41; Reuer, Avoiding lemons in M&A deals; R. M. Di Gregorio, 2003, Making mergers and acquisitions work: What we know and don't know—Part II, *Journal of Change Management,* 3(3): 259–274.
109. D. Mayer & M. Kenney, 2004, Economic action does not take place in a vacuum: Understanding Cisco's acquisition and development strategy, *Industry and Innovation,* 11(4): 299–325.
110. M. A. Hitt, R. D. Ireland, J. S. Harrison, & A. Best, 1998, Attributes of successful and unsuccessful acquisitions of U.S. firms, *British Journal of Management,* 9: 91–114.
111. Harrison, Hitt, Hoskisson, & Ireland, Resource complementarity in business combinations.
112. Uhlenbruck, Hitt, & Semadeni, Market value effects of acquisitions involving Internet firms: A resource-based analysis; J. Hagedoorn & G. Dysters, 2002, External sources of innovative capabilities: The

preference for strategic alliances or mergers and acquisitions, *Journal of Management Studies,* 39: 167–188.

113. J. J. Reuer & R. Ragozzino, 2006, Agency hazards and alliance portfolios, *Strategic Management Journal,* 27: 27–43; P. Porrini, 2004, Can a previous alliance between an acquirer and a target affect acquisition performance? *Journal of Management,* 30: 545–562.
114. R. J. Aiello & M. D. Watkins, 2000, The fine art of friendly acquisition, *Harvard Business Review,* 78(6): 100–107.
115. Krishnan, Hitt, & Park, Acquisition premiums, subsequent workforce reductions and post-acquisition performance; P. Gwynne, 2002, Keeping the right people, *MIT Sloan Management Review,* 43(2): 19; D. D. Bergh, 2001, Executive retention and acquisition outcomes: A test of opposing views on the influence of organizational tenure, *Journal of Management,* 27: 603–622; J. P. Walsh, 1989, Doing a deal: Merger and acquisition negotiations and their impact upon target company top management turnover, *Strategic Management Journal,* 10: 307–322.
116. G. Lodorfos & A. Boateng, 2006, The role of culture in the merger and acquisition process: Evidence from the European chemical industry, *Management Decision,* 44(10):1405–1421; M. L. Marks & P. H. Mirvis, 2001, Making mergers and acquisitions work: Strategic and psychological preparation, *Academy of Management Executive,* 15(2): 80–92.
117. Cullinan, Le Roux, & Weddigen, When to walk away from a deal; S. Rovit & C. Lemire, 2003, Your best M&A strategy, *Harvard Business Review,* 81(3): 16–17.
118. C. Terranova, 2007, Assessing culture during an acquisition, *Organization Development Journal,* 25(2): P43–P48; Hitt, Harrison, & Ireland, *Mergers and Acquisitions;* Q. N. Huy, 2001, Time, temporal capability and planned change, *Academy of Management Review,* 26: 601–623; L. Markoczy, 2001, Consensus formation during strategic change, *Strategic Management Journal,* 22: 1013–1031.
119. Harding & Rouse, Human due diligence.
120. J. B. Steward, 2007, Buffett stake may signal railroad to be corn fed, *Wall Street Journal,* http://www.wsj.com, April 11.
121. J. Anand, 1999, How many matches are made in heaven, Mastering Strategy (Part Five), *Financial Times,* October 25, 6–7.
122. J.-K. Kang, J.-M. Kim, W.-L. Liu, & S. Yi, 2006, Post-takeover restructuring and the sources of gains in foreign takeovers: Evidence from U.S. targets. *Journal of Business,* 79(5): 2503–2537; R. A. Johnson, 1996, Antecedents and outcomes of corporate refocusing, *Journal of Management,* 22: 437–481; J. E. Bethel & J. Liebeskind, 1993, The effects of ownership structure on corporate restructuring, *Strategic Management Journal,* 14 (Special Issue): 15–31.
123. K. E. Meyer, 2006, Globalfocusing: From domestic conglomerates to global specialists, *Journal of Management Studies,* 43: 1109–1144; R. E. Hoskisson, A. A. Cannella, L. Tihanyi, & R. Faraci, 2004. Asset restructuring and business group affiliation in French civil law countries, *Strategic Management Journal,* 25: 525–539.
124. J. L. Morrow Jr., D. G. Sirmon, M. A. Hitt, & T. R. Holcomb, 2007, Creating value in the face of declining performance: Firm strategies and organizational recovery, *Strategic Management Journal,* 28: 271–283; J. L. Morrow Jr., R. A. Johnson, & L. W. Busenitz, 2004, The effects of cost and asset retrenchment on firm performance: The overlooked role of a firm's competitive environment, *Journal of Management,* 30: 189–208.
125. R. D. Nixon, M. A. Hitt, H.-U. Lee, & E. Jeong, 2004, Market reactions to announcements of corporate downsizing actions and implementation strategies, *Strategic Management Journal,* 25: 1121–1129.
126. G. J. Castrogiovanni & G. D. Bruton, 2000, Business turnaround processes following acquisitions: Reconsidering the role of retrenchment, *Journal of Business Research,* 48: 25–34; W. McKinley, J. Zhao, & K. G. Rust, 2000, A sociocognitive interpretation of organizational downsizing, *Academy of Management Review,* 25: 227–243.
127. H. A. Krishnan, M. A. Hitt, & D. Park, 2007, Acquisition premiums, subsequent workforce reductions and post-acquisition performance, *Journal of Management,* 44: 709–732.
128. W. McKinley, C. M. Sanchez, & A. G. Schick, 1995, Organizational downsizing: Constraining, cloning, learning, *Academy of Management Executive,* 9(3): 32–44.
129. P. Patsuris, 2002, Forbes.com layoff tracker surpasses 1M mark, *Forbes,* http://www.forbes.com, January 16.
130. D. Enrich, C. Mollenkamp, & M. Langley, 2007, Citigroup likely to propose cuts of 15,000 jobs; revamp plan may call for charge of $1 billion; high stakes for Prince, *Wall Street Journal,* http://www.wsj.com, March 26, A1, A11.
131. R. E. Hoskisson & M. A. Hitt, 1994, *Downscoping: How to Tame the Diversified Firm,* New York: Oxford University Press.
132. L. Dranikoff, T. Koller, & A. Schneider, 2002, Divestiture: Strategy's missing link, *Harvard Business Review,* 80(5): 74–83.
133. B. Sechler & J. Rose, 2007, American Standard to split businesses, sell unit, *Wall Street Journal,* February 2, A14.
134. Brauer, What have we acquired and what should we acquire in divestiture research; M. Rajand & M. Forsyth, 2002, Hostile bidders, long-term performance, and restructuring methods: Evidence from the UK, *American Business Review,* 20(1): 71–81.
135. Johnson, Hoskisson, & Hitt, Board of director involvement; R. E. Hoskisson & M. A. Hitt, 1990, Antecedents and performance outcomes of diversification: A review and critique of theoretical perspectives, *Journal of Management,* 16: 461–509.
136. R. E. Hoskisson, R. A. Johnson, L. Tihanyi, & R. E. White, 2005, Diversified business groups and corporate refocusing in emerging economies, *Journal of Management,* 31: 941–965.
137. M. Kripalani, 2004, Ratan Tata: No one's doubting now, *Business Week,* July 26, 50–51.
138. Bellman, Tata's Corus deal raises fears about likely heavy debt load.
139. J. Krasoff & J. O'Neill, 2006, The role of distressed investing and hedge funds in turnarounds and buyouts and how this affects middle-market companies, *Journal of Private Equity,* 9(2): 17–23; C. C. Markides & H. Singh, 1997, Corporate restructuring: A symptom of poor governance or a solution to past managerial mistakes? *European Management Journal,* 15: 213–219.
140. J. Mair & C. Moschieri, 2006, Unbundling frees business for take off, *Financial Times,* October 19, 2.
141. M. F. Wiersema & J. P. Liebeskind, 1995, The effects of leveraged buyouts on corporate growth and diversification in large firms, *Strategic Management Journal,* 16: 447–460.
142. R. Harris, D. S. Siegel, & M. Wright, 2005, Assessing the impact of management buyouts on economic efficiency: Plant-level evidence from the United Kingdom, *Review of Economics and Statistics,* 87: 148–153; A. Seth & J. Easterwood, 1995, Strategic redirection in large management buyouts: The evidence from post-buyout restructuring activity, *Strategic Management Journal,* 14: 251–274; P. H. Phan & C. W. L. Hill, 1995, Organizational restructuring and economic performance in leveraged buyouts: An ex-post study, *Academy of Management Journal,* 38: 704–739.
143. C. M. Daily, P. P. McDougall, J. G. Covin, & D. R. Dalton, 2002, Governance and strategic leadership in entrepreneurial firms, *Journal of Management,* 3: 387–412.
144. M. Wright, R. E. Hoskisson, L. W. Busenitz, & J. Dial, 2000, Entrepreneurial growth through privatization: The upside of management buyouts, *Academy of Management Review,* 25: 591–601.
145. W. Kiechel III, 2007, Private equity's long view, *Harvard Business Review,* 85(8): 18–20.; M. Wright, R. E. Hoskisson, & L. W. Busenitz, 2001, Firm rebirth: Buyouts as facilitators of strategic growth and entrepreneurship, *Academy of Management Executive,* 15(1): 111–125.
146. Krishnan, Hitt, & Park, Acquisition premiums, subsequent workforce reductions and post-acquisition performance; Bergh, Executive retention and acquisition outcomes: A test of opposing views on the influence of organizational tenure.

147. H. A. Krishnan & D. Park, 2002, The impact of work force reduction on subsequent performance in major mergers and acquisitions: An exploratory study, *Journal of Business Research,* 55(4): 285–292; P. M. Lee, 1997, A comparative analysis of layoff announcements and stock price reactions in the United States and Japan, *Strategic Management Journal,* 18: 879–894.
148. D. J. Flanagan & K. C. O'Shaughnessy, 2005, The effect of layoffs on firm reputation, *Journal of Management,* 31: 445–463.
149. C. D. Zatzick & R. D. Iverson, 2006, High-involvement management and workforce reduction: Competitive advantage or disadvantage? *Academy of Management Journal,* 49: 999–1015; N. Mirabal & R. DeYoung, 2005, Downsizing as a Strategic Intervention, *Journal of American Academy of Business,* 6(1): 39–45.
150. Brauer, What have we acquired and what should we acquire in divestiture research? K. Shimizu & M. A. Hitt, 2005, What constrains or facilitates divestitures of formerly acquired firms? The effects of organizational inertia, *Journal of Management,* 31: 50–72.
151. S. Toms & M. Wright, 2005, Divergence and convergence within Anglo-American corporate governance systems: Evidence from the US and UK, 1950–2000, *Business History,* 47(2): 267–295.
152. A.-L. Le Nadant & F. Perdreau, 2006, Financial profile of leveraged buy-out targets: Some French evidence, *Review of Accounting and Finance,* (4): 370–392.
153. G. D. Bruton, J. K. Keels, & E. L. Scifres, 2002, Corporate restructuring and performance: An agency perspective on the complete buyout cycle, *Journal of Business Research,* 55: 709–724; W. F. Long & D. J. Ravenscraft, 1993, LBOs, debt, and R&D intensity, *Strategic Management Journal,* 14 (Special Issue): 119–135.
154. Wright, Hoskisson, Busenitz, & Dial, Entrepreneurial growth through privatization; S. A. Zahra, 1995, Corporate entrepreneurship and financial performance: The case of management leveraged buyouts, *Journal of Business Venturing,* 10: 225–248.

International Strategy

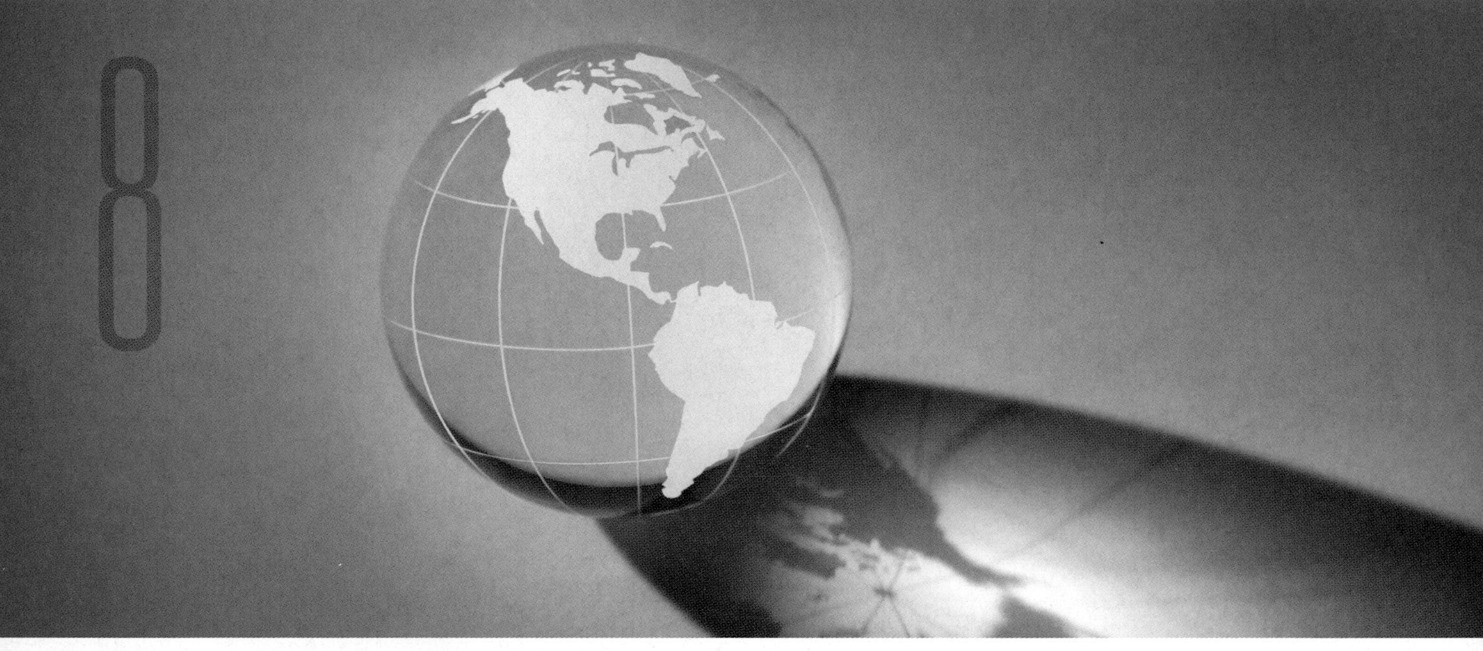

Studying this chapter should provide you with the strategic management knowledge needed to:

1. Explain traditional and emerging motives for firms to pursue international diversification.
2. Identify the four major benefits of an international strategy.
3. Explore the four factors that provide a basis for international business-level strategies.
4. Describe the three international corporate-level strategies: multidomestic, global, and transnational.
5. Discuss the environmental trends affecting international strategy, especially liability of foreignness and regionalization.
6. Name and describe the five alternative modes for entering international markets.
7. Explain the effects of international diversification on firm returns and innovation.
8. Name and describe two major risks of international diversification.

Shanghai Automotive Industry Corporation: Reaching for Global Markets

The Shanghai Automotive Industry Corporation (SAIC) is one of China's oldest and largest automotive companies. The company's 50 manufacturing plants in China produce autos, tractors, motorcycles, trucks, buses, and automobile parts (wholesale and retail). The company is also involved in car leasing and financing. SAIC has had highly successful joint ventures with General Motors and Volkswagen to produce GM and VW automobiles for the growing Chinese automobile market. The majority of SAIC's sales in the 1990s and 2000s have come from these joint ventures. In fact, driving in any major city in China shows the popularity of the GM (e.g., Buick) and VW autos in that country. Yet, some analysts believe that GM and VW may have become too dependent on SAIC.

SAIC also owns almost 51 percent of the Korean automaker, SSangyong, and the intellectual property rights to the Rover 25 and 75 models, as well as the K-series engine. SAIC started manufacturing the Rover 75 (redesigned for the Chinese market) in 2007.

SAIC learned much from its partnerships, and with the licensed technology, it decided to launch and promote its own branded vehicles. The Chinese government is emphasizing the importance of Chinese companies to develop their own brands partly because foreign brands are controlling many of the Chinese markets. Additionally, for these firms to become successful globally competitive companies, they need their own brands. In keeping with this goal, Chinese executives have a favorite term, *zizhu pinpai*, meaning self-owned brand. Actually, *zizhu* means to be one's own master. In 2007, SAIC began selling its own automobile brand, named the Roewe, in Chinese markets.

SAIC is currently among the top three automobile companies in China, and it has a goal of becoming among the top 10 global auto competitors. To do so, it has a goal of entering and competing effectively in the U.S. auto market, which is the largest such market in the world. It hired Philip Murtaugh, former chairman of GM China, to head its Shanghai Motor subsidiary.

This goal represents a major challenge for SAIC because all major automobile companies compete in the U.S. auto market. Hyundai discovered this challenge with its major efforts to compete more successfully in the U.S. market. Despite major improvements in quality and lower prices than competitors for comparable automobiles, Hyundai has been unable to capture the share of the U.S. market that it desires. Although its relative ranking in the market is a little higher than in 2005, its market share has remained stable at just under 3 percent.

Few Chinese autos have been exported in general and even fewer exported to the United States. Although the market share of U.S. automakers has been falling for the last several years, most of the gains in market share have been obtained by Japanese auto manufacturers, especially Toyota. Chinese exports are expected to be about 500,000 autos in 2007, but most are targeted for South America, Southeast Asia, and Eastern Europe. Yet, analysts predict Chinese automakers' success in global markets, including the United States, over time, and SAIC is likely to be one of the leaders.

Sources: A. Webb, 2007, China needs strong automakers—not more. *Automotive News*, http://www.autonews.com, July 20: 2007, China's SAIC says first half sales up 23 percent, Reuters, http://www.reuters.com, July 12; A. K. Gupta & H. Wang, 2007, How to get China and India right: Western companies need to become smarter—and they need to do it quickly, *Wall Street Journal*, April 28, R4; G. Dyer & J. Reed, 2007, SAIC plans to develop five new car classes, *Financial Times*, April 20, 23; C. Isidore, 2007, Cars from China: Not so fast, CNNMoney, http://www.cnnmoney.com, January 27; N. Madden, 2006, Chinese carmaker's push threatens Western rivals, *Advertising Age*, 77(50): 28; M. Vaughn, 2005, Refined Hyundai takes on the big boys, *Globe and Mail Update*, http://www.theglobeandmail.com, August 11.

As the Opening Case indicates, China's firms are building their competitive capabilities and seeking to enter foreign markets. China's entrance into the World Trade Organization (WTO) brought change not only to China and its trading partners but also to industries and firms throughout the world. Despite its underdeveloped market and institutional environment, Chinese firms such as the Shanghai Automotive Industry Corporation (SAIC) are taking advantage of the growing size of the Chinese market to attract foreign partners from whom they can learn new technologies and managerial capabilities.

Many firms choose direct investment in assets (e.g., establishing new subsidiaries, making acquisitions or building joint ventures) over indirect investment because it provides better protection for their assets.[1] Domestic Chinese firms are becoming more competitive and building their capabilities. As indicated in the Opening Case, Chinese firms are developing their manufacturing capabilities and building their own branded products (e.g., SAIC's Roewe auto). As such, the potential global market power of Chinese firms is astounding.[2]

As foreign firms enter China and as Chinese firms enter into other foreign markets, both opportunities and threats for firms competing in global markets are exemplified. This chapter examines opportunities facing firms as they seek to develop and exploit core competencies by diversifying into global markets. In addition, we discuss different problems, complexities, and threats that might accompany a firm's international strategy.[3] Although national boundaries, cultural differences, and geographical distances all pose barriers to entry into many markets, significant opportunities motivate businesses to enter international markets. A business that plans to operate globally must formulate a successful strategy to take advantage of these global opportunities.[4] Furthermore, to mold their firms into truly global companies, managers must develop global mind-sets.[5] As firms move into international markets, they develop relationships with suppliers, customers, and partners, and learn from these relationships. For example, SAIC learned new capabilities from its partnerships with General Motors and Volkswagen.

As illustrated in Figure 1.1, on page 5, we discuss the importance of international strategy as a source of strategic competitiveness and above-average returns. The chapter focuses on the incentives to internationalize. After a firm decides to compete internationally, it must select its strategy and choose a mode of entry into international markets. It may enter international markets by exporting from domestic-based operations, licensing some of its products or services, forming joint ventures with international partners, acquiring a foreign-based firm, or establishing a new subsidiary. Such international diversification can extend product life cycles, provide incentives for more innovation, and produce above-average returns. These benefits are tempered by political and economic risks and the problems of managing a complex international firm with operations in multiple countries.

Figure 8.1 provides an overview of the various choices and outcomes of strategic competitiveness. The relationships among international opportunities, the resources and

Figure 8.1 Opportunities and Outcomes of International Strategy

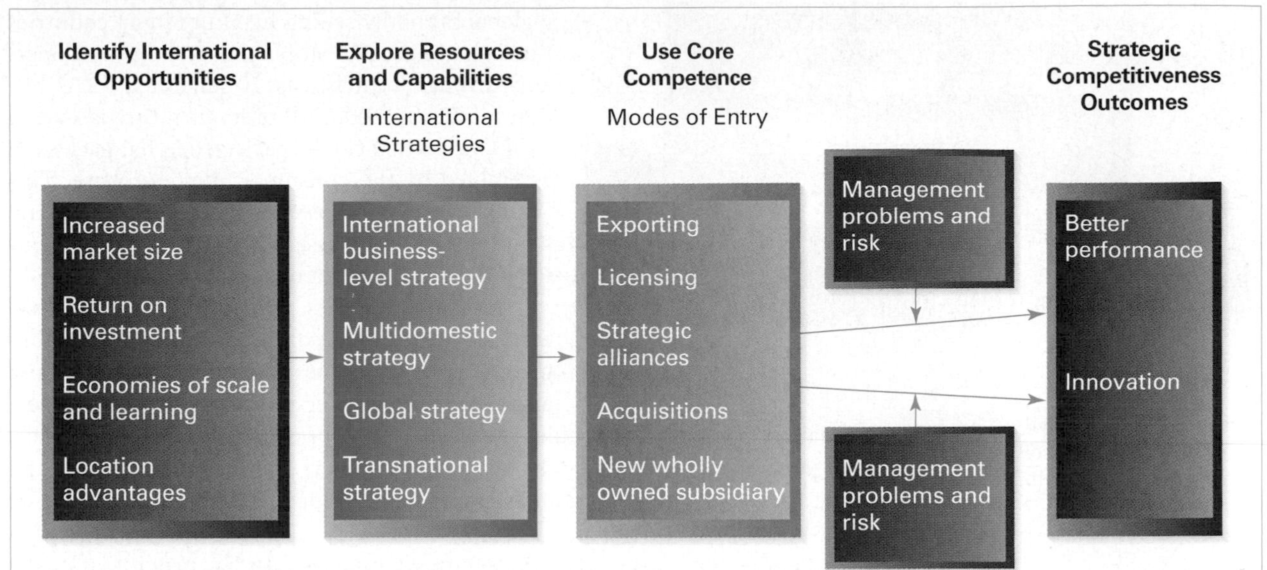

capabilities that result in strategies, and the modes of entry that are based on core competencies are explored in this chapter.

Identifying International Opportunities: Incentives to Use an International Strategy

An **international strategy** is a strategy through which the firm sells its goods or services outside its domestic market.[6] One of the primary reasons for implementing an international strategy (as opposed to a strategy focused on the domestic market) is that international markets yield potential new opportunities.[7]

An **international strategy** is a strategy through which the firm sells its goods or services outside its domestic market.

Raymond Vernon captured the classic rationale for international diversification.[8] He suggested that typically a firm discovers an innovation in its home-country market, especially in an advanced economy such as that of the United States. Often demand for the product then develops in other countries, and exports are provided by domestic operations. Increased demand in foreign countries justifies making investments in foreign operations, especially to fend off foreign competitors. Vernon, therefore, observed that one reason why firms pursue international diversification is to extend a product's life cycle.

Another traditional motive for firms to become multinational is to secure needed resources. Key supplies of raw material—especially minerals and energy—are important in some industries. Other industries, such as clothing, electronics, watch making, and many others, have moved portions of their operations to foreign locations in pursuit of lower production costs. Clearly one of the reasons for Chinese firms' international expansion is to gain access to important resources.[9]

Although these traditional motives persist, other emerging motivations also drive international expansion (see Chapter 1). For instance, pressure has increased for a global integration of operations, mostly driven by more universal product demand. As nations industrialize, the demand for some products and commodities appears to become more similar. This borderless demand for globally branded products may be due to similarities in lifestyle in developed nations. Increases in global communication media also facilitate the ability of people in different countries to visualize and model lifestyles in

IKEA has become a global brand using an international strategy for selling furniture.

different cultures.[10] IKEA, for example, has become a global brand by selling furniture in 44 countries through almost 300 stores that it owns and operates through franchisees. It generated $22.2 billion in sales in 2006. All of its furniture is sold in components that can be packaged in flat packs and assembled by the consumer after purchase. This arrangement has allowed for easier shipping and handling than fully assembled units and has facilitated the development of the global brand.[11]

In some industries, technology drives globalization because the economies of scale necessary to reduce costs to the lowest level often require an investment greater than that needed to meet domestic market demand. Companies also experience pressure for cost reductions, achieved by purchasing from the lowest-cost global suppliers. For instance, research and development expertise for an emerging business start-up may not exist in the domestic market. [12]

New large-scale, emerging markets, such as China and India, provide a strong internationalization incentive based on their high potential demand for consumer products and services.[13] Because of currency fluctuations, firms may also choose to distribute their operations across many countries, including emerging ones, in order to reduce the risk of devaluation in one country.[14] However, the uniqueness of emerging markets presents both opportunities and challenges.[15] Even though India, for example, differs from Western countries in many respects, including culture, politics, and the precepts of its economic system, it also offers a huge potential market and its government is becoming more supportive of foreign direct investment.[16] However, the differences between China and India and Western countries pose serious challenges to Western competitive paradigms that emphasize the skills needed to manage financial, economic, and political risks.[17]

Employment contracts and labor forces differ significantly in international markets. For example, it is more difficult to layoff employees in Europe than in the United States because of employment contract differences. In many cases, host governments demand joint ownership with a local company in order to invest in local operations, which allows the foreign firm to avoid tariffs. Also, host governments frequently require a high percentage of procurements, manufacturing, and R&D to use local sources.[18] These issues increase the need for local investment and responsiveness as opposed to seeking global economies of scale.

We've discussed incentives that influence firms to use international strategies. When these strategies are successful, firms can derive four basic benefits: (1) increased market size; (2) greater returns on major capital investments or on investments in new products and processes; (3) greater economies of scale, scope, or learning; and (4) a competitive advantage through location (e.g., access to low-cost labor, critical resources, or customers). We examine these benefits in terms of both their costs (such as higher coordination expenses and limited access to knowledge about host country political influences[19] and their managerial challenges.

Increased Market Size

Firms can expand the size of their potential market—sometimes dramatically—by moving into international markets. Pharmaceutical firms have been doing significant foreign direct investment into China due to the size of the market. One researcher found that approximately 85 percent of the pharmaceutical firms studied used a joint venture with a local Chinese partner as their entry mode for the Chinese market and the remaining firms established their own subsidiary in China.[20]

Although changing consumer tastes and practices linked to cultural values or traditions is not simple, following an international strategy is a particularly attractive option to firms competing in domestic markets that have limited growth opportunities. For example, firms in the domestic soft drink industry have been searching for growth in foreign markets for some time now. Major competitors Pepsi and Coca-Cola have had relatively stable market shares in the U.S. market for several years. Most of their growth in sales has come from foreign markets. In recent times, Pepsi has been using highly tailored soft drinks to capture more sales and profits in the Japanese market. For example, it introduced a limited run of "Ice Cucumber" and sold 4.8 million bottles of it before withdrawing it from the market. It has introduced several such drinks in Japan (e.g., Pepsi Blue, a berry-flavored soda) and had significant success. The limited edition drinks are designed for the Japanese consumers.[21]

Pepsi's Ice Cucumber drink is sold in the Japanese market.

The size of an international market also affects a firm's willingness to invest in R&D to build competitive advantages in that market.[22] Larger markets usually offer higher potential returns and thus pose less risk for a firm's investments. The strength of the science base in the country in question also can affect a firm's foreign R&D investments. Most firms prefer to invest more heavily in those countries with the scientific knowledge and talent to produce value-creating products and processes from their R&D activities.[23] Research suggests that German multinationals are increasingly investing in international R&D opportunities for resource development and learning purposes as opposed to market-seeking motives.[24]

Return on Investment

Large markets may be crucial for earning a return on significant investments, such as plant and capital equipment or R&D. Therefore, most R&D-intensive industries such as electronics are international. In addition to the need for a large market to recoup heavy investment in R&D, the development pace for new technology is increasing. New products become obsolete more rapidly, and therefore investments need to be recouped more quickly. Moreover, firms' abilities to develop new technologies are expanding, and because of different patent laws across country borders, imitation by competitors is more likely. Through reverse engineering, competitors are able to take apart a product, learn the new technology, and develop a similar product. Because their competitors can imitate the new technology relatively quickly, firms need to recoup new product development costs even more rapidly. Consequently, the larger markets provided by international expansion are particularly attractive in many industries such as pharmaceutical firms, because they expand the opportunity for the firm to recoup significant capital investments and large-scale R&D expenditures.[25]

Regardless of other issues, however, the primary reason for investing in international markets is to generate above-average returns on investments. Still, firms from different countries have different expectations and use different criteria to decide whether to invest in international markets.[26]

Economies of Scale and Learning

By expanding their markets, firms may be able to enjoy economies of scale, particularly in their manufacturing operations. To the extent that a firm can standardize its products across country borders and use the same or similar production facilities, thereby coordinating critical resource functions, it is more likely to achieve optimal economies of scale.[27]

Does General Motors' Survival Depend on International Markets?

For 76 years, General Motors (GM) was the global industry sales leader. In 2006, GM sold approximately 9.1 million vehicles, yet its global market share has been declining for a number of years. In fact, in 2007, Toyota became the world's largest automaker. In addition, GM has been struggling to earn positive returns in recent years. It finally returned to profitability in 2007 after experiencing several years of significant losses. Many of GM's problems stem from its competitive capabilities in the North American market, where Toyota and other foreign automakers have made substantial gains.

Interestingly, GM's return to profitability is not due to success in its North American operations. It continues to lose money there, although the losses are smaller than in past years because of a major program to reduce costs. Its recent profits have come from GM's international operations, especially its sales in the Chinese market. GM invested more than $2 billion in China, and these investments have resulted in positive returns. Sales of 7.2 million light trucks and automobiles were achieved in the Chinese market in 2006. China surpassed Japan to become the second largest vehicle market in the world. GM has the second highest market share in the Chinese market behind Volkswagen.

The Buick Excelle is one of the General Motors cars being produced as part of the General Motors and Shanghai Automotive Industry Corporation (SAIC) joint venture named Shanghai General Motors.

GM's sales in China come from a 50-50 joint venture with the Shanghai Automotive Industry Corporation (SAIC) named Shanghai General Motors. In 2006, this joint venture manufactured more than 400,000 passenger automobiles. GM predicts that Shanghai General Motors will produce 1 million passenger cars by 2010. Of course, the Chinese market for autos continues to grow and is expected to eventually become the largest auto market in the world. Through all of its joint ventures, GM sold more than 875,000 cars in China during 2006. GM's competitive advantage is clear because Toyota sold slightly more than 275,000 cars during the same period. Thus, GM has made large investments in Asia to offset Toyota's gains elsewhere.

GM's operations in Europe have been downsized. To help offset these changes, GM is investing about $500 million in Brazil to build new manufacturing facilities. Even as GM is experiencing success in Asia and is hoping for more in Latin America, it will experience a number of challenges in the next decade. Importantly, its partner in China may become a critical competitor. The transfer to technology and managerial capabilities to SAIC through the joint venture has helped it to develop its own branded auto that will compete with the GM Buicks sold in China. Furthermore, Toyota plans to double its production capacity in China by 2010. As a result, GM must employ effective strategies to maintain its current competitive advantages in China and other Asian markets, and it also must try to stem the tide of lost market share in other markets (e.g., the United States and Western Europe).

Sources: Investing in China, 2007, General Motors, http://www.gm.com, July 31; General Motors gives it stick, 2007, *The Detroit News*, http://www.detroitnews.net, July 31; Rising in the East: General Motors, 2007, *The Economist*, April 28, 82; G. Dyer, 2007, Foreign marks' lead narrows, *Financial Times*, April 25, 15; G. Dyer & J. Reed, 2007, Groups in race to sell alternative fuel cars, *Financial Times*, April 23, 22; G. Fairclough, Passing lane: GM's Chinese partner looms as a new rival; Learning from Detroit, Shanghai Automotive pushes past its own cars, *Wall Street Journal*, April 20, A.1; J. B. White & S. Power, 2007, GM retrenches in Europe, shifts gaze east, *Wall Street Journal*, April 18, A.4.

Economies of scale are critical in the global auto industry. China's decision to join the World Trade Organization has allowed carmakers from other countries to enter the country and for lower tariffs to be charged (in the past, Chinese carmakers have had an advantage over foreign carmakers due to tariffs). Ford, Honda, General Motors, and Volkswagen are each producing an economy car to compete with the existing cars in China. Because of global economies of scale (allowing them to price their products competitively) and local investments in China, all of these companies are likely to obtain significant market share in China. Alternatively, the SAIC is developing its own branded vehicles to compete with the foreign automakers (as explained in the Opening Case). SAIC's joint ventures with both GM and Volkswagen have been highly successful for SAIC and its partners. However as explained in the Opening Case, SAIC is seeking to export vehicles overseas and perhaps enter foreign markets in other ways. It aspires to be one of the 10 largest automakers by 2012 and among the top 6 in the world by 2020.[28]

Firms may also be able to exploit core competencies in international markets through resource and knowledge sharing between units and network partners across country borders.[29] This sharing generates synergy, which helps the firm produce higher-quality goods or services at lower cost. In addition, working across international markets provides the firm with new learning opportunities.[30] Multinational firms have substantial occasions to learn from the different practices they encounter in separate international markets. However, research finds that to take advantage of the international R&D investments, firms need to already have a strong R&D system in place to absorb the knowledge.[31]

Location Advantages

Firms may locate facilities in other countries to lower the basic costs of the goods or services they provide. These facilities may provide easier access to lower-cost labor, energy, and other natural resources. Other location advantages include access to critical supplies and to customers.[32] Once positioned favorably with an attractive location, firms must manage their facilities effectively to gain the full benefit of a location advantage.

Such location advantages can be influenced by costs of production and transportation requirements as well as by the needs of the intended customers.[33] Cultural influences may also affect location advantages and disadvantages. If there is a strong match between the cultures in which international transactions are carried out, the liability of foreignness is lower than if there is high cultural distance.[34] Research also suggests that regulation distances influence the ownership positions of multinational firms as well as their strategies for managing expatriate human resources.[35]

As suggested in the Strategic Focus, General Motors (GM) entered international markets to expand its market size. It is also earning positive returns on its international investments, but primarily in Asia. In fact, GM's recent return to profitability is due to its Asian operations, primarily in China. While GM has lost its position as the world's largest automaker after 76 years in the lead, it has major expansion plans for its China ventures. Still, GM faces a number of challenges from domestic Chinese competitors, such its partner SAIC, and from foreign competitors, such as Toyota and Volkswagen. It will have to formulate and implement a successful strategy for the Chinese market to maintain its current competitive advantage there.

International Strategies

Firms choose to use one or both of two basic types of international strategies: business-level international strategy and corporate-level international strategy. At the business level, firms follow generic strategies: cost leadership, differentiation, focused cost leadership, focused differentiation, or integrated cost leadership/differentiation. The three corporate-level international strategies are multidomestic, global, or transnational (a combination of multidomestic and global). To create competitive advantage, each strategy must utilize a core competence based on difficult-to-imitate resources and capabilities.[36] As discussed in Chapters 4 and 6, firms expect to create value through the implementation of a business-level strategy and a corporate-level strategy.[37]

International Business-Level Strategy

Each business must develop a competitive strategy focused on its own domestic market. We discussed business-level strategies in Chapter 4 and competitive rivalry and competitive dynamics in Chapter 5. International business-level strategies have some unique features. In an international business-level strategy, the home country of operation is often the most important source of competitive advantage.[38] The resources and capabilities established in the home country frequently allow the firm to pursue the strategy into markets located in other countries.[39] However, research indicates that as a firm continues its growth into multiple international locations, the country of origin is less important for competitive advantage.[40]

Michael Porter's model, illustrated in Figure 8.2, describes the factors contributing to the advantage of firms in a dominant global industry and associated with a specific home country or regional environment.[41] The first dimension in Porter's model is the factors of production. This dimension refers to the inputs necessary to compete in any industry—labor, land, natural resources, capital, and infrastructure (such as transportation, postal, and communication systems). There are basic factors (for example, natural and labor resources) and advanced factors (such as digital communication systems and a highly educated workforce). Other production factors are generalized (highway systems and the supply of debt capital) and specialized (skilled personnel in a specific industry, such as the workers in a port that specialize in handling bulk chemicals). If a country has both advanced and specialized production factors, it is likely to serve an industry well by spawning strong home-country competitors that also can be successful global competitors.

Ironically, countries often develop advanced and specialized factors because they lack critical basic resources. For example, some Asian countries, such as South Korea, lack

Figure 8.2 Determinants of National Advantage

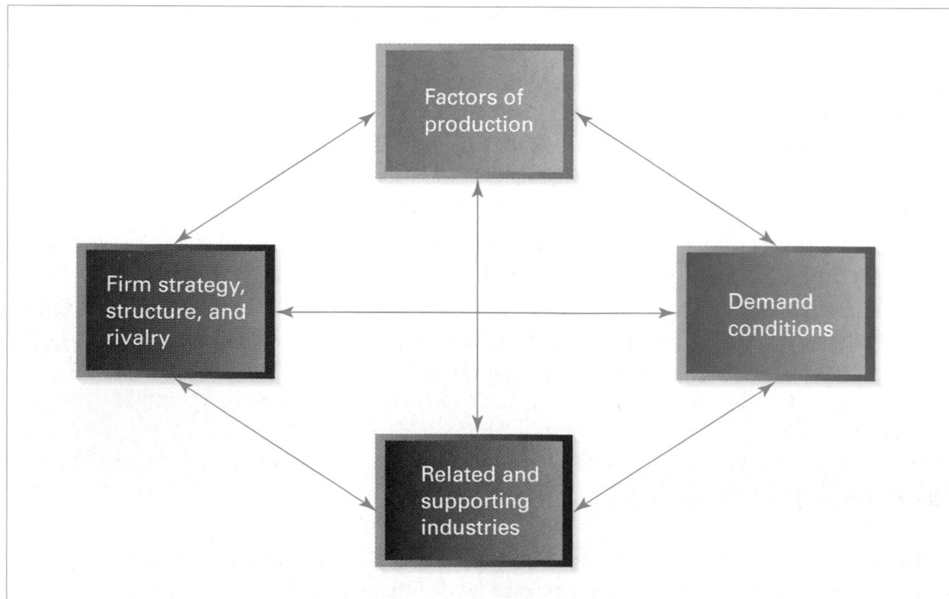

Source: Reprinted with the permission of The Free Press, a Division of Simon & Schuster Adult Publishing Group, from *Competitive Advantage of Nations,* by Michael E. Porter, p. 72.

abundant natural resources but offer a strong work ethic, a large number of engineers, and systems of large firms to create an expertise in manufacturing. Similarly, Germany developed a strong chemical industry, partially because Hoechst and BASF spent years creating a synthetic indigo dye to reduce their dependence on imports, unlike Britain, whose colonies provided large supplies of natural indigo.[42]

The second dimension in Porter's model, demand conditions, is characterized by the nature and size of buyers' needs in the home market for the industry's goods or services. A large market segment can produce the demand necessary to create scale-efficient facilities.

Chinese manufacturing companies have spent years focused on building their businesses in China, but are now beginning to look at markets beyond their borders, as described in the Opening Case about SAIC. As mentioned, SAIC (along with other Chinese firms) has begun the challenging process of building its brand equity in China but especially in other countries. In doing so, most Chinese firms begin in the Far East with the intention to move into Western markets when ready to do so. Companies such as SAIC have been helped by China's entry to the World Trade Organization. Of course, interests of companies such as SAIC in entering international markets are to increase their market share and profits.

Related and supporting industries are the third dimension in Porter's model. Italy has become the leader in the shoe industry because of related and supporting industries; a well-established leather-processing industry provides the leather needed to construct shoes and related products. Also, many people travel to Italy to purchase leather goods, providing support in distribution. Supporting industries in leather-working machinery and design services also contribute to the success of the shoe industry. In fact, the design services industry supports its own related industries, such as ski boots, fashion apparel, and furniture. In Japan, cameras and copiers are related industries. Similarly, it is argued that the "creative resources nurtured by [the] popular cartoons and animation sector, combined with technological knowledge accumulated in the consumer electronics industry, facilitated the emergence of a successful video game industry in Japan."[43]

Firm strategy, structure, and rivalry make up the final country dimension and also foster the growth of certain industries. The types of strategy, structure, and rivalry among firms vary greatly from nation to nation. The excellent technical training system in Germany fosters a strong emphasis on continuous product and process improvements. In Japan, unusual cooperative and competitive systems have facilitated the cross-functional management of complex assembly operations. In Italy, the national pride of the country's designers has spawned strong industries in sports cars, fashion apparel, and furniture. In the United States, competition among computer manufacturers and software producers has contributed to the development of these industries.

The four basic dimensions of the "diamond" model in Figure 8.2 emphasize the environmental or structural attributes of a national economy that contribute to national advantage. Government policy also clearly contributes to the success and failure of many firms and industries. For example, the Chinese government has provided incentives for Chinese firms such as SAIC to develop their own branded products and to develop the capabilities necessary to compete effectively in international markets.

Although each firm must create its own success, not all firms will survive to become global competitors—not even those operating with the same country factors that spawned other successful firms. The actual strategic choices managers make may be the most compelling reason for success or failure. Accordingly, the factors illustrated in Figure 8.2 are likely to produce competitive advantages only when the firm develops and implements an appropriate strategy that takes advantage of distinct country factors. Thus, these distinct country factors must be given thorough consideration when making a decision regarding the business-level strategy to use (i.e., cost leadership, differentiation, focused cost leadership, focused differentiation, and integrated cost leadership/differentiation, discussed in Chapter 4) in an international context. However, pursuing an international strategy leads to more adjustment and learning as the firm adjusts to competition in the host country. Such adjustments are continuous as illustrated by GM's operations in the Chinese market. It must adapt to the increasing competition from its partner, SAIC, and its major competitor in global markets, Toyota.

International Corporate-Level Strategy

The international business-level strategies are based at least partially on the type of international corporate-level strategy the firm has chosen. Some corporate strategies give individual country units the authority to develop their own business-level strategies; other corporate strategies dictate the business-level strategies in order to standardize the firm's products and sharing of resources across countries.[44] International corporate-level strategy focuses on the scope of a firm's operations through both product and geographic diversification.[45] International corporate-level strategy is required when the firm operates in multiple industries and multiple countries or regions.[46] The headquarters unit guides the strategy, although business- or country-level managers can have substantial strategic input, depending on the type of international corporate-level strategy followed. The three international corporate-level strategies are multidomestic, global, and transnational, as shown in Figure 8.3.

Multidomestic Strategy

A **multidomestic strategy** is an international strategy in which strategic and operating decisions are decentralized to the strategic business unit in each country so as to allow that unit to tailor products to the local market.

A **multidomestic strategy** is an international strategy in which strategic and operating decisions are decentralized to the strategic business unit in each country so as to allow that unit to tailor products to the local market.[47] A multidomestic strategy focuses on competition within each country. It assumes that the markets differ and therefore are segmented by country boundaries. The multidomestic strategy uses a highly decentralized approach, allowing each division to focus on a geographic area, region, or country.[48] In other words,

Figure 8.3 International Corporate-Level Strategies

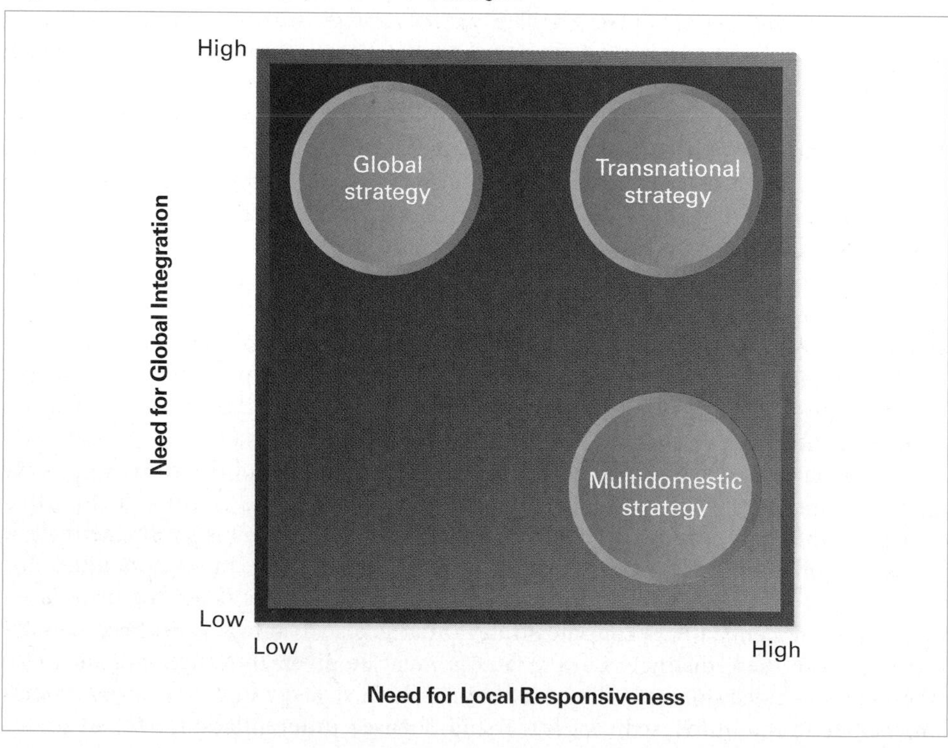

consumer needs and desires, industry conditions (e.g., the number and type of competitors), political and legal structures, and social norms vary by country. With multidomestic strategies, the country managers have the autonomy to customize the firm's products as necessary to meet the specific needs and preferences of local customers. Therefore, these strategies should maximize a firm's competitive response to the idiosyncratic requirements of each market.[49]

The use of multidomestic strategies usually expands the firm's local market share because the firm can pay attention to the needs of the local clientele.[50] However, the use of these strategies results in more uncertainty for the corporation as a whole, because of the differences across markets and thus the different strategies employed by local country units.[51] Moreover, multidomestic strategies do not allow the development of economies of scale and thus can be more costly. As a result, firms employing a multidomestic strategy decentralize their strategic and operating decisions to the business units operating in each country. Historically, Unilever, a large European consumer products firm, has had a highly decentralized approach to managing its international operations. This approach allows regional managers considerable autonomy to adapt the product offerings to fit the market needs.[52]

Global Strategy

In contrast to a multidomestic strategy, a global strategy assumes more standardization of products across country markets.[53] As a result, a global strategy is centralized and controlled by the home office. The strategic business units operating in each country are assumed to be interdependent, and the home office attempts to achieve integration across these businesses.[54] The firm uses a **global strategy** to offer standardized products across country markets, with competitive strategy being dictated by the home office. Thus, a global strategy emphasizes economies of scale and offers greater opportunities to take innovations developed at the corporate level or in one country and utilize them in other markets.[55] Improvements in global accounting and financial reporting standards are facilitating this strategy.[56]

A **global strategy** is an international strategy through which the firm offers standardized products across country markets, with competitive strategy being dictated by the home office.

Although a global strategy produces lower risk, it may cause the firm to forgo growth opportunities in local markets, either because those markets are less likely to be identified as opportunities or because the opportunities require that products be adapted to the local market.[57] The global strategy is not as responsive to local markets and is difficult to manage because of the need to coordinate strategies and operating decisions across country borders. Yahoo! and eBay experienced these challenges when they moved into specific Asian markets. For example, eBay was unsuccessful in both the Japanese and Chinese markets when attempting to export its business model and approach from North America to these two countries. It has reentered China but Meg Whitman, CEO of eBay, suggested that she had no current plans to reenter the Japanese market. Yahoo! has had rough times in China, going through several CEOs and trying to find the right formula to compete effectively in the Chinese market.[58]

Achieving efficient operations with a global strategy requires sharing resources and facilitating coordination and cooperation across country boundaries, which in turn require centralization and headquarters control. Furthermore, research suggests that the performance of the global strategy is enhanced if it deploys in areas where regional integration among countries is occurring, such as the European Union.[59] Many Japanese firms have successfully used the global strategy.[60]

CEMEX is the third largest cement company in the world, behind France's Lafarge and Switzerland's Holcim, and is the largest producer of ready mix, a prepackaged product that contains all the ingredients needed to make localized cement products.

CEMEX has strong market power in the Americas as well as in Europe. CEMEX serves customers in more than 50 countries with more than 50,000 employees globally. Because CEMEX pursues a global strategy effectively, its centralization process has facilitated the integration of several businesses it acquired in the United States,

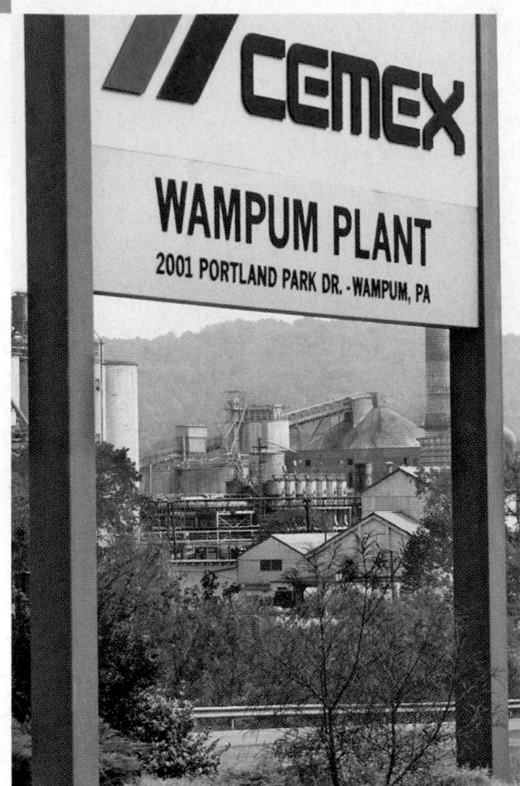

Cemex, a Mexican company, operates successfully all over the world, including in the United States.

Europe, and Asia. To integrate its businesses globally, CEMEX uses the Internet to improve logistics and manage an extensive supply network thereby increasing revenue and reducing costs. Connectivity between the operations in different countries and universal standards dominates its approach.[61] Because of increasing global competition and the need to be cost efficient while simultaneously provide high-quality differentiated products, a number of firms have begun to pursue the transnational strategy, which is described next.

Transnational Strategy

A **transnational strategy** is an international strategy through which the firm seeks to achieve both global efficiency and local responsiveness. Realizing these goals is difficult: One requires close global coordination while the other requires local flexibility. "Flexible coordination"—building a shared vision and individual commitment through an integrated network—is required to implement the transnational strategy. Such integrated networks allow a firm to manage its connections with customers, suppliers, partners, and other parties more efficiently rather than using arm's-length transactions.[62] The transnational strategy is difficult to use because of its conflicting goals (see Chapter 11 for more on the implementation of this and other corporate-level international strategies). On the positive side, the effective implementation of a transnational strategy often produces higher performance than does the implementation of either the multidomestic or global international corporate-level strategies.[63]

A **transnational strategy** is an international strategy through which the firm seeks to achieve both global efficiency and local responsiveness.

Transnational strategies are challenging to implement but are becoming increasingly necessary to compete in international markets. The growing number of global competitors heightens the requirement to hold costs down. However, the increasing sophistication of markets with greater information flow (e.g., based on the diffusion of the Internet) and the desire for specialized products to meet consumers' needs pressures firms to differentiate and even customize their products in local markets. Differences in culture and institutional environments also require firms to adapt their products and approaches to local environments.[64] As a result, more firms are increasingly using a transnational strategy.

Environmental Trends

Although the transnational strategy is difficult to implement, emphasis on global efficiency is increasing as more industries begin to experience global competition. To add to the problem, an increased emphasis on local requirements means that global goods and services often demand some customization to meet government regulations within particular countries or to fit customer tastes and preferences. In addition, most multinational firms desire coordination and sharing of resources across country markets to hold down costs, as illustrated by the CEMEX example.[65] Furthermore, some products and industries may be more suited than others for standardization across country borders.

As a result, some large multinational firms with diverse products employ a multidomestic strategy with certain product lines and a global strategy with others. Many multinational firms may require this type of flexibility if they are to be strategically competitive, in part due to trends that change over time. Two important trends are the liability of foreignness, which has increased since the terrorist attacks and the war in Iraq, and regionalization.

Liability of Foreignness

The dramatic success of Japanese firms such as Toyota and Sony in the United States and other international markets in the 1980s was a powerful jolt to U.S. managers and awakened them to the importance of international competition in markets that were rapidly becoming global markets. In the twenty-first century, China, India, Brazil, and Russia represent potential major international market opportunities for firms from many countries, including the United States, Japan, Korea, and the European Union.[66] However, there are legitimate concerns about the relative attractiveness of global strategies, as illustrated by the experience of Walt Disney Company in opening theme parks in foreign countries. For example, Disney suffered "lawsuits in France, at Disneyland Paris, because of the lack of fit between its transferred personnel policies and the French employees charged to enact them."[67] Disney executives learned from this experience in building the firm's newest theme park in Hong Kong.

Research shows that global strategies are not as prevalent as they once were and are still difficult to implement, even when using Internet-based strategies.[68] The September 11, 2001, attacks and the 2003 war in Iraq are two explanations for these concerns.[69] In addition, the amount of competition vying for a limited amount of resources and customers can limit firms' focus to regional rather than global markets. A regional focus allows firms to marshal their resources to compete effectively in regional markets rather than spreading their limited resources across many international markets.[70]

Lands' End has adapted regionally from a direct-mail catalog to having a presence both online and in retail stores.

As such, firms may focus less on truly global markets and more on regional adaptation. Although parallel developments in the Internet and mobile telecommunication facilitate communications across the globe, as noted earlier, the implementation of Web-based strategies also requires local adaptation.

The globalization of businesses with local strategies is demonstrated by the online operation of Lands' End, Inc., which uses local Internet portals to offer its products for sale. Lands' End, formerly a direct-mail catalog business and now a part of Sears, Roebuck and Co., launched the Web-based portion of its business in 1995. The firm established Web sites in the United Kingdom and Germany in 1999 and in France, Italy, and Ireland in 2000 prior to initiating a catalog business in those countries. With word-of-mouth and limited online advertising, a Web site business can be built in a foreign country without a lot of initial marketing expenses. After the online business becomes large enough, a catalog business can be launched with mailings targeted to customers who have used the business online. Thus, even smaller companies can sell their goods and services globally when facilitated by electronic infrastructure without having significant (brick-and-mortar) facilities outside of their home location. Lands' End and other retailers are going further by creating personal customization for fitting apparel sizes over the Internet. Service can be enhanced by being able to order online and pick up at a store. Even with custom ordering systems, significant local adaptation is still needed in each country or region.[71]

Regionalization

Regionalization is a second trend that has become more common in global markets. Because a firm's location can affect its strategic competitiveness,[72] it must decide whether to compete in all or many global markets, or to focus on a particular region or regions. Competing in all markets provides economies that can be achieved because of the combined market size. Research suggests that firms that compete in risky emerging markets can also have higher performance.[73]

However, a firm that competes in industries where the international markets differ greatly (in which it must employ a multidomestic strategy) may wish to narrow its focus to a particular region of the world. In so doing, it can better understand the cultures, legal and social norms, and other factors that are important for effective competition in those markets. For example, a firm may focus on Far East markets only rather than competing simultaneously in the Middle East, Europe, and the Far East. Or the firm may choose a region of the world where the markets are more similar and some coordination and sharing of resources would be possible. In this way, the firm may be able not only to better understand the markets in which it competes, but also to achieve some economies, even though it may have to employ a multidomestic strategy. For instance, research suggests that most large retailers are better at focusing on a particular region rather than being truly global.[74] Firms commonly focus much of their international market entries into countries adjacent to their home country, which might be referred to as their home region.[75]

Countries that develop trade agreements to increase the economic power of their regions may promote regional strategies. The European Union (EU) and South America's Organization of American States (OAS) are country associations that developed trade agreements to promote the flow of trade across country boundaries within their respective regions.[76] Many European firms acquire and integrate their businesses in Europe to better coordinate pan-European brands as the EU creates more unity in European markets. With this process likely to continue as new countries are added to the agreement, some international firms may prefer to pursue regional strategies versus global strategies because the size of the market is increasing.[77]

The North American Free Trade Agreement (NAFTA), signed by the United States, Canada, and Mexico, facilitates free trade across country borders in North America. NAFTA loosens restrictions on international strategies within this region and provides greater opportunity for regional international strategies. NAFTA does not exist for the sole purpose of U.S. businesses moving across its borders. In fact, Mexico is the number two trading partner of the United States, and NAFTA greatly increased Mexico's exports to the United States. Research suggests that managers of small and medium-sized firms are influenced by the strategy they implement (those with a differentiation strategy are more positively disposed to the agreement than are those pursuing a cost leadership strategy) and by their experience and rivalry with exporting firms.[78]

Most firms enter regional markets sequentially, beginning in markets with which they are more familiar. They also introduce their largest and strongest lines of business into these markets first, followed by their other lines of business once the first lines achieve success. They also usually invest in the same area as their original investment location.[79]

After the firm selects its international strategies and decides whether to employ them in regional or world markets, it must choose a market entry mode.[80]

Choice of International Entry Mode

International expansion is accomplished by exporting products, participating in licensing arrangements, forming strategic alliances, making acquisitions, and establishing new wholly owned subsidiaries. These means of entering international markets and their characteristics are shown in Table 8.1. Each means of market entry has its advantages and disadvantages. Thus, choosing the appropriate mode or path to enter international markets affects the firm's performance in those markets.[81]

Table 8.1 Global Market Entry: Choice of Entry

Type of Entry	Characteristics
Exporting	High cost, low control
Licensing	Low cost, low risk, little control, low returns
Strategic alliances	Shared costs, shared resources, shared risks, problems of integration (e.g., two corporate cultures)
Acquisition	Quick access to new market, high cost, complex negotiations, problems of merging with domestic operations
New wholly owned subsidiary	Complex, often costly, time consuming, high risk, maximum control, potential above-average returns

Exporting

Many industrial firms begin their international expansion by exporting goods or services to other countries.[82] Exporting does not require the expense of establishing operations in the host countries, but exporters must establish some means of marketing and distributing their products. Usually, exporting firms develop contractual arrangements with host-country firms.

The disadvantages of exporting include the often high costs of transportation and tariffs placed on some incoming goods. Furthermore, the exporter has less control over the marketing and distribution of its products in the host country and must either pay the distributor or allow the distributor to add to the price to recoup its costs and earn a profit.[83] As a result, it may be difficult to market a competitive product through exporting or to provide a product that is customized to each international market.[84] However, evidence suggests that cost leadership strategies enhance the performance of exports in developed countries, whereas differentiation strategies are more successful in emerging economies.[85]

Firms export mostly to countries that are closest to their facilities because of the lower transportation costs and the usually greater similarity between geographic neighbors. For example, U.S. NAFTA partners Mexico and Canada account for more than half of the goods exported from Texas. The Internet has also made exporting easier, as illustrated by the Lands' End system described earlier.[86] Even small firms can access critical information about foreign markets, examine a target market, research the competition, and find lists of potential customers.[87] Governments also use the Internet to facilitate applications for export and import licenses. Although the terrorist threat is likely to slow its progress, high-speed technology is still the wave of the future.[88]

Small businesses are most likely to use the exporting mode of international entry.[89] Currency exchange rates are one of the most significant problems small businesses face. The Bush administration has supported a weak dollar against the euro, which makes imports to the United States more expensive to U.S. consumers and U.S. goods less costly to foreign buyers, thus providing some economic relief for U.S. exporters.[90]

Licensing

Licensing is an increasingly common form of organizational network, particularly among smaller firms.[91] A licensing arrangement allows a foreign company to purchase the right to manufacture and sell the firm's products within a host country or set of countries.[92] The licensor is normally paid a royalty on each unit produced and sold. The licensee takes the risks and makes the monetary investments in facilities for manufacturing, marketing, and distributing the goods or services. As a result, licensing is possibly the least costly form of international expansion.

China is a large and growing market for cigarettes, while the U.S. market is shrinking due to health concerns. But U.S. cigarette firms have had trouble entering the Chinese market because state-owned tobacco firms have lobbied against such entry. As such, cigarette firms such as Altria Group, parent company of Philip Morris International, had an incentive to form a deal with these state-owned firms. Such an agreement provides the state-owned firms access to the most famous brand in the world, Marlboro. Accordingly, both the Chinese firms and Philip Morris have formed a licensing agreement to take advantage of the opportunity as China opens its markets more fully.[93] Because it is a licensing agreement rather than a foreign direct investment by Philip Morris, China maintains control of the distribution.

Licensing is also a way to expand returns based on prior innovations.[94] Even if product life cycles are short, licensing may be a useful tool. For instance, because the toy industry faces relentless change and an unpredictable buying public, licensing is used and contracts are often completed in foreign markets where labor may be less expensive.[95] The Sesame Street Workshop, creator of the Muppet figures, has created a large business by licensing figures such as Elmo, Snuffleupagus, and the Count to Target and other specialty stores focused on apparel for "a previously untapped teen/adult market."[96]

Licensing also has disadvantages. For example, it gives the firm little control over the manufacture and marketing of its products in other countries. Thus, license deals must be structured properly.[97] In addition, licensing provides the least potential returns, because returns must be shared between the licensor and the licensee. Additionally, the international firm may learn the technology and produce and sell a similar competitive product after the license expires. Komatsu, for example, first licensed much of its technology from International Harvester, Bucyrus-Erie, and Cummins Engine to compete against Caterpillar in the earthmoving equipment business. Komatsu then dropped these licenses and developed its own products using the technology it had gained from the U.S. companies.[98] Marriott International Inc. has achieved distinction as a franchise licensor of hotel chains. By the middle of 2007, Marriott operated or franchised almost 2,900 lodging properties in the United States and 67 other countries.[99] However, Marriott owns less than 3 percent of the properties, unlike Hilton and Starwood (St. Regis, Sheraton, and Westin hotel chains), which own more than 30 percent. Although Marriott has used franchise licensing successfully, if a firm wants to move to a different ownership arrangement, licensing may create some inflexibility. Thus, it is important that a firm think ahead and consider sequential forms of entry in international markets.[100]

Marriott Hotels, which operates as a franchise licensor, has many hotel properties all over the world but fully owns less than 5 percent of these properties.

© AP Photo/Mark Lennihan

Strategic Alliances

In recent years, strategic alliances have become a popular means of international expansion.[101] Strategic alliances allow firms to share the risks and the resources required to enter international markets.[102] Moreover, strategic alliances can facilitate the development of new core competencies that contribute to the firm's future strategic competitiveness.[103]

As explained in the Opening Case and the recent Strategic Focus, GM formed a joint venture with SAIC to produce Buick and Cadillac autos for the Chinese market. The alliance has been highly successful for both firms. Similar to this example, most international strategic alliances are formed with a host-country firm that knows and understands the competitive conditions, legal and social norms, and cultural idiosyncrasies of the country, which helps the expanding firm manufacture and market a competitive product. Often, firms in emerging economies want to form international alliances and ventures to gain access to sophisticated technologies that are new to them. Gaining access to new technologies was one of SAIC's goals in the alliance with GM. This type of arrangement can benefit the non-emerging economy firm as well, in that it gains access to a new market and doesn't have to pay tariffs to do so (because it is partnering with a local company).[104] In return, the host-country firm may find its new access to the expanding firm's technology and innovative products attractive.

Each partner in an alliance brings knowledge or resources to the partnership.[105] Indeed, partners often enter an alliance with the purpose of learning new capabilities. Common among those desired capabilities are technological skills. However, for technological knowledge to be transferred in an alliance usually requires trust between the partners.[106] Managing these expectations can facilitate improved performance.

The alliance between GM and SAIC has been successful over the years because of the way it was managed. In fact, both firms are pleased with the outcomes. Research suggests that company executives need to know their own firm well, understand factors that determine the norms in different countries, know how the firm is seen by other partners in the venture, and learn to adapt while remaining consistent with their own company cultural values. Such a multifaceted and versatile approach has helped the GM and SAIC alliance succeed.

Not all alliances are successful; in fact, many fail.[107] The primary reasons for failure include incompatible partners and conflict between the partners.[108] International strategic alliances are especially difficult to manage.[109] Several factors may cause a relationship to sour. Trust between the partners is critical and is affected by at least four fundamental issues: the initial condition of the relationship, the negotiation process to arrive at an agreement, partner interactions, and external events.[110] Trust is also influenced by the country cultures involved in the alliance or joint venture.[111]

Research has shown that equity-based alliances, over which a firm has more control, tend to produce more positive returns.[112] (Strategic alliances are discussed in greater depth in Chapter 9.) However, if trust is required to develop new capabilities in a research collaboration, equity can serve as a barrier to the necessary relationship building.[113] If conflict in a strategic alliance or joint venture is not manageable, an acquisition may be a better option.[114] Research suggests that alliances are more favorable in the face of high uncertainty and where cooperation is needed to share knowledge between partners and where strategic flexibility is important, such as with small and medium-sized firms.[115] Acquisitions are better in situations with less need for strategic flexibility and when the transaction is used to maintain economies of scale or scope.[116] Alliances can also lead to an acquisition, which is discussed next.

Acquisitions

As free trade has continued to expand in global markets, cross-border acquisitions have also been increasing significantly. In recent years, cross-border acquisitions have comprised more than 45 percent of all acquisitions completed worldwide.[117] As explained in Chapter 7, acquisitions can provide quick access to a new market. In fact, acquisitions often provide the fastest and the largest initial international expansion of any of the alternatives.[118] Thus, entry is much quicker than by other modes. For example, Wal-Mart entered Germany and the United Kingdom by acquiring local firms. Later, Wal-Mart withdrew from Germany.[119] Also, acquisitions are the mode used by many firms to enter Eastern European markets.

Although acquisitions have become a popular mode of entering international markets, they are not without costs. International acquisitions carry some of the disadvantages of domestic acquisitions (also see Chapter 7). In addition, they can be expensive and also often require debt financing, which carries an extra cost. International negotiations for acquisitions can be exceedingly complex and are generally more complicated than domestic acquisitions. For example, it is estimated that only 20 percent of cross-border bids lead to a completed acquisition, compared with 40 percent of bids for domestic acquisitions.[120]

Interestingly, acquirers make fewer acquisitions in countries with significant corruption. In fact, when they do acquire firms in such countries, acquirers commonly pay smaller premiums to buy the target firms.[121]

Dealing with the legal and regulatory requirements in the target firm's country and obtaining appropriate information to negotiate an agreement frequently present significant problems. Finally, the problems of merging the new firm into the acquiring firm often are more complex than in domestic acquisitions. The acquiring firm must deal not only with different corporate cultures, but also with potentially different social cultures and practices.[122] These differences make the integration of the two firms after the acquisition more challenging; it is difficult to capture the potential synergy when integration is slowed or stymied because of cultural differences.[123] Therefore, while international acquisitions have been popular because of the rapid access to new markets they provide, they also carry with them important costs and multiple risks.

As explained in the Opening Case, SAIC, a China-based automobile producer, acquired assets of the MG Rover Group, a historic British auto producer, which was in insolvency at the time. This acquisition gave the Chinese firm an entry point into Europe and an opportunity to establish its own brand through the MG Rover label. SAIC previously considered a joint venture but decided to make the acquisition bid, worth $104 million.[124] However, SAIC experienced formidable government opposition in the United Kingdom and had to clear extra regulatory hurdles to receive approval.

New Wholly Owned Subsidiary

The establishment of a new wholly owned subsidiary is referred to as a **greenfield venture.**

The establishment of a new wholly owned subsidiary is referred to as a **greenfield venture**. The process of creating such ventures is often complex and potentially costly, but it affords maximum control to the firm and has the most potential to provide above-average returns. This potential is especially true of firms with strong intangible capabilities that might be leveraged through a greenfield venture.[125] A firm maintains full control of its operations with a greenfield venture. More control is especially advantageous if the firm has proprietary technology. Research also suggests that "wholly owned subsidiaries and expatriate staff are preferred" in service industries where "close contacts with end customers" and "high levels of professional skills, specialized know-how, and customization" are required.[126] Other research suggests that greenfield investments are more prominent where physical capital-intensive plants are planned and that acquisitions are more likely preferred when a firm is human capital intensive—that is, where a strong local degree of unionization and high cultural distance would cause difficulty in transferring knowledge to a host nation through a greenfield approach.[127]

The risks are also high, however, because of the costs of establishing a new business operation in a new country. The firm may have to acquire the knowledge and expertise of the existing market by hiring either host-country nationals, possibly from competitors, or consultants, which can be costly. Still, the firm maintains control over the technology, marketing, and distribution of its products.[128] Furthermore, the company must build new manufacturing facilities, establish distribution networks, and learn and implement appropriate marketing strategies to compete in the new market.[129] Research also suggests that when the country risk is high, firms prefer to enter with joint ventures instead of greenfield investments in order to manage the risk. However, if they have previous experience in a country, they prefer to use a wholly owned greenfield venture rather than a joint venture.[130]

The globalization of the air cargo industry has implications for companies such as UPS and FedEx. The impact of this globalization is especially pertinent to the China and the Asia Pacific region. China's air cargo market is expected to grow 11 percent per year through 2023. Accordingly, both UPS and FedEx recently opened new hub operations in Shanghai and Hangzhou, respectively. FedEx opened its Hangzhou subsidiary in late May 2007 serving more than 200 cities throughout China and connecting businesses in China with others across the globe. Almost concurrently, UPS started construction of its

Has the Largest Automaker in the World Made Mistakes with Its International Strategy?

In 2007, three years ahead of its goal, Toyota became the largest automaker in the world. Toyota sold 2.35 million vehicles in the first quarter of 2007, 900,000 more than General Motors. It was the first time in many years that a company other than GM had sold the most vehicles in any one time period. Many analysts praised the automaker for accomplishing its goal. Toyota has many positive attributes. The Toyota brand has come to mean reliability at an affordable price. Furthermore, while sales of Toyota vehicles have leveled off in Europe due to European Union policies designed to limit sales of Toyota products, the company plans to build five more large assembly plants in North America by 2016. That would bring Toyota's total to 13 plants and 50,000 employees in North America.

Though Toyota is now manufacturing and selling its larger automobiles in China—as well as its new hybrid Prius—it is still only third in automobile sales in China behind VW and GM.

Toyota first entered the Chinese market with exported cars built in Japan in the 1960s. Interestingly, it did not begin manufacturing autos in China for the Chinese market until 2002, 10 years after Volkswagen did. The two leaders in the Chinese auto market are VW and GM. Toyota built manufacturing facilities in China as a part of a joint venture with FAW China. Toyota began pushing the sales of a small, modestly priced auto, the Vios, a similar strategy used for many emerging economy countries. Although its initial sales were positive, they weakened as Chinese customers seemed more interested in luxury cars. However, Toyota rebounded quickly with the introduction in 2006 of the Camry, a popular auto in many international markets. Its sales reached 150,000 units in 2007. Toyota also formed other joint ventures in China, such as one with Guangzhou Automotive Group to manufacture engines. Still Toyota must build its brand name in China and also has to fend off anti-Japanese sentiment left over from Japanese government's actions in World War II. For these reasons and its late start, it has a large gap in sales to overtake the market leaders.

Toyota is also experiencing some problems in other international markets. For example, in North America, the number of recalls of its vehicles has tripled in recent years. And customer satisfaction has declined with the J.D. Powers ratings listing Toyota 28th out of 36 in customer experience. Analysts suggest that the reason for these outcomes is Toyota's relentless pressure to increase sales, sometimes at the expense of customer satisfaction. Because of these problems, Toyota has begun a new program in North America named EM^2, Everything Matters Exponentially. The emphasis is on improving product planning, customer service, sales and marketing, along with the car dealerships.

China's major international initiative in the 2000s has been the Chinese market. Thus, it may have "taken its eye off of the North American market a little. However, it cannot afford to slip in the lucrative North American market while it fights for market share in China. Thus, it will be interesting to observe whether Toyota can regain its customer satisfaction in North America, continue to build market share there, and make gains in the Chinese market simultaneously.

Sources: 2007, Toyota, *Hoover's Company Information*, Hoover's, Inc.; D. Welch, 2007, Staying paranoid at Toyota: Fearful of "big-company disease," the No. 1 carmaker keeps scrambling to retool itself, *BusinessWeek*, July 02, 80; R. Regassa & A. Ahmadian, 2007, Comparative study of American and Japanese auto industry: General Motors versus Toyota Motors Corporations, *The Business Review, Cambridge*, Summer, 8(1): 1–11; A. Chozick, 2007, Japan's auto giants steer toward China; Toyota, Nissan, Honda refocus their efforts as U.S. demand slows, *Wall Street Journal*, May 16, A 12; M. Zimmerman, 2007, Autos; Toyota ends GM's reign as car sales leader, *Los Angeles Times*, April 25, C.1; G. Dyer & D. Pilling, 2007, Toyota: Ready to accelerate the Chinese market, *Financial Times*, April 23, 22; M. Dickerson, 2007, Global capital; Picking up steam in Mexico; Japanese automakers are gaining on their U.S. counterparts in what is becoming a key market, *Los Angeles Times*, April 21, C.1; N. Shirouzu, 2006, Toyota speeds up push to expand in China, India; Strategy takes aim at emerging markets with low-cost cars, *Wall Street Journal Asia*, November 13, 1.

new Shanghai subsidiary offices in August 2007. In the five years prior to the establishment of its Shanghai operations, UPS had invested approximately $600 million in China. These investments are wholly owned because these firms need to maintain the integrity of their IT and logistics systems in order to maximize efficiency. Greenfield ventures also help the firms to maintain the proprietary nature of their systems.[131]

Globalization has resulted in UPS signing agreements to open a new hub operation in China. Construction began on the first UPS subsidiary in Shanghai in August of 2007.

© AP Photo/Eugene Hoshiko

As explained in the Strategic Focus, Toyota has become the largest automaker in the world. Its success is because of many positive actions including entry into and effective competition in international markets such as those in Europe and North America. Yet, while it was an early foreign entrant into the Chinese market with exports, it was late to build manufacturing facilities in China. It formed a joint venture with a Chinese firm to manufacture autos in China. It had been reluctant to manufacture cars in China for several reasons. Importantly it wanted to protect its technology and manufacturing processes from falling into the hands of Chinese competitors. Because of its reluctance, Toyota has allowed Volkswagen and General Motors to become the market leaders in the Chinese market. And Toyota faces an uphill battle to gain significant market share in this market. Since 2000, Toyota has invested significant financial resources and effort in China, but doing so may be partly responsible for its problems with quality and customer satisfaction declines in the North American market. Toyota's experiences suggest that operating in international markets can be a substantial challenge, even for a resourceful and powerful multinational company.

Dynamics of Mode of Entry

A firm's choice of mode of entry into international markets is affected by a number of factors.[132] Initially, market entry is often achieved through export, which requires no foreign manufacturing expertise and investment only in distribution. Licensing can facilitate the product improvements necessary to enter foreign markets, as in the Komatsu example. Strategic alliances have been popular because they allow a firm to connect with an experienced partner already in the targeted market. Strategic alliances also reduce risk through the sharing of costs. Therefore, all three modes—export, licensing, and strategic alliance—are good tactics for early market development. Also, the strategic alliance is often used in more uncertain situations, such as an emerging economy where there is significant risk, such as Colombia.[133] However, if intellectual property rights in the emerging economy are not well protected, the number of firms in the industry is growing fast, and the need for global integration is high, the wholly owned subsidiary entry mode is preferred.[134]

To secure a stronger presence in international markets, acquisitions or greenfield ventures may be required. Large aerospace firms Airbus and Boeing have used joint ventures, while military equipment firms such as Thales SA have used acquisitions to build a global presence.[135] Japanese auto manufacturers, such as Toyota, have gained a presence in the United States through both greenfield ventures and joint ventures.[136] Because of Toyota's highly efficient manufacturing process, it wants to maintain control over its auto manufacturing where possible. It has engaged in a joint venture in the United States, but most of its manufacturing facilities are greenfield investments. Therefore, Toyota uses some form of foreign direct investment (e.g., greenfield ventures, joint ventures) rather than another mode of entry (although it may use exporting early in new markets as it did in China). Both acquisitions and greenfield ventures are likely to come at later stages in the development of an international strategy. In addition, both strategies tend to be more successful when the firm making the investment possesses valuable core competencies.[137] Large diversified business groups, often found in emerging economies, not only gain resources through diversification but also have specialized abilities in managing differences in inward and outward flows of foreign direct investment.[138] Multinational firms can engage in substantial competitive rivalry in international markets as evidenced by the battles for market share among GM, Toyota, and VW in China.[139]

Thus, to enter a global market, a firm selects the entry mode that is best suited to the situation at hand. In some instances, the various options will be followed sequentially, beginning with exporting and ending with greenfield ventures. In other cases, the firm may use several, but not all, of the different entry modes, each in different markets. The decision regarding which entry mode to use is primarily a result of the industry's competitive conditions, the country's situation and government policies, and the firm's unique set of resources, capabilities, and core competencies.

Strategic Competitive Outcomes

After its international strategy and mode of entry have been selected, the firm turns its attention to implementation issues (see Chapter 11). Implementation is highly important, because international expansion is risky, making it difficult to achieve a competitive advantage (see Figure 8.1 on p. 213). The probability the firm will be successful with an international strategy increases when it is effectively implemented.

International Diversification and Returns

International diversification is a strategy through which a firm expands the sales of its goods or services across the borders of global regions and countries into different geographic locations or markets.

Firms have numerous reasons to diversify internationally.[140] **International diversification** is a strategy through which a firm expands the sales of its goods or services across the borders of global regions and countries into different geographic locations or markets. Because of its potential advantages, international diversification should be related positively to firms' returns. Research has shown that, as international diversification increases, firms' returns decrease initially but then increase quickly as firms learn to manage international expansion.[141] In fact, the stock market is particularly sensitive to investments in international markets. Firms that are broadly diversified into multiple international markets usually achieve the most positive stock returns, especially when they diversify geographically into core business areas.[142] Many factors contribute to the positive effects of international diversification, such as potential economies of scale and experience, location advantages, increased market size, and the opportunity to stabilize returns. The stabilization of returns helps reduce a firm's overall risk.[143] All of these outcomes can be achieved by smaller and newer ventures, as well as by larger and established firms.

Toyota has found that international diversification allows it to better exploit its core competencies, because sharing knowledge resources across subsidiaries can produce synergy.[144] Also, a firm's returns may affect its decision to diversify internationally. For example, poor returns in a domestic market may encourage a firm to expand internationally in order to enhance its profit potential. In addition, internationally diversified firms may have access to more flexible labor markets, as the Japanese do in the United States, and may thereby benefit from scanning international markets for competition and market opportunities. Also, through global networks with assets in many countries, firms can develop more flexible structures to adjust to changes that might occur. "Offshore outsourcing" has created significant value-creation opportunities for firms engaged in it, especially as firms move into markets with more flexible labor markets. Furthermore, offshoring increases exports to firms that receive the offshoring contract.[145]

International Diversification and Innovation

In Chapter 1, we indicated that the development of new technology is at the heart of strategic competitiveness. As noted in Porter's model (see Figure 8.2 on p. 218), a nation's competitiveness depends, in part, on the capacity of its industry to innovate. Eventually and inevitably, competitors outperform firms that fail to innovate and improve their operations and products. Therefore, the only way to sustain a competitive advantage is to upgrade it continually.[146]

International diversification provides the potential for firms to achieve greater returns on their innovations (through larger or more numerous markets) and reduces the often substantial risks of R&D investments. Therefore, international diversification provides incentives for firms to innovate. Additionally, the firm uses its primary resources and capabilities to diversify internationally and thus earn further returns on these capabilities (e.g., capability to innovate).[147]

In addition, international diversification may be necessary to generate the resources required to sustain a large-scale R&D operation. An environment of rapid technological obsolescence makes it difficult to invest in new technology and the capital-intensive operations necessary to compete in this environment. Firms operating solely in domestic markets may find such investments difficult because of the length of time required to recoup the original investment. If the time is extended, it may not be possible to recover the investment before the technology becomes obsolete.[148] However, international diversification improves a firm's ability to appropriate additional returns from innovation before competitors can overcome the initial competitive advantage created by the innovation. In addition, firms moving into international markets are exposed to new products and processes. If they learn about those products and processes and integrate this knowledge into their operations, further innovation can be developed. To incorporate the learning into their own R&D processes, firms must manage those processes effectively in order to absorb and use the new knowledge to create further innovations.[149]

The relationship among international diversification, innovation, and returns is complex. Some level of performance is necessary to provide the resources to generate international diversification, which in turn provides incentives and resources to invest in research and development. The latter, if done appropriately, should enhance the returns of the firm, which then provides more resources for continued international diversification and investment in R&D.[150]

Because of the potential positive effects of international diversification on performance and innovation, such diversification may even enhance returns in product-diversified firms. International diversification increases market potential in each of these firms' product lines, but the complexity of managing a firm that is both product-diversified and internationally diversified is significant. Research indicates that media firms gain from both product and geographic diversification. However, international diversification often contributes more than product diversification for firms in developed countries.[151] Research also suggests that firms in less developed countries gain more from being product-diversified than firms in developed countries, especially when partnering with multinational firms from a more developed country that desire to enter less developed country markets. [152]

Evidence suggests that more culturally diverse top management teams often have a greater knowledge of international markets and their idiosyncrasies.[153] (Top management teams are discussed further in Chapter 12.) Moreover, an in-depth understanding of diverse markets among top-level managers facilitates intrafirm coordination and the use of long-term, strategically relevant criteria to evaluate the performance of managers and their units.[154] In turn, this approach facilitates improved innovation and performance. [155]

Complexity of Managing Multinational Firms

Although firms can realize many benefits by implementing an international strategy, doing so is complex and can produce greater uncertainty.[156] For example, multiple risks are involved when a firm operates in several different countries. Firms can grow only so large and diverse before becoming unmanageable, or before the costs of managing them exceed their benefits.[157] Managers are constrained by the complexity and sometimes by the culture and institutional systems within which they must operate.[158] The complexities involved in managing diverse international operations are shown in the problems experienced by even high-performing firms such as Toyota. The Strategic Focus explains that Toyota became overly focused on sales in the North American market and began to experience quality problems (i.e., increased number of recalls) and reduced customer satisfaction. It also was late in entering the Chinese market with manufacturing and as a result, it is now behind the market leaders, VW and GM (in the Chinese market).[159] Other complexities include the highly competitive nature of global markets, multiple cultural environments, potentially rapid shifts in the value of different currencies, and the instability of some national governments.

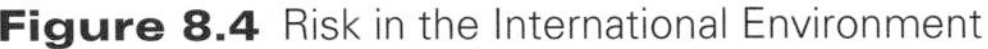

Risks in an International Environment

International diversification carries multiple risks.[160] Because of these risks, international expansion is difficult to implement and manage. The chief risks are political and economic. Specific examples of political and economic risks are shown in Figure 8.4.

Figure 8.4 Risk in the International Environment

Political Risks
- War in Iraq and Afghanistan following the September 11, 2001, terrorist attacks
- Continual warfare between the Palestinians and Israel
- Potential of war between Pakistan and India
- Potential of integration between North and South Korea

Economic Risks
- Failure of the Argentine economy and devaluation of the peso
- Challenges for China in implementing the World Trade Organization agreements
- The proposed constitution as well as entry of new countries into the European Union strengthening the euro currency and uniting Europe more tightly with existing and new partner countries
- Success of privatization and firm restructuring among Eastern European countries

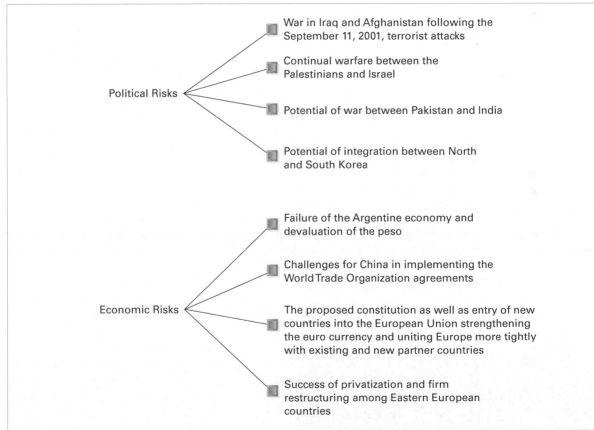

Sources: 2003, Finance and economics: The perils of convergence; Economics focus, *The Economist,* April 5, 71; K. D. Brouthers, 2003, Institutional, cultural and transaction cost influences on entry mode choice and performance, *Journal of International Business Studies,* 33: 203–221; F. Bruni, 2003, With a constitution to ponder, Europeans gather in Greece, *New York Times,* http://www.nytimes.com, June 20; B. Davis, R. Buckman, & C. Rhoads, 2003, A global journal report: For global economy, much rides on how the U. S. war plays out, *Wall Street Journal,* March 20, A1; J. Flint, 2003, China: How big, how fast, how dangerous? *Forbes,* http://www.forbes.com, July 1; G. A. Fowler, 2003, Copies 'R' Us—Pirates in China move fast to pilfer toy makers' ideas, *Wall Street Journal,* January 31, B1; W. Rugg, 2003, A down dollar's lure—and peril, *BusinessWeek Online,* http://www.businessweek.com, May 22; J. H. Zhao, S. H. Kim, & J. Du, 2003, The impact of corruption and transparency on foreign direct investment: An empirical analysis, *Management International Review,* 43(1): 41–62.

Political Risks

Political risks are risks related to instability in national governments and to war, both civil and international. Instability in a national government creates numerous problems, including economic risks and uncertainty created by government regulation; the existence of many, possibly conflicting, legal authorities or corruption; and the potential nationalization of private assets.[161] Foreign firms that invest in another country may have concerns about the stability of the national government and the effects of unrest and government instability on their investments or assets.[162]

Russia has experienced a relatively high level of institutional instability in the years following its revolutionary transition to a more democratic government. Decentralized political control and frequent changes in policies created chaos for many, but especially for those in the business landscape. In an effort to regain more central control and reduce the chaos, Russian leaders took actions such as prosecuting powerful private firm executives, seeking to gain state control of firm assets, and not approving some foreign acquisitions of Russian businesses. The initial institutional instability, followed by the actions of the central government, caused some firms delay or negated significant foreign direct investment in Russia. Although Vladimir Putin, Russia's president, tried to reassure potential investors about their property rights, prior actions, and the fact that other laws (e.g., environmental and employee laws) are weak, many Russian firms keep double books to hide information from tax collectors and the mafia, and the fact that government corruption is common makes firms leery of investing in Russia.[163]

Economic Risks

As illustrated in the example of Russian institutional instability and property rights, economic risks are interdependent with political risks. If firms cannot protect their intellectual property, they are highly unlikely to make foreign direct investments. Countries therefore need to create and sustain strong intellectual property rights and enforce them in order to attract desired foreign direct investment. Another economic risk is the security risk posed by terrorists. For instance, concerns about terrorism in Indonesia have kept firms from investing in the Indonesian economy. Although many foreign investors in the energy and mining sectors have kept their investments in Indonesia through political and economic instability, the nation needs new investors to sustain economic growth. Indonesia has difficulty competing for investment against the comparatively faster growth in China and India, which have fewer security risks.[164]

As noted earlier, foremost among the economic risks of international diversification are the differences and fluctuations in the value of different currencies.[165] The value of the dollar relative to other currencies determines the value of the international assets and earnings of U.S. firms; for example, an increase in the value of the U.S. dollar can reduce the value of U.S. multinational firms' international assets and earnings in other countries. Furthermore, the value of different currencies can also, at times, dramatically affect a firm's competitiveness in global markets because of its effect on the prices of goods manufactured in different countries.[166] An increase in the value of the dollar can harm U.S. firms' exports to international markets because of the price differential of the products. Thus, government oversight and control of economic and financial capital in the country affect not only local economic activity but also foreign investments in the country.[167]

eBay reenters the Chinese market in a joint venture with a Chinese partner, Tom Online Inc.

© AP Photo/Color China Photo

eBay is the market leader in the Internet auction markets in the United States and Europe. However, its expansion to Asian countries has experienced difficulties. As noted earlier, its first ventures into the Japanese and Chinese markets failed and they withdrew. In 2007, Meg Whitman, CEO of eBay, announced that the company planned to reenter the Chinese market with a new partner. It learned from its previous failure and is entering with tighter restrictions to stop the sales of counterfeit goods through eBay's service. So the firm is taking actions to assure trust and safety in the sale and purchase of goods through eBay in the Chinese market.[168]

Limits to International Expansion: Management Problems

After learning how to operate effectively in international markets, firms tend to earn positive returns on international diversification. But, the returns often level off and become negative as the diversification increases past some point.[169] Several reasons explain the limits to the positive effects of international diversification. First, greater geographic dispersion across country borders increases the costs of coordination between units and the distribution of products. Second, trade barriers, logistical costs, cultural diversity, and other differences by country (e.g., access to raw materials and different employee skill levels) greatly complicate the implementation of an international diversification strategy.[170]

Institutional and cultural factors can present strong barriers to the transfer of a firm's competitive advantages from one country to another.[171] Marketing programs often have to be redesigned and new distribution networks established when firms expand into new countries. In addition, firms may encounter different labor costs and capital charges. In general, it is difficult to effectively implement, manage, and control a firm's international operations.[172]

The amount of international diversification that can be managed varies from firm to firm and according to the abilities of each firm's managers. The problems of central coordination and integration are mitigated if the firm diversifies into more friendly countries that are geographically close and have cultures similar to its own country's culture. In that case, the firm is likely to encounter fewer trade barriers, the laws and customs are better understood, and the product is easier to adapt to local markets.[173] For example, U.S. firms may find it less difficult to expand their operations into Mexico, Canada, and Western European countries than into Asian countries.

Companies also do not generally accept poor returns from international expansion. If they experience poor returns, they usually try to change the structure or management approaches to enhance the returns received on foreign investments. For example, IBM reorganized and changed its structure from a multidomestic to a transnational approach. In doing so, it created a more "seamless" organization, allowing it to capitalize on its core competencies.

Management must also be concerned with the relationship between the host government and the multinational corporation.[174] Although government policy and regulations are often barriers, many firms, such as Toyota and General Motors, have turned to strategic alliances, as they did in China, to overcome those barriers. By forming interorganizational networks, such as strategic alliances (see Chapter 9), firms can share resources and risks but also build flexibility. However, large networks can be difficult to manage.[175]

Summary

- The use of international strategies is increasing. Traditional motives include extending the product life cycle, securing key resources, and having access to low-cost labor. Emerging motives include the integration of the Internet and mobile telecommunications, which facilitates global transactions. Also, firms experience increased pressure for global integration as the demand for commodities becomes borderless, and yet they feel simultaneous pressure for local country responsiveness.
- An international strategy is commonly designed primarily to capitalize on four benefits: increased market size; earning a return on large investments; economies of scale and learning; and advantages of location.

- International business-level strategies are usually grounded in one or more home-country advantages, as Porter's model suggests. Porter's model emphasizes four determinants: factors of production; demand conditions; related and supporting industries; and patterns of firm strategy, structure, and rivalry.
- There are three types of international corporate-level strategies. A multidomestic strategy focuses on competition within each country in which the firm competes. Firms using a multidomestic strategy decentralize strategic and operating decisions to the business units operating in each country, so that each unit can tailor its goods and services to the local market. A global strategy assumes more standardization of products across country boundaries; therefore, competitive strategy is centralized and controlled by the home office. A transnational strategy seeks to integrate characteristics of both multidomestic and global strategies to emphasize both local responsiveness and global integration and coordination. This strategy is difficult to implement, requiring an integrated network and a culture of individual commitment.
- Although the transnational strategy's implementation is a challenge, environmental trends are causing many multinational firms to consider the need for both global efficiency and local responsiveness. Many large multinational firms, particularly those with many diverse products, use a multidomestic strategy with some product lines and a global strategy with others.
- The threat of wars and terrorist attacks increase the risks and costs of international strategies. Furthermore, research suggests that the liability of foreignness is more difficult to overcome than once thought.
- Some firms decide to compete only in certain regions of the world, as opposed to viewing all markets in the world as potential opportunities. Competing in regional markets allows firms and managers to focus their learning on specific markets, cultures, locations, resources, and other factors.
- Firms may enter international markets in one of several ways, including exporting, licensing, forming strategic alliances, making acquisitions, and establishing new wholly owned subsidiaries, often referred to as greenfield ventures. Most firms begin with exporting or licensing, because of their lower costs and risks, but later they might use strategic alliances and acquisitions to expand internationally. The most expensive and risky means of entering a new international market is through the establishment of a new wholly owned subsidiary. On the other hand, such subsidiaries provide the advantages of maximum control by the firm and, if it is successful, the greatest returns.
- International diversification facilitates innovation in a firm, because it provides a larger market to gain more and faster returns from investments in innovation. In addition, international diversification may generate the resources necessary to sustain a large-scale R&D program.
- In general, international diversification is related to above average returns, but this assumes that the diversification is effectively implemented and that the firm's international operations are well managed. International diversification provides greater economies of scope and learning, which, along with greater innovation, help produce above-average returns.
- Several risks are involved with managing multinational operations. Among these are political risks (e.g., instability of national governments) and economic risks (e.g., fluctuations in the value of a country's currency).
- Some limits also constrain the ability to manage international expansion effectively. International diversification increases coordination and distribution costs, and management problems are exacerbated by trade barriers, logistical costs, and cultural diversity, among other factors.

Review Questions

1. What are the traditional and emerging motives that cause firms to expand internationally?
2. What are the four primary benefits of an international strategy?
3. What four factors provide a basis for international business-level strategies?
4. What are the three international corporate-level strategies? How do they differ from each other? What factors lead to their development?
5. What environmental trends are affecting international strategy?
6. What five modes of international expansion are available, and what is the normal sequence of their use?
7. What is the relationship between international diversification and innovation? How does international diversification affect innovation? What is the effect of international diversification on a firm's returns?
8. What are the risks of international diversification? What are the challenges of managing multinational firms?

Experiential Exercises

Exercise 1: McDonald's: Global, Multicountry, or Transnational Strategy?

McDonald's is one of the world's best-known brands: The company has approximately 30,000 restaurants located in more than 100 countries and serves 47 million customers *every day*. McDonald's opened its first international restaurant in Japan in 1971. Its Golden Arches are featured prominently in two former bastions of communism: Puskin Square in Moscow and Tiananmen Square in Beijing, China. What strategy has McDonald's used to achieve such visibility? For this exercise, each group will be asked to conduct some background research on the firm and then make a brief presentation to identify the international strategy (i.e., global, multidomestic, or transnational) McDonald's is implementing.

Individual

Use the Internet to find examples of menu variations in different countries. How much do menu items differ for a McDonald's in the United States from other locations outside the United States?

Groups

Review the characteristics of global, multidomestic, and transnational strategies. Conduct additional research to assess what strategy best describes the one McDonald's is using. Prepare a flip chart with a single page of bullet points to explain your reasoning.

Whole Class

Each group should have 5–7 minutes to explain its reasoning. Following Q&A for each group, ask class members to vote for the respective strategy choices.

Exercise 2: Country Analysis

Black Canyon Coffee is a Bangkok-based company that operates a chain of coffee shops. Black Canyon differentiates itself from other coffee chains (e.g., Starbucks, Caribou, Gloria Jeans) by offering a broad menu of "fusion" Asian foods as well as a range of coffee products. Although the company operates primarily in Thailand, it has retail shops in a number of neighboring countries as well.

For this exercise, assume that you have been hired by the Black Canyon management team as consultants. Your group has been retained by management to conduct a preliminary review of several countries. The purpose of this review is to help prioritize the areas that are the most promising targets for international expansion.

Part One

Working in teams of 5–7 persons, select three countries from the following list:

Malaysia	Australia
Singapore	New Zealand
Cambodia	United Arab Emirates
Japan	Taiwan
Indonesia	Philippines

Conduct research on the selected countries for the following criteria:

Economic characteristics: Gross national product, wages, unemployment, inflation, and so on. Trend analysis of this data (e.g., are wages rising or falling, rate of change in wages, etc.) is preferable to single point-in-time snapshots.

Social characteristics: Life expectancy, education norms, income distributions, literacy, and so on.

Risk factors: Economic and political risk assessment.

The following Internet resources may be useful in your research:

- The Library of Congress has a collection of country studies.
- BBC News offers country profiles online.
- *The Economist* offers country profiles.
- Both the United Nations and International Monetary Fund provide statistics and research reports.
- The *CIA World Factbook* has profiles of different regions.
- The Global Entrepreneurship Monitor provides reports with detailed information about economic conditions and social aspects for a number of countries.
- Links can be found at http://www.countryrisk.com to a number of resources that assess both political and economic risk for individual countries.

Part Two

Based on your research, prepare a memorandum (3–4 pages, single-spaced, maximum) that compares and contrasts the attractiveness of the three countries you selected. In your report, include a bullet-point list of other topics that Black Canyon management should consider when evaluating its international expansion opportunities.

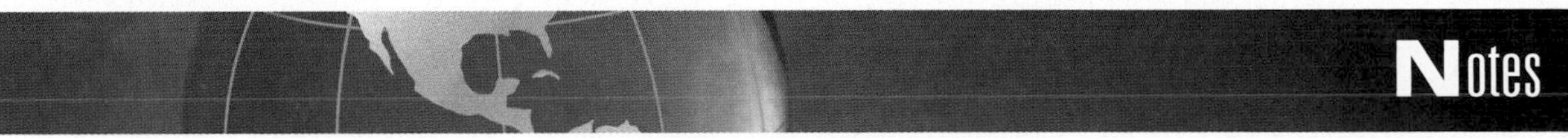

Notes

1. S. Li, 2005, Why a poor governance environment does not deter foreign direct investment: The case of China and its implications for investment protection, *Business Horizons*, 48(4): 297–302.
2. A. K. Gupta & H. Wang, 2007, How to get China and India right: Western companies need to become smarter—and they need to do it quickly, *Wall Street* Journal, April 28, R4.
3. H. J. Sapienza, E. Autio, G. George, & S. A. Zahra, 2006, A capabilities perspective on the effects of early internationalization on firm survival and growth, *Academy of Management Review*, 31: 914–933; W. P. Wan, 2005, Country resource environments, firm capabilities, and corporate diversification strategies. *Journal of Management Studies*, 42: 161–182.

4. F. T. Rothaermel, S. Kotha, & H. K. Steensma, 2006, International market entry by U.S. Internet firms: An empirical analysis of country risk, national culture and market size, *Journal of Management,* 32: 56–82; R. E. Hoskisson, H. Kim, R. E. White, & L. Tihanyi, 2004, A framework for understanding international diversification by business groups from emerging economies, in M. A. Hitt & J. L. C. Cheng (eds.), *Theories of the Multinational Enterprise: Diversity, Complexity, and Relevance. Advances in International Management*, Oxford, UK: Elsevier/JAI Press, 137–163.
5. M. Javidan, R. Steers, & M. A. Hitt (eds.), 2007, *The Global Mindset.* Oxford, UK: Elsevier Publishing; T. M. Begley & D. P. Boyd, 2003, The need for a corporate global mind-set, *MIT Sloan Management Review,* 44(2): 25–32.
6. M. A. Hitt, L. Tihanyi, T. Miller, & B. Connelly, 2006, International diversification: Antecedents, outcomes and moderators, *Journal of Management,* 32: 831–867; L. Tongll, E. J. Ping, & W. K. C. Chiu, 2005, International diversification and performance: Evidence from Singapore, *Asia Pacific Journal of Management* 22: 65–88.
7. Y. Luo & R. L. Tung, 2007, International expansion of emerging market enterprises: A springboard perspective, *Journal of International Business Studies* 38: 481–498; J. E. Ricart, M. J. Enright, P. Ghemawat, S. L. Hart, & T. Khanna, 2004, New frontiers in international strategy, *Journal of International Business Studies,* 35: 175–200.
8. R. Vernon, 1996, International investment and international trade in the product cycle, *Quarterly Journal of Economics,* 80: 190–207.
9. P. J. Buckley, L. J. Clegg, A. R. Cross, X. Liu, H. Voss, & P. Zheng, 2006, The determinants of Chinese outward foreign direct investment, *Journal of International Business Studies,* 38: 499–518.
10. L. Yu, 2003, The global-brand advantage, *MIT Sloan Management Review*, 44(3): 13.
11. IKEA, 2007, Wikipedia, http://en.wikipedia.org.wiki/IKEA, August 1; 2005, IKEA, a household name, *Journal of Commerce*, May 30, 1.
12. D. Rigby & C. Zook, 2003, Open-market innovation, *Harvard Business Review,* 89(10): 80–89; J-R. Lee & J.-S. Chen, 2003, Internationalization, local adaptation and subsidiary's entrepreneurship: An exploratory study on Taiwanese manufacturing firms in Indonesia and Malaysia, *Asia Pacific Journal of Management*, 20: 51–72.
13. Gupta & Wang, How to get China and India right; Y. Luo, 2003, Market-seeking MNEs in an emerging market: How parent-subsidiary links shape overseas success, *Journal of International Business Studies,* 34(3): 290–309.
14. I. Filatotchev, R. Strange, J. Piesse, & Y.-C. Lien, 2007, FDI by firms from newly industrialized economies in emerging markets: Corporate governance, entry mode and location, *Journal of International Business Studies,* 38(4): 556–572; C. C. Y. Kwok & D. M. Reeb, 2000, Internationalization and firm risk: An upstream-downstream hypothesis, *Journal of International Business Studies*, 31: 611–629.
15. M. Wright, I. Filatotchev, R. E. Hoskisson, & M. W. Peng, 2005, Strategy research in emerging economies: Challenging the conventional wisdom, *Journal of Management Studies,* 42: 1–30; T. London & S. Hart, 2004, Reinventing strategies for emerging markets: Beyond the transnational model, *Journal of International Business Studies,* 35: 350–370; R. E. Hoskisson, L. Eden, C. M. Lau, & M. Wright, 2000, Strategy in emerging economies, *Academy of Management Journal*, 43: 249–267.
16. H. Sender, 2005, The economy; the outlook: India comes of age, as focus on returns lures foreign capital, *Wall Street Journal,* June 6, A2.
17. M. A. Witt & A. Y. Lewin, 2007, Outward foreign direct investment as escape to home country institutional constraints, *Journal of International Business Studies,* 38: 579–594; M. W. Peng, S.-H. Lee, & D. Y. L. Wang, 2005, What determines the scope of the firm over time? A focus on institutional relatedness, *Academy of Management Review*, 30: 622–633.
18. J. W. Spencer, T. P. Murtha, & S. A. Lenway, 2005, How governments matter to new industry creation, *Academy of Management Review,* 30: 321–337; I. P. Mahmood & C. Rufin, 2005, Government's dilemma: The role of government in imitation and innovation, *Academy of Management Review*, 30: 338–360.
19. L. Eden & S. Miller, 2004, Distance matters: Liability of foreignness, institutional distance and ownership strategy, in M. A. Hitt & J. L. Cheng (eds.), *Advances in International Management,* Oxford, UK: Elsevier/JAI Press, 187–221; T. Kostova & S. Zaheer, 1999, Organizational legitimacy under conditions of complexity: The case of the multinational enterprise, *Academy of Management Review*, 24: 64–81.
20. F. Jiang, 2005, Driving forces of international pharmaceutical firms' FDI into China, *Journal of Business Research,* 22(1): 21–39.
21. K. Hall, 2007, Fad marketing's balancing act, *BusinessWeek,* August 6, 42.
22. K. Asakawa & M. Lehrer, 2003, Managing local knowledge assets globally: The role of regional innovation relays, *Journal of World Business,* 38: 31–42.
23. J. Cantwell, J. Dunning, & O. Janne, 2004, Towards a technology-seeking explanation of U.S. direct investment in the United Kingdom, *Journal of International Management,* 10: 5–20; W. Chung & J. Alcacer, 2002, Knowledge seeking and location choice of foreign direct investment in the United States, *Management Science*, 48(12): 1534–1554.
24. B. Ambos, 2005, Foreign direct investment in industrial research and development: A study of German MNCs, *Research Policy,* 34: 395–410.
25. Jiang, Driving forces of international pharmaceutical firms' FDI into China.
26. M. D. R. Chari, S. Devaraj, & P. David, 2007, International diversification and firm performance: Role of information technology investments, *Journal of World Business,* 42: 184–197; W. Chung, 2001, Identifying technology transfer in foreign direct investment: Influence of industry conditions and investing firm motives, *Journal of International Business Studies,* 32: 211–229.
27. K. J. Petersen, R. B. Handfield, & G. L. Ragatz, 2005, Supplier integration into new product development: Coordinating product process and supply chain design, *Journal of Operations Management,* 23: 371–388; S. Prasad, J. Tata, & M. Madan, 2005, Build to order supply chains in developed and developing countries, *Journal of Operations Management,* 23: 551–568.
28. A. Webb, 2007, China needs strong automakers—not more. *Automotive News,* http://www.autonews.com, July 20; China's SAIC says first half sales up 23 percent. 2007, Reuters, http://www.reuters.com, July 12; A. Taylor, 2004, Shanghai Auto wants to be the world's next great car company, *Fortune,* October 4, 103–109.
29. L. Zhou, W.-P. Wu, & X. Luo, 2007, Internationalization and the performance of born-global SMEs: The mediating role of social networks, *Journal of International Business Studies*, 38: 673–690; W. Kuemmerle, 2002, Home base and knowledge management in international ventures, *Journal of Business Venturing,* 2: 99–122.
30. H. Berry, 2006, Leaders, laggards, and the pursuit of foreign knowledge, *Strategic Management Journal,* 27: 151–168; Cantwell, Dunning, & Janne, Towards a technology-seeking explanation of U.S. direct investment in the United Kingdom.
31. J. Penner-Hahn & J. M. Shaver, 2005, Does international research increase patent output? An analysis of Japanese pharmaceutical firms, *Strategic Management Journal*, 26: 121–140.
32. G. K. Lee, 2007, The significance of network resources in the race to enter emerging product markets: The convergence of telephony, communications, and computer networking, *Strategic Management Journal,* 28: 17–37; K. Ito & E. L. Rose, 2002, Foreign direct investment location strategies in the tire industry, *Journal of International Business Studies,* 33(3): 593–602.
33. R. Tahir & J. Larimo, 2004, Understanding the location strategies of the European firms in Asian countries, *Journal of*

American Academy of Business, 5: 102–110.
34. D. Xu & O. Shenkar, 2004, Institutional distance and the multinational enterprise, *Academy of Management Review,* 27: 608–618.
35. D. Xu, Y. Pan, & P. W. Beamish, 2004, The effect of regulative and normative distances on MNE ownership and expatriate strategies, *Management International Review,* 44(3): 285–307.
36. Tallman & Fladmoe-Lindquist, Internationalization, globalization, and capability-based strategy; D. A. Griffith & M. G. Harvey, 2001, A resource perspective of global dynamic capabilities, *Journal of International Business Studies,* 32: 597–606; Y. Luo, 2000, Dynamic capabilities in international expansion, *Journal of World Business,* 35(4): 355–378.
37. D. Tan & J. T. Mahoney, 2005, Examining the Penrose effect in an international business context: The dynamics of Japanese firm growth in U.S. industries, *Managerial and Decision Economics,* 26(2): 113–127; K. Uhlenbruck, 2004, Developing acquired foreign subsidiaries: The experience of MNEs for multinationals in transition economies, *Journal of International Business Studies,* 35: 109–123.
38. J. Gimeno, R. E. Hoskisson, B.D. Beal, & W. P. Wan, 2005, Explaining the clustering of international expansion moves: A critical test in the U.S. telecommunications industry, *Academy of Management Journal,* 48: 297–319.
39. M. A. Hitt, L. Bierman, K. Uhlenbruck, & K. Shimizu, 2006, The importance of resources in the internationalization of professional service firms: The good, the bad and the ugly, *Academy of Management Journal,* 49: 1137–1157.
40. L. Nachum, 2001, The impact of home countries on the competitiveness of advertising TNCs, *Management International Review,* 41(1): 77–98.
41. M. E. Porter, 1990, *The Competitive Advantage of Nations,* New York: The Free Press.
42. Ibid., 84.
43. Y. Aoyama & H. Izushi, 2003, Hardware gimmick or cultural innovation? Technological, cultural, and social foundations of the Japanese video game industry, *Research Policy,* 32: 423–443.
44. A. Tempel & P. Walgenbach, 2007, Global standardization of organizational forms and management practices? What new institutionalism and business systems approach can learn from each other, *Journal of Management Studies,* 44: 1–24; P. Ghemawat, 2004, Global standardization vs. localization: A case study and model, in J. A. Quelch & R. Deshpande (eds.), *The Global Market: Developing a Strategy to Manage Across Borders,* New York: Jossey-Bass.
45. W. P. Wan & R. E. Hoskisson, 2003, Home country environments, corporate diversification strategies and firm performance, *Academy of Management Journal,* 46: 27–45; J. M. Geringer, S. Tallman, & D. M. Olsen, 2000, Product and international diversification among Japanese multinational firms, *Strategic Management Journal,* 21: 51–80.
46. Wan & Hoskisson, Home country environments, corporate diversification strategies and firm performance; M. A. Hitt, R. E. Hoskisson, & R. D. Ireland, 1994, A mid-range theory of the interactive effects of international and product diversification on innovation and performance, *Journal of Management,* 20: 297–326.
47. L. Li, 2005, Is regional strategy more effective than global strategy in the U.S. service industries? *Management International Review,* 45: 37–57; B. B. Alred & K. S. Swan, 2004, Global versus multidomestic: Culture's consequences on innovation, *Management International Review,* 44: 81–105.
48. A. Ferner, P. Almond, I. Clark, T. Colling, & T. Edwards, 2004, The dynamics of central control and subsidiary anatomy in the management of human resources: Case study evidence from US MNCs in the UK, *Organization Studies,* 25: 363–392.
49. B. Connelly, M. A. Hitt, A. S. DeNisi, & R. D. Ireland, 2007, Expatriates and corporate-level international strategy: Governing with the knowledge contract, *Management Decision,* 45: 564–581; L. Nachum, 2003, Does nationality of ownership make any difference and if so, under what circumstances? Professional service MNEs in global competition, *Journal of International Management,* 9: 1–32.
50. Y. Luo, 2001, Determinants of local responsiveness: Perspectives from foreign subsidiaries in an emerging market, *Journal of Management,* 27: 451–477.
51. M. Geppert, K. Williams, & D. Matten, 2003, The social construction of contextual rationalities in MNCs: An Anglo-German comparison of subsidiary choice, *Journal of Management Studies,* 40: 617–641; M. Carpenter & J. Fredrickson, 2001, Top management teams, global strategic posture, and the moderating role of uncertainty, *Academy of Management Journal,* 44: 533–545.
52. About the Company, 2007, Unilever, http://www.unilever.com, August 2; G. Jones, 2002, Control, performance, and knowledge transfers in large multinationals: Unilever in the United States, 1945–1980, *Business History Review,* 76(3): 435–478.
53. Tempel & Walgenbach, Global standardization of organizational forms and management practices; Li, Is regional strategy more effective than global strategy in the U.S. service industries?
54. M. Zellmer-Braun & C. Gibson, 2006, Multinational organization context: Implications for team learning and performance, *Academy of Management Journal,* 49:501–518; I. C. MacMillan, A. B. van Putten, & R. G. McGrath, 2003, Global gamesmanship, *Harvard Business Review,* 81(5): 62–71.
55. Connelly, Hitt, DeNisi, & Ireland, Expatriates and corporate-level international strategy; J.F.L. Hong, M. Easterby-Smith, & R.S. Snell, 2006, Transferring organizational learning systems to Japanese subsidiaries in China, *Journal of Management Studies,* 43: 1027–1058.
56. R. G. Barker, 2003, Trend: Global accounting is coming, *Harvard Business Review,* 81 (4): 24–25.
57. A. Yaprak, 2002, Globalization: Strategies to build a great global firm in the new economy, *Thunderbird International Business Review,* 44(2): 297–302; D. G. McKendrick, 2001, Global strategy and population level learning: The case of hard disk drives, *Strategic Management Journal,* 22: 307–334.
58. V. Shannon, 2007, eBay is preparing to re-enter the China auction business, *New York Times,* http://www.nytimes.com, June 22; B Einhorn, 2007, A break in Yahoo's China clouds? *BusinessWeek,* http://wwwbusinessweek.com, June 20.
59. K. E. Meyer, 2006, Globalfocusing: From domestic conglomerates to global specialists, *Journal of Management Studies,* 43: 1109–1144; A. Delios & P. W. Beamish, 2005, Regional and global strategies of Japanese firms, *Management International Review,* 45: 19–36.
60. H. D. Hopkins, 2003, The response strategies of dominant US firms to Japanese challengers, *Journal of Management,* 29: 5–25; S. Massini, A. Y. Lewin, T. Numagami, & A. Pettigrew, 2002, The evolution of organizational routines among large Western and Japanese firms, *Research Policy,* 31(8,9): 1333–1348.
61. 2006 annual report, 2007, CEMEX, http://www.cemex.com, August 2; K. A. Garrett, 2005, Cemex, *Business Mexico,* April 23.
62. B. Elango & C. Pattnaik, 2007, Building capabilities for international operations through networks: A study of Indian firms, *Journal of International Business Studies,* 38: 541–555; T. B. Lawrence, E. A. Morse, & S. W. Fowler, 2005, Managing your portfolio of connections, *MIT Sloan Management Review,* 46(2): 59–65; C. A. Bartlett & S. Ghoshal, 1989, *Managing across Borders: The Transnational Solution,* Boston: Harvard Business School Press.
63. A. Abbott & K. Banerji, 2003, Strategic flexibility and firm performance: The case of US based transnational corporations, *Global Journal of Flexible Systems Management,* 4(1/2): 1–7; J. Child & Y. Van, 2001, National and transnational effects in international business: Indications from Sino-foreign joint ventures, *Management International Review,* 41(1): 53–75.
64. W. Barner-Rasmussen & I. Bjorkman, 2007, Language fluency, socialization and inter-unit relationships in Chinese and Finnish subsidiaries, *Management and*

Organization Review, 3:105–128; A.S. Cui, D.A. Griffith, S.T. Cavusgil, & M. Dabic, 2006, The influence of market and cultural environmental factors on technology transfer between foreign MNCs and local subsidiaries: A Croatian illustration, *Journal of World Business*, 41: 100–111.

65. A. M. Rugman & A. Verbeke, 2003, Extending the theory of the multinational enterprise: Internalization and strategic management perspectives, *Journal of International Business Studies*, 34: 125–137.
66. H. F. Cheng, M. Gutierrez, A. Mahajan, Y. Shachmurove, & M. Shahrokhi, 2007, A future global economy to be built by BRICs, *Global Finance Journal*, in press; Wright, Filatotchev, Hoskisson, & Peng, Strategy research in emerging economies: Challenging the conventional wisdom.
67. N. Y. Brannen, 2004, When Mickey loses face: Recontextualization, semantic fit and semiotics of foreignness, *Academy of Management Review*, 29: 593–616.
68. A. M. Rugman & A. Verbeke, 2007, Liabilities of foreignness and the use of firm-level versus country-level data: A response to Dunning et al. (2007), *Journal of International Business Studies*, 38: 200–205; S. Zaheer & A. Zaheer, 2001, Market microstructure in a global B2B network, *Strategic Management Journal*, 22: 859–873.
69. J. A. Trachtenberg & B. Steinberg, 2003, Plan B for Marketers-in a time of global conflict, companies consider changing how they push products, *Wall Street Journal*, March 20, B7.
70. S. R. Miller & L. Eden, 2006, Local density and foreign subsidiary performance, *Academy of Management Journal*, 49: 341–355.
71. About Lands' End, 2007, Lands' End, http://www.landsend.com, August 2; J. Schlosser, 2004, Cashing in on the new world of me, *Fortune*, December, 13, 244–248.
72. C. H. Oh & A. M. Rugman, 2007, Regional multinationals and the Korean cosmetics industry, *Asia Pacific Journal of Management*, 24: 27–42; A. Rugman & A. Verbeke, 2004, A perspective on regional and global strategies of multinational enterprises, *Journal of International Business Studies*, 35: 3–18.
73. C. Pantzalis, 2001, Does location matter? An empirical analysis of geographic scope and MNC market valuation, *Journal of International Business Studies*, 32: 133–155.
74. A. Rugman & S. Girod, 2003, Retail multinationals and globalization: The evidence is regional, *European Management Journal*, 21(1): 24–37.
75. D. E. Westney, 2006. Review of the regional multinationals: MNEs and global strategic management, *Journal of International Business Studies*, 37: 445–449.
76. R. D. Ludema, 2002, Increasing returns, multinationals and geography of preferential trade agreements, *Journal of International Economics*, 56: 329–358.
77. Meyer, Globalfocusing: From domestic conglomerates to global specialists; Delios & Beamish, Regional and global strategies of Japanese firms.
78. T. L. Pett & J. A. Wolff, 2003, Firm characteristic and managerial perceptions of NAFTA: An assessment of export implications for U.S. SMEs, *Journal of Small Business Management*, 41(2): 117–132.
79. W. Chung & J. Song, 2004, Sequential investment, firm motives, and agglomeration of Japanese electronics firms in the United States, *Journal of Economics and Management Strategy*, 13: 539–560; D. Xu & O. Shenkar, 2002, Institutional distance and the multinational enterprise, *Academy of Management Review*, 27(4): 608–618.
80. K. D. Brouthers, L. E. Brouthers, & S. Werner, 2003, Industrial sector, perceived environmental uncertainty and entry mode strategy, *Journal of Business Research*, 55: 495–507.
81. H. Zhao, Y. Luo, & T. Suh, 2004, Transaction costs determinants and ownership-based entry mode choice: A meta-analytical review, *Journal of International Business Studies*, 35: 524–544; K. D. Brouthers, 2003, Institutional, cultural and transaction cost influences on entry mode choice and performance, *Journal of International Business Studies*, 33: 203–221.
82. C. Lages, C. R. Lages, & L. F. Lages, 2005, The RELQUAL scale: A measure of relationship quality in export market ventures, *Journal of Business Research*, 58: 1040–1048; R. Isaak, 2002, Using trading firms to export: What can the French experience teach us? *Academy of Management Executive*, 16(4): 155–156.
83. Y. Chui, 2002, The structure of the multinational firm: The role of ownership characteristics and technology transfer, *International Journal of Management*, 19(3):472–477.
84. Luo, Determinants of local responsiveness.
85. L. E. Brouthers & K. Xu, 2002, Product stereotypes, strategy and performance satisfaction: The case of Chinese exporters, *Journal of International Business Studies*, 33: 657–677; M. A. Raymond, J. Kim, & A. T. Shao, 2001, Export strategy and performance: A comparison of exporters in a developed market and an emerging market, *Journal of Global Marketing*, 15(2): 5–29.
86. W. Dou, U. Nielsen, & C. M. Tan, 2003, Using corporate Web sites for export marketing, *Journal of Advertising Research*, 42(5): 105–115.
87. A. Haahti, V. Madupu, U. Yavas, & E. Babakus, 2005, Cooperative strategy, knowledge intensity and export performance of small and medium-sized enterprises, *Journal of World Business*, 40(2): 124–138.
88. K. A. Houghton & H. Winklhofer, 2004, The effect of Web site and ecommerce adoption on the relationship between SMEs and their export intermediaries, *International Small Business Journal*, 22: 369–385.
89. P. Westhead, M. Wright, & D. Ucbasaran, 2001, The internationalization of new and small firms: A resource-based view, *Journal of Business Venturing*, 16: 333–358.
90. The U.S. dollar weakened to a new two-year low against the euro, 2007, Union Bank of California, http://www.fxstreet.com, April 17; M. N. Bailey & R. Z. Lawrence, 2005, Don't blame trade for U.S. job losses, *The McKinsey Quarterly*, 1: 86.
91. D. Kline, 2003, Sharing the corporate crown jewels, *MIT Sloan Management Review*, 44(3): 83–88; M. A. Hitt & R. D. Ireland, 2000, The intersection of entrepreneurship and strategic management research, in D. L. Sexton & H. Landstrom (eds.), *Handbook of Entrepreneurship*, Oxford, UK: Blackwell Publishers, 45–63.
92. A. Arora & A. Fosfuri, 2000, Wholly owned subsidiary versus technology licensing in the worldwide chemical industry, *Journal of International Business Studies*, 31: 555–572.
93. N. Zamiska & V. O'Connell, 2005, Philip Morris is in talks to make Marlboros in China, *Wall Street Journal*, April 21, B1, B2.
94. Y. J. Kim, 2005, The impact of firm and industry characteristics on technology licensing, *S.A.M. Advanced Management Journal*, 70(1): 42–49.
95. M. Johnson, 2001, Learning from toys: Lessons in managing supply chain risk from the toy industry, *California Management Review*, 43(3): 106–124.
96. B. Ebenkamp, 2005, Tamra Seldin, *Brandweek*, April 11, 40, 50.
97. Rigby & Zook, Open-market innovation.
98. C. A. Bartlett & S. Rangan, 1992, Komatsu limited, in C. A. Bartlett & S. Ghoshal (eds.), *Transnational Management: Text, Cases and Readings in Cross-Border Management*, Homewood, IL: Irwin, 311–326.
99. Profile: Marriott International, Inc., 2007, Yahoo! Finance, http://finance.yahoo.com, August 2; Fitch, 2004, Soft pillows and sharp elbows, *Forbes*, May 10, 66.
100. J. J. Reuer & T. W. Tong, 2005, Real options in international joint ventures, *Journal of Management* 31: 403–423; B. Petersen, D. E. Welch, & L. S. Welch, 2000, Creating meaningful switching options in international operations, *Long Range Planning*, 33(5): 688–705.
101. M. Nippa, S. Beechler, & A. Klossek, 2007, Success factors for managing international joint ventures: A review and an integrative framework, *Management and Organization Review*, 3: 277–310; R. Larsson, K. R. Brousseau, M. J. Driver, & M. Homqvist, 2003, International growth through cooperation: Brand-driven strategies, leadership, and career development in Sweden,

Academy of Management Executive, 17(1): 7–21.

102. J. S. Harrison, M. A. Hitt, R. E. Hoskisson, & R. D. Ireland, 2001, Resource complementarity in business combinations: Extending the logic to organization alliances, *Journal of Management*, 27: 679–690; T. Das & B. Teng, 2000, A resource-based theory of strategic alliances, *Journal of Management*, 26: 31–61.
103. M. A. Hitt, D. Ahlstrom, M. T. Dacin, E. Levitas, & L. Svobodina, 2004, The institutional effects on strategic alliance partner selection in transition economies: China versus Russia, *Organization Science*, 15: 173–185; M. Peng, 2001, The resource-based view and international business, *Journal of Management*, 27: 803–829.
104. J. Bamford, D. Ernst, & D. G. Fubini, 2004, Launching a world-class joint venture, *Harvard Business Review*, 82(2): 91–100.
105. M. A. Lyles & J. E. Salk, 2007, Knowledge acquisition from foreign parents in international joint ventures: An empirical examination in the Hungarian context, *Journal of International Business Studies*, 38: 3–18; E. W. K. Tsang, 2002, Acquiring knowledge by foreign partners for international joint ventures in a transition economy: Learning-by-doing and learning myopia, *Strategic Management Journal*, 23(9): 835–854; P. J. Lane, J. E. Salk, & M. A. Lyles, 2002, Absorptive capacity learning and performance in international joint ventures, *Strategic Management Journal*, 22: 1139–1161.
106. S. Zaheer & A. Zaheer, 2007, Trust across borders, *Journal of International Business Studies*, 38: 21–29; P. Almeida, J. Song, & R. M. Grant, 2002, Are firms superior to alliances and markets? An empirical test of cross-border knowledge building, *Organization Science*, 13(2): 147–161; M. A. Hitt, M. T. Dacin, E. Levitas, J. L. Arregle, & A. Borza, 2000, Partner selection in emerging and developed market contexts: Resource-based and organizational learning perspectives, *Academy of Management Journal*, 43: 449–467.
107. M. W. Peng & O. Shenkar, 2002, Joint venture dissolution as corporate divorce, *Academy of Management Executive*, 16(2): 92–105; O. Shenkar & A. Van, 2002, Failure as a consequence of partner politics: Learning from the life and death of an international cooperative venture, *Human Relations*, 55: 565–601.
108. J. A. Robins, S. Tallman, & K. Fladmoe-Lindquist, 2002, Autonomy and dependence of international cooperative ventures: An exploration of the strategic performance of U.S. ventures in Mexico, *Strategic Management Journal*, 23(10): 881–901; Y. Gong, O. Shenkar, Y. Luo, & M.-K. Nyaw, 2001, Role conflict and ambiguity of CEOs in international joint ventures: A transaction cost perspective, *Journal of Applied Psychology*. 86: 764–773.
109. P. K. Jagersma, 2005, Cross-border alliances: Advice from the executive suite, *Journal of Business Strategy*, 26(1): 41–50; D. C. Hambrick, J. Li, K. Xin, & A. S. Tsui, 2001, Compositional gaps and downward spirals in international joint venture management groups, *Strategic Management Journal*, 22: 1033–1053.
110. A. Madhok, 2006, Revisiting multinational firms' tolerance for joint ventures: A trust-based approach, *Journal of International Business Studies*, 37: 30–43; J. Child & Y. Van, 2003, Predicting the performance of international joint ventures: An investigation in China, *Journal of Management Studies*, 40(2): 283–320; J. P. Johnson, M. A. Korsgaard, & H. J. Sapienza, 2002, Perceived fairness, decision control, and commitment in international joint venture management teams, *Strategic Management Journal*, 23(12): 1141–1160.
111. L. Huff & L. Kelley, 2003, Levels of organizational trust in individualist versus collectivist societies: A seven-nation study, *Organization Science*, 14(1): 81–90.
112. D. Li, L. Eden, M. A. Hitt, & R. D. Ireland, 2008, Friends, acquaintances and strangers? Partner selection in R&D alliances, *Academy of Management Journal*, in press; Y. Pan & D. K. Tse, 2000, The hierarchical model of market entry modes, *Journal of International Business Studies*, 31: 535–554.
113. J. J. Reuer & M. Zollo, 2005, Termination outcomes of research alliances, *Research Policy*, 34(1): 101–115.
114. P. Porrini, 2004, Can a previous alliance between an acquirer and a target affect acquisition performance? *Journal of Management*, 30: 545–562; J. J. Reuer, 2002, Incremental corporate reconfiguration through international joint venture buyouts and selloffs, *Management International Review*, 42: 237–260.
115. J. J. Reuer, 2005, Avoiding lemons in M&A deals, *MIT Sloan Management Review*; 46(3): 15–17; G. A. Knight & P. W. Liesch, 2002, Information internalization in internationalizing the firm, *Journal of Business Research*, 55(12): 981–995.
116. S. G. Lazzarini, 2007, The impact of membership in competing alliance constellations: Evidence on the operational performance of global airlines, *Strategic Management Journal*, 28: 345–367; J. H. Dyer, P. Kale, & H. Singh, 2004, When to ally and when to acquire, *Harvard Business Review*, 82(7): 108–117.
117. K. Shimizu, M. A. Hitt, D. Vaidyanath, & V. Pisano, 2004, Theoretical foundations of cross-border mergers and acquisitions: A review of current research and recommendations for the future, *Journal of International Management*, 10: 307–353; M. A. Hitt, J. S. Harrison, & R. D. Ireland, 2001, *Mergers and Acquisitions: A Guide to Creating Value for Stakeholders*, New York: Oxford University Press.
118. M. A. Hitt & V. Pisano, 2003, The cross-border merger and acquisition strategy, *Management Research*, 1: 133–144.
119. International operational fact sheet, 2007, http://www.walmartfacts.com, July; J. Levine, 2004, Europe: Gold mines and quicksand, *Forbes*, April 12, 76.
120. 1999, French dressing, *The Economist*, July 10, 53–54.
121. U. Weitzel & S. Berns, 2006, Cross-border takeovers, corruption, and related aspects of governance, *Journal of International Business Studies*, 37: 786–806.
122. A. H. L. Slangen, 2006, National cultural distance and initial foreign acquisition performance: The moderating effect of integration, *Journal of World Business*, 41: 161–170.
123. I. Bjorkman, G. K. Stahl, & E. Vaara, 2007, Cultural differences and capability transfer in cross-border acquisitions: The mediating roles of capability complementarity, absorptive capacity, and social integration, *Journal of International Business Studies*, 38: 658–672.
124. C. Buckley, 2005, SAIC to fund MG Rover bid, *The Times of London*, http://www.timesonline.co.uk, July 18.
125. A.-W. Harzing, 2002, Acquisitions versus greenfield investments: International strategy and management of entry modes, *Strategic Management Journal*, 23: 211–227; K. D. Brouthers & L. E. Brouthers, 2000, Acquisition or greenfield start-up? Institutional, cultural and transaction cost influences, *Strategic Management Journal*, 21: 89–97.
126. C. Bouquet, L. Hebert, & A. Delios, 2004, Foreign expansion in service industries: Separability and human capital intensity, *Journal of Business Research*, 57: 35–46.
127. D. Elango, 2005, The influence of plant characteristics on the entry mode choice of overseas firms, *Journal of Operations Management*, 23(1): 65–79.
128. P. Deng, 2003, Determinants of full-control mode in China: An integrative approach, *American Business Review*, 21(1): 113–123.
129. R. Belderbos, 2003, Entry mode, organizational learning, and R&D in foreign affiliates: Evidence from Japanese firms, *Strategic Management Journal*, 34: 235–259.
130. S. Mani, K. D. Antia & A. Rindfleisch, 2007, Entry mode and equity level: A multilevel examination of foreign direct investment ownership structure, *Strategic Management Journal*, 28: 857–866.
131. Construction starts on UPS air hub in Shanghai, 2007, United Parcel Service, http://ups.com/pressroom, August 9; FedEx announces next-business-day domestic express service in China, 2007, FedEx Corporation, http://home.businesswire.com/portal/site/fedex—corp/index, March 19; B. Stanley, 2005, United Parcel Service to open a hub in Shanghai, *Wall Street Journal*, July 8, B2; B. Stanley, 2005, FedEx plans hub in Guangzhou: Facility to begin operation in 2008 as cargo industry tries to claim turf

in Asia, *Asian Wall Street Journal*, July 14, A3.

132. V. Gaba, Y. Pan, & G. R. Ungson, 2002, Timing of entry in international market: An empirical study of U.S. Fortune 500 firms in China, *Journal of International Business Studies*, 33(1): 39–55; S.-J. Chang & P. Rosenzweig, 2001, The choice of entry mode in sequential foreign direct investment, *Strategic Management Journal*, 22: 747–776.
133. R. Farzad, 2007, Extreme investing: Inside Colombia, *BusinessWeek*, May 28, 50–58; K. E. Myer, 2001, Institutions, transaction costs, and entry mode choice in Eastern Europe, *Journal of International Business Studies*, 32: 357–367.
134. S. Li, 2004, Why are property rights protections lacking in China? An institutional explanation, *California Management Review*, 46(3): 100–115; Y. Luo, 2001, Determinants of entry in an emerging economy: A multilevel approach, *Journal of Management Studies*, 38: 443–472.
135. A. Antoine, C. B. Frank, H. Murata, & E. Roberts, 2003, Acquisitions and alliances in the aerospace industry: An unusual triad, *International Journal of Technology Management*, 25(8): 779–790.
136. M. Zimmerman, 2007, Toyota ends GM's reign as car sales leader, *Los Angeles Times*, April 25, 2007, C.1; L. J. Howell & J. C. Hsu, 2002, Globalization within the auto industry, *Research Technology Management*, 45(4): 43–49.
137. J. Hagedoorn & G. Dysters, 2002, External sources of innovative capabilities: The preference for strategic alliances or mergers and acquisitions, *Journal of Management Studies*, 39: 167–188; H. Chen, 1999, International performance of multinationals: A hybrid model, *Journal of World Business*, 34: 157–170.
138. A. Chacar & B. Vissa, 2005, Are emerging economies less efficient? Performance persistence and the impact of business group affiliation, *Strategic Management Journal*, 26: 933–946; Hoskisson, Kim, Tihanyi, & White, A framework for understanding international diversification by business groups from emerging economies.
139. T. Yu & A. A. Cannella, 2007, Rivalry between multinational enterprises: An event history approach, *Academy of Management Journal*, 50: 665–686.
140. M. F. Wiersma & H. P. Bowen, 2007, Corporate diversification: The impact of foreign competition, industry globalization and product diversification, *Strategic Management Journal*, 28: in press.
141. L. Li, 2007, Multinationality and performance: A synthetic review and research agenda, *International Journal of Management Reviews*, 9: 117–139; J. A. Doukas & O. B. Kan, 2006, Does global diversification destroy firm value, *Journal of International Business Studies*, 37: 352–371; J. W. Lu & P. W. Beamish, 2004, International diversification and firm performance: The S-curve hypothesis, *Academy of Management Journal*, 47: 598–609.
142. S. E. Christophe & H. Lee, 2005, What matters about internationalization: A market-based assessment, *Journal of Business Research*. 58: 536–643; J. A. Doukas & L. H. P. Lang, 2003, Foreign direct investment, diversification and firm performance, *Journal of International Business Studies*, 34: 153–172.
143. Hitt, Tihanyi, Miller, & Connelly, International diversification; Kwok & Reeb, Internationalization and firm risk.
144. Y. Fang, M. Wade, A. Delios, & P. W. Beamish, 2007, International diversification, subsidiary performance, and the mobility of knowledge resources, *Strategic Management Journal*, 28: in press.
145. T. R. Holcomb & M. A. Hitt, 2007, Toward a model of strategic outsourcing, *Journal of Operations Management*, 25: 464–481; J. P. Doh, 2005, Offshore outsourcing: Implications for international business and strategic management theory and practice, *Journal of Management Studies*, 42: 695–704.
146. J. Penner-Hahn & J. M. Shaver, 2005, Does international research and development increase patent output? An analysis of Japanese pharmaceutical firms, *Strategic Management Journal*, 26: 121–140; Hagedoorn & Dysters, External sources of innovative capabilities.
147. Hitt, Bierman, Uhlenbruck, & Shimizu, The importance of resources in the internationalization of professional service firms; L. Tihanyi, R. A. Johnson, R. E. Hoskisson, & M. A. Hitt, 2003, Institutional ownership differences and international diversification: The effects of board of directors and technological opportunity, *Academy of Management Journal*, 46:195–211.
148. Ambos, Foreign direct investment in industrial research and development; F. Bradley & M. Gannon, 2000, Does the firm's technology and marketing profile affect foreign market entry? *Journal of International Marketing*, 8(4): 12–36.
149. B. Ambos & B. B. Schlegelmilch, 2007, Innovation and control in the multinational firm: A comparison of political and contingency approaches, *Strategic Management Journal*, 28: 473–486; Asakawa & Lehrer, Managing local knowledge assets globally: The role of regional innovation relays.
150. O. E. M. Janne, 2002, The emergence of corporate integrated innovation systems across regions: The case of the chemical and pharmaceutical industry in Germany, the UK and Belgium, *Journal of International Management*, 8: 97–119.
151. Wiersema & Bowen, Corporate diversification; J. Jung & S. M. Chan-Olmsted, 2005, Impacts of media conglomerates' dual diversification on financial performance, *Journal of Media Economics*, 18(3): 183–202.
152. Wan & Hoskisson, Home country environments, corporate diversification strategies and firm performance.
153. D. S. Elenkov, W. Judge, & P. Wright, 2005, Strategic leadership and executive innovation influence: An international multi-cluster comparative study, *Strategic Management Journal*, 26: 665–682; P. Herrmann, 2002, The influence of CEO characteristics on the international diversification of manufacturing firms: An empirical study in the United States, *International Journal of Management*, 19(2): 279–289.
154. H. A. Krishnan & D. Park, 2003, Power in acquired top management teams and post-acquisition performance: A conceptual framework, *International Journal of Management*, 20: 75–80; A. McWilliams, D. D. Van Fleet, & P. M. Wright, 2001, Strategic management of human resources for global competitive advantage, *Journal of Business Strategies*, 18(1): 1–24.
155. M. A. Hitt, R. E. Hoskisson, & H. Kim, 1997, International diversification: Effects on innovation and firm performance in product-diversified firms, *Academy of Management Journal*, 40: 767–798.
156. J. Child, L. Chung, & H. Davies, 2003, The performance of cross-border units in China: A test of natural selection, strategic choice and contingency theories, *Journal of International Business Studies*, 34: 242–254.
157. Y.-H. Chiu, 2003, The impact of conglomerate firm diversification on corporate performance: An empirical study in Taiwan, *International Journal of Management*, 19: 231–237; Luo, Market-seeking MNEs in an emerging market: How parent-subsidiary links shape overseas success.
158. C. Crossland & D. C. Hambrick, 2007, How national systems differ in their constraints on corporate executives: A study of CEO effects in three countries, *Strategic Management Journal*, 28: 767–789; M. Javidan, P. W. Dorfman, M. S. de Luque, & R. J. House, 2006, In the eye of the beholder: Cross-cultural lessons in leadership from Project GLOBE, *Academy of Management Perspectives*, 20 (1): 67–90.
159. 2005, Keeping IT together, *Chain Store Age*, June, 48.
160. Y. Paik, 2005, Risk management of strategic alliances and acquisitions between western MNCs and companies in central Europe, *Thunderbird International Business Review*, 47(4): 489–511; A. Delios & W. J. Henisz, 2003, Policy uncertainty and the sequence of entry by Japanese firms, 1980–1998, *Journal of International Business Studies*, 34: 227–241.
161. P. Rodriguez. K. Uhlenbruck, & L. Eden, 2005, Government corruption and the entry strategies of multinationals, *Academy of Management Review*, 30: 383–396; J. H. Zhao, S. H. Kim, & J. Du, 2003, The impact of corruption and transparency on foreign direct investment: An empirical

analysis, *Management International Review*, 43(1): 41–62.
162. P. S. Ring, G. A. Bigley, T. D'aunno, & T. Khanna, 2005, Perspectives on how governments matter, *Academy of Management Review*, 30: 308–320; S. Globerman & D. Shapiro, 2003, Governance infrastructure and U.S. foreign direct investment, *Journal of International Business Studies*, 34(1): 19–39.
163. W. Bailey & A. Spicer, 2007, When does identity matter? Convergence and divergence in international business ethics, *Academy of Management Journal*, 50: in press; Hitt, Ahlstrom, Dacin, Levitas, & Svobodina, The institutional effects on strategic alliance partner selection in transition economies.
164. Y. Lu & J. Yao, 2006, Impact of state ownership and control mechanisms on the performance of group-affiliated companies in China, *Asia Pacific Journal of Management,* 23: 485–503; T. Mapes, 2005, Terror still keeps foreign investors out of Indonesia, *Wall Street Journal,* May 31, A14.
165. T. Vestring, T. Rouse, & U. Reinert, 2005, Hedging your offshoring bets, *MIT Sloan Management Review*, 46(3): 26–29; L. L. Jacque & P. M. Vaaler, 2001, The international control conundrum with exchange risk: An EVA framework, *Journal of International Business Studies*, 32: 813–832.
166. T. G. Andrews & N. Chompusri, 2005, Temporal dynamics of crossvergence: Institutionalizing MNC integration strategies in post-crisis ASEAN, *Asia Pacific Journal of Management,* 22(1): 5–22; S. Mudd, R. Grosse, & J. Mathis, 2002, Dealing with financial crises in emerging markets, *Thunderbird International Business Review*, 44(3): 399–430.
167. L. Tihanyi & W. H. Hegarty, 2007, Political interests and the emergence of commercial banking in transition economies, *Journal of Management Studies,* 44: 789–813.
168. Shannon, eBay is preparing to reenter the Chinese auction business.
169. Lu & Beamish, International diversification and firm performance: The s-curve hypothesis; Wan & Hoskisson, Home country environments, corporate diversification strategies and firm performance; Hitt, Hoskisson, & Kim, International diversification.
170. C. C. Kwok & S. Tadesse, 2006, The MNC as an agent of change for host-country institutions: FDI and corruption, *Journal of International Business Studies*, 37: 767–785; F. J. Contractor, S. K. Kundu, & C. C. Hsu, 2003, A three-stage theory of international expansion: The link between multinationality and performance in the service sector, *Journal of International Business Studies*, 34(1): 5–19.
171. I. Bjorkman, W. Barner-Rasmussen, & L. Li, 2004, Managing knowledge transfer in MNCs: The impact of headquarters control mechanisms, *Journal of International Business Studies,* 35: 443–455.
172. C. M. Chan & S. Makino, 2007, Legitimacy and multi-level institutional environments: Implications for foreign subsidiary ownership structure, *Journal of International Business Studies*, 38:621–638; S. Li & H. Scullion, 2006, Bridging the distance: Managing cross-border knowledge holders, *Asia Pacific Journal of Management,* 23: 71–92.
173. D. W. Yiu, C. M. Lau & G. D. Bruton, 2007, International venturing by emerging economy firms: The effects of firm capabilities, home country networks, and corporate entrepreneurship, *Journal of International Business Studies*, 38: 519–540; P. S. Barr & M. A. Glynn, 2004, Cultural variations in strategic issue interpretation: Relating cultural uncertainty avoidance to controllability in discriminating threat and opportunity, *Strategic Management Journal*, 25: 59–67.
174. W. P. J. Henisz & B. A. Zeiner, 2005, Legitimacy, interest group pressures and change in emergent institutions, the case of foreign investors and host country governments, *Academy of Management Review*, 30: 361–382; T. P. Blumentritt & D. Nigh, 2002, The integration of subsidiary political activities in multinational corporations, *Journal of International Business Studies*, 33: 57–77.
175. S.-J. Chang & S. Park, 2005, Types of firms generating network externalities and MNCs' co-location decisions, *Strategic Management Journal*, 26: 595–616.

Cooperative Strategy

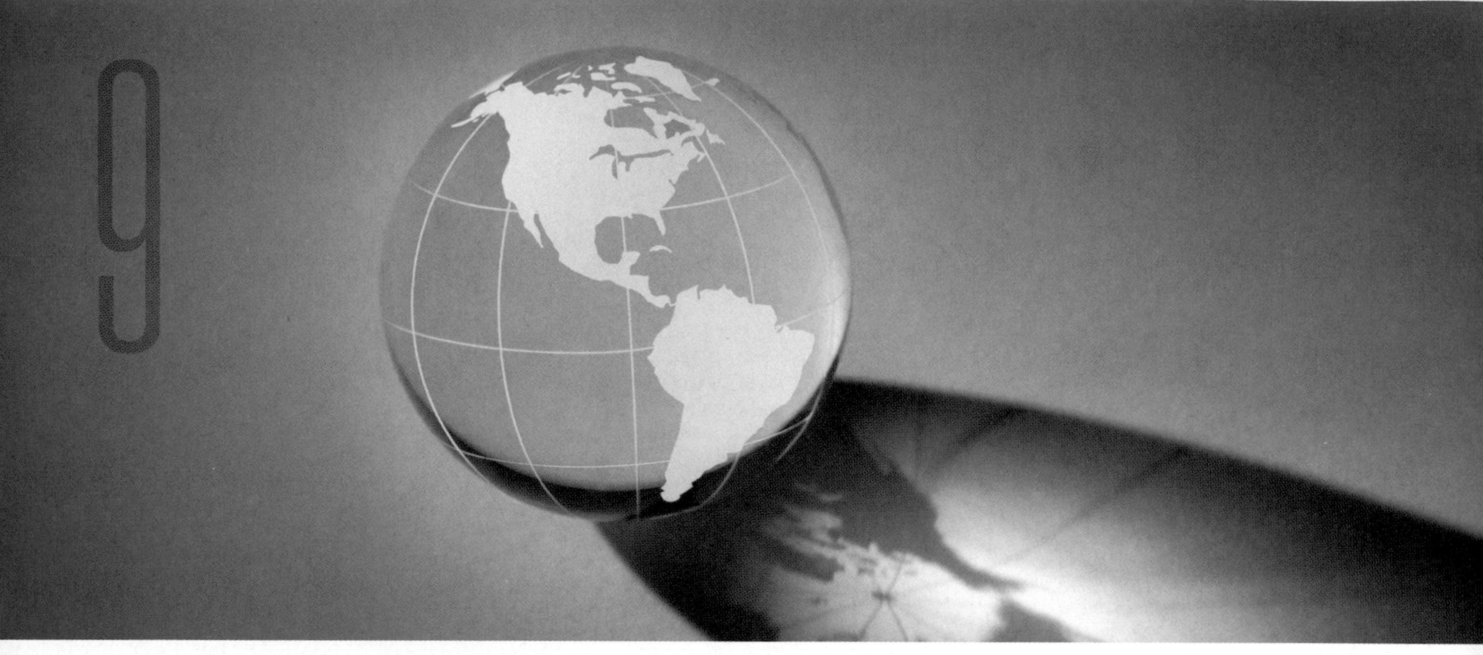

Studying this chapter should provide you with the strategic management knowledge needed to:

1. Define cooperative strategies and explain why firms use them.
2. Define and discuss three types of strategic alliances.
3. Name the business-level cooperative strategies and describe their use.
4. Discuss the use of corporate-level cooperative strategies in diversified firms.
5. Understand the importance of cross-border strategic alliances as an international cooperative strategy.
6. Explain cooperative strategies' risks.
7. Describe two approaches used to manage cooperative strategies.

Using Cooperative Strategies at IBM

A company widely known throughout the world, IBM's 350,000-plus employees design, manufacturer, sell, and service advanced information technologies such as computer systems, storage systems, software, and microelectronics. The firm's extensive lineup of products and services is grouped into three core business units—Systems and Financing, Software, and Services.

As is true for all companies, IBM uses three means to grow—internal developments (primarily through innovation), mergers and acquisitions (such as IBM's recent purchase of Internet Security Systems to boost its ability to deliver security solutions to corporations), and cooperative strategies. By cooperating with other companies, IBM is able to leverage its core competencies to grow and improve its performance.

Through cooperative strategies (e.g., strategic alliances and joint ventures, both of which are defined and discussed in this chapter), IBM finds itself working with a variety of firms in order to deliver products and services. However, IBM has specific performance-related objectives it wants to accomplish as it engages in an array of cooperative arrangements. Some of the firm's cooperative relationships are with competitors. (Actually, deciding to cooperate with a competitor in order to compete in a particular market or market segment is becoming increasingly common.) In late 2007, IBM teamed with longtime computing rival Sun Microsystems. Expectations for this corporate-level cooperative strategy (corporate-level cooperative strategies are discussed later in the chapter) were high in that executives in the two companies labeled it a "comprehensive relationship" that represented a "tectonic shift in the market landscape." Essentially, the firms intended to cooperate on server technologies so that Sun's Solaris operating system could run on IBM's servers and eventually on its mainframes. Gaining ground on Hewlett-Packard in the battle for leadership in the global server market is a key objective for this cooperative arrangement.

In other instances, IBM cooperates with companies to serve the needs of certain-sized firms. For example, IBM's collaboration with SAP (the world's leading provider of business software) seeks to serve the needs that midsized companies in 12 countries have for world-class business applications built on reliable infrastructures. An estimated 80 million small and midsized firms on a global basis can benefit from the joint services of IBM and SAP. These possibilities from working together support the firms' intention of expanding their cooperative relationship. IBM also has a global alliance with Lenovo, the company that purchased its personal computer (PC) business. With a focus on firms in certain industries (health care, financial services, education, retail, and government), IBM and Lenovo are cooperating to deliver end-to-end technology solutions to solve customers' problems. Some of IBM's cooperative arrangements such as the one with Cisco Systems are long-lived. The partners in this strategic alliance, formed in 1997, focus on providing solutions and services to help customers "transform" their businesses by using competitive advantages that result from the interactions of IBM and Cisco personnel.

As one might anticipate, a firm the size and diversity of IBM is involved with a number of cooperative relationships such as those already mentioned. Given the challenges associated with achieving and maintaining superior performance, and in light of its general success with cooperative relationships, one might anticipate that IBM will continue to use cooperative strategies as a path toward growth and enhanced performance.

Sources: B. Bergstein, 2007, IBM and Sun join forces in server technologies, *Houston Chronicle,* http://chron.com, August 17; D. Kawamoto, 2007, IBM to buy ISS for $1.3 billion, http://news.com, May 24; 2007, International Business Machines, *Market Edge Research,* http://marketedgeresearch.com, August 27; 2007, Lenovo and IBM expand global alliance, http://ibm.com, May 22; 2007, IBM and SAP expand partnership to reach midsize companies in Europe and Asia-Pacific, http://ibm.com, April 23; 2007, Cisco and IBM Strategic alliance, http://cisco.com, August 15; 2006, Cognos and IBM form global strategic alliance to deliver integrated solutions to boost customer performance, http://ibm.com, March 7.

As noted in the Opening Case, firms use three means to grow and improve their performance—internal development, mergers and acquisitions, and cooperation. In each of these cases, the firm seeks to use its resources in ways that will create the greatest amount of value for stakeholders.[1]

A **cooperative strategy** is a strategy in which firms work together to achieve a shared objective.

Recognized as a viable engine of firm growth,[2] **cooperative strategy** is a strategy in which firms work together to achieve a shared objective.[3] Thus, cooperating with other firms is another strategy firms use to create value for a customer that exceeds the cost of providing that value and to establish a favorable position relative to competition.[4]

As explained in the Opening Case, IBM is involved with a number of cooperative arrangements. The intention of serving customers better than competitors serve them and of gaining an advantageous position relative to competitors drive this firm's use of cooperative strategies. IBM's corporate-level cooperative strategy with Sun Microsystems, for example, finds it seeking to deliver server technologies in ways that maximize customer value while improving the firm's position relative to Hewlett-Packard as these companies battle for the leadership position in the global server market. The business-level alliance with Lenovo finds IBM and its partner focusing on what the firms believe are the unique personal computer (PC) needs of customers competing in particular industries. The objectives IBM and its various partners seek by working together highlight the reality that in the twenty-first century landscape, firms must develop the skills required to successfully use cooperative strategies as a complement to their abilities to grow and improve performance through internal developments and mergers and acquisitions.[5]

We examine several topics in this chapter. First, we define and offer examples of different strategic alliances as primary types of cooperative strategies. Next, we discuss the extensive use of cooperative strategies in the global economy and reasons for them. In succession, we then describe business-level (including collusive strategies), corporate-level, international, and network cooperative strategies. The chapter closes with discussion of the risks of using cooperative strategies as well as how effective management of them can reduce those risks.

As you will see, we focus on strategic alliances in this chapter because firms use them more frequently than other types of cooperative relationships. Although not frequently used, collusive strategies are another type of cooperative strategy discussed in this chapter. In a *collusive strategy,* two or more firms cooperate to increase prices above the fully competitive level.[6]

Strategic Alliances as a Primary Type of Cooperative Strategy

A **strategic alliance** is a cooperative strategy in which firms combine some of their resources and capabilities to create a competitive advantage.[7] Thus, strategic alliances involve firms with some degree of exchange and sharing of resources and capabilities to co-develop, sell, and service goods or services.[8] Strategic alliances allow firms to leverage their existing resources and capabilities while working with partners to develop additional resources and capabilities as the foundation for new competitive advantages.[9] To be certain, the reality today is that "strategic alliances have become a cornerstone of many firms' competitive strategy."[10]

A **strategic alliance** is a cooperative strategy in which firms combine some of their resources and capabilities to create a competitive advantage.

Consider the case for Kodak. CEO Antonio Perez stated, "Kodak today is involved with partnerships that would have been unthinkable a few short years ago."[11] His comment suggests the breadth and depth of cooperative relationships with which the firm is involved. However, each of the cooperative relationships described in the Strategic Focus is intended to lead to a new competitive advantage as the source of growth and performance improvement.

A competitive advantage developed through a cooperative strategy often is called a *collaborative* or *relational* advantage.[12] As previously discussed, particularly in Chapter 4, competitive advantages enhance the firm's marketplace success. Rapid technological changes and the global economy are examples of factors challenging firms to constantly upgrade current competitive advantages while they develop new ones to maintain strategic competitiveness.[13]

Many firms, especially large global competitors, establish multiple strategic alliances. Although we discussed only a few of them in the Opening Case, the reality is that IBM has formed hundreds of partnerships as it uses cooperative strategies. IBM is not alone in its decision to frequently use cooperative strategies as a means of competition. Focusing on developing advanced technologies, Lockheed Martin has formed more than 250 alliances with firms in more than 30 countries as it concentrates on its primary business of defense modernization and serving the needs of the air transportation industry. Recently, Lockheed Martin and Boeing formed a strategic alliance with the purpose of integrating their capabilities to "accelerate solutions for a growing air traffic capacity problem."[14] Xerox is another large firm relying on hundreds of cooperative arrangements to grow and outperform its rivals as it competes in what the firm sees as a rapidly changing competitive environment.[15] For all cooperative arrangements, including those we are describing here, success is more likely when partners behave cooperatively when interacting with one another. Actively solving problems, being trustworthy, and consistently pursuing ways to combine partners' resources and capabilities to create value are examples of cooperative behavior known to contribute to alliance success.[16]

Increasingly, public-sector agencies are using strategic alliances as well to improve the quality of their work. The recent alliance formed between the Office of the State Comptroller (OSC) and the Division of the Budget (DOB) with the purpose of cooperating to better coordinate the "implementation of a financial system for New York State" is an example of this phenomenon.[17]

Three Types of Strategic Alliances

The three major types of strategic alliances include joint venture, equity strategic alliance, and nonequity strategic alliance.

A **joint venture** is a strategic alliance in which two or more firms create a legally independent company to share some of their resources and capabilities to develop a competitive advantage.[18] Joint ventures, which are often formed to improve firms' abilities to compete in uncertain competitive environments,[19] are effective in establishing long-term relationships and in transferring tacit knowledge. Because it can't be codified, tacit knowledge is learned through experiences[20] such as those taking place when people from

A **joint venture** is a strategic alliance in which two or more firms create a legally independent company to share some of their resources and capabilities to develop a competitive advantage.

Strategic Focus Strategic Focus Strategic Focus

Partnering for Success at Kodak

Founded in 1892, Eastman Kodak Company (Kodak) has a rich history with consumers worldwide for its photographic film products. Currently though, Kodak is focusing its competitive efforts on three main businesses—digital photography, health imaging, and printing. Kodak remains the world's leading producer of silver halide (AgX) paper that is used for printing film and digital images. However, it no longer manufactures or licenses its names to others to produce traditional film cameras. This strategic action highlights Kodak's emphasis on growing in digital markets.

As a large firm, Kodak uses internal development, mergers and acquisitions, and cooperative strategies to grow and enhance its performance. Sony, Canon, and Fuji are just a few of the firms with whom Kodak has developed cooperative relationships. As is common for firms using cooperative strategies, Kodak is also partnering with competitors such as Hewlett-Packard (HP) and Xerox. While competing with Xerox in commercial printing, Kodak partners with that firm to supply the controllers that Xerox uses in its iGen3 digital presses. The Kodak-Creo unit supplies the workflow for HP's Indigo printer as the firms compete in the commercial and home printing markets.

The array of individual cooperative arrangements Kodak has formed is interesting as well as impressive. Recently, Sony Corporation and Kodak entered into a technology cross-license agreement that "will allow broad access to the other's patent portfolio." Simultaneously, Kodak formed another technology alliance with Sony Ericsson. This arrangement called for the sharing of technologies and technological capabilities between the partners. Kodak views these arrangements as validation of the quality of its intellectual property portfolio while allowing it access to technologies that it believes are capable of stimulating digitally oriented innovation and subsequent product developments. Kodak also has formed collaborations with companies (such as Real D and Barco) to effectively serve the worldwide digital camera market with a "full menu of products, systems, and services, including installation and support."

In addition to cooperative relationships with large, well-established companies, Kodak has formed a unit that is responsible for organizing strategic relationships with universities, government labs, and early-stage companies. This unit is considered vital to Kodak's efforts to use cooperative relationships to leverage its innovation and technological capabilities on a global basis. Calling these cooperative relationships Early-Stage Firm Alliances, Kodak believes they will complement its internal development processes while providing access to new technologies, products, and services. Licensing agreements and joint development agreements are examples of the cooperative relationships Kodak is willing to form with early start-up ventures in addition to more traditional strategic alliances and joint ventures.

Although diverse in nature, all of the relationships Kodak is establishing by using cooperative strategies are designed to facilitate its growth and performance as a digitally oriented firm. As we have seen, some of these relationships are with large, established firms while others are being formed with start-up ventures. In all cases though, the focus is on digitalization as the path to Kodak's growth and enhanced performance.

Sources: R. E. Hoskisson, M. A. Hitt, R. D. Ireland, & J. S. Harrison, 2008, *Competing for Advantage,* 2nd ed., Thomson South-Western; 2007, Eastman Kodak, Wikipedia, http://en.wikipedia.org, August 26; 2007, Kodak external alliances, http://kodak.com, August 26; 2005, Kodak and Barco forge strategic alliance to serve the worldwide digital cinema market, *Digital Content Producer.com,* http://digitalcontenproducer.com, June 22; 2005, Kodak and Real D strategic alliance for 3D cinema, http://letsgodigital.org, December 20.

partner firms work together in a joint venture. As discussed in Chapter 3, tacit knowledge is an important source of competitive advantage for many firms.[21]

Typically, partners in a joint venture own equal percentages and contribute equally to the venture's operations. In the joint venture that Polo Ralph Lauren Corp. and Geneva-based watch and jewelry company Compagnie Financiere Richemont AG formed, each firm owns 50 percent of a new entity they are creating. Called Polo Ralph Lauren Watch and Jewelry Co., the partners intend to use this new entity to develop and distribute products through Ralph Lauren boutique stores as well as independent watch and jewelry stores throughout the world. This joint venture is "Polo's first foray into the fine jewelry and luxury watch business and is Richemont's first joint venture with a fashion designer."[22] Overall, evidence suggests that a joint venture may be the optimal type of cooperative arrangement when firms need to combine their resources and capabilities to create a competitive advantage that is substantially different from any they possess individually and when the partners intend to enter highly uncertain markets.[23] These conditions influenced the two independent companies' decision to form the Polo Ralph Lauren Watch and Jewelry Co.

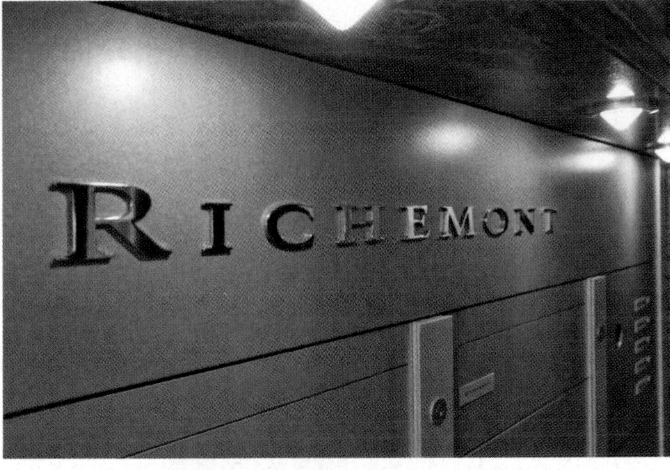

Polo Ralph Lauren Corp. and Geneva-based watch and jewelry company Richemont recently entered into a joint venture, which will be named Polo Ralph Lauren Watch and Jewelry Co. Products will be distributed through Ralph Lauren boutique stores as well as via independent watch and jewelry stores throughout the world.

An **equity strategic alliance** is an alliance in which two or more firms own different percentages of the company they have formed by combining some of their resources and capabilities to create a competitive advantage. Many foreign direct investments, such as those made by Japanese and U.S. companies in China, are completed through equity strategic alliances.[24]

For example, Citigroup Inc. and Nikko Cordial Corporation formed a comprehensive strategic alliance with the intention of creating "one of Japan's leading financial services groups and to enable the combined franchise to pursue important new growth opportunities, giving due respect to Japanese culture and business practices."[25] Citigroup was to have the majority ownership stake in this alliance. Retail businesses, asset management, and capital markets and banking businesses are examples of the product and service domains in which the two firms intend to integrate what they believe are highly complementary capabilities as the foundation for serving many types of customers.

An **equity strategic alliance** is an alliance in which two or more firms own different percentages of the company they have formed by combining some of their resources and capabilities to create a competitive advantage.

A **nonequity strategic alliance** is an alliance in which two or more firms develop a contractual relationship to share some of their unique resources and capabilities to create a competitive advantage.[26] In this type of alliance, firms do not establish a separate independent company and therefore do not take equity positions. For this reason, nonequity strategic alliances are less formal and demand fewer partner commitments than do joint ventures and equity strategic alliances.[27] The relative informality and lower commitment levels characterizing nonequity strategic alliances make them unsuitable for complex projects where success requires effective transfers of tacit knowledge between partners.[28]

A **nonequity strategic alliance** is an alliance in which two or more firms develop a contractual-relationship to share some of their unique resources and capabilities to create a competitive advantage.

Forms of nonequity strategic alliances include licensing agreements, distribution agreements, and supply contracts. Hewlett-Packard (HP), which actively "partners to create new markets . . . and new business models," licenses some of its intellectual property through strategic alliances.[29] Typically, outsourcing commitments are specified in the form of a nonequity strategic alliance. (Discussed in Chapter 3, *outsourcing* is the purchase of a value-creating primary or support activity from another firm.) Dell Inc. and most other computer firms outsource most or all of their production of laptop computers and often form nonequity strategic alliances to detail the nature of the relationship with firms to whom they outsource. Increasingly, state governments in the United States are outsourcing incarceration to private contractors. Corrections Corp. of America and

Geo Group Inc. are two of the largest of these contractors. State governments are forming these relationships to reduce costs and improve services.[30]

Reasons Firms Develop Strategic Alliances

As our discussion to this point implies, cooperative strategies are an integral part of the competitive landscape and are quite important to many companies and even to educational institutions. In educational institutions, for example, the number of libraries cooperating to improve their services continues to expand.[31] In for-profit organizations, many executives believe that strategic alliances are central to their firm's success.[32] One executive's position that "you have to partner today or you will miss the next wave . . . and that . . . you cannot possibly acquire the technology fast enough, so partnering is essential"[33] highlights this belief.

Motorola has recently formed alliances with Suning and Gome Appliances to sell Motorola mobile phones in China. Gome, China's largest electronics retail chain, will open Motorola shop-within-shops inside 30 of its largest stores in China.

Among other benefits, strategic alliances allow partners to create value that they couldn't develop by acting independently[34] and to enter markets more quickly and with greater market penetration possibilities.[35] Moreover, most (if not all) firms lack the full set of resources and capabilities needed to reach their objectives, which indicates that partnering with others will increase the probability of reaching firm-specific performance objectives.[36] Motorola recently formed strategic alliances with Suning, a firm that will be Motorola's first direct supply retailing partner in China, and with Gome Appliances, which will sell Motorola products using a store-within-a-store concept. Through these partnerships, Motorola seeks to increase its share of the Chinese mobile phone market more rapidly than it could as an independent company.[37]

The effects of the greater use of cooperative strategies—particularly in the form of strategic alliances—are noticeable. In large firms, for example, alliances can account for 25 percent or more of sales revenue. And many executives believe that alliances are a prime vehicle for firm growth.[38] In some industries, alliance versus alliance is becoming more prominent than firm versus firm as a point of competition. In the global airline industry, for example, competition is increasingly between large alliances rather than between airlines.[39]

In summary, we can note that firms form strategic alliances to reduce competition, enhance their competitive capabilities, gain access to resources, take advantage of opportunities, build strategic flexibility, and innovate. To achieve these objectives, they must select the right partners and develop trust.[40] Thus, firms attempt to develop a network portfolio of alliances in which they create social capital that affords them flexibility.[41] Because of the social capital, they can call on their partners for help when needed. Of course, social capital means reciprocity exists: Partners can ask them for help as well (and they are expected to provide it).[42]

The individually unique competitive conditions of slow-cycle, fast-cycle, and standard-cycle markets[43] find firms using cooperative strategies to achieve slightly different objectives (see Table 9.1). We discussed these three market types in Chapter 5 while examining competitive rivalry and competitive dynamics. *Slow-cycle markets* are markets where the firm's competitive advantages are shielded from imitation for relatively long periods of time and where imitation is costly. These markets are close to monopolistic conditions. Railroads and, historically, telecommunications, utilities, and financial services are examples of industries characterized as slow-cycle markets. In *fast-cycle markets,* the firm's competitive advantages aren't shielded from imitation, preventing their long-term sustainability. Competitive advantages are moderately shielded from imitation in *standard-cycle markets,* typically allowing them to be sustained for a longer period of time than in fast-cycle market situations, but for a shorter period of time than in slow-cycle markets.

Table 9.1 Reasons for Strategic Alliances by Market Type

Market	Reason
Slow-Cycle	• Gain access to a restricted market • Establish a franchise in a new market • Maintain market stability (e.g., establishing standards)
Fast-Cycle	• Speed up development of new goods or services • Speed up new market entry • Maintain market leadership • Form an industry technology standard • Share risky R&D expenses • Overcome uncertainty
Standard-Cycle	• Gain market power (reduce industry overcapacity) • Gain access to complementary resources • Establish better economies of scale • Overcome trade barriers • Meet competitive challenges from other competitors • Pool resources for very large capital projects • Learn new business techniques

Slow-Cycle Markets

Firms in slow-cycle markets often use strategic alliances to enter restricted markets or to establish franchises in new markets. For example, because of consolidating acquisitions that have occurred over the last dozen or so years, the American steel industry has only two remaining major players: U.S. Steel and Nucor. To improve their ability to compete successfully in the global steel market, these companies are forming cooperative relationships. They have formed strategic alliances in Europe and Asia and are invested in ventures in South America and Australia. Simultaneously however, companies based in countries other than the United States are forming or expanding alliances to enhance their presence in the partially restricted U.S. steel markets. For example, ArcelorMittal, the world's leading steel manufacturer, recently enhanced its strategic alliance with Japan's Nippon Steel Corporation. Expanding the partners' ability to gain share of the automotive sheet steel business in the United States is one of the key objectives of this alliance.[44]

The truth of the matter is that slow-cycle markets are becoming rare in the twenty-first century competitive landscape for several reasons, including the privatization of industries and economies, the rapid expansion of the Internet's capabilities for the quick dissemination of information, and the speed with which advancing technologies make quickly imitating even complex products possible.[45] Firms competing in slow-cycle markets, including steel manufacturers, should recognize the future likelihood that they'll encounter situations in which their competitive advantages become partially sustainable (in the instance of a standard-cycle market) or unsustainable (in the case of a fast-cycle market). Cooperative strategies can be helpful to firms transitioning from relatively sheltered markets to more competitive ones.[46]

Fast-Cycle Markets

Fast-cycle markets are unstable, unpredictable, and complex.[47] Combined, these conditions virtually preclude establishing long-lasting competitive advantages, forcing firms to constantly seek sources of new competitive advantages while creating value by using current ones. Alliances between firms with current excess resources and capabilities and those with promising capabilities help companies competing in fast-cycle markets to effectively transition from the present to the future and to gain rapid entry to new markets.

The information technology (IT) industry is a fast-cycle market, motivating firms to form partnerships as a way to effectively cope with the changes occurring in this market setting. In 2006, Microsoft and Novell (a leader in enterprise-wide operating systems based on Linux) formed a partnership with the intention of building, marketing, and supporting new solutions to improve interoperability and intellectual property assurance. Subsequently, Dell Inc. joined this collaboration in 2007. As the first major systems provider to join the Microsoft/Novell partnership, Dell agreed to "purchase SUSE Linux Enterprise Server certificates from Microsoft and establish a service and marketing program to migrate existing Linux users who are not Dell Linux customers to SUSE Linux Enterprise Server."[48] This expanded partnership was formed because the involved parties believe that Windows and Linux are the platforms on which a majority of applications using hardware will be based in the future.

Standard-Cycle Markets

In standard-cycle markets, alliances are more likely to be made by partners with complementary resources and capabilities. Even though airline alliances were originally set up to increase revenue,[49] airlines have realized that they can also be used to reduce costs. SkyTeam (chaired by Delta and Air France) developed an internal Web site to speed joint buying and let member carriers swap tips on pricing. Managers at Oneworld (American Airlines and British Airways) say the alliance's members have already saved more than $200 million through joint purchasing, and Star Alliance (United and Lufthansa) estimates that its member airlines save up to 25 percent on joint orders.

Given the geographic areas where markets are growing, these global alliances are adding partners from Asia. Recently, China Southern Airlines joined the SkyTeam alliance, Air China and Shanghai Airlines were added to the Star Alliance, and Dragonair joined as an affiliate of Oneworld. The following comment from an Air China executive demonstrates why firms choose to join airline alliances: "In order to survive and develop, airlines have to cooperate with other partners in various forms including multilateral alliance cooperation."[50] As is the case with airline companies, economies of scale are a key objective firms seek when forming alliances in standard-cycle markets.[51] The fact that the Oneworld, SkyTeam, and Star Alliances account for more than 60 percent of the world's airline capacity suggests that firms participating as members of these alliances have gained scale economies.

Business-Level Cooperative Strategy

A firm uses a **business-level cooperative strategy** to grow and improve its performance in individual product markets.

A firm uses a **business-level cooperative strategy** to grow and improve its performance in individual product markets. As discussed in Chapter 4, business-level strategy details what the firm intends to do to gain a competitive advantage in specific product markets. Thus, the firm forms a business-level cooperative strategy when it believes that combining its resources and capabilities with those of one or more partners will create competitive advantages that it can't create by itself and that will lead to success in a specific product market. The four business-level cooperative strategies are listed in Figure 9.1.

Complementary Strategic Alliances

Complementary strategic alliances are business-level alliances in which firms share some of their resources and capabilities in complementary ways to develop competitive advantages.

Complementary strategic alliances are business-level alliances in which firms share some of their resources and capabilities in complementary ways to develop competitive advantages.[52] Vertical and horizontal are the two types of complementary strategic alliances (see Figure 9.1).

Vertical Complementary Strategic Alliance

In a *vertical complementary strategic alliance,* firms share their resources and capabilities from different stages of the value chain to create a competitive advantage

Figure 9.1 Business-Level Cooperative Strategies

- Complementary strategic alliances
  - Vertical
  - Horizontal
- Competition response strategy
- Uncertainty-reducing strategy
- Competition-reducing strategy

(see Figure 9.2).[53] Oftentimes, vertical complementary alliances are formed to adapt to environmental changes;[54] sometimes, as is the case for General Electric (GE) and Konica Minolta, the changes represent an opportunity for partnering firms to innovate while adapting.[55]

GE and Konica Minolta formed an alliance with the intention of combining their "substantial resources and expertise to accelerate the development of this transformational technology."[56] Organic Light Emitting Diodes (OLED), which are thin, organic materials sandwiched between two electronic conductors, is the transformational technology the two firms seek to develop. The firms expect this technology to be capable of driving creative lighting applications. Formed in mid-2007, the partners hoped to introduce OLED-based lighting applications to the marketplace by 2010. Konica Minolta's imaging capabilities were to be combined with GE's lighting products' capabilities for this purpose. Even though both companies had been working on the technology in their own research and development (R&D) laboratories, they concluded that the most promising path was to use their different skills to collaborate to develop superior outcomes in the form of innovative products.

Horizontal Complementary Strategic Alliance

A *horizontal complementary strategic alliance* is an alliance in which firms share some of their resources and capabilities from the same stage (or stages) of the value chain to create a competitive advantage (see Figure 9.2). Commonly, firms use complementary strategic alliances to focus on long-term product development and distribution opportunities.[57] Sprint has formed a number of these alliances as part of its objective of redefining the telecommunications industry.[58] One of these alliances finds Sprint partnering with Lucent to develop wireless data services including mobile broadband and the delivery of network-based VoIP solutions.[59]

The automotive manufacturing industry is one in which many horizontal complementary strategic alliances are formed. In fact, virtually all global automobile manufacturers use cooperative strategies to form scores of cooperative relationships. As we explain in the Strategic Focus, the Renault-Nissan alliance, signed on March 27, 1999, is a prominent example of a horizontal complementary strategic alliance. Thought to be successful, the challenge is to integrate the partners' operations to create value while maintaining their unique cultures.

Competition Response Strategy

As discussed in Chapter 5, competitors initiate competitive actions to attack rivals and launch competitive responses to their competitors' actions. Strategic alliances can be used at the business level to respond to competitors' attacks. Because they can be difficult to reverse and expensive to operate, strategic alliances are primarily formed to take strategic rather than tactical actions and to respond to competitors' actions in a like manner.

Figure 9.2 Vertical and Horizontal Complementary Strategic Alliances

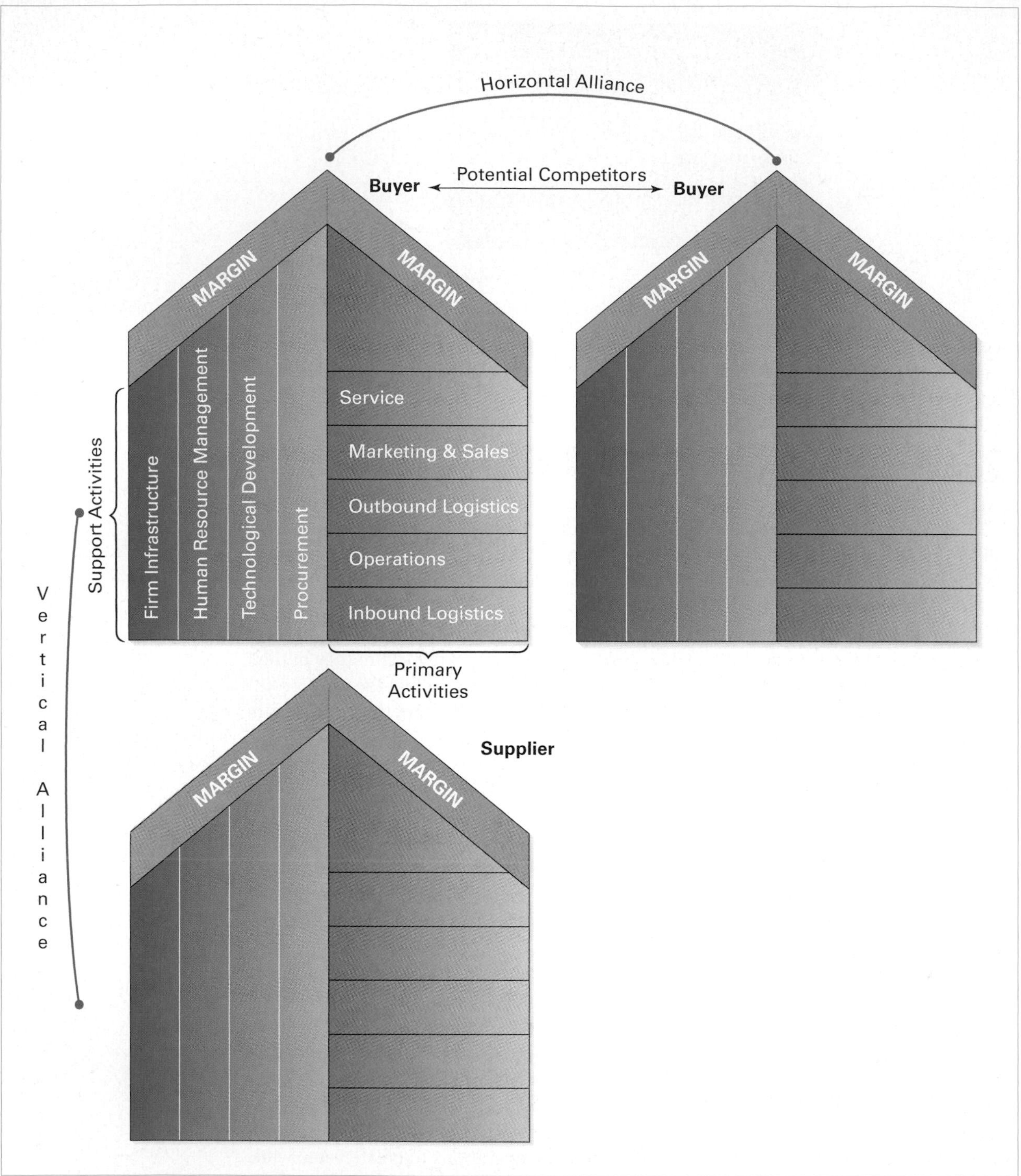

France Telecom and Microsoft, for example, formed an alliance with two initial major projects. The first project found the partners developing a series of phones based on Microsoft technology that uses Internet services. The phones are designed to be used as traditional cell phones or to access the Internet while at home or on the road. This project was a response to the announcement by BT Group PLC of a new hybrid fixed-line and mobile phone service using short-range wireless technology called Bluetooth. The France Telecom–Microsoft alliance will use the more powerful Wireless Fidelity (WiFi)

Using Complementary Resources and Capabilities to Succeed in the Global Automobile Industry

The degree of success a company can achieve as an automobile manufacturer is influenced by its ability to create *economies of scale* (generated when an increase in the scale of the firm's production process causes a decrease in the long-run average cost of each unit produced) and *economies of scope* (generated when the firm earns more sales or reduces its costs by increasing the scope of its activities such as marketing and distribution as well as the number of products sold). Indeed, an inability to generate scale and scope economies places a global automobile manufacturer at a competitive disadvantage. In particular, scale economies can be created by combining firms' resources and capabilities to complete particular activities in the value chain.

The SM3 is one of the new cars that has been produced as a result of the Renault/Nissan alliance.

Because of their relatively small size, the 1990s found Nissan and Renault's cost structures at noncompetitive levels; and their ability to provide multiple innovative products was diminished as well. To deal with their joint and similar problems, these firms finalized the details of a unique strategic alliance in March 1999. This alliance was the first of its kind to involve a Japanese and French company, each with its own corporate culture and brand identity. Horizontal in nature, the Nissan/Renault partnership is an example of an equity strategic alliance. Renault holds a 44.4 percent stake in Nissan which in turn holds 15 percent of Renault's shares. Carlos Ghosn serves as CEO for both companies.

To date, the alliance is deemed successful. "Nissan—Japan's second biggest carmaker and the world's ninth—has produced some hefty profits in recent years, a major turnaround from the late 1990s when the company was in serious financial trouble." Renault is now the world's tenth largest car manufacturer and intends to become Europe's most profitable mass volume producer by 2010. The alliance now accounts for 9.8 percent of the worldwide automobile market.

The firms participate in a number of joint activities to create scale and scope economies. Sharing production platforms (the partners intend to share 10 platforms by 2010) and powertrains (engines and transmissions) are examples of how scale economies are being created as is the alliance's work with Cisco Systems to deliver cost-effective systems and optimized infrastructure capabilities to the partners' IS/IT departments. To generate scope economies, the firms combine their resources and capabilities to cooperate in several activities including sales, purchasing, and the use of common distribution channels in Europe. In a comprehensive and summarized sense, this alliance finds Nissan and Renault cooperating in terms of "global product development, financial policy, and corporate strategy." To facilitate efforts to achieve the alliance's objectives, the partners have formed a number of cross-company teams (employees from both companies looking for ways to create additional synergies in terms of developing new products and manufacturing current ones) and functional task teams (employees from both companies seeking ways to contribute to synergies in support functions such as legal and tax and cost management and control).

The alliance partners continue to seek ways to enhance the performance of their cooperative relationship. For example, the partners examined the possibility of acquiring Ford

Motor Company's Jaguar and Land Rover businesses when those units became available for purchase in 2007. After evaluating the matter, the partners chose not to bid for Jaguar or Land Rover. Across time though, the challenge of managing relationships between partners who are sharing resources and capabilities in various value chain activities remains notable.

Sources: A. English, 2007, No news is bad news, http://telegraphc.co.uk, June 16; S. O'Grady, 2007, Jaguar and Land Rover: Marques on the market, *The Independent on Sunday*, http://news.independent.co.uk, September 2; 2007, The Renault-Nissan alliance, http://renault.com, August 20; 2007, Topics of the alliance, http://nissan.com, August 20; 2006, Q&A: GM-Renault-Nissan alliance, BBC News, http://news.bbc.co.uk, July 4; 2005, Renault and Nissan: Forging a global alliance that is creating more than the sum of its parts, http://cisco.com.

technology. Didier Lombard, CEO of France Telecom, stated that the telecom industry is undergoing rapid changes and current members must also act rapidly to adapt. The partnership with Microsoft is designed to respond to these changes.[60]

Uncertainty-Reducing Strategy

Some firms use business-level strategic alliances to hedge against risk and uncertainty, especially in fast-cycle markets.[61] Also, they are used where uncertainty exists, such as in entering new product markets or emerging economies. The long-term uncertainty about the continuing availability of fossil fuels is a reason ConocoPhillips and Tyson Foods formed a strategic alliance to produce "next generation" renewable diesel fuel. This product is intended to supplement the use of traditional petroleum-based diesel fuel. By-product fats that Tyson generates while processing beef, pork, and poultry are the raw ingredients to be used to create a transportation fuel. This effort is part of the partners' overall goal of collaborating to "leverage Tyson's advanced knowledge in protein chemistry and production with ConocoPhillips' processing and marketing expertise to introduce a renewable diesel to the United States."[62]

In other instances, firms form business-level strategic alliances to reduce the uncertainty associated with developing new products or establishing a technology standard. Interestingly, the alliance between France Telecom and Microsoft (mentioned earlier) is a competition response alliance for France Telecom but is an uncertainty-reducing alliance for Microsoft. Microsoft is using the alliance to learn more about the telecom industry and business. It wants to learn how it can develop software to satisfy needs in this industry. By partnering with a firm in this industry, it is reducing its uncertainty about the market and software needs. And the alliance is clearly designed to develop new products so the alliance reduces the uncertainty for both firms by combining their knowledge and capabilities.

Competition-Reducing Strategy

Used to reduce competition, collusive strategies differ from strategic alliances in that collusive strategies are often an illegal type of cooperative strategy. Two types of collusive strategies are explicit collusion and tacit collusion.

When two or more firms negotiate directly with the intention of jointly agreeing about the amount to produce and the price of the products that are produced, *explicit collusion* exists.[63] Explicit collusion strategies are illegal in the United States and most developed economies (except in regulated industries).

Firms that use explicit collusion strategies may find others challenging their competitive actions. In late 2006, for example, the British Office of Fair Trading and the U.S. Department of Justice joined forces to investigate alleged "price coordination" among American Airlines, United Airlines, and British Airways. The probe was conducted to investigate possible explicit collusion among the airlines in terms of passenger airfares, cargo shipping prices, and various surcharges.[64] In mid-2007, Green Oil, a bio-product company based in Illinois in the United States, alleged that LUKOIL, Russia's largest producer of crude oil, joined forces with Saudi Arabian and Venezuelan companies to manipulate production quotas and the prices of their products in the United States. All companies involved with Green Oil's allegations rejected the charges as baseless and false.[65] As these examples suggest, any firm that may use explicit collusion as a strategy should recognize that competitors and regulatory bodies might challenge the acceptability of their competitive actions.

Tacit collusion exists when several firms in an industry indirectly coordinate their production and pricing decisions by observing each other's competitive actions and responses.[66] Tacit collusion results in production output that is below fully competitive levels and above fully competitive prices. Unlike explicit collusion, firms engaging in tacit collusion do not directly negotiate output and pricing decisions.

Tacit collusion tends to be used as a business-level, competition-reducing strategy in highly concentrated industries, such as breakfast cereals. Firms in these industries recognize that they are interdependent and that their competitive actions and responses significantly affect competitors' behavior toward them. Understanding this interdependence and carefully observing competitors because of it tend to lead to tacit collusion.

Four firms (Kellogg, General Mills, Post, and Quaker) have accounted for as much as 80 percent of sales volume in the ready-to-eat segment of the U.S. cereal market.[67] Some believe that this high degree of concentration results in "prices for branded cereals that are well above [the] costs of production."[68] Prices above the competitive level in this industry suggest the possibility that the dominant firms use a tacit collusion cooperative strategy.

Discussed in Chapter 6, *mutual forbearance* is a form of tacit collusion in which firms do not take competitive actions against rivals they meet in multiple markets. Rivals learn a great deal about each other when engaging in multimarket competition, including how to deter the effects of their rival's competitive attacks and responses. Given what they know about each other as a competitor, firms choose not to engage in what could be destructive competitions in multiple product markets.[69]

In general, governments in free-market economies need to determine how rivals can collaborate to increase their competitiveness without violating established regulations.[70] However, this task is challenging when evaluating collusive strategies, particularly tacit ones. For example, regulation of pharmaceutical and biotech firms who collaborate to meet global competition might lead to too much price fixing and, therefore, regulation is required to make sure that the balance is right, although sometimes the regulation gets in the way of efficient markets.[71] Individual companies must analyze the effect of a competition-reducing strategy on their performance and competitiveness.

Assessment of Business-Level Cooperative Strategies

Firms use business-level strategies to develop competitive advantages that can contribute to successful positions and performance in individual product markets. To develop a competitive advantage using an alliance, the resources and capabilities that are integrated through the alliance must be valuable, rare, imperfectly imitable, and nonsubstitutable (see Chapter 3).

Evidence suggests that complementary business-level strategic alliances, especially vertical ones, have the greatest probability of creating a sustainable competitive advantage.[72] Horizontal complementary alliances are sometimes difficult to maintain because they are often between rivalrous competitors. In this instance, firms may feel a "push" toward and a "pull" from alliances. Airline firms, for example, want to compete aggressively against others serving their markets and target customers. However, the need to develop scale economies and to share resources and capabilities (such as scheduling systems) dictates that alliances be formed so the firms can compete by using cooperative actions and responses while they simultaneously compete against one another through competitive actions and responses. The challenge in these instances is for each firm to find ways to create the greatest amount of value from both their competitive and cooperative actions. It seems that Nissan and Renault have learned how to achieve this balance.

Although strategic alliances designed to respond to competition and to reduce uncertainty can also create competitive advantages, these advantages often are more temporary than those developed through complementary (both vertical and horizontal) strategic alliances. The primary reason is that complementary alliances have a stronger focus on creating value than do competition-reducing and uncertainty-reducing alliances, which are formed to respond to competitors' actions or reduce uncertainty rather than to attack competitors.

Of the four business-level cooperative strategies, the competition-reducing strategy has the lowest probability of creating a sustainable competitive advantage. For example, research suggests that firms following a foreign direct investment strategy using alliances as a follow-the-leader imitation approach may not have strong strategic or learning goals. Thus, such investment could be attributable to tacit collusion among the participating firms rather than to forming a competitive advantage (which should be the core objective).

Corporate-Level Cooperative Strategy

A firm uses a **corporate-level cooperative strategy** to help it diversify in terms of products offered or markets served, or both.

A firm uses a **corporate-level cooperative strategy** to help it diversify in terms of products offered or markets served, or both. Diversifying alliances, synergistic alliances, and franchising are the most commonly used corporate-level cooperative strategies (see Figure 9.3).

Firms use diversifying alliances and synergistic alliances to grow and improve performance by diversifying their operations through a means other than a merger or an acquisition.[73] When a firm seeks to diversify into markets in which the host nation's government prevents mergers and acquisitions, alliances become an especially appropriate option. Corporate-level strategic alliances are also attractive compared with mergers and particularly acquisitions, because they require fewer resource commitments[74] and permit greater flexibility in terms of efforts to diversify partners' operations.[75] An alliance can be used as a way to determine whether the partners might benefit from a future merger or acquisition between them. This "testing" process often characterizes alliances formed to combine firms' unique technological resources and capabilities.[76]

Diversifying Strategic Alliance

A **diversifying strategic alliance** is a corporate-level cooperative strategy in which firms share some of their resources and capabilities to diversify into new product or market areas.

A **diversifying strategic alliance** is a corporate-level cooperative strategy in which firms share some of their resources and capabilities to diversify into new product or market areas. Recently, Marriott International Inc., Miller Global Properties, and Nickelodeon decided to combine some of their resources and capabilities to create value that their firms could not create without each other. In this case, entertainment giant Nickelodeon (which is owned by Viacom International) is providing its brand name to establish Nickelodeon-themed hotels. Marriott's contribution to this diversifying strategic alliance is to manage the hotels

Figure 9.3 Corporate-Level Cooperative Strategies

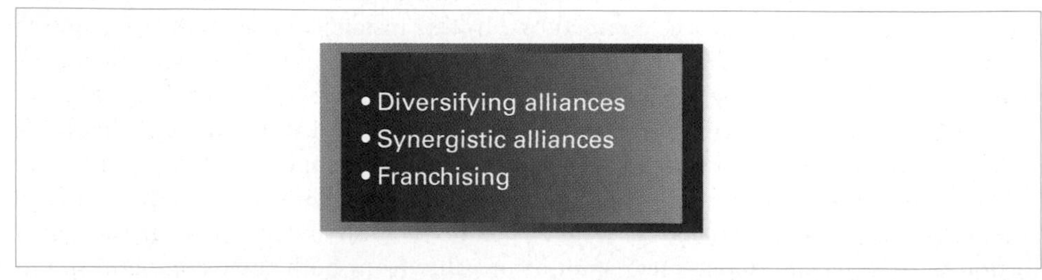

while Miller Global Properties owns them. These partners formed this relationship to take advantage of the growing trend of families desiring to travel to theme-oriented facilities. Nickelodeon believes that it can derive two benefits by its decision to diversity into the hotel business through this alliance: (1) sales of Nickelodeon merchandise (e.g., books, DVDs, toys, and clothes) can be increased by using the hotels as a distribution channel and (2) hotel guests, who are continuously exposed to opportunities to view Nickelodeon programs (e.g., Nick @ Nite), may become loyal watchers of those programs.[77]

Nickelodeon-themed hotels and waterparks are the outcome of the alliance among Marriott Hotels, Miller Global Properities, and Viacom International.

It should be noted that highly diverse networks of alliances can lead to poorer performance by partner firms.[78] However, cooperative ventures are also used to reduce diversification in firms that have overdiversified.[79] Japanese chipmakers Fujitsu, Mitsubishi Electric, Hitachi, NEC, and Toshiba have been using joint ventures to consolidate and then spin off diversified businesses that were performing poorly. For example, Fujitsu, realizing that memory chips were becoming a financial burden, dumped its flash memory business into a joint venture company controlled by Advanced Micro Devices. This alliance helped Fujitsu refocus on its core businesses.[80]

Synergistic Strategic Alliance

A **synergistic strategic alliance** is a corporate-level cooperative strategy in which firms share some of their resources and capabilities to create economies of scope. Similar to the business-level horizontal complementary strategic alliance, synergistic strategic alliances create synergy across multiple functions or multiple businesses between partner firms. The cooperative relationship between IBM and Sun Microsystems we discussed in the Opening Case is a synergistic strategic alliance.

A **synergistic strategic alliance** is a corporate-level cooperative strategy in which firms share some of their resources and capabilities to create economies of scope.

In late 2007, NBC Universal, Viacom, the News Corporation, and CBS were combining forces to establish their own Web site to compete against YouTube. (YouTube "is a video-sharing Web site where users can upload, view, and share video clips."[81]) Launched in 2006, a number of television and entertainment executives dismissed YouTube as a "flash-in-the-pan" business concept (and possibly an illegal one as well, given potential copyright infringement charges concerning content that is posted on YouTube). However, their view changed dramatically in October 2006 when Google Inc. paid $1.65 billion to purchase YouTube. At that point, the media giants decided that YouTube had tapped into customer needs with huge market potential. A number of factors were delaying completion of a cooperative relationship that analysts believed the involved companies almost desperately wanted to form. Ownership percentages and the management structure were among the issues affecting the negotiations. The fact that this type of collaboration among these large firms "would be nearly unprecedented" also increased the complexity of finalizing the proposed alliance's details. In spite of this, analysts expected the alliance to be formed as a means of allowing the media giants to have a competitive platform in what appeared to be an increasingly important distribution channel for their products—online video.[82] Thus, a synergistic strategic alliance such as the one among NBC Universal, Viacom, the News Corporation, and CBS is different from a complementary business-level alliance in that it diversifies the involved firms into a new business, but in a synergistic way.

Franchising is a corporate-level cooperative strategy in which a firm (the franchisor) uses a franchise as a contractual relationship to describe and control the sharing of its resources and capabilities with partners (the franchisees).

Franchising

Franchising is a corporate-level cooperative strategy in which a firm (the franchisor) uses a franchise as a contractual relationship to describe and control the sharing of its resources and capabilities with partners (the franchisees).[83] A *franchise* is a "contractual agreement between two legally independent companies whereby the franchisor grants the right to the franchisee to sell the franchisor's product or do business under its trademarks in a given location for a specified period of time."[84] In strategic management terminology, "franchising is a strategic alliance between groups of people who have specific relationships and responsibilities with a common goal to dominate markets."[85]

Subway, a firm using franchising as a cooperative strategy, is one of the fastest growing businesses in the United States.

Franchising (from the French for honesty or freedom[86]) is a popular strategy. In the United States alone, more than 2,500 franchise systems are located in more than 75 industries; and those operating franchising outlets generate roughly one-third of all U.S. retail sales.[87] Already frequently used in developed nations, franchising is expected to account for significant portions of growth in emerging economies in the twenty-first century as well.[88] As with diversifying and synergistic strategic alliances, franchising is an alternative to pursuing growth through mergers and acquisitions. McDonald's, Hilton International, Mrs. Fields Cookies, Subway, and Ace Hardware are well-known examples of firms using the franchising corporate-level cooperative strategy.

Franchising is a particularly attractive strategy to use in fragmented industries, such as retailing and commercial printing. In fragmented industries, a large number of small and medium-sized firms compete as rivals; however, no firm or small set of firms has a dominant share, making it possible for a company to gain a large market share by consolidating independent companies through contractual relationships.

In the most successful franchising strategy, the partners (the franchisor and the franchisees) work closely together.[89] A primary responsibility of the franchisor is to develop programs to transfer to the franchisees the knowledge and skills that are needed to successfully compete at the local level.[90] In return, franchisees should provide feedback to the franchisor regarding how their units could become more effective and efficient.[91] Working cooperatively, the franchisor and its franchisees find ways to strengthen the core company's brand name, which is often the most important competitive advantage for franchisees operating in their local markets.[92]

Assessment of Corporate-Level Cooperative Strategies

Costs are incurred with each type of cooperative strategy.[93] Compared with those at the business-level, corporate-level cooperative strategies commonly are broader in scope and more complex, making them relatively more costly. Those forming and using cooperative strategies, especially corporate-level ones, should be aware of alliance costs and carefully monitor them.

In spite of these costs, firms can create competitive advantages and value when they effectively form and use corporate-level cooperative strategies.[94] The likelihood of being able to parlay strategy into advantage increases when successful alliance experiences are internalized. In other words, those involved with forming and using corporate-level cooperative strategies can also use them to develop useful knowledge about how to succeed in the future. To gain maximum value from this knowledge, firms should organize it and verify that it is always properly distributed to those involved with forming and using alliances.[95]

We explain in Chapter 6 that firms answer two questions to form a corporate-level strategy—in which businesses will the diversified firm compete and how will those businesses be managed? These questions are also answered as firms form corporate-level cooperative strategies. Thus, firms able to develop corporate-level cooperative strategies and manage them in ways that are valuable, rare, imperfectly imitable, and nonsubstitutable (see Chapter 3) develop a competitive advantage that is in addition to advantages gained through the activities of individual cooperative strategies. (Later in the chapter, we further describe alliance management as another potential competitive advantage.)

International Cooperative Strategy

A **cross-border strategic alliance** is an international cooperative strategy in which firms with headquarters in different nations decide to combine some of their resources and capabilities to create a competitive advantage. Taking place in virtually all industries, the number of cross-border alliances continues to increase.[96] These alliances too are sometimes formed instead of mergers and acquisitions (which can be riskier).[97] Even though cross-border alliances can themselves be complex and hard to manage,[98] they have the potential to help firms use their resources and capabilities to create value in locations outside their home market.

A **cross-border strategic alliance** is an international cooperative strategy in which firms with headquarters in different nations decide to combine some of their resources and capabilities to create a competitive advantage.

The joint venture formed by Sony Corporation and Ericsson is a collaborative relationship through which each company is effectively using its capabilities to create value outside its home market. Founded in 2001, the joint venture is called Sony Ericsson. Combining Sony's consumer electronics expertise with Ericsson's technological leadership in the communications sector, this relationship was formed to make mobile phones. This cross-border alliance has been successful in that at the end of 2006, Sony Ericsson had a 9 percent share of the global mobile phone market, trailing only Nokia, Motorola, and Samsung, and was generating profits.[99]

Several reasons explain the increasing use of cross-border strategic alliances, including the fact that in general, multinational corporations outperform domestic-only firms.[100] What takes place with a cross-border alliance is that a firm leverages core competencies that are the foundation of its domestic success in international markets.[101] Nike provides an example as it leverages its core competence with celebrity marketing to expand globally with its diverse line of athletic goods and apparel. With a $2 billion celebrity endorsement budget, Nike has formed relationships with athletes having global appeal. Tiger Woods, Michael Jordan, seven-time Tour de France winner Lance Armstrong, and Magic Johnson are examples of these types of individuals. In addition, Nike has endorsement relationships with star athletes and organizations outside the United States such as Brazilian soccer star Ronaldo Nazario and Manchester United, the world's most popular soccer team.[102] Coupling these alliances with Nike's powerful global brand name helps the firm apply its marketing competencies in markets outside the United States.

Nike, a U. S.-based company, has endorsement alliances with the Manchester United Soccer team from The United Kingdom.

Limited domestic growth opportunities and foreign government economic policies are additional reasons firms use cross-border alliances. As discussed in Chapter 8, local ownership is an important national policy objective in some nations. In India and China, for example, governmental policies reflect a strong preference to license local companies. Thus, in some countries, the full range of entry mode choices that we described in Chapter 8 may not be available to firms seeking to diversify internationally. Indeed, investment by foreign firms in these instances may be allowed only through a partnership with a local firm, such as in a cross-border alliance. Especially important, strategic alliances with local partners can help firms overcome certain liabilities of moving into a foreign country, such as lack of knowledge of the local culture or institutional norms.[103] A cross-border strategic alliance can also be helpful to foreign partners from an operational perspective, because the local partner has significantly more information about factors contributing to competitive success such as local markets, sources of capital, legal procedures, and politics.[104]

In general, cross-border alliances are more complex and risky than domestic strategic alliances.[105] However, the fact that firms competing internationally tend to outperform domestic-only competitors suggests the importance of learning how to diversify into international markets. Compared with mergers and acquisitions, cross-border alliances may be a better way to learn this process, especially in the early stages of the firms' geographic diversification efforts. Starbucks is a case in point.

When Starbucks sought overseas expansion, it wanted to do so quickly as a means of supporting its strong orientation to continuous growth through expansion. Thus, it agreed to a complex series of joint ventures in many countries in the interest of speed. While the company receives a percentage of the revenues and profits as well as licensing fees for supplying its coffee, controlling costs abroad is more difficult than in the United States. Starbucks is learning from the results achieved from the collaborative relationships it established initially. In light of what it has learned, the firm continues to evaluate its opportunities to collaborate with others in different countries including China, a market that company officials believe "will eventually be the largest international market for Starbucks."[106] Among other actions, Starbucks is seeking to take larger equity positions in some of the joint ventures with which it is now involved in different countries (such as China).

Network Cooperative Strategy

A **network cooperative strategy** is a cooperative strategy wherein several firms agree to form multiple partnerships to achieve shared objectives.

Increasingly, firms use several cooperative strategies. In addition to forming their own alliances with individual companies, a growing number of firms are joining forces in multiple networks.[107] A **network cooperative strategy** is a cooperative strategy wherein several firms agree to form multiple partnerships to achieve shared objectives. IBM and Cisco have multiple cooperative arrangements as do Toyota and General Motors. Demonstrating the complexity of network cooperative strategies is the fact that Cisco also has a set of unique collaborations with both Hewlett-Packard and Dell Inc. The fact is that the number of network cooperative strategies being formed today continues to increase as firms seek to find the best ways to create value by offering multiple goods and services in multiple geographic (domestic and international) locations.

A network cooperative strategy is particularly effective when it is formed by geographically clustered firms,[108] as in California's Silicon Valley (where "the culture of Silicon Valley encourages collaborative webs"[109]) and Singapore's Silicon Island.[110] Effective social relationships and interactions among partners while sharing their resources and capabilities make it more likely that a network cooperative strategy will be successful,[111] as does having a productive *strategic center firm* (we discuss strategic center firms in detail in Chapter 11). Firms involved in networks gain information and knowledge from multiple sources. They can use these heterogeneous knowledge sets to produce more and better innovation. As a result, firms involved in networks of alliances tend to be more innovative.[112] However, there are disadvantages to participating in networks as a firm can be locked in to its partners, precluding the development of alliances with others. In certain types of networks, such as Japanese *keiretsus,* firms in the network are expected to help other firms in the network whenever they need aid. Such expectations can become a burden and reduce the focal firm's performance over time.[113]

Alliance Network Types

SunPower Corp. CEO Thomas Warner is photographed holding a solar panel next to the panels on the roof of SunPower's building in San Jose. Silicon Valley is leveraging its expertise in computer chips to design and manufacture the solar cells needed to convert sunlight into electricity. As prices for fossil fuels rise and demand for renewable energy grows, the region known for its silicon-based semiconductors is emerging as a key center for solar power technology.

© AP Photo/Jeff Chiu

An important advantage of a network cooperative strategy is that firms gain access to their partners' other partners. Having access to multiple collaborations increases the likelihood that additional competitive advantages will be formed as the set of shared resources and capabilities expands.[114] In turn, being able to develop new capabilities further stimulates product innovations that are so critical to strategic competitiveness in the global economy.[115]

The set of strategic alliance partnerships resulting from the use of a network cooperative strategy is commonly called an *alliance network.* The alliance networks that companies develop vary by industry conditions. A *stable alliance network* is formed in mature industries where demand is relatively constant and predictable. Through a stable alliance network, firms try to extend their competitive advantages to other settings while continuing to profit from operations in their core, relatively mature industry. Thus, stable networks are built primarily to *exploit* the economies (scale and/or scope) that exist between the partners.[116] *Dynamic alliance networks* are used in industries characterized by frequent product innovations and short product life cycles.[117] For instance, the pace of innovation in the information technology (IT) industry (as well as other industries that are characterized by fast-cycle markets) is too fast for any one company to be successful across time if it only competes independently. In dynamic alliance networks, partners typically *explore* new ideas and possibilities with the potential to lead to product innovations, entries to new markets, and the development of new markets.[118] Often, large firms in such industries as software and pharmaceuticals create networks of relationships with smaller entrepreneurial start-up firms in their search for innovation-based outcomes.[119] An important outcome for small firms successfully partnering with larger firms in an alliance network is the credibility they build by being associated with their larger collaborators.[120]

Competitive Risks with Cooperative Strategies

Stated simply, many cooperative strategies fail. In fact, evidence shows that two-thirds of cooperative strategies have serious problems in their first two years and that as many as 70 percent of them fail. This failure rate suggests that even when the partnership has potential complementarities and synergies, alliance success is elusive.[121] Although failure is undesirable, it can be a valuable learning experience, meaning that firms should carefully study a cooperative strategy's failure to gain insights with respect to how to form and manage future cooperative arrangements.[122] We show prominent cooperative strategy risks in Figure 9.4.

One cooperative strategy risk is that a partner may act opportunistically. Opportunistic behaviors surface either when formal contracts fail to prevent them or when an alliance is based on a false perception of partner trustworthiness. Not infrequently, the opportunistic firm wants to acquire as much of its partner's tacit knowledge as it can.[123] Full awareness of what a partner wants in a cooperative strategy reduces the likelihood that a firm will suffer from another's opportunistic actions.[124]

The situation in late 2007 with a joint venture British Petroleum (BP) formed in 2003 with oil tycoons Mikhail Fridman, Viktor Vekeselberg, and Len Blavatnik seems to demonstrate opportunistic behavior as well as political risks. Called TNK-BP, the cooperative relationship in question is unique in that BP and the three oilmen each

Figure 9.4 Managing Competitive Risks in Cooperative Strategies

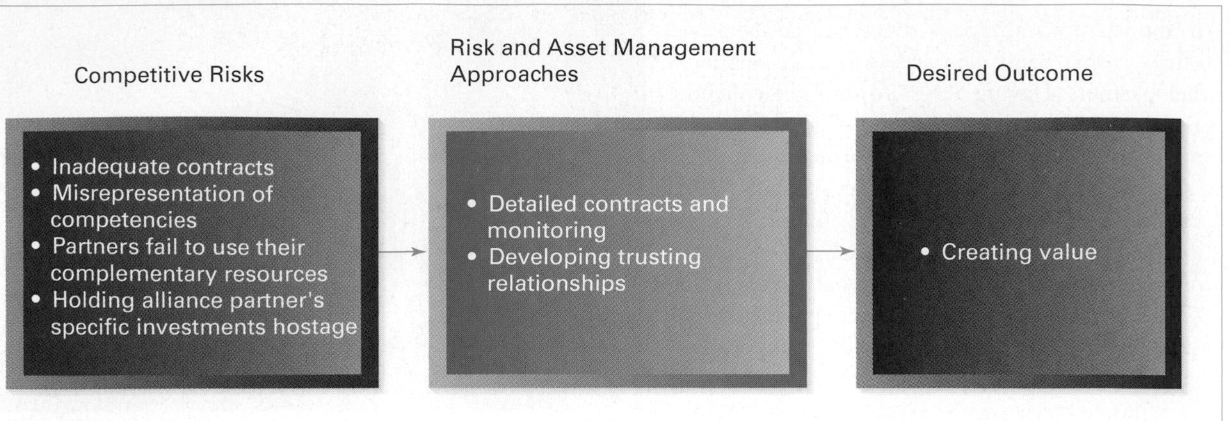

own 50 percent of the venture "that gave the Western company unprecedented access to vital Russian oil and gas." The Kremlin's increasing involvement in the nation's energy production activities and its claim that TNK-BP has failed to fulfill all of the terms of its license regarding production at one field (the Kovykta field) are threatening the venture. Part of the license requires the venture to produce 9 billion cubic meters of gas per year at Kovykta; the actual production is roughly 18 times less than this figure. Some speculate that Gazprom, the state-run gas giant, may join the venture as a partner to deal with the production shortfall. If this were to happen, "the question is what TNK-BP might be able to get for its stake." For its part, BP seeks to maintain good relationships with the Russian government; BP's plan to invest $1.25 billion in TNK-BP in 2007 demonstrates this commitment. Additionally, in light of the available oil and gas reserves in Russia, BP is forming other cooperative relationships including the minority stake it took in 2007 "in a venture with state oil giant Rosneft to drill for crude on Sakhalin Island."[125] Nonetheless, as we see, BP's cooperative strategies with Russian companies are not risk free.

Some cooperative strategies fail when it is discovered that a firm has misrepresented the competencies it can bring to the partnership. The risk of competence misrepresentation is more common when the partner's contribution is grounded in some of its intangible assets. Superior knowledge of local conditions is an example of an intangible asset that partners often fail to deliver. Asking the partner to provide evidence that it does possess the resources and capabilities (even when they are largely intangible) it is to share in the cooperative strategy may be an effective way to deal with this risk.

Another risk is a firm failing to make available to its partners the resources and capabilities (such as the most sophisticated technologies) that it committed to the cooperative strategy. This risk surfaces most commonly when firms form an international cooperative strategy.[126] In these instances, different cultures and languages can cause misinterpretations of contractual terms or trust-based expectations.

A final risk is that one firm may make investments that are specific to the alliance while its partner does not. For example, the firm might commit resources and capabilities to develop manufacturing equipment that can be used only to produce items coming from the alliance. If the partner isn't also making alliance-specific investments, the firm is at a relative disadvantage in terms of returns earned from the alliance compared with investments made to earn the returns. Issues such as these led to problems with the cooperative relationship that was formed between Pixar and Walt Disney Company.

Pixar (a computer animation studio) and entertainment giant Walt Disney Company partnered to develop and market several computer-animated features, including *Toy Story, Monsters Inc.,* and *Cars,* all of which were box-office hits. However, Disney perceived risks in its partnership with Pixar, largely because the films Pixar made without Disney were greater successes at the box office than were the films Disney made through its own studio operations. Moreover, the films Disney made with Pixar accounted for a substantial percentage of the profits Disney earned from its studio operations (35 percent in 2002). Thus, it seemed that Disney may have been making more alliance-specific commitments to the relationship than was Pixar.

Subsequently, ineffective communications between Pixar's chairman, Steve Jobs, and then-current Disney CEO (Michael Eisner) led to a breakdown of negotiations for a revised partnership arrangement in mid-2004. After some time and Eisner's departure as Disney's CEO, negotiations between the two firms resumed in September 2005. These negotiations led to Disney's purchase of Pixar in January 2006. The purchase was an all-stock transaction valued at $7.4 billion. Given that he owned 50.1 percent of Pixar, this transaction made Steve Jobs Disney's largest single shareholder. Currently, Disney is working on sequels to some of the box office successes that it had with Pixar (*Toy Story 3*, for example, will be in theaters in 2010).[127]

Managing Cooperative Strategies

Although cooperative strategies are an important means of firm growth and enhanced performance, managing these strategies is challenging. Learning how to effectively manage cooperative strategies is important however, in that being able to do so can be a source of competitive advantage.[128] Because the ability to effectively manage cooperative strategies is unevenly distributed across organizations in general, assigning managerial responsibility for a firm's cooperative strategies to a high-level executive or to a team improves the likelihood that the strategies will be well managed.

Those responsible for managing the firm's set of cooperative strategies should take the actions necessary to coordinate activities, categorize knowledge learned from previous experiences, and make certain that what the firm knows about how to effectively form and use cooperative strategies is in the hands of the right people at the right time. And firms must learn how to manage both the tangible assets and the intangible assets (such as knowledge) that are involved with a cooperative arrangement. Too often, partners concentrate on managing tangible assets at the expense of taking action to also manage a cooperative relationship's intangible assets.[129]

Two primary approaches are used to manage cooperative strategies—cost minimization and opportunity maximization[130] (see Figure 9.4). In the *cost minimization* management approach, the firm develops formal contracts with its partners. These contracts specify how the cooperative strategy is to be monitored and how partner behavior is to be controlled. The TNK-BP joint venture discussed previously is managed through contractual agreements. The goal of the cost minimization approach is to minimize the cooperative strategy's cost and to prevent opportunistic behavior by a partner. The focus of the second managerial approach—*opportunity maximization*—is on maximizing a partnership's value-creation opportunities. In this case, partners are prepared to take advantage of unexpected opportunities to learn from each other and to explore additional marketplace possibilities. Less formal contracts, with fewer constraints on partners' behaviors, make it possible for partners to explore how their resources and capabilities can be shared in multiple value-creating ways.

Firms can successfully use both approaches to manage cooperative strategies. However, the costs to monitor the cooperative strategy are greater with cost minimization, in that writing detailed contracts and using extensive monitoring mechanisms is expensive, even though the approach is intended to reduce alliance costs. Although monitoring systems may prevent partners from acting in their own best interests, they also often preclude positive responses to new opportunities that surface to use the alliance's competitive advantages. Thus, formal contracts and extensive monitoring systems tend to stifle partners' efforts to gain maximum value from their participation in a cooperative strategy and require significant resources to put into place and use.[131]

The relative lack of detail and formality that is a part of the contract developed by firms using the second management approach of opportunity maximization means that firms need to trust each other to act in the partnership's best interests. A psychological state, *trust* in the context of cooperative arrangements is "the expectation held by one firm that another will not exploit its vulnerabilities when faced with the opportunity to do so."[132] When partners trust each other, there is less need to write detailed formal contracts to specify each firm's alliance behaviors,[133] and the cooperative relationship tends to be more stable.[134] On a relative basis, trust tends to be more difficult to establish in international cooperative strategies compared with domestic ones. Differences in trade policies, cultures, laws, and politics that are part of cross-border alliances account for the increased difficulty. When trust exists, partners' monitoring costs are reduced and opportunities to create value are maximized. Essentially, in these cases, the firms have built social capital.[135] According to company officials, the alliance between Renault and Nissan that we examined in the Strategic Focus on page 255 is built on "mutual trust between the two partners . . . together with operating and confidentiality rules."[136]

Research showing that trust between partners increases the likelihood of alliance success seems to highlight the benefits of the opportunity maximization approach to managing cooperative strategies. Trust may also be the most efficient way to influence and control alliance partners' behaviors. Research indicates that trust can be a capability that is valuable, rare, imperfectly imitable, and often nonsubstitutable.[137] Thus, firms known to be trustworthy can have a competitive advantage in terms of how they develop and use cooperative strategies.[138] One reason is that it is impossible to specify all operational details of a cooperative strategy in a formal contract. Confidence that its partner can be trusted reduces the firm's concern about the inability to contractually control all alliance details.

Summary

- A cooperative strategy is one where firms work together to achieve a shared objective. Strategic alliances, where firms combine some of their resources and capabilities to create a competitive advantage, are the primary form of cooperative strategies. Joint ventures (where firms create and own equal shares of a new venture that is intended to develop competitive advantages), equity strategic alliances (where firms own different shares of a newly created venture), and nonequity strategic alliances (where firms cooperate through a contractual relationship) are the three basic types of strategic alliances. Outsourcing, discussed in Chapter 3, commonly occurs as firms form nonequity strategic alliances.
- Collusive strategies are the second type of cooperative strategies (with strategic alliances being the other). In many economies, explicit collusive strategies are illegal unless sanctioned by government policies. Increasing globalization has led to fewer government-sanctioned situations of explicit collusion. Tacit collusion, also called mutual forbearance, is a cooperative strategy through which firms tacitly cooperate to reduce industry output below the potential competitive output level, thereby raising prices above the competitive level.
- The reasons firms use cooperative strategies vary by slow-cycle, fast-cycle, and standard-cycle market conditions. To enter restricted markets (slow-cycle), to move quickly from one competitive advantage to another (fast-cycle), and to gain market power (standard-cycle) are among the reasons why firms choose to use cooperative strategies.
- Four business-level cooperative strategies are used to help the firm improve its performance in individual product markets. (1) Through vertical and horizontal complementary alliances, companies combine their resources and capabilities to create value in different parts (vertical) or the same parts (horizontal) of the value chain. (2) Competition-responding strategies are formed to respond to competitors' actions, especially strategic ones. (3) Competition-reducing strategies are used to avoid excessive competition while the firm marshals its resources and capabilities to improve its competitiveness. (4) Uncertainty-reducing strategies are used to hedge against the risks created by the conditions of uncertain competitive environments (such as new product markets). Complementary alliances have the highest probability of yielding a sustainable competitive advantage; competition-reducing alliances have the lowest probability of doing so.
- Firms use corporate-level cooperative strategies to engage in product and/or geographic diversification. Through diversifying strategic alliances, firms agree to share some of their resources and capabilities to enter new markets

or produce new products. Synergistic alliances are ones where firms share resources and capabilities to develop economies of scope. This alliance is similar to the business-level horizontal complementary alliance where firms try to develop operational synergy, except that synergistic alliances are used to develop synergy at the corporate level. Franchising is a corporate-level cooperative strategy where the franchisor uses a franchise as a contractual relationship to specify how resources and capabilities will be shared with franchisees.

- As an international cooperative strategy, a cross-border alliance is used for several reasons, including the performance superiority of firms competing in markets outside their domestic market and governmental restrictions on growth through mergers and acquisitions. Commonly, cross-border alliances are riskier than their domestic counterparts, particularly when partners aren't fully aware of each other's purpose for participating in the partnership.
- In a network cooperative strategy, several firms agree to form multiple partnerships to achieve shared objectives. A primary benefit of a network cooperative strategy is the firm's opportunity to gain access "to its partner's other partnerships." When this happens, the probability greatly increases that partners will find unique ways to share their resources and capabilities to form competitive advantages. Network cooperative strategies are used to form either a stable alliance network or a dynamic alliance network. Used in mature industries, partners use stable networks to extend competitive advantages into new areas. In rapidly changing environments where frequent product innovations occur, dynamic networks are primarily used as a tool of innovation.
- Cooperative strategies aren't risk free. If a contract is not developed appropriately, or if a partner misrepresents its competencies or fails to make them available, failure is likely. Furthermore, a firm may be held hostage through asset-specific investments made in conjunction with a partner, which may be exploited.
- Trust is an increasingly important aspect of successful cooperative strategies. Firms recognize the value of partnering with companies known for their trustworthiness. When trust exists, a cooperative strategy is managed to maximize the pursuit of opportunities between partners. Without trust, formal contracts and extensive monitoring systems are used to manage cooperative strategies. In this case, the interest is to minimize costs rather than to maximize opportunities by participating in a cooperative strategy.

Review Questions

1. What is the definition of cooperative strategy, and why is this strategy important to firms competing in the twenty-first century competitive landscape?
2. What is a strategic alliance? What are the three types of strategic alliances firms use to develop a competitive advantage?
3. What are the four business-level cooperative strategies, and what are the differences among them?
4. What are the three corporate-level cooperative strategies? How do firms use each one to create a competitive advantage?
5. Why do firms use cross-border strategic alliances?
6. What risks are firms likely to experience as they use cooperative strategies?
7. What are the differences between the cost-minimization approach and the opportunity-maximization approach to managing cooperative strategies?

Experiential Exercises

Exercise 1: Starbucks and Dreyers

The United States is the largest producer of frozen dairy desserts in the world. Although many of these products are destined for export, a substantial quantity of them is consumed within the United States as well. As evidence, the U.S. Department of Agriculture reports that the average American consumes between 15 and 16 pounds of ice cream each year. Additionally, Americans consume another 10 pounds per year of other frozen dairy desserts, including lowfat ice cream, yogurt, and related products.

In 1996, Starbucks and Dreyers Ice Cream (a subsidiary of Nestle) launched a series of coffee-flavored ice cream products. These products, with names such as Java Chip, Italian Roast Coffee, and Caffe Almond Fudge, contained actual coffee and were sold in supermarkets.

Group

Working in groups of 5–7 persons, answer the following questions:

1. What type of strategic alliance did Starbucks and Dreyers form?

2. In what type of market are they competing?
3. What is the rationale for the alliance between these two firms?

Exercise 2: The Swatchmobile

Swatch is well known for its line of stylish, affordable wristwatches. In the early 1990s, Swatch CEO Nicholas Hayek had a novel idea to diversify his company's product offerings: a stylish, affordable automobile. His vision was to create a two-seater car with minimal storage space. Fuel-efficient, he expected these cars would be highly attractive to younger European car buyers. Drawing on the company's watch designs, the Swatch car was intended to have removable body panels so that owners could change the car's look on a whim.

Swatch initially partnered with Volkswagen, but the alliance never reached production. In 1994, Swatch partnered with Mercedes-Benz. The vehicle was named SMART, which stood for "Swatch Mercedes Art."

Using Internet resources, answer the following questions:

1. What resources did each partner bring to the partnership?
2. How successful has the partnership been for each company?
3. Which company seems to be deriving the greatest benefit from the partnership and why?

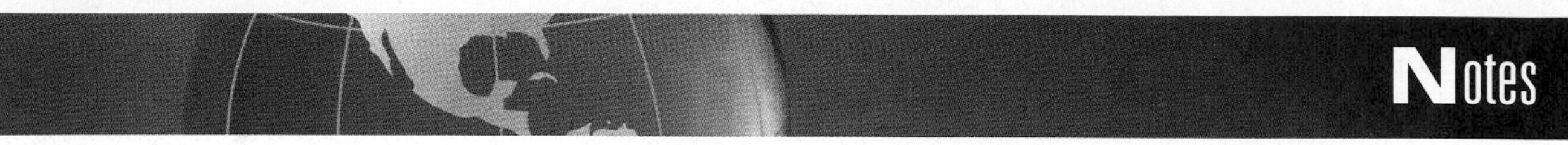

Notes

1. J. L. Morrow, Jr., D. G. Sirmon, M. A. Hitt, & T. R. Holcomb, 2007, Creating value in the face of declining performance: Firm strategies and organizational recovery, *Strategic Management Journal,* 28: 271–283.
2. 2007, Small-to-midsize firms often form alliances to kick start growth, *The Conference Board,* Release #5149, July 12.
3. R. C. Fink, L. F. Edelman, & K. J. Hatten, 2007, Supplier performance improvements in relational exchanges, *Journal of Business & Industrial Marketing,* 22: 29–40.
4. P. E. Bierly, III & S. Gallagher, 2007, Explaining alliance partner selection: Fit, trust and strategic expediency, *Long Range Planning,* 40: 134–153; K. Singh & W. Mitchell, 2005, Growth dynamics: The bidirectional relationship between interfirm collaboration and business sales in entrant and incumbent alliances, *Strategic Management Journal,* 26: 497–521.
5. P. M. Senge, B. B. Lichtenstein, K. Kaeufer, H. Bradbury, & J. Carroll, 2007, Collaborating for systemic change, *MIT Sloan Management Review,* 48(2): 44–53; C. Hardy, T. B. Lawrence, & D. Grant, 2005, Discourse and collaboration: The role of conversations and collective identity, *Academy of Management Review,* 30: 58–77; R. Vassolo, J. Anand, & T. B. Folta, 2004, Non-additivity in portfolios of exploration activities: A real options-based analysis of equity alliances in biotechnology, *Strategic Management Journal,* 25: 1045–1061.
6. T. L. Sorenson, 2007, Credible collusion in multimarket oligopoly, *Managerial and Decision Economics,* 28: 115–128.
7. R. D. Ireland, M. A. Hitt, & D. Vaidyanath, 2002, Alliance management as a source of competitive advantage, *Journal of Management,* 28: 413–446; J. G. Coombs & D. J. Ketchen, 1999, Exploring interfirm cooperation and performance: Toward a reconciliation of predictions from the resource-based view and organizational economics, *Strategic Management Journal,* 20: 867–888.
8. J. J. Reuer & A. Arino, 2007, Strategic alliance contracts: Dimensions and determinants of contractual complexity, *Strategic Management Journal,* 28: 313–330; M. R. Subramani & N. Venkatraman, 2003, Safeguarding investments in asymmetric interorganizational relationships: Theory and evidence, *Academy of Management Journal,* 46(1): 46–62.
9. R. Krishnan, X Martin, & N. G. Noorderhaven, 2007, When does trust matter to alliance performance? *Academy of Management Journal,* 49: 894–917; P. Kale, J. H. Dyer, & H. Singh, 2002, Alliance capability, stock market response, and long-term alliance success: The role of the alliance function, *Strategic Management Journal,* 23: 747–767.
10. K. H. Heimeriks & G. Duysters, 2007, Alliance capability as a mediator between experience and alliance performance: An empirical investigation into the alliance capability development process, *Journal of Management Studies,* 44: 25–49.
11. R. E. Hoskisson, M. A. Hitt, R. D. Ireland, & J. S. Harrison, 2008, *Competing for Advantage,* 2nd ed., Thomson/Southwestern, 184.
12. R. Seppanen, K. Blomqvist, & S. Sundqvist, 2007, Measuring interorganizational trust—A critical review of the empirical research in 1990–2003, *Industrial Marketing Management,* 36: 249–265; T. K. Das & B.-S. Teng, 2001, A risk perception model of alliance structuring, *Journal of International Management,* 7: 1–29.
13. F. F. Suarez & G. Lanzolla, 2007, The role of environmental dynamics in building a first mover advantage theory, *Academy of Management Review,* 32: 377–392; M. A. Geletkanycz & S. S. Black, 2001, Bound by the past? Experience-based effects on commitment to the strategic status quo, *Journal of Management,* 27: 3–21.
14. 2007, Lockheed Martin and Boeing form strategic alliance, http://www.lockheedmartin.com, January 22.
15. T. Wailgum & D. Kleiman, 2007, Picture perfect, *Continental.com Magazine,* June, 76–79.
16. D. Gerwin, 2004, Coordinating new product development in strategic alliances, *Academy of Management Review,* 29: 241–257; Ireland, Hitt, & Vaidyanath, Alliance management as a source of competitive advantage.
17. 2007, Strategic alliance formed between OSC and DOB, http://www.nyfms.state.ny.us, April 23.
18. 2007, Strategic alliances and joint ventures: A how to guide, *New Zealand Trade & Enterprise,* http://exportyear.co.nz, March.
19. Y. Luo, 2007, Are joint venture partners more opportunistic in a more volatile environment? *Strategic Management Journal,* 28: 39–60.
20. S. L. Berman, J. Down, & C. W. L. Hill, 2002, Tacit knowledge as a source of competitive advantage in the National Basketball Association, *Academy of Management Journal,* 45: 13–31.
21. R. W. Coff, D. C. Coff & R. Eastvold, 2007, The knowledge-leveraging paradox: How to achieve scale without making knowledge imitable, *Academy of Management Review,* 31: 452-465; H. Hoang & F. T. Rothaermel, 2005, The effect of general and partner-specific alliance experience on joint R&D project performance, *Academy of Management Journal,* 48: 332–345.
22. T. Agins, 2007, Polo, Richemont team up in watch and jewelry venture, *Wall Street Journal Online,* http://online.wsj.com, March 5.
23. L. G. Zucker, M. R. Darby, J. Furner, & R. C. Liu, 2007, Minerva unbound:

Knowledge flows and new knowledge production, *Research Policy,* 36: 850–863; R. E. Hoskisson & L. W. Busenitz, 2002, Market uncertainty and learning distance in corporate entrepreneurship entry mode choice, in M. A. Hitt, R. D. Ireland, S. M. Camp, & D. L. Sexton (eds.), *Strategic Entrepreneurship: Creating a New Mindset,* Oxford, UK: Blackwell Publishers, 151–172.

24. D. Greenaway & R. Kneller, 2007, Firm heterogeneity, exporting and foreign direct investment, *The Economic Journal,* 117: F134–F161; A.-W. Harzing, 2002, Acquisitions versus greenfield investments: International strategy and management of entry modes, *Strategic Management Journal,* 23: 211–227.
25. 2007, Citigroup and Nikko Cordial agree on comprehensive strategic alliance, http://www.citi.com/domain/index.htm, March 6.
26. Y. Wang & S. Nicholas, 2007, The formation and evolution of nonequity strategic alliances in China, *Asia Pacific Journal of Management,* 24: 131–150.
27. R. Kumar & T. K. Das, 2007, Interpartner legitimacy in the alliance development process, *Journal of Management Studies,* in press.
28. S. Comino, P. Mariel, & J. Sandonis, 2007, Joint ventures versus contractual agreements: An empirical investigation, *Spanish Economic Journal,* 9: 159–175.
29. 2007, Intellectual property licensing, http://hp.com, August 30.
30. M. Lifsher, 2007, Companies say they can build prisons cheaper, faster than government, *Bryan-College Station Eagle,* September 2, E1, E2.
31. L. M. Anglada, 2007, Collaborations and alliances: Social intelligence applied to academic libraries, *Library Management,* 28: 406–415.
32. M. J. Kelly, J.-L. Schaan, & H. Jonacas, 2002, Managing alliance relationships: Key challenges in the early stages of collaboration, *R&D Management,* 32(1): 11–22.
33. A. C. Inkpen & J. Ross, 2001, Why do some strategic alliances persist beyond their useful life? *California Management Review,* 44(1): 132–148.
34. M. Haiken, Innovative partnering, 2007, http://money.cnn.com, February 28; C. Hardy, N. Phillips, & T. B. Lawrence, 2003, Resources, knowledge and influence: The organizational effects of interorganizational collaboration, *Journal of Management Studies,* 40(2): 321–347.
35. F. Rothaermel & D. L. Deeds, 2006, Alliance type, alliance experience and alliance management capability in high-technology ventures, *Journal of Business Venturing,* 21: 429–460; L. Fuentelsaz, J. Gomez, & Y. Polo, 2002, Followers' entry timing: Evidence from the Spanish banking sector after deregulation, *Strategic Management Journal,* 23: 245–264.
36. B. L. Bourdeau, J. J. Cronink, Jr., & C. M. Voorhees, 2007, Modeling service alliances: An exploratory investigation of spillover effects in service partnerships, *Strategic Management Journal,* 28: 609–622.
37. 2007, Motorola enters strategic alliance with Suning, *ChinaTechNews,* http://chinatechnews.com, April 17.
38. A. Arino, P. Olk, & J. J. Reuer, 2008, *Entrepreneurial Strategic Alliances,* Prentice Hall, in press.
39. S. G. Lazzarini, 2007, The impact of membership in competing alliance constellations: Evidence on the operational performance of global airlines, *Strategic Management Journal,* 28: 345–367.
40. M. A. Hitt, D. Ahlstrom, M. T. Dacin, E. Levitas, & L. Svobodina, 2004, The institutional effects of strategic alliance partner selection in transition economies: China versus Russia, *Organization Science,* 15: 173–185; P. A. Saparito, C. C. Chen, & H. J. Sapienza, 2004, The role of relational trust in bank-small firm relationships, *Academy of Management Journal,* 47: 400–410.
41. A. C. Inkpen & E. W. K. Tsang, 2005, Social capital, networks and knowledge transfer, *Academy of Management Review,* 30: 146–165.
42. M. Hughes, R. D. Ireland, & R. E. Morgan, 2007, Stimulating dynamic value: Social capital and business incubation as a pathway to competitive success, *Long Range Planning,* 40(2): 154-177; T. G. Pollock, J. F. Porac, & J. B. Wade, 2004, Constructing deal networks: Brokers as network "architects" in the U.S. IPO market and other examples, *Academy of Management Review,* 29: 50–72.
43. J. R. Williams, 1998, *Renewable Advantage: Crafting Strategy Through Economic Time,* New York: The Free Press.
44. 2007, ArcelorMittal broadens strategic alliance with Nippon Steel, http://reuters.com, July 12.
45. S. A. Zahra, R. D. Ireland, I. Gutierrez, & M. A. Hitt, 2000, Privatization and entrepreneurial transformation: Emerging issues and a future research agenda, *Academy of Management Review,* 25: 509–524.
46. I. Filatotchev, M. Wright, K. Uhlenbruck, L. Tihanyi, & R. E. Hoskisson, 2003, Governance, organizational capabilities, and restructuring in transition economies, *Journal of World Business,* 38(4): 331–347.
47. J. Lash & F. Wellington, 2007, Competitive advantage on a warming planet, *Harvard Business Review,* 85(3): 94–102; K. M. Eisenhardt, 2002, Has strategy changed? *MIT Sloan Management Review,* 43(2): 88–91.
48. 2007, Dell joins Microsoft and Novell collaboration, http://novell.com, May 7.
49. C. Czipura & D. R. Jolly, 2007, Global airline alliances: Sparking profitability for a troubled industry, *Journal of Business Strategy,* 28(2): 57–64.
50. 2007, Tourism futures international, http://tourismfuturesintl.com, August 26.
51. 2007, Airline alliance, Wikipedia, http://en.wikipedia.org, August 26; D. Michaels & J. L. Lunsford, 2003, Airlines move toward buying planes jointly, *Wall Street Journal,* May 20, A3.
52. D. R. King, J. G. Covin, & H. Hegarty, 2003, Complementary resources and the exploitation of technological innovations, *Journal of Management,* 29: 589–606; J. S. Harrison, M. A. Hitt, R. E. Hoskisson, & R. D. Ireland, 2001, Resource complementarity in business combinations: Extending the logic to organizational alliances, *Journal of Management,* 27: 679–699.
53. F. T. Rothaermel, M. A. Hitt, & L. A. Jobe, 2006, Balancing vertical integration and strategic outsourcing: Effects on product portfolio, product success, and firm performance, *Strategic Management Journal,* 27: 1033–1056.
54. R. Gulati, P. R. Lawrence, & P. Puranam, 2005, Adaptation in vertical relationships beyond incentive conflict, *Strategic Management Journal,* 26: 415–440.
55. B.-S. Teng, 2007, Corporate entrepreneurship activities through strategic alliances: A resource-based approach toward competitive advantage, *Journal of Management Studies,* 44: 119–142.
56. 2007, Konica Minolta and GE form strategic alliance to accelerate the commercialization of OLED lighting, http://konicaminolta.com, March 27.
57. F. T. Rothaermel & M. Thursby, 2007, The nanotech versus the biotech revolution: Sources of productivity in incumbent firm research, *Research Policy,* 36: 832–849; T. H. Oum, J.-H. Park, K. Kim & C. Yu, 2004, The effect of horizontal alliances on firm productivity and profitability: Evidence from the global airline industry; *Journal of Business Research,* 57: 844–853.
58. S. Nelson, 2007, Strategic alliances are channels for innovation at Sprint Nextel, *Global Business and Organizational Excellence,* 26(5): 6–12.
59. 2007, Strategic alliances, http://sprint.com, August 30.
60. C. Bryan-Low & B. Lagrotteria, 2005, France Telecom and Microsoft forge product alliance, *Wall Street Journal Online,* http://online.wsj.com, July 7.
61. J. J. Reuer & T. W. Tong, 2005, Real options in international joint ventures, *Journal of Management,* 31: 403–423; S. Chatterjee, R. M. Wiseman, A. Fiegenbaum, & C. E. Devers, 2003, Integrating behavioral and economic concepts of risk into strategic management: The twain shall meet, *Long Range Planning,* 36(1), 61–80.
62. 2007, ConocoPhillips and Tyson Foods announce strategic alliance, http://conocophillips.com, April 16.
63. L. Tesfatsion, 2007, Agents come to bits: Toward a constructive comprehensive taxonomy of economic entities, *Journal*

of Economic Behavior & Organization, 63: 333–346.

64. M. Adams, 2006, Airline price-fixing allegations raised, *USA Today,* http://usatoday.com, June 23.
65. 2007, LUKOIL dismisses charges of price fixing in U.S., RIA Novosti, http://en.rian.ru/business.com, June 8.
66. C. d'Aspremont, R. D. S. Ferreira & L.-A. Gerard-Varet, 2007, Competition for market share or for market size: Oligopolistic equilibria with varying competitive toughness, *International Economic Review,* 48: 761–784.
67. G. K. Price & J. M. Connor, 2003, Modeling coupon values for ready-to-eat breakfast cereals, *Agribusiness,* 19(2): 223–244.
68. G. K. Price, 2000, Cereal sales soggy despite price cuts and reduced couponing, *Food Review,* 23(2): 21–28.
69. J. Hagedoorn & G. Hesen, 2007, Contract law and the governance of interfirm technology partnerships—An analysis of different modes of partnering and their contractual implications, *Journal of Management Studies,* 44: 342–366; B. R. Golden & H. Ma, 2003, Mutual forbearance: The role of intrafirm integration and rewards, *Academy of Management Review,* 28: 479–493.
70. J. Apesteguia, M. Dufwenberg, & R. Selton, 2007, Blowing the whistle, *Economic Theory,* 31: 127–142.
71. J. H. Johnson & G. K. Leonard, 2007, Economics and the rigorous analysis of class certification in antitrust cases, *Journal of Competition Law and Economics,* http://jcle.oxfordjournals.org, June 26.
72. P. Dussauge, B. Garrette, & W. Mitchell, 2004, Asymmetric performances: The market share impact of scale ad link alliances in global auto industry, *Strategic Management Journal,* 25: 701–711.
73. Harrison, Hitt, Hoskisson, & Ireland, Resource complementarity, 684–685.
74. R. Grunwald & A. Kieser, 2007, Learning to reduce interorganizational learning: An analysis of architectural product innovation in strategic alliances, *Journal of Product Innovation Management,* 24: 369–391; A. E. Bernardo & B. Chowdhry, 2002, Resources, real options, and corporate strategy, *Journal of Financial Economics,* 63: 211–234; Inkpen, Strategic alliances, 413.
75. J. L. Johnson, R. P.-W. Lee, A. Saini, & B. Grohmann, 2003, Market-focused strategic flexibility: Conceptual advances and an integrative model, *Academy of Marketing Science Journal,* 31: 74–90.
76. C. C. Pegels & Y. I. Song, 2007, Market competition and cooperation: Identifying competitive/cooperative interaction groups, *International Journal of Services Technology and Management,* 2/3: 139–154; Folta & Miller, Real options in equity partnerships, 77.
77. S. Berfield, 2007, Room service, send up some slime, *BusinessWeek,* June 11, 38.
78. A. Goerzen & P. W. Beamish, 2005, The effect of alliance network diversity on multinational enterprise performance, *Strategic Management Journal,* 333–354.
79. M. V. Shyam Kumar, 2005, The value from acquiring and divesting a joint venture: A real options approach, *Strategic Management Journal,* 26: 321–331.
80. J. Yang, 2003, One step forward for Japan's chipmakers, *BusinessWeek Online,* http://www.businessweek.com, July 7.
81. 2007, YouTube, Wikipedia, http://en.wikipedia.org, August 31.
82. R. Siklos & B. Carter, 2006, Old model versus a speedster, *New York Times Online,* http://nytimes.com, December 18.
83. M. Tuunanen & F. Hoy, 2007, Franchising—multifaceted form of entrepreneurship, *International Journal of Entrepreneurship and Small Business,* 4: 52–67; J. G. Combs & D. J. Ketchen Jr., 2003, Why do firms use franchising as an entrepreneurial strategy? A meta-analysis, *Journal of Management,* 29: 427–443.
84. F. Lafontaine, 1999, Myths and strengths of franchising, "Mastering Strategy" (Part Nine), *Financial Times,* November 22, 8–10.
85. 2007, What is franchising? *Franchising.com,* http://franchising.com, August 31.
86. 2007, Franchising, Wikipedia, http://en.wikipedia.org, August 31.
87. B. Barringer & R. D. Ireland, 2008, *Entrepreneurship: Successfully Launching New Ventures,* 2nd ed., Prentice Hall, 440.
88. 2007, Global trends in franchising, *DCStrategy,* http://dcstrategy.com, August 23.
89. R. B. DiPietro, D. H. B. Welsh, P. V. Raven, & D. Severt, 2007, A message of hope in franchises systems: Assessing franchisees, top executives, and franchisors, *Journal of Leadership & Organizational Studies,* 13(3): 59–66; S. C. Michael, 2002, Can a franchise chain coordinate? *Journal of Business Venturing,* 17: 325–342.
90. J. Barthelemy, 2004, The administrative productivity of U.S. franchisors: An empirical investigation, *Economics Letters,* 83(1): 115–121.
91. J. Torikka, 2007, Franchisees can be made: Empirical evidence from a follow-up study, *International Journal of Entrepreneurship and Small Business,* 4: 68–96; P. J. Kaufmann & S. Eroglu, 1999, Standardization and adaptation in business format franchising, *Journal of Business Venturing,* 14: 69–85.
92. S. C. Michael, 2002, First mover advantage through franchising, *Journal of Business Venturing,* 18: 61–81.
93. M. Zollo, J. J. Reuer, & H. Singh, 2002, Interorganizational routines and performance in strategic alliances, *Organization Science,* 13: 701–714.
94. Ireland, Hitt, & Vaidyanath, Alliance management.
95. A. V. Shipilov, 2007, Network strategies and performance of Canadian investment banks, *Academy of Management Journal,* 49: 590–604; P. Almeida, G. Dokko, & L. Rosenkopf, 2003, Startup size and the mechanisms of external learning: Increasing opportunity and decreasing ability? *Research Policy,* 32(2): 301–316.
96. R. Narula & G. Duysters, 2004, Globalization and trends in international R&D alliances, *Journal of International Management,* 10: 199–218; M. A. Hitt, M. T. Dacin, E. Levitas, J.-L. Arregle, & A. Borza, 2000, Partner selection in emerging and developed market contexts: Resource-based and organizational learning perspectives, *Academy of Management Journal,* 43: 449–467.
97. J. H. Dyer, P. Kale, & H. Singh, 2004, When to ally & when to acquire, *Harvard Business Review,* 81(7/8): 109–115.
98. P. Ghemawat, 2007, Managing differences: The central challenge of global strategy, *Harvard Business Review,* 85(3): 59–68.
99. 2007, Sony Ericsson, *Wikipedia,* http://en.wikipedia.org, August 28.
100. L. Dong & K.W. Glaister, 2007, National and corporate culture differences in international strategic alliances: Perceptions of Chinese partners, *Asia Pacific Journal of Management,* 24: 191–205; I. M. Manev, 2003, The managerial network in a multinational enterprise and the resource profiles of subsidiaries, *Journal of International Management,* 9: 133–152.
101. P. H. Dickson, K. M. Weaver, & F. Hoy, 2006, Opportunism in the R&D alliances of SMEs: The roles of the institutional environment and SME size, *Journal of Business Venturing,* 21: 487–513; H. K. Steensma, L. Tihanyi, M. A. Lyles, & C. Dhanaraj, 2005, The evolving value of foreign partnerships in transitioning economies, *Academy of Management Journal,* 48: 213–235.
102. 2007, Branding and celebrity endorsements, *VentureRepublic,* http://venturerepublic.com, August 31.
103. Y. Luo, O. Shenkar, & M.-K. Nyaw, 2002, Mitigating the liabilities of foreignness: Defensive versus offensive approaches, *Journal of International Management,* 8: 283–300.
104. S. R. Miller & A. Parkhe, 2002, Is there a liability of foreignness in global banking? An empirical test of banks' x-efficiency, *Strategic Management Journal,* 23: 55–75; Y. Luo, 2001, Determinants of local responsiveness: Perspectives from foreign subsidiaries in an emerging market, *Journal of Management,* 27: 451–477.
105. D. Li, L. E. Eden, M. A. Hitt, & R. D. Ireland, 2008, Friends, acquaintances or strangers? Partner selection in R&D alliances, *Academy of Management Journal,* in press; J. E. Oxley & R. C. Sampson, 2004, The scope and governance of international R&D alliances, *Strategic Management Journal,* 25: 723–749.

106. 2006, Starbucks acquires control of China joint venture, *Apostille US*, http://apostille.us.com, October 25.
107. D. Lavie, C. Lechner, & H. Singh, 2007, The performance implications of timing of entry and involvement in multipartner alliances, *Academy of Management Journal*, 49: 569–604; Z. Zhao, J. Anand, & W. Mitchell, 2005, A dual networks perspective on inter-organizational transfer of R&D capabilities: International joint ventures in the Chinese automotive industry, *Journal of Management Studies*, 42: 127–160.
108. A. Nosella & G. Petroni, 2007, Multiple network leadership as a strategic asset: The Carlo Gavazzi space case, *Long Range Planning*, 40: 178–201.
109. K. Sawyer, 2007, Strength in webs, *The Conference Board*, July/August, 9–11.
110. A. H. Van de Ven & H. J. Sapienza, 2008, Entrepreneurial pursuits of self and collective interests in resource mobilization and running in packs, *Strategic Entrepreneurship Journal*, in press; M. Ferrary, 2003, Managing the disruptive technologies life cycle by externalizing the research: Social network and corporate venturing in the Silicon Valley, *International Journal of Technology Management*, 25(1,2): 165–180.
111. G. K. Lee, 2007, The significance of network resources in the race to enter emerging product markets: The convergence of telephony communications and computer networking, 1989–2001, *Strategic Management Journal*, 28: 17–37; A. C. Cooper, 2002, Networks, alliances, and entrepreneurship, in M. A. Hitt, R. D. Ireland, S. M. Camp, & D. L. Sexton (eds.), *Strategic Entrepreneurship: Creating a New Mindset*, Oxford, UK: Blackwell Publishers, 203–222.
112. G. G. Bell, 2005, Clusters, networks, and firm innovativeness, *Strategic Management Journal*, 26: 287–295.
113. H. Kim, R. E. Hoskisson, & W. P. Wan, 2004, Power, dependence, diversification strategy and performance in keiretsu member firms, *Strategic Management Journal*, 25: 613–636.
114. M. Rudberg & J. Olhager, 2003, Manufacturing networks and supply chains: An operations strategy perspective, *Omega*, 31(1): 29–39.
115. E. J. Kleinschmidt, U. de Brentani, & S. Salomo, 2007, Programs: A resource-based view, *Journal of Product Innovation Management*, 24: 419–441; G. J. Young, M. P. Charns, & S. M. Shortell, 2001, Top manager and network effects on the adoption of innovative management practices: A study of TQM in a public hospital system, *Strategic Management Journal*, 22: 935–951.
116. E. Garcia-Canal, C. L. Duarte, J. R. Criado, & A. V. Llaneza, 2002, Accelerating international expansion through global alliances: A typology of cooperative strategies, *Journal of World Business*, 37(2): 91–107; F. T. Rothaermel, 2001, Complementary assets, strategic alliances, and the incumbent's advantage: An empirical study of industry and firm effects in the biopharmaceutical industry, *Research Policy*, 30: 1235–1251.
117. V. Shankar & B. L. Bayus, 2003, Network effects and competition: An empirical analysis of the home video game industry, *Strategic Management Journal*, 24: 375–384.
118. Z. Simsek, M. H. Lubatkin, & D. Kandemir, 2003, Inter-firm networks and entrepreneurial behavior: A structural embeddedness perspective, *Journal of Management*, 29: 401–426.
119. P. Puranam & K. Srikanth, 2007, What they know vs. what they do: How acquirers leverage technology acquisitions, *Strategic Management Journal*, 28: 805–825; M. Moensted, 2007, Strategic networking in small high-tech firms, *The International Entrepreneurship and Management Journal*, 3: 15–27.
120. C. T. Street & A.-F. Cameron, 2007, External relationships and the small business: A review of small business alliance and network research, *Journal of Small Business Management*, 45: 239–266.
121. T. K. Das & R. Kumar, 2007, Learning dynamics in the alliance development process, *Management Decision*, 45: 684–707.
122. J.-Y. Kim & A. S. Miner, 2007, Vicarious learning from the failures and near-failures of others: Evidence from the U.S. commercial banking industry, *Academy of Management Journal*, 49: 687–714.
123. P. M. Norman, 2002, Protecting knowledge in strategic alliances—Resource and relational characteristics, *Journal of High Technology Management Research*, 13(2): 177–202; P. M. Norman, 2001, Are your secrets safe? Knowledge protection in strategic alliances, *Business Horizons*, November–December, 51–60.
124. J. Connell & R. Voola, 2007, Strategic alliances and knowledge sharing: Synergies or silos? *Journal of Knowledge Management*, 11: 52–66.
125. J. Bush, 2007, The Kremlin's big squeeze, *BusinessWeek*, April 30, 42–43.
126. P. D. Cousins & B. Lawson, 2007, Sourcing strategy, supplier relationships and firm performance: An empirical investigation of UK organizations, *British Journal of Management*, 18(2): 123–137; P. Lane, J. E. Salk, & M. A. Lyles, 2001, Absorptive capacity, learning, and performance in international joint ventures, *Strategic Management Journal*, 22: 1139–1161.
127. 2007, Pixar, *Wikipedia*, http://en.wikipedia.org, September 2.
128. K. G. Provan & P. Kenis, 2007, Modes of network governance: Structure, management, and effectiveness, *Journal of Public Administration Research and Theory*, in press; J. H. Dyer, P. Kale, & H. Singh, 2001, How to make strategic alliances work, *MIT Sloan Management Review*, 42(4): 37–43.
129. Connell & Voola, Strategic alliances and knowledge sharing.
130. J. H. Dyer, 1997, Effective interfirm collaboration: How firms minimize transaction costs and maximize transaction value, *Strategic Management Journal*, 18: 535–556.
131. J. H. Dyer & C. Wujin, 2003, The role of trustworthiness in reducing transaction costs and improving performance: Empirical evidence from the United States, Japan, and Korea, *Organization Science*, 14: 57–69.
132. Krishnan, Martin, & Noorderhaven, When does trust matter to alliance performance?
133. M. Lundin, 2007, Explaining cooperation: How resource interdependence, goal congruence, and trust affect joint actions in policy implementation, *Journal of Public Administration Research and Theory*, in press.
134. V. Perrone, A. Zaheer, & B. McEvily, 2003, Free to be trusted? Boundary constraints on trust in boundary spanners, *Organization Science*, 14: 422–439; H. K. Steensma, L. Marino, & K. M. Weaver, 2000, Attitudes toward cooperative strategies: A cross-cultural analysis of entrepreneurs, *Journal of International Business Studies*, 31: 591–609.
135. R. D. Ireland & J. W. Webb, 2007, A multi-theoretic perspective on trust and power in strategic supply chains, *Journal of Operations Management*, 25: 482–497.
136. 2007, The principles of the alliance, http://renault.com, August 26.
137. F. D. Schoorman, R. C. Mayer, & J. H. Davis, 2007, An integrative model of organizational trust: Past, present, and future, *Academy of Management Review*, 344–354; J. H. Davis, F. D. Schoorman, R. C. Mayer, & H. H. Tan, 2000, The trusted general manager and business unit performance: Empirical evidence of a competitive advantage, *Strategic Management Journal*, 21: 563–576.
138. B. Hillebrand & W. G. Biemans, 2003, The relationship between internal and external cooperation: Literature review and propositions, *Journal of Business Research*, 56: 735–744.

Part 3 Strategic Actions: Strategy Implementation

Corporate Governance

Studying this chapter should provide you with the strategic management knowledge needed to:

1. Define corporate governance and explain why it is used to monitor and control managers' strategic decisions.
2. Explain why ownership has been largely separated from managerial control in the modern corporation.
3. Define an agency relationship and managerial opportunism and describe their strategic implications.
4. Explain how three internal governance mechanisms—ownership concentration, the board of directors, and executive compensation—are used to monitor and control managerial decisions.
5. Discuss the types of compensation executives receive and their effects on strategic decisions.
6. Describe how the external corporate governance mechanism—the market for corporate control—acts as a restraint on top-level managers' strategic decisions.
7. Discuss the use of corporate governance in international settings, especially in Germany and Japan.
8. Describe how corporate governance fosters ethical strategic decisions and the importance of such behaviors on the part of top-level executives.

How Has Increasingly Intensive Corporate Governance Affected the Lives of CEOs?

© AP Photo/Gail Burton

In 2006, a record number of CEOs left their jobs through dismissal, retirement, or recruitment to another firm. This notable exodus is due in part to increasing scrutiny by boards, governance activists, and increased pressure from the market for corporate control (other firms considering an ownership position or outright purchase of an underperforming target firm), especially by private equity firms and activist hedge funds. Although many CEOs still hold the title of chair and chief executive officer, the day of the "Imperial CEO" is over as board members are pressured to challenge the views of the CEO if they appear to be headed in a direction that will not benefit all stakeholders. As such, outside directors are also more forthright. Nell Minow, a corporate governance expert, indicated, "It used to be that it was considered somehow impolite or improper (for a board member) to ask a tough question, now it is considered irresponsible not to ask a tough question."

Also, the controversy and scrutiny in the media, by government agencies such as the Security and Exchange Commission (SEC), and from activist shareholders (e.g., pension funds) over executive pay is increasing. The Sarbanes-Oxley legislation (passed in 2002) caused U.S. corporate governance policies to be more intense. This scrutiny translates into a zero tolerance for any form of corruption, conflict of interest, or other forms of wrongdoing or inappropriate behavior.

On the other hand, all of this scrutiny may have a price. Interestingly, the average tenure of CEOs is now down to 18–24 months because so many new CEOs have been appointed. An article in the *Harvard Business Review* reported, "At the current rate, almost 50 percent of the largest U.S. firms will have a new CEO in the next four years." This trend presents a true challenge for a CEO who comes from the outside to make the business profitable in a short period of time without inside knowledge of how to run the business. Because of the high turnover and shorter tenures, CEOs are focusing more and more on short-term turnaround corporate strategies and contractually looking to their inevitable departure. Ironically, the increases in governance controls have led to an increase in CEO pay and severance perks, including golden parachutes that often pay three years of annual salary if a CEO exits before his/her contract expires because the firm is taken over. If the SEC sets a limit on exit pay, CEOs will likely arrange more pay upfront to compensate for the risks they are taking, given the shorter CEO tenures in most firms.

Additionally, CEOs are now serving on fewer external boards in order to focus on their own firms' activities. However, the result is less external governance experience for CEOs to understand a large complex operation associated with most S&P 500 or *Fortune* 500–type firms. Author of the book *Built to Last,* Jim Collins, found that inside CEOs are able to provide information that is idiosyncratic and allows the firm to experience longer-term profitability and above-average returns. The problem, he argues, is that on average it took about seven years into a CEO's tenure to help a firm achieve profitability, which does not bode well for most CEOs who are "resigning" much sooner than seven years. Collins suggests, "If we're systematically looking for saviors and shortening the amount of time a CEO gets, we're on a systematic path toward increased mediocrity."

In summary, corporate governance is a double-edged sword. On the one hand, it is necessary to put an end to scandals such as the Enron disaster, which led to a significant loss for all of the stakeholders involved, including employees. Also, CEO compensation is quite excessive relative to other managers and employees. On the other hand, governance that is overly restrictive can reduce managerial risk taking and increase governance costs excessively as well as constrain the CEO's decision-making authority. Ironically, it inadvertently leads to increased pay for CEOs, which many governance activists rail against. Although corporate governance is a necessity, it is also important to make sure that it is executed properly to avoid the problems noted here.

Sources: N. Byrnes & J. Sasseen, 2007, Board of hard knocks: Activist shareholders, tougher rules and anger over CEO pay have put directors on the hot seat, *BusinessWeek*, January 22, 37–39; K. P. Coyne & E. J. Coyne, Sr., 2007, Surviving your CEO, *Harvard Business Review*, 85(5): 1–9; D. R. Dalton & C. M. Dalton, 2007, CEO succession: Best practices in a changing environment, *Journal of Business Strategy*, 28(2): 11–13; L. Dittmar, 2007, Raising the bar on governance: Are boards up to the task? *Financial Executive*, 23(2): 50–53; D. Eichinger, 2007, Do you know where your next CEO is? *BusinessWeek*, http://www.businessweek.com, July 31; F. Guerrera, 2007, Once-mighty U.S. chiefs feel the heat, *Financial Times*, January 3, 22; C. Hymowitz, 2007, Personal boundaries shrink as companies punish bad behavior, *Wall Street Journal*, June 18, B1; K. Kelly, 2007, Roller coaster leadership, *Business Strategy Review*, 18(1): 22–27; 2006, Why corporate boardrooms are in turmoil, *Wall Street Journal*, September 16, A7; N. Byrnes, D. Kiley, R. O. Crockett, & T. Lowry, 2006, The great CEO exodus, *BusinessWeek*, October 30, 78.

As the Opening Case illustrates, making sure that the governance devices used to oversee firms are appropriately applied is an increasingly important part of the strategic management process.[1] If the board makes the wrong decisions in selecting, governing, and compensating the firm's strategic leader (e.g., CEO), the shareholders and the firm suffer. When CEOs are motivated to act in the best interest of the firm—in particular, the shareholders—the firm's value should increase.

Although some critics argue that CEOs in the United States are paid too much, the hefty increases in their incentive compensation in recent years ostensibly come from linking pay to their firms' performance, and U.S. firms have performed better than many companies in other countries. However, research also suggests that firms with a smaller pay gap between the CEO and other top executives perform better, especially when collaboration among top management team members is more important.[2] The performance improvement is attributed to better cooperation among the top management team members. Other research suggests that CEOs receive excessive compensation when corporate governance is the weakest.[3]

Corporate governance is the set of mechanisms used to manage the relationship among stakeholders and to determine and control the strategic direction and performance of organizations.

Corporate governance is the set of mechanisms used to manage the relationship among stakeholders and to determine and control the strategic direction and performance of organizations.[4] At its core, corporate governance is concerned with identifying ways to ensure that strategic decisions are made effectively.[5] Governance can also be thought of as a means corporations use to establish order between parties (the firm's owners and its top-level managers) whose interests may conflict. Thus, corporate governance reflects and enforces the company's values.[6] In modern corporations—especially those in the United States and the United Kingdom—a primary objective of corporate governance is to ensure that the interests of top-level managers are aligned with the interests of the shareholders. Corporate governance involves oversight in areas where owners, managers, and members of boards of directors may have conflicts of interest. As the Opening Case illustrates, these areas include the election of directors, the general supervision of CEO pay and more focused supervision of director pay, and the corporation's overall structure and strategic direction.[7]

Recent emphasis on corporate governance stems mainly from the occasional failure of corporate governance mechanisms to adequately monitor and control top-level managers' decisions. This situation results in changes in governance mechanisms in corporations throughout the world, especially with respect to efforts intended to improve the performance of boards of directors. These changes often cause confusion about the proper role of the board. According to one observer, "Depending on the company, you get very different perspectives: Some boards are settling for checking the boxes on compliance regulations, while others are thinking about changing the fundamental way they govern, and some worry that they've gotten themselves into micromanaging the CEO and company. There's a fair amount of turmoil and collective searching going on."[8] A second and more positive reason for this interest comes from evidence that suggests that a well-functioning corporate governance and control system can create a competitive advantage for an individual firm.[9] For example, one governance mechanism—the board of directors—has been suggested to be rapidly evolving into a major strategic force in U.S. business firms.[10] Thus, in this chapter, we describe actions designed to implement strategies that focus on monitoring and controlling mechanisms, which can help to ensure that top-level managerial actions contribute to the firm's strategic competitiveness and its ability to earn above-average returns.

Effective corporate governance is also of interest to nations.[11] Although corporate governance reflects company standards, it also collectively reflects country societal standards.[12] As with these firms and their boards, nations that effectively govern their corporations may gain a competitive advantage over rival countries. In a range of countries, but especially in the United States and the United Kingdom, the fundamental goal of business organizations is to maximize shareholder value.[13] Traditionally, shareholders are treated as the firm's key stakeholders, because they are the company's legal owners. The firm's owners expect top-level managers and others influencing the corporation's actions (e.g., the board of directors) to make decisions that will maximize the company's value and, hence, the owners' wealth.[14] Interestingly, research shows that in cross-border acquisitions target firms from countries with weak governance (e.g., lower shareholder protections) are devalued relative to targets from countries with stronger governance regimes.[15]

In the first section of this chapter, we describe the relationship that is the foundation on which the modern corporation is built: the relationship between owners and managers. The majority of this chapter is used to explain various mechanisms owners use to govern managers and to ensure that they comply with their responsibility to maximize shareholder value.

Three internal governance mechanisms and a single external one are used in the modern corporation. The three internal governance mechanisms we describe in this chapter are (1) ownership concentration, as represented by types of shareholders and their different incentives to monitor managers; (2) the board of directors; and (3) executive compensation. We then consider the market for corporate control, an external corporate governance mechanism. Essentially, this market is a set of potential owners seeking to acquire undervalued firms and earn above-average returns on their investments by replacing ineffective top-level management teams.[16] The chapter's focus then shifts to the issue of international corporate governance. We briefly describe governance approaches used in German and Japanese firms whose traditional governance structures are being affected by the realities of global competition. In part, this discussion suggests that the structures used to govern global companies in many different countries, including Germany, Japan, the United Kingdom, and the United States, as well as emerging economies, are becoming more, rather than less, similar. Closing our analysis of corporate governance is a consideration of the need for these control mechanisms to encourage and support ethical behavior in organizations.

Importantly, the mechanisms discussed in this chapter can positively influence the governance of the modern corporation, which has placed significant responsibility and authority in the hands of top-level managers. With multiple governance mechanisms operating simultaneously, however, it is also possible for some of the governance mechanisms to be in conflict.[17] Later, we review how these conflicts can occur.

Separation of Ownership and Managerial Control

Historically, U.S. firms were managed by the founder-owners and their descendants. In these cases, corporate ownership and control resided in the same persons. As firms grew larger, "the managerial revolution led to a separation of ownership and control in most large corporations, where control of the firm shifted from entrepreneurs to professional managers while ownership became dispersed among thousands of unorganized stockholders who were removed from the day-to-day management of the firm."[18] These changes created the modern public corporation, which is based on the efficient separation of ownership and managerial control. Supporting the separation is a basic legal premise suggesting that the primary objective of a firm's activities is to increase the corporation's profit and, thereby, the financial gains of the owners (the shareholders).[19]

The separation of ownership and managerial control allows shareholders to purchase stock, which entitles them to income (residual returns) from the firm's operations after paying expenses. This right, however, requires that they also take a risk that the firm's expenses may exceed its revenues. To manage this investment risk, shareholders maintain a diversified portfolio by investing in several companies to reduce their overall risk.[20] As shareholders diversify their investments over a number of corporations, their risk declines. The poor performance or failure of any one firm in which they invest has less overall effect. Thus, shareholders specialize in managing their investment risk.

In small firms, managers often are high percentage owners, which means less separation between ownership and managerial control. In fact, in a large number of family-owned firms, ownership and managerial control are not separated. In the United States, at least one-third of the S&P 500 firms have substantial family ownership, holding on average about 18 percent of the outstanding equity. And family-owned firms perform better when a member of the family is the CEO than when the CEO is an outsider.[21] In many countries outside the United States, such as in Latin America, Asia, and some European countries, family-owned firms represent the dominant form.[22] The primary purpose of most of these firms is to increase the family's wealth, which explains why a family CEO often is better than an outside CEO.

Family-controlled firms face at least two critical issues. First, as they grow, they may not have access to all of the skills needed to effectively manage the firm and maximize its returns for the family. Thus, they may need outsiders. Also, as they grow, they may need to seek outside capital and thus give up some of the ownership. In these cases, protection of the minority owners' rights becomes important.[23] To avoid these potential problems, when these firms grow and become more complex, their owner-managers may contract with managerial specialists. These managers make major decisions in the owners' firm and are compensated on the basis of their decision-making skills. As decision-making specialists, managers are agents of the firm's owners and are expected to use their decision-making skills to operate the owners' firm in ways that will maximize the return on their investment.[24]

Without owner (shareholder) specialization in risk bearing and management specialization in decision making, a firm may be limited by the abilities of its owners to manage and make effective strategic decisions. Thus, the separation and specialization of ownership (risk bearing) and managerial control (decision making) should produce the highest returns for the firm's owners.

Shareholder value is reflected by the price of the firm's stock. As stated earlier, corporate governance mechanisms, such as the board of directors, or compensation based on the performance of a firm is the reason that CEOs show general concern about the firm's stock price.

Agency Relationships

The separation between owners and managers creates an agency relationship. An **agency relationship** exists when one or more persons (the principal or principals) hire another person or persons (the agent or agents) as decision-making specialists to perform a service.[25] Thus, an agency relationship exists when one party delegates decision-making responsibility to a second party for compensation (see Figure 10.1).[26] In addition to shareholders and top executives, other examples of agency relationships are consultants and clients and insured and insurer. Moreover, within organizations, an agency relationship exists between managers and their employees, as well as between top executives and the firm's owners.[27] In the modern corporation, managers must understand the links between these relationships and the firm's effectiveness.[28] Although the agency relationship between managers and their employees is important, in this chapter we focus on the agency relationship between the firm's owners (the principals) and top-level managers (the principals' agents), because this relationship is related directly to how the firm's strategies are implemented.[29]

An **agency relationship** exists when one or more persons (the principal or principals) hire another person or persons (the agent or agents) as decision-making specialists to perform a service.

The separation between ownership and managerial control can be problematic. Research evidence documents a variety of agency problems in the modern corporation.[30] Problems can surface because the principal and the agent have different interests and goals, or because shareholders lack direct control of large publicly traded corporations. Problems also arise when an agent makes decisions that result in the pursuit of goals that conflict with those of the principals. Thus, the separation of ownership and control potentially allows divergent interests (between principals and agents) to surface, which can lead to managerial opportunism.

Managerial opportunism is the seeking of self-interest with guile (i.e., cunning or deceit).[31] Opportunism is both an attitude (e.g., an inclination) and a set of behaviors (i.e., specific acts of self-interest).[32] It is not possible for principals to know beforehand which

Managerial opportunism is the seeking of self-interest with guile (i.e., cunning or deceit).

Figure 10.1 An Agency Relationship

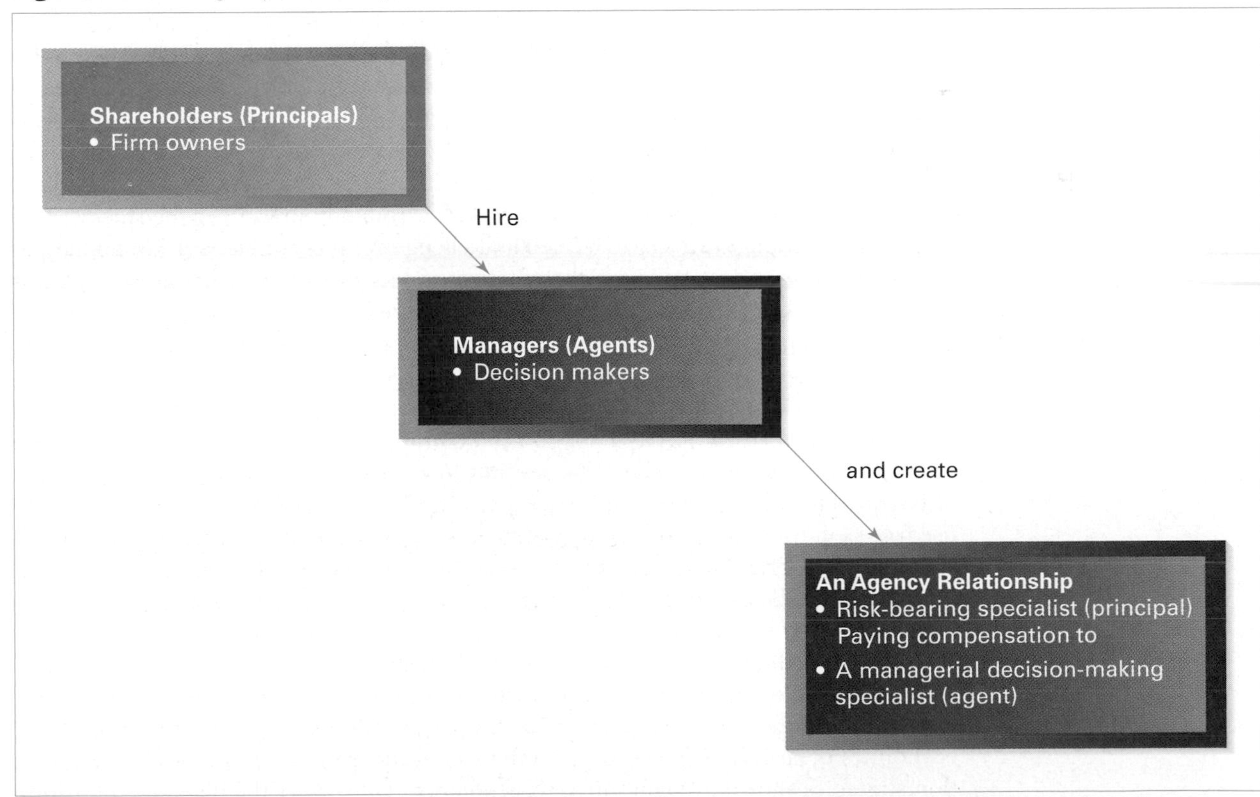

agents will or will not act opportunistically. The reputations of top executives are an imperfect predictor, and opportunistic behavior cannot be observed until it has occurred. Thus, principals establish governance and control mechanisms to prevent agents from acting opportunistically, even though only a few are likely to do so. Any time that principals delegate decision-making responsibilities to agents, the opportunity for conflicts of interest exists. Top executives, for example, may make strategic decisions that maximize their personal welfare and minimize their personal risk.[33] Decisions such as these prevent the maximization of shareholder wealth. Decisions regarding product diversification demonstrate these possibilities.

Product Diversification as an Example of an Agency Problem

As explained in Chapter 6, a corporate-level strategy to diversify the firm's product lines can enhance a firm's strategic competitiveness and increase its returns, both of which serve the interests of shareholders and the top executives. However, product diversification can result in two benefits to managers that shareholders do not enjoy, so top executives may prefer product diversification more than shareholders do.[34]

First, diversification usually increases the size of a firm, and size is positively related to executive compensation. Also, diversification increases the complexity of managing a firm and its network of businesses, possibly requiring more pay because of this complexity.[35] Thus, increased product diversification provides an opportunity for top executives to increase their compensation.[36]

Second, product diversification and the resulting diversification of the firm's portfolio of businesses can reduce top executives' employment risk. Managerial employment risk is the risk of job loss, loss of compensation, and loss of managerial reputation.[37] These risks are reduced with increased diversification, because a firm and its upper-level managers are less vulnerable to the reduction in demand associated with a single or limited number of product lines or businesses. For example, Kellogg Co. was almost entirely focused on breakfast cereal in 2001 when it suffered its first-ever market share leadership loss to perennial number two, General Mills, Inc. Upon appointing Carlos Gutierrez, a longtime manager at Kellogg, to the CEO position, the company embarked on a new strategy to overcome its poor performance. A *BusinessWeek* article outlined his strategy results as follows: "To drive sales, Gutierrez unveiled such novel products as Special K snack bars, bought cookie maker Keebler Co., and ramped up Kellogg's health-foods presence by snapping up Worthington Foods Inc., a maker of soy and vegetarian products, and cereal maker Kashi. He pushed net earnings up 77 percent, to $890.6 million, from 1998 to 2004, as sales rose 42 percent, to $9.6 billion; no wonder the stock soared 54 percent, to some $42 a share."[38] In 2006, Kellogg revenues were at $10.9 billion a year and the stock was close to $52. Kellogg's diversified scope increased, and through this strategy the CEO's risk of job loss was substantially reduced.

Another concern that may represent an agency problem is a firm's free cash flows over which top executives have control. Free cash flows are resources remaining after the firm has invested in all projects that have positive net present value within its current businesses.[39] In anticipation of positive returns, managers may decide to invest these funds in products that are not associated with the firm's current lines of business to increase the firm's level of diversification. The managerial decision to use free cash flows to overdiversify the firm is an example of self-serving and opportunistic managerial behavior. In contrast to managers, shareholders may prefer that free cash flows be distributed to them as dividends, so they can control how the cash is invested.[40]

Curve *S* in Figure 10.2 depicts the shareholders' optimal level of diversification. Owners seek the level of diversification that reduces the risk of the firm's total failure while simultaneously increasing the company's value through the development of economies of scale and scope (see Chapter 6). Of the four corporate-level diversification strategies shown in Figure 10.2, shareholders likely prefer the diversified position

Figure 10.2 Manager and Shareholder Risk and Diversification

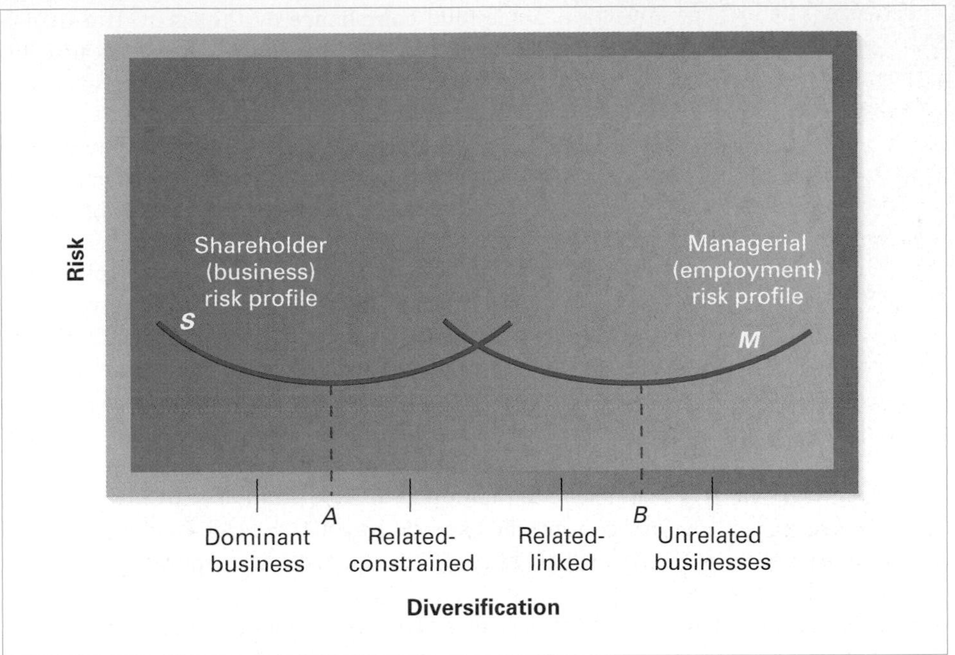

noted by point *A* on curve *S*—a position that is located between the dominant business and related-constrained diversification strategies. Of course, the optimum level of diversification owners seek varies from firm to firm.[41] Factors that affect shareholders' preferences include the firm's primary industry, the intensity of rivalry among competitors in that industry, and the top management team's experience with implementing diversification strategies.

As do principals, upper-level executives—as agents—also seek an optimal level of diversification. Declining performance resulting from too much product diversification increases the probability that corporate control of the firm will be acquired in the market. After a firm is acquired, the employment risk for the firm's top executives increases substantially. Furthermore, a manager's employment opportunities in the external managerial labor market (discussed in Chapter 12) are affected negatively by a firm's poor performance. Therefore, top executives prefer diversification, but not to a point that it increases their employment risk and reduces their employment opportunities.[42] Curve *M* in Figure 10.2 shows that executives prefer higher levels of product diversification than do shareholders. Top executives might prefer the level of diversification shown by point *B* on curve *M*.

In general, shareholders prefer riskier strategies and more focused diversification. They reduce their risk through holding a diversified portfolio of equity investments. Alternatively, managers obviously cannot balance their employment risk by working for a diverse portfolio of firms. Therefore, top executives may prefer a level of diversification that maximizes firm size and their compensation and that reduces their employment risk. Product diversification, therefore, is a potential agency problem that could result in principals incurring costs to control their agents' behaviors.

Agency Costs and Governance Mechanisms

Agency costs are the sum of incentive costs, monitoring costs, enforcement costs, and individual financial losses incurred by principals because governance mechanisms cannot guarantee total compliance by the agent.

The potential conflict illustrated by Figure 10.2, coupled with the fact that principals do not know which managers might act opportunistically, demonstrates why principals establish governance mechanisms. However, the firm incurs costs when it uses one or more governance mechanisms. **Agency costs** are the sum of incentive costs, monitoring costs, enforcement costs, and individual financial losses incurred by principals

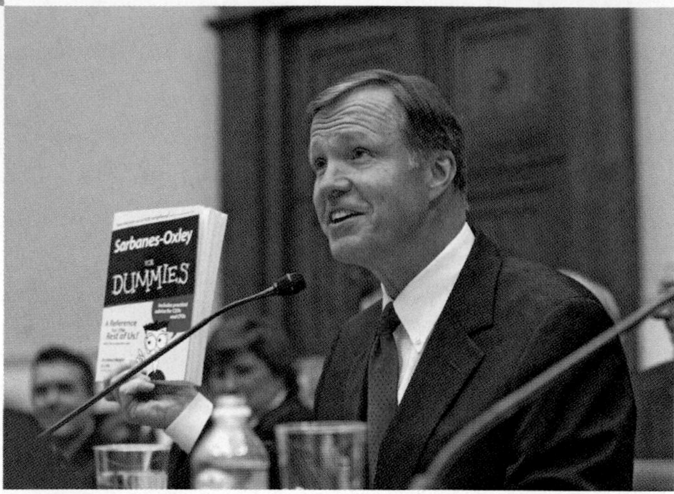

Securities and Exchange Commission Chairman Christopher Cox holds up a copy of the "Sarbanes-Oxley for Dummies" book while testifying on Capitol Hill in Washington, before the House Financial Services Committee.

because governance mechanisms cannot guarantee total compliance by the agent. If a firm is diversified, governance costs increase because it is more difficult to monitor what is going on inside the firm.[43]

In general, managerial interests may prevail when governance mechanisms are weak, as is exemplified by allowing managers a significant amount of autonomy to make strategic decisions. If, however, the board of directors controls managerial autonomy, or if other strong governance mechanisms are used, the firm's strategies should better reflect the interests of the shareholders. More recently, governance observers have been concerned about more egregious behavior beyond inefficient corporate strategy.

Due to fraudulent behavior such as that found at Enron and WorldCom, concerns regarding corporate governance continue to grow. In 2002, the U.S. Congress enacted the Sarbanes-Oxley (SOX) Act, which increased the intensity of corporate governance mechanisms.[44]

Since the implementation of the Sarbanes-Oxley Act in 2002 a significant controversy centers around whether its effect on the economy is positive or negative. On the positive side, many analysts argue that it is a set of regulations that is being copied in democracies and other economies throughout the world. Furthermore, the stock market value increased dramatically since the implementation of SOX because the act helps increase confidence in the stock market due to the reduced possibility of fraud by corporate executives. Section 404 of SOX, which prescribes significant transparency improvement on internal controls associated with accounting and auditing, has arguably improved the internal auditing scrutiny and thereby trust in such financial reporting. In fact a recent study indicated that internal controls associated with Section 404 have increased shareholder value.[45]

On the other hand, many argue that the act, especially Section 404, creates excessive costs for firms. Certainly, information systems audit corporations experience increased revenues, and it has been a boon for such firms.[46] Others also argue that a decrease in foreign firms listing on U.S. stock exchanges occurred at the same time as listing on foreign exchanges increased. In part, this shift may be due to the costs associated with listing on U.S. exchanges associated with requirements of SOX. In fact, figures show that fewer foreign companies are listed on both their domestic and the U.S. exchange, and that more listings have been done in countries where there are less restrictive regulations. Interestingly, this view was supported by Henry Paulson, U.S. Treasury Secretary.[47]

These criticisms led the Bush administration to seek to lessen the affects of the Sarbanes-Oxley Act by adjusting the legislation. As such Bush indicated, "Government should not decide the compensation for America's corporate executives." However he did note that "the salaries and bonuses of CEOs should be based on their success in improving the companies and bringing value to their shareholders."[48]

More intensive application of governance mechanisms may produce significant changes in strategies. For example, because of more intense governance, firms may take on fewer risky projects and thus decrease potential shareholder wealth significantly. As the Opening Case indicates, CEOs and directors have been distracted from more important strategic issues in order to meet detailed compliance deadlines provided by the Sarbanes-Oxley Act and increased governance intensity and media scrutiny. Next, we explain the effects of different governance mechanisms on the decisions managers make about the choice and the use of the firm's strategies.

Ownership Concentration

Both the number of large-block shareholders and the total percentage of shares they own define **ownership concentration. Large-block shareholders** typically own at least 5 percent of a corporation's issued shares. Ownership concentration as a governance mechanism has received considerable interest because large-block shareholders are increasingly active in their demands that corporations adopt effective governance mechanisms to control managerial decisions.[49]

Both the number of large-block shareholders and the total percentage of shares they own define **ownership concentration.**

Large-block shareholders typically own at least 5 percent of a corporation's issued shares.

In general, diffuse ownership (a large number of shareholders with small holdings and few, if any, large-block shareholders) produces weak monitoring of managers' decisions. Among other problems, diffuse ownership makes it difficult for owners to effectively coordinate their actions. Diversification of the firm's product lines beyond the shareholders' optimum level can result from ineffective monitoring of managers' decisions. Higher levels of monitoring could encourage managers to avoid strategic decisions that harm shareholder value. In fact, research evidence shows that ownership concentration is associated with lower levels of firm product diversification.[50] Thus, with high degrees of ownership concentration, the probability is greater that managers' strategic decisions will be intended to maximize shareholder value.[51]

As noted, such concentration of ownership has an influence on strategies and firm value. Interestingly, research in Spain showed a curvilinear relationship between shareholder concentration and firm value. At moderate levels of shareholder concentration, firm value increased; at high levels of concentration, firm value decreased for shareholders, especially minority shareholders.[52] When large shareholders have a high degree of wealth, they have power relative to minority shareholders in extracting wealth from the firm, especially when they are in managerial positions. The importance of boards of directors in mitigating expropriation of minority shareholder value has been found in the United States relative to strong family ownership wherein lays incentive to appropriate shareholder wealth, especially in the second generation after the founder has left.[53] Such expropriation is often found in countries such as Korea where minority shareholder rights are not as protected as they are in the United States.[54] However, in the United States much of this concentration has come from increasing equity ownership by institutional investors.

The Growing Influence of Institutional Owners

A classic work published in the 1930s argued that the "modern" corporation had become characterized by a separation of ownership and control.[55] This change occurred primarily because growth prevented founders-owners from maintaining their dual positions in their increasingly complex companies. More recently, another shift has occurred: Ownership of many modern corporations is now concentrated in the hands of institutional investors rather than individual shareholders.[56]

Institutional owners are financial institutions such as stock mutual funds and pension funds that control large-block shareholder positions. Because of their prominent ownership positions, institutional owners, as large-block shareholders, are a powerful governance mechanism. Institutions of these types now own more than 50 percent of the stock in large U.S. corporations, and of the top 1,000 corporations, they own, on average, 56 percent of the stock. Pension funds alone control at least one-half of corporate equity.[57]

Institutional owners are financial institutions such as stock mutual funds and pension funds that control large-block shareholder positions.

These ownership percentages suggest that as investors, institutional owners have both the size and the incentive to discipline ineffective top-level managers and can significantly influence a firm's choice of strategies and overall strategic decisions.[58] Research evidence indicates that institutional and other large-block shareholders are becoming more active in their efforts to influence a corporation's strategic decisions, unless they have a business relationship with the firm. Initially, these shareholder activists and institutional investors concentrated on the performance and accountability of CEOs and contributed

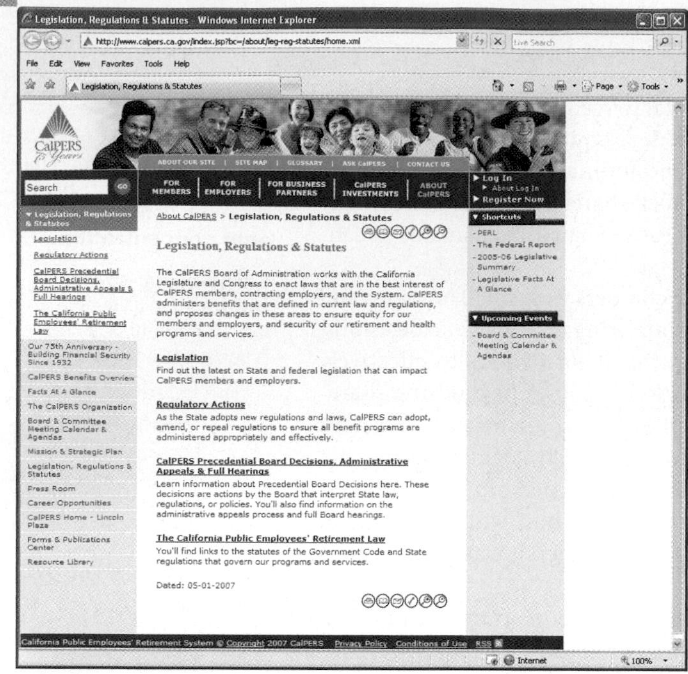

CalPERS, the largest public employee pension fund in the United States, acts boldly to promote regulations and improve firm governance that it believes will enhance shareholder value in companies in which it invests.

to the dismissal of a number of them. They are now targeting actions of boards more directly via proxy vote proposals that are intended to give shareholders more decision rights because they believe board processes have been ineffective.[59]

For example, CalPERS provides retirement and health coverage to more than 1.3 million current and retired public employees. As the largest public employee pension fund in the United States, CalPERS is generally thought to act aggressively to promote governance decisions and actions that it believes will enhance shareholder value in companies in which it invests. For instance, the *Financial Times* indicated that CalPERS "filed 33 'shareowner proposals' as of June 30 [2007], compared with 17 for the previous year [2006]."[60] The shareholder proposals referred to are usually proposed governance changes (say on executive compensation) put forward and supported by significant shareholders on annual proxy ballots that also include new board member nominations. Six of CalPERS's proposals that appeared on proxy ballots in the first half of 2007 received shareholder votes averaging more than 60 percent. The largest institutional investor, TIAA-CREF, has taken actions similar to those of CalPERS, but with a less publicly aggressive stance. To date, research suggests that this institutional activism may not have a direct effect on firm performance, but that its influence may be indirect through its effects on important strategic decisions, such as those concerned with international diversification and innovation.[61] With the increased intensity of governance associated with the passage of the SOX Act, institutional investors as well as other groups have been emboldened in their activism. But this activism may also depend on the country context. For example, one analyst was disappointed in the activism of Indian institutional investors who were also on the board of key firms.[62]

Board of Directors

Typically, shareholders monitor the managerial decisions and actions of a firm through the board of directors. Shareholders elect members to their firm's board. Those who are elected are expected to oversee managers and to ensure that the corporation is operated in ways that will maximize its shareholders' wealth. Even with large institutional investors having major equity ownership in U.S. firms, diffuse ownership continues to exist in most firms, which means that in large corporations, monitoring and control of managers by individual shareholders is limited. Furthermore, large financial institutions, such as banks, are prevented from directly owning stock in firms and from having representatives on companies' boards of directors, although this restriction is not the case in Europe and elsewhere.[63] These conditions highlight the importance of the board of directors for corporate governance. Unfortunately, over time, boards of directors have not been highly effective in monitoring and controlling top management's actions.[64] As noted in the Opening Case, boards are experiencing increasing pressure from shareholders, lawmakers, and regulators to become more forceful in their oversight role and thereby forestall inappropriate actions by top executives. Furthermore, boards not only serve a monitoring role, but they also provide resources to firms. These resources include their personal knowledge and expertise as well as their access to resources of other firms through their external contacts and relationships.[65]

Table 10.1 Classifications of Board of Director Members

Insiders

- The firm's CEO and other top-level managers

Related outsiders

- Individuals not involved with the firm's day-to-day operations, but who have a relationship with the company

Outsiders

- Individuals who are independent of the firm in terms of day-to-day operations and other relationships

The **board of directors** is a group of elected individuals whose primary responsibility is to act in the owners' best interests by formally monitoring and controlling the corporation's top-level executives.[66] Boards have the power to direct the affairs of the organization, punish and reward managers, and protect shareholders' rights and interests. Thus, an appropriately structured and effective board of directors protects owners from managerial opportunism such as that found at Enron and WorldCom where shareholders and employees encountered significant losses. Board members are seen as stewards of their company's resources, and the way they carry out these responsibilities affects the society in which their firm operates. For instance, research suggests that better governance encourages increased flow of foreign direct investment into emerging economies.[67]

The **board of directors** is a group of elected individuals whose primary responsibility is to act in the owners' interests by formally monitoring and controlling the corporation's top-level executives.

Generally, board members (often called directors) are classified into one of three groups (see Table 10.1). *Insiders* are active top-level managers in the corporation who are elected to the board because they are a source of information about the firm's day-to-day operations.[68] *Related outsiders* have some relationship with the firm, contractual or otherwise, that may create questions about their independence, but these individuals are not involved with the corporation's day-to-day activities. *Outsiders* provide independent counsel to the firm and may hold top-level managerial positions in other companies or may have been elected to the board prior to the beginning of the current CEO's tenure.[69]

Historically boards of directors were primarily dominated by inside managers. A widely accepted view is that a board with a significant percentage of its membership drawn from the firm's top executives tends to provide relatively weak monitoring and control of managerial decisions.[70] Managers have been suspected of using their power to select and compensate directors and exploit their personal ties with them. In response to the SEC's proposal to require audit committees to be made up of outside directors, in 1984, the New York Stock Exchange, possibly to preempt formal legislation, implemented an audit committee rule requiring outside directors to head the audit committee. Subsequently, other rules required important committees such as the compensation committee and the nomination committee to be headed by independent outside directors.[71] These other requirements were instituted after the Sarbanes-Oxley Act was passed, and policies of the New York Stock Exchange as well as the American Exchange now require companies to maintain boards of directors that are composed of a majority of outside independent directors and to maintain full independent audit committees. Thus one can clearly see that corporate governance is becoming more intense through the board of directors mechanism.

Critics advocate reforms to ensure that independent outside directors represent a significant majority of the total membership of a board, which research suggests has been accomplished.[72] On the other hand, others argue that having outside directors is not enough to resolve the problems; it depends on the power of the CEO. One proposal to reduce the power of the CEO is to separate the chairperson's role and the CEO's role on the board so that the same person does not hold both positions.[73]

Because of previous scandals in board rooms, the trend toward separating the roles of the CEO and the chairperson continues, which provides more power and independence to the independent outside directors relative to the CEOs. As the Opening Case indicates, this shift has led to more CEO dismissals when things go wrong, such as the dismissal of Robert Nardelli (see the Strategic Focus on page 288). Because of recent problems associated with the egregious use of CEO power, CEOs now must meet tougher standards.[74] Although the Sarbanes-Oxley Act has created stronger scrutiny in regard to finances, the legislation and concern in the media have heightened scrutiny on a range of candidate traits beyond the leader's actual ability to run the company's businesses.[75]

Alternatively, having a large number of outside board members can also create some problems. Outsiders do not have contact with the firm's day-to-day operations and typically do not have easy access to the level of information about managers and their skills that is required to effectively evaluate managerial decisions and initiatives.[76] Outsiders can, however, obtain valuable information through frequent interactions with inside board members, during board meetings and otherwise. Insiders possess such information by virtue of their organizational positions. Thus, boards with a critical mass of insiders typically are better informed about intended strategic initiatives, the reasons for the initiatives, and the outcomes expected from them.[77] Without this type of information, outsider-dominated boards may emphasize the use of financial, as opposed to strategic, controls to gather performance information to evaluate managers' and business units' performances. A virtually exclusive reliance on financial evaluations shifts risk to top-level managers, who, in turn, may make decisions to maximize their interests and reduce their employment risk. Reductions in R&D investments, additional diversification of the firm, and the pursuit of greater levels of compensation are some of the results of managers' actions to achieve financial goals set by outsider-dominated boards.[78]

Enhancing the Effectiveness of the Board of Directors

Because of the importance of boards of directors in corporate governance and as a result of increased scrutiny from shareholders—in particular, large institutional investors—the performances of individual board members and of entire boards are being evaluated more formally and with greater intensity.[79] Given the demand for greater accountability and improved performance, many boards have initiated voluntary changes. Among these changes are (1) increases in the diversity of the backgrounds of board members (e.g., a greater number of directors from public service, academic, and scientific settings; a greater percentage of ethnic minorities and women; and members from different countries on boards of U.S. firms), (2) the strengthening of internal management and accounting control systems, and (3) the establishment and consistent use of formal processes to evaluate the board's performance.[80] Additional changes include (4) the creation of a "lead director" role that has strong powers with regard to the board agenda and oversight of nonmanagement board member activities, and (5) modification of the compensation of directors, especially reducing or eliminating stock options as a part of the package. Activists shareholders such as CalPERS are also lobbying that "directors be elected by a majority of votes cast rather than by a plurality."[81]

Boards have become more involved in the strategic decision-making process, so they must work collaboratively. Some argue that improving the processes used by boards to make decisions and monitor managers and firm outcomes is the key to increasing board effectiveness.[82] Moreover, because of the increased pressure from owners and the potential conflict among board members, procedures are necessary to help boards function effectively in facilitating the strategic decision-making process.

Increasingly, outside directors are being required to own significant equity stakes as a prerequisite to holding a board seat. In fact, some research suggests that firms perform better if outside directors have such a stake; the trend is toward higher pay for directors with more stock ownership, but less stock options.[83] However, other research suggests that too much ownership can cause problems of less independence and lead to problems for the firm.[84] Additionally, other research suggests that diverse boards help firms make more effective strategic decisions and perform better over time.[85] Although questions remain about whether more independent and diverse boards are more effective, it is likely that board independence and increasing diversity are likely to continue. Also, activist shareholders are likely to continue to put forward shareholder proposals as evidenced by their increased level of activity in the Opening Case. As such, boards need to work on being more effective under this situation.

Executive Compensation

As the Opening Case and Strategic Focus illustrate, the compensation of top-level managers, and especially of CEOs, generates a great deal of interest and strongly held opinions. One reason for this widespread interest can be traced to a natural curiosity about extremes and excesses. For example, the *Los Angeles Times* reported that "CEO compensation tripled from 1990 to 2004, rising at more than three times the rate of corporate earnings. CEOs at 11 of the largest U.S. companies received $865 million in a five-year period while presiding over losses in shareholder value."[86] Another stems from a more substantive view that CEO pay is tied in an indirect but tangible way to the fundamental governance processes in large corporations: Who has power? What are the bases of power? How and when do owners and managers exert their relative preferences? How vigilant are boards? Who is taking advantage of whom?[87]

Executive compensation is a governance mechanism that seeks to align the interests of managers and owners through salaries, bonuses, and long-term incentive compensation, such as stock awards and options.[88] Long-term incentive plans have become a critical part of compensation packages in U.S. firms. The use of longer-term pay theoretically helps firms cope with or avoid potential agency problems by linking managerial wealth to the wealth of common shareholders.[89]

Executive compensation is a governance mechanism that seeks to align the interests of managers and owners through salaries, bonuses, and long-term incentive compensation, such as stock awards and options.

Sometimes the use of a long-term incentive plan prevents major stockholders (e.g., institutional investors) from pressing for changes in the composition of the board of directors, because they assume that the long-term incentives will ensure that top executives will act in shareholders' best interests. Alternatively, stockholders largely assume that top-executive pay and the performance of a firm are more closely aligned when firms have boards that are dominated by outside members. However, research shows that fraudulent behavior can be associated with stock option incentives, especially if board members also hold stock options and the CEO also holds the board chair position.[90]

Recently, the persistence of institutional investors has paid off in regard to questioning actions of boards regarding executive pay packages. As the Strategic Focus on executive compensation indicates, the persistent questions of activists and the media led to the dismissal of CEO Robert Nardelli at Home Depot.

Effectively using executive compensation as a governance mechanism is particularly challenging to firms implementing international strategies. For example, the interests of owners of multinational corporations may be best served by less uniformity among the firm's foreign subsidiaries' compensation plans.[91] Developing an array of unique compensation plans requires additional monitoring and increases the firm's potential agency costs. Importantly, levels of pay vary by regions of the world. For example, managerial pay is highest in the United States and much lower in Asia. Compensation is lower in India partly because many of the largest firms have strong family ownership and control.[92] As corporations acquire firms in other countries, the managerial compensation puzzle for boards becomes more complex and may cause additional governance problems.[93]

Strategic Focus Strategic Focus Strategic Focus

Executive Compensation Is Increasingly Becoming a Target for Media, Activist Shareholders, and Government Regulators

In April 2007 the *Wall Street Journal* developed a special report on executive compensation. The lead article was entitled "Ten ways to restore investor confidence in compensation: What words can do to ease shareholder anger over pay packages." Amid growing outrage over excessive executive compensation, a number of outside entities, including the media, shareholder activists, and government regulators, are seeking to reduce the increases in CEO and other executive compensation pay packages.

The reason for this outrage can be illustrated by the compensation package for former Home Depot CEO Robert Nardelli. Home Depot awarded Mr. Nardelli $245 million over his five-year stint. However during his tenure the company's stock price slid 12 percent, while the stock price of its most important rival, Lowe's, increased 173 percent. When Nardelli was hired by Home Depot, he successfully negotiated a package relative to what his future earnings would have been at General Electric (GE). As such, he was awarded $25 million in vested shares on his start date. Additionally, he received a new car every three years (similar price to a Mercedes-Benz S series), the opportunity to use the company jet for personal trips, as well as a $10 million loan at an annual interest of 5.8 percent that would be forgiven over five years.

The board argued that to hire such a high-profile candidate as Nardelli was a significant achievement for Home Depot because he could move to another job quite readily as indicated by Gerard R. Roche, a high-profile recruiter who brought Nardelli to the attention of Home Depot's board: "I can tell you there are a number of companies telling me to find them another Nardelli." In part, due to his perception as a top-level executive, when Mr. Nardelli did not reach his performance goals, the board changed the long-term incentive plan and lowered his target goals in order for him to reach his goals and obtain his negotiated compensation.

Besides the competition for high-profile CEOs such as Nardelli, what are other reasons that a board would approve such compensation packages as received by Robert Nardelli? A *New York Times* article suggested that the six-member compensation committee was composed of other CEOs, one of which had an even higher compensation package than Nardelli. Others were suggested to have had associations with Nardelli, directly or indirectly, through his previous employer GE. As such, it would be hard for his associates to lower Nardelli's pay, especially when one board member was making more than he was.

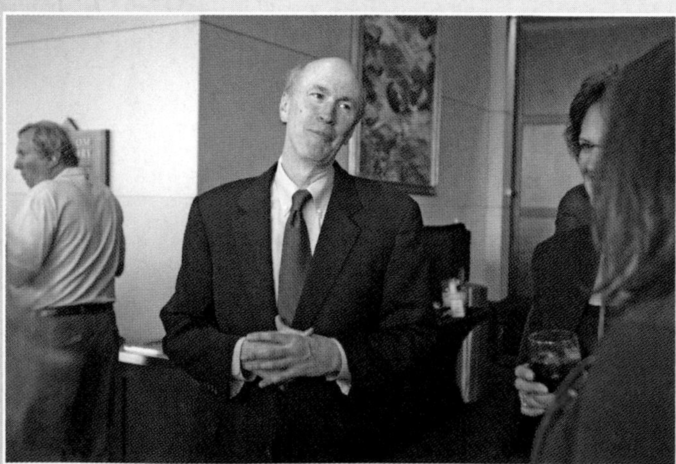

Frank Blake, the new CEO at Home Depot received a salary and long-term incentive package much less than that of his predecessor, Robert Nardelli.

However, increased pressure comes from a number of sources, as noted previously, including the media, the government, and activist shareholders. In July 2006 the Securities and Exchange Commission overhauled the rules regarding requirements for disclosure of information provided to shareholders in proxy statements about executive compensation. This increased information disclosure as well as the number of scandals associated with backdating options (using hindsight to set an option price at the lowest or near the lowest stock price during the year, which is illegal) have made board executive compensation committees (and boards in general) a focus of activist investors and have increased government scrutiny. Certainly Home Depot was a target for much of this scrutiny, which forced the board to oust Nardelli from his position when he would not accept a lower pay package.

The new Home Depot CEO, Frank Blake, has a pay package that is significantly less than his predecessor. Interestingly, Blake rejected the retailer's first offer because it included too much pay. He refused getting restricted stock that retains value even if the share price declines. In other words, he wanted to make sure that his pay package was in line with the desires of Home Depot shareholders. In the end, Blake received a pay package worth as much as $8 million, which is roughly one third of the $24 million (excluding stock options) that Robert Nardelli earned annually during his six-year term at the home improvement chain. At least in the case of Home Depot, it appears that increased scrutiny, activist shareholder monitoring, and executive pay disclosure rules are having a significant effect in bringing CEO pay in line.

However, a large discrepancy still remains between executive and other nonunion employee pay increases. In 2006 salary and bonus compensation increased 7.1 percent in the largest 350 U.S. corporations while it increased 3.6 percent for nonunion employees. However, executive long-term incentive pay increased 8.1 percent, even more than the salary and bonus increase. It is important to note that corporate profits jumped 14.4 percent in 2006. At least it appears that overall compensation is keeping pace with profits in the latest year available.

Sources: M. Byrnes & J. Sasseen, 2007, Board of hard knocks, activists shareholders, tough rules and anger over CEO pay have the directors on the hot seat, *BusinessWeek*, January 22, 37; G. Colvin, 2007, A tie goes to the Managers, *Fortune*, May 28, 34; G. Colvin, A gadfly in the ivory tower, 2007, *Fortune*, April 16, 40; J. S. Lublin, 2007, Ten ways to restore investor confidence in compensation: What boards can do to ease shareholder anger over pay packages, *Wall Street Journal*, April 9, R1, R3; J. S. Lublin, 2007, The pace of pay gains: A survey overview, *Wall Street Journal*, April 9, R1; J. S. Lublin & A. Zimmerman, 2007, Home Depot CEO takes stand on pay, *Wall Street Journal*, B7; S. Lueck, 2007, Executive pay looks to take hit, *Wall Street Journal*, January 30, A4; J. McGregor, 2007, Activist investors get more respect, *BusinessWeek*, June 11, 34; G. Morgenson, 2007, Panel to look at conflicts in consulting, *New York Times*, http://www.nyt.com, May 11; M. Orey & M. Arndt, 2007, Jumping without a parachute, *BusinessWeek*, April 16, 16; J. Sasseen, 2007, A better look at the bosses pay: New SEC rules require greater disclosure but don't expect CEOs to take a hit, *BusinessWeek*, February 26, 44; E. White & A. O. Patrick, 2007, Shareholders push for vote on executive pay, *Wall Street Journal*, February 26, B1, B3; G. Wright, 2007, Home Depot reports pay for its CEOs, *Wall Street Journal*, April 16, B5; J. Creswell, 2006, With links to board, Chief saw his pay soar, *New York Times*, http://www.nyt.com, May 24.

The Effectiveness of Executive Compensation

Executive compensation—especially long-term incentive compensation—is complicated for several reasons. First, the strategic decisions made by top-level managers are typically complex and nonroutine, so direct supervision of executives is inappropriate for judging the quality of their decisions. The result is a tendency to link the compensation of top-level managers to measurable outcomes, such as the firm's financial performance. Second, an executive's decision often affects a firm's financial outcomes over an extended period, making it difficult to assess the effect of current decisions on the corporation's performance. In fact, strategic decisions are more likely to have long-term, rather than short-term, effects on a company's strategic outcomes. Third, a number of other factors affect a firm's performance besides top-level managerial decisions and behavior. Unpredictable economic, social, or legal changes (see Chapter 2) make it difficult to discern the effects of strategic decisions. Thus, as indicated in the Strategic Focus, although performance-based compensation may provide incentives to top management teams to make decisions that best serve shareholders' interests, such compensation plans alone are imperfect in their ability to monitor and control managers. Still, incentive compensation represents a significant portion of many executives' total pay.

Although incentive compensation plans may increase the value of a firm in line with shareholder expectations, such plans are subject to managerial manipulation as the Home Depot example illustrates. Additionally, annual bonuses may provide incentives to pursue short-run objectives at the expense of the firm's long-term interests. Although long-term, performance-based incentives may reduce the temptation to under-invest in the short run, they increase executive exposure to risks associated with uncontrollable events, such as market fluctuations and industry decline. The longer term the focus of incentive compensation, the greater are the long-term risks borne by top-level managers. Also, because long-term incentives tie a manager's overall wealth to the firm in a way that is inflexible, such incentives and ownership may not be valued as highly by a manager as by outside investors who have the opportunity to diversify their wealth in a number of other financial investments.[94] Thus, firms may have to overcompensate for managers using long-term incentives.

Even though some stock option–based compensation plans are well designed with option strike prices substantially higher than current stock prices, too many have been designed simply to give executives more wealth. Research of stock option repricing where the strike price value of the option has been lowered from its original position suggests that action is taken more frequently in high-risk situations.[95] However, repricing also happens when firm performance is poor, to restore the incentive effect for the option. Evidence also suggests that politics are often involved, which has resulted in "option backdating."[96] Interestingly, institutional investors prefer compensation schemes that link pay with performance, including the use of stock options.[97] Again, this evidence shows that no internal governance mechanism is perfect.

Stock options became highly popular as a means of compensating top executives and linking pay with performance, but they also have become controversial of late as indicated in the Opening Case. Because all internal governance mechanisms are imperfect, external mechanisms are also needed. One such governance device is discussed next.

Market for Corporate Control

The **market for corporate control** is an external governance mechanism that becomes active when a firm's internal controls fail.

The **market for corporate control** is an external governance mechanism that becomes active when a firm's internal controls fail.[98] The market for corporate control is composed of individuals and firms that buy ownership positions in or take over potentially undervalued corporations so they can form new divisions in established diversified companies or merge two previously separate firms. Because the undervalued firm's executives are assumed to be responsible for formulating and implementing the strategy that led to poor performance, they are usually replaced. Thus, when the market for corporate control operates effectively, it ensures that managers who are ineffective or act opportunistically are disciplined.[99]

The market for corporate control is often viewed as a "court of last resort."[100] The takeover market as a source of external discipline is used only when internal governance mechanisms are relatively weak and have proven to be ineffective. Alternatively, other research suggests that the rationale for takeovers as a corporate governance strategy is not as strong as the rationale for takeovers as an ownership investment in target candidates where the firm is performing well and does not need discipline.[101] A study of active corporate raiders in the 1980s showed that takeover attempts often were focused on above-average performance firms in an industry.[102] Taken together, this research suggests that takeover targets are not always low performers with weak governance. As such, it also suggests that the market for corporate control may not be as efficient as a governance device as theory suggests. At the very least, internal governance controls would be much more precise relative to this external control mechanism.

Hedge funds are also becoming a source of activist investors as noted in Chapter 7 and in the Opening Case. An enormous amount of money is invested in hedge funds, and because it is becoming significantly more difficult to gain high returns in the market, hedge funds have turned to activism. Likewise in a competitive environment characterized by a greater willingness on part of investors to hold under-performing managers accountable, hedge funds have been given license for increased activity.[103] Traditionally, hedge funds are a portfolio of stocks or bonds, or both, managed by an individual or a team on behalf of a large number of investors. Hedge funds usually engage in faster turnaround investments than traditional mutual funds. Hedge fund managers often invest in futures, derivatives, and other riskier investment strategies to take advantage of rapid changes in the market. Activism allows them to influence the market by taking a large position in seeking to drive the stock price up in a short period of time and then sell. More recently this activity is done through proxy votes, where they seek to get a fund representative voted to be a member of the board of directors. Hedge fund managers are allowed to sit on boards because they do not manage a traditional mutual or pension fund (whereas mutual fund managers or financial institutions do not have this privilege by law). Most hedge funds are unregulated relative to the Securities and Exchange Commission because they represent a set of private investors. However, more recently these private investors represent large public pension funds. Many pension funds have an average of 6 percent of their portfolio invested in hedge funds as well as private equity funds.[104]

Although the market for corporate control may be a blunt instrument as far as corporate governance is concerned, the takeover market has continued to be active as noted in Chapter 7. In fact, research suggests that the more intense governance environment may have fostered an increasingly active takeover market. Because institutional investors have more concentrated ownership, they may be interested in firms that are targeted for acquisition. Target firms earn a substantial premium over the acquiring firm.[105] At the same time, managers who have ownership positions or stock options are likely to gain in making a transaction with an acquiring firm. Even more evidence indicates that this type of gain may be the case, given the increasing number of firms that have golden parachutes that allow up to three years of additional compensation plus other incentives if a firm is taken over. These compensation contracts reduce the risk for managers if a firm is taken over. Private equity firms often seek to obtain a lower price in the market through initiating friendly takeover deals. The target firm's executives may be amenable to such "friendly" deals because not only do they get the payout through a golden parachute, but at their next firm they may get a "golden hello" as a signing bonus to work for the new firm.[106] Golden parachutes help them leave, but "golden hellos are increasingly needed to get them in the door" of the next firm.[107] For instance, W. James McNerney Jr., a former executive of General Electric received such outsized pay packages by moving to 3M in 2000 and then again to Boeing in 2005. When he moved from 3M to Boeing he received "a pay package worth more than $52 million, which included $25.3 million of restricted shares and $22 million to replace his 3M pension."[108] Although the 1980s had more defenses put up against hostile takeovers, the current environment has been much friendlier, most likely due to the increased intensity of the governance devices on both the buyer (institutional investor) side as well as the corporate management side. The idea that CEOs who have substantial ownership or stock options in the target firm do well in the friendly transactions in the 1990s and into the twenty-first century is also supported by research.[109]

The market for corporate control governance mechanisms should be triggered by a firm's poor performance relative to industry competitors. A firm's poor performance, often demonstrated by the firm's below-average returns, is an indicator that internal governance mechanisms have failed; that is, their use did not result in managerial decisions that maximized shareholder value. This market has been active for some time. As noted in Chapter 7, the years 2005 and 2006 produced the largest number and value of mergers and acquisitions. Additionally, the number of mergers and acquisitions began to increase and the market for corporate control has become increasingly international, with more than 40 percent of the merger and acquisition activity involving firms from different countries.[110]

Although some acquisition attempts are intended to obtain resources important to the acquiring firm, most *hostile* takeover attempts are due to the target firm's poor performance.[111] Therefore, target firm managers and members of the boards of directors are highly sensitive about hostile takeover bids. It frequently means that they have not done an effective job in managing the company. If they accept the offer, they are likely to lose their jobs; the acquiring firm will insert its own management. If they reject the offer and fend off the takeover attempt, they must improve the performance of the firm or risk losing their jobs as well.[112]

Managerial Defense Tactics

Hostile takeovers are the major activity in the market for corporate control governance mechanism. Not all hostile takeovers are prompted by poorly performing targets, and firms targeted for hostile takeovers may use multiple defense tactics to fend off the takeover attempt. Historically, the increased use of the market for corporate control has enhanced the sophistication and variety of managerial defense tactics that are used to reduce the influence of this governance mechanism. The market for corporate control tends to increase risk for managers. As a result, managerial pay is often augmented indirectly through golden parachutes (wherein, as mentioned, a CEO can receive up to three years' salary if his or her firm is taken over). Golden parachutes, similar to most other defense tactics, are controversial.

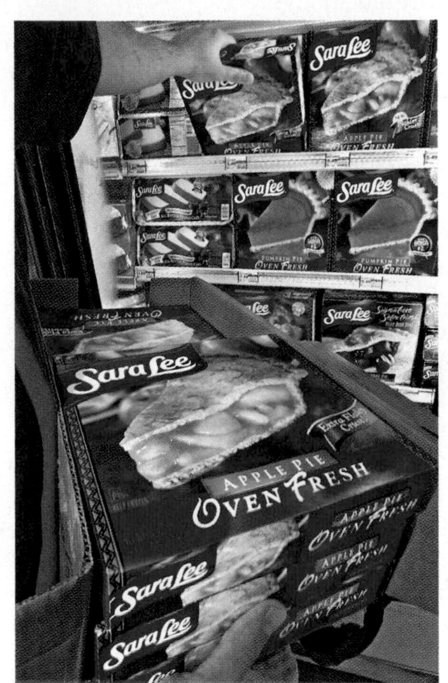

Sara Lee Corporation is currently using managerial defense tactics to restructure its capital structure and operations for the purpose of increased shareholder benefits in the event that a bid is made for the company.

Among other outcomes, takeover defenses increase the costs of mounting a takeover, causing the incumbent management to become entrenched, while reducing the chances of introducing a new management team.[113] One takeover defense is traditionally known as a "poison pill." This defense mechanism usually allows shareholders (other than the acquirer) to convert "shareholders' rights" into a large number of common shares if anyone acquires more than a set amount of the target's stock (typically 10–20%.) This move dilutes the percentage of shares that the acquiring firm must purchase at a premium and in effect raises the cost of the deal for the acquiring firm.

Many firms have been pressured to reduce such takeover defenses. Sara Lee Corporation restructured its operations, as noted in Chapter 7, and shed approximately 40 percent of its revenue through divestitures and spinoffs. It also has a plan to buy back its own stock worth approximately $3 billion to facilitate an increase in share price. In addition, shareholders voted to terminate Sara Lee's "poison pill" takeover defense in an effort to increase shareholder benefits if a bid for the firm is presented.[114]

Table 10.2 lists a number of additional takeover defense strategies. Some defense tactics necessitate only changes in the financial structure of the firm, such as repurchasing shares of the firm's outstanding stock.[115] Some tactics (e.g., reincorporation of the firm in another state) require shareholder approval, but the greenmail tactic, wherein money is used to repurchase stock from a corporate raider to avoid the takeover of the firm, does not. Some firms use rotating board member elections as a defense tactic where only one third of members are up for reelection each year. Research shows that this results in managerial entrenchment and reduced vulnerability to hostile takeovers.[116] These defense tactics are controversial, and the research on their effects is inconclusive.

Most institutional investors oppose the use of defense tactics. TIAA-CREF and CalPERS have taken actions to have several firms' poison pills eliminated. Many institutional investors also oppose severance packages (golden parachutes), and the opposition is growing significantly in Europe as well.[117] But, as previously noted, an advantage to severance packages is that they may encourage executives to accept takeover bids that are attractive to shareholders.[118] Also, as in the case of Robert Nardelli at Home Depot, a severance package may encourage a CEO doing a poor job to depart.[119]

A potential problem with the market for corporate control is that it may not be totally efficient. A study of several of the most active corporate raiders in the 1980s showed that approximately 50 percent of their takeover attempts targeted firms with above-average

Table 10.2 Hostile Takeover Defense Strategies

Defense strategy	Category	Popularity among firms	Effectiveness as a defense	Stockholder wealth effects
Poison pill Preferred stock in the merged firm offered to shareholders at a highly attractive rate of exchange.	Preventive	High	High	Positive
Corporate charter amendment An amendment to stagger the elections of members to the board of directors of the attacked firm so that all are not elected during the same year, which prevents a bidder from installing a completely new board in the same year.	Preventive	Medium	Very low	Negative
Golden parachute Lump-sum payments of cash that are distributed to a select group of senior executives when the firm is acquired in a takeover bid.	Preventive	Medium	Low	Negligible
Litigation Lawsuits that help a target company stall hostile attacks; areas may include antitrust, fraud, inadequate disclosure.	Reactive	Medium	Low	Positive
Greenmail The repurchase of shares of stock that have been acquired by the aggressor at a premium in exchange for an agreement that the aggressor will no longer target the company for takeover.	Reactive	Very low	Medium	Negative
Standstill agreement Contract between the parties in which the pursuer agrees not to acquire any more stock of the target firm for a specified period of time in exchange for the firm paying the pursuer a fee.	Reactive	Low	Low	Negative
Capital structure change Dilution of stock, making it more costly for a bidder to acquire; may include employee stock option plans (ESOPs), recapitalization, new debt, stock selling, share buybacks.	Reactive	Medium	Medium	Inconclusive

Source: J. A. Pearce II & R. B. Robinson, Jr., 2004, Hostile takeover defenses that maximize shareholder wealth, *Business Horizons,* 47(5): 15–24.

performance in their industry—corporations that were neither undervalued nor poorly managed.[120] The targeting of high-performance businesses may lead to acquisitions at premium prices and to decisions by managers of the targeted firm to establish what may prove to be costly takeover defense tactics to protect their corporate positions.[121]

Although the market for corporate control lacks the precision of internal governance mechanisms, the fear of acquisition and influence by corporate raiders is an effective constraint on the managerial-growth motive. The market for corporate control has been responsible for significant changes in many firms' strategies and, when used appropriately, has served shareholders' interests. But this market and other means of corporate governance vary by region of the world and by country. Accordingly, we next address the topic of international corporate governance.

International Corporate Governance

Understanding the corporate governance structure of the United Kingdom and the United States is inadequate for a multinational firm in today's global economy.[122] The stability associated with German and Japanese governance structures has historically been viewed as an asset, but the governance systems in these countries are changing, just as they are in other parts of the world.[123] These changes are partly the result of multinational firms operating in many different countries and attempting to develop a more global governance system.[124] Although the similarity among national governance systems is increasing, significant differences remain evident, and firms employing an international strategy must understand these differences in order to operate effectively in different international markets.[125]

Corporate Governance in Germany

In many private German firms, the owner and manager may still be the same individual. In these instances, agency problems are not present.[126] Even in publicly traded German corporations, a single shareholder is often dominant. Thus, the concentration of ownership is an important means of corporate governance in Germany, as it is in the United States.[127]

Historically, banks occupied the center of the German corporate governance structure, as is also the case in many other European countries, such as Italy and France. As lenders, banks become major shareholders when companies they financed earlier seek funding on the stock market or default on loans. Although the stakes are usually less than 10 percent, the only legal limit on how much of a firm's stock banks can hold is that a single ownership position cannot exceed 15 percent of the bank's capital. Through their shareholdings, and by casting proxy votes for individual shareholders who retain their shares with the banks, three banks in particular—Deutsche, Dresdner, and Commerzbank—exercise significant power. Although shareholders can tell the banks how to vote their ownership position, they generally do not do so. A combination of their own holdings and their proxies results in majority positions for these three banks in many German companies. Those banks, along with others, monitor and control managers, both as lenders and as shareholders, by electing representatives to supervisory boards.

German firms with more than 2,000 employees are required to have a two-tiered board structure that places the responsibility for monitoring and controlling managerial (or supervisory) decisions and actions in the hands of a separate group.[128] All the functions of direction and management are the responsibility of the management board (the Vorstand), but appointment to the Vorstand is the responsibility of the supervisory tier (the Aufsichtsrat). Employees, union members, and shareholders appoint members to the Aufsichtsrat. Proponents of the German structure suggest that it helps prevent corporate wrongdoing and rash decisions by "dictatorial CEOs." However, critics maintain that it slows decision making and often ties a CEO's hands. In Germany the power sharing may have gone too far because it includes representation from the local community as well as unions. Accordingly, the corporate governance framework in Germany has made it difficult to restructure companies as quickly as can be done in the United States when performance suffers. Such is the case with EADS, the parent of Airbus. Part of Airbus's difficulties stem from the challenges it encountered in restructuring due to the complexities of corporate governance not only in Germany, but also in France.[129]

Because of the role of local government (through the board structure) and the power of banks in Germany's corporate governance structure, private shareholders rarely have major ownership positions in German firms. Large institutional investors, such as pension funds and insurance companies, are also relatively insignificant owners of corporate stock. Thus, at least historically, German executives generally have not been dedicated to the maximization of shareholder value that occurs in many countries.[130]

However, corporate governance in Germany is changing, at least partially, because of the increasing globalization of business. Many German firms are beginning to gravitate toward the U.S. system. Recent research suggests that the traditional system produced some agency costs because of a lack of external ownership power. According to research, countries that traditionally have more relationship-oriented capital markets such as Germany whose firms are exposed and required to meet governance aspects of financial capitalism due stock exchange listing requirements (perhaps in the United States) often begin to adopt such governance requirements. For example, German firms with such exposure have increasingly adopted executive stock option compensation as a long-term incentive pay policy.[131]

Corporate Governance in Japan

Attitudes toward corporate governance in Japan are affected by the concepts of obligation, family, and consensus.[132] In Japan, an obligation "may be to return a service for one rendered or it may derive from a more general relationship, for example, to one's family or old alumni, or one's company (or Ministry), or the country. This sense of particular obligation is common elsewhere but it feels stronger in Japan."[133] As part of a company family, individuals are members of a unit that envelops their lives; families command the attention and allegiance of parties throughout corporations. Moreover, a *keiretsu* (a group of firms tied together by cross-shareholdings) is more than an economic concept; it, too, is a family. Consensus, an important influence in Japanese corporate governance, calls for the expenditure of significant amounts of energy to win the hearts and minds of people whenever possible, as opposed to top executives issuing edicts.[134] Consensus is highly valued, even when it results in a slow and cumbersome decision-making process.

As in Germany, banks in Japan play an important role in financing and monitoring large public firms.[135] The bank owning the largest share of stocks and the largest amount of debt—the main bank—has the closest relationship with the company's top executives. The main bank provides financial advice to the firm and also closely monitors managers. Thus, Japan has a bank-based financial and corporate governance structure, whereas the United States has a market-based financial and governance structure.[136]

Aside from lending money, a Japanese bank can hold up to 5 percent of a firm's total stock; a group of related financial institutions can hold up to 40 percent. In many cases, main-bank relationships are part of a horizontal keiretsu. A keiretsu firm usually owns less than 2 percent of any other member firm; however, each company typically has a stake of that size in every firm in the keiretsu. As a result, somewhere between 30 and 90 percent of a firm is owned by other members of the keiretsu. Thus, a keiretsu is a system of relationship investments.

As is the case in Germany, Japan's structure of corporate governance is changing. For example, because of Japanese banks' continuing development as economic organizations, their role in the monitoring and control of managerial behavior and firm outcomes is less significant than in the past.[137] In fact, research indicates that it increased the cost of governance due the entrenchment of poor management. Also, deregulation in the financial sector reduced the cost of mounting hostile takeovers.[138] As such, deregulation facilitated more activity in Japan's market for corporate control, which was nonexistent in past years.[139]

Also, as noted in the following Strategic Focus, activist shareholders have also been lobbying for governance changes. With foreign shareholders accounting for 28 percent of the overall ownership among Japanese firms, their opinions are being heard in shareholder meetings where votes on proposition for change are voiced. Outside directors are increasing their influence, and activist shareholders have become aggressive with their increased ownership positions as illustrated in the Strategic Focus.

It will be interesting to see how this activism influences the long-term orientation of Japanese firms. Research suggests that the Japanese stewardship-management approach, historically dominated by inside managers, produces greater investments in long-term R&D projects than does the more financially oriented system in the United States.[140] As the potential for a stronger takeover market increases, some Japanese firms are considering delisting and taking their firms private in order to maintain long-term "strategic flexibility."[141] Interestingly, research suggests that the SOX Act in the United States has created an increase in delisting.[142]

Strategic Focus

Shareholder Activists Invade Japan's Large Firms Traditionally Focused on "Stakeholder" Capitalism

Japanese firms have recently begun experiencing activist shareholders who seek to increase returns through improved dividend policy.

Japan has traditionally focused on relationship-capitalism, built on the premise that firms help each other when they are weak and facilitate each other's success when they are strong. This relationship-capitalism created a system of protection against "outside" owners by having a close-knit group of insiders who manage the firm as well as a larger set of interlocking shareholders who are mutually bonded by owning each other's stock. This arrangement largely prevented outsiders from "taking over" Japanese corporations. In the 1980s such cross-shareholdings between banks, companies, and insurers accounted for approximately 50 percent of equity. Over the recent term, however, ownership has changed with cross-shareholdings currently accounting for only about 20 percent. As this change occurred and with deregulation allowing more foreign ownership, foreign ownership of Japanese firms has increased from approximately 4.7 percent in 1990 to 28 percent in 2007.

A parallel trend is the increase in activist foreign shareholders making proposals in governing the firms differently. Many of the publicly traded firms in Japan hold their annual shareholder meetings in the latter part of June. In 2007, at many of the shareholder meetings, Japanese managers faced increasing activism, especially by foreign shareholders. Interestingly, in Japan, shareholders can vote directly on dividends and executive pay. Thus, on the surface it would appear that Japanese stock market policies are more shareholder-friendly than those in the United States or the United Kingdom. Furthermore, shareholders can vote to dismiss the entire board without cause. However, Japanese investors do not take up this power readily and most often defer to executive proposals.

These practices are changing now that 28 percent of Japanese shares are held by foreign institutional investors. At the June 2007 annual shareholders' meeting, companies faced 30 shareholder resolutions, nearly twice as many as in 2006, which is threatening to Japanese managers who are seeking to maintain the tight-knit business culture that exists in Japan. For example, the activist shareholders brought to light the large cash reserves that sizeable corporations hold as well as a reluctance to restructure operations that would require layoffs. The large cash reserves are sought by the activist shareholders to increase returns through improved dividend policy and increase overall stock prices by restructuring operations to improve return on equity. For example, returns have languished in Japan at about 9 percent compared to 14 percent and 17 percent in the United States and Europe, respectively. In fact, these figures suggest that Japanese managers could profitably put their cash reserves to better use or return the money to shareholders through stock buybacks or improved dividends.

Not surprisingly many of the large Japanese firms are fighting back by encouraging politicians and media outlets to "demonize" the activists as "financial criminals" who seek short-term gain over long-term health. Similar accusations were made in the European press in 2005 when private equity firms were making hostile acquisitions called *locusts.* However, it appears that the long-term health of Japanese firms might be improved, given that Japanese firms hold cash and securities equivalent to 16 percent of GDP, whereas American firms' long-term average of cash and securities is about 5 percent. Although these slack resources in Japan may facilitate a longer-term view, from the eyes of the

© Don Hammond/Design Pics/Corbis

activist shareholders they represents underutilization of potential capital, which, if not utilized, should be returned to shareholders through dividends or stock buybacks.

Sources: 2007, Business: In the locust position; shareholder activism in Japan, *Economist*, June 30, 80; S. Moffett, 2007, Signs of hope for Japan's activists, *Wall Street Journal*, July 13, C3; M. Nakamoto, 2007, Corporate Japan needs the activist touch, *Financial Times*, June 25, 13; D. Pilling, 2007, Japan's outsiders can come in from the cold, *Financial Times*, June 28, 9; A. Scott, Japanese companies get an ear full; activist funds try to muscle cash out of big firms, *Wall Street Journal*, March 27, C5; L. Santini, 2006, Investor activism grows globally, but wins are rare, *Wall Street Journal*, July 3, C1.

Global Corporate Governance

As noted in the Strategic Focus, foreign investors are becoming increasingly important to shareholders in economies around the world, even in emerging economies. Although many times domestic shareholders will vote with management, as activist foreign investors enter a country it gives domestic institutional investors courage to become more active in shareholder proposals, which will increase shareholder welfare.

For example, Steel Partners, LLC, focused its attention on Korean cigarette maker KT&G. Warren Lichtenstein of Steel Partners and Carl Icahn pressured KT&G to increase its market value. Lichtenstein and Icahn began their activism in February 2006, by nominating a slate of board directors as well as pushing KT&G to sell off its lucrative Ginseng unit, which manufactures popular herbal products in Korea. They also demanded that the company sell off its real estate assets, raise its dividends, and buy back common shares. Lichtenstein and Icahn threatened a hostile tender offer if their demands were not met. Shareholders showed support for Steel Partners' activism such that they elected Mr. Lichtenstein to KT&G's board. In 2006 Mr. Icahn sold his 4.74 percent ownership in KT&G and received a 33 percent return. Mr. Lichtenstein opposed KT&G's offer in 2007 to acquire 1 percent of Korea's Shinhan Financial Group, Korea's second-largest banking institution. However, it was approved by 11 of KT&G's 12 other board members, thus Lichtenstein threatened to remove the CEO, Kwak Young-kyoon, if KT&G completed the deal. Interestingly, in support of Mr. Lichtenstein's opposition, the stock price decreased by 2.2 percent. Activist hedge funds, such as Steel Partners, have found fertile ground in Korean companies and other emerging economies because of low valuations relative to their global peers.[143]

The trends toward improved governance are reaching even Chinese firms, which are primarily government owned. China has been seeking to demonstrate increased openness in advance of the Olympic Games in Beijing in August 2008. Accordingly it has created regulations for greater firm transparency that will go into effect May 1, 2008. Although this regulatory action is meant to broaden the transparency of all aspects of Chinese society, it does have an impact on corporate governance aspects to allow better disclosure of financial information. However, because of the dominance of a central communist party system in China, some areas are considered "too sensitive" to disclose and the government has a "screening" system for protecting certain information. Many government-owned firms will find cover using these means and not disclose more information.[144]

Not only has the legislation that produced the Sarbanes-Oxley Act in 2002 increased the intensity of corporate governance in the United States,[145] but other governments around the world are seeking to increase the transparency and intensity of corporate governance to prevent the type of scandals found in the United States and other places around the world. For example, the British government in 2003 implemented the findings of the Derek Higgs report, which increased governance intensity mandated by the United Kingdom's Combined Code on Corporate Governance. Similarly, Japan is considering drafting legislation entitled "Financial Instruments and Exchange Law," which will be dubbed "J-Sox" because of its similarity to the U.S. Sarbanes-Oxley Act. This legislation is expected to pass by the middle of 2008. Also the European Union enacted what is known as the Transparency Directive, which is aimed at enhancing reporting and the disclosure of financial reports by firms within the European capital markets. Another European Union initiative labeled "Modernizing Company Law and Enhancing Corporate Governance" promises to improve the responsibility and liability of executive officers, board members, and others to important stakeholders such as shareholders, creditors, and members of the public at large.[146] Thus, governance is becoming more intense around the world.

Governance Mechanisms and Ethical Behavior

The governance mechanisms described in this chapter are designed to ensure that the agents of the firm's owners—the corporation's top executives—make strategic decisions that best serve the interests of the entire group of stakeholders, as described in Chapter 1. In the United States, shareholders are recognized as a company's most significant stakeholder. Thus, governance mechanisms focus on the control of managerial decisions to ensure that shareholders' interests will be served, but product market stakeholders (e.g., customers, suppliers, and host communities) and organizational stakeholders (e.g., managerial and nonmanagerial employees) are important as well.[147] Therefore, at least the minimal interests or needs of all stakeholders must be satisfied through the firm's actions. Otherwise, dissatisfied stakeholders will withdraw their support from one firm and provide it to another (e.g., customers will purchase products from a supplier offering an acceptable substitute).

The firm's strategic competitiveness is enhanced when its governance mechanisms take into consideration the interests of all stakeholders. Although the idea is subject to debate, some believe that ethically responsible companies design and use governance mechanisms that serve all stakeholders' interests. The more critical relationship, however, is found between ethical behavior and corporate governance mechanisms. The Enron disaster illustrates the devastating effect of poor ethical behavior not only on a firm's stakeholders, but also on other firms. This issue is being taken seriously in other countries. The trend toward increased governance scrutiny continues to spread around the world.[148]

For instance, SK Corporation in South Korea faced a shareholder-led proposal to oust or significantly reshape the company's CEO position. Although the CEO was not replaced (despite being convicted of accounting fraud) because he is the dominant family owner, they did force change in some of the ways that the corporation was governed.[149]

In addition to Enron, scandals at WorldCom, HealthSouth, and Tyco show that all corporate owners are vulnerable to unethical behaviors by their employees, including top-level managers—the agents who have been hired to make decisions that are in shareholders' best interests. The decisions and actions of a corporation's board of directors can be an effective deterrent to these behaviors. In fact, some believe that the most effective boards participate actively to set boundaries for their firms' business ethics and values.[150] Once formulated, the board's expectations related to ethical decisions and actions of all of the firm's stakeholders must be clearly communicated to its top-level managers. Moreover, as shareholders' agents, these managers must understand that the board will hold them fully accountable for the development and support of an organizational culture that allows unethical decisions and behaviors. As will be explained in Chapter 12, CEOs can be positive role models for improved ethical behavior.

Dennis Kozlowski was sentenced to up to 25 years in prison and fined $70 million for his fraudulent behavior when he was the CEO of Tyco.

Only when the proper corporate governance is exercised can strategies be formulated and implemented that will help the firm achieve strategic competitiveness and earn above-average returns. As the discussion in this chapter suggests, corporate governance mechanisms are a vital, yet imperfect, part of firms' efforts to select and successfully use strategies.

Summary

- Corporate governance is a relationship among stakeholders that is used to determine a firm's direction and control its performance. How firms monitor and control top-level managers' decisions and actions affects the implementation of strategies. Effective governance that aligns managers' decisions with shareholders' interests can help produce a competitive advantage.
- Three internal governance mechanisms in the modern corporation include (1) ownership concentration, (2) the board of directors, and (3) executive compensation. The market for corporate control is the single external governance mechanism influencing managers' decisions and the outcomes resulting from them.
- Ownership is separated from control in the modern corporation. Owners (principals) hire managers (agents) to make decisions that maximize the firm's value. As risk-bearing specialists, owners diversify their risk by investing in multiple corporations with different risk profiles. As decision-making specialists, owners expect their agents (the firm's top-level managers) to make decisions that will lead to maximization of the value of their firm. Thus, modern corporations are characterized by an agency relationship that is created when one party (the firm's owners) hires and pays another party (top-level managers) to use its decision-making skills.
- Separation of ownership and control creates an agency problem when an agent pursues goals that conflict with principals' goals. Principals establish and use governance mechanisms to control this problem.
- Ownership concentration is based on the number of large-block shareholders and the percentage of shares they own. With significant ownership percentages, such as those held by large mutual funds and pension funds, institutional investors often are able to influence top executives' strategic decisions and actions. Thus, unlike diffuse ownership, which tends to result in relatively weak monitoring and control of managerial decisions, concentrated ownership produces more active and effective monitoring. Institutional investors are an increasingly powerful force in corporate America and actively use their positions of concentrated ownership to force managers and boards of directors to make decisions that maximize a firm's value.
- In the United States and the United Kingdom, a firm's board of directors, composed of insiders, related outsiders, and outsiders, is a governance mechanism expected to represent shareholders' collective interests. The percentage of outside directors on many boards now exceeds the percentage of inside directors. Through the implementation of the SOX Act, outsiders are expected to be more independent of a firm's top-level managers compared with directors selected from inside the firm.
- Executive compensation is a highly visible and often criticized governance mechanism. Salary, bonuses, and long-term incentives are used to strengthen the alignment between managers' and shareholders' interests. A firm's board of directors is responsible for determining the effectiveness of the firm's executive compensation system. An effective system elicits managerial decisions that are in shareholders' best interests.
- In general, evidence suggests that shareholders and boards of directors have become more vigilant in their control of managerial decisions. Nonetheless, these mechanisms are insufficient to govern managerial behavior in many large companies. Therefore, the market for corporate control is an important governance mechanism. Although it, too, is imperfect, the market for corporate control has been effective in causing corporations to combat inefficient diversification and to implement more effective strategic decisions.
- Corporate governance structures used in Germany and Japan differ from each other and from the structure used in the United States. Historically, the U.S. governance structure focused on maximizing shareholder value. In Germany, employees, as a stakeholder group, take a more prominent role in governance. By contrast, until recently, Japanese shareholders played virtually no role in the monitoring and control of top-level managers. However, now Japanese firms are being challenged by "activist" shareholders. Internationally, all these systems are becoming increasingly similar, as are many governance systems both in developed countries, such as France and Spain, and in transitional economies, such as Russia and China.
- Effective governance mechanisms ensure that the interests of all stakeholders are served. Thus, long-term strategic success results when firms are governed in ways that permit at least minimal satisfaction of capital market stakeholders (e.g., shareholders), product market stakeholders (e.g., customers and suppliers), and organizational stakeholders (managerial and nonmanagerial employees; see Chapter 2). Moreover, effective governance produces ethical behavior in the formulation and implementation of strategies.

Review Questions

1. What is corporate governance? What factors account for the considerable amount of attention corporate governance receives from several parties, including shareholder activists, business press writers, and academic scholars? Why is governance necessary to control managers' decisions?
2. What does it mean to say that ownership is separated from managerial control in the modern corporation? Why does this separation exist?
3. What is an agency relationship? What is managerial opportunism? What assumptions do owners of modern corporations make about managers as agents?
4. How is each of the three internal governance mechanisms—ownership concentration, boards of directors, and executive compensation—used to align the interests of managerial agents with those of the firm's owners?
5. What trends exist regarding executive compensation? What is the effect of the increased use of long-term incentives on executives' strategic decisions?
6. What is the market for corporate control? What conditions generally cause this external governance mechanism to become active? How does the mechanism constrain top executives' decisions and actions?
7. What is the nature of corporate governance in Germany and Japan as well as in emerging economies?
8. How can corporate governance foster ethical strategic decisions and behaviors on the part of managers as agents?

Experiential Exercises

Exercise 1: International Governance Codes

As described in the chapter, passage of the Sarbanes-Oxley Act in 2002 has drawn attention to the importance of corporate governance. Similar legislation is pending in other nations as well. However, interest in improved governance predated SOX by a decade in the form of governance codes or guidelines. These codes established sets of "best practices" for both board composition and processes. The first such code was developed by the Cadbury Committee for the London Stock Exchange in 1992. The Australian Stock Exchange developed its guidelines in the Hilmer Report, released in 1993. The Toronto Stock Exchange developed its guidelines the following year in the Dey Report. Today, most major stock exchanges have governance codes.

Working in small groups, find the governance codes of two stock exchanges. Prepare a short (2–3 pages, single-spaced) bullet point comparison of the similarities and differences between the two codes. Be sure to include the following topics in your analysis:

- How are the guidelines structured? Are they rules (i.e., required) or recommendations (i.e., suggestions)? What mechanism is included to monitor or enforce the guidelines?
- What board roles are addressed in the guidelines? For example, some codes may place most or all of their emphasis on functions derived from the importance of the agency relationship illustrated in Figure 10.1 on p. 279, such as monitoring, oversight, and reporting. Codes might also mention the board's role in supporting strategy, or their contribution to firm performance and shareholder wealth.
- What aspects of board composition and structure are covered in the guidelines? For instance, items included in different codes include the balance of insiders and outsiders, committees, whether the CEO also serves as board chair, director education and/or evaluation, compensation of officers and directors, and ownership by board members.

Exercise 2: Governance and Personal Investments

Governance mechanisms are considered to be effective if they meet the needs of all stakeholders, including shareholders. As an investor, how much weight, if any, do you place on a firm's corporate governance? If you currently own any stocks, select a firm that you have invested in. If you do not own any stocks, select a publicly traded company that you consider an attractive potential investment. Working individually, complete the following research on your target firm:

- Find a copy of the company's most recent proxy statement. Proxy statements are mailed to shareholders prior to each year's annual meeting and contain detailed information about the company's governance and present issues on which a shareholder vote might be held. Proxy statements are typically available from a firm's Web site (look for an "Investors" submenu). You can also access proxy statements and other government filings such as the 10-K from the SEC's EDGAR database (http://www.sec.gov/edgar.shtml).
- Conduct a search for news articles that address the governance of your target company. Using different keywords (e.g., *governance, directors,* or *board of directors*) in combination with the company name may be helpful.

Some of the topics that you should examine include:

- Compensation plans (for both the CEO and board members)
- Board composition (e.g., board size, insiders and outsiders)
- Committees
- Stock ownership by officers and directors
- Whether the CEO holds both CEO and board chairperson positions
- Is there a lead director who is not an officer of the company?
- Board seats held by blockholders or institutional investors
- Activities by activist shareholders regarding corporate governance issues of concern

Prepare a one-page single-spaced memo that summarizes the results of your findings. Your memo should include the following topics:

- Summarize what you consider to be the key aspects of the firm's governance mechanisms.
- Based on your review of the firm's governance, did you change your opinion of the firm's desirability as an investment? Why or why not?

Notes

1. C. Thomas, D. Kidd, & C. Fernández-Aráoz, 2007, Are you underutilizing your board? *MIT Sloan Management Review*, 48(2): 71–76; D. C. Carey &, M. Patsalos-Fox, 2006, Shaping strategy from the boardroom. *McKinsey Quarterly*, (3): 90–94; K. Hendry & G. C. Kiel, 2004, The role of the board in firm strategy: Integrating agency and organizational control perspectives, *Corporate Governance*, 12(4), 500–520.
2. J. B. Wade, C. A. O'Reilly, & T. G. Pollock, 2006, Overpaid CEOs and underpaid managers: Fairness and executive compensation, *Organization Science*, 17: 527–544; A. Henderson & J. Fredrickson, 2001, Top management team coordination needs and the CEO pay gap: A competitive test of economic and behavioral views, *Academy of Management Journal*, 44: 96–117.
3. A. D. F. Penalva, 2006, Governance structure and the weighting of performance measures in CEO compensation, *Review of Accounting Studies*, 11: 463–493; S. Werner, H. L. Tosi, & L. Gomez-Mejia, 2005, Organizational governance and employee pay: How ownership structure affects the firm's compensation strategy, *Strategic Management Journal*, 26: 377–384.
4. C. Crossland & D. C. Hambrick, 2007, How national systems differ in their constraints on corporate executives: A study of CEO effects in three countries, *Strategic Management Journal*, 28: 767–789; M. D. Lynall, B. R. Golden, & A. J. Hillman, 2003, Board composition from adolescence to maturity: A multitheoretic view, *Academy of Management Review*, 28: 416–431.
5. M. A. Rutherford, A. K. Buchholtz, & J. A. Brown, 2007, Examining the relationships between monitoring and incentives in corporate governance, *Journal of Management Studies* 44: 414–430; C. M. Daily, D. R. Dalton, & A. A. Cannella, 2003, Corporate governance: Decades of dialogue and data, *Academy of Management Review*, 28: 371–382; P. Stiles, 2001, The impact of the board on strategy: An empirical examination, *Journal of Management Studies*, 38: 627–650.
6. C. J. Prince, 2006, When bad things happen to good CEOs, *Chief Executive*, October, 52–55; M. S. Schwartz, T. W. Dunfee, & M. J. Kline, 2005, Tone at the top: An ethics code for directors? *Journal of Business Ethics*, 58: 79–100; D. Finegold, E. E. Lawler III, & J. Conger, 2001, Building a better board, *Journal of Business Strategy*, 22(6): 33–37.
7. E. F. Fama & M. C. Jensen, 1983, Separation of ownership and control, *Journal of Law and Economics*, 26: 301–325.
8. C. Hymowitz, 2004, Corporate Governance (a special report); Experiments in corporate governance: Finding the right way to improve board oversight isn't easy; but plenty of companies are trying, *Wall Street Journal*, June 21, R1.
9. I. Le Breton-Miller & D. Miller, 2006, Why do some family businesses out-compete? Governance, long-term orientations, and sustainable capability, *Entrepreneurship Theory and Practice*, 30: 731–746; M. Carney, 2005, Corporate governance and competitive advantage in family-controlled firms, *Entrepreneurship Theory and Practice*, 29: 249–265; R. Charan, 1998, *How Corporate Boards Create Competitive Advantage*, San Francisco: Jossey-Bass.
10. G. J. Nicholson & G. C. Kiel, 2007, Can directors impact performance? A case-based test of three theories of corporate governance, *Corporate Governance*, 15(4): 585–608; G. J. Nicholson & G. C. Kiel, 2004, Breakthrough board performance: How to harness your board's intellectual capital, *Corporate Governance*, 4(1): 5–23; A. Cannella Jr., A. Pettigrew, & D. Hambrick, 2001, Upper echelons: Donald Hambrick on executives and strategy, *Academy of Management Executive*, 15(3): 36–52.
11. X. Wu, 2005, Corporate governance and corruption: A cross-country analysis, *Governance*, 18(2): 151–170; J. McGuire & S. Dow, 2002, The Japanese keiretsu system: An empirical analysis, *Journal of Business Research*, 55: 33–40.
12. R. E. Hoskisson, D. Yiu, & H. Kim, 2004, Corporate governance systems: Effects of capital and labor market congruency on corporate Innovation and global competitiveness, *Journal of High Technology Management*, 15: 293–315.
13. Crossland & Hambrick, How national systems differ in their constraints on corporate executives; R. Aguilera & G. Jackson, 2003, The cross-national diversity of corporate governance: Dimensions and determinants, *Academy of Management Review*, 28: 447–465.
14. R. P. Wright, 2004, Top managers' strategic cognitions of the strategy making process: Differences between high and low performing firms, *Journal of General Management*, 30(1): 61–78.
15. A. Bris & C. Cabous, 2006, In a merger, two companies come together and integrate their distribution lines, brands, work forces, management teams, strategies and cultures, *Financial Times*, October 6, 1.
16. S. Sudarsanam & A. A. Mahate, 2006, Are friendly acquisitions too bad for shareholders and managers? Long-term value creation and top management turnover in hostile and friendly acquirers, *British Journal of Management: Supplement*, 17(1): S7–S30; T. Moeller, 2005, Let's make a deal! How shareholder control impacts merger payoffs, *Journal of Financial Economics*, 76(1): 167–190; M. A. Hitt, R. E. Hoskisson, R. A. Johnson, & D. D. Moesel, 1996, The market for corporate control and firm innovation, *Academy of Management Journal*, 39: 1084–1119.
17. R. E. Hoskisson, M. A. Hitt, R. A. Johnson, & W. Grossman, 2002, Conflicting voices: The effects of ownership heterogeneity and internal governance on corporate strategy, *Academy of Management Journal*, 45: 697–716.
18. G. E. Davis & T. A. Thompson, 1994, A social movement perspective on corporate control, *Administrative Science Quarterly*, 39: 141–173.
19. R. Bricker & N. Chandar, 2000, Where Berle and Means went wrong: A reassessment of capital market agency and financial reporting, *Accounting, Organizations, and Society*, 25: 529–554; M. A. Eisenberg, 1989, The structure of corporation law, *Columbia Law Review*, 89(7): 1461, as cited in R. A. G. Monks & N. Minow, 1995, *Corporate Governance*, Cambridge, MA: Blackwell Business, 7.
20. R. M. Wiseman & L. R. Gomez-Mejia, 1999, A behavioral agency model of managerial risk taking, *Academy of Management Review*, 23: 133–153.
21. T. Zellweger, 2007, Time horizon, costs of equity capital, and generic investment strategies of firms, *Family Business Review*, 20(1): 1–15; R. C. Anderson & D. M. Reeb, 2004, Board composition: Balancing family influence in S&P 500 firms, *Administrative Science Quarterly*, 49: 209–237.
22. Carney, Corporate governance and competitive advantage in family-controlled firms; N. Anthanassiou, W. F. Crittenden, L. M. Kelly, & P. Marquez, 2002, Founder centrality effects on the Mexican family

firm's top management group: Firm culture, strategic vision and goals and firm performance, *Journal of World Business,* 37: 139–150.

23. M. Santiago-Castro & C. J. Brown, 2007, Ownership structure and minority rights: A Latin American view, *Journal of Economics and Business*, 59: 430–442; M. Carney & E. Gedajlovic, 2003, Strategic innovation and the administrative heritage of East Asian family business groups, *Asia Pacific Journal of Management,* 20: 5–26; D. Miller & I. Le Breton-Miller, 2003, Challenge versus advantage in family business, *Strategic Organization,* 1: 127–134.
24. E. E. Fama, 1980, Agency problems and the theory of the firm, *Journal of Political Economy,* 88: 288–307.
25. Rutherford, Buchholtz, & Brown, Examining the relationships between monitoring and incentives in corporate governance; D. Dalton, C. Daily, T. Certo, & R. Roengpitya, 2003, Meta-analyses of financial performance and equity: Fusion or confusion? *Academy of Management Journal,* 46: 13–26; M. Jensen & W. Meckling, 1976, Theory of the firm: Managerial behavior, agency costs, and ownership structure, *Journal of Financial Economics,* 11: 305–360.
26. G. C. Rodríguez, C. A.-D. Espejo, & R. Valle Cabrera, 2007, Incentives management during privatization: An agency perspective, *Journal of Management Studies*, 44: 536–560; D. C. Hambrick, S. Finkelstein, & A. C. Mooney, 2005, Executive job demands: New insights for explaining strategic decisions and leader behaviors, *Academy of Management Review,* 30: 472–491.
27. T. G. Habbershon, 2006, Commentary: A framework for managing the familiness and agency advantages in family firms, *Entrepreneurship Theory and Practice*, 30: 879–886; M. G. Jacobides & D. C. Croson, 2001, Information policy: Shaping the value of agency relationships, *Academy of Management Review,* 26: 202–223.
28. S.-H. Kang, P. Kumar, & H. Lee, 2006, Agency and corporate investment: The role of executive compensation and corporate governance, *Journal of Business*, 79: 1127–1147; H. E. Ryan Jr. & R. A. Wiggins III, 2004, Who is in whose pocket? Director compensation, board independence, and barriers to effective monitoring, *Journal of Financial Economics,* 73: 497–524.
29. Y. Y. Kor, 2006, Direct and interaction effects of top management team and board compositions on R&D investment strategy, *Strategic Management Journal*, 27: 1081–1099.
30. A. Ghosh, D. Moon, & K. Tandon, 2007, CEO ownership and discretionary investments, *Journal of Business Finance & Accounting,* 34: 819–839; M. W. Peng, 2004, Outside directors and firm performance during institutional transitions, *Strategic Management Journal,* 25: 453–471; A. J. Hillman & T. Dalziel, 2003, Boards of directors and firm performance: Integrating agency and resource dependence perspectives, *Academy of Management Review,* 28: 383–396.
31. S. Ghoshal & P. Moran, 1996, Bad for practice: A critique of the transaction cost theory, *Academy of Management Review,* 21: 13–47; O. E. Williamson, 1996, *The Mechanisms of Governance,* New York: Oxford University Press, 6.
32. E. Kang, 2006, Investors' perceptions of managerial opportunism in corporate acquisitions: The moderating role of environmental condition, *Corporate Governance,* 14: 377–387; R. W. Coff & P. M. Lee, 2003, Insider trading as a vehicle to appropriate rent from R&D. *Strategic Management Journal,* 24: 183–190; C. C. Chen, M. W. Peng, & P. A. Saparito, 2002, Individualism, collectivism, and opportunism: A cultural perspective on transaction cost economics, *Journal of Management,* 28: 567–583.
33. Fama, Agency problems and the theory of the firm.
34. P. Jiraporn, Y. Sang Kim, W. N. Davidson, & M. Singh, 2006, Corporate governance, shareholder rights and firm diversification: An empirical analysis, *Journal of Banking & Finance*, 30: 947–963; R. C. Anderson, T. W. Bates, J. M. Bizjak, & M. L. Lemmon, 2000, Corporate governance and firm diversification, *Financial Management,* 29(1): 5–22; R. E. Hoskisson & T. A. Turk, 1990, Corporate restructuring: Governance and control limits of the internal market, *Academy of Management Review,* 15: 459–477.
35. G. P. Baker & B. J. Hall, 2004, CEO incentives and firm size, *Journal of Labor Economics*, 22: 767–798; R. Bushman, Q. Chen, E. Engel, & A. Smith, 2004, Financial accounting information, organizational complexity and corporate governance systems, *Journal of Accounting & Economics,* 7: 167–201; M. A. Geletkanycz, B. K. Boyd, & S. Finkelstein, 2001, The strategic value of CEO external directorate networks: Implications for CEO compensation, *Strategic Management Journal,* 9: 889–898.
36. S. W. Geiger & L. H. Cashen, 2007, Organizational size and CEO compensation: The moderating effect of diversification in downscoping organizations, *Journal of Managerial Issues,* 9(2): 233–252; Y. Grinstein & P. Hribar, 2004, CEO compensation and incentives: Evidence from M&A bonuses, *Journal of Financial Economics,* 73: 119–143; P. Wright, M. Kroll, & D. Elenkov, 2002, Acquisition returns, increase in firm size and chief executive officer compensation: The moderating role of monitoring, *Academy of Management Journal,* 45: 599–608.
37. S. Rajgopal, T. Shevlin, & V. Zamora, 2006, CEOs' outside employment opportunities and the lack of relative performance evaluation in compensation contracts, *Journal of Finance*, 61: 1813–1844; Gomez-Mejia, Nunez-Nickel, & Gutierrez, The role of family ties in agency contracts.
38. J. Weber, 2007, The accidental CEO (well, not really); Kellogg needed a new boss, fast. Here's how it groomed insider David Mackay, *BusinessWeek*, April 23, 65.
39. M. S. Jensen, 1986, Agency costs of free cash flow, corporate finance, and takeovers, *American Economic Review,* 76: 323–329.
40. A. V. Douglas, 2007, Managerial opportunism and proportional corporate payout policies, *Managerial Finance,* 33(1): 26–42; M. Jensen & E. Zajac, 2004, Corporate elites and corporate strategy: How demographic preferences and structural position shape the scope of the firm, *Strategic Management Journal,* 25: 507–524; T. H. Brush, P. Bromiley, & M. Hendrickx, 2000, The free cash flow hypothesis for sales growth and firm performance, *Strategic Management Journal,* 21: 455–472.
41. J. Lunsford & B. Steinberg, 2006, Conglomerates' conundrum, *Wall Street Journal,* September 14, B1, B7; K. Ramaswamy, M. Li, & B. S. P. Petitt, 2004, Who drives unrelated diversification? A study of Indian manufacturing firms, *Asia Pacific Journal of Management,* 21: 403–423; Ramaswamy, Li, & Veliyath, Variations in ownership behavior and propensity to diversify.
42. K. B. Lee, M. W. Peng & K. Lee, 2007, From diversification premium to diversification discount during institutional transitions, *Journal of World Business,* forthcoming; A. Desai, M. Kroll, & P. Wright, 2005, Outside board monitoring and the economic outcomes of acquisitions: A test of the substitution hypothesis, *Journal of Business Research,* 58: 926–934; P. Wright, M. Kroll, A. Lado, & B. Van Ness, 2002, The structure of ownership and corporate acquisition strategies, *Strategic Management Journal,* 23: 41–53.
43. T. K. Berry, J. M. Bizjak, M. L. Lemmon, & L. Naveen, 2006, Organizational complexity and CEO labor markets: Evidence from diversified firms, *Journal of Corporate Finance,* 12: 797–817; R. Rajan, H. Servaes, & L. Zingales, 2001, The cost of diversity: The diversification discount and inefficient investment, *Journal of Finance,* 55: 35–79; A. Sharma, 1997, Professional as agent: Knowledge asymmetry in agency exchange, *Academy of Management Review,* 22: 758–798.
44. V. Chhaochharia & Y. Grinstein, 2007, Corporate governance and firm value: The impact of the 2002 governance rules, *Journal of Finance,* 62: 1789–1825; A. Borrus, L. Lavelle, D. Brady, M. Arndt, & J. Weber, 2005, Death, taxes and Sarbanes-Oxley? Executives may be frustrated with the law's burdens, but corporate performance is here to stay, *BusinessWeek,* January 17, 28–31.
45. D. Reilly, 2006, Checks on internal controls pay off, *Wall Street Journal,* August 10, C3.
46. S. E. Needleman, 2006, Sarbanes-Oxley creates special demand, *Wall Street Journal,* May 16, B8; T. J. Healey, 2007, Sarbox was the right medicine, *Wall Street Journal,* August 9, A13.
47. G. Ip, 2006, Is a U.S. listing worth the effort?; Premiums paid for shares in foreign firms are reduced since crackdown, study finds, *Wall Street Journal,* November 28, C1.
48. J. D. McKinnon & C. Conkey, 2007, Bush gives hope to foes of Sarbanes-Oxley law, *Wall Street Journal,* February 1, A4.
49. F. Navissi & V. Naiker, 2006, Institutional ownership and corporate value, *Managerial*

Finance, 32: 247–256; A. de Miguel, J. Pindado, & C. de la Torre, 2004, Ownership structure and firm value: New evidence from Spain, *Strategic Management Journal*, 25: 1199–1207; J. Coles, N. Sen, & V. McWilliams, 2001, An examination of the relationship of governance mechanisms to performance, *Journal of Management*, 27: 23–50.

50. Jiraporn, Kim, Davidson, & Singh, Corporate governance, shareholder rights and firm diversification; M. Singh, I. Mathur, & K. C. Gleason, 2004, Governance and performance implications of diversification strategies: Evidence from large U.S. firms, *Financial Review*, 39: 489–526; R. E. Hoskisson, R. A. Johnson, & D. D. Moesel, 1994, Corporate divestiture intensity in restructuring firms: Effects of governance, strategy, and performance, *Academy of Management Journal*, 37: 1207–1251.
51. G. Iannotta, G. Nocera, & A. Sironi, 2007, Ownership structure, risk and performance in the European banking industry, *Journal of Banking & Finance*, 31: 2127–2149.
52. De Miguel, Pindado, & de la Torre, Ownership structure and firm value: New evidence from Spain.
53. B. Villalonga & R. Amit, 2006, How do family ownership, control and management affect firm value? *Journal of Financial Economics*, 80: 385–417; R. C. Anderson & D. M. Reeb, 2004, Board composition: Balancing family influence in S&P 500 firms, *Administrative Science Quarterly*, 49: 209–237.
54. S. J. Chang, 2003, Ownership structure, expropriation and performance of group-affiliated companies in Korea, *Academy of Management Journal*, 46: 238–253.
55. A. Berle & G. Means, 1932, *The Modern Corporation and Private Property*, New York: Macmillan.
56. M. Gietzmann, 2006, Disclosure of timely and forward-looking statements and strategic management of major institutional ownership, *Long Range Planning*, 39(4): 409–427; B. Ajinkya, S. Bhojraj, & P. Sengupta, 2005, The association between outside directors, institutional investors and the properties of management earnings forecasts, *Journal of Accounting Research*, 43: 343–376; M. P. Smith, 1996, Shareholder activism by institutional investors: Evidence from CalPERS, *Journal of Finance*, 51: 227–252.
57. Hoskisson, Hitt, Johnson, & Grossman, Conflicting voices; C. M. Daily, 1996, Governance patterns in bankruptcy reorganizations, *Strategic Management Journal*, 17: 355–375.
58. M. M. Cornett, A. J. Marcus, A. Saunders, & H. Tehranian, 2007, The impact of institutional ownership on corporate operating performance, *Journal of Banking & Finance*, 3: 1771–1794; A. Picou & M. J. Rubach, 2006, Does good governance matter to institutional investors? Evidence from the enactment of corporate governance guidelines, *Journal of Business Ethics*, 65(1), 55–67.
59. T. W. Briggs, 2007, Corporate governance and the new hedge fund activism: An empirical analysis. *Journal of Corporation Law*, 32(4): 681–723,725–738; K. Rebeiz, 2001, Corporate governance effectiveness in American corporations: A survey, *International Management Journal*, 18(1): 74–80.
60. J. Grant & F. Guerrera, 2007, CalPERS files twice as many "shareholder proposals," *Financial Times*, August 14, 19.
61. S. Thurm, When investor activism doesn't pay, *Wall Street Journal*, September 12, A2; S. M. Jacoby, 2007, Principles and agents: CalPERS and corporate governance in Japan, *Corporate Governance*, 15(1): 5–15; L. Tihanyi, R. A. Johnson, R. E. Hoskisson, & M. A. Hitt, 2003, Institutional ownership differences and international diversification: The effects of boards of directors and technological opportunity, *Academy of Management Journal*, 46: 195–211; Hoskisson, Hitt, Johnson, & Grossman, Conflicting voices; P. David, M. A. Hitt, & J. Gimeno, 2001, The role of institutional investors in influencing R&D, *Academy of Management Journal*, 44: 144–157.
62. M. A. A. Khan, 2006, Corporate governance and the role of institutional investors in India, *Journal of Asia-Pacific Business*, 7(2): 37–54.
63. V. Krivogorsky, 2006, Ownership, board structure, and performance in continental Europe, *International Journal of Accounting*, 41(2): 176–197; S. Thomsen & T. Pedersen, 2000, Ownership structure and economic performance in the largest European companies, *Strategic Management Journal*, 21: 689–705.
64. C. M. Dalton & D. R. Dalton, 2006, Corporate governance best practices: The proof is in the process, *Journal of Business Strategy*, 27(4), 5–7; R. V. Aguilera, 2005, Corporate governance and director accountability: An institutional comparative perspective, *British Journal of Management*, 16(S1), S39–S53; E. H. Fram, 2004, Governance reform: It's only just begun, *Business Horizons*, 47(6): 10–14.
65. Thomas, Kidd, & Fernández-Aráoz, Are you underutilizing your board?; Hillman & Dalziel, Boards of directors and firm performance.
66. L. Bonazzi, & S. M. N. Islam, 2007, Agency theory and corporate governance: A study of the effectiveness of board in their monitoring of the CEO, *Journal of Modeling in Management*, 2(1): 7–23; Rebeiz, Corporate governance effectiveness in American corporations.
67. N. Chipalkatti, Q. V. Le, & M. Rishi, 2007, Portfolio flows to emerging capital markets: Do corporate transparency and public governance matter? *Business and Society Review*, 112(2): 227–249; J. Chidley, 2001, Why boards matter, *Canadian Business*, October 29, 6; D. P. Forbes & F. J. Milliken, 1999, Cognition and corporate governance: Understanding boards of directors as strategic decision-making groups, *Academy of Management Review*, 24: 489–505.
68. Krivogorsky, Ownership, board structure, and performance in continental Europe; Hoskisson, Hitt, Johnson, & Grossman, Conflicting voices; B. D. Baysinger & R. E. Hoskisson, 1990, The composition of boards of directors and strategic control: Effects on corporate strategy, *Academy of Management Review*, 15: 72–87.
69. E. E. Lawler III & D. Finegold, 2006, Who's in the boardroom and does it matter: The impact of having non-director executives attend board meetings, *Organizational Dynamics*, 35(1): 106–115; M. Carpenter & J. Westphal, 2001, Strategic context of external network ties: Examining the impact of director appointments on board involvement in strategic decision making, *Academy of Management Journal*, 44: 639–660; E. J. Zajac & J. D. Westphal, 1996, Director reputation, CEO-board power, and the dynamics of board interlocks, *Administrative Science Quarterly*, 41: 507–529.
70. E. M. Fich & A. Shivdasani, 2006, Are busy boards effective monitors? *Journal of Finance*, 61: 689–724; J. Westphal & L. Milton, 2000, How experience and network ties affect the influence of demographic minorities on corporate boards, *Administrative Science Quarterly*, 45(2): 366–398.
71. Fich & Shivdasani, Are busy boards effective monitors; S. T. Petra, 2005, Do outside independent directors strengthen corporate boards? *Corporate Governance*, 5(1): 55–65.
72. S. K. Lee & L. R. Carlson, 2007, The changing board of directors: Board independence in S & P 500 Firm, *Journal of Organizational Culture, Communication and Conflict*, 11(1): 31–41.
73. R. C. Pozen, 2006, Before you split that CEO/Chair, *Harvard Business Review*, 84(4): 26–28; J. W. Lorsch & A. Zelleke, 2005, Should the CEO be the Chairman, *MIT Sloan Management Review*, 46(2): 71–74.
74. A. Murray, 2007, *Revolt in the Boardroom: The New Rules of Power in Corporate America*, New York: HarperCollins.
75. E. White & T. Herrick, 2006, Ethical breaches pose dilemma for boards: When to fire a CEO? *Wall Street Journal*, February 16, B1.
76. Fich & Shivdasani, Are busy boards effective monitors; J. Roberts, T. McNulty, &, P. Stiles, 2005, Beyond agency conceptions of the work of the non-executive director: Creating accountability in the boardroom, *British Journal of Management*, 16(S1): S5–S26.
77. Fich & Shivdasani, Are busy boards effective monitors; S. Zahra, 1996, Governance, ownership and corporate entrepreneurship among the *Fortune* 500: The moderating impact of industry technological opportunity, *Academy of Management Journal*, 39: 1713–1735.
78. Baysinger, & Hoskisson, Board composition and strategic control: The effect on corporate strategy.
79. Lawler & Finegold, Who's in the boardroom and does it matter?; E. E. Lawler III & D. L. Finegold, 2005, The changing face of corporate boards, *MIT Sloan Management Review*, 46(2): 67–70; A. Conger, E. E. Lawler, & D. L. Finegold, 2001, *Corporate Boards: New Strategies for Adding Value at the Top*, San Francisco: Jossey-Bass; J. A. Conger, D. Finegold, & E. E. Lawler III, 1998, Appraising boardroom performance, *Harvard Business Review*, 76(1): 136–148.

80. A. L. Boone, L. C. Field, J. M. Karpoff, & C. G. Raheja, 2007, The determinants of corporate board size and composition: An empirical analysis, *Journal of Financial Economics*, 85(1): 66–101; J. Marshall, 2001, As boards shrink, responsibilities grow, *Financial Executive*, 17(4): 36–39.
81. L. Brannen, 2007, A center lane for governance, *Business Finance*, August, 25.
82. T. Long, 2007, The evolution of FTSE 250 boards of directors: Key factors influencing board performance and effectiveness, *Journal of General Management*, 32(3): 45–60; S. Finkelstein & A. C. Mooney, 2003, Not the usual suspects: How to use board process to make boards better, *Academy of Management Executive*, 17: 101–113.
83. J. L. Koors, 2006 Director pay: A work in progress, *The Corporate Governance Advisor*, 14(5): 25–31; W. Shen, 2005, Improve board effectiveness: The need for incentives, *British Journal of Management*, 16(S1): S81–S89; M. Gerety, C. Hoi, & A. Robin, 2001, Do shareholders benefit from the adoption of incentive pay for directors? *Financial Management*, 30: 45–61; D. C. Hambrick & E. M. Jackson, 2000, Outside directors with a stake: The linchpin in improving governance, *California Management Review*, 42(4): 108–127.
84. Y. Deutsch, T. Keil, & T. Laamanen, 2007, Decision making in acquisitions: the effect of outside directors' compensation on acquisition patterns, *Journal of Management*, 33(1): 30–56.
85. A. J. Hillman, C. Shropshire, & A. A. Cannella, Jr. 2007, Organizational predictors of women on corporate boards, *Academy of Management Journal*, 50: 941–952; I. Filatotchev & S. Toms, 2003, Corporate governance, strategy and survival in a declining industry: A study of UK cotton textile companies, *Journal of Management Studies*, 40: 895–920.
86. 2007, Wall St. Roundup; pay increases for CEOs fall below 10% in 2006, *Los Angeles Times*, April 3, C4.
87. L. A. Bebchuk & J. M. Fried, 2006, Pay without performance: Overview of the issues, *Academy of Management Perspectives*, 20(1): 5–24; L. A. Bebchuk & J. M. Fried, 2004, *Pay Without Performance: The Unfulfilled Promise of Executive Compensation*, Cambridge, MA: Harvard University Press; M. A. Carpenter & W. G. Sanders, 2002, Top management team compensation: The missing link between CEO pay and firm performance, *Strategic Management Journal*, 23: 367–375.
88. K. Rehbein, 2007, Explaining CEO compensation: How do talent, governance, and markets fit in? *Academy of Management Perspectives*, 21(1): 75–77; J. S. Miller, R. M. Wiseman, & L. R. Gomez-Mejia, 2002, The fit between CEO compensation design and firm risk, *Academy of Management Journal*, 45: 745–756; L. Gomez-Mejia & R. M. Wiseman, 1997, Reframing executive compensation: An assessment and outlook, *Journal of Management*, 23: 291–374.
89. M. Larraza-Kintana, R. M. Wiseman, L. R. Gomez-Mejia, & T. M. Welbourne, 2007, Disentangling compensation and employment risks using the behavioral agency model, *Strategic Management Journal*, 28: 1001–1019; J. McGuire & E. Matta, 2003, CEO stock options: The silent dimension of ownership, *Academy of Management Journal*, 46: 255–265; W. G. Sanders & M. A. Carpenter, 1998, Internationalization and firm governance: The roles of CEO compensation, top team composition and board structure, *Academy of Management Journal*, 41: 158–178.
90. J. P. O'Connor, R. L. Priem, J. E. Coombs, & K. M. Gilley, 2006, Do CEO stock options prevent or promote fraudulent financial reporting? *Academy of Management Journal*, 49: 483–500.
91. S. O'Donnell, 2000, Managing foreign subsidiaries: Agents of headquarters, or an interdependent network? *Strategic Management Journal*, 21: 521–548; K. Roth & S. O'Donnell, 1996, Foreign subsidiary compensation: An agency theory perspective, *Academy of Management Journal*, 39: 678–703.
92. A. Ghosh, 2006, Determination of executive compensation in an emerging economy: Evidence from India, *Emerging Markets, Finance & Trade*, 42(3): 66–90; K. Ramaswamy, R. Veliyath, & L. Gomes, 2000, A study of the determinants of CEO compensation in India, *Management International Review*, 40(2): 167–191.
93. C. L. Staples, 2007, Board globalization in the world's largest TNCs 1993–2005, *Corporate Governance*, 15(2): 311–32.
94. L. K. Meulbroek, 2001, The efficiency of equity-linked compensation: Understanding the full cost of awarding executive stock options, *Financial Management*, 30(2): 5–44.
95. C. E. Devers, R. M. Wiseman, & R. M. Holmes Jr., 2007, The effects of endowment and loss aversion in managerial stock option valuation, *Academy of Management Journal*, 50: 191–208; J. C. Bettis, J. M. Biziak, & M. L. Lemmon, 2005, Exercise behavior, valuation and the incentive effects of employee stock options, *Journal of Financial Economics*, 76: 445–470.
96. M. Klausner, 2007, Reducing directors' legal risk, *Harvard Business Review*, 85(4), 28; T. G. Pollock, H. M. Fischer, & J. B. Wade, 2002, The role of politics in repricing executive options, *Academy of Management Journal*, 45: 1172–1182; M. E. Carter & L. J. Lynch, 2001, An examination of executive stock option repricing, *Journal of Financial Economics*, 59: 207–225; D. Chance, R. Kumar, & R. Todd, 2001, The "repricing" of executive stock options, *Journal of Financial Economics*, 59: 129–154.
97. Picou & Rubach, Does good governance matter to institutional investors? Evidence from the enactment of corporate governance guidelines; J. C. Hartzell & L. T. Starks, 2003, Institutional investors and executive compensation, *Journal of Finance*, 58: 2351–2374.
98. R. Sinha, 2006, Regulation: The market for corporate control and corporate governance, *Global Finance Journal*, 16(3): 264–282; R. Coff, 2002, Bidding wars over R&D intensive firms: Knowledge, opportunism and the market for corporate control, *Academy of Management Journal*, 46: 74–85; Hitt, Hoskisson, Johnson, & Moesel, The market for corporate control and firm innovation.
99. R. W. Masulis, C. Wang, & F. Xie, 2007, Corporate governance and acquirer returns, *Journal of Finance*, 62(4), 1851–1889; R. Sinha, 2004, The role of hostile takeovers in corporate governance, *Applied Financial Economics*, 14: 1291–1305; D. Goldstein, 2000, Hostile takeovers as corporate governance? Evidence from 1980s, *Review of Political Economy*, 12: 381–402.
100. O. Kini, W. Kracaw, & S. Mian, 2004, The nature of discipline by corporate takeovers, *Journal of Finance*, 59: 1511–1551.
101. Masulis, Wang, & Xie, Corporate governance and acquirer returns.
102. J. P. Walsh & R. Kosnik, 1993, Corporate raiders and their disciplinary role in the market for corporate control, *Academy of Management Journal*, 36: 671–700.
103. T. W. Briggs, 2007, Corporate governance and a new hedge fund activism: *Empirical Analysis*, 32(4): 681–723.
104. N. Naik & M. Tapley, 2007, Demystifying hedge funds, *Business Strategy Review*, 18(2): 68–72.
105. Thurm, When investor activism doesn't pay.
106. R. B. Adams & D. Ferreira, 2007, A theory of friendly boards, *Journal of Finance*, 62: 217–250.
107. J Cresswell, 2006, Gilded paychecks: Pay packages allow executives to jump ship with less risk, *New York Times*, http://www.nyt.com, December 29.
108. Ibid.
109. M. Maremont, 2007, Scholars link success of firms to lives of CEOs, *Wall Street Journal*, September 5, A1, A15; J. Hartzell, E. Ofek, & D. Yermack, 2004, What's in it for me? CEOs whose firms are acquired, *Review of Financial Studies*, 17: 37–61.
110. J. McCary, 2007, Foreign investments rise, *Wall Street Journal*, June 6, A5; K. Shimizu, M. A. Hitt, D. Vaidyanath, & P. Vincenzo, 2004, Theoretical foundations of cross-border mergers and acquisitions: A review of current research and recommendations for the future, *Journal of International Management*, 10: 307–353; M. A. Hitt & V. Pisano, 2003, The cross-border merger and acquisition strategy, *Management Research*, 1: 133–144.
111. Sinha, Regulation: The market for corporate control and corporate governance; J. Anand & A. Delios, 2002, Absolute and relative resources as determinants of international acquisitions, *Strategic Management Journal*, 23: 119–134.
112. J. Harford, 2003, Takeover bids and target directors' incentives: The impact of a bid on directors' wealth and board seats, *Journal of Financial Economics*, 69: 51–83; S. Chatterjee, J. S. Harrison, & D. D. Bergh, 2003, Failed takeover attempts, corporate

governance, and refocusing, *Strategic Management Journal,* 24: 87–96.

113. E. Webb, 2006, Relationships between board structure and takeover defenses, *Corporate Governance,* 6(3): 268–180; C. Sundaramurthy, J. M. Mahoney, & J. T. Mahoney, 1997, Board structure, antitakeover provisions, and stockholder wealth, *Strategic Management Journal,* 18: 231–246.
114. J. Jargon & J. Vuocolo, 2007, Sara Lee CEO challenged on anti-takeover defenses, *Wall Street Journal,* May 11, B4.
115. W. G. Sanders & M. A. Carpenter, 2003, Strategic satisficing? A behavioral-agency theory perspective on stock repurchase program announcements, *Academy of Management Journal,* 46: 160–178; J. Westphal & E. Zajac, 2001, Decoupling policy from practice: The case of stock repurchase programs, *Administrative Science Quarterly,* 46: 202–228.
116. O. Faleye, 2007, Classified boards, firm value, and managerial entrenchment, *Journal of Financial Economics,* 83: 501–529.
117. 2007, Leaders: Pay slips; management in Europe, *Economist,* June 23, 14: A. Cala, 2005, Carrying golden parachutes; France joins EU trend to reign in executive severance deals, *Wall Street Journal,* June 8, A13.
118. J. A. Pearce II & R. B. Robinson Jr., 2004, Hostile takeover defenses that maximize shareholder wealth, *Business Horizons,* 47(5): 15–24.
119. G. Wright, 2007, Home Depot reports pay for its CEOs, *Wall Street Journal,* April 16, B5.
120. Walsh & Kosnik, Corporate raiders.
121. A. Chakraborty & R. Arnott, 2001, Takeover defenses and dilution: A welfare analysis, *Journal of Financial and Quantitative Analysis,* 36: 311–334.
122. M Wolf, 2007, The new capitalism: How unfettered finance is fast reshaping the global economy, *Financial Times,* June 19, 13: C. Millar, T. I. Eldomiaty, C. J. Choi, & B. Hilton, 2005, Corporate governance and institutional transparency in emerging markets, *Journal of Business Ethics,* 59: 163–174; D. Norburn, B. K. Boyd, M. Fox, & M. Muth, 2000, International corporate governance reform, *European Business Journal,* 12(3): 116–133; M. Useem, 1998, Corporate leadership in a globalizing equity market, *Academy of Management Executive,* 12(3): 43–59.
123. S. M. Jacoby, 2004, *The Embedded Corporation: Corporate Governance and Employment Relations in Japan and the United States,* Princeton, NJ: Princeton University Press.
124. P. Witt, 2004, The competition of international corporate governance systems—A German perspective, *Management International Review,* 44: 309–333; L. Nachum, 2003, Does nationality of ownership make any difference and if so, under what circumstances? Professional service MNEs in global competition, *Journal of International Management,* 9: 1–32.
125. Crossland & Hambrick, How national systems differ in their constraints on corporate executives; Aguilera & Jackson, The cross-national diversity of corporate governance: Dimensions and determinants.
126. Carney, Corporate governance and competitive advantage in family-controlled firms; S. Klein, 2000, Family businesses in Germany: Significance and structure, *Family Business Review,* 13: 157–181.
127. A. Tuschke & W. G. Sanders, 2003, Antecedents and consequences of corporate governance reform: The case of Germany, *Strategic Management Journal,* 24: 631–649; J. Edwards & M. Nibler, 2000, Corporate governance in Germany: The role of banks and ownership concentration, *Economic Policy,* 31: 237–268; E. R. Gedajlovic & D. M. Shapiro, 1998, Management and ownership effects: Evidence from five countries, *Strategic Management Journal,* 19: 533–553.
128. P. C. Fiss, 2006, Social influence effects and managerial compensation evidence from Germany, *Strategic Management Journal,* 27: 1013–1031; S. Douma, 1997, The two-tier system of corporate governance, *Long Range Planning,* 30(4): 612–615.
129. K Done, 2007, Tackling the many challenges of Airbus, *Financial Times,* July 17, 22.
130. P. C. Fiss & E. J. Zajac, 2004, The diffusion of ideas over contested terrain: The (non) adoption of a shareholder value orientation among German firms, *Administrative Science Quarterly,* 49: 501–534.
131. W. G. Sanders & A. C. Tuschke, 2007, The adoption of the institutionally contested organizational practices: The emergence of stock option pay in Germany, *Academy of Management Journal,* 57: 33–56.
132. T. Hoshi, A. K. Kashyap, & S. Fischer, 2001, *Corporate Financing and Governance in Japan,* Boston: MIT Press.
133. J. P. Charkham, 1994. *Keeping Good Companies: A Study of Corporate Governance in Five Countries.* New York: Oxford University Press, 70.
134. M. A. Hitt, H. Lee, & E. Yucel, 2002, The importance of social capital to the management of multinational enterprises: Relational networks among Asian and Western Firms, *Asia Pacific Journal of Management,* 19: 353–372.
135. W. P. Wan, D. W. Yiu, R. E. Hoskisson, & H. Kim, 2008, The performance implications of relationship banking during macroeconomic expansion and contraction: A study of Japanese banks' social relationships and overseas expansion, *Journal of International Business Studies,* forthcoming.
136. Jacoby, *The embedded corporation;* P. M. Lee & H. M. O'Neill, 2003, Ownership structures and R&D investments of U.S. and Japanese firms: Agency and stewardship perspectives, *Academy of Management Journal,* 46: 212–225.
137. I. S. Dinc, 2006, Monitoring the monitors: The corporate governance in Japanese banks and their real estate lending in the 1980s, *Journal of Business,* 79(6): 3057–3081; A. Kawaura, 2004, Deregulation and governance: Plight of Japanese banks in the 1990s, *Applied Economics,* 36: 479–484; B. Bremner, 2001, Cleaning up the banks—finally, *BusinessWeek,* December 17, 86; 2000, Business: Japan's corporate-governance U-turn, *The Economist,* November 18, 73.
138. N. Isagawa, 2007, A theory of unwinding of cross-shareholding under managerial entrenchment, *Journal of Financial Research,* 30: 163–179.
139. C. L. Ahmadjian & G. E. Robbins, 2005, A clash of capitalisms: Foreign shareholders and corporate restructuring in 1990s Japan, *American Sociological Review,* 70: 451–471.
140. P. M. Lee, 2004, A comparison of ownership structures and innovations of U.S. and Japanese firms, *Managerial and Decision Economics,* 26(1): 39–50; Lee & O'Neill, Ownership structures and R&D investments of U.S. and Japanese firms.
141. Y. Hayashi, 2005, Japan firms ponder private life, *Wall Street Journal,* August 1, C14.
142. E. Engel, R. M. Hayes, & X. Wang, 2007, The Sarbanes-Oxley Act and firms' going-private decisions, *Journal of Accounting & Economics,* 44(1/2): 116–145.
143. L. Santini, 2007, Rematch: KT&G vs. Steel Partners: Korean cigarette maker again angers an activist fund, *Wall Street Journal,* June 22, C5.
144. G. A. Fowler & J. Quin, 2007, China moves to boost transparency, but much is kept hidden, *Wall Street Journal,* April 25, A6.
145. T. J. Healey, 2007, Sarbox was the right medicine, *Wall Street Journal,* August 9, A13.
146. J. D. Hughes & J. H. Lee, 2007, The changing landscape of D & O liability, *Risk Management Journal,* January, 18–22.
147. C. Shropshire & A. J. Hillman, 2007, A longitudinal study of significant change in stakeholder management, *Business and Society,* 46(1): 63–87; S. Sharma & I. Henriques, 2005, Stakeholder influences on sustainability practices in the Canadian Forest products industry, *Strategic Management Journal,* 26: 159–180; A. J. Hillman, G. D. Keim, & R. A. Luce, 2001, Board composition and stakeholder performance: Do stakeholder directors make a difference? *Business and Society,* 40: 295–314.
148. D. L. Gold & J. W. Dienhart, 2007, Business ethics in the corporate governance era: Domestic and international trends in transparency, regulation, and corporate governance, *Business and Society Review,* 112(2): 163–170; N. Demise, 2005, Business ethics and corporate governance in Japan, *Business and Society,* 44: 211–217.
149. L. Santini, 2006, Investor activism grows globally, but wins are rare, *Wall Street Journal,* July 3, C1.
150. R. V. Aguilera, D. E. Rupp, C. A. Williams, & J. Ganapathi, 2007, Putting the S back in corporate social responsibility: A multilevel theory of social change in organizations, *Academy of Management Review,* 32(3): 836–863; Caldwell & Karri, Organizational governance and ethical systems: A covenantal approach to building trust; A. Felo, 2001, Ethics programs, board involvement, and potential conflicts of interest in corporate governance, *Journal of Business Ethics,* 32: 205–218.

Organizational Structure and Controls

Studying this chapter should provide you with the strategic management knowledge needed to:

1. Define organizational structure and controls and discuss the difference between strategic and financial controls.
2. Describe the relationship between strategy and structure.
3. Discuss the functional structures used to implement business-level strategies.
4. Explain the use of three versions of the multidivisional (M-form) structure to implement different diversification strategies.
5. Discuss the organizational structures used to implement three international strategies.
6. Define strategic networks and discuss how strategic center firms implement such networks at the business, corporate, and international levels.

Are Strategy and Structural Changes in the Cards for GE?

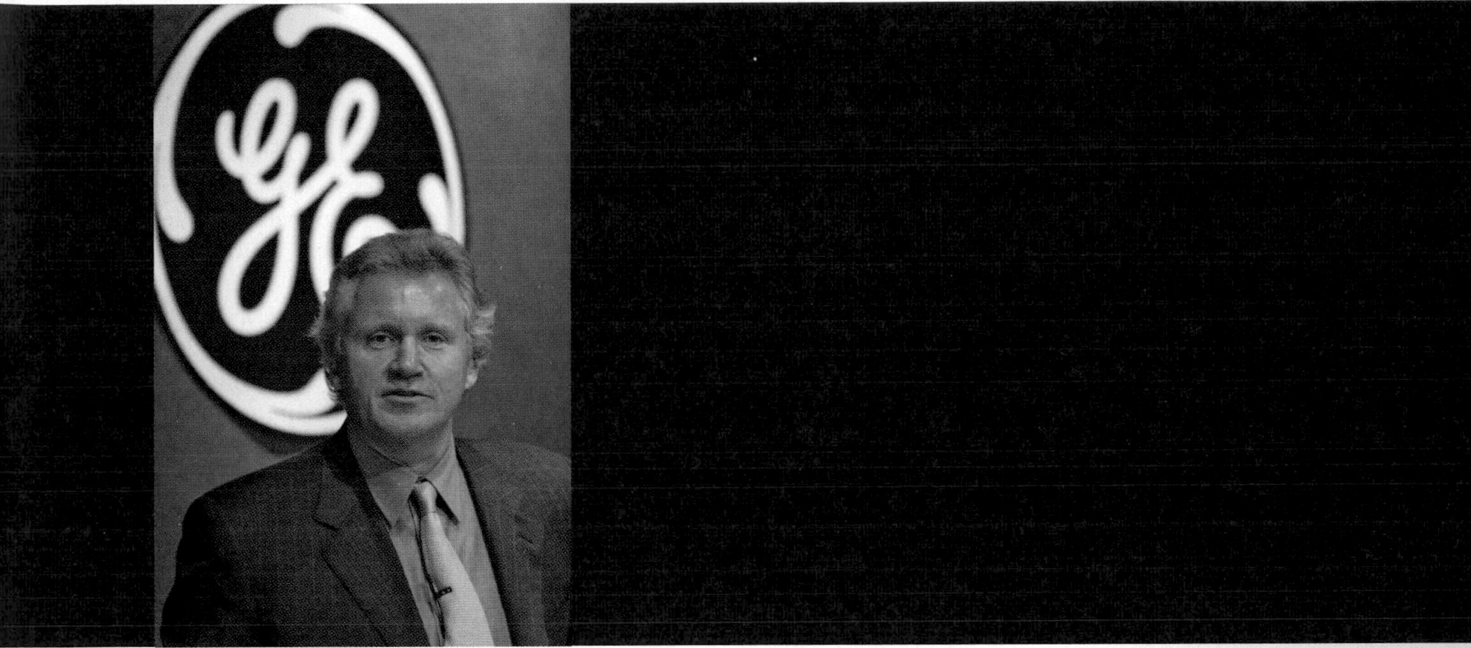

GE is the only company listed in the Dow Jones Industrial Index today that was also included in the original index in 1896. This fact highlights the quality of General Electric's performance for more than a century. The firm's 2006 financial results ($163 billion in revenue and $20.7 billion of earnings) also appear to validate the view that GE is performing extremely well. Today, GE serves customers in more than 100 countries, employs more than 300,000 people worldwide, and generates in excess of 50 percent of its revenues from outside the United States. Committed to innovation as an important source of profitable growth, GE spent $5.7 billion in research and development (R&D) in 2006. But in some analysts' and investors' eyes, all is not well at GE. To respond to these concerns, changes to GE's corporate-level strategy and structure may be in the making.

In mid-2005, slightly less than four years after taking over from Jack Welch as CEO, Jeffrey Immelt changed GE's structure so that the firm operated with 6 rather than 11 business units. (Commercial Finance, Healthcare, Industrial, Infrastructure, Money, and NBC Universal were the six businesses forming the new structure. Infrastructure accounts for the largest percentage of total firm revenue with NBC Universal generating the smallest percentage of total revenue.) In announcing his decision, Immelt said that "these changes will accelerate GE's growth in key industries" while simultaneously helping the firm become more focused on emerging technologies with significant commercial potential. Even with this reorganization, GE continued using the related-linked diversification strategy at the corporate level (see Chapter 6); the SBU form of the multidivisional structure (discussed in this chapter) remained the structure in place to facilitate use of the related-linked strategy.

Let's move forward to mid-2007, a time when a prominent analyst appeared to speak for many of his peers and some investors when he called for GE to sell one or more of its six businesses. Specifically, the call was for GE to sell noncore businesses such as NBC Universal and Money (formerly called Consumer Finance) to "raise billions (and) make this colossus a heck of a lot easier for one man to manage." The thought is that these two businesses have relatively little in common with the other four, and having them in GE's portfolio of businesses takes attention away from developing additional synergies (primarily in the form of economies of scope—see Chapter 6) across the four businesses with greater similarities. Immelt and Welch both reacted less than positively to this suggestion with Welch saying that following this advice "would be a tragedy of enormous proportions."

If these two businesses were sold, GE's corporate-level strategy would change from related linked to related constrained. If this change in strategy were to occur, the firm's structure would also need to be changed from the SBU form of the multidivisional structure to the cooperative form of the multidivisional structure. From the perspective of strategic management, the important outcome is that a change to organizational structure accompany a decision to change a firm's strategy. The reason for making such a change is that a mismatch between strategy and structure negatively affects performance.

Sources: 2007, Our businesses, http://www.ge.com, September 2; 2007, The weight of one observer's words, *New York Times Online*, http://www.nytimes.com, July 22; N. D. Schwartz, 2007, Is GE too big for its own good? *New York Times Online*, http://www.nytimes.com, July 22; G. Colvin, 2006, Lafley and Immelt: In search of billions, *Fortune*, December 11, 70–82.

As we explain in Chapter 4, all firms use one or more business-level strategies. In Chapters 6–9, we discuss other strategies firms may choose to use (corporate-level, international, and cooperative). Once selected, strategies are not implemented in a vacuum. Organizational structure and controls, this chapter's topic, provide the framework within which strategies are used in both for-profit organizations and not-for-profit agencies.[1] However, as we explain, separate structures and controls are required to successfully implement different strategies. In all organizations, top-level managers have the final responsibility for ensuring that the firm has matched each of its strategies with the appropriate organizational structure and that changes to both occur when necessary. Thus, Jeffrey Immelt is responsible for changing GE's organizational structure if the firm decides to use a different corporate-level strategy. The match or degree of fit between strategy and structure influences the firm's attempts to earn above-average returns.[2] Thus, the ability to select an appropriate strategy and match it with the appropriate structure is an important characteristic of effective strategic leadership.[3]

This chapter opens with an introduction to organizational structure and controls. We then provide more details about the need for the firm's strategy and structure to be properly matched. Affecting firms' efforts to match strategy and structure is their influence on each other.[4] As we discuss, strategy has a more important influence on structure, although once in place, structure influences strategy.[5] Next, we describe the relationship between growth and structural change successful firms experience. We then discuss the different organizational structures firms use to implement the separate business-level, corporate-level, international, and cooperative strategies. A series of figures highlights the different structures firms match with strategies. Across time and based on their experiences, organizations, especially large and complex ones, customize these general structures to meet their unique needs.[6] Typically, the firm tries to form a structure that is complex enough to facilitate use of its strategies but simple enough for all parties to understand and implement.[7] When structures become too complicated, firms try to reduce that complexity. This process is happening at Yahoo! through its efforts to flatten the organization's hierarchies so the firm will be closer to the customer as it battles rivals such as Google.[8]

Organizational Structure and Controls

Research shows that organizational structure and the controls that are a part of the structure affect firm performance.[9] In particular, evidence suggests that performance declines when the firm's strategy is not matched with the most appropriate structure and controls.[10] Even though mismatches between strategy and structure do occur, research indicates that managers try to act rationally when forming or changing their firm's structure.[11] His record of success at GE suggests that Jeffrey Immelt will pay close attention to the need to make certain that strategy and structure remained matched in his firm if a decision is made to divest one or more businesses.

Organizational Structure

Organizational structure specifies the firm's formal reporting relationships, procedures, controls, and authority and decision-making processes.[12] Developing an organizational structure that effectively supports the firm's strategy is difficult,[13] especially because of the uncertainty (or unpredictable variation[14]) about cause-effect relationships in the global economy's rapidly changing and dynamic competitive environments.[15] When a structure's elements (e.g., reporting relationships, procedures, etc.) are properly aligned with one another, the structure facilitates effective use of the firm's strategies.[16] Thus, organizational structure is a critical component of effective strategy implementation processes.[17]

Organizational structure specifies the firm's formal reporting relationships, procedures, controls, and authority and decision-making processes.

A firm's structure specifies the work to be done and how to do it, given the firm's strategy or strategies.[18] Thus, organizational structure influences how managers work and the decisions resulting from that work.[19] Supporting the implementation of strategies, structure is concerned with processes used to complete organizational tasks.[20] Sometimes, firms develop creative processes for employees to use while completing their work. This appears to be the case at Best Buy. As we explain in the Strategic Focus, the firm's ROWE (Results-Only Work Environment) program is unique and is generating positive outcomes for Best Buy as a company and for participating employees. However, Best Buy and all firms must recognize that in general, changing processes detailing how work is to be performed is challenging and may be resisted for a variety of reasons.[21]

Effective structures provide the stability a firm needs to successfully implement its strategies and maintain its current competitive advantages while simultaneously providing the flexibility to develop advantages it will need in the future.[22] *Structural stability* provides the capacity the firm requires to consistently and predictably manage its daily work routines[23] while *structural flexibility* provides the opportunity to explore competitive possibilities and then allocate resources to activities that will shape the competitive advantages the firm will need to be successful in the future.[24] An effectively flexible organizational structure allows the firm to *exploit* current competitive advantages while *developing* new ones[25] that can potentially be used in the future.[26] For example, at Bavarian Motor Works (BMW) the firm's structure is thought to be "flat, flexible, entrepreneurial, and fast";[27] these structural characteristics contribute positively to efforts to exploit current advantages while exploring for new ones. For Best Buy, the long-term success of its ROWE program may be a function of the degree to which its use simultaneously enhances the firm's structural stability and structural flexibility.

Modifications to the firm's current strategy or selection of a new strategy call for changes to its organizational structure. However, research shows that once in place, organizational inertia often inhibits efforts to change structure, even when the firm's performance suggests that it is time to do so.[28] In his pioneering work, Alfred Chandler found that organizations change their structures when inefficiencies force them to do so.[29] Firms seem to prefer the structural status quo and its familiar working relationships until the firm's performance declines to the point where change is absolutely necessary.[30] Necessity may be the case at Samsung Electronics Co. Some analysts think that "Samsung is at a crossroads." A faltering corporate-level strategy and the use of the structure supporting that strategy may be contributing to the firm's difficulties.[31]

In addition to the issues we already mentioned, it is important to note that top-level managers hesitate to conclude that the firm's structure (or its strategy, for that matter) are the problem, in that doing so suggests that their previous choices were not the best ones. Because of these inertial tendencies, structural change is often induced instead by actions from stakeholders (e.g., those from the capital market and customers—see Chapter 2) who are no longer willing to tolerate the firm's performance. Evidence shows that appropriate timing of structural change happens when top-level managers recognize that a current organizational structure no longer provides the coordination and direction needed for the firm to successfully implement its strategies.[32]

Strategic Focus Strategic Focus Strategic Focus

Increased Job Autonomy: A Structural Approach to Increased Performance and Job Satisfaction?

Best Buy is the largest U.S. consumer electronics retailer with more than 100,000 employees and roughly 800 stores. In addition to its well-known flagship stores, Best Buy owns Future Shop (Canada's largest and fastest-growing retailer of consumer electronics) and Magnolia (a high-end electronics retailer concentrating on audio and video packages for homes, cars, and businesses). The firm's Geek Squads are located in each Best Buy store and are offered as self-standing units in some cities such as Atlanta, Dallas, and Minneapolis (the firm's headquarters).

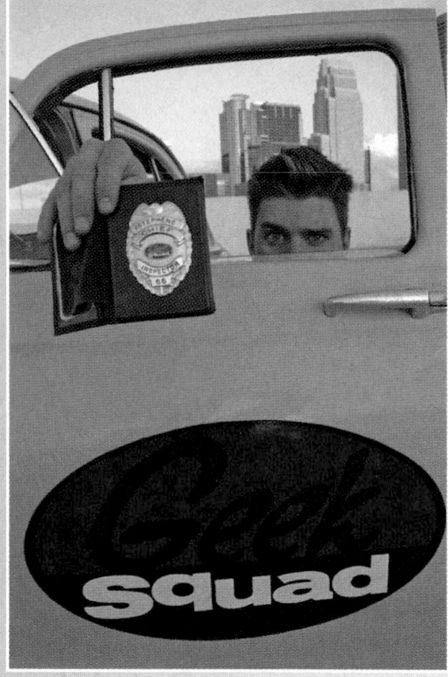

The Results-Only Work Environment (ROWE) program, created to improve job satisfaction and productivity, is being used in multiple parts of Best Buy's operations, including the Geek Squad.

To improve job satisfaction, employee productivity, and the firm's performance, Best Buy continues to experiment with ROWE (Results-Only Work Environment). Developed in-house, ROWE was rolled out in 2002 with approximately 4,000 headquarters' employees participating in the experiment. Results achieved through this program are impressive in that "Productivity has increased an average of 35 percent within six to nine months in Best Buy units implementing ROWE, a figure based on metrics reported or estimated by managers using the new system. Voluntary turnover has dropped between 52 percent and 90 percent in three Best Buy locations being studied." Survey results also indicate that employees take more ownership of their work and express much greater satisfaction with what they do as well as how they complete the tasks associated with their jobs.

Redesigns of how work activities are performed are at the core of ROWE. Essentially, employees have the freedom and responsibility to decide when and where they will work. Those supervising employees empowered in this manner believe that they are managing outcomes rather than directly managing the people expected to reach the desired outcomes. A designer of the program describes one of ROWE's objectives in this manner: "We want people to stop thinking of work as someplace you go to, five days a week from 8 to 5, and start thinking of work as something you do."

This paradigm shift in work activities that is becoming a more central part of Best Buy's organizational structure is guided by 13 commandments. Because Best Buy has established a division (CultureRX) that is selling the ROWE program to other companies, only three of the commandments, as follows, are public information: "(1) There are no work schedules, (2) Every meeting is optional, and (3) Employees should render no judgment about how colleagues spend their time." Employee performance is judged strictly on the basis of tasks completed, even if none of them were handled in the office. In this results-only environment, the work design allows people to come and go as they please. But the trade-off is that employees are clearly held accountable for their work to be completed successfully and on time. Excuses are not tolerated; and, for employees, it is important to understand that the "guidelines that signal where work ends and leisure begins" become blurred.

Given its success, the challenge for Best Buy's executives is to determine how to adapt ROWE for use across other tasks that are a part of its organizational structure. Can the results-only approach be adapted to all of Best Buy's work processes? This important question remains unanswered.

Sources: J. Brandon, 2007, Rethinking the clock, *Business 2.0,* March, 24–29; F. Jossi, 2007, Clocking out, *HR Magazine,* June, 47–50; C. Penttila, 2007, Flexibility is the workstyle of the future, *Entrepreneur,* May, 47; M. Conlin, 2006, Smashing the clock, *BusinessWeek,* December 11, 60–68; P. J. Kiger, 2006, Throwing out the rules of work, *WorkForce Management,* September 25, 16–23.

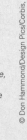

Chandler's contributions to our understanding of organizational structure and its relationship to strategies and performance are quite significant. Indeed, some believe that Chandler's emphasis on "organizational structure so transformed the field of business history that some call the period before Dr. Chandler's publications "B.C.," meaning "before Chandler." [33] As we discuss next, effective organizational controls help managers recognize when it is time to adjust the firm's structure.

Organizational Controls

Organizational controls are an important aspect of structure.[34] **Organizational controls** guide the use of strategy, indicate how to compare actual results with expected results, and suggest corrective actions to take when the difference is unacceptable. When fewer differences separate actual from expected outcomes, the organization's controls are more effective.[35] It is difficult for the company to successfully exploit its competitive advantages without effective organizational controls.[36] Properly designed organizational controls provide clear insights regarding behaviors that enhance firm performance.[37] Firms use both strategic controls and financial controls to support using their strategies.

Organizational controls guide the use of strategy, indicate how to compare actual results with expected results, and suggest corrective actions to take when the difference is unacceptable.

Strategic controls are largely subjective criteria intended to verify that the firm is using appropriate strategies for the conditions in the external environment and the company's competitive advantages. Thus, strategic controls are concerned with examining the fit between what the firm *might do* (as suggested by opportunities in its external environment) and what it *can do* (as indicated by its competitive advantages). Effective strategic controls help the firm understand what it takes to be successful.[38] Strategic controls demand rich communications between managers responsible for using them to judge the firm's performance and those with primary responsibility for implementing the firm's strategies (such as middle and first-level managers). These frequent exchanges are both formal and informal in nature.[39]

Strategic controls are largely subjective criteria intended to verify that the firm is using appropriate strategies for the conditions in the external environment and the company's competitive advantages.

Strategic controls are also used to evaluate the degree to which the firm focuses on the requirements to implement its strategies. For a business-level strategy, for example, the strategic controls are used to study primary and support activities (see Tables 3.6 and 3.7, on page 86) to verify that the critical activities are being emphasized and properly executed. With related corporate-level strategies, strategic controls are used to verify the sharing of appropriate strategic factors such as knowledge, markets, and technologies across businesses. To effectively use strategic controls when evaluating related diversification strategies, executives must have a deep understanding of each unit's business-level strategy.[40]

P&G's recent acquisition of Gillette, a giant in the personal grooming arena, is a result of restructuring efforts designed to exert strategic controls on P&G's future growth.

As we described in the Opening Case, GE's CEO Jeffrey Immelt allocates a great deal of his time and energy to issues related to strategic control. Constantly challenged to "deliver profitable growth," executives rely on innovative strategies and appropriate organizational structures as the path to improved performance. To facilitate a focus on what he believes are key technologies (e.g., renewable energy and nanotechnology), Immelt has changed GE's structure by jettisoning "much of GE's insurance business while bulking up in health care, water, security, and other areas." Similarly, Procter & Gamble's CEO A. G. Lafley is restructuring parts of P&G. Deciding to work with external partners to develop innovative products while divesting well-known brands such as Crisco, Jif, Pert Plus, and Sure while acquiring giants Gillette, Clairol, and Wella are products of this restructuring effort. The exact structural changes necessary to accommodate these acquisitions remain a work in progress at P&G. In both firms though, the CEOs are using strategic controls to support their chosen strategies.[41]

Financial controls are largely objective criteria used to measure the firm's performance against previously established quantitative standards. Accounting-based measures

Financial controls are largely objective criteria used to measure the firm's performance against previously established quantitative standards.

such as return on investment (ROI) and return on assets (ROA) as well as market-based measures such as economic value added are examples of financial controls. Partly because strategic controls are difficult to use with extensive diversification,[42] financial controls are emphasized to evaluate the performance of the firm using the unrelated diversification strategy. The unrelated diversification strategy's focus on financial outcomes (see Chapter 6) requires using standardized financial controls to compare performances between units and managers.[43]

When using financial controls, firms evaluate their current performance against previous outcomes as well as against competitors' performance and industry averages. In the global economy, technological advances are being used to develop highly sophisticated financial controls, making it possible for firms to more thoroughly analyze their performance results and to assure compliance with regulations. Companies such as Oracle and SAP sell software tools that automate processes firms can use to meet the financial reporting requirements specified by the Sarbanes-Oxley Act. (As noted in Chapter 10, this act requires a firm's principal executive and financial officers to certify corporate financial and related information in quarterly and annual reports submitted to the Securities and Exchange Commission.)

Both strategic and financial controls are important aspects of each organizational structure, and as we noted previously, any structure's effectiveness is determined by using a combination of strategic and financial controls. However, the relative use of controls varies by type of strategy. For example, companies and business units of large diversified firms using the cost leadership strategy emphasize financial controls (such as quantitative cost goals), while companies and business units using the differentiation strategy emphasize strategic controls (such as subjective measures of the effectiveness of product development teams).[44] As previously explained, a corporate-wide emphasis on sharing among business units (as called for by related diversification strategies) results in an emphasis on strategic controls, while financial controls are emphasized for strategies in which activities or capabilities are not shared (e.g., in an unrelated diversification strategy).

As firms consider controls, the important point is to properly balance the use of strategic and financial controls. Indeed, overemphasizing one at the expense of the other can lead to performance declines. According to Michael Dell, an overemphasis on financial controls to produce attractive short-term results contributed to recent performance difficulties at Dell Inc. In addressing this issue, Dell said the following: "The company was too focused on the short term, and the balance of priorities was way too leaning toward things that deliver short-term results."[45] Dell is now restructuring his firm to achieve a proper emphasis on the long term as well as the short term. A greater emphasis on strategic controls is resulting from this restructuring.

Relationships between Strategy and Structure

Strategy and structure have a reciprocal relationship.[46] This relationship highlights the interconnectedness between strategy formulation (Chapters 4, 6–9) and strategy implementation (Chapters 10–13). In general, this reciprocal relationship finds structure flowing from or following selection of the firm's strategy. Once in place though, structure can influence current strategic actions as well as choices about future strategies. Consider, for example, the possible influences of the ROWE program on Best Buy's current and future strategies (see the Strategic Focus).

The general nature of the strategy/structure relationship means that changes to the firm's strategy create the need to change how the organization completes its work. In the "structure influences strategy" direction, firms must be vigilant in their efforts to verify that how their structure calls for work to be completed remains consistent with the implementation requirements of chosen strategies. Research shows, however, that "strategy has a much more important influence on structure than the reverse."[47]

Regardless of the strength of the reciprocal relationships between strategy and structure, those choosing the firm's strategy and structure should be committed to matching each strategy with a structure that provides the stability needed to use current competitive advantages as well as the flexibility required to develop future advantages. Therefore, when changing strategies, the firm should simultaneously consider the structure that will be needed to support use of the new strategy; properly matching strategy and structure can create a competitive advantage.[48]

Evolutionary Patterns of Strategy and Organizational Structure

Research suggests that most firms experience a certain pattern of relationships between strategy and structure. Chandler[49] found that firms tend to grow in somewhat predictable patterns: "first by volume, then by geography, then integration (vertical, horizontal), and finally through product/business diversification"[50] (see Figure 11.1). Chandler interpreted his findings as an indication that firms' growth patterns determine their structural form.

As shown in Figure 11.1, sales growth creates coordination and control problems the existing organizational structure cannot efficiently handle. Organizational growth

Figure 11.1 Strategy and Structure Growth Pattern

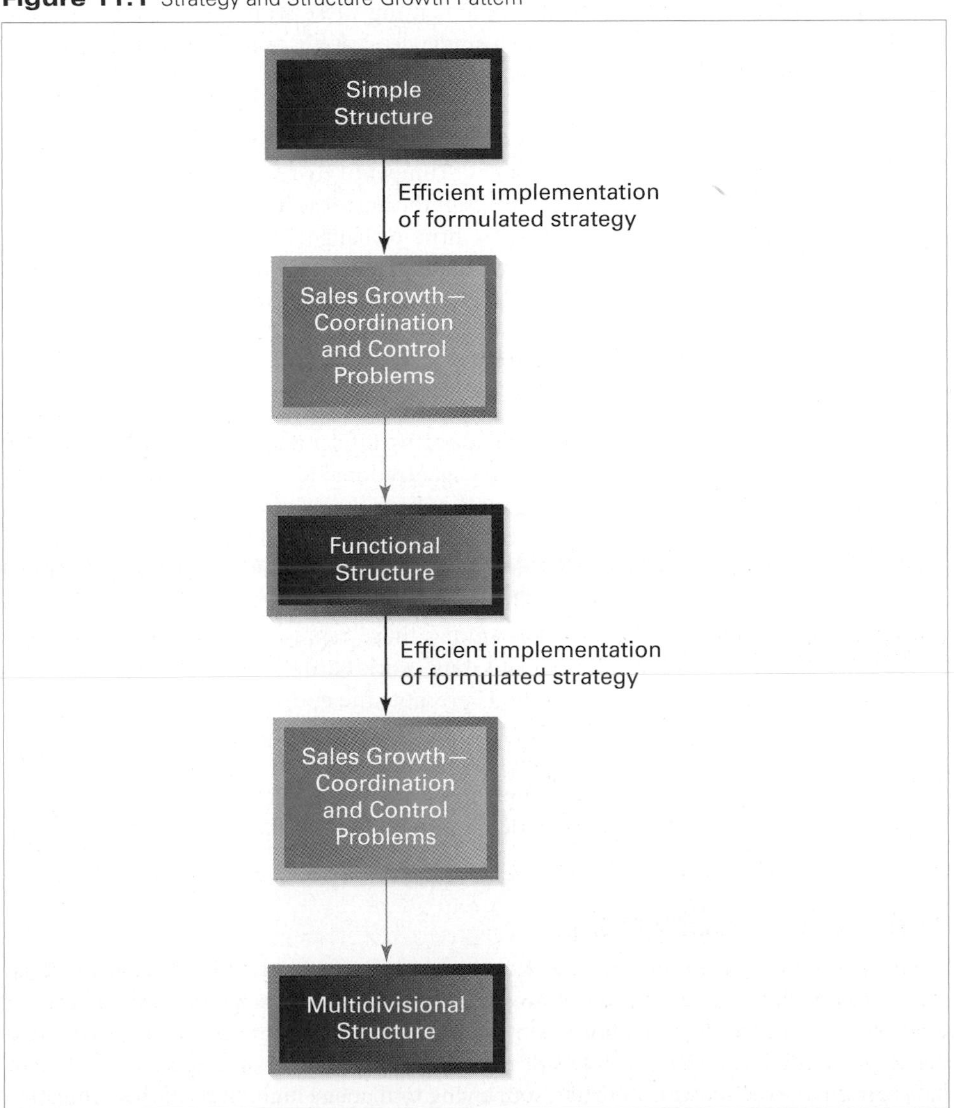

creates the opportunity for the firm to change its strategy to try to become even more successful. However, the existing structure's formal reporting relationships, procedures, controls, and authority and decision-making processes lack the sophistication required to support using the new strategy.[51] A new structure is needed to help decision makers gain access to the knowledge and understanding required to effectively integrate and coordinate actions to implement the new strategy.[52]

Firms choose from among three major types of organizational structures—simple, functional, and multidivisional—to implement strategies. Across time, successful firms move from the simple to the functional to the multidivisional structure to support changes in their growth strategies.[53]

Simple Structure

The **simple structure** is a structure in which the owner-manager makes all major decisions and monitors all activities while the staff serves as an extension of the manager's supervisory authority.

The **simple structure** is a structure in which the owner-manager makes all major decisions and monitors all activities while the staff serves as an extension of the manager's supervisory authority.[54] Typically, the owner-manager actively works in the business on a daily basis. Informal relationships, few rules, limited task specialization, and unsophisticated information systems characterize this structure. Frequent and informal communications between the owner-manager and employees make coordinating the work to be done relatively easy. The simple structure is matched with focus strategies and business-level strategies, as firms implementing these strategies commonly compete by offering a single product line in a single geographic market. Local restaurants, repair businesses, and other specialized enterprises are examples of firms using the simple structure.

As the small firm grows larger and becomes more complex, managerial and structural challenges emerge. For example, the amount of competitively relevant information requiring analysis substantially increases, placing significant pressure on the owner-manager. Additional growth and success may cause the firm to change its strategy. Even if the strategy remains the same, the firm's larger size dictates the need for more sophisticated workflows and integrating mechanisms. At this evolutionary point, firms tend to move from the simple structure to a functional organizational structure.[55]

Functional Structure

The **functional structure** consists of a chief executive officer and a limited corporate staff, with functional line managers in dominant organizational areas such as production, accounting, marketing, R&D, engineering, and human resources.

The **functional structure** consists of a chief executive officer and a limited corporate staff, with functional line managers in dominant organizational areas such as production, accounting, marketing, R&D, engineering, and human resources.[56] This structure allows for functional specialization,[57] thereby facilitating active sharing of knowledge within each functional area. Knowledge sharing facilitates career paths as well as professional development of functional specialists. However, a functional orientation can negatively affect communication and coordination among those representing different organizational functions. For this reason, the CEO must work hard to verify that the decisions and actions of individual business functions promote the entire firm rather than a single function.[58] The functional structure supports implementing business-level strategies and some corporate-level strategies (e.g., single or dominant business) with low levels of diversification. When changing from a simple to a functional structure, firms want to avoid introducing value-destroying bureaucratic procedures such as failing to promote innovation and creativity.[59]

Multidivisional Structure

With continuing growth and success, firms often consider greater levels of diversification. Successfully using a diversification strategy requires analyzing substantially greater amounts of data and information when the firm offers the same products in different markets (market or geographic diversification) or offers different products in several markets (product diversification). In addition, trying to manage high levels of diversification through functional structures creates serious coordination and control problems,[60] a fact that commonly leads to a new structural form.[61]

The **multidivisional (M-form) structure** consists of operating divisions, each representing a separate business or profit center in which the top corporate officer delegates responsibilities for day-to-day operations and business-unit strategy to division managers. Each division represents a distinct, self-contained business with its own functional hierarchy.[62] As initially designed, the M-form was thought to have three major benefits: "(1) it enabled corporate officers to more accurately monitor the performance of each business, which simplified the problem of control; (2) it facilitated comparisons between divisions, which improved the resource allocation process; and (3) it stimulated managers of poorly performing divisions to look for ways of improving performance."[63] Active monitoring of performance through the M-form increases the likelihood that decisions made by managers heading individual units will be in stakeholders' best interests. Because diversification is a dominant corporate-level strategy used in the global economy, the M-form is a widely adopted organizational structure.[64]

The **multidivisional (M-form) structure** consists of operating divisions, each representing a separate business or profit center in which the top corporate officer delegates responsibilities for day-to-day operations and business-unit strategy to division managers.

Used to support implementation of related and unrelated diversification strategies, the M-form helps firms successfully manage diversification's many demands.[65] Chandler viewed the M-form as an innovative response to coordination and control problems that surfaced during the 1920s in the functional structures then used by large firms such as DuPont and General Motors.[66] Research shows that the M-form is appropriate when the firm grows through diversification.[67] Partly because of its value to diversified corporations, some consider the multidivisional structure to be one of the twentieth century's most significant organizational innovations.[68]

No one organizational structure (simple, functional, or multidivisional) is inherently superior to the others.[69] Peter Drucker says the following about this matter: "There is no one right organization. . . . Rather the task . . . is to select the organization for the particular task and mission at hand."[70] In our context, Drucker is saying that the firm must select a structure that is "right" for successfully using the chosen strategy. Because no single structure is optimal in all instances, managers concentrate on developing proper matches between strategies and organizational structures rather than searching for an "optimal" structure. This matching of structure and strategy is taking place at Pfizer, Inc. Noting that the firm's current organizational structure was not serving it well, CEO David Shedlarz is changing the firm's structure so it will be easier for company personnel to openly collaborate to develop new products, form effective alliances, and identify ideal companies to acquire (all of these actions are necessary to implement the firm's strategies).[71]

Pfizer CEO David Shedlarz is working to change Pfizer's corporate structure for more effective sharing of ideas, resources, and personnel.

We now describe the strategy/structure matches that evidence shows positively contribute to firm performance.

Matches between Business-Level Strategies and the Functional Structure

Firms use different forms of the functional organizational structure to support implementing the cost leadership, differentiation, and integrated cost leadership/differentiation strategies. The differences in these forms are accounted for primarily by different uses of three important structural characteristics: *specialization* (concerned with the type and number of jobs required to complete work[72]), *centralization* (the degree to which decision-making authority is retained at higher managerial levels[73]), and *formalization* (the degree to which formal rules and procedures govern work[74]).

Using the Functional Structure to Implement the Cost Leadership Strategy

Firms using the cost leadership strategy sell large quantities of standardized products to an industry's typical customer. Simple reporting relationships, few layers in the decision-making and authority structure, a centralized corporate staff, and a strong focus on process improvements through the manufacturing function rather than the development of new products by emphasizing product R&D characterize the cost leadership form of the functional structure[75] (see Figure 11.2). This structure contributes to the emergence of a low-cost culture—a culture in which employees constantly try to find ways to reduce the costs incurred to complete their work.[76]

In terms of centralization, decision-making authority is centralized in a staff function to maintain a cost-reducing emphasis within each organizational function (engineering, marketing, etc.). While encouraging continuous cost reductions, the centralized staff also verifies that further cuts in costs in one function won't adversely affect the productivity levels in other functions.[77]

Jobs are highly specialized in the cost leadership functional structure; work is divided into homogeneous subgroups. Organizational functions are the most common subgroup, although work is sometimes batched on the basis of products produced or clients served. Specializing in their work allows employees to increase their efficiency, reducing costs as a result. Guiding individuals' work in this structure are highly formalized rules and procedures, which often emanate from the centralized staff.

Wal-Mart Stores Inc. uses the functional structure to implement cost leadership strategies in each of its three segments (Wal-Mart Stores, Sam's Clubs, and International). In the Wal-Mart Stores segment (which generates the largest share of the firm's total sales), the cost leadership strategy is used in the firm's Supercenter, Discount, and Neighborhood Market retailing formats.[78] Long known for its "Always Low Prices" slogan (which was used for 19 years), Wal-Mart recently changed to a new slogan—"Save Money, Live

Figure 11.2 Functional Structure for Implementing a Cost Leadership Strategy

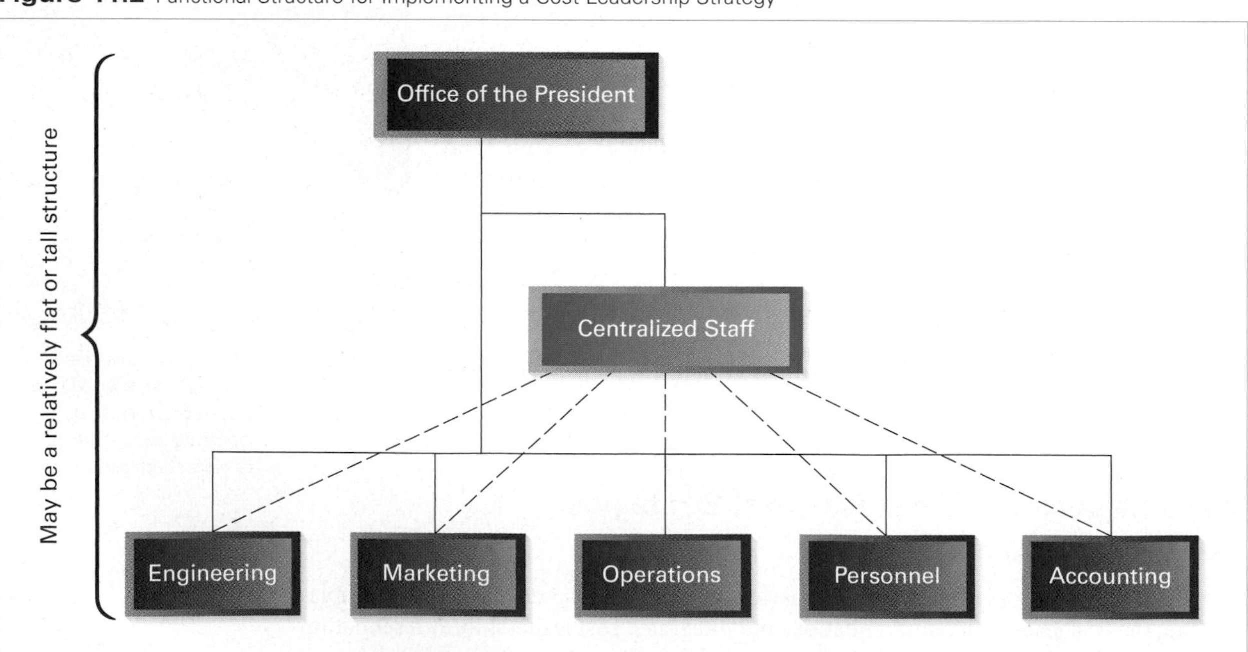

Notes:
- Operations is the main function
- Process engineering is emphasized rather than new product R&D
- Relatively large centralized staff coordinates functions
- Formalized procedures allow for emergence of a low-cost culture
- Overall structure is mechanistic; job roles are highly structured

Better."[79] Although the slogan is new, Wal-Mart continues using the functional organizational structure in its divisions to drive costs lower. As discussed in Chapter 4, competitors' efforts to duplicate the success of Wal-Mart's cost leadership strategies have generally failed, partly because of the effective strategy/structure matches in each of the firm's segments.

Wal-Mart Stores Inc. uses the functional structure to implement cost leadership strategies in each of its three segments (ASDA is part of Wal-Mart's International segment).

Using the Functional Structure to Implement the Differentiation Strategy

Firms using the differentiation strategy produce products customers perceive as being different in ways that create value for them. With this strategy, the firm wants to sell nonstandardized products to customers with unique needs. Relatively complex and flexible reporting relationships, frequent use of cross-functional product development teams, and a strong focus on marketing and product R&D rather than manufacturing and process R&D (as with the cost leadership form of the functional structure) characterize the differentiation form of the functional structure (see Figure 11.3). From this structure emerges a development-oriented culture in which employees try to find ways to further differentiate current products and to develop new, highly differentiated products.[80]

Continuous product innovation demands that people throughout the firm interpret and take action based on information that is often ambiguous, incomplete, and uncertain. Following a strong focus on the external environment to identify new opportunities, employees often gather this information from people outside the firm (e.g., customers and suppliers). Commonly, rapid responses to the possibilities indicated by the collected

Figure 11.3 Functional Structure for Implementing a Differentiation Strategy

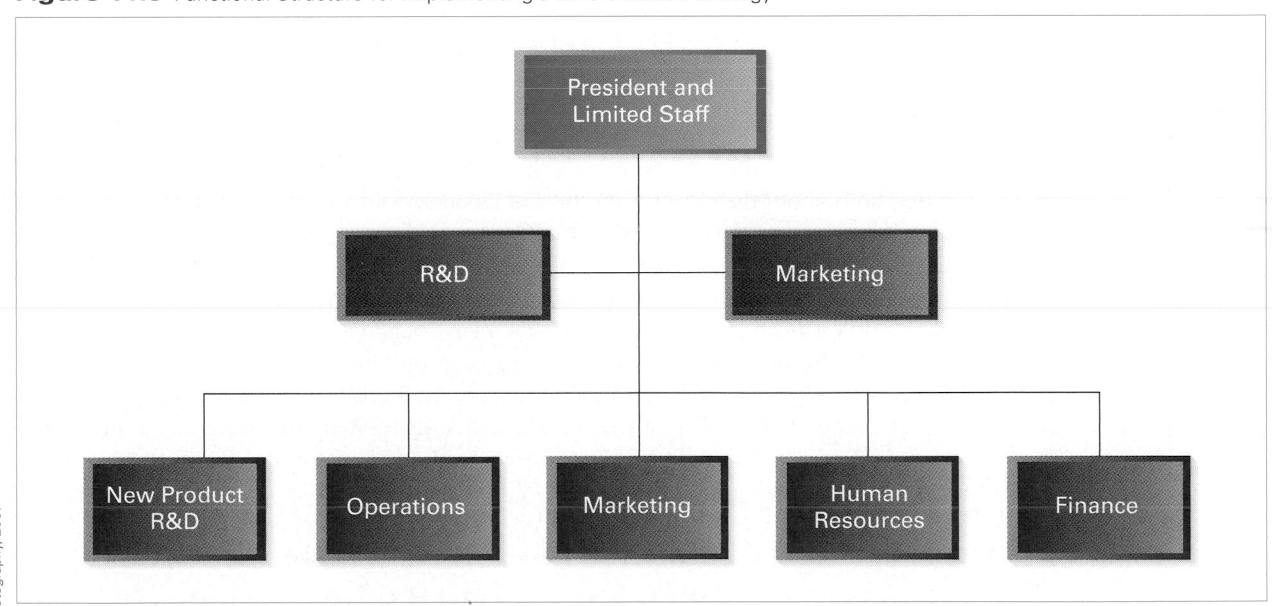

Notes:
- Marketing is the main function for keeping track of new product ideas
- New product R&D is emphasized
- Most functions are decentralized, but R&D and marketing may have centralized staffs that work closely with each other
- Formalization is limited so that new product ideas can emerge easily and change is more readily accomplished
- Overall structure is organic; job roles are less structured

information are necessary, suggesting the need for decentralized decision-making responsibility and authority. To support creativity and the continuous pursuit of new sources of differentiation and new products, jobs in this structure are not highly specialized. This lack of specialization means that workers have a relatively large number of tasks in their job descriptions. Few formal rules and procedures also characterize this structure. Low formalization, decentralization of decision-making authority and responsibility, and low specialization of work tasks combine to create a structure in which people interact frequently to exchange ideas about how to further differentiate current products while developing ideas for new products that can be crisply differentiated.

Using the Functional Structure to Implement the Integrated Cost Leadership/Differentiation Strategy

Firms using the integrated cost leadership/differentiation strategy sell products that create value because of their relatively low cost and reasonable sources of differentiation. The cost of these products is low "relative" to the cost leader's prices while their differentiation is "reasonable" when compared with the clearly unique features of the differentiator's products.

Although challenging to implement, the integrated cost leadership/differentiation strategy is used frequently in the global economy. The challenge of using this structure is due largely to the fact that different primary and support activities (see Chapter 3) are emphasized when using the cost leadership and differentiation strategies. To achieve the cost leadership position, production and process engineering are emphasized, with infrequent product changes. To achieve a differentiated position, marketing and new product R&D are emphasized while production and process engineering are not. Thus, effective use of the integrated strategy depends on the firm's successful combination of activities intended to reduce costs with activities intended to create additional differentiation features. As a result, the integrated form of the functional structure must have decision-making patterns that are partially centralized and partially decentralized. Additionally, jobs are semispecialized, and rules and procedures call for some formal and some informal job behavior.

Matches between Corporate-Level Strategies and the Multidivisional Structure

As explained earlier, Chandler's research shows that the firm's continuing success leads to product or market diversification or both.[81] The firm's level of diversification is a function of decisions about the number and type of businesses in which it will compete as well as how it will manage the businesses (see Chapter 6). Geared to managing individual organizational functions, increasing diversification eventually creates information processing, coordination, and control problems that the functional structure cannot handle. Thus, using a diversification strategy requires the firm to change from the functional structure to the multidivisional structure to develop an appropriate strategy/structure match.

As defined in Figure 6.1, on page 156, corporate-level strategies have different degrees of product and market diversification. The demands created by different levels of diversification highlight the need for a unique organizational structure to effectively implement each strategy (see Figure 11.4).

Using the Cooperative Form of the Multidivisional Structure to Implement the Related Constrained Strategy

The **cooperative form** is a structure in which horizontal integration is used to bring about interdivisional cooperation.

The **cooperative form** is a structure in which horizontal integration is used to bring about interdivisional cooperation. Divisions in a firm using the related constrained diversification strategy commonly are formed around products, markets, or both. In Figure 11.5, we use product divisions as part of the representation of the cooperative form of the multidivisional

Figure 11.4 Three Variations of the Multidivisional Structure

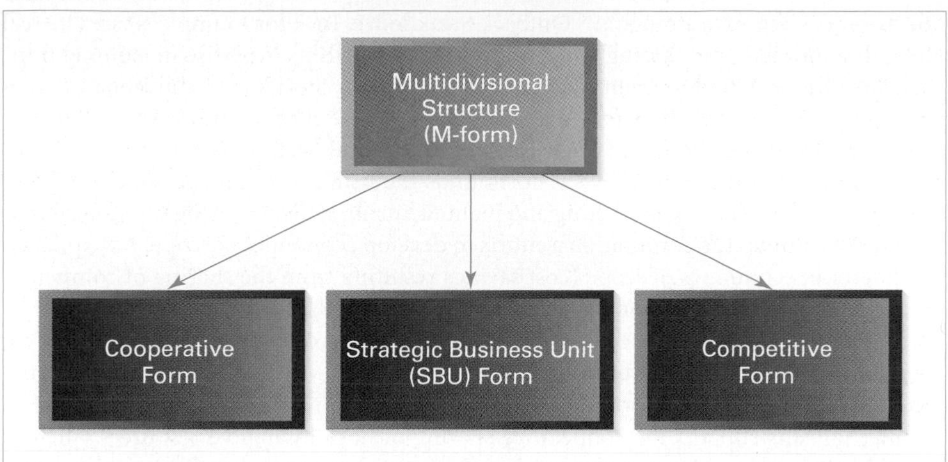

structure, although market divisions could be used instead of or in addition to product divisions to develop the figure.

Using this structure, Harley-Davidson, Inc., has two divisions or segments: Motorcycles & Related Products and Financial Services. These divisions "are managed separately based on the fundamental differences in their operations." However, the divisions are "related" because they share the firm's brand name and reputation.[82]

Figure 11.5 Cooperative Form of the Multidivisional Structure for Implementing a Related Constrained Strategy

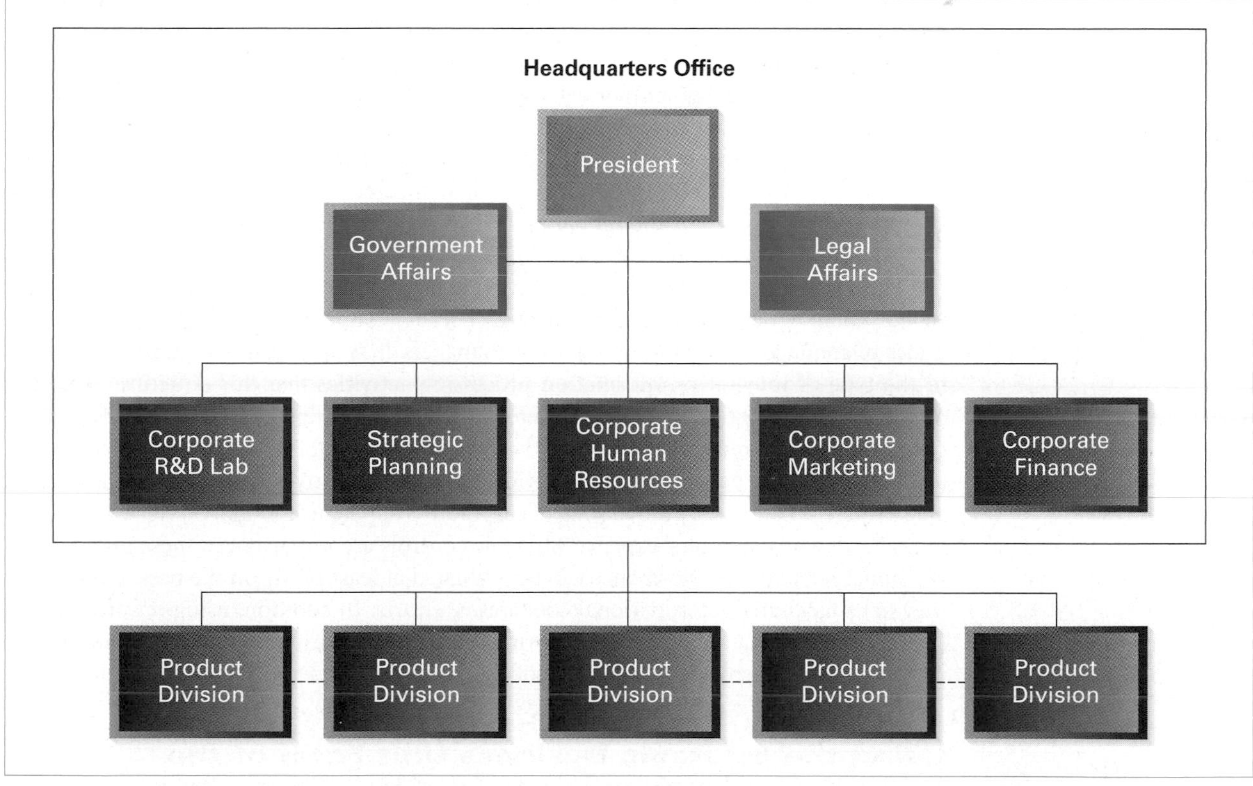

Notes:
- Structural integration devices create tight links among all divisions
- Corporate office emphasizes centralized strategic planning, human resources, and marketing to foster cooperation between divisions
- R&D is likely to be centralized
- Rewards are subjective and tend to emphasize overall corporate performance in addition to divisional performance
- Culture emphasizes cooperative sharing

As is the case at Harley-Davidson, all divisions in a related constrained firm share one or more corporate strengths.[83] Outback Steakhouse, Inc., for example, shares its real estate development, purchasing and leasing strengths, and its expertise in running franchise operations across its eight food concepts (Outback Steakhouse, Carrabba's Italian Grill, Roy's Restaurant, Bonefish Grill, Fleming's Prime Steakhouse & Wine Bar, Lee Roy Selmon's, Cheeseburger in Paradise, and Blue Coral Seafood & Spirits).[84] Colgate-Palmolive's use of the cooperative M-form finds the firm's oral care, personal care, and pet food divisions sharing marketing and manufacturing skills.[85] Sharing divisional competencies facilitates the corporation's efforts to develop economies of scope. As explained in Chapter 6, economies of scope (cost savings resulting from the sharing of competencies developed in one division with another division) are linked with successful use of the related constrained strategy. Interdivisional sharing of competencies depends on cooperation, suggesting the use of the cooperative form of the multidivisional structure.[86] Increasingly, it is important that the links resulting from effectively using integrating mechanisms support the cooperative sharing of both intangible resources (such as knowledge) and tangible resources (such as facilities and equipment).[87]

The cooperative structure uses different characteristics of structure (centralization, standardization, and formalization) as integrating mechanisms to facilitate interdivisional cooperation. Centralizing real estate development at the corporate level allows Outback Steakhouse, Inc., for example, to use these skills across its eight food concepts.[88] Frequent, direct contact between division managers, another integrating mechanism, encourages and supports cooperation and the sharing of competencies or resources that could be used to create new advantages. Sometimes, liaison roles are established in each division to reduce the time division managers spend integrating and coordinating their unit's work with the work occurring in other divisions. Temporary teams or task forces may be formed around projects whose success depends on sharing competencies that are embedded within several divisions. Formal integration departments might be established in firms frequently using temporary teams or task forces.

Ultimately, a matrix organization may evolve in firms implementing the related constrained strategy. A *matrix organization* is an organizational structure in which there is a dual structure combining both functional specialization and business product or project specialization.[89] Although complicated, an effective matrix structure can lead to improved coordination among a firm's divisions.[90]

The success of the cooperative multidivisional structure is significantly affected by how well divisions process information. However, because cooperation among divisions implies a loss of managerial autonomy, division managers may not readily commit themselves to the type of integrative information-processing activities that this structure demands. Moreover, coordination among divisions sometimes results in an unequal flow of positive outcomes to divisional managers. In other words, when managerial rewards are based at least in part on the performance of individual divisions, the manager of the division that is able to benefit the most by the sharing of corporate competencies might be viewed as receiving relative gains at others' expense. Strategic controls are important in these instances, as divisional managers' performance can be evaluated at least partly on the basis of how well they have facilitated interdivisional cooperative efforts. In addition, using reward systems that emphasize overall company performance, besides outcomes achieved by individual divisions, helps overcome problems associated with the cooperative form.

Using the Strategic Business Unit Form of the Multidivisional Structure to Implement the Related Linked Strategy

The **strategic business unit (SBU) form** consists of three levels: corporate headquarters, strategic business units (SBUs), and SBU divisions.

Firms with fewer links or less constrained links among their divisions use the related linked diversification strategy. The strategic business unit form of the multidivisional structure supports implementation of this strategy. The **strategic business unit (SBU) form** consists of three levels: corporate headquarters, strategic business units (SBUs), and SBU divisions (see Figure 11.6). The SBU structure is used by large firms and can be complex, with the complexity reflected by the organization's size and product and market diversity.

The divisions within each SBU are related in terms of shared products or markets or both, but the divisions of one SBU have little in common with the divisions of the other SBUs. Divisions within each SBU share product or market competencies to develop economies of scope and possibly economies of scale. The integrating mechanisms used by the divisions in this structure can be equally well used by the divisions within the individual strategic business units that are part of the SBU form of the multidivisional structure. In this structure, each SBU is a profit center that is controlled and evaluated by the headquarters office. Although both financial and strategic controls are important, on a relative basis financial controls are vital to headquarters' evaluation of each SBU; strategic controls are critical when the heads of SBUs evaluate their divisions' performances. Strategic controls are also critical to the headquarters' efforts to determine whether the company has formed an effective portfolio of businesses and whether those businesses are being successfully managed.

Sharing competencies among units within an SBU is an important characteristic of the SBU form of the multidivisional structure (see the notes to Figure 11.6). A drawback to the SBU structure is that multifaceted businesses often have difficulties in communicating this complex business model to stockholders.[91] Furthermore, if coordination between SBUs is needed, problems can arise because the SBU structure, similar to the competitive form discussed next, does not readily foster cooperation across SBUs.

Figure 11.6 SBU Form of the Multidivisional Structure for Implementing a Related Linked Strategy

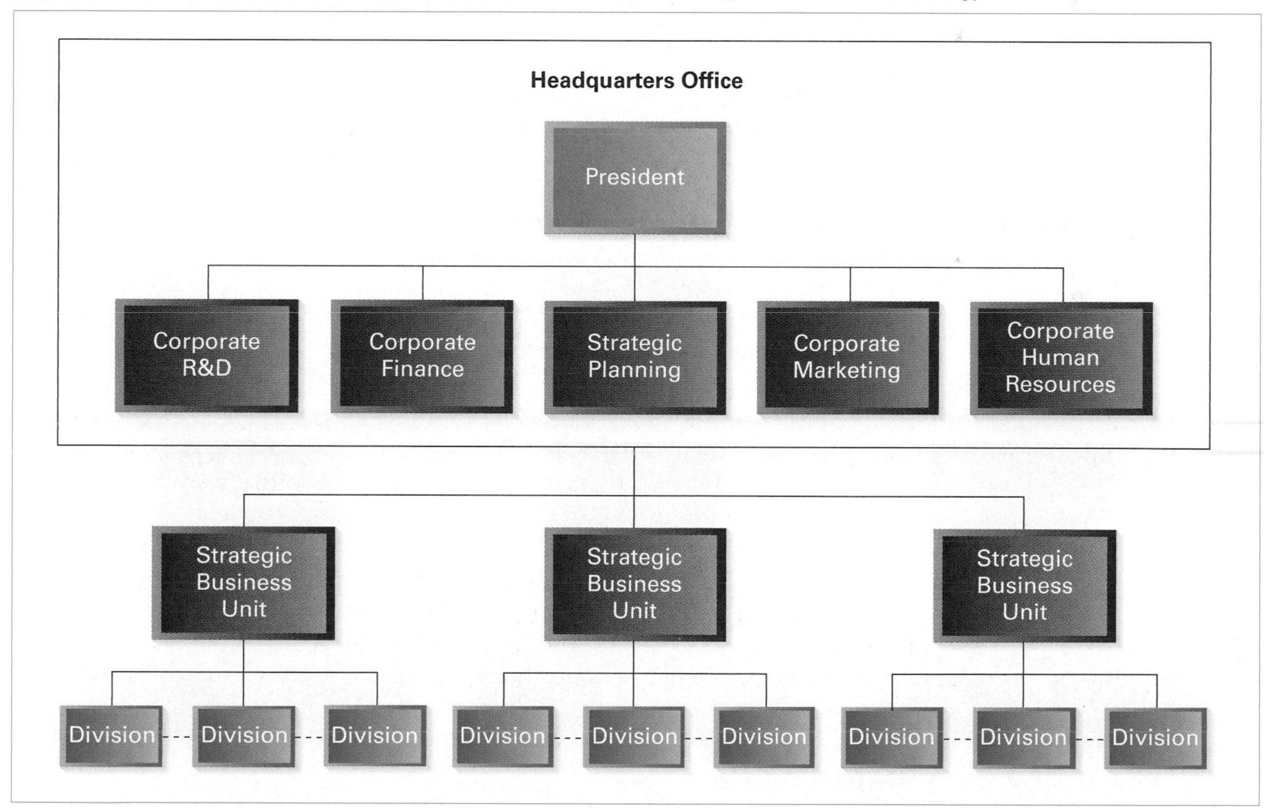

Notes:
- Structural integration among divisions within SBUs, but independence across SBUs
- Strategic planning may be the most prominent function in headquarters for managing the strategic planning approval process of SBUs for the president
- Each SBU may have its own budget for staff to foster integration
- Corporate headquarters staff serve as consultants to SBUs and divisions, rather than having direct input to product strategy, as in the cooperative form

Using the Competitive Form of the Multidivisional Structure to Implement the Unrelated Diversification Strategy

The **competitive form** is a structure characterized by complete independence among the firm's divisions.

Firms using the unrelated diversification strategy want to create value through efficient internal capital allocations or by restructuring, buying, and selling businesses.[92] The competitive form of the multidivisional structure supports implementation of this strategy.

The **competitive form** is a structure characterized by complete independence among the firm's divisions (see Figure 11.7). Unlike the divisions included in the cooperative structure, divisions that are part of the competitive structure do not share common corporate strengths. Because strengths are not shared, integrating devices are not developed for use by the divisions included in the competitive structure.

The efficient internal capital market that is the foundation for using the unrelated diversification strategy requires organizational arrangements emphasizing divisional competition rather than cooperation.[93] Three benefits are expected from the internal competition. First, internal competition creates flexibility (e.g., corporate headquarters can have divisions working on different technologies and projects to identify those with the greatest potential). Resources can then be allocated to the division appearing to have the most potential to fuel the entire firm's success. Second, internal competition challenges the status quo and inertia, because division heads know that future resource allocations are a product of excellent current performance as well as superior positioning in terms of future performance. Last, internal competition motivates effort in that the challenge of competing against internal peers can be as great as the challenge of competing against external rivals.[94] In this structure, organizational controls (primarily financial controls) are used to emphasize and support internal competition among separate divisions and as the basis for allocating corporate capital based on divisions' performances.

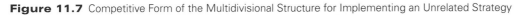

Figure 11.7 Competitive Form of the Multidivisional Structure for Implementing an Unrelated Strategy

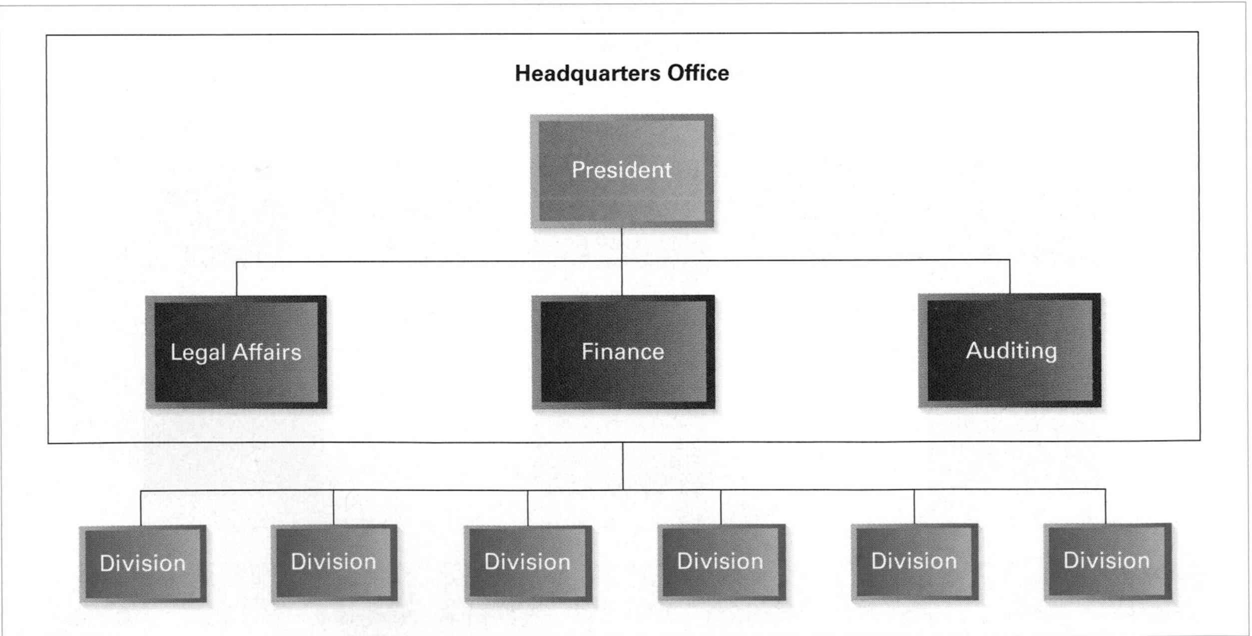

Notes:
- Corporate headquarters has a small staff
- Finance and auditing are the most prominent functions in the headquarters office to manage cash flow and assure the accuracy of performance data coming from divisions
- The legal affairs function becomes important when the firm acquires or divests assets
- Divisions are independent and separate for financial evaluation purposes
- Divisions retain strategic control, but cash is managed by the corporate office
- Divisions compete for corporate resources

Textron Inc., a large "multi-industry" company seeks "to identify, research, select, acquire and integrate companies, and has developed a set of rigorous criteria to guide decision making." Textron continuously looks "to enhance and reshape its portfolio by divesting non-core assets and acquiring branded businesses in attractive industries with substantial long-term growth potential." Textron operates four independent businesses—Bell Helicopter (29% of revenue), Cessna Aircraft (35%), Finance (6%), and Industrial (30%). The firm uses return on invested capital (ROIC) as the "compass for guiding" the evaluation of its diversified set of businesses as they compete internally for resources.[95]

Textron, Inc., owner of Bell Helicopter, uses the competitive form of the multidivisional structure to encourage the best performance from its four business units.

To emphasize competitiveness among divisions, the headquarters office maintains an arm's-length relationship with them, intervening in divisional affairs only to audit operations and discipline managers whose divisions perform poorly. In emphasizing competition between divisions, the headquarters office relies on strategic controls to set rate-of-return targets and financial controls to monitor divisional performance relative to those targets. The headquarters office then allocates cash flow on a competitive basis, rather than automatically returning cash to the division that produced it. Thus, the focus of the headquarters' work is on performance appraisal, resource allocation, and long-range planning to verify that the firm's portfolio of businesses will lead to financial success.[96]

The three major forms of the multidivisional structure should each be paired with a particular corporate-level strategy. Table 11.1 shows these structures' characteristics. Differences exist in the degree of centralization, the focus of the performance appraisal, the horizontal structures (integrating mechanisms), and the incentive compensation schemes. The most centralized and most costly structural form is the cooperative structure. The least centralized, with the lowest bureaucratic costs, is the competitive structure. The SBU structure requires partial centralization and involves some of the mechanisms

Table 11.1 Characteristics of the Structures Necessary to Implement the Related Constrained, Related Linked, and Unrelated Diversification Strategies

	Overall Structural Form		
Structural Characteristics	**Cooperative M-Form (Related Constrained Strategy)[a]**	**SBU M-Form (Related Linked Strategy)[a]**	**Competitive M-Form (Unrelated Diversification Strategy)[a]**
Centralization of operations	Centralized at corporate office	Partially centralized (in SBUs)	Decentralized to divisions
Use of integration mechanisms	Extensive	Moderate	Nonexistent
Divisional performance appraisals	Emphasize subjective (strategic) criteria	Use a mixture of subjective (strategic) and objective (financial) criteria	Emphasize objective (financial) criteria
Divisional incentive compensation	Linked to overall corporate performance	Mixed linkage to corporate, SBU, and divisional performance	Linked to divisional performance

[a]Strategy implemented with structural form.

necessary to implement the relatedness between divisions. Also, the divisional incentive compensation awards are allocated according to both SBUs and corporate performance.

Matches between International Strategies and Worldwide Structure

As explained in Chapter 8, international strategies are becoming increasingly important for long-term competitive success[97] in what continues to become an increasingly borderless global economy.[98] Among other benefits, international strategies allow the firm to search for new markets, resources, core competencies, and technologies as part of its efforts to outperform competitors.[99]

As with business-level and corporate-level strategies, unique organizational structures are necessary to successfully implement the different international strategies.[100] Forming proper matches between international strategies and organizational structures facilitates the firm's efforts to effectively coordinate and control its global operations. More importantly, research findings confirm the validity of the international strategy/structure matches we discuss here.[101]

Using the Worldwide Geographic Area Structure to Implement the Multidomestic Strategy

The *multidomestic strategy* decentralizes the firm's strategic and operating decisions to business units in each country so that product characteristics can be tailored to local preferences. Firms using this strategy try to isolate themselves from global competitive forces by establishing protected market positions or by competing in industry segments that are most affected by differences among local countries. The worldwide geographic area structure is used to implement this strategy. The **worldwide geographic area structure** emphasizes national interests and facilitates the firm's efforts to satisfy local differences (see Figure 11.8).

The **worldwide geographic area structure** emphasizes national interests and facilitates the firm's efforts to satisfy local differences.

Figure 11.8 Worldwide Geographic Area Structure for Implementing a Multidomestic Strategy

Notes:
- The perimeter circles indicate decentralization of operations
- Emphasis is on differentiation by local demand to fit an area or country culture
- Corporate headquarters coordinates financial resources among independent subsidiaries
- The organization is like a decentralized federation

Strategic Focus Strategic Focus Strategic Focus

Using the Worldwide Geographic Area Structure at Xerox Corporation

Xerox Corporation is a technology and services company helping "businesses deploy smart document management strategies and find better ways to work." The firm emphasizes product innovation to best serve customers' needs and process innovations to simultaneously improve quality and reduce its production costs. Allocating more than 6 percent of total revenues to research and development (R&D), Xerox's Innovation Group collaborates with personnel across the firm's business units to facilitate development of product and process innovations.

Xerox focuses its efforts on three primary markets: (1) high-end production and commercial print environments, (2) networked offices from small to large and (3) value-added services. Document color and solutions "that tailor Xerox devices to solve a customer's problem" are the unifying themes that guide the firm's actions in these three markets.

Xerox is using the multidomestic strategy to serve customers in its three primary markets. One reason for using this strategy is so the firm can apply its service capabilities to solve the unique problems of customers in different geographic locations. Although customers throughout the world have needs for documents and document services, the specific nature of their needs varies on the basis of business culture and the sophistication of the local business environment. Because of this reality, Xerox uses the worldwide geographic area structure to support its multidomestic strategy. Global Services, North America, Europe, and Developing Markets Operations are the four business groups that make up Xerox's organizational structure. Supporting these units' efforts to serve the unique needs of customers in different regions are groups such as Innovation, Corporate Strategy/Alliances, and Human Resources/Ethics. Xerox relies on the match between its international strategy and structure as a key driver of profitable growth.

Sources: M. Bushman, 2007, Functional, divisional and matrix organizational structures, *The People's Media Company*, http://www.associatedcontent.com, January 18; 2007, Xerox fact sheet, http://www.xerox.com, September 14; 2006, Aligning the organization with the market: Focusing on the customer's total experience, *Knowledge@Wharton*, http://knowledge.wharton.upenn.edu, May 31; 2006, Xerox annual report, http://www.xerox.com.

As explained in the Strategic Focus, Xerox Corporation uses the worldwide geographic area structure to support implementation of its multidomestic strategy. In 2006, 52 percent of the firm's revenue was generated in the United States while 34 percent was earned in Europe. The remaining 13.2 percent of Xerox's 2006 revenue came from sales in developing markets.

Using the multidomestic strategy requires little coordination between different country markets, meaning that integrating mechanisms among divisions in the worldwide geographic area structure are not needed. Hence, formalization is low, and coordination among units in a firm's worldwide geographic area structure is often informal.

The multidomestic strategy/worldwide geographic area structure match evolved as a natural outgrowth of the multicultural European marketplace. Friends and family members of the main business who were sent as expatriates into foreign countries to develop the independent country subsidiary often used this structure for the main business. The relationship to corporate headquarters by divisions took place through informal communication among "family members."[102]

Just as Xerox Corporation does, SABMiller uses the worldwide geographic area structure. SABMiller is one of the world's largest brewers with distribution agreements and brewing interests in more than 60 countries involving six continents. It is also one of the world's largest bottlers of Coca-Cola products. SABMiller was created in 2002 through a

SABMiller, created by a merger of two companies in 2002, uses a multidomestic strategy to sell its premium beers around the world.

merger of South African Breweries and Miller Brewing. Currently, SABMiller owns several premium international beers including Pilsner Urquell, Peroni Nastro Azzurro, and Miller Genuine Draft. Six of its brands are among the world's top 50 beer brands. In late 2007, the firm planned to launch its premium Italian beer (Peroni Nastro Azzurro) in Japan (its first foray into the East Asian market). Complementing these international brands are dominant locally prominent beers such as Aquila, Snow, and Tyskie, which are also part of SABMiller's product lines. Committed to profitable growth, SABMiller uses the multidomestic strategy to expand its product offerings and geographic locations. Acquisitions and cooperative strategies figure prominently in the firm's use of this strategy. In late 2007, for example, SABMiller's joint venture with China Resources Enterprises, Limited (called CRE), announced that it was acquiring four breweries in China.[103] Global brewers Inbev and Heineken have also acquired firms and formed cooperative relationships as a means of implementing their multidomestic strategies.[104]

To implement its multidomestic strategy, SABMiller uses the worldwide geographic area structure with regional and country division headquarters throughout the world. Decentralization to these regional and country headquarters allows for strong marketing to adapt the acquired brands to the local cultures and for some improved cost structures, especially in avoiding significant transportation costs across geographic regions. SABMiller expects to make further acquisitions in developing markets, such as India, to contribute to future growth. The strategy/structure match we are describing likely contributes to this firm's positive financial performance.[105]

A key disadvantage of the multidomestic strategy/worldwide geographic area structure match is the inability to create strong global efficiency. With an increasing emphasis on lower-cost products in international markets, the need to pursue worldwide economies of scale has also increased. These changes foster use of the global strategy and its structural match, the worldwide product divisional structure.

Using the Worldwide Product Divisional Structure to Implement the Global Strategy

With the corporation's home office dictating competitive strategy, the *global strategy* is one through which the firm offers standardized products across country markets. The firm's success depends on its ability to develop economies of scope and economies of scale on a global level. Decisions to outsource some primary or support activities to the world's best providers are particularly helpful when the firm tries to develop economies of scale.[106]

In the **worldwide product divisional structure,** decision-making authority is centralized in the worldwide division headquarters to coordinate and integrate decisions and actions among divisional business units.

The worldwide product divisional structure supports use of the global strategy. In the **worldwide product divisional structure,** decision-making authority is centralized in the worldwide division headquarters to coordinate and integrate decisions and actions among divisional business units (see Figure 11.9). This structure is often used in rapidly growing firms seeking to manage their diversified product lines effectively. Avon Products, Inc. is an example of a firm using the worldwide product divisional structure.

Avon is a global brand leader in products for women such as lipsticks, fragrances, and anti-aging skincare. Committed to "empowering women all over the world since 1886," Avon relies on product innovation to be a first-mover in its markets. For years, Avon used the multidomestic strategy. However, the firm's growth came to a screeching halt in 2006. Contributing to this decline were simultaneous stumbles in sales revenues in emerging markets (e.g., Russia and Central Europe), the United States, and Mexico. To cope with its problems, the firm changed to a global strategy and to the worldwide product divisional structure to support its use. Commenting on this change, CEO Andrea Jung noted that, "Previously, Avon managers from Poland to Mexico ran their own plants,

Figure 11.9 Worldwide Product Divisional Structure for Implementing a Global Strategy

Notes:

- The headquarters'circle indicates centralization to coordinate information flow among worldwide products
- Corporate headquarters uses many intercoordination devices to facilitate global economies of scale and scope
- Corporate headquarters also allocates financial resources in a cooperative way
- The organization is like a centralized federation

developed new products, and created their own ads, often relying as much on gut as numbers."[107] Today, Avon is organized around product divisions including Avon Color, the firm's "flagship global color cosmetics brand, which offers a variety of color cosmetics products, including foundations, powders, lips, eye, and nail products," Skincare, Bath & Body, Hair Care, Wellness, and Fragrance. The analysis of these product divisions' performances is conducted by individuals in the firm's New York headquarters. One of the purposes of changing strategy and structure is for Avon to control its costs and gain additional scale economies as paths to performance improvements.[108]

Avon has recently moved from a multidomestic strategy to a global strategy and to the worldwide product divisional structure in order to control costs and develop economies of scale.

Integrating mechanisms are important in the effective use of the worldwide product divisional structure. Direct contact between managers, liaison roles between departments, and temporary task forces as well as permanent teams are examples of these mechanisms. One researcher describes the use of these mechanisms in the worldwide structure: "There is extensive and formal use of task forces and operating committees to supplement communication and coordination of worldwide operations."[109] The disadvantages of the global strategy/worldwide structure combination are the difficulty involved with coordinating decisions and actions across country borders and the inability to quickly respond to local needs and preferences.

To deal with these types of disadvantages, Avon takes several actions including completing surveys with women on a global basis. In 2005, for example, Avon surveyed more than 20,000 women in 22 countries to better understand their opinions about skincare, physical appearance, and self-indulgence. With this information, the firm is better able to develop innovative products that will appeal to women on a global basis.[110]

Using the Combination Structure to Implement the Transnational Strategy

The **combination structure** is a structure drawing characteristics and mechanisms from both the worldwide geographic area structure and the worldwide product divisional structure.

The *transnational strategy* calls for the firm to combine the multidomestic strategy's local responsiveness with the global strategy's efficiency. Firms using this strategy are trying to gain the advantages of both local responsiveness and global efficiency. The combination structure is used to implement the transnational strategy. The **combination structure** is a structure drawing characteristics and mechanisms from both the worldwide geographic area structure and the worldwide product divisional structure. The transnational strategy is often implemented through two possible combination structures: a global matrix structure and a hybrid global design.[111]

The global matrix design brings together both local market and product expertise into teams that develop and respond to the global marketplace. The global matrix design (the basic matrix structure was defined earlier) promotes flexibility in designing products and responding to customer needs. However, it has severe limitations in that it places employees in a position of being accountable to more than one manager. At any given time, an employee may be a member of several functional or product group teams. Relationships that evolve from multiple memberships can make it difficult for employees to be simultaneously loyal to all of them. Although the matrix places authority in the hands of managers who are most able to use it, it creates problems in regard to corporate reporting relationships that are so complex and vague that it is difficult and time-consuming to receive approval for major decisions.

We illustrate the hybrid structure in Figure 11.10. In this design, some divisions are oriented toward products while others are oriented toward market areas. Thus, in some cases when the geographic area is more important, the division managers are area-oriented. In other divisions where worldwide product coordination and efficiencies are more important, the division manager is more product oriented.

Individual managers seek synergies as they simultaneously work to discharge their geographic- or product-centered responsibilities. In the case of Procter & Gamble (P&G), the firm's structure includes global business units (product focused) and market development organizations (geography or location focused). At P&G, those managing these units seek to define the brand's equity while at the same time applying that equity within the context of different tastes in various geographic regions.[112]

The fits between the multidomestic strategy and the worldwide geographic area structure and between the global strategy and the worldwide product divisional structure are apparent. However, when a firm wants to implement the multidomestic and the global strategies simultaneously through a combination structure, the appropriate integrating

Figure 11.10 Hybrid Form of the Combination Structure for Implementing a Transnational Strategy

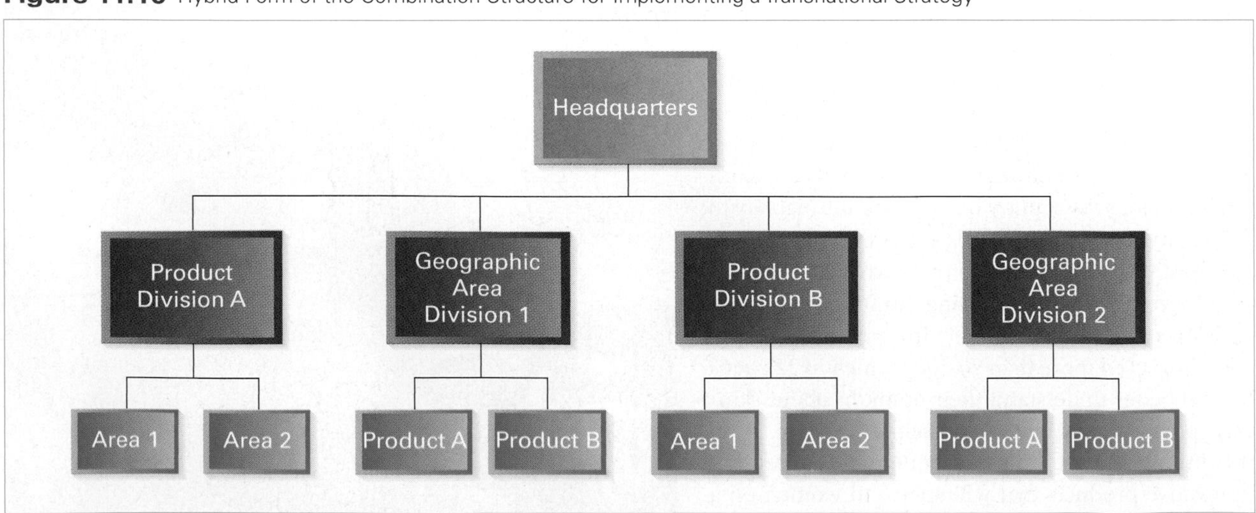

mechanisms are less obvious. The structure used to implement the transnational strategy must be simultaneously centralized and decentralized; integrated and nonintegrated; formalized and nonformalized. These seemingly opposite characteristics must be managed by an overall structure that is capable of encouraging all employees to understand the effects of cultural and geographic diversity on a firm's operations.

Matches between Cooperative Strategies and Network Structures

As discussed in Chapter 9, a network strategy exists when partners form several alliances in order to improve the performance of the alliance network itself through cooperative endeavors.[113] The greater levels of environmental complexity and uncertainty facing companies in today's competitive environment are causing more firms to use cooperative strategies such as strategic alliances and joint ventures.[114]

The breadth and scope of firms' operations in the global economy create many opportunities for firms to cooperate.[115] In fact, a firm can develop cooperative relationships with many of its stakeholders, including customers, suppliers, and competitors. When a firm becomes involved with combinations of cooperative relationships, it is part of a strategic network, or what others call an alliance constellation.[116]

A *strategic network* is a group of firms that has been formed to create value by participating in multiple cooperative arrangements. An effective strategic network facilitates discovering opportunities beyond those identified by individual network participants.[117] A strategic network can be a source of competitive advantage for its members when its operations create value that is difficult for competitors to duplicate and that network members can't create by themselves.[118] Strategic networks are used to implement business-level, corporate-level, and international cooperative strategies.

Commonly, a strategic network is a loose federation of partners participating in the network's operations on a flexible basis. At the core or center of the strategic network, the *strategic center firm* is the one around which the network's cooperative relationships revolve (see Figure 11.11).

Figure 11.11 A Strategic Network

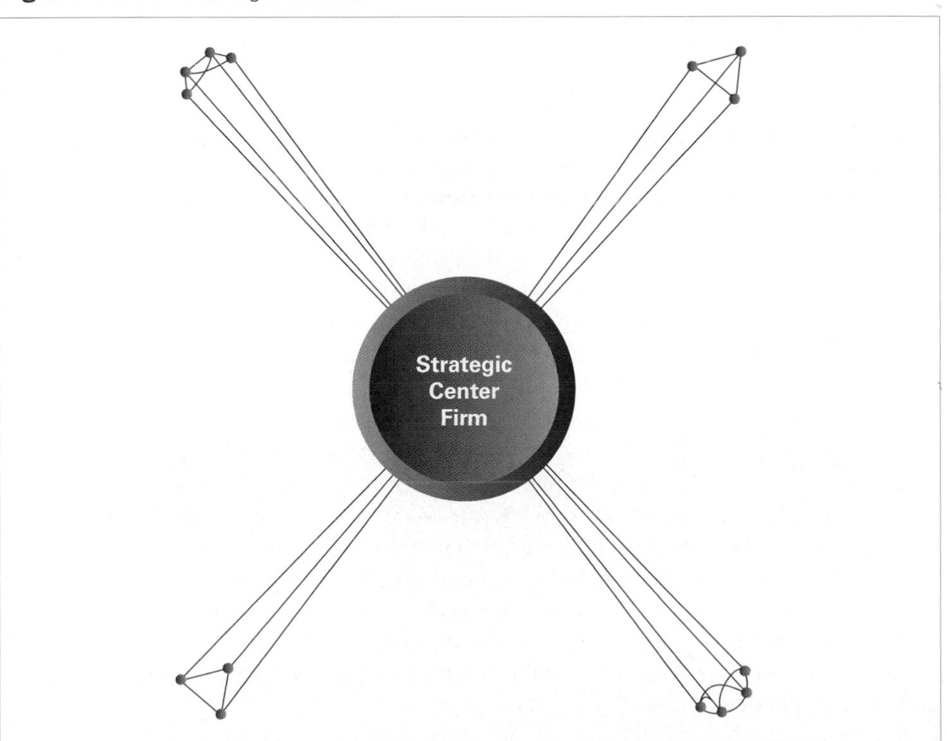

Because of its central position, the strategic center firm is the foundation for the strategic network's structure. Concerned with various aspects of organizational structure, such as formal reporting relationships and procedures, the strategic center firm manages what are often complex, cooperative interactions among network partners. To perform the tasks discussed next, the strategic center firm must make sure that incentives for participating in the network are aligned so that network firms continue to have a reason to remain connected.[119] The strategic center firm is engaged in four primary tasks as it manages the strategic network and controls its operations:[120]

Strategic outsourcing. The strategic center firm outsources and partners with more firms than do other network members. At the same time, the strategic center firm requires network partners to be more than contractors. Members are expected to find opportunities for the network to create value through its cooperative work.

Competencies. To increase network effectiveness, the strategic center firm seeks ways to support each member's efforts to develop core competencies with the potential of benefiting the network.

Technology. The strategic center firm is responsible for managing the development and sharing of technology-based ideas among network members. The structural requirement that members submit formal reports detailing the technology-oriented outcomes of their efforts to the strategic center firm facilitates this activity.[121]

Race to learn. The strategic center firm emphasizes that the principal dimensions of competition are between value chains and between networks of value chains. Because of this interconnection, the strategic network is only as strong as its weakest value-chain link. With its centralized decision-making authority and responsibility, the strategic center firm guides participants in efforts to form network-specific competitive advantages. The need for each participant to have capabilities that can be the foundation for the network's competitive advantages encourages friendly rivalry among participants seeking to develop the skills needed to quickly form new capabilities that create value for the network.[122]

Interestingly, strategic networks are being used more frequently, partly because of the ability of a strategic center firm to execute a strategy that effectively and efficiently links partner firms. Improved information systems and communication capabilities (e.g., the Internet) make such networks possible.[123]

Implementing Business-Level Cooperative Strategies

As noted in Chapter 9, the two types of business-level complementary alliances are vertical and horizontal. Firms with competencies in different stages of the value chain form a vertical alliance to cooperatively integrate their different, but complementary, skills. Firms combining their competencies to create value in the same stage of the value chain are using a horizontal alliance. Vertical complementary strategic alliances such as those developed by Toyota Motor Company are formed more frequently than horizontal alliances.[124]

A strategic network of vertical relationships such as the network in Japan between Toyota and its suppliers often involves a number of implementation issues.[125] First, the strategic center firm encourages subcontractors to modernize their facilities and provides them with technical and financial assistance to do so, if necessary. Second, the strategic center firm reduces its transaction costs by promoting longer-term contracts with subcontractors, so that supplier-partners increase their long-term productivity. This approach is diametrically opposed to that of continually negotiating short-term contracts based on unit pricing. Third, the strategic center firm enables engineers in upstream companies (suppliers) to have better communication with those companies with whom it has contracts for services. As a result, suppliers and the strategic center firm become more interdependent and less independent.[126]

The lean production system (a vertical complementary strategic alliance) pioneered by Toyota and others has been diffused throughout the global auto industry.[127] However, no auto company has learned how to duplicate the manufacturing effectiveness and efficiency Toyota derives from the cooperative arrangements in its strategic network.[128] A key factor accounting for Toyota's manufacturing-based competitive advantage is the cost other firms would incur to imitate the structural form used to support Toyota's application. In part, then, the structure of Toyota's strategic network that it created as the strategic center firm facilitates cooperative actions among network participants that competitors can't fully understand or duplicate.

In vertical complementary strategic alliances, such as the one between Toyota and its suppliers, the strategic center firm is obvious, as is the structure that firm establishes. However, the same is not always true with horizontal complementary strategic alliances where firms try to create value in the same part of the value chain, as with airline alliances that are commonly formed to create value in the marketing and sales primary activity segment of the value chain (see Table 3.6). Because air carriers commonly participate in multiple horizontal complementary alliances such as the Star Alliance between Lufthansa, United, Thai, Air Canada, SAS, and others, it is difficult to determine the strategic center firm. Moreover, participating in several alliances can cause firms to question partners' true loyalties and intentions. Also, if rivals band together in too many collaborative activities, one or more governments may suspect the possibility of illegal collusive activities. For these reasons, horizontal complementary alliances are used less frequently than their vertical counterpart.

Implementing Corporate-Level Cooperative Strategies

Corporate-level cooperative strategies (such as franchising) are used to facilitate product and market diversification. As a cooperative strategy, franchising allows the firm to use its competencies to extend or diversify its product or market reach, but without completing a merger or an acquisition.[129] Research suggests that knowledge embedded in corporate-level cooperative strategies facilitates synergy.[130] For example, "McDonald's Corporation primarily franchises and operates McDonald's restaurants in the food service industry. These restaurants serve a varied, yet limited value-priced menu in more than 100 countries around the world."[131] The McDonald's franchising system is a strategic network. McDonald's headquarters office serves as the strategic center firm for the network's franchisees. The headquarters office uses strategic controls and financial controls to verify that the franchisees' operations create the greatest value for the entire network.

An important strategic control issue for McDonald's is the location of its franchisee units. Because it believes that its greatest expansion opportunities are outside the United States, the firm has decided to continue expanding in countries such as China where it is a "partner of the 2008 Summer Olympic Games in Beijing."[132] Thus, as the strategic center firm around the globe for its restaurants, McDonald's is devoting the majority of its capital expenditures to develop units in non–U.S. markets.

Implementing International Cooperative Strategies

Strategic networks formed to implement international cooperative strategies result in firms competing in several countries.[133] Differences among countries' regulatory environments increase the challenge of managing international networks and verifying that at a minimum, the network's operations comply with all legal requirements.[134]

Distributed strategic networks are the organizational structure used to manage international cooperative strategies. As shown in Figure 11.12, several regional strategic center firms are included in the distributed network to manage partner firms' multiple cooperative arrangements.[135]

Figure 11.12 A Distributed Strategic Network

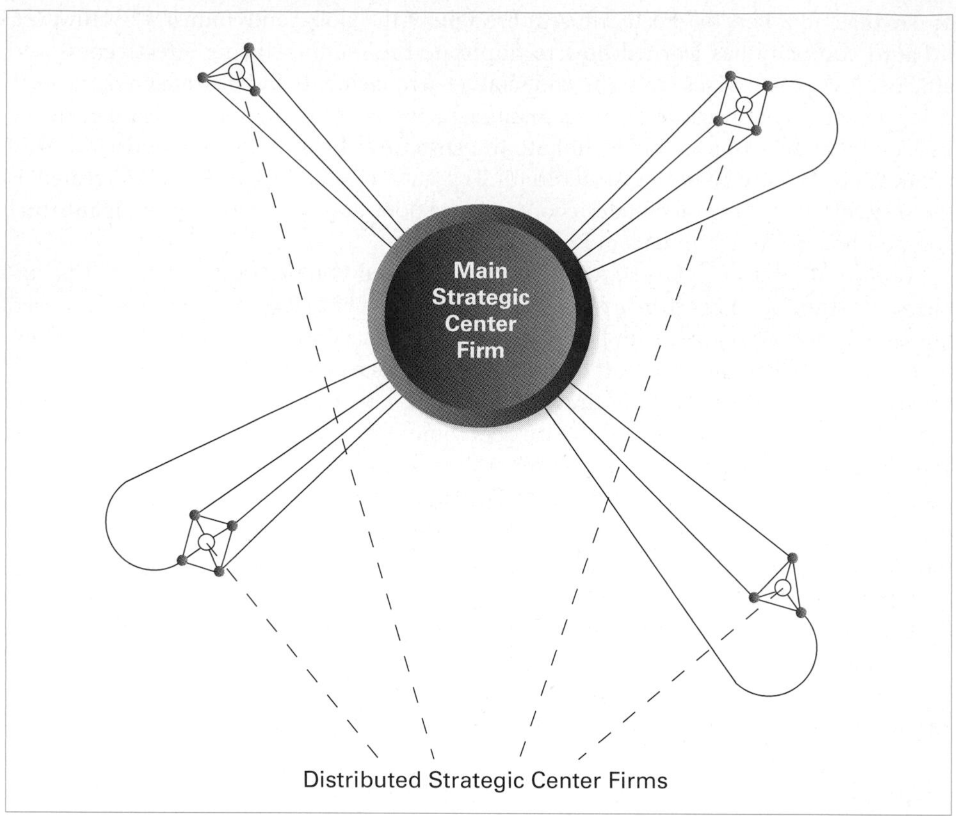

The EDS Agility Alliance is an example of a distributed strategic network. This alliance is "built on the basis that all of the Alliance members will jointly deliver solutions—committing resources to a project and collaborating with each other to get the job done."[136] EDS is the main strategic center firm in this alliance and has two dedicated centers that are the hubs for jointly developing initiatives with its partners. Cisco, SAP, Sun, Xerox, Oracle, EMC, and Microsoft are members of this distributed strategic network. Working together, EDS and its partners "collaborate to design, build and run a market-leading services platform and develop technology-based services that deliver tangible results to clients."[137] EDS's partners each work with their own networks to complete projects that are a part of the Agility Alliance. As this example demonstrates, the structure used to implement the international cooperative strategy is complex and demands careful attention to be used successfully.

Summary

- Organizational structure specifies the firm's formal reporting relationships, procedures, controls, and authority and decision-making processes. Essentially, organizational structure details the work to be done in a firm and how that work is to be accomplished. Organizational controls guide the use of strategy, indicate how to compare actual and expected results, and suggest actions to take to improve performance when it falls below expectations. A proper match between strategy and structure can lead to a competitive advantage.
- Strategic controls (largely subjective criteria) and financial controls (largely objective criteria) are the two types of organizational controls used to implement a strategy. Both controls are critical, although their degree of emphasis varies based on individual matches between strategy and structure.
- Strategy and structure influence each other; overall though, strategy has a stronger influence on structure. Research indicates that firms tend to change structure when declining performance forces them to do so. Effective managers

anticipate the need for structural change and quickly modify structure to better accommodate the firm's strategy when evidence calls for that action.

- The functional structure is used to implement business-level strategies. The cost leadership strategy requires a centralized functional structure—one in which manufacturing efficiency and process engineering are emphasized. The differentiation strategy's functional structure decentralizes implementation-related decisions, especially those concerned with marketing, to those involved with individual organizational functions. Focus strategies, often used in small firms, require a simple structure until such time that the firm diversifies in terms of products and/or markets.
- Unique combinations of different forms of the multidivisional structure are matched with different corporate-level diversification strategies to properly implement these strategies. The cooperative M-form, used to implement the related constrained corporate-level strategy, has a centralized corporate office and extensive integrating mechanisms. Divisional incentives are linked to overall corporate performance. The related linked SBU M-form structure establishes separate profit centers within the diversified firm. Each profit center may have divisions offering similar products, but the centers are unrelated to each other. The competitive M-form structure, used to implement the unrelated diversification strategy, is highly decentralized, lacks integrating mechanisms, and utilizes objective financial criteria to evaluate each unit's performance.
- The multidomestic strategy, implemented through the worldwide geographic area structure, emphasizes decentralization and locates all functional activities in the host country or geographic area. The worldwide product divisional structure is used to implement the global strategy. This structure is centralized in order to coordinate and integrate different functions' activities so as to gain global economies of scope and economies of scale. Decision-making authority is centralized in the firm's worldwide division headquarters.
- The transnational strategy—a strategy through which the firm seeks the local responsiveness of the multidomestic strategy and the global efficiency of the global strategy—is implemented through the combination structure. Because it must be simultaneously centralized and decentralized, integrated and nonintegrated, and formalized and nonformalized, the combination structure is difficult to organize and successfully manage. However, two structural designs are suggested: the matrix and the hybrid structure with both geographic and product-oriented divisions.
- Increasingly important to competitive success, cooperative strategies are implemented through organizational structures framed around strategic networks. Strategic center firms play a critical role in managing strategic networks.

Review Questions

1. What is organizational structure and what are organizational controls? What are the differences between strategic controls and financial controls? What is the importance of these differences?
2. What does it mean to say that strategy and structure have a reciprocal relationship?
3. What are the characteristics of the functional structures used to implement the cost leadership, differentiation, integrated cost leadership/differentiation, and focused business-level strategies?
4. What are the differences among the three versions of the multidivisional (M-form) organizational structures that are used to implement the related constrained, the related linked, and the unrelated corporate-level diversification strategies?
5. What organizational structures are used to implement the multidomestic, global, and transnational international strategies?
6. What is a strategic network? What is a strategic center firm?

Experiential Exercises

Exercise 1: The Merits of ROWE (Results-Only Work Environment)

For this exercise, you and your classmates will debate the merits of Best Buy's ROWE initiative. To complete this exercise, your instructor will divide the class into five groups of roughly equal size. The groups will have these responsibilities:

Team 1 will present arguments why ROWE is desirable and should be implemented in other organizations.

Team 2 will present a counterargument why ROWE is undesirable and hence should not be implemented in other organizations.

Team 3 will cross-examine Team 1.

Team 4 will cross-examine Team 2.

Team 5 will decide which of the two arguments is most convincing.

Exercise 2: Burger Buddy and Ma Maison

Assume that it is a few months before your college graduation. You and some classmates have decided to become entrepreneurs. The group has agreed on the restaurant industry, but your discussions thus far have gone back and forth between two different dining concepts—Burger Buddy and Ma Masion. Details about these two concepts follow:

The idea for Burger Buddy is to operate near campus in order to serve the student market. Burger Buddy will be a 1950s-themed hamburger joint, emphasizing large portions and affordable prices.

Ma Maison is the alternate concept. One of your partners has attended cooking school and has proposed the idea of a small, upscale French restaurant. The menu would have no set items, but would vary on a daily basis instead. Ma Maison would position itself as a boutique restaurant that provides superb customer service and unique offerings.

Working in small groups, answer the following questions:

1. What is the underlying strategy for each restaurant concept?
2. How would the organizational structure of the two restaurant concepts differ?
3. How would the nature of work vary between the two restaurants?
4. If the business concept is successful, how might you expect items 2 and 3 to change in the next 5–7 years?

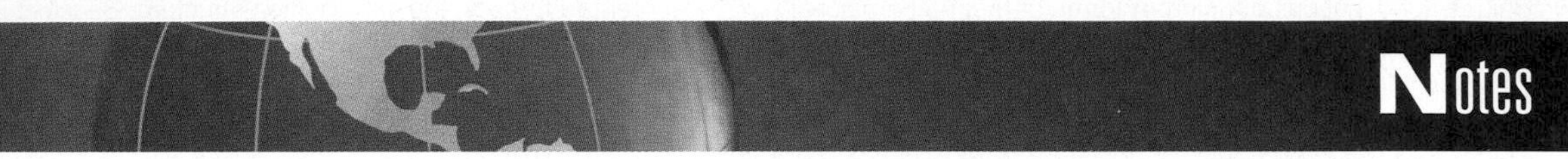

Notes

1. B. Ambos & B. B. Schlegelmilch, 2007, Innovation and control in the multinational firm: A comparison of political and contingency approaches, *Strategic Management Journal,* 28: 473–486; S. Kumar, S. Kant, & T. L. Amburgey, 2007, Pubic agencies and collaborative management approaches, *Administration & Society,* 39: 569–610.
2. R. C. Sampson, 2007, R&D alliances and firm performance: The impact of technological diversity and alliance organization on innovation, *Academy of Management Journal,* 50: 364–386; R. E. Miles & C. C. Snow, 1978, *Organizational Strategy, Structure and Process,* New York: McGraw-Hill.
3. E. M. Olson, S. F. Slater, & G. T. M. Hult, 2007, The importance of structure and process to strategy implementation, *Business Horizons,* 48(1): 47–54; D. N. Sull & C. Spinosa, 2007, Promise-based management, *Harvard Business Review,* 85(4):79–86.
4. T. Amburgey & T. Dacin, 1994, As the left foot follows the right? The dynamics of strategic and structural change, *Academy of Management Journal,* 37: 1427–1452.
5. P. Ghemawat, 2007, Managing differences: The central challenge of global strategy, *Harvard BusinessReview,* 85(3): 59–68; B. Keats & H. O'Neill, 2001, Organizational structure: Looking through a strategy lens, in M. A. Hitt, R. E. Freeman, & J. S. Harrison (eds.), *Handbook of Strategic Management,* Oxford, UK: Blackwell Publishers, 520–542.
6. P. J. Brews & C. L. Tucci, 2007, The structural and performance effects of internetworking, *Long Range Planning,* 40: 223–243; R. E. Hoskisson, C. W. L. Hill, & H. Kim, 1993, The multidivisional structure: Organizational fossil or source of value? *Journal of Management,* 19: 269–298.
7. E. M. Olson, S. F. Slater, G. Tomas, & G. T. M. Hult, 2005, The performance implications of fit among business strategy, marketing organization structure, and strategic behavior, *Journal of Marketing,* 69(3): 49–65.
8. R. D. Hof, 2007, Back to the future at Yahoo! *BusinessWeek,* July 2, 35–36.
9. T. Burns & G. M. Stalker, 1961, *The Management of Innovation,* London: Tavistok; P. R. Lawrence & J. W. Lorsch, 1967, *Organization and Environment,* Homewood, IL: Richard D. Irwin; J. Woodward, 1965, *Industrial Organization: Theory and Practice,* London: Oxford University Press.
10. H. Kim, R. E. Hoskisson, L. Tihanyi, & J. Hong, 2004, Evolution and restructuring of diversified business groups in emerging markets: The lessons from chaebols in Korea, *Asia Pacific Journal of Management,* 21: 25–48.
11. R. Kathuria, M. P. Joshi, & S. J. Porth, 2007, Organizational alignment and performance: Past, present and future, *Management Decision,* 45: 503–517.
12. A. Tempel & P. Walgenbach, 2007, Global standardization of organizational forms and management practices: What new institutionalism and the business-systems approach can learn from each other, *Journal of Management Studies,* 44: 1–24; Keats & O'Neill, Organizational structure, 533.
13. M. Buchanan, 2007, Questioning authority, *The Conference Board Review,* July/August, 59; H. J. Leavitt, 2003, Why hierarchies thrive, *Harvard Business Review,* 81(3): 96–102.
14. J. S. McMullen & D. A. Shepherd, 2006, Entrepreneurial action and the role of uncertainty in the theory of the entrepreneur, *Academy of Management Review,* 31: 132–152; R. L. Priem, L. G. Love, & M. A. Shaffer, 2002, Executives' perceptions of uncertainty sources: A numerical taxonomy and underlying dimensions, *Journal of Management,* 28: 725–746.
15. W. R. Chen & K. D. Miller, 2007, Situational and institutional determinants of firms' R&D search intensity, *Strategic Management Journal,* 28: 369–381; S. K. Ethiraj & D. Levinthal, 2004, Bounded rationality and the search for organizational architecture: An evolutionary perspective on the design of organizations and their evolvability, *Administrative Science Quarterly,* 49: 404–437.
16. J. G. Covin, D. P. Slevin, & M. B. Heeley, 2001, Strategic decision making in an intuitive vs. technocratic mode: Structural and environmental consideration, *Journal of Business Research,* 52: 51–67.
17. E. M. Olson, S. F. Slater, & G. T. M. Hult, 2005, The importance of structure and process to strategy implementation, *Business Horizons,* 48(1): 47–54; H. Barkema, J. A. C. Baum, & E. A. Mannix, 2002, Management challenges in a new time, *Academy of Management Journal,* 45: 916–930.
18. L. Donaldson, 2001, *The contingency theory of organizations,* Thousand Oaks, CA: Sage; Jenster & Hussey, *Company Analysis,* 169.
19. M. A. Schilling & H. K. Steensma, 2001, The use of modular organizational forms: An industry-level analysis, *Academy of Management Journal,* 44: 1149–1168.
20. C. B. Dobni & G. Luffman, 2003, Determining the scope and impact of market orientation profiles on strategy implementation and performance, *Strategic Management Journal,* 24: 577–585; D. C. Hambrick & J. W. Fredrickson, 2001, Are you sure you have a strategy? *Academy of Management Executive,* 15(4): 48–59.
21. M. Hammer, 2007, The process audit, *Harvard Business Review,* 85(4): 111–123.
22. R. D. Ireland & J. W. Webb, 2007, Strategic entrepreneurship: Creating competitive advantage through streams of innovation, *Business Horizons,* 50: 49–59; T. J. Andersen, 2004, Integrating decentralized strategy making and strategic planning processes in dynamic

environments, *Journal of Management Studies,* 41: 1271–1299.
23. J. Rivkin & N. Siggelkow, 2003, Balancing search and stability: Interdependencies among elements of organizational design, *Management Science,* 49: 290–321; G. A. Bigley & K. H. Roberts, 2001, The incident command system: High-reliability organizing for complex and volatile task environments, *Academy of Management Journal,* 44: 1281–1299.
24. S. Nadkarni & V. K. Narayanan, 2007, Strategic schemas, strategic flexibility, and firm performance: The moderating role of industry clockspeed, *Strategic Management Journal,* 28: 243–270; K. D. Miller & A. T. Arikan, 2004, Technology search investments: Evolutionary, option reasoning, and option pricing approaches, *Strategic Management Journal,* 25: 473–485.
25. S. K. Ethiraj & D. Levinthal, 2004, Modularity and innovation in complex systems, *Management Science,* 50: 159–173; T. W. Malnight, 2001, Emerging structural patterns within multinational corporations: Toward process-based structures, *Academy of Management Journal,* 44: 1187–1210; H. A. Simon, 1991, Bounded rationality and organizational learning, *Organization Science,* 2: 125–134.
26. C. Zook, 2007, Finding your next core business, *Harvard Business Review,* 85(4): 66–75.
27. G. Edmondson, 2006, BMW's dream factory, *BusinessWeek,* October 16, 70–78.
28. S. K. Maheshwari & D. Ahlstrom, 2004, Turning around a state owned enterprise: The case of Scooters India Limited, *Asia Pacific Journal of Management,* 21(1–2): 75–101; B. W. Keats & M. A. Hitt, 1988, A causal model of linkages among environmental dimensions, macroorganizational characteristics, and performance, *Academy of Management Journal,* 31: 570–598.
29. A. Chandler, 1962, *Strategy and Structure,* Cambridge, MA: MIT Press.
30. R. E. Hoskisson, R. A. Johnson, L. Tihanyi, & R. E. White, 2005, Diversified business groups and corporate refocusing in emerging economies, *Journal of Management,* 31: 941–965; J. D. Day, E. Lawson, & K. Leslie, 2003, When reorganization works, *The McKinsey Quarterly,* (2), 20–29.
31. M. Ihlwan, 2007, Samsung is having a Sony moment, *BusinessWeek,* July 30, 38.
32. S. K. Ethiraj, 2007, Allocation of inventive effort in complex product systems, *Strategic Management Journal,* 28: 563–584.
33. D. Martin, 2007, Alfred D. Chandler, Jr., a business historian, dies at 88, *New York Times Online,* http://www.nytimes.com, May 12.
34. A. Weibel, 2007, Formal control and trustworthiness, *Group & Organization Management,* 32: 500–517; P. K. Mills & G. R. Ungson, 2003, Reassessing the limits of structural empowerment: Organizational constitution and trust as controls, *Academy of Management Review,* 28: 143–153.
35. M. Santala & P. Parvinen, 2007, From strategic fit to customer fit, *Management Decision,* 45: 582–601; R. Reed, W. J. Donoher, & S. F. Barnes, 2004, Predicting misleading disclosures: The effects of control, pressure, and compensation, *Journal of Managerial Issues,* 16: 322–336.
36. T. Galpin, R. Hilpirt, & B. Evans, 2007, The connected enterprise: Beyond division of labor, *Journal of Business Strategy,* 28(2): 38–47; C. Sundaramurthy & M. Lewis, 2003, Control and collaboration: Paradoxes of governance, *Academy of Management Review,* 28: 397–415.
37. Y. Li, L. Li, Y. Liu, & L. Wang, 2005, Linking management control system with product development and process decisions to cope with environment complexity, *International Journal of Production Research,* 43: 2577–2591; D. F. Kuratko, R. D. Ireland, & J. S. Hornsby, 2001, Improving firm performance through entrepreneurial actions: Acordia's corporate entrepreneurship strategy, *Academy of Management Executive,* 15(4): 60–71.
38. G. J. M. Braam & E. J. Nijssen, 2004, Performance effects of using the Balanced Scorecard: A note on the Dutch experience, *Long Range Planning,* 37: 335–349; S. D. Julian & E. Scifres, 2002, An interpretive perspective on the role of strategic control in triggering strategic change, *Journal of Business Strategies,* 19: 141–159.
39. D. F. Kuratko, R. D. Ireland, & J. S. Hornsby, 2004, Corporate entrepreneurship behavior among managers: A review of theory, research, and practice, in J. A. Katz & D. A. Shepherd (Eds.), *Advances in Entrepreneurship: Firm Emergence and Growth: Corporate Entrepreneurship,* Oxford, UK: Elsevier Publishing, 7–45; R. E. Hoskisson, M. A. Hitt, & R. D. Ireland, 1994, The effects of acquisitions and restructuring strategies (strategic refocusing) on innovation, in G. von Krogh, A. Sinatra, & H. Singh (eds.), *Managing Corporate Acquisition,* London: MacMillan, 144–169.
40. K. L. Turner & M. V. Makhija, 2006, The role of organizational controls in managing knowledge, *Academy of Management Review,* 31: 197–217; M. A. Hitt, R. E. Hoskisson, R. A. Johnson, & D. D. Moesel, 1996, The market for corporate control and firm innovation, *Academy of Management Journal,* 39: 1084–1119.
41. C. Witkin, 2006, Lafley and Immelt: In search of billions, *Fortune,* December 11, 70–81.
42. M. A. Hitt, L. Tihanyi, T. Miller, & B. Connelly, 2006, Internatioanl diversification: Antecedents, outcomes, and moderators, *Journal of Management,* 32:831–867; R. E. Hoskisson & M. A. Hitt, 1988, Strategic control and relative R&D investment in multiproduct firms, *Strategic Management Journal,* 9: 605–621.
43. D. Collis, D. Young, & M. Goold, 2007, The size, structure, and performance of corporate headquarters, *Strategic Management Journal,* 28: 383–405.
44. K. Chaharbaghi, 2007, The problematic of strategy: A way of seeing is also a way of not seeing, *Management Decision,* 45: 327–339; J. B. Barney, 2002, *Gaining and Sustaining Competitive Advantage,* 2nd ed., Upper Saddle River, NJ: Prentice Hall.
45. S. Lohr, 2007, Can Michael Dell refocus his namesake? *New York Times Online,* http://www.nytimes.com, September 9.
46. X. Yin & E. J. Zajac, 2004, The strategy/governance structure fit relationship: Theory and evidence in franchising arrangements, *Strategic Management Journal,* 25: 365–383.
47. Keats & O'Neill, Organizational structure, 531.
48. Olson, Slater, & Hult, The importance of structure and process to strategy implementation; D. Miller & J. O. Whitney, 1999, Beyond strategy: Configuration as a pillar of competitive advantage, *Business Horizons,* 42(3): 5–17.
49. Chandler, *Strategy and Structure.*
50. Keats & O'Neill, Organizational structure, 524.
51. M. E. Sosa, S. D. Eppinger, & C. M. Rowles, 2004, The misalignment of product architecture and organizational structure in complex product development, *Management Science,* 50: 1674–1689.
52. S. Karim & W. Mitchell, 2004, Innovating through acquisition and internal development: A quarter-century of boundary evolution at Johnson & Johnson, *Long Range Planning,* 37: 525–547; C. Williams & W. Mitchell, 2004, Focusing firm evolution: The impact of information infrastructure on market entry by U.S. telecommunications companies, 1984–1998, *Management Science,* 50: 1561–1575.
53. I. Daizadeh, 2006, Using intellectual property to map the organizational evolution of firms: Tracing a biotechnology company from startup to bureaucracy to a multidivisional firm, *Journal of Commercial Biotechnology,* 13: 28–36.
54. C. Levicki, 1999, *The Interactive Strategy Workout,* 2nd ed., London: Prentice Hall.
55. E. E. Entin, F. J. Diedrich, & B. Rubineau, 2003, Adaptive communication patterns in different organizational structures, *Human Factors and Ergonomics Society Annual Meeting Proceedings,* 405–409; H. M. O'Neill, R. W. Pouder, & A. K. Buchholtz, 1998, Patterns in the diffusion of strategies across organizations: Insights from the innovation diffusion literature, *Academy of Management Review,* 23: 98–114.
56. 2007, Organizational structure, *Wikipedia,* http://en.wikipedia.org; Gallbraith, *Designing Organizations,* 25.
57. Keats & O'Neill, Organizational structure, 539.
58. T. J. Andersen & A. H. Segars, 2001, The impact of IT on decision structure and firm performance: Evidence from the textile and apparel industry, *Information & Management,* 39: 85–100; Lawrence & Lorsch, *Organization and Environment.*

59. J. Welch & S. Welch, 2006, Growing up but staying young, *BusinessWeek,* December 11, 112.
60. O. E. Williamson, 1975, *Markets and Hierarchies: Analysis and Anti-Trust Implications,* New York: The Free Press.
61. B. Harstad, 2007, Organizational form and the market for talent, *Journal of Labor Economics,* 25: 581–611; Chandler, *Strategy and Structure.*
62. R. Inderst, H. M. Muller, & K. Warneryd, 2007, Distributional conflict in organizations, *European Economic Review,* 51: 385–402; J. Greco, 1999, Alfred P. Sloan Jr. (1875–1966): The original organizational man, *Journal of Business Strategy,* 20(5): 30–31.
63. Hoskisson, Hill, & Kim, The multidivisional structure, 269–298.
64. H. Zhou, 2005, Market structure and organizational form, *Southern Economic Journal,* 71: 705–719; W. G. Rowe & P. M. Wright, 1997, Related and unrelated diversification and their effect on human resource management controls, *Strategic Management Journal,* 18: 329–338.
65. C. E. Helfat & K. M. Eisenhardt, 2004, Inter-temporal economies of scope, organizational modularity, and the dynamics of diversification, *Strategic Management Journal,* 25: 1217–1232; A. D. Chandler, 1994, The functions of the HQ unit in the multibusiness firm, in R. P. Rumelt, D. E. Schendel, & D. J. Teece (eds.), *Fundamental Issues in Strategy,* Cambridge, MA: Harvard Business School Press, 327.
66. O. E. Williamson, 1994, Strategizing, economizing, and economic organization, in R. P. Rumelt, D. E. Schendel, & D. J. Teece (eds.), *Fundamental Issues in Strategy,* Cambridge, MA: Harvard Business School Press, 361–401.
67. R. M. Burton & B. Obel, 1980, A computer simulation test of the M-form hypothesis, *Administrative Science Quarterly,* 25: 457–476.
68. O. E. Williamson, 1985, *The Economic Institutions of Capitalism: Firms, Markets, and Relational Contracting,* New York: Macmillan.
69. Keats & O'Neill, Organizational structure, 532.
70. M. F. Wolff, 1999, In the organization of the future, competitive advantage will be inspired, *Research Technology Management,* 42(4): 2–4.
71. A. Weintraub, 2006, The big rethink at Pfizer, *BusinessWeek,* December 18, 42.
72. R. H. Hall, 1996, *Organizations: Structures, Processes, and Outcomes,* 6th ed., Englewood Cliffs, NJ: Prentice Hall, 13; S. Baiman, D. F. Larcker, & M. V. Rajan, 1995, Organizational design for business units, *Journal of Accounting Research,* 33: 205–229.
73. L. G. Love, R. L. Priem, & G. T. Lumpkin, 2002, Explicitly articulated strategy and firm performance under alternative levels of centralization, *Journal of Management,* 28: 611–627.
74. Hall, *Organizations,* 64–75.
75. Barney, *Gaining and Sustaining Competitive Advantage,* 257.
76. H. Karandikar & S. Nidamarthi, 2007, Implementing a platform strategy for a systems business via standardization, *Journal of Manufacturing Technology Management,* 18: 267–280.
77. Olson, Slater, Tomas, & Hult, The performance implications of fit.
78. 2007, Wal-Mart Stores, Inc, *New York Times Online,* http://www.nytimes.com, July 21.
79. 2007, Wal-Mart rolling out new company slogan, *New York Times Online,* http://www.nytimes.com, July 12.
80. Olson, Slater, Tomas & Hult, The performance implications of fit.
81. Chandler, *Strategy and Structure.*
82. 2007, Harley-Davidson, Inc., *New York Times Online,* http://www.nytimes.com, July 19.
83. R. Rumelt, 1974, *Strategy, Structure and Economic Performance,* Boston: Harvard University Press.
84. 2007, Outback Steakhouse, http://www.outback.com, September 21; R. Gibson, 2005, Outback tries to diversify in new strategy, *Wall Street Journal,* April 27, B8.
85. 2007, Restructuring boosts Colgate profit, *CNNMoney.com,* http://cnnmoney.com, July 25.
86. C. C. Markides & P. J. Williamson, 1996, Corporate diversification and organizational structure: A resource-based view, *Academy of Management Journal,* 39: 340–367; C. W. L. Hill, M. A. Hitt, & R. E. Hoskisson, 1992, Cooperative versus competitive structures in related and unrelated diversified firms, *Organization Science,* 3: 501–521.
87. P. F. Drucker, 2002, They're not employees, they're people, *Harvard Business Review,* 80(2): 70–77; J. Robins & M. E. Wiersema, 1995, A resource-based approach to the multibusiness firm: Empirical analysis of portfolio interrelationships and corporate financial performance, *Strategic Management Journal,* 16: 277–299.
88. J. R. Baum & S. Wally, 2003, Strategic decision speed and firm performance, *Strategic Management Journal,* 24: 1107–1129.
89. J. G. March, 1994, *A Primer on Decision Making: How Decisions Happen,* New York: The Free Press, 117–118.
90. M. Goold & A. Campbell, 2003, Structured networks: Towards the well designed matrix, *Long Range Planning,* 36(5): 427–439.
91. P. A. Argenti, R. A. Howell, & K. A. Beck, 2005, The strategic communication imperative, *MIT Sloan Management Review,* 46(3): 84–89.
92. R. E. Hoskisson & M. A. Hitt, 1990, Antecedents and performance outcomes of diversification: A review and critique of theoretical perspectives, *Journal of Management,* 16: 461–509.
93. Hill, Hitt, & Hoskisson, Cooperative versus competitive structures, 512.
94. J. Birkinshaw, 2001, Strategies for managing internal competition, *California Management Review,* 44(1): 21–38.
95. 2007, Textron Inc., *Wikipedia,* http://en.wikipedia.org, September 21; 2007, Textron profile, http://www.textron.com, September 21.
96. M. Maremont, 2004, Leadership; more can be more: Is the conglomerate a dinosaur from a bygone era? The answer is no—with a caveat, *Wall Street Journal,* October 24, R4; T. R. Eisenmann & J. L. Bower, 2000, The entrepreneurial M-form: Strategic integration in global media firms, *Organization Science,* 11: 348–355.
97. T. Yu & A. A. Cannella, Jr., 2007, Rivalry bwetween multinational enterprises: An event history approach, *Academy of Management Journal,* 50: 665–686; S. E. Christophe & H. Lee, 2005, What matters about internationalization: A market-based assessment, *Journal of Business Research,* 58: 636–643; Y. Luo, 2002, Product diversification in international joint ventures: Performance implications in an emerging market, *Strategic Management Journal,* 23: 1–20.
98. M. Mandel, 2007, Globalization vs. immigration reform, *BusinessWeek,* June 4, 40.
99. T. M. Begley & D. P. Boyd, 2003, The need for a corporate global mind-set, *MIT Sloan Management Review,* 44(2): 25–32; Tallman, Global strategic management, 467.
100. T. Kostova & K. Roth, 2003, Social capital in multinational corporations and a micro-macro model of its formation, *Academy of Management Review,* 28: 297–317.
101. J. Jermias & L. Gani, 2005, Ownership structure, contingent-fit, and business-unit performance: A research model and evidence, *The International Journal of Accounting,* 40: 65–85; J. Wolf & W. G. Egelhoff, 2002, A reexamination and extension of international strategy-structure theory, *Strategic Management Journal,* 23: 181–189.
102. C. A. Bartlett & S. Ghoshal, 1989, *Managing Across Borders: The Transnational Solution,* Boston: Harvard Business School Press.
103. 2007, SABMiller joint venture to buy 4 Chinese breweries for $79M, *St. Louis Buisness Journal,* http://www.mlive.com, August 24.
104. 2007, Netherlands: Heineken, InBev, SABMiller benefit from coverge review, *Just-Drinks,* http://www.just-drinks.com, September 18.
105. 2007, About SABMiller, http://www.sabmiller.com, September 21.
106. S. T. Cavusgil, S. Yeniyurt, & J. D. Townsend, 2004, The framework of a global company: A conceptualization and preliminary validation, *Industrial Marketing Management,* 33: 711–716.
107. N. Byrnes, 2007, Avon: More than cosmetic changes, *BusinessWeek,* March 12, 62–63.
108. 2007, Avon's Products, http://www.avon.com, September 20.
109. Malnight, Emerging structural patterns, 1197.
110. 2007, Avon 2005 Global Women's Survey, http://www.avon.com, September 22.

111. B. Connelly, M. A. Hitt, A. DeNisi, & R. D. Ireland, 2007, Expatriates and corporate-level international strategy: Governing with the knowledge contract, *Management Decision,* 45: 564–581.
112. 2007, P&G Corporate information—Structure, http://www.pg.com, September 21.
113. S. G. Lazzarini, 2007, The impact of membership in competing alliance constellations: Evidence on the operational performance of global airlines, *Strategic Management Journal,* 28: 345–367; Y. L. Doz & G. Hamel, 1998, *Alliance Advantage: The Art of Creating Value through Partnering,* Boston: Harvard Business School Press, 222.
114. Y. Luo, 2007, Are joint venture partners more opportunistic in a more volatile environment? *Strategic Management Journal,* 28: 39–60; K. Moller, A. Rajala, & S. Svahn, 2005, Strategic business nets—their type and management, *Journal of Business Research,* 58: 1274–1284.
115. D. Li, L. E. Eden, M. A. Hitt, & R. D. Ireland, 2008, Friends, acquaintances or strangers? *Academy of Management Journal,* in press.
116. B. Comes-Casseres, 2003, Competitive advantage in alliance constellations, *Strategic Organization,* 1: 327–335; T. K. Das & B. S. Teng, 2002, Alliance constellations: A social exchange perspective, *Academy of Management Review,* 27: 445–456.
117. S. Tallman, M. Jenkins, N. Henry, & S. Pinch, 2004, Knowledge, clusters, and competitive advantage, *Academy of Management Review,* 29: 258–271; C. Lee, K. Lee, & J. M. Pennings, 2001, Internal capabilities, external networks, and performance: A study on technology-based ventures, *Strategic Management Journal,* 22: 615–640.
118. A. Capaldo, 2007, Network structure and innovation: The leveraging of a dualnetwork as a distnictive relational capability, *Strategic Management Journal,* 28: 585–608; A. Zaheer & G. G. Bell, 2005, Benefiting from network position: Firm capabilities, structural holes, and performance, *Strategic Management Journal,* 26: 809–825; M. B. Sarkar, R. Echambadi, & J. S. Harrison, 2001, Alliance entrepreneurship and firm market performance, *Strategic Management Journal,* 22: 701–711.
119. R. D. Ireland & J. W. Webb, 2007, A multi-theoretic perspective on trust and power in strategic supply chains, *Journal of Operations Management,* 25: 482–497; V. G. Narayanan & A. Raman, 2004, Aligning incentives in supply chains, *Harvard Business Review,* 82(11): 94–102.
120. S. Harrison, 1998, *Japanese Technology and Innovation Management,* Northampton, MA: Edward Elgar.
121. T. Keil, 2004, Building external corporate venturing capability, *Journal of Management Studies,* 41: 799–825.
122. P. Dussauge, B. Garrette, & W. Mitchell, 2004, Learning from competing partners: Outcomes and duration of scale and link alliances in Europe, North America and Asia, *Strategic Management Journal,* 21: 99–126; G. Lorenzoni & C. Baden-Fuller, 1995, Creating a strategic center to manage a web of partners, *California Management Review,* 37(3): 146–163.
123. N. C. Carr, 2005, In praise of walls, *MIT Sloan Management Review,* 45(3): 10–13.
124. T. A. Stewart & A. P. Raman, 2007, Lessons from Toyota's long drive, *Harvard Business Review,* 85(7/8): 74–83; J. H. Dyer & K. Nobeoka, 2000, Creating and managing a high-performance knowledge-sharing network: The Toyota case, *Strategic Management Journal,* 21: 345–367.
125. K. G. Provan & P. Kenis, 2007, Modes of network governance: Structure, management, and effectiveness, *Journal of Public Administration Research and Theory,* http://www.oxfordjournals.org, September 21; M. Kotabe, X. Martin, & H. Domoto, 2003, Gaining from vertical partnerships: Knowledge transfer, relationship duration and supplier performance improvement in the U.S. and Japanese automotive industries, *Strategic Management Journal,* 24: 293–316.
126. T. Nishiguchi, 1994, *Strategic Industrial Sourcing: The Japanese Advantage,* New York: Oxford University Press.
127. P. Dussauge, B. Garrette, & W. Mitchell, 2004, Asymmetric performance: The market share impact of scale and link alliances in the global auto industry, *Strategic Management Journal,* 25: 701–711.
128. C. Dawson & K. N. Anhalt, 2005, A "China price" for Toyota, *BusinessWeek,* February 21, 50–51; W. M. Fruin, 1992, *The Japanese Enterprise System,* New York: Oxford University Press.
129. M. Tuunanen & F. Hoy, 2007, Franchising: Multifaceted form of entrepreneurship, *International Journal of Entrepreneurship and Small Business,* 4: 52–67.
130. B. B. Nielsen, 2005, The role of knowledge embeddedness in the creation of synergies in strategic alliances, *Journal of Business Research,* 58: 1194–1204.
131. 2007, McDonald's Corporation, http://www.reuters.com, September 21.
132. 2007, McDonald's: China Olympics, http://www.mcchronicles.blogspot.com, September 21.
133. P. H. Andersen & P. R. Christensen, 2005, Bridges over troubled water: Suppliers as connective nodes in global supply networks, *Journal of Business Research,* 58: 1261–1273; C. Jones, W. S. Hesterly, & S. P. Borgatti, 1997, A general theory of network governance: Exchange conditions and social mechanisms, *Academy of Management Review,* 22: 911–945.
134. A. Goerzen, 2005, Managing alliance networks: Emerging practices of multinational corporations, *Academy of Management Executive,* 19(2): 94–107; J. M. Mezias, 2002, Identifying liabilities of foreignness and strategies to minimize their effects: The case of labor lawsuit judgments in the United States, *Strategic Management Journal,* 23: 229–244.
135. R. E. Miles, C. C. Snow, J. A. Mathews, G. Miles, & J. J. Coleman Jr., 1997, Organizing in the knowledge age: Anticipating the cellular form, *Academy of Management Executive,* 11(4): 7–20.
136. 2005, EDS and the ability alliance, http://www.ovum.com.
137. 2007, EDG Agility Alliance, http://www.eds.com, September 21.

Strategic Leadership

Studying this chapter should provide you with the strategic management knowledge needed to:

1. Define strategic leadership and describe top-level managers' importance.
2. Define top management teams and explain their effects on firm performance.
3. Describe the managerial succession process using internal and external managerial labor markets.
4. Discuss the value of strategic leadership in determining the firm's strategic direction.
5. Describe the importance of strategic leaders in managing the firm's resources.
6. Define organizational culture and explain what must be done to sustain an effective culture.
7. Explain what strategic leaders can do to establish and emphasize ethical practices.
8. Discuss the importance and use of organizational controls.

How Long Can I Have the Job? The Short Lives of CEOs and Top-Level Strategic Leaders

Evidence shows that the shelf life of a CEO is not long, and it continues to get shorter. In 1995, the average CEO tenure was 9.5 years. This average fell to 7.3 years in 2005 and is becoming even shorter today.

In ways, these averages dealing with CEO tenure do not tell the full story in that other top-level leaders sometimes last for only a short amount of time as well. Consider the following tenures as examples of this phenomenon: (1) Craig Monaghan, Sears CFO, five months, (2) Tom Taylor, Home Depot Marketing and Merchandising Chief, 11 months, (3) Catherine West, JCPenny COO, 7 months, (4) Charles Champion, Airbus Chief Operating Officer, 13 months, and (5) Xie Wen, Yahoo! China President, 42 days. Thus, short tenure for some top-level leaders is not specific to an industry, a job title, or duties.

What accounts for the brevity of some CEOs and top-level managers' tenure as strategic leaders? Without a doubt, the high stress levels and significant performance expectations cause some CEOs and top-level managers to voluntarily resign their positions more rapidly than historically was the case (we say more about this issue in the chapter's last Strategic Focus). However, other reasons play a role as well.

Peter Boneparth recently resigned as CEO of Jones Apparel Group, which owns brands such as Anne Klein, Jones New York, and Nine West. Disagreements between Boneparth and the firm's board of directors about the firm's strategy (and the future Boneparth envisioned for Jones using different strategies) led to his resignation. Chosen from the external managerial labor market (described in this chapter), Boneparth "spent much of his six years at Jones diversifying its clothing offerings through acquisitions, including a hostile takeover of the Maxwell Shoe Company, the purchase of Gloria Vanderbilt, and later, Barneys New York." The firm's board of directors seemingly felt that the company had lost contact with its core customers and that it had become too diversified through actions Boneparth took and championed. Accordingly, Jones sold Barneys New York and considered selling itself to a private equity firm. No search was conducted to replace Boneparth; instead, an insider who had been at Jones since 1990 was chosen as the new CEO.

Lasting roughly five years, Paul Pressler was tapped from Disney in the fall of 2002 to become Gap Inc.'s new CEO. In part, Pressler was chosen because he was known to be a "hard-nosed operations wizard," the type of disciplined leader Gap's board believed would reign in the firm's cost structure and improve its performance. As it turned out though, critics contend that Pressler never learned to appreciate the nuances of the fashion business. For this reason, Gap's creative artists and designers felt constrained by what they thought was an overemphasis on controlling costs and using strict financial controls. After the departure, a former Gap executive said that although talented, Pressler may have been "the wrong guy at the wrong time."

These examples appear to imply the superiority of internal successions to top-level positions; but, such an assumption is not the case. Selecting people from inside the company, with rich experience and even deep understandings of the firm's traditions as top-level strategic leaders can also lead to quick departures and less-than-expected outcomes.

Sources: N. Byrnes & D. Kiley, 2007, Hello, you must be going, *BusinessWeek*, February 12, 30–32; L. Lee, 2007, Paul Pressler's fall from the Gap, *BusinessWeek*, February 26, 80–84; J. L. Story, 2007, Chief executive steps down at Jones Apparel, *New York Times Online*, http://www.nytimes.com, July 13.

As the Opening Case implies, strategic leaders' work is demanding, challenging, and may end rapidly. Regardless of how long they remain in their positions though, strategic leaders (and most prominently CEOs) can make a major difference in how a firm performs. If a strategic leader can create a strategic vision for the firm using forward thinking, she may be able to energize the firm's human capital and achieve positive outcomes. However, the challenge of strategic leadership is significant. For example, a great deal of publicity accompanied Hewlett-Packard's (HP) hiring of Carly Fiorina; and she operated under the media spotlight during much of the six years she served as HP's CEO. The controversial acquisition of Compaq and the attempts to change the company appeared to be unsuccessful as the firm suffered weakening performance. Fiorina paid the ultimate price: losing her job. Her replacement (Mark Hurd) is unlike Fiorina in many ways and is focusing on improving HP's operational performance—a task some believe is necessary to realize benefits from acquiring Compaq. In late 2007 though, HP was outperforming major rival Dell Inc. in the PC business (see Chapter 5's Opening Case). An intriguing question to consider is the amount of credit that should go to Fiorina rather than to Hurd for this turnaround.

A major message in this chapter is that effective strategic leadership is the foundation for successfully using the strategic management process. As is implied in Figure 1.1 (on page 5), strategic leaders guide the firm in ways that result in forming a vision and mission (see Chapter 1). Often, this guidance finds leaders thinking of ways to create goals that stretch everyone in the organization to improve performance.[1] Moreover, strategic leaders facilitate the development of appropriate strategic actions and determine how to implement them. As we show in Figure 12.1, these actions are the path to strategic competitiveness and above-average returns.[2]

We begin this chapter with a definition of strategic leadership; we then discuss its importance as a potential source of competitive advantage as well as effective strategic leadership styles. Next, we examine top management teams and their effects on innovation, strategic change, and firm performance. Following this discussion, we analyze the internal and external managerial labor markets from which strategic leaders are selected. Closing the chapter are descriptions of the five key components of effective strategic leadership: determining a strategic direction, effectively managing the firm's resource portfolio (which includes exploiting and maintaining core competencies along with developing human capital and social capital), sustaining an effective organizational culture, emphasizing ethical practices, and establishing balanced organizational controls.

Strategic Leadership and Style

Strategic leadership is the ability to anticipate, envision, maintain flexibility, and empower others to create strategic change as necessary.

Strategic leadership is the ability to anticipate, envision, maintain flexibility, and empower others to create strategic change as necessary. Multifunctional in nature, strategic leadership involves managing through others, managing an entire enterprise rather than a functional subunit, and coping with change that continues to increase in the global

Figure 12.1 Strategic Leadership and the Strategic Management Process

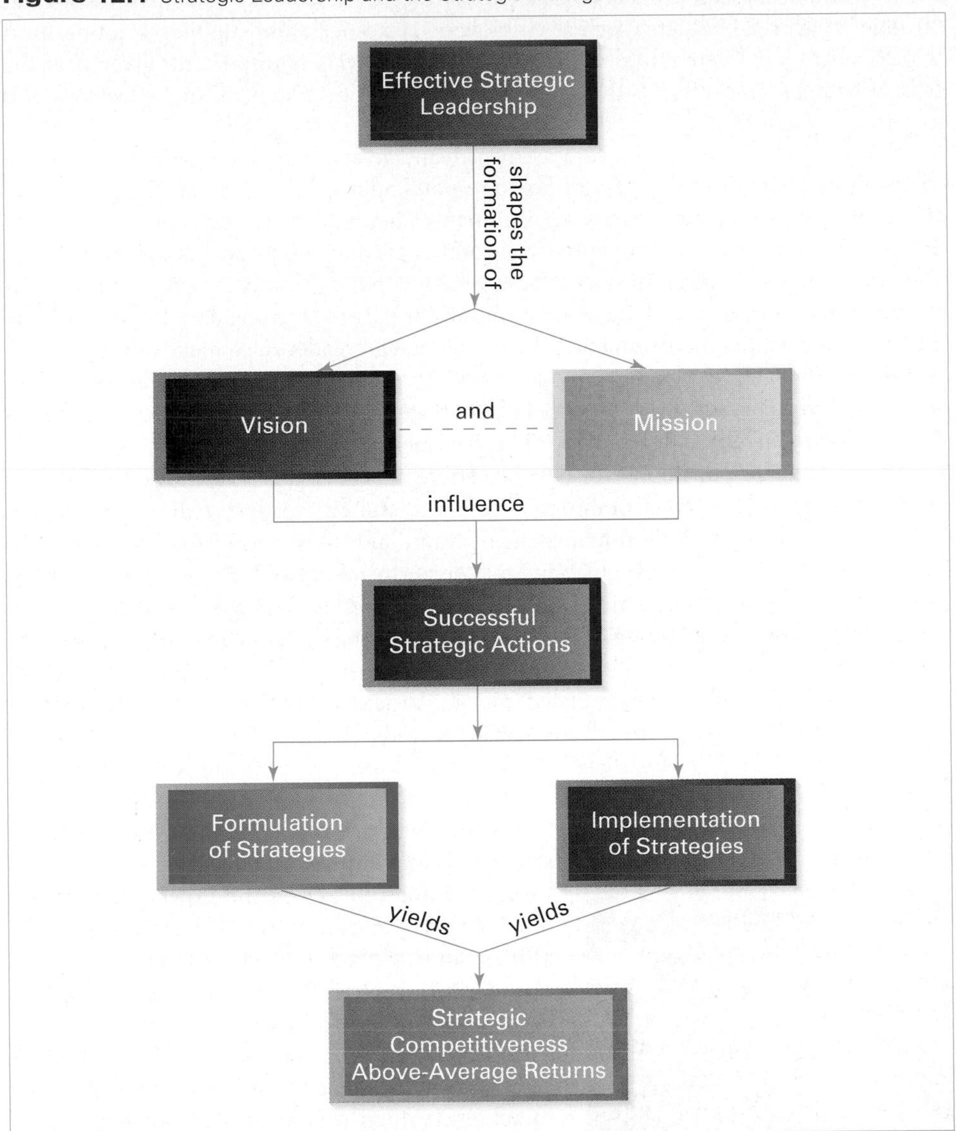

economy. Because of the global economy's complexity, strategic leaders must learn how to effectively influence human behavior, often in uncertain environments. By word or by personal example, and through their ability to envision the future, effective strategic leaders meaningfully influence the behaviors, thoughts, and feelings of those with whom they work.[3]

The ability to attract and then manage human capital may be the most critical of the strategic leader's skills,[4] especially in light of the fact that not being able to fill key positions with talented human capital constrains firm growth.[5] Increasingly, leaders throughout the global economy possess or are developing this skill. Some believe, for example, that leaders now surfacing in Chinese companies understand the rules of competition in market-based economies and are leading in ways that will develop their firm's human capital.[6] However, for some of these leaders, learning how to successfully compete in market-based economies creates a great deal of stress, causing some analysts to say that "progress, as always, comes with a price."[7]

In the twenty-first century, intellectual capital that the firm's human capital possesses, including the ability to manage knowledge and create and commercialize innovation, affects a strategic leader's success.[8] Effective strategic leaders also establish the context through which stakeholders (such as employees, customers, and suppliers) can perform at peak efficiency.[9] Being able to demonstrate these skills is important, given that the crux of strategic leadership is the ability to manage the firm's operations effectively and sustain high performance over time.[10]

A firm's ability to achieve a competitive advantage and earn above-average returns is compromised when strategic leaders fail to respond appropriately and quickly to changes in the complex global competitive environment. The inability to respond or to identify the need for change in the competitive environment is one of the reasons some CEOs fail. Therefore, strategic leaders must learn how to deal with diverse and complex environmental situations. Individual judgment is an important part of learning about and analyzing the firm's competitive environment.[11] However, strategic leaders also make mistakes when evaluating competitive conditions in their firm's external environment. Effective strategic leaders have the courage to admit to and accept responsibility for such decision errors and then to ask for corrective feedback from peers, superiors, and employees.[12]

The primary responsibility for effective strategic leadership rests at the top, in particular with the CEO. Other commonly recognized strategic leaders include members of the board of directors, the top management team, and divisional general managers. In truth, any individual with responsibility for the performance of human capital and/or a part of the firm (e.g., a production unit) is a strategic leader. Regardless of their title and organizational function, strategic leaders have substantial decision-making responsibilities that cannot be delegated.[13] Strategic leadership is a complex but critical form of leadership. Strategies cannot be formulated and implemented for the purpose of achieving above-average returns without effective strategic leaders.

McDonald's founder, Ray Kroc, was a strategic leader known for his high degree of integrity.

© AP Photo

The styles used to provide leadership often affect the productivity of those being led. Transformational leadership is the most effective strategic leadership style. This style entails motivating followers to exceed the expectations others have of them, to continuously enrich their capabilities, and to place the interests of the organization above their own.[14] Transformational leaders develop and communicate a vision for the organization and formulate a strategy to achieve the vision. They make followers aware of the need to achieve valued organizational outcomes. And they encourage followers to continuously strive for higher levels of achievement. These types of leaders have a high degree of integrity (Roy Kroc, founder of McDonald's was a strategic leader valued for his high degree of integrity)[15] and character. Speaking about character, one CEO said the following: "Leaders are shaped and defined by character. Leaders inspire and enable others to do excellent work and realize their potential. As a result, they build successful, enduring organizations."[16] Additionally, transformational leaders have emotional intelligence. Emotionally intelligent leaders understand themselves well, have strong motivation, are empathetic with others, and have effective interpersonal skills.[17] At Procter & Gamble (P&G), emotional intelligence is thought of as having an "in-touch capability."[18]

STRATEGY RIGHT NOW

Doug Conant, CEO of Campbell Soup Co., appears to be a transformational leader. We present evidence supporting this possibility in the Strategic Focus. Notice that among other characteristics of a transformational leader, Conant has established a vision and mission for the firm and is committed to supporting the firm's employees—a resource that he believes is critical to his firm's continuing success. While reading the Strategic Focus, make a list of the characteristics or qualities that allow you to conclude that Conant is a transformational leader.

Strategic Focus Strategic Focus Strategic Focus

Doug Conant: Providing Effective Strategic Leadership at Campbell Soup Co.

"In just under six years since he came on board, Conant, 55, has transformed Campbell from a beleaguered old brand rumored to be on the auction block to one of the food industry's best performers." Obviously, the accomplishments these words suggest are quite noteworthy. Although cutting costs contributed to this positive outcome, smart product innovations and actions to empower and reinvigorate the workforce are playing a more important role in the Conant-led turnaround at Campbell. Additionally, Conant constantly evaluates the synergies within his firm's portfolio of consumer goods. Recently, he concluded that the Godiva unit no longer fits with Campbell's "strategic focus on simple meals, including soup, baked snacks, and vegetable-based beverages." As a result, Godiva became available for sale in the third quarter of 2007.

Many of the actions Conant is taking as well as how he takes those actions are consistent with the attributes of transformational leadership. Consider that he happily gives credit to others for the firm's achievements and continuously deflects praise about his role in Campbell's turnaround. During his tenure, he sent (to date) more than 16,000 handwritten thank you notes to employees and others to highlight an achievement. He makes this effort to celebrate "what's right" about a person's work or attitudes. He readily admits mistakes (saying "I can do better"), largely because he realizes he doesn't have all the answers. Framing an inspiring vision and mission statements were among the first actions he took as CEO. He believes strongly in workforce diversity, saying that "Our goal as a company is to cultivate a diverse employee population that brings new and richer perspectives to their jobs and enables us to better understand, anticipate and respond to the changed marketplace." Part of the reason for announcing that Campbell would expand its corporate headquarters building (as well as construct other facilities at its headquarters site) in Camden, New Jersey, is Conant's belief that companies need to be good citizens in the communities in which they are located.

Several principles guide Conant's work as a strategic leader. Using a personal touch to interact with people, working with individuals to jointly set their performance expectations, and creating opportunities for every person to succeed are some of the direction-providing principles Conant follows as a strategic leader.

Sources: 2007, Diversity, passion, innovation, growth, http://www.campbellsoupcompany.com, September 30; 2007, Executive team, http://www.campbellsoupcompany.com, September 30; 2007, Doug Conant remarks to press announcing plan for Campbell to expand world headquarters facilities, http://www.campbellsoupcompany.com, September 30; B. Dorman, 2007, Campbell Soup considers selling Godiva unit, *USA Today Online*, http://www.usatoday.com, August 9; A. Carter, 2006, Lighting a fire under Campbell, *BusinessWeek*, December 4, 96–100.

The Role of Top-Level Managers

Top-level managers play a critical role in that they are charged to make certain their firm is able to effectively formulate and implement strategies.[19] Top-level managers' strategic decisions influence how the firm is designed and goals will be achieved. Thus, a critical element of organizational success is having a top management team with superior managerial skills.[20]

Managers often use their discretion (or latitude for action) when making strategic decisions, including those concerned with effectively implementing strategies.[21] Managerial discretion differs significantly across industries. The primary factors that determine the amount of decision-making discretion held by a manager (especially a top-level manager) are (1) external environmental sources such as the industry structure, the rate of market growth in the firm's primary industry, and the degree to which products can be differentiated; (2) characteristics of the organization, including its size, age, resources, and culture; and (3) characteristics of the manager, including commitment to the firm and its strategic outcomes, tolerance for ambiguity, skills in working with different people, and aspiration levels (see Figure 12.2). Because strategic leaders' decisions are intended to help the firm gain a competitive advantage, how managers exercise discretion when determining appropriate strategic actions is critical to the firm's success.[22]

In addition to determining new strategic initiatives, top-level managers develop a firm's organizational structure and reward systems. Top executives also have a major effect on a firm's culture. Evidence suggests that managers' values are critical in shaping a firm's cultural values.[23] Accordingly, top-level managers have an important effect on organizational activities and performance.[24] Because of the challenges top executives face, they often are more effective when they operate as top management teams.

Top Management Teams

In most firms, the complexity of challenges and the need for substantial amounts of information and knowledge require strategic leadership by a team of executives. Using a team to make strategic decisions also helps to avoid another potential problem when these decisions are made by the CEO alone: managerial hubris. Research evidence

Figure 12.2 Factors Affecting Managerial Discretion

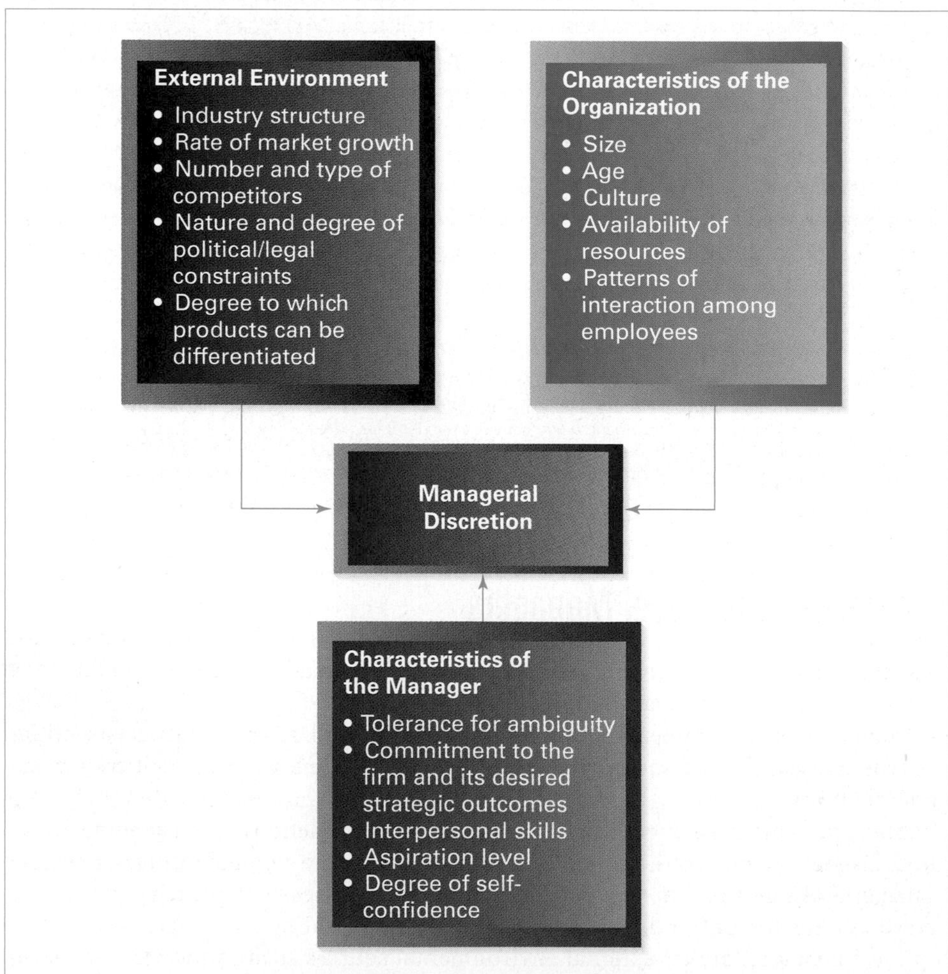

Source: Adapted from S.Finkelstein & D. C. Hambrick, 1996, *Strategic Leadership: Top Executives and Their Effects on Organizations,* St. Paul, MN: West Publishing Company.

shows that when CEOs begin to believe glowing press accounts and to feel that they are unlikely to make errors, they are more likely to make poor strategic decisions.[25] Top executives need to have self-confidence but must guard against allowing it to become arrogance and a false belief in their own invincibility.[26] To guard against CEO overconfidence and poor strategic decisions, firms often use the top management team to consider strategic opportunities and problems and to make strategic decisions. The **top management team** is composed of the key individuals who are responsible for selecting and implementing the firm's strategies. Typically, the top management team includes the officers of the corporation, defined by the title of vice president and above or by service as a member of the board of directors.[27] The quality of the strategic decisions made by a top management team affects the firm's ability to innovate and engage in effective strategic change.[28]

The **top management team** is composed of the key individuals who are responsible for selecting and implementing the firm's strategies.

Top Management Team, Firm Performance, and Strategic Change

The job of top-level executives is complex and requires a broad knowledge of the firm's operations, as well as the three key parts of the firm's external environment—the general, industry, and competitor environments, as discussed in Chapter 2. Therefore, firms try to form a top management team with knowledge and expertise needed to operate the internal organization, yet that also can deal with all the firm's stakeholders as well as its competitors.[29] To have these characteristics normally requires a heterogeneous top management team. A **heterogeneous top management team** is composed of individuals with different functional backgrounds, experience, and education.

A **heterogeneous top management team** is composed of individuals with different functional backgrounds, experience, and education.

Members of a heterogeneous top management team benefit from discussing the different perspectives advanced by team members.[30] In many cases, these discussions increase the quality of the team's decisions, especially when a synthesis emerges within the team after evaluating the diverse perspectives.[31] The net benefit of such actions by heterogeneous teams has been positive in terms of market share and above-average returns. Research shows that more heterogeneity among top management team members promotes debate, which often leads to better strategic decisions. In turn, better strategic decisions produce higher firm performance.[32]

It is also important for top management team members to function cohesively. In general, the more heterogeneous and larger the top management team is, the more difficult it is for the team to effectively implement strategies.[33] Comprehensive and long-term strategic plans can be inhibited by communication difficulties among top executives who have different backgrounds and different cognitive skills.[34] Alternatively, communication among diverse top management team members can be facilitated through electronic communications, sometimes reducing the barriers before face-to-face meetings.[35] However, a group of top executives with diverse backgrounds may inhibit the process of decision making if it is not effectively managed. In these cases, top management teams may fail to comprehensively examine threats and opportunities, leading to a suboptimal strategic decision. Thus, the CEO must attempt to achieve behavioral integration among the team members.[36]

Having members with substantive expertise in the firm's core functions and businesses is also important to a top management team's effectiveness. In a high-technology industry, it may be critical for a firm's top management team members to have R&D expertise, particularly when growth strategies are being implemented.[37] Yet their eventual effect on strategic decisions depends not only on their expertise and the way the team is managed but also on the context in which they make the decisions (the governance structure, incentive compensation, etc.).[38]

The characteristics of top management teams are related to innovation and strategic change.[39] For example, more heterogeneous top management teams are positively associated with innovation and strategic change. The heterogeneity may force the team or some of its members to "think outside of the box" and thus be more creative in making decisions. Therefore, firms that need to change their strategies are more likely to do so if they have top management teams with diverse backgrounds and expertise. When a new CEO is hired from outside the industry, the probability of strategic change is greater than if the new CEO is from inside the firm or inside the industry.[40] Although hiring a new CEO from outside the industry adds diversity to the team, the top management team must be managed effectively to use the diversity in a positive way. Thus, to successfully create strategic change, the CEO should exercise transformational leadership.[41] A top management team with various areas of expertise is more likely to identify environmental changes (opportunities and threats) or changes within the firm, suggesting the need for a different strategic direction.

The CEO and Top Management Team Power

As noted in Chapter 10, the board of directors is an important governance mechanism for monitoring a firm's strategic direction and for representing stakeholders' interests, especially those of shareholders.[42] In fact, higher performance normally is achieved when the board of directors is more directly involved in shaping a firm's strategic direction.[43]

Boards of directors, however, may find it difficult to direct the strategic actions of powerful CEOs and top management teams.[44] Often, a powerful CEO appoints a number of sympathetic outside members to the board or may have inside board members who are also on the top management team and report to her or him.[45] In either case, the CEO may significantly influence the board's actions. Thus, the amount of discretion a CEO has in making strategic decisions is related to the board of directors and how it chooses to oversee the actions of the CEO and the top management team.[46]

CEOs and top management team members can achieve power in other ways. A CEO who also holds the position of chairperson of the board usually has more power than the CEO who does not.[47] Some analysts and corporate "watchdogs" criticize the practice of CEO duality (when the CEO and the chairperson of the board are the same). A reason for this criticism is that CEO duality has been blamed for poor performance and slow response to change in a number of firms.[48]

Although it varies across industries, CEO duality occurs most commonly in larger firms. Increased shareholder activism, however, has brought CEO duality under scrutiny and attack in both U.S. and European firms. Historically, an independent board leadership structure in which the same person did not hold the positions of CEO and chair was believed to enhance a board's ability to monitor top-level managers' decisions and actions, particularly with respect to financial performance.[49] And, as reported in Chapter 10, many believe these two positions should be separate in most companies to make the board more independent from the CEO. Stewardship theory, on the other hand, suggests that CEO duality facilitates effective decisions and actions. In these instances, the increased effectiveness gained through CEO duality accrues from the individual who wants to perform effectively and desires to be the best possible steward of the firm's assets. Because of this person's positive orientation and actions, extra governance and the coordination costs resulting from an independent board leadership structure would be unnecessary.[50]

Top management team members and CEOs who have long tenure—on the team and in the organization—have a greater influence on board decisions. And CEOs with greater influence may take actions in their own best interests, the outcomes of which increase their compensation from the company.[51] In response to this concern, U.S. lawmakers voted in the latter part of 2007 to "require public companies to put executive pay packages before shareholders for an advisory vote." Most analysts expected the bill to face an uphill battle, meaning that the final outcome for this proposed legislation was uncertain.[52]

In general, long tenure is thought to constrain the breadth of an executive's knowledge base. Some evidence suggests that with the limited perspectives associated with a restricted knowledge base, long-tenured top executives typically develop fewer alternatives to evaluate in making strategic decisions.[53] However, long-tenured managers also may be able to exercise more effective strategic control, thereby obviating the need for board members' involvement because effective strategic control generally produces higher performance.[54] Intriguingly, recent findings suggest that "the liabilities of short tenure . . . appear to exceed the advantages, while the advantages of long tenure—firm-specific human and social capital, knowledge, and power—seem to outweigh the disadvantages of rigidity and maintaining the status quo."[55] Overall then the relationship between CEO tenure and firm performance is complex, indicating that to strengthen the firm, boards of directors should develop an effective relationship with the top management team.

In summary, the relative degrees of power held by the board and top management team members should be examined in light of an individual firm's situation. For example, the abundance of resources in a firm's external environment and the volatility of that environment may affect the ideal balance of power between the board and the top management teams. Moreover, a volatile and uncertain environment may create a situation where a powerful CEO is needed to move quickly, but a diverse top management team may create less cohesion among team members and prevent or stall necessary strategic actions. With effective working relationships, boards, CEOs, and other top management team members have the foundation required to select arrangements with the highest probability of best serving stakeholders' interests.[56]

Managerial Succession

The choice of top executives—especially CEOs—is a critical decision with important implications for the firm's performance.[57] Many companies use leadership screening systems to identify individuals with managerial and strategic leadership potential as well as to determine the criteria individuals should satisfy to be candidates for the CEO position.[58] The most effective of these systems assess people within the firm and gain valuable information about the capabilities of other companies' managers, particularly their strategic leaders.[59] Based on the results of these assessments, training and development programs are provided for current individuals in an attempt to preselect and shape the skills of people who may become tomorrow's leaders. Because of the quality of its programs, General Electric "is famous for developing leaders who are dedicated to turning imaginative ideas into leading products and services."[60]

Organizations select managers and strategic leaders from two types of managerial labor markets—internal and external.[61] An **internal managerial labor market** consists of a firm's opportunities for managerial positions and the qualified employees within that firm. An **external managerial labor market** is the collection of managerial career opportunities and the qualified people who are external to the organization in which the opportunities exist.

An **internal managerial labor market** consists of a firm's opportunities for managerial positions and the qualified employees within that firm.

An **external managerial labor market** is the collection of managerial career opportunities and the qualified people who are external to the organization in which the opportunities exist.

Several benefits are thought to accrue to a firm when the internal labor market is used to select an insider as the new CEO. Because of their experience with the firm and the industry environment in which it competes, insiders are familiar with company products, markets, technologies, and operating procedures. Also, internal hiring produces lower turnover among existing personnel, many of whom possess valuable firm-specific knowledge. When the firm is performing well, internal succession is favored to sustain high performance. It is assumed that hiring from inside keeps the important knowledge necessary to sustain performance.

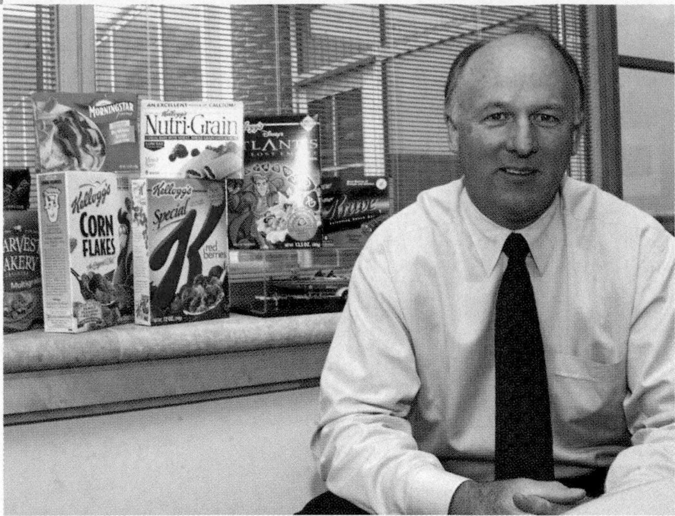

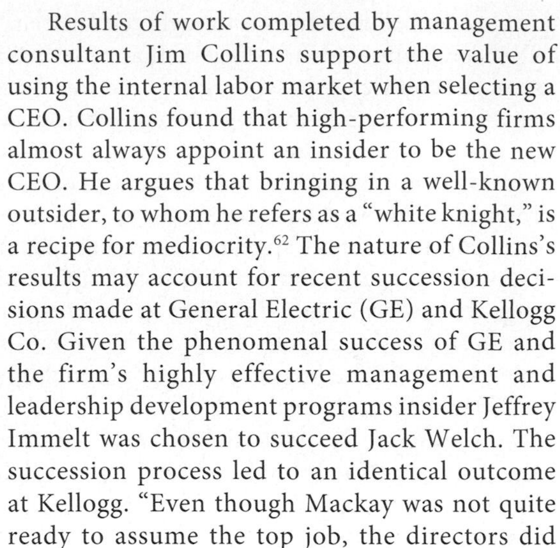

Kellogg's has consistently been named one of the most ethical companies in the world. David Mackay, CEO of Kellogg's, has worked hard to maintain founder W. K. Kellogg's philosophy of integrity and doing good things for people through good nutrition.

Results of work completed by management consultant Jim Collins support the value of using the internal labor market when selecting a CEO. Collins found that high-performing firms almost always appoint an insider to be the new CEO. He argues that bringing in a well-known outsider, to whom he refers as a "white knight," is a recipe for mediocrity.[62] The nature of Collins's results may account for recent succession decisions made at General Electric (GE) and Kellogg Co. Given the phenomenal success of GE and the firm's highly effective management and leadership development programs insider Jeffrey Immelt was chosen to succeed Jack Welch. The succession process led to an identical outcome at Kellogg. "Even though Mackay was not quite ready to assume the top job, the directors did not want to entrust the nearly 100-year-old company to someone who hadn't spent his professional life hip-deep in corn flakes, Rice Krispies, and Froot Loops." Given their view, Kellogg's board of directors chose insider David Mackay as its new CEO. However, one of its own board members served as interim CEO for two years, a time period during which Mackay fully acquainted himself with the nature and rigors of his new position.[63]

It is not unusual for employees to strongly prefer using the internal managerial labor market when selecting top management team members and the CEO. In the past, companies have also had a preference for insiders to fill top-level management positions because of a desire for continuity and a continuing commitment to the firm's current vision, mission, and chosen strategies.[64] However, because of a changing competitive landscape and varying levels of performance, an increasing number of boards of directors are turning to outsiders to succeed CEOs. A firm often has valid reasons to select an outsider as its new CEO: In some situations for example, long tenure with a firm may reduce strategic leaders' level of commitment to push innovation throughout the firm. Given innovation's importance to firm success (see Chapter 13), this hesitation could be a liability for a strategic leader.

Alan Mulally (pictured here), Ford's new CEO, was an outside hire. In fact, all of Detroit's big three car companies are now headed by new CEOs hired from outside their organizations.

In a break from tradition, the recent choices of CEOs in U.S. automobile manufacturers (Chrysler, Ford, and General Motors) have come from the external labor market. Some analysts see these choices as an indication that "it is no longer a requirement to have 'motor oil in your veins'. . . to run a car company."[65] However, as is the case with using the internal market, deciding to select top-level leaders from the external market does not guarantee success. Consider Wal-Mart's recent experiences. Facing a "mid-life" crisis,[66] Wal-Mart recruited Claire Watts from the external market and appointed her as senior vice president for merchandising. Having worked at Limited Brands and May Department Stores, Watts was asked to lead Wal-Mart's foray into fashionable clothing and home décor. Stated simply, this effort never approached the levels of success Wal-Mart envisioned, resulting in Watts's decision to resign.[67] Although the exact causes of this failure are probably many, some who have worked at Wal-Mart allege that the firm's culture is too resistant to new programs[68] and that the resistance likely created problems for Watts and those working with her.

Figure 12.3 Effects of CEO Succession and Top Management Team Composition on Strategy

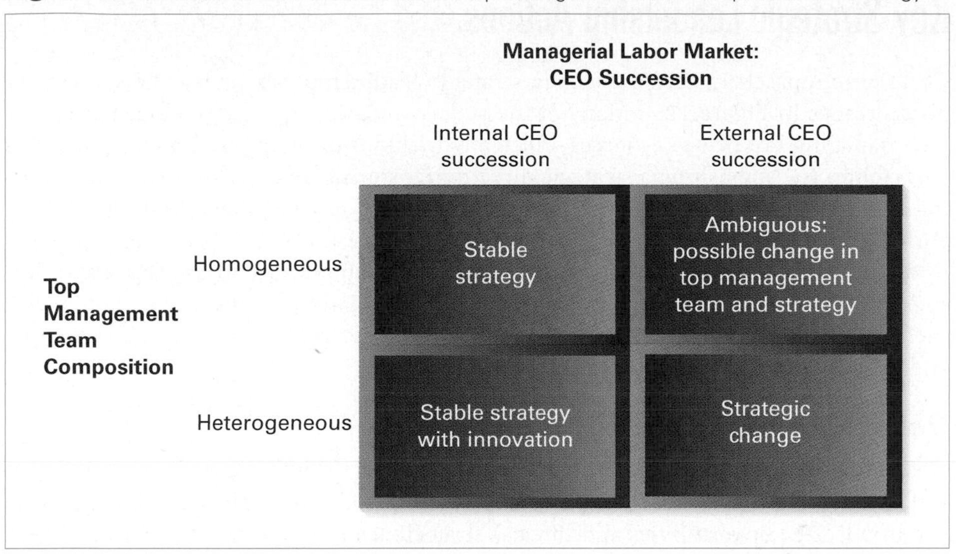

In Figure 12.3, we show how the composition of the top management team and the CEO succession (managerial labor market) interact to affect strategy. For example, when the top management team is homogeneous (its members have similar functional experiences and educational backgrounds) and a new CEO is selected from inside the firm, the firm's current strategy is unlikely to change. Alternatively, when a new CEO is selected from outside the firm and the top management team is heterogeneous, the probability is high that strategy will change. When the new CEO is from inside the firm and a heterogeneous top management team is in place, the strategy may not change, but innovation is likely to continue. An external CEO succession with a homogeneous team creates a more ambiguous situation. The recent selection of Sir Howard Stringer as CEO of Sony suggests changes in that firm's future. He is not only an outsider but also a foreigner. His selection as Sony's new CEO may be a result of increasing globalization and may be a harbinger of future appointments.[69]

Including talent from all parts of both the internal and external labor markets increases the likelihood that the firm will be able to form an effective top-management team. Evidence suggests that women are a qualified source of talent as strategic leaders that have been somewhat overlooked. In light of the success of a growing number of female executives, the foundation for change may be established. Trailblazers such as Catherine Elizabeth Hughes (the first African-American woman to head a firm that was publicly traded on a U.S. stock exchange), Muriel Siebert (the first woman to purchase a seat on the New York Stock Exchange), and publisher Judith Regan have made important contributions as strategic leaders. Prominent female CEOs are also receiving deserved recognition for their accomplishments. Anne Mulcahy (Xerox Corporation), Meg Whitman (eBay), and Andrea Jung (Avon Products) are examples of these individuals.

Despite the progress already made, work remains. Recent evidence shows, for example, "that investor reactions to the announcements of female CEOs are significantly more negative than those of their male counterparts."[70] Other evidence suggests that "women continue to be markedly underrepresented in leadership positions in organizations."[71] The important point for strategic leaders to recall is that empowering all individuals in the workforce increases the opportunities for them to fully develop their skills, expanding the size of the internal and external managerial labor markets as a result of doing so.[72]

Key Strategic Leadership Actions

Certain actions characterize effective strategic leadership; we present the most important ones in Figure 12.4. Many of the actions interact with each other. For example, managing the firm's resources effectively includes developing human capital and contributes to establishing a strategic direction, fostering an effective culture, exploiting core competencies, using effective organizational control systems, and establishing ethical practices. While studying these actions, notice that all of them find strategic leaders making decisions about the firm's direction, about how to use resources, and so forth.[73] The most effective strategic leaders create viable options when dealing with each of the key strategic leadership action situations as the foundation for making effective decisions.[74]

Determining Strategic Direction

Determining the strategic direction involves specifying the image and character the firm seeks to develop over time.

Determining the strategic direction involves specifying the image and character the firm seeks to develop over time.[75] The strategic direction is framed within the context of the conditions (i.e., opportunities and threats) strategic leaders expect their firm to face in roughly the next three to five years.

The ideal long-term strategic direction has two parts: a core ideology and an envisioned future. The core ideology motivates employees through the company's heritage, but the envisioned future encourages employees to stretch beyond their expectations of accomplishment and requires significant change and progress to be realized.[76] The envisioned future serves as a guide to many aspects of a firm's strategy implementation process, including motivation, leadership, employee empowerment, and organizational design.

Most changes in strategic direction are difficult to design and implement; however, CEO Jeffrey Immelt has an even greater challenge at GE. GE performed exceptionally well under Jack Welch's leadership. Although change is necessary because the competitive landscape is shifting, stakeholders accustomed to Jack Welch and high performance may not readily accept Immelt's changes (e.g., changes to the firm's corporate-level strategy and structure we discussed in Chapter 11). Immelt is trying to effect critical changes in the firm's culture, strategy, and governance and simultaneously gain stakeholders'

Figure 12.4 Exercise of Effective Strategic Leadership

commitment to them. As is true for all leaders trying to change a firm's strategic direction, Immelt needs to win people's hearts and minds while encouraging them to "tackle unscalable heights and make them understand why change is necessary, passionately explaining what's in it for the company—and employees."[77] Additionally, information regarding the firm's strategic direction must be consistently and clearly communicated to all affected parties.[78]

A charismatic CEO may foster stakeholders' commitment to a new vision and strategic direction. Nonetheless, it is important not to lose sight of the organization's strengths when making changes required by a new strategic direction. Immelt, for example, needs to use GE's strengths to ensure continued positive performance. The goal is to pursue the firm's short-term need to adjust to a new vision and strategic direction while maintaining its long-term survivability by effectively managing its portfolio of resources.

Effectively Managing the Firm's Resource Portfolio

Effectively managing the firm's portfolio of resources may be the most important strategic leadership task. The firm's resources are categorized as financial capital, human capital, social capital, and organizational capital (including organizational culture).[79]

Clearly, financial capital is critical to organizational success; strategic leaders understand this reality.[80] However, the most effective strategic leaders recognize the equivalent importance of managing each remaining type of resource as well as managing the integration of resources (e.g., using financial capital to provide training opportunities through which human capital is able to learn and maximize its performance). Most importantly, effective strategic leaders manage the firm's resource portfolio by organizing them into capabilities, structuring the firm to facilitate using those capabilities, and choosing strategies through which the capabilities are successfully leveraged to create value for customers. Exploiting and maintaining core competencies and developing and retaining the firm's human and social capital are actions taken to reach these important objectives.

Exploiting and Maintaining Core Competencies

Examined in Chapters 1 and 3, *core competencies* are capabilities that serve as a source of competitive advantage for a firm over its rivals. Typically, core competencies relate to an organization's functional skills, such as manufacturing, finance, marketing, and research and development. Strategic leaders must verify that the firm's competencies are emphasized when implementing strategies. Intel, for example, has core competencies of *competitive agility* (an ability to act in a variety of competitively relevant ways) and *competitive speed* (an ability to act quickly when facing environmental and competitive pressures).[81] Capabilities are developed over time as firms learn from their actions and enhance their knowledge about specific actions needed. For example, through repeated interactions, some firms have formed a capability allowing them to fully understand customers' needs as they change.[82] Firms with capabilities in R&D that develop into core competencies are rewarded by the market because of the critical nature of innovation in many industries.[83]

In many large firms, and certainly in related diversified ones, core competencies are effectively exploited when they are developed and applied across different organizational units (see Chapter 6). For example, PepsiCo purchased Quaker Oats (now called Quaker Foods), which makes the

Through its purchase of Quaker Foods (which owned Gatorade), PepsiCo was able to use its competence in distribution systems to exploit the Quaker assets and to increase the nutritional value of all of its food offerings.

sports drink Gatorade. PepsiCo uses its competence in distribution systems to exploit the Quaker assets. In this instance, Pepsi soft drinks (e.g., Pepsi Cola and Mountain Dew) and Gatorade share the logistics activity. Similarly, PepsiCo uses this competence to distribute Quaker's healthy snacks and Frito-Lay salty snacks through the same channels. Today, PepsiCo seeks to increase the nutritional value of all of its food items while trying to "ensure consumers never have to trade off nutrition and taste."[84]

Firms must continuously develop and when appropriate, change their core competencies to outperform rivals. If they have a competence that provides an advantage but do not change it, competitors will eventually imitate that competence and reduce or eliminate the firm's competitive advantage. Additionally, firms must guard against the competence becoming a liability, thereby preventing change.

As we discuss next, human capital is critical to a firm's success. One reason it's so critical is that human capital is the resource through which core competencies are developed and used.

Developing Human Capital and Social Capital

Human capital refers to the knowledge and skills of a firm's entire workforce.

Human capital refers to the knowledge and skills of a firm's entire workforce. From the perspective of human capital, employees are viewed as a capital resource requiring continuous investment.[85] At PepsiCo, people are identified as the key to the firm's continuing success. Given the need to "sustain its talent," PepsiCo invests in its human capital in the form of a host of programs and development-oriented experiences.[86]

Investments such as those being made at PepsiCo are productive, in that much of the development of U.S. industry can be attributed to the effectiveness of its human capital. This fact suggests that "as the dynamics of competition accelerate, people are perhaps the only truly sustainable source of competitive advantage."[87] In all types of organizations—large and small, new and established, and so forth—human capital's increasing importance suggests a significant role for the firm's human resource management activities.[88] As a support activity (see Chapter 3), human resource management practices facilitate people's efforts to successfully select and especially to use the firm's strategies.[89]

Effective training and development programs increase the probability of individuals becoming successful strategic leaders.[90] These programs are increasingly linked to firm success as knowledge becomes more integral to gaining and sustaining a competitive advantage.[91] Additionally, such programs build knowledge and skills, inculcate a common set of core values, and offer a systematic view of the organization, thus promoting the firm's vision and organizational cohesion. At McDonald's, the firm is trying to build an "employment brand," which suggests that individuals can begin their McDonald's career as a teenager and, through hard work and the company's training programs, become a strategic leader. This career path is the one Karen King, who is the president of McDonald's USA East Division, has experienced.[92]

Effective training and development programs also contribute positively to the firm's efforts to form core competencies.[93] Furthermore, they help strategic leaders improve skills that are critical to completing other tasks associated with effective strategic leadership, such as determining the firm's strategic direction, exploiting and maintaining the firm's core competencies, and developing an organizational culture that supports ethical practices. Thus, building human capital is vital to the effective execution of strategic leadership. Indeed, some argue that the world's "best companies are realizing that no matter what business they're in, their real business is building leaders."[94]

Strategic leaders must acquire the skills necessary to help develop human capital in their areas of responsibility.[95] When human capital investments are successful, the result is a workforce capable of learning continuously. Continuous learning and leveraging the firm's expanding knowledge base are linked with strategic success.[96]

An important aspect of leveraging a firm's knowledge is for retiring employees to convey their knowledge to their successors. Increasingly, firms are putting formal programs into place through which knowledge from human capital that is retiring is successfully transferred to human capital that is the firm's future.[97]

Learning also can preclude making errors. Strategic leaders tend to learn more from their failures than their successes because they sometimes make the wrong attributions for the successes.[98] For example, the effectiveness of certain approaches and knowledge can be context specific.[99] Some "best practices," for example, may not work well in all situations. We know that using teams to make decisions can be effective, but sometimes it is better for leaders to make decisions alone, especially when the decisions must be made and implemented quickly (e.g., in crisis situations).[100]

Walt Disney's strategic leaders learned that trying to sell cell phone service directly to customers was difficult and would not work.

Thus, effective strategic leaders recognize the importance of learning from success *and* from failure. Although Disney Co.'s strategic leaders have learned from many successes, they have a current opportunity to learn from failure. Only briefly after launching Disney cell phone service and the ESPN cell phone company, Disney closed both businesses. The decision to rely on brand names to sell cell phones and cell phone services directly to customers simply did not work as efforts to compete against the major carriers and to use big box retailers such as Best Buy as distribution channels were unsuccessful. Learning from these failures, Disney is now seeking to partner with others (e.g., Verizon Wireless) to find ways to distribute its content.[101]

Learning and building knowledge are important for creating innovation in firms.[102] Innovation leads to competitive advantage.[103] Overall, firms that create and maintain greater knowledge usually achieve and maintain competitive advantages. However, as noted with core competencies, strategic leaders must guard against allowing high levels of knowledge in one area to lead to myopia and overlooking knowledge development opportunities in other important areas of the business.[104]

When facing challenging conditions, firms sometimes decide to lay off some of their human capital. Strategic leaders must recognize though that layoffs can result in a significant loss of the knowledge possessed by the firm's human capital. Research evidence shows that moderate-sized layoffs may improve firm performance, but large layoffs produce stronger performance downturns in firms because of the loss of human capital.[105] Although it is also not uncommon for restructuring firms to reduce their expenditures on or investments in training and development programs, restructuring may actually be an important time to increase investments in these programs. The reason for increased focus on training and development is that restructuring firms have less slack and cannot absorb as many errors; moreover, the employees who remain after layoffs may find themselves in positions without all the skills or knowledge they need to perform the required tasks effectively.

Viewing employees as a resource to be maximized rather than as a cost to be minimized facilitates successful implementation of a firm's strategies as does the strategic leader's ability to approach layoffs in a manner that employees believe is fair and equitable.[106]A critical issue for employees is the fairness in the layoffs and in treatment in their jobs.[107]

Social capital involves relationships inside and outside the firm that help the firm accomplish tasks and create value for customers and shareholders.[108] Social capital is a critical asset for a firm. Inside the firm, employees and units must cooperate to get the work done. In multinational organizations, employees often find themselves cooperating across country boundaries on activities such as R&D to achieve performance objectives (e.g., developing new products).[109]

Social capital involves relationships inside and outside the firm that help the firm accomplish tasks and create value for customers and shareholders.

External social capital is increasingly critical to firm success. The reason for this is that few if any companies have all of the resources they need to successfully compete against their rivals. Firms can use cooperative strategies such as strategic alliances (see Chapter 9) to develop social capital. Social capital can develop in strategic alliances as firms share complementary resources. Resource sharing must be effectively managed, though, to ensure that the partner trusts the firm and is willing to share the desired resources.[110]

Research evidence suggests that the success of many types of firms may partially depend on social capital. Large multinational firms often must establish alliances in order to enter new foreign markets. Likewise, entrepreneurial firms often must establish alliances to gain access to resources, venture capital, or other types of resources (e.g., special expertise that the entrepreneurial firm cannot afford to maintain in-house).[111] Retaining quality human capital and maintaining strong internal social capital can be affected strongly by the firm's culture.

Sustaining an Effective Organizational Culture

An **organizational culture** consists of a complex set of ideologies, symbols, and core values that are shared throughout the firm and influence the way business is conducted.

In Chapter 1, we define **organizational culture** as a complex set of ideologies, symbols, and core values that are shared throughout the firm and influence the way business is conducted. Evidence suggests that a firm can develop core competencies in terms of both the capabilities it possesses and the way the capabilities are leveraged when implementing strategies to produce desired outcomes. In other words, because the organizational culture influences how the firm conducts its business and helps regulate and control employees' behavior, it can be a source of competitive advantage[112] and is a "critical factor in promoting innovation."[113] Given its importance, it may be that a vibrant organizational culture is the most valuable competitive differentiator for business organizations.[114] Thus, shaping the context within which the firm formulates and implements its strategies—that is, shaping the organizational culture—is an essential strategic leadership action.[115]

Entrepreneurial Mind-Set

Especially in large organizations, an organizational culture often encourages (or discourages) strategic leaders from pursuing (or not pursuing) entrepreneurial opportunities.[116] This issue is important because entrepreneurial opportunities are a vital source of growth and innovation.[117] Therefore, a key role of strategic leaders is to encourage and promote innovation by pursuing entrepreneurial opportunities.[118]

One way to encourage innovation is to invest in opportunities as real options—that is, invest in an opportunity in order to provide the potential option of taking advantage of the opportunity at some point in the future.[119] For example, a firm might buy a piece of land to have the option to build on it at some time in the future should the company need more space and should that location increase in value to the company. Firms might enter strategic alliances for similar reasons. In this instance, a firm might form an alliance to have the option of acquiring the partner later or of building a stronger relationship with it (e.g., developing a joint new venture).[120]

In Chapter 13, we describe how large firms use strategic entrepreneurship to pursue entrepreneurial opportunities and to gain first-mover advantages. Small and medium-sized firms also rely on strategic entrepreneurship when trying to develop innovations as the foundation for profitable growth. In firms of all sizes, strategic entrepreneurship is more likely to be successful when employees have an entrepreneurial mind-set.[121] Five dimensions characterize a firm's entrepreneurial mind-set: autonomy, innovativeness, risk taking, proactiveness, and competitive aggressiveness.[122] In combination, these dimensions influence the actions a firm takes to be innovative and launch new ventures. In sum, strategic leaders with an entrepreneurial mind-set are committed to pursuing profitable growth.[123]

Autonomy, the first of an entrepreneurial orientation's five dimensions, allows employees to take actions that are free of organizational constraints and permits individuals and groups to be self-directed. The second dimension, *innovativeness,* "reflects a firm's tendency to engage in and support new ideas, novelty, experimentation, and creative processes that may result in new products, services, or technological processes."[124] Cultures with a tendency toward innovativeness encourage employees to think beyond existing knowledge, technologies, and parameters to find creative ways to add value. *Risk taking* reflects a willingness by employees and their firm to accept risks when pursuing entrepreneurial opportunities. Assuming significant levels of debt and allocating large amounts of other resources (e.g., people) to projects that may not be completed are examples of these risks. The fourth dimension of an entrepreneurial orientation, *proactiveness,* describes a firm's ability to be a market leader rather than a follower. Proactive organizational cultures constantly use processes to anticipate future market needs and to satisfy them before competitors learn how to do so. Finally, *competitive aggressiveness* is a firm's propensity to take actions that allow it to consistently and substantially outperform its rivals.[125]

Changing the Organizational Culture and Restructuring

Changing a firm's organizational culture is more difficult than maintaining it; however, effective strategic leaders recognize when change is needed. Incremental changes to the firm's culture typically are used to implement strategies.[126] More significant and sometimes even radical changes to organizational culture support selecting strategies that differ from those the firm has implemented historically. Regardless of the reasons for change, shaping and reinforcing a new culture require effective communication and problem solving, along with selecting the right people (those who have the values desired for the organization), engaging in effective performance appraisals (establishing goals and measuring individual performance toward goals that fit in with the new core values), and using appropriate reward systems (rewarding the desired behaviors that reflect the new core values).[127]

Evidence suggests that cultural changes succeed only when the firm's CEO, other key top management team members, and middle-level managers actively support them.[128] To effect change, middle-level managers in particular need to be highly disciplined to energize the culture and foster alignment with the strategic vision.[129]

Emphasizing Ethical Practices

The effectiveness of processes used to implement the firm's strategies increases when they are based on ethical practices. Ethical companies encourage and enable people at all organizational levels to act ethically when doing what is necessary to implement strategies. In turn, ethical practices and the judgment on which they are based create "social capital" in the organization, increasing the "goodwill available to individuals and groups" in the organization.[130] Alternatively, when unethical practices evolve in an organization, they may become acceptable to many managers and employees. One study found that in these circumstances, managers were particularly likely to engage in unethical practices to meet their goals when current efforts to meet them were insufficient.[131]

To properly influence employees' judgment and behavior, ethical practices must shape the firm's decision-making process and must be an integral part of organizational culture. In fact, research evidence suggests that a value-based culture is the most effective means of ensuring that employees comply with the firm's ethical requirements.[132] As we explained in Chapter 10, managers may act opportunistically, making decisions that are in their own best interests but not in the firm's best interests when facing lax expectations regarding ethical behavior. In other words, managers acting opportunistically take advantage of their positions, making decisions that benefit themselves to the detriment of the firm's stakeholders.[133] But strategic leaders are most likely to integrate ethical values into their decisions when the company has explicit ethics codes, the code is integrated into the business through extensive ethics training, and shareholders expect ethical behavior.[134]

Firms should employ ethical strategic leaders—leaders who include ethical practices as part of their strategic direction for the firm, who desire to do the right thing, and for whom honesty, trust, and integrity are important.[135] Strategic leaders who consistently display these qualities inspire employees as they work with others to develop and support an organizational culture in which ethical practices are the expected behavioral norms.[136]

Strategic leaders can take several actions to develop an ethical organizational culture. Examples of these actions include (1) establishing and communicating specific goals to describe the firm's ethical standards (e.g., developing and disseminating a code of conduct); (2) continuously revising and updating the code of conduct, based on inputs from people throughout the firm and from other stakeholders (e.g., customers and suppliers); (3) disseminating the code of conduct to all stakeholders to inform them of the firm's ethical standards and practices; (4) developing and implementing methods and procedures to use in achieving the firm's ethical standards (e.g., using internal auditing practices that are consistent with the standards); (5) creating and using explicit reward systems that recognize acts of courage (e.g., rewarding those who use proper channels and procedures to report observed wrongdoings); and (6) creating a work environment in which all people are treated with dignity.[137] The effectiveness of these actions increases when they are taken simultaneously and thereby are mutually supportive. When strategic leaders and others throughout the firm fail to take actions such as these—perhaps because an ethical culture has not been created—problems are likely to occur. As we discuss next, formal organizational controls can help prevent further problems and reinforce better ethical practices.[138]

Establishing Balanced Organizational Controls

Organizational controls are basic to a capitalistic system and have long been viewed as an important part of strategy implementation processes.[139] Controls are necessary to help ensure that firms achieve their desired outcomes.[140] Defined as the "formal, information-based . . . procedures used by managers to maintain or alter patterns in organizational activities," controls help strategic leaders build credibility, demonstrate the value of strategies to the firm's stakeholders, and promote and support strategic change.[141] Most critically, controls provide the parameters for implementing strategies as well as the corrective actions to be taken when implementation-related adjustments are required.

In this chapter, we focus on two organizational controls—strategic and financial—that were introduced in Chapter 11. Our discussion of organizational controls here emphasizes strategic and financial controls because strategic leaders, especially those at the top of the organization, are responsible for their development and effective use.

As we explained in Chapter 11, financial control focuses on short-term financial outcomes. In contrast, strategic control focuses on the *content* of strategic actions rather than their *outcomes.* Some strategic actions can be correct but still result in poor financial outcomes because of external conditions such as a recession in the economy, unexpected domestic or foreign government actions, or natural disasters. Therefore, emphasizing financial controls often produces more short-term and risk-averse managerial decisions, because financial outcomes may be caused by events beyond managers' direct control. Alternatively, strategic control encourages lower-level managers to make decisions that incorporate moderate and acceptable levels of risk because outcomes are shared between the business-level executives making strategic proposals and the corporate-level executives evaluating them.

The challenge strategic leaders face is to verify that their firm is emphasizing financial and strategic controls so that firm performance improves. The Balanced Scorecard is a tool that helps strategic leaders assess the effectiveness of the controls.

The Balanced Scorecard

The **balanced scorecard** is a framework firms can use to verify that they have established both strategic and financial controls to assess their performance.[142] This technique is most appropriate for use when dealing with business-level strategies; however, it can also be used with the other strategies firms may choose to implement (e.g., corporate level, international, and cooperative).

The **balanced scorecard** is a framework firms can use to verify that they have established both strategic and financial controls to assess their performance.

The underlying premise of the balanced scorecard is that firms jeopardize their future performance possibilities when financial controls are emphasized at the expense of strategic controls,[143] in that financial controls provide feedback about outcomes achieved from past actions, but do not communicate the drivers of future performance.[144] Thus, an overemphasis on financial controls has the potential to promote managerial behavior that sacrifices the firm's long-term, value-creating potential for short-term performance gains.[145] An appropriate balance of strategic controls and financial controls, rather than an overemphasis on either, allows firms to effectively monitor their performance.

Four perspectives are integrated to form the balanced scorecard framework: *financial* (concerned with growth, profitability, and risk from the shareholders' perspective), *customer* (concerned with the amount of value customers perceive was created by the firm's products), *internal business processes* (with a focus on the priorities for various business processes that create customer and shareholder satisfaction), and *learning and growth* (concerned with the firm's effort to create a climate that supports change, innovation, and growth). Thus, using the balanced scorecard framework allows the firm to understand how it looks to shareholders (financial perspective), how customers view it (customer perspective), the processes it must emphasize to successfully use its competitive advantage (internal perspective), and what it can do to improve its performance in order to grow (learning and growth perspective).[146] Generally speaking, strategic controls tend to be emphasized when the firm assesses its performance relative to the learning and growth perspective, whereas financial controls are emphasized when assessing performance in terms of the financial perspective.

Firms use different criteria to measure their standing relative to the scorecard's four perspectives. We show sample criteria in Figure 12.5. The firm should select the number of criteria that will allow it to have both a strategic understanding and a financial understanding of its performance without becoming immersed in too many details.[147] For example, we know from research that a firm's innovation, quality of its goods and services, growth of its sales, and its profitability are all interrelated.[148]

Strategic leaders play an important role in determining a proper balance between strategic controls and financial controls, whether they are in single-business firms or large diversified firms. A proper balance between controls is important, in that "wealth creation for organizations where strategic leadership is exercised is possible because these leaders make appropriate investments for future viability [through strategic control], while maintaining an appropriate level of financial stability in the present [through financial control]."[149] In fact, most corporate restructuring is designed to refocus the firm on its core businesses, thereby allowing top executives to reestablish strategic control of their separate business units.[150]

Successfully using strategic control frequently is integrated with appropriate autonomy for the various subunits so that they can gain a competitive advantage in their respective markets.[151] Strategic control can be used to promote the sharing of both tangible and intangible resources among interdependent businesses within a firm's portfolio. In addition, the autonomy provided allows the flexibility necessary to take advantage of

Figure 12.5 Strategic Controls and Financial Controls in a Balanced Scorecard Framework

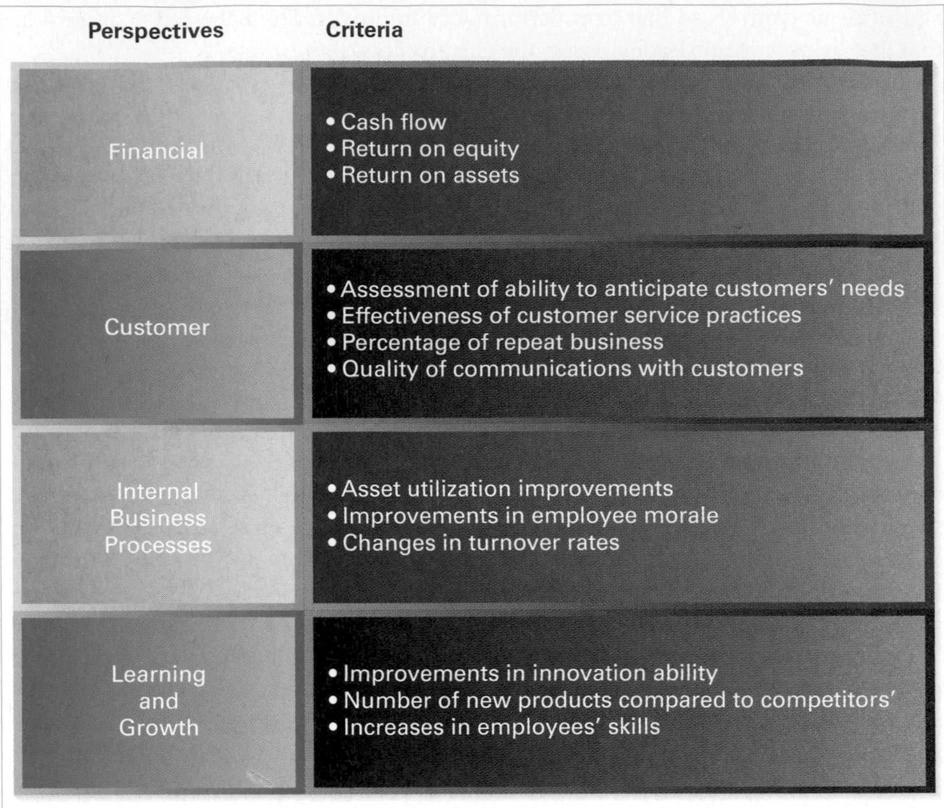

Perspectives	Criteria
Financial	• Cash flow • Return on equity • Return on assets
Customer	• Assessment of ability to anticipate customers' needs • Effectiveness of customer service practices • Percentage of repeat business • Quality of communications with customers
Internal Business Processes	• Asset utilization improvements • Improvements in employee morale • Changes in turnover rates
Learning and Growth	• Improvements in innovation ability • Number of new products compared to competitors' • Increases in employees' skills

specific marketplace opportunities. As a result, strategic leadership promotes simultaneous use of strategic control and autonomy.[152]

The balanced scorecard is being used by car manufacturer Porsche. After this manufacturer of sought-after sports cars regained its market-leading position, it implemented a balanced scorecard approach in an effort to maintain this position. In particular, Porsche used the balanced scorecard to promote learning and continuously improve the business. For example, knowledge was collected from all Porsche dealerships throughout the world. The instrument used to collect the information was referred to as "Porsche Key Performance Indicators." The fact that Porsche is now the world's most profitable automaker suggests the value the firm gained and is gaining by using the balanced scorecard as a foundation for simultaneously emphasizing strategic and financial controls.[153]

Porsche used the balanced scorecard to promote learning and continuously improve the business.

As we have explained, strategic leaders are critical to a firm's ability to successfully use all parts of the strategic management process. What does the future hold for strategic leaders? We try to describe that future in the Strategic Focus. As you will see, the future for strategic leaders is likely to be challenging. At the same time, the work of strategic leaders will remain exciting and will still be a set of actions that, when executed successfully, has a strong possibility of creating positive outcomes for all of a firm's stakeholders.

Strategic Focus Strategic Focus **Strategic Focus**

What's Next? Strategic Leadership in the Future

The essence of the expectations for a firm's key strategic leaders is captured by the details of the strategic management process. Stated simply, strategic leaders must design a process (such as the one shown in Figure 1.1, on page 5) their firm will use as the foundation for earning above-average returns and consistently outperforming rivals. The simplicity of this statement belies its complexity though, whether we are talking about strategic management today or strategic management for tomorrow.

What do we know about the future of strategic leadership and the tasks future strategic leaders may encounter? Even though predicting the future is risky, several realities and expectations seem likely.

First, it is likely that tomorrow's strategic leaders will feel even more stress than do their counterparts of today. One reason for this expectation is that those for whom a firm's key strategic leaders work (the board of directors in the case of the CEO and the CEO in the instance of top-level executives) rightfully have significant expectations of strategic leaders. The past successes of individuals chosen as strategic leaders are assumed to predict even greater success in the future. Strategic leadership's demands create stress that leaders must acknowledge and with which they must learn how to cope if they are to successfully discharge their responsibilities.

Another reasonably safe prediction is that all stakeholders will continue to expect the firm's board of directors to better represent their interests. Even today, board members are on the "hot seat" to improve their performance as agents for each stakeholder group. In turn, the expectation of better board performance will find board members holding strategic leaders more accountable for achieving positive outcomes with respect to (1) strategy formulation and execution, (2) the effective handling of crises, particularly financial ones, (3) being able to meaningfully link top-level managerial pay to performance, and (4) representing the company's best interests at all times. Tomorrow's board members and a firm's strategic leaders will undoubtedly continue to face high levels of accountability for their actions and the outcomes they achieve or fail to achieve.

What can individuals do to enhance their ability to be an effective strategic leader in tomorrow's organizations? We'll identify a few actions here. First, strategic leaders should be continuously curious so that they will have the foundation for seeking to learn everything they can from every person with whom they have contact. Greater diversity of what a person "knows" increases the likelihood an individual will examine the widest possible range of issues when making decisions related to effective strategic management. Strategic leaders should rely on their curiosity to spot patterns that suggest future conditions. Once spotted, these individuals should think deeply about the implications of those patterns for their firm's success. Additionally, tomorrow's strategic leaders should place even greater emphasis on the "simple rules" of effective strategic leadership than is the case today. These simply yet vital rules are the following:

1. Leaders make work about others, not about themselves. Once a person becomes a strategic leader, everything that person does is about "them" (the stakeholders, but especially employees) while nothing is about the leader.
2. Leaders learn everything possible about their company from both strategic and tactical perspectives.
3. Leaders hold individuals accountable for their outcomes. However, leaders must make themselves the most accountable for overall performance.
4. Leaders shoulder all responsibility for all parts of their job; they always take the blame for mistakes and distribute the credit for successes to others.

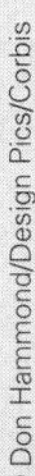

Sources: N. Byrnes & J. Sasseen, 2007, Board of hard knocks, *BusinessWeek*, January 22, 36–39; K. Sulkowicz, 2007, Stressed for success, *BusinessWeek*, May 21, 18; J. Useem, 2007, What's next? *Fortune*, February 5, 44–54; M. Heffernan, 2006, Lessons from a great thinker, *Fast Company Online*, http://www.fastcompany.com, January 2; L. Lavelle, 2005, Three simple rules Carly ignored, *BusinessWeek*, February 28, 46.

Summary

- Effective strategic leadership is a prerequisite to successfully using the strategic management process. Strategic leadership entails the ability to anticipate events, envision possibilities, maintain flexibility, and empower others to create strategic change.
- Top-level managers are an important resource for firms to develop and exploit competitive advantages. In addition, when they and their work are valuable, rare, imperfectly imitable, and nonsubstitutable, strategic leaders can themselves be a source of competitive advantage.
- The top management team is composed of key managers who play a critical role in selecting and implementing the firm's strategies. Generally, they are officers of the corporation or members of the board of directors.
- The top management team's characteristics, a firm's strategies, and its performance are all interrelated. For example, a top management team with significant marketing and R&D knowledge positively contributes to the firm's use of growth strategies. Overall, having diverse skills increases most top management teams' effectiveness.
- Typically, performance improves when the board of directors is involved in shaping a firm's strategic direction. However, when the CEO has a great deal of power, the board may be less involved in decisions about strategy formulation and implementation. By appointing people to the board and simultaneously serving as CEO and chair of the board, CEOs increase their power.
- In managerial succession, strategic leaders are selected from either the internal or the external managerial labor market. Because of the effect on performance, selection of strategic leaders has implications for a firm's effectiveness. Companies use a variety of reasons for looking either internally or externally when choosing the firm's strategic leaders. In most instances, the internal market is used to select the CEO; but the number of outsiders chosen is increasing. Outsiders often are selected to initiate changes.
- Effective strategic leadership has five major components: determining the firm's strategic direction, effectively managing the firm's resource portfolio (including exploiting and maintaining core competencies and managing human capital and social capital), sustaining an effective organizational culture, emphasizing ethical practices, and establishing balanced organizational controls.
- Strategic leaders must develop the firm's strategic direction. The strategic direction specifies the image and character the firm wants to develop over time. To form the strategic direction, strategic leaders evaluate the conditions (e.g., opportunities and threats in the external environment) they expect their firm to face over the next three to five years.
- Strategic leaders must ensure that their firm exploits its core competencies, which are used to produce and deliver products that create value for customers, when implementing its strategies. In related diversified and large firms in particular, core competencies are exploited by sharing them across units and products.
- The abililty to manage the firm's resource portfolio is a critical element of strategic leadership and processes used to effectively implement the firm's strategy. Managing the resource portfolio includes integrating resources to create capabilities and leveraging those capabilities through strategies to build competitive advantages. Human capital and social capital are perhaps the most important resources.
- As a part of managing the firm's resources, strategic leaders must develop a firm's human capital. Effective strategic leaders view human capital as a resource to be maximized—not as a cost to be minimized. Resulting from this perspective is the development and use of programs intended to train current and future strategic leaders to build the skills needed to nurture the rest of the firm's human capital.
- Effective strategic leaders also build and maintain internal and external social capital. Internal social capital promotes cooperation and coordination within and across units in the firm. External social capital provides access to resources the firm needs to compete effectively.
- Shaping the firm's culture is a central task of effective strategic leadership. An appropriate organizational culture encourages the development of an entrepreneurial orientation among employees and an ability to change the culture as necessary.
- In ethical organizations, employees are encouraged to exercise ethical judgment and to always act ethically. Improved ethical practices foster social capital. Setting specific goals to describe the firm's ethical standards, using a code of conduct, rewarding ethical behaviors, and creating a work environment where all people are treated with dignity are examples of actions facilitating and supporting ethical behavior.
- Developing and using balanced organizational controls is the final component of effective strategic leadership. The balanced scorecard is a tool that measures the effectiveness of the firm's strategic and financial controls. An effective balance between strategic and financial controls allows for flexible use of core competencies, but within the parameters of the firm's financial position.

Review Questions

1. What is strategic leadership? In what ways are top executives considered important resources for an organization?
2. What is a top management team, and how does it affect a firm's performance and its abilities to innovate and make effective strategic changes?
3. How do the internal and external managerial labor markets affect the managerial succession process?
4. What is the effect of strategic leadership on determining the firm's strategic direction?
5. How do strategic leaders effectively manage their firm's resource portfolio such that its core competencies are exploited and the human capital and social capital are leveraged to achieve a competitive advantage?
6. What is organizational culture? What must strategic leaders do to develop and sustain an effective organizational culture?
7. As a strategic leader, what actions could you take to establish and emphasize ethical practices in your firm?
8. What are organizational controls? Why are strategic controls and financial controls important aspects of the strategic management process?

Experiential Exercises

Exercise 1: Executive succession

For this exercise, you will identify and analyze a case of CEO succession. Working in small groups, find a publicly held firm that has changed CEOs. The turnover event must have happened at least twelve months ago but no more than twenty-four months ago. Use a combination of company documents and news articles to answer the following questions:

1. Why did the CEO leave? Common reasons for CEO turnover include death or illness, retirement, accepting a new position, change in ownership or control, or termination. In cases of termination, there is often no official statement as to why the CEO departed. Consequently, you may have to rely on news articles that may speculate that a CEO was fired or forced to resign.
2. Did the replacement CEO come from inside the organization or outside?
3. What are the similarities and differences between the new CEO and the CEO who was replaced? Possible comparison items could include functional experience, industry experience, etc. If your library has a subscription to Hoovers Online, you can find information on top managers through this resource.
4. At the time of the succession event, how did the firm's financial performance compare to industry norms? Has the firm's standing relative to the industry changed since the new CEO took over?
5. Has the firm made major strategic changes since the succession event? For example, has the firm made major acquisitions or divestitures since the succession event? Launched or closed down product lines?

Create a PowerPoint presentation that presents your answers to each of the above questions. Your presentation should be brief, consisting of no more than five to seven slides.

Exercise 2: Balanced Scorecard and the Baldridge Quality Award

The chapter described the role of the business scorecard in facilitating effective strategic leadership practices. For this exercise, you will be asked to compare and contrast the balanced scorecard against the Baldridge Quality Award Criteria. The Baldridge Award was created in 1988 to recognize firms that were leaders in global competitiveness through product and process quality initiatives. The Award is named in honor of Malcolm Baldridge, who was Secretary of Commerce in the United States during the 1980s. The Web site of the Baldridge Award can be found at:

http://www.quality.nist.gov/

Working in small groups, prepare a brief write-up (2–3 pages maximum) that answers the following questions:

1. What similarities and differences exist in the goals of the balanced scorecard and Baldridge Award frameworks?
2. What are the similarities and differences in the evaluation metrics used in these frameworks?
3. From your analysis, are these competing or complementary frameworks? Or does one have no relevance to the other? What recommendation would you make to a firm that was considering implementing both frameworks concurrently?

Notes

1. E. F. Goldman, 2007, Strategic thinking at the top, *MIT Sloan Management Review,* 48(4): 75–81.
2. L. Bassi & D. McMurrer, 2007, Maximizing your return on people, *Harvard Business Review,* 85(3): 115–123; R. D. Ireland & M. A. Hitt, 2005, Achieving and maintaining strategic competitiveness in the 21st century: The role of strategic leadership, *Academy of Management Executive,* 19: 63–77.
3. J. P. Kotter, 2007, Leading change: Why transformation efforts fail, *Harvard Business Review,* 85(1): 96–103.
4. M. A. Hitt, C. Miller, & A. Collella, 2009, *Organizational Behavior: A Strategic Approach,* 2nd ed., New York: John Wiley & Sons; M. A. Hitt & R. D. Ireland, 2002, The essence of strategic leadership: Managing human and social capital, *Journal of Leadership and Organizational Studies,* 9: 3–14.
5. D. A. Ready & J. A. Conger, 2007, Make your company a talent factory, *Harvard Business Review,* 85(6): 69–77.
6. D. Roberts & C.-C. Tschang, 2007, China's rising leaders, *BusinessWeek,* October 1, 33–35.
7. M. Conlin, 2007, Go-go—going to pieces in China, *BusinessWeek,* April 23, 88.
8. P. A. Gloor & S. M. Cooper, 2007, The new principles of a swarm business, *MIT Sloan Management Review,* 48(3): 81–85; A. S. DeNisi, M. A. Hitt, & S. E. Jackson, 2003, The knowledge-based approach to sustainable competitive advantage, in S. E. Jackson, M. A. Hitt, & A. S. DeNisi (eds.), *Managing Knowledge for Sustained Competitive Advantage,* San Francisco: Jossey-Bass, 3–33.
9. L. Bossidy, 2007, What your leader expects of you: And what you should expect in return, *Harvard Business Review,* 85(4): 58–65; J. E. Post, L. E. Preston, & S. Sachs, 2002, Managing the extended enterprise: The new stakeholder view, *California Management Review,* 45(1): 6–28.
10. A. McKee & D. Massimilian, 2007, Resonant leadership: A new kind of leadership for the digital age, *Journal of Business Strategy,* 27(5): 45–49.
11. E. Baraldi, R. Brennan, D. Harrison, A. Tunisini, & J. Zolkiewski, 2007, Strategic thinking and the IMP approach: A comparative analysis, *Industrial Marketing Management,* 36: 879–894; C. L. Shook, R. L. Priem, & J. E. McGee, 2003, Venture creation and the enterprising individual: A review and synthesis, *Journal of Management,* 29: 379–399.
12. K. K. Reardon, 2007, Courage as a skill, *Harvard Business Review,* 85(1): 48–564.
13. R. A. Burgleman & A. S. Grove, 2007, Let chaos reign, then rein in chaos—repeatedly: Managing strategic dynamics for corporate longevity, *Strategic Management Journal,* 28: 965–979.
14. S. Borener, S. A. Eisenbeliss, & D. Griesser, 2007, Follower behavior and organizational performance: The impact of transformational leaders, *Journal of Leadership & Organizational Studies,* 13(3): 15–26; D. Vera & M. Crossan, 2004, Strategic leadership and organizational learning, *Academy of Management Review,* 29: 222–240.
15. T. G. Buchholz, 2007, The Kroc legacy at McDonald's, *The Conference Review Board,* July/August, 14–15.
16. H. S. Givray, 2007, When CEOs aren't leaders, *BusinessWeek,* September 3, 102.
17. D. Goleman, 2004, What makes a leader? *Harvard Business Review,* 82(1): 82–91.
18. 2007, How they do it, *Fortune,* October 1, 111.
19. J. L. Morrow, Jr., D. G. Sirmon, M. A. Hitt, & T. R. Holcomb, 2007, Creating value in the face of declining performance: Firm strategies and organizational recovery, *Strategic Management Journal,* 28: 271–283; R. Castanias & C. Helfat, 2001, The managerial rents model: Theory and empirical analysis, *Journal of Management,* 27: 661–678.
20. H. G. Barkema & O. Shvyrkov, 2007, Does top management team diversity promote or hamper foreign expansion? *Strategic Management Journal,* 28: 663–680; M. Beer & R. Eisenstat, 2000, The silent killers of strategy implementation and learning, *Sloan Management Review,* 41(4): 29–40.
21. V. Santos & T. Garcia, 2007, The complexity of the organizational renewal decision: The management role, *Leadership & Organization Development Journal,* 28: 336–355; M. Wright, R. E. Hoskisson, L. W. Busenitz, & J. Dial, 2000, Entrepreneurial growth through privatization: The upside of management buyouts, *Academy of Management Review,* 25: 591–601; N. Rajagopalan, A. M. Rasheed, & D. K. Datta, 1993, Strategic decision processes: Critical review and future directions, *Journal of Management,* 19: 349–384.
22. Y. L. Doz & M. Kosonen, 2007, The new deal at the top, *Harvard Business Review,* 85(6): 98–104; W. G. Rowe, 2001, Creating wealth in organizations: The role of strategic leadership, *Academy of Management Executive,* 15(1): 81–94.
23. A. S. Tsui, Z.-X. Zhang, H. Wang, K. R. Xin, & J. B. Wu, 2006, Unpacking the relationship between CEO leadership behavior and organizational culture, *The Leadership Quarterly,* 17: 113–137; J. A. Petrick & J. F. Quinn, 2001, The challenge of leadership accountability for integrity capacity as a strategic asset, *Journal of Business Ethics,* 34: 331–343.
24. D. G. Sirmon, S. Gove, & M. A. Hitt, 2008, Resource management in dyadic competitive rivalry: The effects of resource bundling and deployment, *Academy of Management Journal,* in press; R. Martin, 2007, How successful leaders think, *Harvard Business Review,* 85(6): 60–67.
25. M. L. A. Hayward, V. P. Rindova, & T. G. Pollock, 2004, Believing one's own press: The causes and consequences of CEO celebrity, *Strategic Management Journal,* 25: 637–653.
26. N. J. Hiller & D. C. Hambrick, 2005, Conceptualizing executive hubris: The role of (hyper-) core self-evaluations in strategic decision making, *Strategic Management Journal,* 26: 297–319.
27. A. M. L. Raes, U. Glunk, M. G. Heijitjes, & R. A. Roe, 2007, Top management team and middle managers, *Small Group Research,* 38: 360–386; I. Goll, R. Sambharya, & L. Tucci, 2001, Top management team composition, corporate ideology, and firm performance, *Management International Review,* 41(2): 109–129.
28. J. Bunderson, 2003, Team member functional background and involvement in management teams: Direct effects and the moderating role of power and centralization, *Academy of Management Journal,* 46: 458–474; L. Markoczy, 2001, Consensus formation during strategic change, *Strategic Management Journal,* 22: 1013–1031.
29. C. Pegels, Y. Song, & B. Yang, 2000, Management heterogeneity, competitive interaction groups, and firm performance, *Strategic Management Journal,* 21: 911–923.
30. R. Rico, E. Molleman, M. Sanchez-Manzanares, & G. S. Van der Vegt, 2007, The effects of diversity faultlines and team task autonomy on decision quality and social integration, *Journal of Management,* 33: 111–132.
31. A. Srivastava, K. M. Bartol, & E. A. Locke, 2006, Empowering leadership in management teams: Effects on knowledge sharing, efficacy, and performance, *Academy of Management Journal,* 49: 1239–1251; D. Knight, C. L. Pearce, K. G. Smith, J. D. Olian, H. P. Sims, K. A. Smith, & P. Flood, 1999, Top management team diversity, group process, and strategic consensus, *Strategic Management Journal,* 20: 446–465.
32. B. J. Olson, S. Parayitam, & Y. Bao, 2007, Strategic decision making: The effects of cognitive diversity, conflict, and trust on decision outcomes, *Journal of Management,* 33: 196–222; T. Simons, L. H. Pelled, & K. A. Smith, 1999, Making use of difference, diversity, debate, and decision comprehensiveness in top management teams, *Academy of Management Journal,* 42: 662–673.

33. S. Finkelstein, D. C. Hambrick, & A. A. Cannella, Jr., 2008, *Strategic Leadership: Top Executives and Their Effects on Organizations,* New York: Oxford University Press.
34. S. Barsade, A. Ward, J. Turner, & J. Sonnenfeld, 2000, To your heart's content: A model of affective diversity in top management teams, *Administrative Science Quarterly,* 45: 802–836; C. C. Miller, L. M. Burke, & W. H. Glick, 1998, Cognitive diversity among upper-echelon executives: Implications for strategic decision processes, *Strategic Management Journal,* 19: 39–58.
35. B. J. Avolio & S. S. Kahai, 2002, Adding the "e" to e-leadership: How it may impact your leadership, *Organizational Dynamics,* 31: 325–338.
36. Z. Simsek, J. F. Veiga, M. L. Lubatkin, & R. H. Dino, 2005, Modeling the multilevel determinants of top management team behavioral integration, *Academy of Management Journal,* 48: 69–84.
37. U. Daellenbach, A. McCarthy, & T. Schoenecker, 1999, Commitment to innovation: The impact of top management team characteristics, *R&D Management,* 29(3): 199–208; D. K. Datta & J. P. Guthrie, 1994, Executive succession: Organizational antecedents of CEO characteristics, *Strategic Management Journal,* 15: 569–577.
38. M. Jensen & E. J. Zajac, 2004, Corporate elites and corporate strategy: How demographic preferences and structural position shape the scope of the firm, *Strategic Management Journal,* 25: 507–524.
39. W. B. Werther, 2003, Strategic change and leader-follower alignment, *Organizational Dynamics,* 32: 32–45; S. Wally & M. Becerra, 2001, Top management team characteristics and strategic changes in international diversification: The case of U.S. multinationals in the European community, *Group & Organization Management,* 26: 165–188.
40. Y. Zhang & N. Rajagopalan, 2003, Explaining the new CEO origin: Firm versus industry antecedents, *Academy of Management Journal,* 46: 327–338.
41. T. Dvir, D. Eden, B. J. Avolio, & B. Shamir, 2002, Impact of transformational leadership on follower development and performance: A field experiment, *Academy of Management Journal,* 45: 735–744.
42. C. Thomas, D. Kidd, & C. Fernandez-Araoz, 2007, Are you underutilizing your board? *MIT Sloan Management Review,* 48(2): 71–76.
43. F. Adjaoud, D. Zeghal & S. Andaleeb, 2007, The effect of board's quality on performance: A study of Canadian firms, *Corporate Governance: An International Review,* 15: 623–635; L. Tihanyi, R. A. Johnson, R. E. Hoskisson, & M. A. Hitt, 2003, Institutional ownership and international diversification: The effects of boards of directors and technological opportunity, *Academy of Management Journal,* 46: 195–211.
44. B. R. Golden & E. J. Zajac, 2001, When will boards influence strategy? Inclination times power equals strategic change, *Strategic Management Journal,* 22: 1087–1111.
45. M. Carpenter & J. Westphal, 2001, Strategic context of external network ties: Examining the impact of director appointments on board involvement in strategic decision making, *Academy of Management Journal,* 44: 639–660.
46. M. A. Rutherford & A. K. Buchholtz, 2007, Investigating the relationship between board characteristics and board information, *Corporate Governance: An International Review,* 15: 576–584.
47. X. Huafang & Y. Jianguo, 2007, Ownership structure, board composition and corporate voluntary disclosure: Evidence from listed companies in China, *Managerial Auditing Journal,* 22: 604–619.
48. J. Coles, N. Sen, & V. McWilliams, 2001, An examination of the relationship of governance mechanisms to performance, *Journal of Management,* 27: 23–50; J. Coles & W. Hesterly, 2000, Independence of the chairman and board composition: Firm choices and shareholder value, *Journal of Management,* 26: 195–214.
49. C. M. Daily & D. R. Dalton, 1995, CEO and director turnover in failing firms: An illusion of change? *Strategic Management Journal,* 16: 393–400.
50. D. Miller, I. LeBreton-Miller, & B. Scholnick, 2007, Stewardship vs. stagnation: An empirical comparison of small family and non-family businesses, *Journal of Management Studies,* in press; G. J. Nicholson & G. C. Kiel, 2007, Can directors impact performance? A case-based test of three theories of corporate governance, *Corporate Govenance: An International Review,* 15: 585–608; J. H. Davis, F. D. Schoorman, & L. Donaldson, 1997, Toward a stewardship theory of management, *Academy of Management Review,* 22: 20–47.
51. J. G. Combs & M. S. Skill, 2003, Managerialist and human capital explanations for key executive pay premiums: A contingency perspective, *Academy of Management Journal,* 46: 63–73.
52. J. Peterson, 2007, House wants investors to vote on executive pay, *Los Angeles Times Online,* http://www.latimes.com, April 27.
53. N. Rajagopalan & D. Datta, 1996, CEO characteristics: Does industry matter? *Academy of Management Journal,* 39: 197–215.
54. R. A. Johnson, R. E. Hoskisson, & M. A. Hitt, 1993, Board involvement in restructuring: The effect of board versus managerial controls and characteristics, *Strategic Management Journal,* 14 (Special Issue): 33–50.
55. Z. Simsek, 2007, CEO tenure and organizational performance: An intervening model, *Strategic Management Journal,* 28: 653–662.
56. M. Schneider, 2002, A stakeholder model of organizational leadership, *Organization Science,* 13: 209–220.
57. M. Sorcher & J. Brant, 2002, Are you picking the right leaders? *Harvard Business Review,* 80(2): 78–85; D. A. Waldman, G. G. Ramirez, R. J. House, & P. Puranam, 2001, Does leadership matter? CEO leadership attributes and profitability under conditions of perceived environmental uncertainty, *Academy of Management Journal,* 44: 134–143.
58. J. Werdigier, 2007, UBS not willing to talk about departure of chief, *New York Times Online,* http://www.nytimes.com, July 7.
59. W. Shen & A. A. Cannella, 2002, Revisiting the performance consequences of CEO succession: The impacts of successor type, postsuccession senior executive turnover, and departing CEO tenure, *Academy of Management Journal,* 45: 717–734.
60. D. Ulrich & N. Smallwood, 2007, Building a leadership brand, *Harvard Business Review,* 85(7/8): 93–100.
61. G. A. Ballinger & F. D. Schoorman, 2007, Individual reactions to leadership succession in workgroups, *Academy of Management Review,* 32: 116–136; R. E. Hoskisson, D. Yiu, & H. Kim, 2000, Capital and labor market congruence and corporate governance: Effects on corporate innovation and global competitiveness, in S. S. Cohen & G. Boyd (eds.), *Corporate Governance and Globalization,* Northampton, MA: Edward Elgar, 129–154.
62. M. Hurlbert, 2005, Lo! A white knight! So why isn't the market cheering? *New York Times Online,* http://www.nytimes.com, March 27.
63. J. Weber, 2007, The accidental CEO, *BusinessWeek,* April 23, 64–72.
64. W. Shen & A. A. Cannella, 2003, Will succession planning increase shareholder wealth? Evidence from investor reactions to relay CEO successions, *Strategic Management Journal,* 24: 191–198.
65. M. Maynard, 2007, Importing chiefs, Detroit reflects in its "car guys," *New York Times Online,* http;//www.nytimes.com, August 12.
66. A. Bianco, 2007, Wal-Mart's midlife crisis, *BusinessWeek,* April 30, 46–56.
67. M. Barbaro, 2007, Wal-Mart apparel chief resigns as sales lag, *New York Times Online,* http://nytimes.com, July 21.
68. R. Berner, 2007, My year at Wal-Mart, *BusinessWeek,* February 12, 70–73.
69. K. Belson & T. Zaun, 2005, Land of the rising gaijin chief executive, *New York Times Online,* http://www.nytimes.com, March 27.
70. P. M. Lee & E. H. James, 2007, She'-E-Os: Gender effects and investor reactions to the announcements of top executive appointments, *Strategic Management Journal,* 28: 227–41.
71. M. K. Ryan & S. A. Haslam, 2007, The glass cliff: Exploring the dynamics surrounding the appointment of women to precarious leadership positions, *Academy of Management Review,* 32: 549–572.
72. D. Brady, 2007, Getting to the corner office, *BusinessWeek,* March 12, 104.

73. J. Welch & S. Welch, 2007, Bosses who get it all wrong, *BusinessWeek,* July 23, 88.
74. J. O'Toole & E. E. Lawler, Jr., 2006, The choices managers make—or don't make, *The Conference Board,* September/October, 24–29.
75. M. A. Hitt, B. W. Keats, & E. Yucel, 2003, Strategic leadership in global business organizations, in W. H. Mobley & P. W. Dorfman (eds.), *Advances in Global Leadership,* Oxford, UK: Elsevier Science, Ltd., 9–35.
76. I. M. Levin, 2000, Vision revisited, *Journal of Applied Behavioral Science,* 36: 91–107.
77. J. Welch & S. Welch, 2006, It's not about empty suits, *BusinessWeek,* October 16, 132.
78. J. Welch & S. Welch, 2007, When to talk, when to balk, *BusinessWeek,* April 30, 102.
79. J. Barney & A. M. Arikan, 2001, The resource-based view: Origins and implications, in M. A. Hitt, R. E. Freeman, & J. S. Harrison (eds.), *Handbook of Strategic Management,* Oxford, UK: Blackwell Publishers, 124–188.
80. E. T. Prince, 2005, The fiscal behavior of CEOs, *Managerial Economics,* 46(3): 23–26.
81. R. A. Burgelman, 2001, *Strategy Is Destiny: How Strategy-Making Shapes a Company's Future,* New York: The Free Press.
82. D. J. Ketchen, Jr., G. T. M. Hult, & S. F. Slater, 2007, Toward greater understanding of market orientation and the resource-based view, *Strategic Management Journal,* 28: 961–964; S. K. Ethiraj, P. Kale, M. S. Krishnan, & J. V. Singh, 2005, Where do capabilities come from and how do they matter? A study in the software services industry, *Strategic Management Journal,* 26: 25–45.
83. S. K. Ethiraj, 2007, Allocation of inventive effort in complex product systems, *Strategic Management Journal,* 28: 563–584; S. Dutta, O. Narasimhan, & S. Rajiv, 2005, Conceptualizing and measuring capabilities: Methodology and empirical application, *Strategic Management Journal,* 26: 277–285.
84. 2006, PepsiCo Annual Report, http://www.pepsico.com, September.
85. M. Larson & F. Luthans, 2006, Potential added value of psychological capital in predicting work attitudes, *Journal of Leadership & Organizational Studies,* 13: 45–62; N. W. Hatch & J. H. Dyer, 2004, Human capital and learning as a source of sustainable competitive advantage, *Strategic Management Journal,* 25: 1155–1178.
86. 2006, PepsiCo Annual Report, http://www.pepsico.com, September.
87. M. A. Hitt, L. Bierman, K. Shimizu, & R. Kochhar, 2001, Direct and moderating effects of human capital on strategy and performance in professional service firms: A resource-based perspective, *Academy of Management Journal,* 44: 13–28.
88. S. E. Jackson, M. A. Hitt, & A. S. DeNisi (eds.), 2003, *Managing Knowledge for Sustained Competitive Advantage: Designing Strategies for Effective Human Resource Management,* Oxford, UK: Elsevier Science, Ltd.
89. B. E. Becker & M. A. Huselid, 2007, Strategic human resources management: Where do we go from here? *Journal of Management,* 32: 898–925.
90. R. E. Ployhart, 2007, Staffing in the 21st century: New challenges and strategic opportunities, *Journal of Management,* 32: 868–897.
91. R. A. Noe, J. A. Colquitt, M. J. Simmering, & S. A. Alvarez, 2003, Knowledge management: Developing intellectual and social capital, in S. E. Jackson, M. A. Hitt, & A. S. DeNisi (eds.), 2003, *Managing Knowledge for Sustained Competitive Advantage: Designing Strategies for Effective Human Resource Management,* Oxford, UK: Elsevier Science, Ltd., 209–242.
92. B. Helm & M. Arndt, 2007, It's not a McJob, it's a McCalling, *BusinessWeek,* June 4, 13.
93. G. P. Hollenbeck & M. W. McCall Jr. 2003, Competence, not competencies: Making a global executive development work, in W. H. Mobley & P. W. Dorfman (eds.), *Advances in Global Leadership,* Oxford, UK: Elsevier Science, Ltd., 101–119; J. Sandberg, 2000, Understanding human competence at work: An interpretative approach, *Academy of Management Journal,* 43: 9–25.
94. G. Colvin, 2007, Leader machines, *Fortune,* October 1, 100–106.
95. Y. Liu, J. G. Combs, D. A. Ketchen, Jr., & R. D. Ireland, 2007, The value of human resource management for organizational performance, *Business Horizons,* in press.
96. J. S. Bunderson & K. M. Sutcliffe, 2003, Management team learning orientation and business unit performance, *Journal of Applied Psychology,* 88: 552–560; C. R. James, 2003, Designing learning organizations, *Organizational Dynamics,* 32(1): 46–61.
97. A. Fisher, 2006, Retain your brains, *Fortune,* July 24, 49.
98. J. D. Bragger, D. A. Hantula, D. Bragger, J. Kirnan, & E. Kutcher, 2003, When success breeds failure: History, hysteresis, and delayed exit decisions, *Journal of Applied Psychology,* 88: 6–14.
99. M. R. Haas & M. T. Hansen, 2005, When using knowledge can hurt performance: The value of organizational capabilities in a management consulting company, *Strategic Management Journal,* 26: 1–24; G. Ahuja & R. Katila, 2004, Where do resources come from? The role of idiosyncratic situations, *Strategic Management Journal,* 25: 887–907.
100. Hitt, Miller, & Colella, *Organizational Behavior.*
101. M. Marr, 2007, Disney will shut down cellphone service, *Wall Street Journal,* September 28, B3.
102. J. W. Spencer, 2003, Firms' knowledge-sharing strategies in the global innovation system: Empirical evidence from the flat-panel display industry, *Strategic Management Journal,* 24: 217–233; M. Harvey & M. M. Novicevic, 2002, The hypercompetitive global marketplace: The importance of intuition and creativity in expatriate managers, *Journal of World Business,* 37: 127–138.
103. S. Rodan & C. Galunic, 2004, More than network structure: How knowledge heterogeneity influences managerial performance and innovativeness, *Strategic Management Journal,* 25: 541–562; S. K. McEvily & B. Charavarthy, 2002, The persistence of knowledge-based advantage: An empirical test for product performance and technological knowledge, *Strategic Management Journal,* 23: 285–305.
104. K. D. Miller, 2002, Knowledge inventories and managerial myopia, *Strategic Management Journal,* 23: 689–706.
105. R. D. Nixon, M. A. Hitt, H. Lee, & E. Jeong, 2004, Market reactions to corporate announcements of downsizing actions and implementation strategies, *Strategic Management Journal,* 25: 1121–1129.
106. Nixon, Hitt, Lee, & Jeong, Market reactions to corporate announcements of downsizing actions.
107. T. Simons & Q. Roberson, 2003, Why managers should care about fairness: The effects of aggregate justice perceptions on organizational outcomes, *Journal of Applied Psychology,* 88: 432–443; M. L. Ambrose & R. Cropanzano, 2003, A longitudinal analysis of organizational fairness: An examination of reactions to tenure and promotion decisions, *Journal of Applied Psychology,* 88: 266–275.
108. P. S. Adler & S.-W. Kwon, 2002, Social capital: Prospects for a new concept, *Academy of Management Review,* 27: 17–40.
109. C. Williams, 2007, Transfer in context: Replication and adaptation in knowledge transfer relationships, *Strategic Management Journal,* 28: 867–889; A. Mendez, 2003, The coordination of globalized R&D activities through project teams organization: An exploratory empirical study, *Journal of World Business,* 38: 96–109.
110. W. H. Hoffmann, 2007, Strategies for managing a portfolio of alliances, *Strategic Management Journal,* 28: 827–856; R. D. Ireland, M. A. Hitt, & D. Vaidyanath, 2002, Managing strategic alliances to achieve a competitive advantage, *Journal of Management,* 28: 413–446.
111. J. Florin, M. Lubatkin, & W. Schulze, 2003, *Academy of Management Journal,* 46: 374–384; P. Davidsson & B. Honig, 2003, The role of social and human capital among nascent entrepreneurs, *Journal of Business Venturing,* 18: 301–331.
112. C. M. Fiol, 1991, Managing culture as a competitive resource: An identity-based view of sustainable competitive advantage, *Journal of Management,* 17: 191–211; J. B. Barney, 1986, Organizational culture: Can it be a source of sustained competitive advantage? *Academy of Management Review,* 11: 656–665.
113. 2006, Connecting the dots between innovation and leadership, *Knowledge@wharton,* http: //www.knowledge.wharton.upenn.edu, October 4.
114. S. Cawood, 2007, Culture as a competitive advantage, *Talent Management,* http://www.talentmgt.com, July.

115. M.-F. Lai & G.-G Lee, Relationships of organizational culture toward knowledge activities, *Business Process Management Journal,* 13: 306–322; V. Govindarajan & A. K. Gupta, 2001, Building an effective global business team, *Sloan Management Review,* 42(4): 63–71; S. Ghoshal & C. A. Bartlett, 1994, Linking organizational context and managerial action: The dimensions of quality of management, *Strategic Management Journal,* 15: 91–112.
116. R. D. Ireland, J. G. Covin, & D. F. Kuratko, 2008, Conceptualizing corporate entrepreneurship strategy, *Entrepreneurship Theory and Practice,* in press; D. F. Kuratko, R. D. Ireland, & J. S. Hornsby, 2001, Improving firm performance through entrepreneurial actions: Acordia's corporate entrepreneurship strategy, *Academy of Management Executive,* 15(4): 60–71.
117. R. D. Ireland & J. W. Webb, 2007, Strategic entrepreneurship: Creating competitive advantage through streams of innovation, *Business Horizons,* 50: 49–49; T. E. Brown, P. Davidsson, & J. Wiklund, 2001, An operationalization of Stevenson's conceptualization of entepreneurship as opportunity-based firm behavior, *Strategic Management Journal,* 2: 953–968.
118. S. Ko & J. E. Butler, 2007, Creativity: A key to entrepreneurial behavior, *Business Horizons,* 50: 365–372; D S. Elenkov, W. Judge, & P. Wright, 2005, Strategic leadership and executive innovation influence: An international multi-cluster comparative study, *Strategic Management Journal,* 26: 665–682.
119. R. E. Hoskisson, M. A. Hitt, R. D. Ireland, & J. S. Harrison, 2008, *Competing for Advantage,* 2nd ed., Thomson Publishing; R. G. McGrath, W. J. Ferrier & A. L. Mendelow, 2004, Real options as engines of choice and heterogeneity, *Academy of Management Review,* 29: 86–101.
120. R. S. Vassolo, J. Anand, & T. B. Folta, 2004, Non-additivity in portfolios of exploration activities: A real options analysis of equity alliances in biotechnology, *Strategic Management Journal,* 25: 1045–1061.
121. R. D. Ireland, M. A. Hitt, & D. Simon, 2003, A model of strategic entrepreneurship: The construct and its dimensions, *Journal of Management,* 29: 963–989.
122. G. T. Lumpkin & G. G. Dess, 1996, Clarifying the entrepreneurial orientation construct and linking it to performance, *Academy of Management Review,* 21: 135–172; R. G. McGrath & I. MacMillan, 2000, *The Entrepreneurial Mindset,* Boston: Harvard Business School Press.
123. C. Heath & D. Heath, 2007, Leadership is a muscle, *Fast Company,* July/August, 62–63.
124. Lumpkin & Dess, Clarifying the entrepreneurial orientation construct, 142.
125. Ibid., 137.
126. P. Pyoria, 2007, Informal organization culture: The foundation of knowledge workers' performance, *Journal of Knowledge Management,* 11(3): 16–; R. R. Sims, 2000, Changing an organization's culture under new leadership, *Journal of Business Ethics,* 25: 65–78.
127. C. M. Christensen & S. D. Anthony, 2007, Put investors in their place, *BusinessWeek,* May 28, 108; R. A. Burgelman & Y. L. Doz, 2001, The power of strategic integration, *Sloan Management Review,* 42(3): 28–38.
128. J. S. Hornsby, D. F. Kuratko, & S. A. Zahra, 2002, Middle managers' perception of the internal environment for corporate entrepreneurship: Assessing a measurement scale, *Journal of Business Venturing,* 17: 253–273.
129. D. F Kuratko, R. D. Ireland, J. G. Covin, & J. S. Hornsby, 2005, A model of middle-level managers' entrepreneurial behavior, *Entrepreneurship Theory and Practice,* 29: 699–716.
130. Adler & Kwon, Social capital.
131. M. E. Scheitzer, L. Ordonez, & M. Hoegl, 2004, Goal setting as a motivator of unethical behavior, *Academy of Management Journal,* 47: 422–432.
132. D. C. Kayes, D. Stirling, & T. M. Nielsen, 2007, Building organizational integrity, *Business Horizons,* 50: 61–70; L. K. Trevino, G. R. Weaver, D. G. Toffler, & B. Ley, 1999, Managing ethics and legal compliance: What works and what hurts, *California Management Review,* 41(2): 131–151.
133. M. A. Hitt & J. D. Collins, 2007, Business ethics, strategic decision making, and firm performance, *Business Horizons,* 50: 353–357; C. W. L. Hill, 1990, Cooperation, opportunism, and the invisible hand: Implications for transaction cost theory, *Academy of Management Review,* 15: 500–513.
134. J. M. Stevens, H. K. Steensma, D. A. Harrison, & P. L. Cochran, 2005, Symbolic or substantive document? Influence of ethics codes on financial executives' decisions, *Strategic Management Journal,* 26: 181–195.
135. C. Driscoll & M. McKee, 2007, Restorying a culture of ethical and spiritual values: A role for leader storytelling, *Journal of Business Ethics,* 73: 205–217; C. J. Robertson & W. F. Crittenden, 2003, Mapping moral philosophies: Strategic implications for multinational firms, *Strategic Management Journal,* 24: 385–392; E. Soule, 2002, Managerial moral strategies—In search of a few good principles, *Academy of Management Review,* 27: 114–124.
136. C. Caldwell & L. A. Hayes, 2007, Leadership, trustworthiness, and the mediating lens, *Journal of Management Development,* 26: 261–281.
137. M. Schminke, A. Arnaud, & M. Kuenzi, 2007, The power of ethical work climates, *Organizational Dynamics,* 36: 171–186; L. B. Ncube & M. H. Wasburn, 2006, Strategic collaboration for ethical leadership: A mentoring framework for business and organizational decision making, *Journal of Leadership & Organizational Studies,* 13: 77–92; P. E. Murphy, 1995, Corporate ethics statements: Current status and future prospects, *Journal of Business Ethics,* 14: 727–740.
138. J. Welch & S. Welch, 2007, Flying solo: A reality check, *BusinessWeek,* June 4, 116.
139. A. Weibel, 2007, Formal control and trustworthiness, *Group & Organization Management,* 32: 500–517; G. Redding, 2002, The capitalistic business system of China and its rationale, *Asia Pacific Journal of Management,* 19: 221–249.
140. A. C. Costa, 2007, Trust and control interrelations, *Group & Organization Management,* 32: 392–406; J. H. Gittell, 2000, Paradox of coordination and control, *California Management Review,* 42(3): 101–117.
141. M. D. Shields, F. J. Deng, & Y. Kato, 2000, The design and effects of control systems: Tests of direct- and indirect-effects models, *Accounting, Organizations and Society,* 25: 185–202.
142. R. S. Kaplan & D. P. Norton, 2001, The strategy-focused organization, *Strategy & Leadership,* 29(3): 41–42; R. S. Kaplan & D. P. Norton, 2000, *The Strategy-Focused Organization: How Balanced Scorecard Companies Thrive in the New Business Environment,* Boston: Harvard Business School Press.
143. B. E. Becker, M. A. Huselid, & D. Ulrich, 2001, *The HR Scorecard: Linking People, Strategy, and Performance,* Boston: Harvard Business School Press, 21.
144. Kaplan & Norton, The strategy-focused organization.
145. R. S. Kaplan & D. P. Norton, 2001, Transforming the balanced scorecard from performance measurement to strategic management: Part I, *Accounting Horizons,* 15(1): 87–104.
146. R. S. Kaplan & D. P. Norton, 1992, The balanced scorecard—measures that drive performance, *Harvard Business Review,* 70(1): 71–79.
147. M. A. Mische, 2001, *Strategic Renewal: Becoming a High-Performance Organization,* Upper Saddle River, NJ: Prentice Hall, 181.
148. H.-J. Cho & V. Pucik, 2005, Relationship between innovativeness, quality, growth, profitability and market value, *Strategic Management Journal,* 26: 555–575.
149. Rowe, Creating wealth in organizations: The role of strategic leadership.
150. R. E. Hoskisson, R. A. Johnson, D. Yiu, & W. P. Wan, 2001, Restructuring strategies of diversified business groups: Differences associated with country institutional environments, in M. A. Hitt, R. E. Freeman, & J. S. Harrison (eds.), *Handbook of Strategic Management,* Oxford, UK: Blackwell Publishers, 433–463.
151. J. Birkinshaw & N. Hood, 2001, Unleash innovation in foreign subsidiaries, *Harvard Business Review,* 79(3): 131–137.
152. Ireland & Hitt, Achieving and maintaining strategic competitiveness.
153. G. Edmondson, 2007, Pedal to the metal at Porsche, *BusinessWeek,* September 3, 68; J. D. Gunkel & G. Probst, 2003, Implementation of the balanced scorecard as a means of corporate learning: The Porsche case, European Case Clearing House, Cranfield, UK.

Strategic Entrepreneurship

13

Studying this chapter should provide you with the strategic management knowledge needed to:

1. Define strategic entrepreneurship and corporate entrepreneurship.
2. Define entrepreneurship and entrepreneurial opportunities and explain their importance.
3. Define invention, innovation, and imitation, and describe the relationship among them.
4. Describe entrepreneurs and the entrepreneurial mind-set.
5. Explain international entrepreneurship and its importance.
6. Describe how firms internally develop innovations.
7. Explain how firms use cooperative strategies to innovate.
8. Describe how firms use acquisitions as a means of innovation.
9. Explain how strategic entrepreneurship helps firms create value.

© Don Hammond/Design Pics/Corbis

Googling Innovation!

© AP Photo/Paul Sakuma

Google has become an entrepreneurial sensation with rapid and phenomenal success as an Internet search engine. In 2007 it had more than 380 million people accessing its services in 35 different languages globally. It has become so popular that a new term has entered our lexicon. People refer to searching for information on the Internet using a Google search engine as *googling*.

Google actually provides a number of services. In addition to its well-known search engines, it also provides Web portal services such as Webmail, blogging, photo sharing, and instant messaging. It also provides a number of other tools such as interactive maps, discussion groups, comparison shopping, and an image library. Google has expanded the services that it provides through acquisitions (e.g., YouTube, DoubleClick) and extended its reach to different markets through strategic alliances (e.g., with Sun Microsystems, MTV, News Corporation's Fox Interactive Media).

However, Google is perhaps best known as an innovative company because it constantly develops and introduces to the market new services. Google has a corporate culture that promotes creativity and innovation. For example, all employees are allowed 20 percent of their time to work on projects of their choosing. Also, Google has a flat organization structure and few managers. Even project teams have no permanent leader. Team members rotate as the project leader. Google is a relaxed and fun place to work with free snacks and meals and video games available for break times. The attractiveness of its culture is shown by the fact that Google has almost no turnover.

Google has found a way to harness all of the ideas created by its employees and its motivational workplace. First, to harness the many ideas, Google established an internal Web page for tracking new ideas. Each "idea creator" set up a special Web page for her/his new idea. This information was posted on the intranet, which allowed others in the company to test the idea. Second, Marissa Mayer was made vice president of search products and user experience. Her responsibility is to recommend if and when a particular product is ready for release to the market. Thus, she has an internal gatekeeper role. Marissa also plays a role in helping to develop good ideas. She is able to span the boundary between the technical ("geeks") and the markets (marketing and sales). One former colleague described it as "her clothes match but she is also a geek." She helps to determine when projects are adequately developed and tested to present to the company's other top managers. To further test new "product" ideas, Google launched Google Labs where the public was invited to test new product ideas, providing feedback on new technology and service prototypes.

Google Labs also provides an initial way to build demand for a new product so that it has a customer base when the product is formally introduced to the market.

Google has launched what some analysts refer to as "category killers," such as Google Checkout, which have become major successes. This phenomenon is especially true for its new search products. Some believe that the best services it offers outside of search have come through acquisitions and strategic alliances. Regardless, Google uses innovation as a way to beat its competition even in international markets such as China. The market leader in China is Baidu.com. But Google developed a research center in Beijing to develop new products for the Chinese market and introduced a Chinese-language brand name to compete effectively in this market.

Sources: 2007, Marissa Mayer, *Wikipedia*, http://wikipedia.org, September 2; 2007, It's not journalism; Google's latest effort highlights the difference between what it does and what newspapers and magazines do, *Los Angeles Times*, August 17, 30; D. Clark, 2007, Google begins to distribute Sun's Staroffice software, *Wall Street Journal*, August 16, B4; K. J. Delaney & A. LaVallee, 2007, Google news offers rebuttal time; Articles' subjects, sources allowed to post comments; Verifying identity an issue, *Wall Street Journal*. August 9, B2; L. Garrigues, 2007, Surui partner with Google Earth to map territory, *Indian Country Today*, July 4, *27*(4): A5; 2007, Reclaiming the web from YouTube, *Investors Chronicle*, May 29, 1; J. Murphy, 2007, Google prepares to fend off army of "YouTube killers," *Media*, April 20, 14; A. Pham, 2007, Google spends oodles again; The Internet behemoth agrees to pay $3.1 billion for ad firm and once more uses its financial strength to head off rivals, *Los Angeles Times*, April 14, C1; A. Schein, 2007, Google, Inc. (NASDAQ (GS): GOOG), http://www.google.com; 2006. Inside Google's new-product process. *BusinessWeek*, http://businessweek.com, June 30; 2006, Google, BSkyB plan online video deal, *Wall Street Journal* (Eastern edition), December 6, B4; M. Hitt, C. Miller, & A. Collela, 2006, *Organizational Behavior*, New York: John Wiley & Sons, 469–476; B. Elgin, 2005, Managing Google's idea factory, *BusinessWeek*, http://businessweek.com, October 3.

In Chapter 1, we indicated that *organizational culture* refers to the complex set of ideologies, symbols, and core values that are shared throughout the firm and that influence how the firm conducts business. Thus, culture is the social energy that drives—or fails to drive—the organization. This chapter's Opening Case explains that Google's culture encourages and supports continuous product innovations. Increasingly, a firm's ability to engage in innovation makes the difference in gaining and maintaining a competitive advantage and achieving performance targets.[1]

Google is clearly an entrepreneurial and innovative company. Not only is Google the leading Internet search engine in the world, but it also consistently produces product innovations. In addition to the internal development of new products, Google has diversified its product offerings and the markets served by making carefully planned acquisitions and participating in strategic alliances. From reading this chapter, you will understand that Google's ability to innovate shows that it successfully practices strategic entrepreneurship.

Strategic entrepreneurship is taking entrepreneurial actions using a strategic perspective.

Strategic entrepreneurship is taking entrepreneurial actions using a strategic perspective. When engaging in strategic entrepreneurship, the firm simultaneously focuses on finding opportunities in its external environment that it can try to exploit through innovations. Identifying opportunities to exploit through innovations is the *entrepreneurship* dimension of strategic entrepreneurship, while determining the best way to manage the firm's innovation efforts is the *strategic* dimension. Thus, firms engaging in strategic entrepreneurship integrate their actions to find opportunities and to successfully innovate as a primary means of pursuing them.[2] In the twenty-first–century competitive landscape, firm survival and success depend on a firm's ability to continuously find new opportunities and quickly produce innovations to pursue them.[3]

To examine strategic entrepreneurship, we consider several topics in this chapter. First, we examine entrepreneurship and innovation in a strategic context. Definitions of entrepreneurship, entrepreneurial opportunities, and entrepreneurs as those who engage in entrepreneurship to pursue entrepreneurial opportunities are included as parts of this analysis. We then describe international entrepreneurship, a phenomenon reflecting the increased use of entrepreneurship in economies throughout the world. After this discussion, the chapter shifts to descriptions of the three ways firms innovate. Internally, firms innovate through either autonomous or induced strategic behavior. We then describe actions firms take to implement the innovations resulting from those two types of strategic behavior.

In addition to innovating through internal activities, firms can develop innovations by using cooperative strategies, such as strategic alliances, and by acquiring other companies to gain access to their innovations and innovative capabilities. Most large, complex firms use all three methods to innovate. The method the firm chooses to innovate can be affected by the firm's governance mechanisms. Research evidence suggests, for example, that inside board directors with equity positions favor internal innovation while outside directors with equity positions prefer acquiring innovation.[4] The chapter closes with summary comments about how firms use strategic entrepreneurship to create value and earn above-average returns.

As you will see from studying this chapter, innovation and entrepreneurship are vital for young and old and for large and small firms, for service companies as well as manufacturing firms, and for high-technology ventures.[5] In the global competitive landscape, the long-term success of new ventures and established firms is a function of the ability to meld entrepreneurship with strategic management.[6]

A major portion of the material in this chapter is on innovation and entrepreneurship within established organizations. This phenomenon is called **corporate entrepreneurship**, which is the use or application of entrepreneurship within an established firm.[7] An important part of the entrepreneurship discipline, corporate entrepreneurship increasingly is thought to be linked to survival and success of established organizations.[8] Indeed, established firms use entrepreneurship to strengthen their performance and to enhance growth opportunities.[9] Of course, innovation and entrepreneurship play a critical role in the degree of success achieved by start-up entrepreneurial ventures as well. Much of the content examined in this chapter is equally important in entrepreneurial ventures (sometimes called "start-ups") and established organizations.[10]

Corporate entrepreneurship is the use or application of entrepreneurship within an established firm.

Entrepreneurship and Entrepreneurial Opportunities

Entrepreneurship is the process by which individuals or groups identify and pursue entrepreneurial opportunities without being immediately constrained by the resources they currently control.[11] **Entrepreneurial opportunities** are conditions in which new goods or services can satisfy a need in the market. These opportunities exist because of competitive imperfections in markets and among the factors of production used to produce them[12] and when information about these imperfections is distributed asymmetrically (i.e., not equally) among individuals.[13] Entrepreneurial opportunities come in a host of forms such as the chance to develop and sell a new product and the chance to sell an existing product in a new market.[14] Firms should be receptive to pursuing entrepreneurial opportunities whenever and wherever they may surface.[15]

Entrepreneurship is the process by which individuals or groups identify and pursue entrepreneurial opportunities without being immediately constrained by the resources they currently control.

Entrepreneurial opportunities are conditions in which new goods or services can satisfy a need in the market.

As these two definitions suggest, the essence of entrepreneurship is to identify and exploit entrepreneurial opportunities—that is, opportunities others do not see or for which they do not recognize the commercial potential.[16] As a process, entrepreneurship results in the "creative destruction" of existing products (goods or services) or methods of producing them and replaces them with new products and production methods.[17] Thus, firms engaging in entrepreneurship place high value on individual innovations as well as the ability to continuously innovate across time.[18]

We study entrepreneurship at the level of the individual firm. However, evidence suggests that entrepreneurship is the economic engine driving many nations' economies in the global competitive landscape.[19] Thus, entrepreneurship, and the innovation it spawns, is important for companies competing in the global economy and for countries seeking to stimulate economic climates with the potential to enhance the living standard of their citizens.[20] A recent study conducted by the Boston Consulting Group and the Small Business Division of Intuit found that 10 million people in the United States were considering starting a new business. About one-third of those who do will expand into international markets. The study suggested that by 2017 the number of entrepreneurs will increase, and the entrepreneurs will be younger and include more women and immigrants. Thus, even though the importance of entrepreneurship continues to grow, the "face" of those who start new ventures is also changing.[21]

Innovation

Peter Drucker argued that "innovation is the specific function of entrepreneurship, whether in an existing business, a public service institution, or a new venture started by a lone individual."[22] Moreover, Drucker suggested that innovation is "the means by which the entrepreneur either creates new wealth-producing resources or endows existing resources with enhanced potential for creating wealth."[23] Thus, entrepreneurship and the innovation resulting from it are important for large and small firms, as well as for start-up ventures, as they compete in the twenty-first–century competitive landscape. In fact, some argue that firms failing to innovate will stagnate.[24] The realities of competition in the competitive landscape of the twenty-first century suggest that to be market leaders, companies must regularly develop innovative products desired by customers. This means that innovation should be an intrinsic part of virtually all of a firm's activities.[25]

Innovation is a key outcome firms seek through entrepreneurship and is often the source of competitive success, especially in turbulent, highly competitive environments.[26] For example, research results show that firms competing in global industries that invest more in innovation also achieve the highest returns.[27] In fact, investors often react positively to the introduction of a new product, thereby increasing the price of a firm's stock. Furthermore, "innovation may be required to maintain or achieve competitive parity, much less a competitive advantage in many global markets."[28] Investing in the development of new technologies can increase the performance of firms that operate in different but related product markets (refer to the discussion of related diversification in Chapter 6). In this way, the innovations can be used in multiple markets, and return on the investments is earned more quickly.[29]

Invention is the act of creating or developing a new product or process.

Innovation is the process of creating a commercial product from an invention.

Imitation is the adoption of a similar innovation by different firms.

In his classic work, Schumpeter argued that firms engage in three types of innovative activity.[30] **Invention** is the act of creating or developing a new product or process. **Innovation** is the process of creating a commercial product from an invention. Innovation begins after an invention is chosen for development.[31] Thus, an invention brings something new into being, while an innovation brings something new into use. Accordingly, technical criteria are used to determine the success of an invention, whereas commercial criteria are used to determine the success of an innovation.[32] Finally, **imitation** is the adoption of a similar innovation by different firms. Imitation usually leads to product or process standardization, and products based on imitation often are offered at lower prices, but without as many features. Entrepreneurship is critical to innovative activity in that it acts as the linchpin between invention and innovation.[33]

In the United States in particular, innovation is the most critical of the three types of innovative activity. Many companies are able to create ideas that lead to inventions, but commercializing those inventions has, at times, proved difficult. This difficulty is suggested by the fact that approximately 80 percent of R&D occurs in large firms, but these same firms produce fewer than 50 percent of the patents.[34] Patents are a strategic asset and the ability to regularly produce them can be an important source of competitive advantage, especially for firms competing in knowledge-intensive industries (e.g., pharmaceuticals).[35]

Entrepreneurs

Entrepreneurs are individuals, acting independently or as part of an organization, who see an entrepreneurial opportunity and then take risks to develop an innovation to pursue it. Entrepreneurs are found throughout an organization—from top-level managers to those working to produce a firm's goods or services. Entrepreneurs are found throughout Google, for example. Recall from the Opening Case that all Google employees are encouraged to use roughly 20 percent of their time to develop innovations. Entrepreneurs tend to demonstrate several characteristics: They are highly motivated, willing to take responsibility for their projects, and self-confident.[36] In addition, entrepreneurs tend to be passionate and emotional about the value and importance of their innovation-based ideas.[37] They are able to deal with uncertainty and are more alert to opportunities than others.[38]

Entrepreneurs are individuals, acting independently or as part of an organization, who see an entrepreneurial opportunity and then take risks to develop an innovation to exploit it.

Evidence suggests that successful entrepreneurs have an entrepreneurial mind-set. The person with an **entrepreneurial mind-set** values uncertainty in the marketplace and seeks to continuously identify opportunities with the potential to lead to important innovations.[39] Because it has the potential to lead to continuous innovations, an individual's entrepreneurial mind-set can be a source of competitive advantage for a firm.[40] Howard Schultz, founder of Starbucks, and his management team at the company have an entrepreneurial mind-set. Making music a meaningful part of Starbucks' customers' experiences is an example of an evolving product offering resulting from an entrepreneurial mind-set. In Schultz's words: "The music world is changing, and Starbucks and Starbucks Hear Music will continue to be an innovator in the industry. It takes passion, commitment, and even a bit of experimentation to maintain that position."[41] Expanding its reach into the music market, Starbucks formed an alliance with Concord Music Group to help market its new Hear Music label. The alliance seems to be successful: Paul McCartney's new album on this label sold more than 1 million copies in the first two months after its release. Starbucks is also extending its package of products to other forms of entertainment, including movies. It signed a deal to jointly distribute the family movie, *Akeelah and the Bee*.[42]

The person with an **entrepreneurial mind-set** values uncertainty in the marketplace and seeks to continuously identify opportunities with the potential to lead to important innovations.

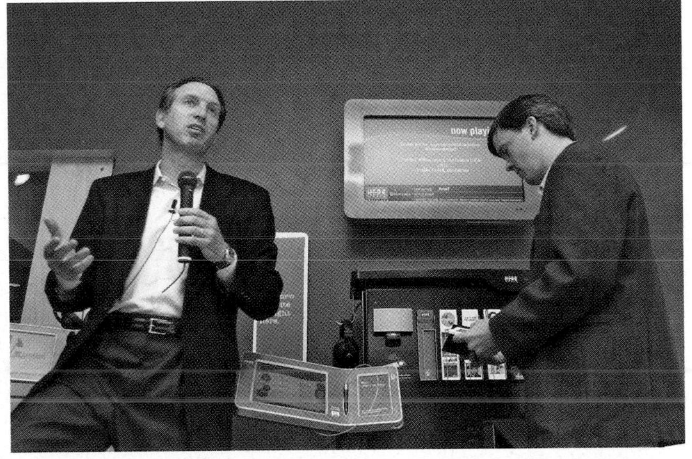

Starbucks Hear Music™ is a result of the entrepreneurial mindset of Starbucks Chairman Howard Schultz and his management team. Here Schultz and executive Don MacKinnon unveil the first Hear Music media bar.

Entrepreneurial mind-sets are fostered and supported when knowledge is readily available throughout a firm. Indeed, research has shown that units within firms are more innovative when they have access to new knowledge.[43] Transferring knowledge, however, can be difficult, often because the receiving party must have adequate absorptive capacity (or the ability) to learn the knowledge.[44] Learning requires that the new knowledge be linked to the existing knowledge. Thus, managers need to develop the capabilities of their human capital to build on their current knowledge base while incrementally expanding that knowledge.[45]

Recent actions at Coca-Cola are designed to acquire and better use knowledge to enter new product markets. In 2007, Coca-Cola announced a reorganization of its North American operations, with special focus on its beverage units. It created a special unit with the purpose of developing new products outside the soft drink market. It also acquired Fuze Beverages, maker of teas and juices, to enlarge its product portfolio and to gain knowledge about other beverage markets.[46]

International Entrepreneurship

International entrepreneurship is a process in which firms creatively discover and exploit opportunities that are outside their domestic markets in order to develop a competitive advantage.

International entrepreneurship is a process in which firms creatively discover and exploit opportunities that are outside their domestic markets in order to develop a competitive advantage.[47] As the practices suggested by this definition show, entrepreneurship is a global phenomenon.[48] As noted earlier, approximately one-third of new ventures move into international markets early in their life cycle. Most large established companies have significant foreign operations and often start new ventures in domestic and international markets. Large multinational companies, for example, generate approximately 54 percent of their sales outside their domestic market, and more than 50 percent of their employees work outside of the company's home country.[49]

A key reason that entrepreneurship has become a global phenomenon is that in general, internationalization leads to improved firm performance.[50] Nonetheless, decision makers should recognize that the decision to internationalize exposes their firms to various risks, including those of unstable foreign currencies, problems with market efficiencies, insufficient infrastructures to support businesses, and limitations on market size.[51] Thus, the decision to engage in international entrepreneurship should be a product of careful analysis.

Because of its positive benefits, entrepreneurship is at the top of public policy agendas in many of the world's countries, including Finland, Germany, Ireland, and Israel. Some argue that placing entrepreneurship on these agendas may be appropriate in that regulation hindering innovation and entrepreneurship is the root cause of Europe's productivity problems.[52] In Ireland, for example, the government is "particularly focused on encouraging new innovative enterprises that have growth potential and are export oriented."[53]

Even though entrepreneurship is a global phenomenon, the rate of entrepreneurship differs across countries. A study of 42 countries found that the percentage of adults involved in entrepreneurial activity ranged from a high of more than 40 percent in Peru to a low of approximately 3 percent in Belgium. The United States had a rate slightly more than 10 percent. Importantly, this study also found a strong positive relationship between the rate of entrepreneurial activity and economic development in a country.[54]

Culture is one of the reasons for the differences in rates of entrepreneurship among different countries. The research suggests that a balance between individual initiative and a spirit of cooperation and group ownership of innovation is needed to encourage entrepreneurial behavior. For firms to be entrepreneurial, they must provide appropriate autonomy and incentives for individual initiative to surface, but also promote cooperation and group ownership of an innovation if it is to be implemented successfully. Thus, international entrepreneurship often requires teams of people with unique skills and resources, especially in cultures that highly value individualism or collectivism. In addition to a balance of values for individual initiative and cooperative behaviors, firms must build the capabilities to be innovative and acquire the resources needed to support innovative activities.[55]

The level of investment outside of the home country made by young ventures is also an important dimension of international entrepreneurship. In fact, with increasing globalization, a greater number of new ventures have been "born global."[56] Research has shown that new ventures that enter international markets increase their learning of new technological knowledge and thereby enhance their performance.[57] Because of the positive outcomes associated with its use, the amount of international entrepreneurship has been increasing in recent years.[58]

The probability of entering international markets increases when the firm has top executives with international experience, which increases the likelihood of the firm successfully competing in those markets.[59] Because of the learning and economies of scale and scope afforded by operating in international markets, both young and established internationally diversified firms often are stronger competitors in their domestic market as well. Additionally, as research has shown, internationally diversified firms are generally more innovative.[60]

Next, we discuss the three ways firms innovate.

Internal Innovation

In established organizations, most innovation comes from efforts in research and development (R&D). Effective R&D often leads to firms' filing for patents to protect their innovative work. Increasingly, successful R&D results from integrating the skills available in the global workforce. Firms seeking internal innovations through their R&D must understand that "Talent and ideas are flourishing everywhere—from Bangalore to Shanghai to Kiev—and no company, regardless of geography, can hesitate to go wherever those ideas are."[61] Thus, in the years to come, the ability to have a competitive advantage based on innovation may accrue to firms able to meld the talent of human capital from countries around the world.

Motorola has been a highly innovative firm over time as explained in the Strategic Focus on page 374. In fact, because of its significant innovation efforts, it was awarded the National Medal of Technology. It has created many radical (handheld cellular phone) and incremental (e.g., Razr2) innovations. And its Razr cell phone sold more units than any cell phone in history. Additionally, it has R&D operations all over the world. Yet, it was caught with an incomplete product portfolio recently and competitors took market share away from it. This example suggests the critical nature and importance of innovation to firm success.

Increasingly, it seems possible that in the twenty-first century competitive landscape, R&D may be the most critical factor in gaining and sustaining a competitive advantage in some industries, such as pharmaceuticals. Larger, established firms, certainly those competing globally, often try to use their R&D labs to create competence-destroying new technologies and products.[62] Being able to innovate in this manner can create a competitive advantage for a firm in many industries.[63] Although critical to long-term corporate success, the outcomes of R&D investments are uncertain and often not achieved in the short term,[64] meaning that patience is required as firms evaluate the outcomes of their R&D efforts.

Incremental and Radical Innovation

Firms produce two types of internal innovations—incremental and radical innovations—when using their R&D activities. Most innovations are *incremental*—that is, they build on existing knowledge bases and provide small improvements in the current product lines. Incremental innovations are evolutionary and linear in nature.[65] "The markets for incremental innovations are well-defined, product characteristics are well understood, profit margins tend to be lower, production technologies are efficient, and competition is primarily on the basis of price."[66] Adding a different kind of whitening agent to a soap detergent is an example of an incremental innovation, as are improvements in televisions over the last few decades (moving from black-and-white to color, improving existing audio capabilities, etc.). Motorola's launch of the Razr2 is an example of incremental innovation. Companies launch far more incremental innovations than radical innovations.[67]

In contrast to incremental innovations, *radical innovations* usually provide significant technological breakthroughs and create new knowledge.[68] Radical innovations, which are revolutionary and nonlinear in nature typically use new technologies to serve newly created markets. The development of the original personal computer (PC) is an example of a radical innovation. Reinventing the computer by developing a "radically new computer-brain chip" (e.g., with the capability to process a trillion calculations per second) is an example of what could be a radical innovation. Obviously, such a radical innovation would seem to have the capacity to revolutionize the tasks computers could perform.

The Razr's Edge: R&D and Innovation at Motorola

Motorola has been known for its innovative products since its inception as Galvin Manufacturing Corporation. In fact, it introduced the first car radios in 1930. Importantly, Motorola developed the first handheld cellular phone in 1984. It is a *Fortune* 100 company with $42.6 billion of sales in 2006. It has received many awards for its innovations, including these recent ones:

2004 National Medal of Technology

2006 IEEE-Standards Association Corporate Award

2006 CES Mark of Excellence Award (for the best home wireless product)

2006 Best of ITS Award for Research and Innovation

2006 Nano 50th Award for Nano Emissive Display Technology

The National Medal of Technology is presented by the White House and is the highest honor in the United States for technological innovation. This medal was awarded "for over 75 years of technological achievement and leadership in the development of innovation in electronic solutions, which have enabled portable and mobile communications to become the standard across society."

In recent years, however, Motorola is perhaps best known to the mass markets for its Razr wireless cell phone introduced in 2005. The Razr is an ultraslim phone with a highly attractive design. In fact, it became popular as a fashion item and at one time sold for more than $500 per phone. Its popularity led to Motorola selling its 100 millionth Razr in the summer of 2007, only three years after its introduction. The Razr helped Motorola to increase its market share in this market from 13 percent in 2003 to 22 percent in 2006. To produce products such as the Razr, Motorola has a labyrinth of R&D laboratories and complementary units. These units work in a cross-functional manner to develop new product ideas, test them, and then commercialize the best ones. The company makes use of the best technology minds globally with research units in North, Central, and South America, Europe, and Asia. These research units are operating on the cutting edge of technology and may have some radical new products on the horizon (e.g., a special writing keypad).

In 2004, Motorola received the National Medal of Technology for over 75 years of technological achievement and leadership. Recently however, Motorola's market share has declined because they were not putting enough money into R&D. Motorola is again emphasizing the R&D process and has already introduced 5 new products.

Although Motorola has been a technology leader, it has also suffered from some strategic errors in the past. Most recently, Motorola's market share declined and it was supplanted as the number two handset manufacturer by Samsung. It posted a loss in the first quarter of 2007. The reason for this drop in the market was a move to gain market share by cutting costs and prices rather than continuing to introduce new products to the market. Motorola's CEO Ed Zander admitted this mistake. As a result, the company was caught with a weak product portfolio at a time when competitors were introducing a host of new products.

Motorola moved its R&D processes into high gear to correct these problems. In May 2007, Motorola introduced five new handset products. The most important of its new products is the Razr2. Even more sleek than the Razr, the Razr2 has the most up-to-date technology including the 3G network technology.

Because of the negative outcomes it experienced, Motorola took other actions to solidify its position. For example, Motorola acquired Symbol Technologies, Inc., to gain access to products and systems for enterprise mobility solutions, advanced data capture, and radio frequency identification. Additionally, it acquired Good Technology to move into the markets for "smartphones." Finally, it acquired Terayon to build Motorola's capabilities to provide next-generation services (e.g., targeted advertising).

Sources: Motorola Technology: Global R&D and Software Development Organization, http://www.motorola.com/innovators/pdfs/Motorola-Technology-FactSheet05142007.pdf, fact sheet, accessed September 7; J. Palmer, 2007, Our gadget of the week: A better Razr, *Barron's*, August 27, 87(35): 40; M. Palmer & P. Taylor, 2007, Loss of market share adds to pressure on Motorola chief, *Financial Times*, August 23, 21; P. Taylor, 2007, Gloom over Motorola's results, *Financial Times*, July 19, 23; R. O. Crockett, 2007, Honing the Razr edge: Motorola stops trying to reinvent the wheel, *BusinessWeek*, May 28, 38; R. Martin, 2007, With Razr2, Motorola returns to what's worked before, *Information Week*, May 21, 36; M. Reardon, 2007, Is Motorola's cell phone revamp enough? CNET.com, http://www.news.com, May 15.

Because they establish new functionalities for users, radical innovations have strong potential to lead to significant growth in revenue and profits.[69] Developing new processes is a critical part of producing radical innovations. Both types of innovation can create value, meaning that firms should determine when it is appropriate to emphasize either incremental or radical innovation.[70] However, radical innovations have the potential to contribute more significantly to a firm's efforts to earn above-average returns.

Radical innovations are rare because of the difficulty and risk involved in developing them. The value of the technology and the market opportunities are highly uncertain.[71] Because radical innovation creates new knowledge and uses only some or little of a firm's current product or technological knowledge, creativity is required. However, creativity does not produce something from nothing. Rather, creativity discovers, combines, or synthesizes current knowledge, often from diverse areas.[72] This knowledge is then used to develop new products that can be used in an entrepreneurial manner to move into new markets, capture new customers, and gain access to new resources.[73] Such innovations are often developed in separate business units that start internal ventures.[74]

Internally developed incremental and radical innovations result from deliberate efforts. These deliberate efforts are called *internal corporate venturing*, which is the set of activities firms use to develop internal inventions and especially innovations.[75] As shown in Figure 13.1, autonomous and induced strategic behaviors are the two types of internal corporate venturing. Each venturing type facilitates incremental and radical innovations. However, a larger number of radical innovations spring from autonomous

Figure 13.1 Model of Internal Corporate Venturing

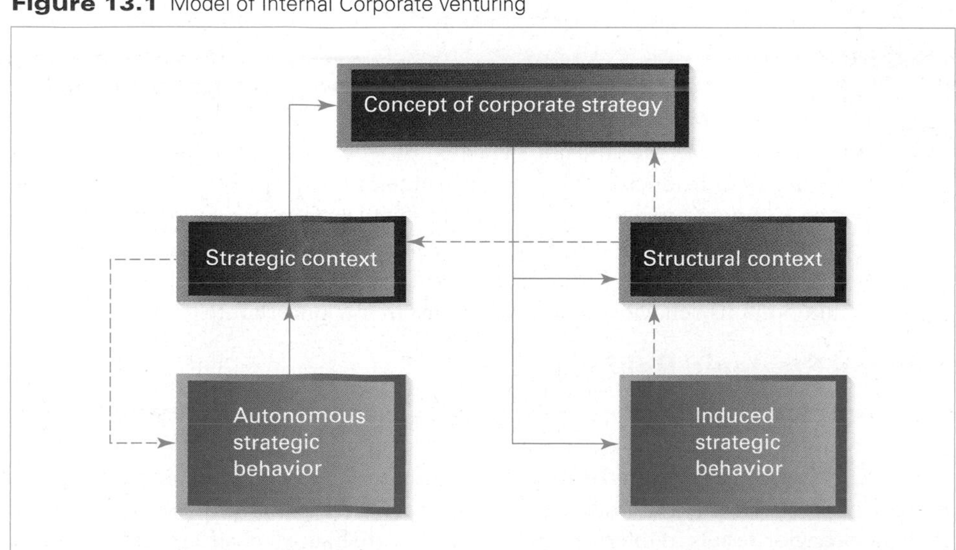

Source: Adapted from R. A. Burgelman, 1983, A model of the interactions of strategic behavior, corporate context, and the concept of strategy, *Academy of Management Review*, 8: 65.

strategic behavior while the greatest percentage of incremental innovations come from induced strategic behavior.

Autonomous Strategic Behavior

Autonomous strategic behavior is a bottom-up process in which product champions pursue new ideas, often through a political process, by means of which they develop and coordinate the commercialization of a new good or service until it achieves success in the marketplace. A *product champion* is an organizational member with an entrepreneurial vision of a new good or service who seeks to create support for its commercialization. Product champions play critical roles in moving innovations forward.[76] Indeed, in many corporations, "Champions are widely acknowledged as pivotal to innovation speed and success."[77] Champions are vital to sell the ideas to others in the organization so that the innovations will be commercialized. Commonly, product champions use their social capital to develop informal networks within the firm. As progress is made, these networks become more formal as a means of pushing an innovation to the point of successful commercialization.[78] Internal innovations springing from autonomous strategic behavior frequently differ from the firm's current strategy, taking it into new markets and perhaps new ways of creating value for customers and other stakeholders.

Autonomous strategic behavior is based on a firm's wellspring of knowledge and resources that are the sources of the firm's innovation. Thus, a firm's technological capabilities and competencies are the basis for new products and processes.[79] Obviously, Motorola has depended to a degree on autonomous strategic behavior over the years to identify new technologies and products that can better serve its customers. The iPod likely resulted from autonomous strategic behavior in Apple. Yet, the development of the iPhone likely was more the result of induced strategic behavior discussed in the next section.

While the iPod likely resulted from autonomous strategic behavior, the iPhone is probably a result of induced strategic behavior.

© AP Photo/fls/Jason DeCrow

Changing the concept of corporate-level strategy through autonomous strategic behavior results when a product is championed within strategic and structural contexts (see Figure 13.1). Such a transformation occurred with the development of the iPod and introduction of iTunes at Apple. The strategic context is the process used to arrive at strategic decisions (often requiring political processes to gain acceptance). The best firms keep changing their strategic context and strategies because of the continuous changes in the current competitive landscape. Thus, some believe that the most competitively successful firms reinvent their industry or develop a completely new one across time as they compete with current and future rivals.[80]

To be effective, an autonomous process for developing new products requires that new knowledge be continuously diffused throughout the firm. In particular, the diffusion of tacit knowledge is important for development of more effective new products.[81] Interestingly, some of the processes important for the promotion of autonomous new product development behavior vary by the environment and country in which a firm operates. For example, the Japanese culture is high on uncertainty avoidance. As such, research has found that Japanese firms are more likely to engage in autonomous behaviors under conditions of low uncertainty.[82]

Induced Strategic Behavior

The second of the two forms of internal corporate venturing, *induced strategic behavior,* is a top-down process whereby the firm's current strategy and structure foster innovations that are closely associated with that strategy and structure.[83] In this form of venturing, the strategy in place is filtered through a matching structural hierarchy. In essence, induced strategic behavior results in internal innovations that are highly consistent with the firm's current strategy.

Nokia, one of Motorola's chief competitors in the global cell phone market, is using an induced strategic approach to developing new mobile phones. For example, its strategic goal is to add 2 billion new customers by the end of 2010 by focusing on emerging markets. Thus, its decentralized R&D units in China, Brazil, and India are integrating attributes that are important and attractive to the local culture (e.g., design features) with major technologies developed in the Finnish R&D laboratories at its headquarters. Interestingly, these design teams include not only engineers but also anthropologists and psychologists who study cultures and behaviors in the search for early signals of changes in behavior patterns that may be important for the design of cell phones (or even the need for new technologies). They are especially sensitive to country-specific trends. These actions and approaches at Nokia are intended to keep the firm number one in the global market.[84]

Implementing Internal Innovations

An entrepreneurial mind-set is required to be innovative and to develop successful internal corporate ventures. When valuing environmental and market uncertainty, which are key parts of an entrepreneurial mind-set, individuals and firms demonstrate their willingness to take risks to commercialize innovations. Although they must continuously attempt to identify opportunities, they must also select and pursue the best opportunities and do so with discipline. Employing an entrepreneurial mind-set entails not only developing new products and markets but also placing an emphasis on execution. Often, firms provide incentives to managers to be entrepreneurial and to commercialize innovations.[85]

Having processes and structures in place through which a firm can successfully implement the outcomes of internal corporate ventures and commercialize the innovations is critical. Indeed, the successful introduction of innovations into the marketplace reflects implementation effectiveness.[86] In the context of internal corporate ventures, managers must allocate resources, coordinate activities, communicate with many different parties in the organization, and make a series of decisions to convert the innovations resulting from either autonomous or induced strategic behaviors into successful market entries.[87] As we describe in Chapter 11, organizational structures are the sets of formal relationships that support processes managers use to commercialize innovations.

Effective integration of the various functions involved in innovation processes—from engineering to manufacturing and, ultimately, market distribution—is required to implement the incremental and radical innovations resulting from internal corporate ventures.[88] Increasingly, product development teams are being used to integrate the activities associated with different organizational functions. Such integration involves coordinating and applying the knowledge and skills of different functional areas in order to maximize innovation.[89] Teams must help to make decisions as to which projects should be commercialized and which ones should end. Although ending a project is difficult, sometimes because of emotional commitments to innovation-based projects, effective teams recognize when conditions change such that the innovation cannot create value as originally anticipated.

Cross-Functional Product Development Teams

Cross-functional teams facilitate efforts to integrate activities associated with different organizational functions, such as design, manufacturing, and marketing.[90] In addition, new product development processes can be completed more quickly and the products more easily commercialized when cross-functional teams work effectively.[91] Using cross-functional teams, product development stages are grouped into parallel or overlapping processes to allow the firm to tailor its product development efforts to its unique core competencies and to the needs of the market.

Horizontal organizational structures support the use of cross-functional teams in their efforts to integrate innovation-based activities across organizational functions.[92] Therefore, instead of being designed around vertical hierarchical functions or departments, the organization is built around core horizontal processes that are used to produce and manage innovations. Some of the core horizontal processes that are critical to innovation efforts are formal; they may be defined and documented as procedures and practices. More commonly, however, these processes are informal: "They are routines or ways of working that evolve over time."[93] Often invisible, informal processes are critical to successful innovations and are supported properly through horizontal organizational structures more so than through vertical organizational structures.

Two primary barriers that may prevent the successful use of cross-functional teams as a means of integrating organizational functions are independent frames of reference of team members and organizational politics.[94] Team members working within a distinct specialization (e.g., a particular organizational function) may have an independent frame of reference typically based on common backgrounds and experiences. They are likely to use the same decision criteria to evaluate issues such as product development efforts as they do within their functional units. Research suggests that functional departments vary along four dimensions: time orientation, interpersonal orientation, goal orientation, and formality of structure.[95] Thus, individuals from different functional departments having different orientations on these dimensions can be expected to perceive product development activities in different ways. For example, a design engineer may consider the characteristics that make a product functional and workable to be the most important of the product's characteristics. Alternatively, a person from the marketing function may hold characteristics that satisfy customer needs most important. These different orientations can create barriers to effective communication across functions and even produce conflict in the team at times.[96]

Organizational politics is the second potential barrier to effective integration in cross-functional teams. In some organizations, considerable political activity may center on allocating resources to different functions. Interunit conflict may result from aggressive competition for resources among those representing different organizational functions. This dysfunctional conflict between functions creates a barrier to their integration.[97] Methods must be found to achieve cross-functional integration without excessive political conflict and without changing the basic structural characteristics necessary for task specialization and efficiency.

Facilitating Integration and Innovation

Shared values and effective leadership are important for achieving cross-functional integration and implementing innovation.[98] Highly effective shared values are framed around the firm's vision and mission, and become the glue that promotes integration between functional units. Thus, the firm's culture promotes unity and internal innovation.[99]

Strategic leadership is also highly important for achieving cross-functional integration and promoting innovation. Leaders set the goals and allocate resources. The goals include integrated development and commercialization of new goods and services. Effective strategic leaders also ensure a high-quality communication system to facilitate cross-functional integration. A critical benefit of effective communication is the sharing of knowledge among team members. Effective communication thus helps create synergy and gains team members' commitment to an innovation throughout the organization. Shared values and leadership practices shape the communication systems that are formed to support the development and commercialization of new products.[100]

Creating Value from Internal Innovation

The model in Figure 13.2 shows how firms can create value from the internal corporate venturing processes they use to develop and commercialize new goods and services. An

Figure 13.2 Creating Value Through Internal Innovation Processes

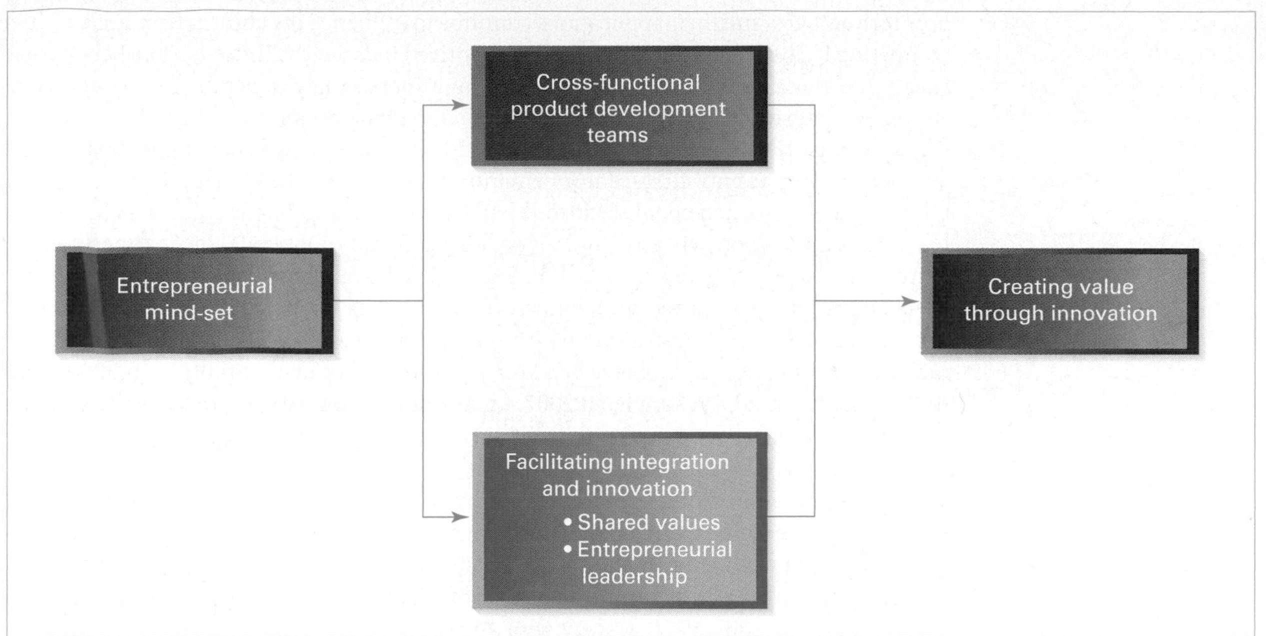

entrepreneurial mind-set is necessary so that managers and employees will consistently try to identify entrepreneurial opportunities the firm can pursue by developing new goods and services and new markets. Cross-functional teams are important for promoting integrated new product design ideas and commitment to their subsequent implementation. Effective leadership and shared values promote integration and vision for innovation and commitment to it. The end result for the firm is the creation of value for the customers and shareholders by developing and commercializing new products.[101] We should acknowledge that not all entrepreneurial efforts succeed, even with effective management. Sometimes managers must decide to exit the market as well to avoid value decline.[102]

In the next two sections, we discuss the other ways firms innovate—by using cooperative strategies and by acquiring companies.

Innovation Through Cooperative Strategies

Virtually all firms lack the breadth and depth of resources (e.g., human capital and social capital) in their R&D activities needed to internally develop a sufficient number of innovations to meet the needs of the market and remain competitive. As such, firms must be open to using external resources to help produce innovations.[103] Alliances with other firms can contribute to innovations in several ways. First, they provide information on new business opportunities and how to exploit them.[104] In other instances, firms use cooperative strategies to align what they believe are complementary assets with the potential to lead to future innovations.[105]

The rapidly changing technologies of the twenty-first-century competitive landscape, globalization, and the need to innovate at world-class levels are primary influences on firms' decisions to innovate by cooperating with other companies. Evidence shows that the skills and knowledge contributed by firms

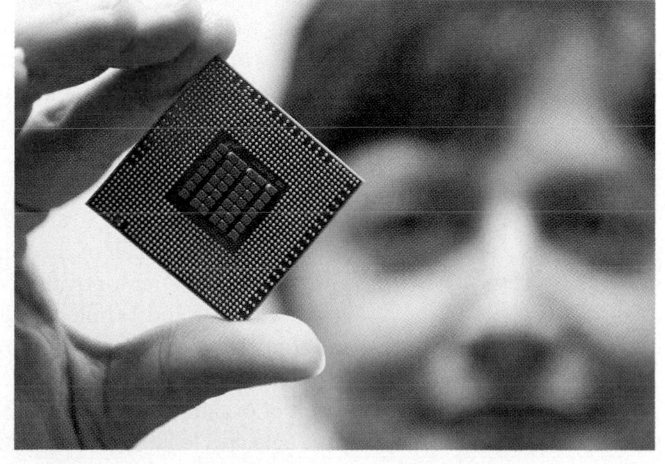

IBM now has full partnerships with several companies to research, develop, and manufacture, next generation computer chips.

forming a cooperative strategy to innovate tend to be technology-based, a fact suggesting how technologies and their applications continue to influence the choices firms make while competing in the twenty-first–century competitive landscape.[106] Indeed, some believe that because of these conditions, firms are becoming increasingly dependent on cooperative strategies as a path to successful competition in the global economy.[107] Even venerable old firms such as IBM have learned that they need help to create innovations necessary to be competitive in a twenty-first–century environment. In 2002, IBM's chip business lost $1 billion and IBM management decided it had to make major changes. As such, it decided to open its innovation processes and invite full partners to cooperate. It is partnering with Sony, Toshiba, and Albany Nanotech in R&D on cell chips. It is working with AMD and Freescale on R&D to develop manufacturing processes for high-performance chips. It also has a number of partners with which it is doing research to produce next-generation materials and processes to achieve breakthroughs in science on computer chips. Although the process has not been simple, in 2007 it had a number of partners that invested almost $1 billion of their resources in working with IBM to produce innovations.[108]

Both entrepreneurial firms and established firms use cooperative strategies (e.g., strategic alliances and joint ventures) to innovate. An entrepreneurial firm, for example, may seek investment capital as well as established firms' distribution capabilities to successfully introduce one of its innovative products to the market.[109] Alternatively, more-established companies may need new technological knowledge and can gain access to it by forming a cooperative strategy with entrepreneurial ventures.[110] Alliances between large pharmaceutical firms and biotechnology companies increasingly have been formed to integrate the knowledge and resources of both to develop new products and bring them to market.[111]

Because of the importance of strategic alliances, particularly in the development of new technology and in commercializing innovations, firms are beginning to build networks of alliances that represent a form of social capital to them.[112] Building social capital in the form of relationships with other firms provides access to the knowledge and other resources necessary to develop innovations.[113] Knowledge from these alliances helps firms develop new capabilities.[114] Some firms now even allow other companies to participate in their internal new product development processes. It is not uncommon, for example, for firms to have supplier representatives on their cross-functional innovation teams because of the importance of the suppliers' input to ensure quality materials for any new product developed.[115]

However, alliances formed for the purpose of innovation are not without risks. In addition to conflict that is natural when firms try to work together to reach a mutual goal,[116] cooperative strategy participants also take a risk that a partner will appropriate a firm's technology or knowledge and use it to enhance its own competitive abilities.[117] To prevent or at least minimize this risk, firms, particularly new ventures, need to select their partners carefully. The ideal partnership is one in which the firms have complementary skills as well as compatible strategic goals.[118] However, because companies are operating in a network of firms and thus may be participating in multiple alliances simultaneously, they encounter challenges in managing the alliances.[119] Research has shown that firms can become involved in too many alliances, which can harm rather than facilitate their innovation capabilities.[120] Thus, effectively managing a cooperative strategy to produce innovation is critical.

As explained in the Strategic Focus, Whole Foods is a successful and innovative company. However, not all of the innovation is developed solely by Whole Foods' employees and managers. One innovative concept introduced is the result of an alliance between Lord & Taylor and Whole Foods. Located in the same redevelopment, they are working on opportunities for cross-selling goods. Whole Foods has made a number of acquisitions as listed in the Strategic Focus. Thus, Whole Foods' offerings to customers are the result of organic growth (internal innovation), shared resources (alliances), and acquired products and locations (acquisitions).

Does Whole Foods Really Obtain Innovation in Unnatural Ways?

Whole Foods pioneered the natural and organic food supermarket and almost single-handedly made organic food a household term. Whole Foods started as a small organic food retailer in Austin, Texas, in 1980. In 2006, it operated more than 300 stores and had sales of $5.6 billion. It has become the world's largest natural food retailer. It markets more than 1,500 items, two-thirds of which are perishable.

Over the years, Whole Foods introduced a number of unique products and concepts, and it stands alone at the top of its industry. Most of the new products and concepts introduced in its stores were developed from internal ideas. For example, in 2005, Whole Foods developed a new stand-alone store named Lifestyle Store. It sells environment-friendly goods ranging from clothes to housewares. The products are composed of all organic materials. For example, Lenore Bags and Totes are made from old phone books and other recycled materials. The stores also have organic clothing for babies, and departments that serve other personal and home needs of customers.

Yet, not all of its new product introductions come from internal ideas. For example, Whole Foods acquired Allegro Coffee Company and entered the specialty coffee market. Allegro Coffee is sold in all of the Whole Foods stores. Likewise in 2007 Whole Foods formed an alliance with Lord & Taylor to serve as anchors of a redevelopment project in Stamford, Connecticut. They are promoting it as a distinctive shopping experience that integrates department store *chic* with supermarket *hip.* They believe that both have unique cross-selling opportunities.

Interestingly for a natural food retailer that has grown largely through organic (internal) means, it has completed an interesting number of acquisitions over time. In addition to Allegro, Whole Foods acquired Wellspring Grocery, Bread & Circus, Mrs. Gooch's, Fresh Fields, Bread of Life, Amrion, Merchant of Vino, WholePeople.com (e-commerce subsidiary), Nature's Heartland, Food For Thought, Harry's Farmers Market, Select Fish, Fresh & Wild, Tiny Trapeze, and most recently, Wild Oats. Undoubtedly, these businesses provide not only growth, new customers and outlets, but also add new products to the Whole Foods portfolio. Whole Foods used acquisitions as a means to enter international markets, buying a small natural food chain in the United Kingdom. It then opened its first large new retail outlet in London in 2007.

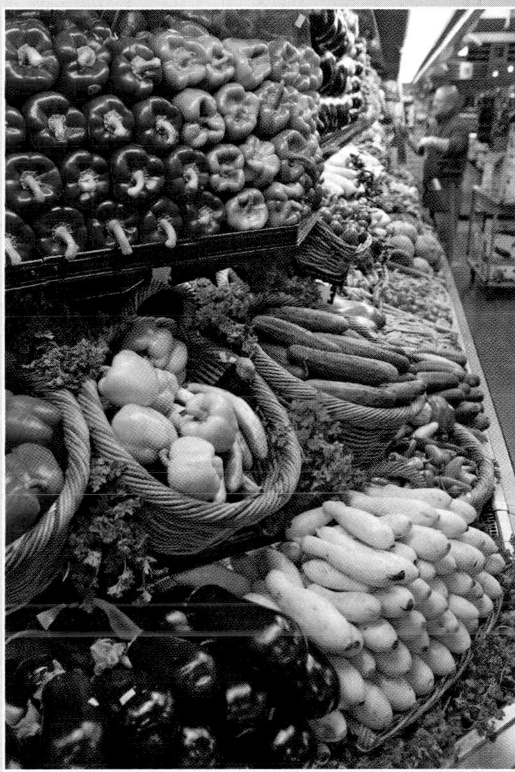

While Whole Foods began as a natural and organic food supermarket, they have continued to expand through innovation, acquisition, and strategic alliances.

Regardless of the use of alliances and acquisitions, Whole Foods continues to be innovative. It opened a restaurant in its Chicago store and it became so popular for dinner among customers that it has now opened restaurants in other store locations. The restaurants promote the organic foods sold in the stores. Interestingly, Whole Foods has been listed on the best companies to work for during the period of 1998–2007.

Sources: 2007, Whole Foods Market, Inc., http://www.hoovers.com/company-information, September 2; 2007, Whole Foods Market, Inc., http://www.wikipedia.org, September 2; 2007, Whole Foods, http://www.wholefoodsmarket.com, September 2; K. Field, 2007, Vertically championed, *Chain Store Age*, August, 83(8): 158; S. Armstrong, 2007, Make way for Big Organic, *New Statesman*, April 2, 136(4838): 32; D. Desjardins, 2005, Whole Foods goes Hollywood with Lifestyle store, *DSN Retailing Today*, November 7, 44(21): 4; D. Howell, 2005, Whole Foods goes whole hog with landmark Austin store, *DSN Retailing Today*, October 10, 44(5): 3.

Innovation Through Acquisitions

Firms sometimes acquire companies to gain access to their innovations and to their innovative capabilities. One reason companies make these acquisitions is that the capital market values growth; acquisitions provide a means to rapidly extend one or more product lines and increase the firm's revenues. Acquisitions pursued for this reason should, nonetheless, have a strategic rationale. For example, several large pharmaceutical firms have made acquisitions in recent years for several reasons such as enhancing growth. However, a primary reason for acquisitions in this industry has been to acquire innovation, new drugs that can be commercialized. In this way they strengthen their new product pipeline.[121]

Similar to internal corporate venturing and strategic alliances, acquisitions are not a risk-free approach to innovating. A key risk of acquisitions is that a firm may substitute an ability to buy innovations for an ability to produce innovations internally. In support of this contention, research shows that firms engaging in acquisitions introduce fewer new products into the market.[122] This substitution may take place because firms lose strategic control and focus instead on financial control of their original and especially of their acquired business units.

We note in Chapter 7 that companies can also learn new capabilities from firms they acquire. Thus, firms may gain capabilities to produce innovation from an acquired company. Additionally, firms that emphasize innovation and carefully select companies for acquisition that also emphasize innovation are likely to remain innovative.[123] Likewise, firms must manage well the integration of the acquired firms' technical capabilities so that they remain productive and continue to produce innovation after the acquired firm is merged into the acquiring firm.[124] Cisco has been highly successful with the integration of acquired technology firms. Cisco managers take great care not to lose key personnel in the acquired firm, realizing they are the source of many innovations.

This chapter closes with an assessment of how strategic entrepreneurship, as we have discussed it, helps firms create value for stakeholders through its operations.

Creating Value Through Strategic Entrepreneurship

Newer entrepreneurial firms often are more effective than larger established firms in the identification of entrepreneurial opportunities.[125] As a consequence, entrepreneurial ventures produce more radical innovations than do their larger, more established counterparts. Entrepreneurial ventures' strategic flexibility and willingness to take risks at least partially account for their ability to identify opportunities and then develop radical innovations to exploit them.

Alternatively, larger and well-established firms often have more resources and capabilities to exploit identified opportunities.[126] Younger, entrepreneurial firms generally excel in the opportunity-seeking dimension of strategic entrepreneurship while more established firms generally excel in the advantage-seeking dimension. However, to compete effectively in the twenty-first–century competitive landscape, firms must not only identify and exploit opportunities but do so while achieving and sustaining a competitive advantage.[127] Thus, on a relative basis, newer entrepreneurial firms must learn how to gain a competitive advantage (advantage-seeking behaviors), and older, more established firms must relearn how to identify entrepreneurial opportunities (opportunity-seeking skills).

In some large organizations, action is being taken to deal with these matters. For example, an increasing number of widely known, large firms, including Williams-Sonoma, Inc., Wendy's International, AstraZeneca, and Choice Hotels, have created a new, top-level managerial position commonly called president or executive vice president of emerging brands. The essential responsibility for people holding these positions is to find entrepreneurial opportunities for their firms. If a decision is made to pursue one or more of the identified opportunities, this person also leads the analysis to determine whether the innovations should be internally developed, pursued through a cooperative venture, or acquired. The objective is to help firms develop successful incremental and radical innovations.

To be entrepreneurial, firms must develop an entrepreneurial mind-set among their managers and employees. Managers must emphasize the management of their resources, particularly human capital and social capital.[128] The importance of knowledge to identify and exploit opportunities as well as to gain and sustain a competitive advantage suggests that firms must have strong human capital.[129] Social capital is critical for access to complementary resources from partners in order to compete effectively in domestic and international markets.[130]

Many entrepreneurial opportunities continue to surface in international markets, a reality that is contributing to firms' willingness to engage in international entrepreneurship. By entering global markets that are new to them, firms can learn new technologies and management practices and diffuse this knowledge throughout the entire enterprise. Furthermore, the knowledge firms gain can contribute to their innovations. Research has shown that firms operating in international markets tend to be more innovative.[131] Entrepreneurial ventures and large firms now regularly enter international markets. Both types of firms must also be innovative to compete effectively. Thus, by developing resources (human and social capital), taking advantage of opportunities in domestic and international markets, and using the resources and knowledge gained in these markets to be innovative, firms achieve competitive advantages.[132] In so doing, they create value for their customers and shareholders.

Firms practicing strategic entrepreneurship contribute to a country's economic development. In fact, some countries such as Ireland have made dramatic economic progress by changing the institutional rules for businesses operating in the country. This approach could be construed as a form of institutional entrepreneurship. Likewise, firms that seek to establish their technology as a standard, also representing institutional entrepreneurship, are engaging in strategic entrepreneurship because creating a standard produces a competitive advantage for the firm.[133]

Research shows that because of its economic importance and individual motives, entrepreneurial activity is increasing around the globe. Furthermore, more women are becoming entrepreneurs because of the economic opportunity entrepreneurship provides and the individual independence it affords. Recent research showed that about one-third of all entrepreneurs are now women[134] In the United States, for example, women are the nation's fastest-growing group of entrepreneurs.[135] In future years, entrepreneurial activity may increase the wealth of less-affluent countries and continue to contribute to the economic development of the more-affluent countries. Regardless, the entrepreneurial ventures and large, established firms that choose to practice strategic entrepreneurship are likely to be the winners in the twenty-first century.[136]

After identifying opportunities, entrepreneurs must act to develop capabilities that will become the basis of their firm's core competencies and competitive advantages. The process of identifying opportunities is entrepreneurial, but this activity alone is not sufficient to create maximum wealth or even to survive over time.[137] As we learned in Chapter 3, to successfully exploit opportunities, a firm must develop capabilities that are valuable, rare, difficult to imitate, and nonsubstitutable. When capabilities satisfy these four criteria, the firm has one or more competitive advantages to exploit the identified opportunities (as described in Chapter 3). Without a competitive advantage, the firm's success will be only temporary (as explained in Chapter 1). An innovation may be valuable and rare early in its life, if a market perspective is used in its development. However, competitive actions must be taken to introduce the new product to the market and protect its position in the market against competitors to gain a competitive advantage. These actions combined represent strategic entrepreneurship.

Summary

- Strategic entrepreneurship is taking entrepreneurial actions using a strategic perspective. Firms engaging in strategic entrepreneurship simultaneously engage in opportunity-seeking and advantage-seeking behaviors. The purpose is to continuously find new opportunities and quickly develop innovations to exploit them.
- Entrepreneurship is a process used by individuals and groups to identify entrepreneurial opportunities without being immediately constrained by the resources they control. Corporate entrepreneurship is the application of entrepreneurship (including the identification of entrepreneurial opportunities) within ongoing, established organizations. Entrepreneurial opportunities are conditions in which new goods or services can satisfy a need in the market. Increasingly, entrepreneurship positively contributes to individual firms' performance and stimulates growth in countries' economies.
- Firms engage in three types of innovative activity: (1) invention, which is the act of creating a new good or process, (2) innovation, or the process of creating a commercial product from an invention, and (3) imitation, which is the adoption of similar innovations by different firms. Invention brings something new into being while innovation brings something new into use.
- Entrepreneurs see or envision entrepreneurial opportunities and then take actions to develop innovations to exploit them. The most successful entrepreneurs (whether they are establishing their own venture or are working in an ongoing organization) have an entrepreneurial mind-set, which is an orientation that values the potential opportunities available because of marketplace uncertainties.
- International entrepreneurship, or the process of identifying and exploiting entrepreneurial opportunities outside the firm's domestic markets, has become important to firms around the globe. Evidence suggests that firms capable of effectively engaging in international entrepreneurship outperform those competing only in their domestic markets.
- Three basic approaches are used to produce innovation: (1) internal innovation, which involves R&D and forming internal corporate ventures, (2) cooperative strategies such as strategic alliances, and (3) acquisitions. Autonomous strategic behavior and induced strategic behavior are the two forms of internal corporate venturing. Autonomous strategic behavior is a bottom-up process through which a product champion facilitates the commercialization of an innovative good or service. Induced strategic behavior is a top-down process in which a firm's current strategy and structure facilitate the development and implementation of product or process innovations. Thus, induced strategic behavior is driven by the organization's current corporate strategy and structure while autonomous strategic behavior can result in a change to the firm's current strategy and structure arrangements.
- Firms create two types of innovation—incremental and radical—through internal innovation that takes place in the form of autonomous strategic behavior or induced strategic behavior. Overall, firms produce more incremental innovations although radical innovations have a higher probability of significantly increasing sales revenue and profits. Increasingly, cross-functional integration is vital to a firm's efforts to develop and implement internal corporate venturing activities and to commercialize the resulting innovation. Additionally, integration and innovation can be facilitated by developing shared values and effectively using strategic leadership.
- To gain access to the specialized knowledge that often is required to innovate in the complex global economy, firms may form a cooperative relationship such as a strategic alliance with other companies, some of which may be competitors.
- Acquisitions are another means firms use to obtain innovation. Innovation can be acquired through direct acquisition, or firms can learn new capabilities from an acquisition, thereby enriching their internal innovation abilities.
- The practice of strategic entrepreneurship by all types of firms, large and small, new and more established, creates value for all stakeholders, especially for shareholders and customers. Strategic entrepreneurship also contributes to the economic development of countries.

Review Questions

1. What is strategic entrepreneurship? What is corporate entrepreneurship?
2. What is entrepreneurship, and what are entrepreneurial opportunities? Why are they important for firms competing in the twenty-first–century competitive landscape?
3. What are invention, innovation, and imitation? How are these concepts interrelated?
4. What is an entrepreneur, and what is an entrepreneurial mind-set?
5. What is international entrepreneurship? Why is it important?
6. How do firms develop innovations internally?
7. How do firms use cooperative strategies to innovate and to have access to innovative capabilities?
8. How does a firm acquire other companies to increase the number of innovations it produces and improve its capability to produce innovations?
9. How does strategic entrepreneurship help firms to create value?

Experiential Exercises

Exercise 1: Do You Want to Be an Entrepreneur?

Would you make a good entrepreneur? In this exercise, we will explore how individual attributes and characteristics contribute to entrepreneurial success. If you believe that you have the traits of a successful entrepreneur, would you be more effective working within a large firm or starting your own business? Complete the first stage of the exercise individually, then meet in small groups to discuss your answers.

Individual

Brainstorm a list of personal attributes or characteristics that could help (or hinder) a person's success as an entrepreneur.

Next, evaluate the importance of each item on your list.

Finally, compare your prioritized list against your personal characteristics. Do you think that you are a good candidate to be an entrepreneur? Why or why not?

Group

First, compare each person's list of attributes and characteristics. Combine similar items and create a composite list.

Second, as a group, evaluate the importance of each item on the list. It is not important to rank order the characteristics. Rather, sort them into categories "very important," "somewhat important," and "minimally important."

Then, discuss within your group which team member seems to be the best suited to be an entrepreneur. Create a brief profile of how to describe that person if he or she were applying for a job at an innovative company such as Google, Intel, or Motorola.

Whole Class

The instructor will ask for student volunteers to present their interview profiles.

Exercise 2: Global Differences in Entrepreneurial Activity

As described in the chapter, entrepreneurship is a global phenomenon. However, innovativeness varies from country to country, as does the infrastructure to support new business development. These differences have substantial implications for both persons wishing to start new businesses, as well as for companies seeking local partners in different regions.

This exercise will acquaint you with the Global Entrepreneurship Monitor (GEM), an annual series of studies that evaluate entrepreneurial activity in different regions of the world. GEM is a collaborative initiative between the London Business School and Babson College. Working with experts in multiple countries, they produce a series of annual reviews of entrepreneurial activity, both at the country level and in a summary global report. Publications from the GEM Consortium are available online at http://www.gemconsortium.org. GEM started in 1999 with reports on 10 countries. By 2001 the scope had broadened to 29 countries. The 2007 reports will include 43 countries.

Working in teams, complete either Assignment A or Assignment B.

Assignment A

Compare entrepreneurial activities across countries.

1. Pick two countries that are located in the same region of the world (i.e., the Americas, Europe, Asia-Pacific, or the Middle East).
2. Review the most recent GEM country reports for your two selections.
3. Prepare a brief PowerPoint presentation that identifies the similarities and differences between the two countries. Include the levels of entrepreneurial activity, infrastructure, and challenges/problems facing both nations.

Assignment B

Compare entrepreneurial activities over time.

1. Select one country that was included in both the 2001 and the most recent GEM surveys.
2. Review the GEM reports for that country for both years.
3. Prepare a brief PowerPoint presentation that identifies the similarities and differences within the country over time. Include the levels of entrepreneurial activity, infrastructure, and challenges/problems. Overall, is the climate for entrepreneurship improving or worsening?

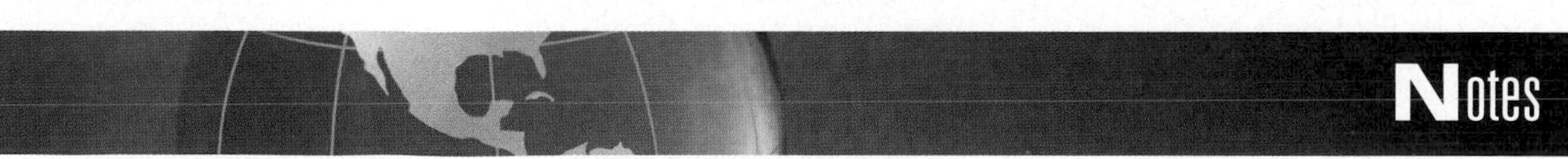

Notes

1. D. J. Miller, M. J. Fern, & L. B. Cardinal, 2007, The use of knowledge for technological innovation within diversified firms, *Academy of Management Journal,* 50: 308–326; D. S. Elenkov & I. M. Manev, 2005, Top management leadership and influence on innovation: The role of sociocultural context, *Journal of Management,* 31: 381–402.
2. R. D. Ireland & J. W. Webb, 2007, Strategic entrepreneurship: Creating competitive advantage through streams of innovation, *Business Horizons,* 50(4): 49–59; M. A. Hitt, R. D. Ireland, S. M. Camp, & D. L. Sexton, 2002, Strategic entrepreneurship: Integrating entrepreneurial and strategic management perspectives, in M. A. Hitt, R. D. Ireland, S. M. Camp, & D. L. Sexton (eds.), *Strategic Entrepreneurship: Creating a New Mindset,* Oxford, UK: Blackwell Publishers, 1–16; M. A. Hitt, R. D. Ireland, S. M. Camp, & D. L. Sexton, 2001, Strategic entrepreneurship: Entrepreneurial strategies for wealth creation, *Strategic Management Journal,* 22 (Special Issue): 479–491.
3. C. E. Helfat, 2006, Review of Open innovation: The new imperative for creating and profiting from technology, *Academy of Management Perspectives,* 20(2): 86–88; D. A. Shepherd & D. R. DeTienne, 2005, Prior knowledge, potential financial reward, and opportunity identification, *Entrepreneurship Theory and Practice,* 29(1): 91–112.

4. R. E. Hoskisson, M. A. Hitt, R. A. Johnson, & W. Grossman, 2002, Conflicting voices: The effects of institutional ownership heterogeneity and internal governance on corporate innovation strategies, *Academy of Management Journal,* 45: 697–716.
5. J. L. Morrow, D. G. Sirmon, M. A. Hitt & T. R. Holcomb, 2007, Creating value in the face of declining performance: Firm strategies and organizational recovery, *Strategic Management Journal,* 28: 271–283; K. G. Smith, C. J. Collins, & K. D. Clark, 2005, Existing knowledge, knowledge creation capability, and the rate of new product introduction in high-technology firms, *Academy of Management Journal,* 48: 346–357.
6. D. F. Kuratko, 2007, Entrepreneurial leadership in the 21st century, *Journal of Leadership and Organizational Studies,* 13(4): 1–11; R. D. Ireland, M. A. Hitt, & D. G. Sirmon, 2003, A model of strategic entrepreneurship: The construct and its dimensions, *Journal of Management,* 29: 963–989.
7. B. R. Barringer & R. D. Ireland, 2008, *Entrepreneurship: Successfully Launching New Ventures,* Upper Saddle River, NJ: Pearson Prentice Hall, 5; D. T. Holt, M. W. Rutherford, & G. R. Clohessy, 2007, Corporate entrepreneurship: An empirical look at individual characteristics, context and process, *Journal of Leadership and Organizational Studies,* 13(4): 40–54.
8. M. H. Morris, S. Coombes, & M. Schindehutte, 2007, Antecedents and outcomes of entrepreneurial and market orientations in a non-profit context: Theoretical and empirical insights, *Journal of Leadership and Organizational Studies,* 13(4): 12–39; H. A. Schildt, M. V. J. Maula, & T. Keil, 2005, Explorative and exploitative learning from external corporate ventures, *Entrepreneurship Theory and Practice,* 29: 493–515.
9. G. T. Lumpkin & B. B. Lichtenstein, 2005, The role of organizational learning in the opportunity-recognition process, *Entrepreneurship Theory and Practice,* 29: 451–472.
10. B. A. Gilbert, P. P. McDougall, & D. B. Audretsch, 2006, New venture growth: A review and extension, *Journal of Management,* 32: 926–950.
11. Barringer & Ireland, *Entrepreneurship;* S. A. Zahra, H. J. Sapienza, & P. Davidsson, 2006, Entrepreneurship and dynamic capabilities: A review, model and research agenda, *Journal of Management Studies,* 43: 917–955.
12. S. A. Alvarez & J. B. Barney, 2005, Organizing rent generation and appropriation: Toward a theory of the entrepreneurial firm, *Journal of Business Venturing,* 19: 621–635.
13. M. Minniti, 2005, Entrepreneurial alertness and asymmetric information in a spin-glass model, *Journal of Business Venturing,* 19: 637–658.
14. W. Kuemmerle, 2005, The entrepreneur's path to global expansion, *MIT Sloan Management Review,* 46(2): 42–49.
15. C. Marquis & M. Lounsbury, 2007, Vive la resistance: Competing logics and the consolidation of U.S. community banking, *Academy of Management Journal,* 50: 799–820; S.-H. Lee, M. W. Peng, & J. B. Barney, 2007, Bankruptcy law and entrepreneurship development: A real-options perspective, *Academy of Management Review,* 32: 257–272.
16. N. Wasserman, 2006, Stewards, agents, and the founder discount: Executive compensation in new ventures, *Academy of Management Journal,* 49: 960–976; S. Shane & S. Venkataraman, 2000, The promise of entrepreneurship as a field of research, *Academy of Management Review,* 25: 217–226.
17. J. Schumpeter, 1934, *The Theory of Economic Development,* Cambridge, MA: Harvard University Press.
18. R. Greenwood & R. Suddaby, 2006, Institutional entrepreneurship in mature fields: The big five accounting firms, *Academy of Management Journal,* 49: 27–48; R. Katila, 2002, New product search over time: Past ideas in their prime? *Academy of Management Journal,* 45: 995–1010.
19. W. J. Baumol, R. E. Litan, & C. J. Schramm, 2007, *Good capitalism, bad capitalism, and the economics of growth and prosperity,* New Haven: Yale University Press; R. G. Holcombe, 2003, The origins of entrepreneurial opportunities, *Review of Austrian Economics,* 16: 25–54.
20. R. D. Ireland, J. W. Webb, & J. E. Coombs, 2005, Theory and methodology in entrepreneurship research, in D. J. Ketchen Jr. & D. D. Bergh (eds.), *Research Methodology in Strategy and Management* (Volume 2), San Diego: Elsevier Publishers, 111–141; S. D. Sarasvathy, 2005, The questions we ask and the questions we care about: Reformulating some problems in entrepreneurship research, *Journal of Business Venturing,* 19: 707–717.
21. K. E. Klein, 2007, The face of entrepreneurship in 2017, *BusinessWeek,* http://www.businessweek.com, January 31.
22. P. F. Drucker, 1998, The discipline of innovation, *Harvard Business Review,* 76(6): 149–157.
23. Ibid.
24. K. Karnik, 2005, Innovation's importance: Powering economic growth, *National Association of Software and Service Companies,* http://www.nasscom.org, January 24.
25. M. Subramaniam & M. A. Youndt, 2005, The influence of intellectual capital on the types of innovative capabilities, *Academy of Management Journal,* 48: 450–463.
26. F. F. Suarez & G. Lanzolla, 2007, The role of environmental dynamics in building a first mover advantage theory, *Academy of Management Review,* 32: 377–392.
27. R. Price, 1996, Technology and strategic advantage, *California Management Review,* 38(3): 38–56; L. G. Franko, 1989, Global corporate competition: Who's winning, who's losing and the R&D factor as one reason why, *Strategic Management Journal,* 10: 449–474.
28. M. A. Hitt, R. D. Nixon, R. E. Hoskisson, & R. Kochhar, 1999, Corporate entrepreneurship and cross-functional fertilization: Activation, process and disintegration of a new product design team, *Entrepreneurship: Theory and Practice,* 23(3): 145–167.
29. D. J. Miller, 2006, Technological diversity, related diversification, and firm performance, *Strategic Management Journal,* 27: 601–619.
30. Schumpeter, *The Theory of Economic Development.*
31. R. Katila & S. Shane, 2005, When does lack of resources make new firms innovative? *Academy of Management Journal,* 48: 814–829.
32. P. Sharma & J. L. Chrisman, 1999, Toward a reconciliation of the definitional issues in the field of corporate entrepreneurship, *Entrepreneurship: Theory and Practice,* 23(3): 11–27; R. A. Burgelman & L. R. Sayles, 1986, *Inside Corporate Innovation: Strategy, Structure, and Managerial Skills,* New York: Free Press.
33. D. K. Dutta & M. M. Crossan, 2005, The nature of entrepreneurial opportunities: Understanding the process using the 4I organizational learning framework, *Entrepreneurship Theory and Practice* 29: 425–449.
34. R. E. Hoskisson & L. W. Busenitz, 2002, Market uncertainty and learning distance in corporate entrepreneurship entry mode choice, in M. A. Hitt, R. D. Ireland, S. M. Camp, & D. L. Sexton (eds.), *Strategic Entrepreneurship: Creating a New Mindset,* Oxford, UK: Blackwell Publishers, 151–172.
35. S. Thornhill, 2006, Knowledge, innovation, and firm performance in high- and low-technology regimes, *Journal of Business Venturing,* 21: 687–703; D. Somaya, 2003, Strategic determinants of decisions not to settle patent litigation, *Strategic Management Journal,* 24: 17–38.
36. F. Luthans & E. S. Ibrayeva, 2006, Entrepreneurial self-efficacy in central Asian transition economies: Quantitative and qualitative analyses, *Journal of International Business Studies,* 37: 92–110; D. Duffy, 2004, Corporate entrepreneurship: Entrepreneurial skills for personal and corporate success, *Center for Excellence,* http://www.centerforexcellence.net, June 14.
37. M. S. Cardon, C. Zietsma, P. Saparito, B. P. Matheren, & C. Davis, 2005, A tale of passion: New insights into entrepreneurship from a parenthood metaphor, *Journal of Business Venturing,* 19: 23–45.
38. J. O. Fiet, 2007, A prescriptive analysis of search and discovery, *Journal of Management Studies,* 44: 592–611; J. S. McMullen & D. A. Shepherd, 2006, Entrepreneurial action and the role of uncertainty in the theory of the entrepreneur, *Academy of Management Review,* 31: 132–152.

39. R. A. Baron, 2006, Opportunity recognition as pattern recognition: How entrepreneurs "connect the dots" to identify new business opportunities, *Academy of Management Perspectives,* 20(1): 104–119; R. G. McGrath & I. MacMillan, 2000, *The Entrepreneurial Mindset,* Boston, MA: Harvard Business School Press.
40. R. D. Ireland, M. A. Hitt, & J. W. Webb, 2005, Entrepreneurial alliances and networks, in O. Shenkar and J. J. Reuer (eds.), *Handbook of Strategic Alliances,* Thousand Oaks, CA: Sage Publications, 333–352; T. M. Begley & D. P. Boyd, 2003, The need for a corporate global mind-set, *MIT Sloan Management Review,* 44(2): 25–32.
41. H. D. Schultz, 2005, Starbucks' founder on innovation in the music biz, *BusinessWeek,* July 4, 16–17.
42. P. Sexton, 2007, Mocha and music as Starbucks serves up a record label, *Financial Times,* http://www.ft.com, August 27; Starbucks to launch music label, 2007, CBC Arts, http://www.cbc.ca/consumer story, March 13.
43. W. Tsai, 2001, Knowledge transfer in intraorganizational networks: Effects of network position and absorptive capacity on business unit innovation and performance, *Academy of Management Journal,* 44: 996–1004.
44. S. A. Zahra & G. George, 2002, Absorptive capacity: A review, reconceptualization, and extension, *Academy of Management Review,* 27: 185–203.
45. M. A. Hitt, L. Bierman, K. Uhlenbruck, & K. Shimizu, 2006, The importance of resources in the internationalization of professional service firms: The good, the bad and the ugly, *Academy of Management Journal,* 49: 1137–1157; M. A. Hitt, L. Bierman, K. Shimizu, & R. Kochhar, 2001, Direct and moderating effects of human capital on strategy and performance in professional service firms, *Academy of Management Journal,* 44: 13–28.
46. A. Ward, 2007, Coca-Cola looks beyond the fizz, *Financial Times,* http://www.ft.com, March 10.
47. Zahra & George, Absorptive capacity: 261.
48. H. J. Sapienza, E. Autio, G. George, & S. A. Zahra, 2006, A capabilities perspective on the effects of early internationalization on firm survival and growth, *Academy of Management Review,* 31: 914–933; T. M. Begley, W.-L. Tan, & H. Schoch, 2005, Politico-economic factors associated with interest in starting a business: A multi-country study, *Entrepreneurship Theory and Practice,* 29: 35–52.
49. M. Javidan, R. M. Steers, & M. A. Hitt, 2007, *The Global Mindset,* Amsterdam: Elsevier Ltd.
50. Hitt, Bierman, Uhlenbruck, Shimizu, The importance of resources in the internationalization of professional service firms; L. Tihanyi, R. A. Johnson, R. E. Hoskisson, & M. A. Hitt, 2003, Institutional ownership differences and international diversification: The effects of boards of directors and technological opportunity, *Academy of Management Journal,* 46: 195–211.
51. Q. Yang & C. X. Jiang, 2007, Location advantages and subsidiaries' R&D activities in emerging economies: Exploring the effect of employee mobility, *Asia Pacific Journal of Management,* 24: 341–358; R. D. Ireland & J. W. Webb, 2006, International entrepreneurship in emerging economies: A resource-based perspective, in S. Alvarez, A. Carrera, L. Mesquita, & R. Vassolo (eds.), *Entrepreneurship and Innovation in Emerging Economies,* Oxford, UK: Blackwell Publishers, in press.
52. D. Farrell, H. Fassbender, T. Kneip, S. Kriesel, & E. Labaye, 2003, Reviving French and German productivity, *The McKinsey Quarterly,* (1), 40–53.
53. 2004, *GEM 2004 Irish Report,* http://www.gemconsortium.org/download, July 13.
54. N. Bosma & R. Harding, 2007, 2006 *Global Entrepreneurship Monitor,* Babson College, http://www3.babson.edu/ESHIP/research-publications/gem.cfm, March 1.
55. D. W. Yiu, C. M. Lau, & G. D. Bruton, 2007, International venturing by emerging economy firms: The effects of firm capabilities, home country networks, and corporate entrepreneurship, *Journal of International Business Studies,* 38: 519–540; M. H. Morris, 1998, *Entrepreneurial Intensity: Sustainable Advantages for Individuals, Organizations, and Societies,* Westport, CT: Quorum Books, 85–86.
56. N. Nummeia, S. Saarenketo, & K. Puumalainen, 2005, Rapidly with a rifle or more slowly with a shotgun? Stretching the company boundaries of internationalizing ICT firms, *Journal of International Entrepreneurship,* 2: 275–288; S. A. Zahra & G. George, 2002, International entrepreneurship: The state of the field and future research agenda, in M. A. Hitt, R. D. Ireland, S. M. Camp, & D. L. Sexton (eds.), *Strategic Entrepreneurship: Creating a New Mindset,* Oxford, UK: Blackwell Publishers, 255–288.
57. S. A. Zahra, R. D. Ireland, & M. A. Hitt, 2000, International expansion by new venture firms: International diversity, mode of market entry, technological learning and performance, *Academy of Management Journal,* 43: 925–950.
58. R. Mudambi & S.A. Zahra, 2007, The survival of international new ventures, *Journal of International Business Studies,* 38: 333-352; P. P. McDougall & B. M. Oviatt, 2000, International entrepreneurship: The intersection of two paths, *Academy of Management Journal,* 43: 902–908.
59. H. Barkema, & O. Chvyrkov, 2007, Does top management team diversity promote or hamper foreign expansion? *Strategic Management Journal,* 28: 663–680; A. Yan, G. Zhu, & D. T. Hall, 2002, International assignments for career building: A model of agency relationships and psychological contracts, *Academy of Management Review,* 27: 373–391.
60. T. S. Frost, 2001, The geographic sources of foreign subsidiaries' innovations, *Strategic Management Journal,* 22: 101–122.
61. R. Underwood, 2005, Walking the talk? *Fast Company,* March, 25–26.
62. J. Battelle, 2005, Turning the page, *Business 2.0,* July, 98–100.
63. J. Santos, Y. Doz, & P. Williamson, 2004, Is your innovation process global? *MIT Sloan Management Review,* 45(4): 31–37; C. D. Charitou & C. C. Markides, 2003, Responses to disruptive strategic innovation, *MIT Sloan Management Review,* 44(2): 55–63.
64. J. A. Fraser, 2004, A return to basics at Kellogg, *MIT Sloan Management Review,* 45(4): 27–30; P. M. Lee & H. M. O'Neill, 2003, Ownership structures and R&D investments of U.S. and Japanese firms: Agency and stewardship perspectives, *Academy of Management Journal,* 46: 212–225.
65. F. K. Pil & S. K. Cohen, 2006, Modularity: Implications for imitation, innovation, and sustained advantage, *Academy of Management Review,* 31: 995–1011; S. Kola-Nystrom, 2003, Theory of conceptualizing the challenge of corporate renewal, Lappeenranta University of Technology, working paper.
66. 2005, Radical and incremental innovation styles, *Strategies 2 innovate,* http://www.strategies2innovate.com, July 12.
67. W. C. Kim & R. Mauborgne, 2005, Navigating toward blue oceans, *Optimize,* February, 44–52.
68. G. Ahuja & M. Lampert, 2001, Entrepreneurship in the large corporation: A longitudinal study of how established firms create breakthrough inventions, *Strategic Management Journal,* 22 (Special Issue): 521–543.
69. 2005, Getting an edge on innovation, *BusinessWeek,* March 21, 124.
70. J. E. Ashton, F. X. Cook Jr., & P. Schmitz, 2003, Uncovering hidden value in a midsize manufacturing company, *Harvard Business Review,* 81(6): 111–119; L. Fleming & O. Sorenson, 2003, Navigating the technology landscape of innovation, *MIT Sloan Management Review,* 44(2): 15–23.
71. J. Goldenberg, R. Horowitz, A. Levav, & D. Mazursky, 2003, Finding your innovation sweet spot, *Harvard Business Review,* 81(3): 120–129; G. C. O'Connor, R. Hendricks, & M. P. Rice, 2002, Assessing transition readiness for radical innovation, *Research Technology Management,* 45(6): 50–56.
72. C. E. Shalley & J. E. Perry-Smith, 2008, Team creativity and creative cognition: Interactive effects of social and cognitive networks, *Strategic Entrepreneurship Journal,* 1: in press; R. I. Sutton, 2002, Weird ideas that spark innovation, *MIT Sloan Management Review,* 43(2): 83–87.
73. K. G. Smith & D. Di Gregorio, 2002, Bisociation, discovery, and the role of entrepreneurial action, in M. A. Hitt, R. D. Ireland, S. M. Camp, & D. L. Sexton (eds.), *Strategic Entrepreneurship: Creating*

a New Mindset, Oxford, UK: Blackwell Publishers, 129–150.

74. J. G. Covin, R. D. Ireland, & D. F. Kuratko, 2005, Exploration through internal corporate ventures, Indiana University, working paper; Hoskisson & Busenitz, Market uncertainty and learning distance.
75. R. A. Burgelman, 1995, *Strategic Management of Technology and Innovation,* Boston: Irwin.
76. S. K. Markham, 2002, Moving technologies from lab to market, *Research Technology Management,* 45(6): 31–42.
77. J. M. Howell, 2005, The right stuff: Identifying and developing effective champions of innovation, *Academy of Management Executive,* 19(2): 108–119.
78. M. D. Hutt & T. W. Seph, 2004, *Business Marketing Management,* 8th ed., Cincinnati, OH: Thomson South-Western.
79. S. K. Ethiraj, 2007, Allocation of inventive effort in complex product systems, *Strategic Management Journal,* 28: 563–584; M. A. Hitt, R. D. Ireland, & H. Lee, 2000, Technological learning, knowledge management, firm growth and performance, *Journal of Engineering and Technology Management,* 17: 231–246.
80. H. W. Chesbrough, 2002, Making sense of corporate venture capital, *Harvard Business Review,* 80(3): 90–99.
81. M. Subramaniam & N. Venkatraman, 2001, Determinants of transnational new product development capability: Testing the influence of transferring and deploying tacit overseas knowledge, *Strategic Management Journal,* 22: 359–378.
82. M. Song & M. M. Montoya-Weiss, 2001, The effect of perceived technological uncertainty on Japanese new product development, *Academy of Management Journal,* 44: 61–80.
83. B. Ambos & B. B. Schegelmilch, 2007, Innovation and control in the multinational firm: A comparison of political and contingency approaches, *Strategic Management Journal,* 28: 473–486.
84. N. Lakshman, 2007, Nokia: It takes a village to design a phone for emerging markets, *BusinessWeek,* September, 12–14.
85. M. Makri, P. J. Lane, & L. R. Gomez-Mejia, 2006, CEO incentives, innovation and performance in technology-intensive firms: A reconciliation of outcome and behavior-based incentive schemes, *Strategic Management Journal,* 27: 1057–1080.
86. Multinational knowledge spillovers with decentralized R&D: A game theoretic approach, *Journal of International Business Studies,* 2007, 38: 47–63; 2002, Building scientific networks for effective innovation, *MIT Sloan Management Review,* 43(3): 14.
87. E. Danneels, 2007, The process of technological competence leveraging, *Strategic Management Journal,* 28: 511–533; C. M. Christensen & M. Overdorf, 2000, Meeting the challenge of disruptive change, *Harvard Business Review,* 78(2): 66–77.
88. L. Yu, 2002, Marketers and engineers: Why can't we just get along? *MIT Sloan Management Review,* 43(1): 13.
89. A. Somech, 2006, The effects of leadership style and team process on performance and innovation in functionally hetergeneous teams, *Journal of Management,* 32: 132–157.
90. P. Evans & B. Wolf, 2005, Collaboration rules, *Harvard Business Review,* 83(7): 96–104.
91. B. Fischer & A. Boynton, 2005, Virtuoso teams, *Harvard Business Review,* 83(7): 116–123.
92. Hitt, Nixon, Hoskisson, & Kochhar, Corporate entrepreneurship.
93. Christensen & Overdorf, Meeting the challenge of disruptive change.
94. Hitt, Nixon, Hoskisson, & Kochhar, Corporate entrepreneurship.
95. A. C. Amason, 1996, Distinguishing the effects of functional and dysfunctional conflict on strategic decision making: Resolving a paradox for top management teams, *Academy of Management Journal,* 39: 123–148; P. R. Lawrence & J. W. Lorsch, 1969, *Organization and Environment,* Homewood, IL: Richard D. Irwin.
96. M. A. Cronin & L. R. Weingart, 2007, Representational gaps, information processing, and conflict in functionally heterogeneous teams, *Academy of Management Review,* 32: 761–773; D. Dougherty, L. Borrelli, K. Muncir, & A. O'Sullivan, 2000, Systems of organizational sensemaking for sustained product innovation, *Journal of Engineering and Technology Management,* 17: 321–355.
97. Hitt, Nixon, Hoskisson, & Kochhar, Corporate entrepreneurship.
98. E. C. Wenger & W. M. Snyder, 2000, Communities of practice: The organizational frontier, *Harvard Business Review,* 78(1): 139–144.
99. Gary Hamel, 2000, *Leading the Revolution,* Boston: Harvard Business School Press.
100. Q. M. Roberson & J. A. Colquitt, 2005, Shared and configural justice: A social network model of justice in teams, *Academy of Management Review,* 30: 595–607.
101. N. Stieglitz & L. Heine, 2007, Innovations and the role of complementarities in a strategic theory of the firm, *Strategic Management Journal,* 28: 1–15; S. W. Fowler, A. W. King, S. J. Marsh, & B. Victor, 2000, Beyond products: New strategic imperatives for developing competencies in dynamic environments, *Journal of Engineering and Technology Management,* 17: 357–377.
102. M. B. Sarkar, R. Echamabadi, R. Agarwal, & B. Sen, 2006, The effect of the innovative environment on exit of entrepreneurial firms, *Strategic Management Journal,* 27: 519–539.
103. K. Larsen & A. Salter, 2006, Open for innovation: The role of openness in explaining innovation performance among U.K. manufacturing firms, *Strategic Management Journal,* 27: 131–150.
104. A. Tiwana & M. Keil, 2007, Does peripheral knowledge complement control? An empirical test in technology outsourcing alliances, *Strategic Management Journal,* 28: 623–634; A.V. Shipilov, 2006, Network strategies and performance of Canadian investment banks, *Academy of Management Journal,* 49: 590–604.
105. C. Dhanaraj & A. Parkhe, 2006, Orchestrating innovation networks, *Academy of Management Review,* 31: 659–669.
106. F. T. Rothaermel & D. L. Deeds, 2004, Exploration and exploitation alliances in biotechnology: A system of new product development, *Strategic Management Journal,* 25: 201–221; R. Gulati & M. C. Higgins, 2003, Which ties matter when? The contingent effects of interorganizational partnerships on IPO success, *Strategic Management Journal,* 24: 127–144.
107. F. T. Rothaermel, M. A. Hitt & L. A. Jobe, 2006, Balancing vertical integration and strategic outsourcing: Effects on product portfolio, product success and firm performance, *Strategic Management Journal,* 27: 1033–1056; J. Hagel III & J. S. Brown, 2005, Productive friction, *Harvard Business Review,* 83(2): 82–91.
108. S. Hamm, 2007, Radical Collaboration: Lessons from IBM's innovation factory, *BusinessWeek,* September 10, 17–22.
109. A. C. Cooper, 2002, Networks, alliances and entrepreneurship, in M. A. Hitt, R. D. Ireland, S. M. Camp, & D. L. Sexton (eds.), *Strategic Entrepreneurship: Creating a New Mindset,* Oxford, UK: Blackwell Publishers, 204–222.
110. B.-S. Teng, 2007, Corporate entrepreneurship activities through strategic alliances: A resource-based approach toward competitive advantage, *Journal of Management Studies,* 44: 119–142; S. A. Alvarez & J. B. Barney, 2001, How entrepreneurial firms can benefit from alliances with large partners, *Academy of Management Executive,* 15(1): 139–148.
111. F. T. Rothaermel, 2001, Incumbent's advantage through exploiting complementary assets via interfirm cooperation, *Strategic Management Journal,* 22 (Special Issue): 687–699.
112. A. Capaldo, 2007, Network structure and innovation: The leveraging of a dual network as a distinctive capability, *Strategic Management Journal,* 28: 585–608.
113. H. Yli-Renko, E. Autio, & H. J. Sapienza, 2001, Social capital, knowledge acquisition and knowledge exploitation in young technology-based firms, *Strategic Management Journal,* 22 (Special Issue): 587–613.
114. C. Lee, K. Lee, & J. M. Pennings, 2001, Internal capabilities, external networks and performance: A study of technology-based ventures, *Strategic Management Journal,* 22 (Special Issue): 615–640.
115. A. Takeishi, 2001, Bridging inter- and intra-firm boundaries: Management of supplier involvement in automobile product development, *Strategic Management Journal,* 22: 403–433.
116. R. C. Sampson, 2007, R&D alliances and firm performance: The impact of

technological diversity and alliance organization on innovation, *Academy of Management Journal,* 50: 364–386; J. Weiss & J. Hughes, 2005, Want collaboration? Accept—and actively manage—conflict, *Harvard Business Review,* 83(3): 92–101.

117. R. D. Ireland, M. A. Hitt, & D. Vaidyanath, 2002, Strategic alliances as a pathway to competitive success, *Journal of Management,* 28: 413–446.
118. M. A. Hitt, M. T. Dacin, E. Levitas, J. -L. Arregle, & A. Borza, 2000, Partner selection in emerging and developed market contexts: Resource-based and organizational learning perspectives, *Academy of Management Journal,* 43: 449–467.
119. J. J. Reuer, M. Zollo, & H. Singh, 2002, Post-formation dynamics in strategic alliances, *Strategic Management Journal,* 23: 135–151.
120. F. Rothaermel & D. Deeds, 2002, More good things are not always necessarily better: An empirical study of strategic alliances, experience effects, and new product development in high-technology start-ups, in M. A. Hitt, R. Amit, C. Lucier, & R. Nixon (eds.), *Creating Value: Winners in the New Business Environment,* Oxford, UK: Blackwell Publishers, 85–103.
121. 2005, Novartis announces completion of Hexal AG acquisition, http://www.novartis.com, June 6; 2005, Pfizer sees sustained long-term growth, http://www.pfizer.com, April 5.
122. M. A. Hitt, R. E. Hoskisson, R. A. Johnson, & D. D. Moesel, 1996, The market for corporate control and firm innovation, *Academy of Management Journal,* 39: 1084–1119.
123. P. Puranam & K. Srikanth, 2007, What they know vs. what they do: How acquirers leverage technology acquisitions, *Strategic Management Journal,* 28: 805–825; M. A. Hitt, J. S. Harrison, & R. D. Ireland, 2001, *Mergers and Acquisitions: A Guide to Creating Value for Stakeholders,* New York: Oxford University Press.
124. P. Puranam, H. Singh & M. Zollo, 2006, Organizing for innovation: Managing the coordination-autonomy dilemma in technology, *Academy of Management Journal,* 49: 263–280.
125. Ireland, Hitt, & Sirmon, A model of strategic entrepreneurship.
126. Ibid.
127. Hitt, Ireland, Camp, & Sexton, Strategic entrepreneurship.
128. D. G. Sirmon, M. A. Hitt, & R. D. Ireland, 2007, Managing firm resources in dynamic environment to create value: Looking inside the black box, *Academy of Management Review,* 32: 273–292.
129. Hitt, Bierman, Shimizu, & Kochhar, Direct and moderating effects of human capital.
130. Hitt, Bierman, Uhlenbruck, & Shimizu, The importance of resources in the internationalization of professional service firms; M. A. Hitt, H. Lee, & E. Yucel, 2002, The importance of social capital to the management of multinational enterprises: Relational networks among Asian and Western firms, *Asia Pacific Journal of Management,* 19: 353–372.
131. M. A. Hitt, R. E. Hoskisson, & H. Kim, 1997, International diversification: Effects on innovation and firm performance in product diversified firms, *Academy of Management Journal,* 40: 767–798.
132. M. A. Hitt & R. D. Ireland, 2002, The essence of strategic leadership: Managing human and social capital, *Journal of Leadership and Organization Studies,* 9(1): 3–14.
133. Baumol, Litan, & Schramm, *Good capitalism, bad capitalism*; R. Garud, S. Jain, & A. Kumaraswamy, 2002, Institutional entrepreneurship in the sponsorship of common technological standards: The case of Sun Microsystems and JAVA, *Academy of Management Journal,* 45: 196–214.
134. I. E. Allen, N. Langowitz, & M. Minniti, 2007, Global entrepreneurship monitor: 2006 report on women in entrepreneurship, Babson College, http://www3.babson.edu/ESHIP/research-publications/gem.cfm, March 1.
135. J. D. Jardins, 2005, I am woman (I think), *Fast Company,* May, 25–26.
136. Hitt, Ireland, Camp, & Sexton, Strategic entrepreneurship.
137. C. W. L. Hill & F. T. Rothaermel, 2003, The performance of incumbent firms in the face of radical technological innovation, *Academy of Management Review,* 28: 257–274.

Name Index

C

N

O

P

Q

R

S

X

Y

Z

Company Index

Subject Index

DB51451165